MALT
WHISKY
YEARBOOK
2012

First published in Great Britain in 2011 by
MagDig Media Limited

© MagDig Media Limited 2011

ISBN 978-0-9552607-8-0

MagDig Media Limited
1 Brassey Road
Old Potts Way, Shrewsbury
Shropshire SY3 7FA
ENGLAND

E-mail: info@maltwhiskyyearbook.com
www.maltwhiskyyearbook.com

Previous editions

Contents

Introduction

This is the seventh edition of Malt Whisky Yearbook and for the first six editions, my biggest problem has been how to be able to fit in everything that happens in the world of whisky during one year. I knew I had to do something about it so this year, I have added another 24 pages making the **Malt Whisky Yearbook 2012** the largest ever!

My excellent team of whisky writers have excelled themselves this year and contribute with some fascinating articles;
   The Prohibition in the 1920s stopped a nation from drinking. Or did it? *Charles Maclean* has the truth behind the dry days of USA and how it helped shape the whisky world of today.
   The young guns of whisky blenders are taking over. *Dominic Roskrow* has met with a whole new generation of whisky creators who are eager to leave their stamp on your daily dram.
   Are there any blended malts out there? *Gavin Smith* asks the question if a whole category of Scotch whiskies is about to be abandoned by the industry.
   Same drink but completely different cultures. Follow *Neil Ridley* around the world to see the differences in how whisky is enjoyed.
   The hot shots of the global whisky industry gather. *Ian Buxton* was listening to their discussions and lets you in on the secrets.
   The emotional side of whisky drinking! Try a new way of experiencing and describing your whiskies. *Colin Dunn* helps you get in touch with your emotions.
   Sales of Irish whiskey have increased dramatically. *Iorwerth Griffiths* met with some happy producers to find out why.
   How did the Japanese whisky industry cope after the earthquake and what is the future for Japanese whisky on the global scene? Living in Japan, *Chris Bunting* definitely has the best view.

In **Malt Whisky Yearbook 2012** you will also find the unique, detailed and much appreciated section on Scottish and Irish malt whisky distilleries. It has been thoroughly revised and updated, not just in text, but also including numerous, new pictures and tasting notes for all the core brands. The chapter on Japanese whisky is completely revised and the presentation of distilleries from the rest of the world is larger than ever. You will also find a list of 130 of the best whisky shops in the world with their full details and a comprehensive list of 500 new bottlings. The summary of The Whisky Year That Was has been expanded again this year, in order to reflect on the exciting times. A special chapter describes the various steps in whisky production and you will also meet the people behind the whiskies - the distillery managers. Finally, the very latest statistics, gives you all the answers to your questions on production and consumption.

Thank you for buying **Malt Whisky Yearbook 2012**. I hope that you will have many enjoyable moments reading it and we can assure you that we will be back with a new edition in 2013.

Great care has been taken to ensure the accuracy of the information presented in this book. MagDig Media Ltd can, however, not be held liable for inaccuracies.

**Malt Whisky Yearbook 2013 will be published in October 2012.
To make sure you will be able to order it directly, please register at
www.maltwhiskyyearbook.com.**

**If you need any of the previous six volumes of Malt Whisky Yearbook,
they are available for purchase (in limited numbers) from the website
www.maltwhiskyyearbook.com**

Acknowledgments

First of all I wish to thank the writers who have shared their great specialist knowledge on the subject in a brilliant and entertaining way – Chris Bunting, Ian Buxton, Colin Dunn, Iorwerth Griffiths, Charles MacLean, Neil Ridley, Dominic Roskrow and Gavin D. Smith.

A special thanks goes to Gavin and Dominic who put in a lot of effort nosing, tasting and writing notes for more than 100 different whiskies. Thanks also to Ian for the tasting notes for independent bottlings and to Chris for the Japanese notes.

The following persons have also made important photographic or editorial contributions and I am grateful to all of them:

Alistair Abbott, Iain Allan, Rob Allanson, Alasdair Anderson, Bobby Anderson, Russel Anderson, David Baker, Duncan Baldwin, Nicola Ball, Nick Ballard, Keith Batt, Jan Beckers, Kirsteen Beeston, Darek Bell, Benny Borgh, Stephen Bremner, Andrew Brown, Graham Brown, Alex Bruce, Gordon Bruce, Stephen Burnett, Pär Caldenby, Mike Cameron, Douglas Campbell, Peter Campbell, Ian Chang, Ian Chapman, Yuseff Cherney, Ashok Chokalingam, Stewart Christine, Margaret Mary Clarke, Doug Clement, Willie Cochrane, Michael Cockram, Susan Colville, Neal Corbett, Graham Coull, Jeremy Cunnington, Francis Cuthbert, Kirsty Dagnan, Susie Davidson, Stephen Davies, David Doig, Jean Donnay, Dennis Downing, Frances Dupuy, Gavin Durnin, Ben Ellefsen, Graham Eunson, Joanna Fearnside, Berle Figgins Jr, Hannah Fisher, Douglas Fitchett, Erik Fitchett, Robert Fleming, Tim Forbes, Robert Fullarton, Didier Ghorbanzadeh, Gillian Gibson, Gregg Glass, John Glass, Kenny Grant, Gary Haggart, Mike Haldane, Andy Hannah, Michael Heads, Shane Healy, Paul Hooper, Robbie Hughes, Jill Inglis, Anne Jack, Richard Jansson, Pat Jones, Jens-Erik Jörgensen, Moritz Kallmeyer, Marko Karakasevic, Jenny Karlsson, Davin de Kergommeaux, Ruedi Käser, Cara Laing, Bill Lark, Charles Leclef, Claudia Liebl, Karl Locher, Mark Lochhead, Ian Logan, Jim Long, Alistair Longwell, Conn Lynch, Deborah Lynch, Horst Lüning, Eddie McAffer, Iain MacAllister, Des McCagherty, Brendan McCarron, Andy Macdonald, Gillian Macdonald, John MacDonald, Polly MacDonald, Willie MacDougall, Frank McHardy, Doug McIvor, Ian Mackay, Bruce Mackenzie, Ewen Mackintosh, Ian MacMillan, Grant MacPherson, Patrick Maguire, David Mair, Dennis Malcolm, Martin Markvardsen, Stephen Marshall, Lee Medoff, Annabel Meikle, Roger Melander, Jean Metzger, Dai Minato, Euan Mitchell, Henric Molin, Nick Morgan, John Mullen, Jayne Murphy, Douglas Murray, Andrew Nelstrop, Stuart Nickerson, Graham Nicolson, Linda Outterson, Casey Overeem, Richard A Pelletier, Sean Phillips, Stuart Pirie, Olivia Plunkett, Phil Prichard, Anssi Pyysing, Rachel Quinn, Robert Ransom, Joanne Reavley, Donald Renwick, Damian Riley-Smith, Patrick Roberts, James Robertson, Niels Römer, Torsten Römer, Tyler Schramm, Bryan Schultz, Jacqui Seargeant, Andrew Shand, Sam Simmons, Sukhinder Singh, Alison Spowart, Jolanda Stadelmann, Jeremy Stephens, Vicky Stevens, Karen Stewart, Thomas Sundblom, Mark Tayburn, Elizabeth Teape, Stephen Teeling, Marcel Telser, David Thomson, Erkin Tuzmuhamedov, Paul Verbruggen, Lasse Vesterby, Alistair Walker, Malcolm Waring, Chris Watt, Mark Watt, Andy Watts, Stuart Watts, Iain Weir, James Whelan, Nick White, Ronald Whiteford, Robert Whitehead, Cristina Wilkie, Anthony Wills, Anna Wilson, Allan Winchester, Gordon Winton, Stephen Woodcock, Patrick van Zuidam.

Finally, to my wife Pernilla and our daughter Alice,
thank you for your patience and your love and to Vilda,
the lab, my faithful companion during long working hours.

Ingvar Ronde
Editor
Malt Whisky Yearbook

The dry years

When Prohibition hit the USA in the 1920s, things did not go as the legislators had hoped for. Consumption was booming and the producers found alternative ways of dealing with the new order. Charles Maclean explains how this has affected the whisky industry of today.

O n 17th January 1920 America went dry. The 18th Amendment to the Constitution, which banned the manufacture, transportation, import, export and sale of alcohol, had been passed the year before – presented by an obscure congressman from Minnesota named Andrew J. Volstead (who was not, himself, a prohibitionist), and thus often referred to as 'The Volstead Act'. It would remain in place for thirteen years, and would have far-reaching effects on the Scotch whisky industry.

The industry's first reaction was surprise – the general view was that a well co-ordinated minority lobby had imposed its will on the majority: think of the smoking bans of modern times. But, like the anti-smoking lobby, the temperance/prohibition faction had already showed considerable political cunning. In 1917, when President Wilson declared war on Germany, his war programme included a Food Control Bill. Led by the ruthless and unscrupulous Wayne Wheeler, the temperance lobby managed to have the Bill amended to prevent all foodstuffs being used in the manufacture of alcohol.

The Cincinnati Enquirer remarked trenchantly: "For brazen affrontery, unmitigated gall, super-egoism, transcendent audacity, supreme impudence, commend us to the legislative committee of the prohibition lobby…Here we have the President of the United States under orders from an officious and offensive lobby".

Surprise was immediately followed by dismay at the closure of a market on which the Scotch whisky trade pinned a lot of hope, and fear that the 'dry rot' would spread. The home market was in poor shape. The British government raised duty three times between 1918 and 1920, increasing it over 500%. The price of a bottle rose from 9/- (45p) to 12/6d (62.5p). At the same time, the economy was sliding swiftly into recession, where it would remain for the rest of the decade. The only hope was to increase exports, yet there was a significant move towards temperance in many Western countries in the post-War years. Australia, New Zealand, South Africa and Canada imposed tariffs and trade restrictions on imported liquor (Canada had introduced

Photo: Library of Congress/Archive Photos/Getty Images

prohibition in 1918, but repealed it in 1920). Sweden and Norway imposed restrictions on the sale of all spirits, while Finland went completely dry.

Rum Runners and Bootleggers

However, it did not take long for the industry to realise that America's thirst for alcohol had not diminished, and that by making use of ports in countries adjacent to the U.S., cargoes could be brought within striking distance of their market. A blind eye was cast on just how they reached the prohibited country.

Mexico and Canada, Latin America and British Guyana, the West Indies (particularly the Bahamas, where the government spent a fortune dredging the entrance to Nassau to allow larger ships access to the harbour) and off-lying islands like St. Pierre and Miquelon in the Gulf of St. Lawrence all became points of access. The latter imported 119,000 gallons of Scotch in 1922, which was described laconically as "quite a respectful quantity for an island of 6,000 people"!

From these entrepôts, ships loaded with whisky and gin sailed to just outside American territorial waters (originally three miles off-shore, soon increased to twelve miles) and off-loaded their cargoes onto speedboats which then dodged the blockade attempted by the U.S. Coastguard Agency to run the liquor ashore. Upwards of a hundred ships might be found in the 'rum row' off the New Jersey coast, and twenty U.S. Navy destroyers were seconded to the Coastguard to catch the smugglers. On land fast cars and trucks were used, and railway cars with false floors.

It was a highly lucrative trade: Scotch fetched 100% more than it did in the home market, while 'rum runners' and 'bootleggers' could make upwards of $100,000 a year. By comparison, a Coastguard Commander earned $6,000 a year, and seamen $30 a week. It was worth the risk, and appealed to many de-mobbed servicemen who found in whisky-running the excitement and danger of wartime action.

One British newspaper remarked: "With American whiskey out of the way and an ever-increasing demand for good Scotch brands, there must be a greatly increased business, seeing that prior to Prohibition the amount of Scotch whisky consumed in the States in comparison with American was, we believe, somewhere in the region of 5 per cent".

The problem confronting the industry was how to exploit the opportunity without upsetting the American and British governments – the latter under pressure from the former to curtail exports. There was also the problem of becoming too closely involved with the criminal elements – the Mafia, and mobsters like Al Capone – which rapidly came to control the illicit market for alcoholic beverages. Some distillers refused to participate (Macdonald & Muir, for example, owners of Glenmorangie Distillery and the popular Highland Queen blend); more than one distiller failed to obtain payment for shipments; one committed suicide as a result.

The solution was proposed by Thomas Herd, Managing Director of the Distillers Company Limited (DCL), which, by 1925 when it amalgamated with the 'Big Three' whisky companies (John Walker & Sons, John Dewar & Sons and James Buchanan & Co), was the largest player in the game. In April 1925 he proposed the establishment of a discreet body to be known as 'The Scheduled Area Organisation'.

The proposal was originally to ensure that DCL's standard brands did not lose out to cheap blends made especially to supply the bootleggers, but with the increased market clout following the Big Amalgamation, the Organisation's control tightened. Prices, quality and lines of credit were regulated and customers vetted. An intelligence network made sure that interlopers were excluded and that whisky bought for other markets did not find its way to America. Companies which breached the regulations were deprived of supplies of whisky or credit.

It was an ingenious solution. Herd and others in the industry knew that Prohibition could not last for ever, and that if America could be supplied with good quality Scotch the market, post repeal, would be immense. Brands were graded and priced accordingly; bulk shipments were discouraged since bottled goods were less easily adulterated. The risks of doing business with gangsters was reduced by curtailing competition among suppliers. And since the whole Organisation was secret, American pressure on the British government was reduced.

Captain Bill McCoy (right) and his crew landing a shipload of whisky in the Bahamas

By 1930 the industry was less secretive. When questioned by the Royal Commission on Licensing that year, Sir Alexander Walker made the famous reply:

> Q: *Could you, if you would, as whisky distillers, stop a large proportion of the export of liquors to the United States?*
>
> A: *Certainly not.*
>
> Q: *You could not?*
>
> A: *We would not if we could.*

Whisky as Medicine

The only exceptions allowed under the Volstead Act were, 1) alcohol for sacramental purposes in churches and synagogues, 2) industrial alcohol and 3) liquor made, imported or exported for medicinal purposes and bought under a doctor's prescription. All three were ruthlessly exploited, especially the last.

In the first five months of 1920, 15,000 doctors and 57,000 druggists in Chicago alone applied for licenses to sell medicinal liquor; by the end of the year the Prohibition Bureau reckoned that 30 million gallons of 'medicinal liquor' had been released. Legal shipments of Scotch increased, marked as being 'for medicinal purposes' and imported under license.

It is not known just how much Scotch was exported in this way, although an article in the Saturday Evening Post (August 1920) commented: "A nation that has developed enough sickness in eighteen months to require 18 million gallons, or thereabouts, of whisky to alleviate its suffering may be depended upon to remain sick indefinitely"!

Ian Hunter, owner of Laphroaig Distillery, used the medicinal loophole to sell his whisky in the U.S. (and very soon after Prohibition was repealed, registered a trade mark); the irrepressible Tommy Dewar, by this time Lord Dewar of Homestall, recorded in his memoirs:

"I was going through a 'prohibition' State and tried to get some whisky from the conductor of the train, but without success. 'Can't do it boss; we're in a prohibition State.'

A prescription for whisky to be used as medicine

However, he eventually advised me to try at a store at the next stopping place, and this I did.

"Do you sell whisky?"

"Are you sick, mister, or got a medical certificate?"

"No".

"Then I can't do it. See this is a prohibition State, so I can't sell it; but I reckon our cholera mixture'll about fix you. Try a bottle of that."

I did, but to my great astonishment received a very familiar bottle which, although it was labelled on one side 'Cholera Mixture: a wine-glassful to be taken every two hours', had upon the other side the well-known label of a firm of Scotch whisky distillers, whose name modesty requires me to suppress!"

American distillers were also allowed to export their products if they were to be used 'for medicinal purposes', although, once clearance certificates had been issued most were redirected back to the States.

"Does anybody believe," wrote Roy Haynes, the first Prohibition Commissioner, "that Scotland, the home of whisky, is really in need of 66,000 gallons of American whiskey for non-beverage purposes?"

The Brands

The secret nature of the Scheduled Area Organisation makes it impossible to know just how much Scotch was exported to the U.S. during Prohibition, or which brands. It is likely that the leading names will have been available. Other well-known brands were ear-marked specifically for export markets – Haig & Haig and Haig's Pinch, for example: in 1927, Haigs shipped 37,233 gallons to America, which was by now its third largest export market. A raft of previously unknown whiskies were developed for the Scheduled Area.

The most famous and enduring of the latter was Cutty Sark, created for Berry Bros & Rudd, the long-established London wine merchants. Francis Berry went to Nassau in

1921 to investigate the phenomenal trade that was being conducted from there. He met Captain Bill McCoy, one of the leading and more reputable rum-runners; they discussed what style of whisky would most appeal to the American palate, and on his return specified a blend that was to be "light but smooth, never darker than pale sherry".

A regular visitor to the United States during Prohibition was Jimmy Barclay, owner of Ballantine's (which he managed to have listed on the Queen Mary and the Mauritania) and Old Smuggler. He appointed Charlie Berns and his cousin, Jack Kriendler, owners of the legendary speakeasy, Club 21 at 21 West 57th Street, New York, as his agents. The Club was raided many times during Prohibition, but the owners were never caught: as soon as a raid began, a system of levers tipped the shelves of the bar, sweeping the liquor bottles through a chute and into the city's sewers!

Barclay never spoke of his adventures in America during Prohibition, except once. Graham Nown records in his Story of Ballantine's 17YO that when pressed to say "whether there was any truth in the rumours of beatings and shootouts in the scramble to deliver whisky consignments to

SNARE OF PUSSYFOOTISM.

LORD DEWAR TELLS OF ITS TRAGIC RESULTS IN AMERICA—DEATH AND CRIME.

FACTS THAT ARE NOT TOLD.

(Special to " THE GLOBE.")

Lord Dewar, who has just returned from a tour in the U.S.A., has come back " with the goods " so far as Prohibition is concerned.

He has seen evidence, facts, conditions, situations which prove all that has been written in " The Globe " on the failure of " Pussyfootism " to establish temperance conditions in America, or prove that Prohibition is the blessing which Scotland is being told at present is the case.

" From what I have just seen in the United States," said Lord Dewar to a " Globe " representative to-day, " I think " The Globe " ought to be thanked for the public service it is doing in waking up England to the dangers of ' Pussyfootism.'

" Prohibition has proved a fraud, a delusion, and a snare, and it always has been in any State where it has been tried.

ILLICIT STILLS.

" It has caused illicit stills to spring up in the towns, backwoods, and in the wild and woolly West like mushrooms.

" The Californian fruit growers are getting more money for their fruit now because they are selling it in retail quantities.

" More concrete basements are being built in houses throughout America now than ever before, and liquor is being stored therein. Many people who signed for Prohibition immediately afterwards stocked their wine cellars.

" It has caused a new fashion, whereby men carry bottles in their hip pockets instead of going to a saloon or a hotel for a drink.

SMUGGLING.

" Let it be remembered that the border lines of U.S.A. on the Atlantic and Pacific coasts and the 3,000 miles

MUST BE FOUGHT.

" No, these agitations are no novelty, but they must be fought for the sake of the liberty of the people and those who desire to choose for themselves.

"Prohibition has been moving in cycles. The Licensing Bill here gives ample powers, and by it the authorities have power to abolish redundant public houses at the rate of 1,200 per year.

"No one wants drinking dens; but Pussyfoot won his way in America because the people did not take him seriously, and the danger here is that he may win if the people are not aroused to the results which follow Prohibition.

ENGLAND SOON.

"That is the danger in Scotland, and it will be England's turn soon. Pussyfoot must be fought, and the inattentive and irresponsible public should be warned against a campaign, the individuals of which are going moth-like through the country as they did in the United States.

" Fancy, the ' Pussyfooters ' even have a Mormon Elder to come over to teach people temperance.

" This Mormon, the adherent to a religion which has canonised Brigham Young, the husband of 27 wives and father of 56 children, has arrived to tell British women the benefits of peaceful Pussyfoot homes.

"It is not generally known, I suppose, that until recently the Mormons sold liquor from their store, Zion Co-operative Mercantile Institute in Salt Lake City, and the Church was the owner of the institute.

LEAVE IT TO THE WOMEN.

"Well, I fancy that the British women will be able to deal with that aspect of the question.

The Globe quotes Tommy Dewar upon his return from America in 1920 "Prohibition has proved a fraud, a delusion, and a snare, and it always has been in any State where it has been tried."

Photo: John Dewar & Sons Archive

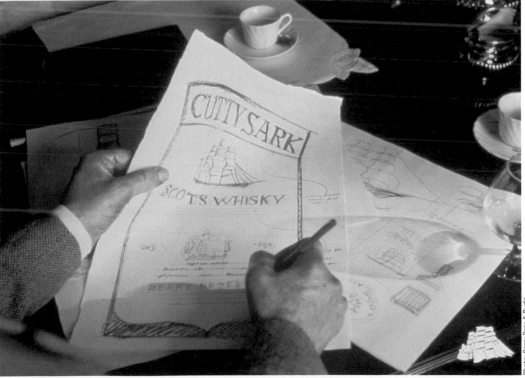

James McBey sketching on what would become the logo of Cutty Sark - a blended Scotch tailormade for the American market

Photo: Berry Bros & Rudd

America, Barclay said nothing, but removed his jacket and shirt to reveal a mass of scars across his back".

Post Repeal

By the time Prohibition was repealed in 1933, or very soon thereafter, the leading Scotch whisky companies appointed agents in the U.S. – often men who had been involved either in bootlegging or on the other side of the fence, supressing the illicit trade.

Berry Bros. appointed the Buckingham Corporation, established in 1933 by Charlie Guttman, a former prohibition officer, and Jay Culhane, an Irish real estate dealer to handle Cutty Sark. When the partners quarrelled four years later, Guttman set up another company, the Paddington Corporation, and obtained the agency from "the other wine merchant in St. James", Justerini & Brooks, who, like Berry Bros., had just created J&B Rare specifically for the U.S. market.

The DCL used a number of distributors, including Joseph Kennedy's Somerset Importers. Joe Kennedy (father of John F. and Bobby) had won an impressive reputation for his selling ability during Prohibition and was now heavily engaged in politics. Among others, he was responsible for selling Dewar's White Label. It is said that within hours of repeal Somerset unloaded substantial quantities of Dewar's in New York, from ships that had been waiting on rum row for Joe's order. The company later held the agencies for Johnnie Walker and Gordon's Gin.

As well as distributing Scotch, a number of Canadian distillers who had made fortunes during Prohibition, turned their attention to buying Scotch whisky brands and distilleries, including 'The Big Three': Hiram Walker, the Seagram Corporation and Schenley Industries. "If there was a turning point in DCL's history", wrote Dr. Ron Wier, "and of the twentieth century Scotch whisky industry, it was 1934. Profits made in the U.S. domestic whisky trade underwrote North American investment in the 'Old Country'".

Hiram Walker Gooderham & Worts, had been created through amalgamation by Harry Hatch, and was, by 1933, the largest distiller in Canada – owner, among other brands, of Canadian Club. In 1935 Hatch bought Ballantine's and Old Smuggler from

The end of Prohibition - the first legal beer cases arrive at the White House in April 1933

Jimmy Barclay, then commissioned him to buy Scotch whisky distilleries. The first two were Miltonduff and Glenburgie. In 1938 Hiram Walker built the largest distillery in Europe, at Dumbarton on the River Clyde.

Harry Hatch's opposite number at Seagram was the redoubtable Sam Bronfman, who preferred to draw a veil over the company's activities during Prohibition: "We loaded a car load of goods, got our cash and shipped it. Of course we knew where it went, but we had no legal proof. And I never went to the other side of the border to count the empty Seagram bottles".

During Prohibition Sam and his brothers had established a grain whisky distillery, and approached DCL for malt fillings to blend a 'Scotch style' Canadian whisky. This led to a collaborative venture, Distillers Corporation of Canada. Post 1933, Seagrams went on a 'rampage of acquisitions', buying distilling companies in the U.S. and Canada, rum distilleries in the West Indies, wineries in California and Venezuela, champagne houses in France, and in 1935 the Glasgow blender Robert Brown Ltd. – the first of many acquisitions in Scotland.

Lew Rosenstiel, founder, chairman and chief stock-holder in Schenley Industries Inc., made a fortune from medicinal alcohol during the 1920s and then bought up all the whisky he could lay his hands on. Within a year of repeal his company had sales of $40 million, and had launched the prominent Canadian whisky Black Velvet. Sam Bronfman proposed to DCL that Schenley join Distillers Corporation, but DCL would hear nothing of this – although Schenley was later appointed agent for Dewar's, and looked towards acquisitions in England and Scotland.

The Boom Years

In January 1940 rationing was introduced to the U.K. and the Ministry of Food cut malt whisky distilling by one-third, in order to preserve barley. The Whisky Association reduced supplies to the Home Market by 20% (increased to 50% in 1941) in order to release more for export, particularly to the U.S.A., so as to improve the U.K. dollar earnings and offset the cost of war materials bought there. In 1940 nearly 7 million proof gallons were shipped to America – 2.2mpg more than in 1939 – a last gasp by overseas agents to secure as much Scotch as

they could before enemy action closed the seaways.

The War Cabinet's decision to give whisky priority in post-war planning was not endorsed by the Labour Government, which was elected in the summer of 1945. Barley was allocated to distillers only on the understanding that three-quarters of the whisky made would be sold in export markets.

Led by America, there was a phenomenal increase in the demand during the 1960s, but it was impossible to meet this. Scotch was now 'the drink of the Free World' – the embodiment of style and fashion, made even more attractive by being in short supply. Stocks of mature whisky remained very low owing to wartime restrictions, and when it was finally taken 'off-quota' in the home market in 1954 (at the same time as food rationing finally ceased), the industry was obliged to continue some form of quota system until 1959.

Although the U.K. remained the largest market, sales were depressed by increases in duty: by 1970 it was twice what it had been in 1960. So export markets were crucial. In 1960 exports to the U.S. stood at 12 million proof gallons; by 1968 it was 33 mpg. Two mpg of Scotch was exported to Italy in 1970, and the amounts to France and Germany were even higher. To meet the current and expected future demand, new distilleries were built and existing distilleries modernised and enlarged. Output of malt whisky doubled during the decade, and stocks under bond rose from 2.2 million litres in 1965 to a staggering 4.5 billion litres in 1975. Fortunately this was mostly taken up by export orders (which tripled between 1960 and 1971, from 23.13 to 70.32 mpg).

North American companies were not slow to see the opportunity, and continued to expand their Scotch whisky interests.

Sam Bronfman attempted to buy Robertson & Baxter in 1947, then switched his attention to Chivas Bros. of Aberdeen, which he acquired in 1950 in a deal arranged by Jimmy Barclay, who also sold him Strathisla Distillery (which he had bought from the receiver for a knock-down price the same year). It was Mr. Sam's avowed intention to make Chivas Regal (which he was himself involved in blending) into "the greatest name in Scotch whisky', and he threw a lot of money behind the brand. One of his colleagues remarked: "This was not just a man

Sam Bronfman, the legendary founder of Seagrams,
played his cards well during Prohibition

Photo: Arthur Schatz/TIME & LIFE Images/Getty Images

Bottling at Hiram Walker's Dumbarton Distillery in the fifties

Photo: Keystone-France/Gamma-Keystone/Getty Images

marketing a new product – it was an artist producing his chef d'oevre".

Hiram Walker bought Glencadam and Scapa Distilleries in 1954, to secure malt whisky fillings, and Pulteney Distillery in 1955. That same year it also developed a method at Dumbarton Distillery, built in 1938, which allowed the production of different styles of spirit from a single still – the Lomond still.

Schenley bought the London distiller, Seager Evans (owner of Strathclyde and Glenugie Distilleries, and Long John blended Scotch) in 1956, built Kinclaith Distillery (in 1957, within Strathclyde Distillery) and Tormore (completed 1960), and bought Black Bottle (1959) and gradually acquired Laphroaig Distillery between 1962 and 1972. By this time sales of Long John had quadrupled in the U.K. alone.

Barton Brands of Chicago took full control

of Littlemill Distillery in 1971; Inver House Distillers was incorporated in 1964 as a subsidiary of Publicker Industries of Philadelphia, and immediately began to convert a mill on the outskirts of Airdrie into a distillery complex making both grain and malt whisky, with the largest maltings in Europe at that time – employing, it is said, 1,000 people in the early 1970s.

The Dark Years

The post-war boom, driven by America – where a taste for Scotch had been nurtured during Prohibition – was equalled only by the 'Whisky Boom' of the 1890s, and like that era, ended in tears.

In the mid-1970s there was a severe economic slump, prompted by an oil crisis and the end of the Vietnam War, which had stimulated the American economy. Sterling fell

The many whisky festivals (here at Whisky Show in London 2010) give evidence to how enthusiasm for whisky has grown dramatically

against the dollar from $2.33 in September 1974 to $1.66 in September 1976 (since 1970 Scotch had been invoiced in dollars).

But production remained at an all-time high: by 1980 the amount of whisky under bond was four times what it had been in 1960. To make matters worse, whisky was no longer as fashionable as it had been during the past two decades, and many consumers were switching to vodka or white rum, or wine. Orders for fillings and mature whisky began to drop, and malt distillers' traditional customer base – the blenders – began to shrink.

The slump in 1975 encouraged feverish amalgamation. Indeed there were rumours in the Stock Market that all independent whisky companies might be taken over. The impetus towards amalgamation came from North America, and from large U.K. brewing groups.

Justerini & Brooks (now part of Independent Distillers & Vintners) went to the English brewers Watney Mann. Long John International was bought by Whitbread and

William Teacher & Sons by Allied Breweries. In 1977 the prestigious The Glenlivet Distillers sold to Seagram, its U.S. distributor and principal customer, while Seagram's old rival, Hiram Walker, attempted to buy Invergordon Distillers, then Highland Distilleries, then sold out to Allied Lyons in 1988.

The Renaissance

These amalgamations drastically narrowed the independent distillers' customer base – the blenders to whom they sold fillings – and encouraged them to seek a way out by promoting their makes as singe malts.

The 'Renaissance' of malt whisky, which began during the 1960s, pioneered by Glenfiddich, The Glenlivet and Glen Grant (in Italy) – all of which were selling over 5,000 cases of single malt per annum by 1970 – has been much written about. Suffice to say that during the 1970s and 80s there was a steady growth in the availability of single malt bottlings.

In 1970 only around thirty makes were available as singles, and many of these in

18

small quantities from independent bottlers, notably Gordon & Macphail. By 1980 this figure had doubled, but sales of single malt still represented less than 1% of the world market for Scotch. That year a symposium of whisky companies estimated that exports of single malts would rise by 8% to 10% per annum in the coming five years. In fact growth was twice that, and continued to remain steady at around 10%.

Demand was driven by consumers. Malt whisky was a new discovery, and quickly generated enthusiasm, even passion, among consumers. Publishers were not short to spot this trend: three times as many books about Scotch whisky were published in the 1970s and 80s than had appeared 1900-1970 – over sixty titles. Newspapers and magazines carried consumer articles about malt whisky, where blended Scotch had always been relegated to the business pages.

The industry responded by making more malts available, sometimes in a range of ages, increasing promotional budgets and making their products more widely available. By the end of the decade around 200 single malts were available (half of them bottled by independents).

During the past twenty years, enthusiasm for malt whisky has grown dramatically all over the world. Double the number of books about the subject have been published (over 120 titles) in the U.K. alone. Magazines dedicated to whisky appear regularly in the U.S.A., U.K., Germany, Switzerland, France, Japan, Russia. Large annual whisky fairs and festivals are now held in over twenty countries. Clubs and societies proliferate, and more recently websites and blogs.

In his introduction to 'New Bottlings' in last year's edition of The Malt Whisky Yearbook, the editor wrote: "It is virtually impossible to list all new bottlings during a year, there are simply too many… In this list we have selected 500."

industry aware for the first time of the crucial importance of other export markets.

2. Post-WWII, whisky (both Scotch and Bourbon) became 'the drink of the free world' – "introduced by Allied troops, and advertised by Hollywood", as one Italian importer told me.

3. In order to meet demand, distilling capacity was dramatically increased, often with the support of American distillers.

4. But this led to a surfeit of whisky by the mid-1970s, when Scotch ceased to be fashionable, and this in turn led to increased amalgamation within the industry, making many distillers nervous about the shrinking number of blenders, their key customers.

5. They found salvation in malt whisky, enthusiastically embraced by consumers around the world, and the halo-effect of this was to introduce (or re-introduce) them to blended Scotch, the backbone of the industry.

Charles MacLean has spent the past twenty-five years researching and writing about Scotch whisky and is one of the leading authorities. He spends his time sharing his knowledge around the world, in articles and publications, lectures and tastings, and on TV and radio. His first book (Scotch Whisky) was published in 1993 and since then he has published nine books on the subject, his most recent being Charles MacLean's Whiskypedia, published in 2009. He was elected a Keeper of the Quaich in 1992, in 1997 Malt Whisky won the Glenfiddich Award and in 2003 A Liquid History won 'Best Drinks Book' in the James Beard Awards.

Conclusion

Is it fanciful to put all this down to Prohibition? Not entirely. The logical steps in my argument are:

1. Prohibition introduced Americans to good Scotch, and following repeal the U.S. soon became the largest export market. It also made the Scotch whisky

Blended Malts

- an entry point to single malts or just a footnote in whisky history

What used to be known as vatted malts enjoyed a triumphant rennaisance during the last decade. Now sales are slipping and the producers seem uncertain which way to go. Gavin D Smith takes a closer look at a whisky category struggling to find its place.

The Scotch Whisky Regulations 2009 (SWR) which came into force on 23 November 2009 declare that "'Blended Malt Scotch Whisky' means a blend of two or more Single Malt Scotch Whiskies that have been distilled at more than one distillery."

The new regulations outlawed official use of the terms 'vatted' malt and 'pure' malt, a move which proved contentious within the Scotch whisky industry. Many people argued that far from enlightening the consumer as to the true nature of the product in question, employment of the word 'blended' in relation to malt whiskies really only served to muddy the waters further.

Opponents to the new terminology argued that many years and much money had been spent in educating drinkers about the difference between a 'blend' and a 'malt,' and now the two terms were being placed side by side.

However, it has also been suggested that some of the opposition was due to concerns that if producers were forced to label their whiskies as 'blended malts' then they would no longer be able to charge single malt prices!

Deliberations regarding the change of name had begun in June 2005, when the Scotch Whisky Association (SWA) circulated a Consultation Document to the industry regarding terminology.

Glen Barclay, Director of Legal Affairs at the SWA says that "As regards 'Vatted Malts', we could find very few labels which bore that description. A wide variety of other descriptions were used, with many products bottled in France in particular being described as 'Pure Malt.' However, the description 'Pure Malt' had been widely used on single malt Scotch whiskies as well. As a result, it was not surprising that consumers were confused as to the different types of Scotch whisky available."

Barclay adds that "The SWA Working Group, which consisted of representatives from a wide variety of companies, debated at length what description should be used for Vatted Malts. The term 'Vatted Malt' was rejected because everyone accepted that it was meaningless to consumers and market research indicated that it was an unattractive description for consumers. A number of other alternatives were considered, but 'Blended Malt Scotch Whisky' was selected." Among the reasons for choosing the term

Glen Barclay, Director of Legal Affairs at SWA

Photo: SWA

was an indication from market research that consumers understood the term 'blend' to mean 'more than one'. In other words, the description 'Blended Malt' would convey to consumers that this was a product containing more than one malt.

Additionally, as Glen Barclay says, "There are two types of 'single' Scotch whisky produced – Single Malts and Single Grains. From these two types of single whisky, three blends can be made, namely Blended Scotch whisky (malt and grain), Blended Malt Scotch Whisky (malt and malt) and Blended Grain Scotch Whisky (grain and grain). There is logic in calling a blend a blend."

The forerunner of blended Scotch

Whether we choose to call it vatted malt, pure malt or blended malt, this genre of Scotch whisky has its origins in the mid-19th century and was effectively the forerunner of blended Scotch whisky. One of the acknowledged 'founding fathers' of blending was Andrew Usher of Edinburgh, and before beginning to combine malt and grain spirit to create blended Scotch, he spent many years vatting together samples of The Glenlivet, one of the most highly-regarded whiskies of the day.

As RJS McDowall wrote in The Whiskies of Scotland (1967), "The blending of whiskies began about 1853 when the firm of Ushers in Edinburgh , who were agents for Smith's Glenlivet whiskies, mixed several, some no doubt better than others, to make Ushers Old Vatted Glenlivet whisky. The idea proba-

bly came from the blenders in France who mix especially old and new brandies. Ushers blending, no doubt, added considerably to the amount of Glenlivet whiskies available and produced a more standardised product."

Although blended malts have become much more visible during the last decade or so, the genre was not entirely swept aside by the rising tide of blended Scotch whisky that commenced in the Usher era. In the 1986 revised version of McDowall's The Whiskies of Scotland, it was noted that John Walker & Sons were selling Cardhu Vatted Malt during the 1890s, and speculating on the raison d'être for vatted malts, the author declared that "It might possibly be a matter of cost. The cheapest whisky is grain whisky, which is rarely drunk on its own. The most expensive is a single malt."

He singled out Strathconan for particular praise – "produced by Buchanan and consisting of four 12 year old malts" – and noted that Gordon & MacPhail have marketed "…high class vatted malts such as Pride of Stathspey 25 years old, Pride of Orkney 12 years old and so on." Others singled out for approval were the 8 year old trio of Mar Lodge, Glen Drummond and Glencoe, along with Glenforres and Glenleven 12 year olds.

However, the author generally took a slightly condescending approach to blended malts, as embodied in his conclusion. "Commercial vatted malts are now here to stay and there seems little doubt they satisfy a need as there is a demand for them. Many will, however, prefer to stay with what they know best – their favourite single malts." Three years earlier, in The Schweppes Guide

to Scotch (1983), Philip Morrice had written tellingly that 'vatted malts' were "…an available option when the entire production of an unspectacular malt has not been sold for blending, and the distiller is doubtful that it will hold its own against very strong competition in the single malt field."

Despite that comment, he also noted that "A good vatted malt has much to commend it, provided the marrying of the malts has been done with care and expertise, since an unhappy combination of single malts can produce an unsatisfactory result.

"Sometimes a particular single malt predominates, as in the case where the proprietor of the whisky distillery does not usually market his malt bottled in single form: an example is Glenforres, which is Edradour malt vatted with one other malt. The number of vatted malts is on the increase as malt whisky takes on a wider appeal, and new brands appear regularly."

Morrice also observed that "Many new [vatted malts] have come on the market recently but have been labeled in such a way as to blur the distinction between single and vatted malts. The Duart Castle label states that it is 'finest single malt Scotch whisky' with Isle of Mull under the name. Tobermory Distillery is the only distillery on the Isle of Mull but there is no obvious connection between it and Duart Castle, which is certainly not a distillery."

This neatly brings us back to where we started out – with confusion and controversy surrounding terminology. The most high profile example of such confusion and controversy actually came in 2003, and was partly responsible for precipitating the Scotch Whisky Association's category-related deliberations.

In that year, Diageo announced that due to increasing demand, particularly from Spain, its Cardhu single malt was in future to be labeled as 'Pure Malt' and was to be a vatting of Cardhu, Glendullan and other Speyside single malts. This initiative became the subject of heated and public debate, with William Grant & Sons Ltd leading opposition to the changes, arguing that maintaining the distillery name, and applying it to a 'vatted' malt, was misleading for consumers and potentially damaging for the reputation of single malts. Ultimately, Diageo backed down, and Cardhu was once again marketed as a single malt in 2006.

Whisky growth in Asia sparked sales of blended malts

Despite the divisions caused by the provisions of the Scotch Whisky Regulations 2009, it seems that most producers and promoters of blended malts are now relatively sanguine about the situation. Susan Colville of niche bottler Wemyss Malts, which focuses on a range of blended malts, along with some single cask bottlings, says that "For the uneducated or novice drinker 'blended malt' can seem confusing. However, if the industry as a whole continues to use the term, then people will get used to it."

At the opposite end of the scale, Diageo occupies the number one spot in terms of global blended malt sales courtesy of its Johnnie Walker Green Label brand, which accounted for over 220,000 cases in 2009.

Dr. Nicholas Morgan, Scotch Knowledge and Heritage Director for Diageo, declares that "Diageo was heavily involved in the new regulations. We support the product descriptions and are happy with the change."

By the time the new terminology came into force, there had been a major expansion of the blended malt category, which, to a large extent, was driven by the growth of markets for Scotch whisky in Asia, and particularly in Taiwan.

Johnnie Walker Green Label dates from 1997, and Nick Morgan says that "Around 10 years ago blended malts took off hugely in Taiwan, at the same time as The Macallan, and they are still extremely vibrant there. Taiwan is a major market for Scotch, but it's not attracted to 'big' whisky flavours like Islays. It's into things like The Macallan, Singleton of Glen Ord – whiskies with very accessible flavour profiles. That is what consumers are looking for."

He notes that "Single malts are very expensive in Taiwan, so having blended malts, which cost less, gave consumers two entry points to the malt market. Green Label was aimed at offering something for people who were comfortable with their favourite blend, but not sure how to get into single malts. It meant you would get the Johnnie

Susan Colville - regional sales manager for Wemyss malts

Walker guarantee of quality but with no big surprises. Single malts tend to be polarised in flavour – light or heavy, smoky, and so on. Johnnie Walker Green Label is right in the middle of our 'flavour map.' It has very wide appeal."

If Johnnie Walker Green Label is an established blended malt which performs well in Taiwan, then Prime Blue is a more recent example of the genre, and one that was created specifically to target that market. Prime Blue is produced by the Suntory subsidiary Morrison Bowmore Distillers Ltd and a spokesperson for the brand says that "The product was developed for Taiwan, to offer premium quality whisky to consumers and was launched in 2004. It targets the mainstream Scotch market and has developed a strong presence today.

"We see Scottish Leader, The Famous Grouse and Matisse Old Blended as our main competitors in Taiwan. According to the

IWSR [International Wine & Spirits Research], Prime Blue is the sixth largest brand in the Taiwanese whisky arena, following Johnnie Walker, The Macallan, Scottish Leader, Famous Grouse and Singleton of Glen Ord."

Prime Blue comes in 12, 17 and 21 year old variants, as well as a version with no age statement, and while around 90 per cent of sales is of the no-age statement variety, the company spokesperson notes that "Taiwanese consumers appreciate age statements, and Prime Blue offers alternatives to customers to satisfy each preference."

According to Diageo's Nick Morgan, "If you want über-flexibility you don't put on an age statement, but if you are pitching your blended malt against single malts, then an age statement helps, because single malts almost invariably carry age statements. In Taiwan you are competing against 10 and 12 year old Macallan, Singleton of Glen Ord, Glenfiddich and so on."

The Famous Grouse 15 year old

Monkey Shoulder

Prime Blue 12 year old

The Famous Grouse currently offers the widest spectrum of age-specific variants, with a non-age statement bottling plus 10, 12, 15, 18, 21 and 30 year old expressions of its blended malt in various markets, with the line up having been introduced in 2004. As with Johnnie Walker, the principal purpose of developing a Famous Grouse blended malt was to allow loyal consumers to move 'up' to malts without leaving the brand.

If blended malts offer an accessible way into malts for many consumers, there are also some obvious advantages for producers, who have far greater freedom when it comes to assembling them.

As Nick Morgan observes, "If you can make your blended malt from a combination of malts – if you are heading for a specific flavour profile – then you can get there in various ways. If you are using, say, eight malts out of an available total of 12 to 15 that suit the flavour profile, you have a guarantee of consistent flavour and you can continue to produce it."

Flexibility is particularly important in the case of smaller bottlers without the 'clout' of major distillers such as Diageo and Chivas Brothers, with their vast inventories of stock. Susan Colville of Wemyss Malts declares that "Blended malts were always the first choice as a result of our experience and background in the wine industry.

"All premium wines, even Bordeaux and Burgundy, are blended together, creating a fine blend. We use this practice in the recipes for the blended malts. We are hand-selecting the best single casks from the Speyside, Highland and Islay categories to create our blended malts, allowing the final result to showcase the best from each region. Blended malts also offer us the consistency that un-named single malts are unable to offer."

Nikka Taketsuru 21 year old   Wemyss Spice King   Matisse 12 year old

Wemyss has three blended malts in its regular line-up, namely Spice King, Peat Chimney and Smooth Gentleman. According to company Managing Director William Wemyss, "Up to sixteen different single malt whiskies are expertly blended together before introducing the 'signature' malts to create three distinct taste profiles: 'Spicy' (Spice King), 'Peaty' (Peat Chimney) and 'Smooth' (Smooth Gentleman).

"For Spice King, our signature malt is from the Highlands, to produce a whisky with rich, full and spicy top notes. For Smooth Gentleman we use a signature malt from Speyside, giving sweet, floral and honeyed top notes and Peat Chimney uses an Islay signature to give top notes of sweet smoke, iodine and peat."

By contrast, Nick Morgan of Diageo says that "There is no 'signature' malt in Johnnie Walker Green Label. There are six to eight single malts in it, including Linkwood, Cragganmore, Caol Ila, and Talisker. Producing a blended malt is a very different piece of work to the complexities of putting together a blend. There are fewer malts and obviously no grain element to integrate, so it's a less complex process for a blender."

Sometimes the 'fewer malts' referred to by Morgan become merely the produce of two distilleries, as in the case of the Japanese blended malt Taketsuru from the Nikka Whisky Distilling Co Ltd. Taketsuru is offered in 12, 17 and 21 year old expressions, and although it comprises only two malts, it effectively contains a far greater range of malt styles, since Nikka's two distilleries, Yoichi and Miyagikyo, were both designed to produce a wide permutation of spirit types. Yoichi continues to use direct-fired stills, fuelled by coal, making both unpeated and peated spirit, while Miyagikyo is equipped with four pairs of pot stills, as well as Coffey stills, which are sometimes used to distil malted barley.

As we have seen, in many instances Asian markets are the principal target for blended malts, but this is not always the case, as evidenced by William Grant & Sons' Monkey Shoulder.

According to Master Blender Brian Kinsman, "The original concept for Monkey Shoulder was the cocktail/mixologist market. We developed a flavour profile that appealed as very mixable, but retained malt credentials. In other words, it is light and fruity without being overly oaky. It was originally

sold just in the UK and only recently have we started to distribute in other international markets."

Sometimes, producers and bottlers are reluctant to divulge the 'palate' of component malts which they use to create their blended malts, but Grants are quite open about the contents of Monkey Shoulder, which they describe as 'Triple Malt,' and which features spirit from the company's three Speyside malt distilleries of Glenfiddich, Balvenie and Kininvie.

More money to be made in single malts and luxury blends

Conversations with most promoters of blended malts produce positive noises about the sector, with several pointing out that the economic devastation wrought on the USA and much of Europe during the past few years has largely by-passed the key Asian markets and duty-free arenas where blended malt sales are strongest.

However, recorded figures tend to show that optimism about blended malts may well be misplaced on a global basis. The 2010 edition of The Scotch Whisky Industry Record reveals volume sales of the leading four blended malts (Johnnie Walker Green Label, Glen Turner, Ballantine's and The Famous Grouse) falling by a total of 31% from 2008 to 2009, though Glen Turner's sales held up relatively well. Green Label's volumes peaked in 2007, by which time The Famous Grouse blended malts were already on the decline.

Scotch Whisky Association figures for the three months to March 2010 claim that blended malts accounted for three million litres of Scotch whisky sales, but in the parallel period for 2011 they comprised just 1.06 million litres; in other words, a dramatic decline of 65%.

Alan Gray is a specialist whisky analyst and author of The Scotch Whisky Industry Record and his personal take on blended malts is instructive. "Blended malts, to my way of thinking, were a relatively short-term development," he claims. "In terms of perception, blended or vatted malts just didn't have the sex appeal of single malts.

"At the time when blended malts were in the ascendency, producers were trying to use up stocks of malt. It was before single malts really took off in such a big way. Now stocks of malt are tight, and producers are holding on to it rather than getting rid of it at almost any price – a practice which had fed the blended malts growth."

Gray adds that "The industry has become more focused on value than previously, and there is now more money to be made in single malts than in blended malts. Taking all categories of Scotch whisky, volume sales fell by 2.3% in 2010 over 2009, but value grew by 12%. Single malts and deluxe blends are doing very well as categories, so why sell blended malts for less than single malts, especially when you need the stock of malts?

"I think the industry has re-focused. In 2007, single malt sales fell by 5%, while blends rose by 31%. By 2010 single malts had risen by 30% on parallel 2009 figures, and blends by nearly 7%. This shows the trend."

Sales volumes of The Famous Grouse 'family' of blended malts have fallen from a peak of 180,000 cases in 2006 to just 30,000 in 2009, leading to speculation that owners The Edrington Group has lacked real commitment to the category in recent years. There is little doubt that The Famous Grouse blended malt has also been 'squeezed' by the growing number of competitors in the sector.

As a result, with the exception of Taiwan, where the non-age statement variant and the 12 year old will remain, Edrington is planning to phase out The Famous Grouse blended malt across all other territories. Marketing energy and expenditure will be focused on The Famous Grouse blend and its Black Grouse and Snow Grouse extensions.

Whether we perceive blended malts to be a 'poor relation' of single malts, lacking their prestige and provenance, or a significant category in its own right, providing value for money and catering for a real consumer need, there look to be hard times ahead.

Perhaps the passage of time will show that the first few years of the 21st century were a golden age for blended malts, which ultimately went back to being little more than a footnote in the long history of Scotch whisky.

Gavin D Smith is one of Scotland's leading whisky writers and Contributing Editor to www.whisky-pages.com He hosts whisky presentations and tastings and produces feature material for a wide range of publications, including Whisky Magazine, The Malt Advocate, Whiskeria, Drinks International *and* Whisky Etc. *He is the author of more than 20 books, including* Whisky, Wit & Wisdom, The A-Z of Whisky, Worts, Worms & Washbacks, The Secret Still, The Whisky Men, Ardbeg: A Peaty Provenance *and* Goodness Nose *(with Richard Paterson). He collaborated with Dominic Roscrow to produce a new edition of the iconic title* Michael Jackson's Malt Whisky Companion *in 2010, and his latest book is* Discovering Scotland's Distilleries. *He is currently working on two new whisky titles. He is a Keeper of the Quaich and lives in the Scottish Borders.*

Tasting notes

Matisse Blended Malt, 12 year old
Sweet and balanced, with caramel, vanilla, orange juice and a wisp of smoke on the nose. Developing molasses. Initially sweet on the palate, slightly nutty, drying to cocoa powder and oak in the medium-length finish.

Johnnie Walker Green Label, 15 year old
A sweet, vanilla and floral nose, vibrant and full-bodied in the mouth, spicy, with gentle smoke from the Talisker and Caol Ila components, and a lingering malty aftertaste. Smooth, sophisticated and well-balanced.

Wemyss Spice King, 8 year old
Initially spicy aromas, ginger, pepper and nutmeg, with a gently smoky background and a whiff of soy sauce. Approachable on the palate, with angelica, Sherry, a tang of Islay and cough syrup. The finish is drying and nutty, with mild peat and oak.

The Famous Grouse Blended Malt, 15 year old
A soft, fragrant and floral nose, with candy floss and sweet sherry notes, plus a pinch of salt. Quite full-bodied, rich and rounded. Stewed fruits, sherry and mild spice, plus a hint of black pepper. Drying to liquorice in the finish.

Prime Blue Blended Malt, 21 year old
Soft fudge and Bramley apples on the nose. Pleasing and distinctive. Robust, yet smooth, with good mouth presence. Sleek sherry notes, spice and almonds. The finish is spicy, with aniseed and liquorice.

Taketsuru Blended Malt, 21 year old
A sweet, rich nose, with figs, sultanas and sherry. Smoky molasses develops, and beyond that, an icing sugar note. Ripe oranges and plums, plus ginger and discreet wood smoke on the palate. Lingering smoke and cinnamon in the finish.

World Whiskies Conference

*Every year hot shots of the global whisky industry
gather from all over the world for a two day summit.
A lot of the things discussed there will have an impact on you
as a whisky lover so why not eavesdrop on what they had to say.
Our guide is of course the Conference Director Ian Buxton.*

As I have reported here before, and regular readers of the Malt Whisky Yearbook will know, I started the World Whiskies Conference in 2006 and act as its Conference Director. It's my job to recruit the speakers, trying always for a varied yet balanced programme; stroke and encourage the vitally important sponsors and even, if time permits, sell a few more delegate tickets: I like to think of myself as the Conference's Master Blender!

So this isn't an impartial report on the 2011 proceedings. Consider it rather as an inside view of an exclusive, senior-level, trade-only event that is rapidly gaining a reputation as the global whisky business summit. As whisky drinkers you're naturally concerned to eavesdrop on what was discussed and learn who was there.

But to begin at the beginning: once again, the Conference this year was a two day session, held on 12-13th April 2011, and once again we returned to Glasgow's Radisson Hotel and Conference Centre. I aimed to design this year's programme to avoid an insular discussion limited to just whisk(e)y but tried to introduce relevant topics and

informative speakers who looked at other categories such as gin and champagne to see what could be learned there. In addition, I looked for speakers who would stimulate and provoke, even at the risk of some controversy. It all makes for good debate!

Build the brand but not through price promotion

"Would you rather be marketing Monkey Nuts or Monkey Shoulder?" asked Steven Sturgeon, addressing delegates as Head of Marketing & Communications for Speedo International. Sturgeon was, of course, better known to the room as the former Marketing Director of William Grant & Sons but at the conclusion of a lively presentation, answered his own question by revealing that he had just returned to the whisky industry as Group Marketing Director for CL World Brands (owners of Bunnahabhain, Tobermory and Black Bottle).

His theme was "To see oursel's as others see us" and, speaking with the benefit of a period of reflection from outside the industry, he warned that the spirits business is "beginning to sell its soul" by relying too heavily on price promotions to gain sales.

Ian Chang - Kavalan´s Master Blender

"As an industry you are beginning to change the way consumers view brands," he told delegates.

Citing Apple as a positive example of how companies can sell branded products without resort to constant cut price offers, Sturgeon continued: "When brands are consistently promoted on price, consumers eventually see the promotional price as the absolute price of the product."

"The UK is the worst example of this. So when as a producer you want to put in a price increase, retailers are simply saying no, we can't do it," he went on. This was part of "the good, the bad and the ugly" face of drinks marketing but, despite this, "appreciating brands" was something Sturgeon believed the whisky business, in general, did well. Strong portfolio management, exemplified by the Johnnie Walker line-up, was an under-valued and under-appreciated asset of the global spirits industry.

But, if brand management was the positive face, Sturgeon was unsparing of the industry's failure to attract the best new talent.

"So far as I can see," he said "the industry is male dominated with little interest in attracting women." There was, he continued, "no reason why the drinks industry should not attract people like P&G and Unilever, but that doesn't seem to be the case." Ouch!

And the industry has lost control of the debate on alcohol abuse, very much "the ugly" side of the drinks industry. "The discussion is led by a media agenda focusing on binge drinking." But it can't be all bad, as he himself admitted when announcing a return to an industry he clearly loves. And that was greeted with a warm round of applause.

Next up was Mark Gorman, Senior V-P for Government Affairs at US industry association DISCUS and, encouragingly, he subtitled his presentation on the US Whisk(e)y Market "On the Path to Economic Recovery".

Whisky of all types, he explained, accounted for 29% of all spirits sales in the USA, some 47 million cases, or $5.6 billion of revenue. Within the overall total, volume was up 1.4% in 2010; 'value brands' declined by 2.0%, premium styles were flat, but there was a strong offsetting performance among high end (5%) and super premium whiskies (8.1%). Within the different categories of whisky, Irish whiskey grew a remarkable 21.5% (Jameson has been a particular success); Single Malt Scotch was up 11.7%; Bourbon and Tennessee whiskies were up 2.5% (with the luxury super premium styles up 16.2%), while Blended Scotch declined 1.4%. The respective category share of market is shown below.

But, by contrast, vodka had grown overall by over 6% and now accounted for 31% of the industry's volumes – a topic that was to be discussed in greater depth later in the day. Tequila also saw an increase ahead of whisky, with a 3.6% volume growth and premium styles particularly successful. In other words, with growth of less than 1.5% whisky lost share and slipped back in comparison to other spirits.

Gorman then turned to the fast-growing

2010 U.S. Whisk(e)y Market

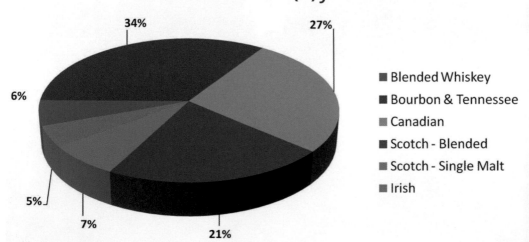

- Blended Whiskey
- Bourbon & Tennessee
- Canadian
- Scotch - Blended
- Scotch - Single Malt
- Irish

34% 27% 6% 5% 7% 21%

phenomenon of craft distilling in the USA with the number of licensed distilleries more than doubling in the past decade from 300 to more than 725. In recognition of the importance of this growth and the dynamism of this sector DISCUS will now admit micro-distillers into its ranks, a significant vote of confidence in this sector and a way for the craft distilling movement to get more attention and respect from Government – something that should be good for the small distillers and their customers alike.

Like Steven Sturgeon before him, Mark Gorman also discussed the adverse effects of alcohol and described the industry's efforts to stay ahead of the debate. Noting that parental influence was by far the most significant factor in under-age drinking (21 being the age for legal consumption in the USA) he also encouraged delegates with the dramatic downward trend in alcohol-related driving fatalities – down 49% in the years since 1982, with particularly encouraging falls in 2008 and 2009.

Has Scotch whisky failed Scotland?

Following this presentation, Donald Blair took on the vexed topic of "Why Scotch has failed Scotland". Donald Blair is a persistent critic of the Scotch whisky industry and its long-term economic performance. Now largely retired, he worked for many years in the industry first with Seagrams/Chivas

Brothers and then with United Distillers/Diageo and was responsible for setting up and running for four years the company that is today Diageo Poland.

His presentation was a detailed and complex one, intended to provide "an evidence-based analysis of the industry's global performance over the last 35 years; a comparison of that global performance compared to global macro-economic indicators and thus an estimate of unrealised economic and employment opportunities within Scotland."

Using independent data from a variety of sources, he presented the "things people don't want you to know". In summary, his argument states that while global Scotch whisky volumes have increased by around 11% in the past 35 years, the global economy has expanded by almost 190% – more than 17 times faster than Scotch whisky during the same period. This under-performance, he argues, has cost Scotland 40,000 jobs and a revenue loss of £4.7 billion every year.

While you may not accept a direct correlation of employment with volumes, it is harder to escape the data on Scotch whisky's performance vs. vodka, and Blair made much of the fact that vodka's growth and global volume now out-stripped Scotch whisky. The chart below makes unpleasant reading for whisky's sales and marketing community.

Global Scotch volumes v. Global Vodka volumes
(million litres of pure alcohol)

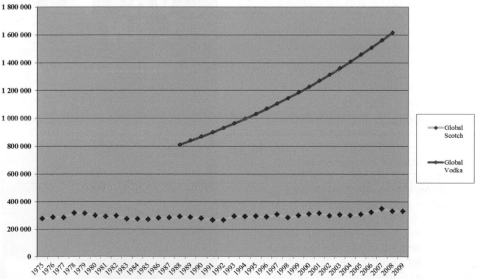

Donald Blair was being critical of the Scotch whisky industry

Photo: World Whiskies Conference

Following on from Donald Blair's provocative end to the opening session, Day 2 of the conference centred around positive developments in world whisky: the opening of Diageo's Roseisle; a progress report from Taiwan on the remarkable Kavalan distillery; discussions on the retail challenges of BRIC markets; new research on whisky innovation and a review of recent trends in social media.

Delegates also debated the whisky industry's PR skills with a media panel of writers (Gavin Smith and myself), bloggers (Neil Ridley of caskstrength.net) and journalists (Rob Allanson, Whisky Magazine and Chris Brook-Carter, Just-Drinks.com) looking to suggest improvements in communication and mutual understanding. The prevailing tone was positive, with the conference concluding on a high note with a witty presentation from AT&T's new media specialist, New York-based David Polinchock featuring live web links and YouTube footage.

A distillery with one million visitors per year

But many delegates were eagerly looking forward to hearing about Kavalan. Established as recently as 2005, the Kavalan

The relentless analysis continued. While vodka had doubled its global volume since 1988 (a compound annual growth rate of 3.5%), the equivalent figure for Scotch whisky was 0.29%. Over the same period, world GDP grew at over 3% and GDP per capita at 1.6%.

In a world that was growing richer Scotch was being left behind, argued Blair, and this was costing Scotland jobs and investment. Government agencies, the Scottish Parliament and the Scotch Whisky Association all simply ignored the statistics, he claimed.

He was heard in what might be described as polite silence. Many delegates seemed either stunned or disbelieving, though there were some energetic exchanges when the time came for questions!

Outside of the conference I have been criticised for giving Mr Blair a platform. However, I do not believe that it was a mistake. If he is wrong then the industry should present the data that shows him to have misunderstood the situation; if he is correct, even partly so, then everyone – including the consumers who love Scotch whisky and care about its future (you, I presume, as you have bought this book) – should be demanding answers and taking action to reverse these trends. Raising these issues is what the World Whiskies Conference is all about.

Distillery in Taiwan is part of the King Car group of companies, who also produce instant noodles, coffee, chewing gum, detergents and insecticides. So why whisky?

Basically, because the company's owner and Chairman Mr T T Lee loves whisky and his country and determined that if Scotland could make whisky, so could his homeland. Master Blender and Head of R&D Ian Chang explained that Kavalan is the name of the tribe indigenous to the land of I-Lan, the county where the distillery is located. Hence the old name of the I-Lan county was also Kavalan: exactly the same as calling your distillery Glenlivet, in fact.

He went on to describe the genesis of the distillery and its rapid development, to the point where in January 2010 its 2 year old single malt came top of a blind tasting in The Times (beating some well-known Scotch single malts). Since the official launch their whiskies have gone on to be very well received as they continue to mature in Taiwan's hot and humid climate. It is thought that 3 to 4 years in Taiwan will be roughly equivalent to 10-12 years in Scotland so while the whisky may mature very quickly we are unlikely to see many great ages ever being offered due to the high rate of evaporation. The distillery has also invested heavily in high quality casks, being advised by their consultant Dr Jim Swan, who also attended the conference.

Ian Chang went on to outline Kavalan's current range which includes a 'standard' single malt; a port finish and two non-chill filtered, naturally coloured, cask strength expressions under the Solist label. The offering will further evolve as stocks age. He also emphasised the educational role played by the more than 1 million annual consumer visits to the distillery, which, to put it in context, is as many visits as all the distilleries in Scotland put together. "But," stressed Chang paying generous tribute to the work of distillery consultant Dr Jim Swan and the inspiration King Car derived from Scotch, "though Kavalan is a good whisky in its own right, we are not here to compete or to copy but to join the community."

Kavalan's whiskies are currently only available in the Far East but they are actively seeking distribution in the UK, EU and North America and it is expected that they will have launched in all three of these major markets by Spring 2012, marking a further step in the development of this exciting new brand and confirming the scale of their ambition. Though Ian Chang was at pains to

The still room at Roseisle Distillery

Nick Morgan from Diageo says his company is making malt whisky for the company's blending team - not for the whisky aficionados

stress that Kavalan wanted to "join the community", with an annual production of close to 4 million litres per annum it may have occurred to more than one delegate that someone will have to move over to make room for this precocious newcomer.

Will Roseisle mean the closure of smaller distilleries?

That someone will not be Diageo. So much was clear from Dr Nick Morgan, the company's Knowledge & Heritage Director, reviewing the opening of the giant Roseisle distillery (at 10 million litres annually, the equivalent of around two and a half Kavalans).

As readers will know there has been a great deal of commentary on blog sites, some of it less than well informed and some downright mischievous as to the potential impact of Roseisle on Diageo's smaller single malt distilleries. Dr Morgan was at great pains to rebut those claims, pointing to Diageo's further investment plans at Caol Ila, Dailuaine and Glen Ord and demonstrating at length the research and analysis behind the planned future expansion of the company's major brands of blended Scotch whisky.

In addition, Diageo has other proposals which would see production capacity increa-

sed at their existing distilleries by over 10 million litres per annum over the next two to three years – the equivalent capacity to another Roseisle – with an investment of around £10 million. The details of these plans are still being developed and will be announced gradually, subject to the relevant planning processes.

"Roseisle is a considered and confident response to the current and predicted growth trends of Scotch," he stated, emphasising that the entire output was required for rapidly growing premium brands such as Johnnie Walker. His message was blunt:

"Diageo is a blended whisky company. Diageo does not make single malts for me to enjoy. We do not make single malts for the aficionado to enjoy. We make single malts for our blending team."

From the sound of it they will shortly be making a lot more and the word amongst industry insiders is that Diageo may even have under-estimated future demand and will consider a further Roseisle-style project.

Discussion of whisky innovation – or the lack of it – might have proved controversial. But the presentation of a unique new survey by Just-Drinks.com for the conference passed off relatively quietly in the hall despite some provocative responses to the questionnaire. Chris Brook-Carter posed the question in the following terms:

Chris Brook-Carter discussed innovation in the whisky business

whisky marketers have to think and work a little bit harder when it comes to innovation."

Mr Brook-Carter did throw out one intriguing suggestion however, remarking cryptically that "Senior figures within the Scotch whisky industry – while wary of going on the record for political reasons – admit to Just-Drinks to having misgivings about the tightness of the current regulations."
Who they are, delegates may have to wait until 2012 to learn!

Could this indicate some future change in industry attitudes – and thus a further round of Scotch whisky legislation? It seems unlikely but would undoubtedly be exciting.

The conference closed for 2011 with a lively discussion of social media, increasingly important in the direct marketing of many whiskies to their consumer 'fans' and a media panel considering the communication between writers and journalists and the industry itself. Despite the apparent danger to the future of print journalism of brands' use of social media to talk direct to the consumer, it was felt that conventional media still lent authority and credibility to the message and that the future remained bright for the 'scribbling classes' (or 'Fourth Estate' as they prefer to be known!).

"The fact that neither Red Stag nor Compass Box's The Spice Tree is permitted under current SWA regulations is at the heart of this debate. Is this a sound means of protecting the identity of a hugely valuable spirits category – or a reactionary check on the sector's innate natural creativity and dynamism?"

The survey showed that Scotch producers certainly rate innovation very highly, with close to 80% of the 500+ respondents considering it a 'high' or 'very high' priority for their business. If that's any indication of what's planned, consumers can expect more new brands and products, more redesigned packaging and more brand extensions from the whisky industry in the next 12 months. Despite the controversy over Compass Box's Spice Tree, many replies to the survey picked this out as a positive example, perhaps inspired by Compass Box's flexible and imaginative response to the initial SWA ruling.

Innovation in the vodka category was seen as better than in whisky but, despite that, the idea of flavoured whiskies, changes in age legislation or the use of alternative raw materials were all comprehensively rejected by the survey. One senior marketer Neil MacDonald, Chivas Brothers' Marketing Director for Malt Whiskies summed it up:

"The Scotch whisky regulations restrict and guide innovation, but they also provide a very clear framework which means that

Keeper of the Quaich and Liveryman of the Worshipful Company of Distillers, Ian Buxton is well-placed to write or talk about whisky, not least because he lives on the site of a former distillery!
Ian began work in the Scotch Whisky industry in 1987 and, since 1991, has run his own strategic marketing consultancy business. In addition, he gives lectures, presentations and tastings and writes regular columns for Whisky Magazine, WhiskyEtc, The Tasting Panel, Malt Advocate and various other titles.
During 2011 he has written or contributed to three new books on whisky: The Famous Grouse Whisky Companion (Ebury, contributor); Cutty Sark: The Making of a Whisky Brand (Birlinn, Editor and contributor) and Glenfarclas 175 (author). He is working on a follow-up to his best-selling 101 Whiskies to Try Before You Die (Hachette).

I Second That Emotion

Many whisky enthusiasts approach their dram almost like a scientist would – with dissection, analysis and evaluation as the key words. What they miss is the emotional side of whisky drinking. Colin Dunn takes us on a different journey where whisky opens up our minds and souls.

The definition of emotion in Merriam - Websters medical dictionary states: *"a conscious mental reaction subjectively experienced as strong feeling usually directed toward a specific object and typically accompanied by physiological and behavioral changes in the body* (compare affect*)."*

My first whisky tasting I attended way back in the eighties, was in London while I was sitting an exam on Wines & Spirits. I, until then, had sampled some whisky as a young man growing up in a seaside town, and mainly I drunk it as a shot, instant gratification that gave me a strange kind of feeling akin to shocking my sense of taste. I had seen older men in the public houses shooting whisky and it seemed that it was a manly drink, to be drunk after indulging in large quantities of ale.

And so to my first ever whisky tasting. The tutor that day talked about the past, the present, and in his view, the future of whisky. He conjured up images of this liquid from its humble beginnings to being drunk by Kings and Queens. His words drew me into his world of *aqua vitae, uisge beatha* or, as he called it, the water of life .

By the time I got to touch and hold the glasses in front of me, and to smell and taste the liquid, I had entered unknown territory. Emotionally and physically I had entered the "zone" of whisky appreciation and I was hooked. I wanted to know more about taste and flavour and I felt like I had taken the first step on what could be a very long journey.

Fast forward into the 21st century and I find myself in front of diverse audiences of people from around the world, from different age groups and sexes, talking and introducing single malt whisky to their palates, many attending (just like me all those years ago) their very first whisky tasting.

Now, when I first got into whisky, single malts were just growing in ascendency and I went to every tasting I could. I tried to learn everything from this small but growing band of whisky ambassadors, until one day I felt that I had the confidence to conduct my own tastings, and that's when the fun really began. I found that it was not enough to have the historical knowledge, I had to find different ways of making the liquid come alive. Tasting and drinking whisky neat was fine but with younger palates in the

Fingal's Cave on the island of Staffa

audiences in front of me, sometimes it was having a negative effect, and before long I was introducing the same whisky in X different ways. With water, with ice, with water and ice, with frozen rocks, in a cocktail, with canapes and even with a whole four course dinner! I was looking to find ways to excite everyone and tasting neat (which in my case is still my favourite way of drinking malts) was not the only way to win people over.

This got me thinking of Henri Cartier-Bresson, the french photographer, considered by many to be the father of photojournalism. He said that when he was working his craft he was a pack of nerves waiting for that perfect "moment" to capture the photograph, and that this feeling grows and grows and then it explodes, like a physical joy, a dance, space and time reunited.

Tasting single malt whisky can be a unique experience, whether singular or with a group. It can give a feeling of complete enjoyment of the senses if explored correctly and in my view whisky is more than just a drink. Often in the tastings I do now, if it's possible, I take the people away from the tasting room, outside into the fresh air and, as a group, we taste malt whisky as a cultural/communal drink and what often happens is that people start talking together, laughing, smiling, and having a different perspective of themselves as individuals, where they are taken away from the expected and enter a part of their psyche that influences their thought, behavior and personality.

I call it getting into their soul. When this happens I can see in their faces that they are experiencing something totally new, a new kind of heightened awareness where sight, sound, touch, smell and taste all come together for that perfect moment that becomes etched in their memory.

In the footsteps of Tennyson and Mendelssohn

Don't get me wrong here, I'm no psycologist, I'm a guy that has fallen for a spirit that is more than just a "drink" and I am lucky enough to be in a profession where I can create something special for people, so, I am always exploring new avenues trying to give a whisky tasting experience.

Last year I was privileged to be asked to host some journalists on a cruise to the Isle of Skye. These chaps were not interested in tasting whisky on the boat, and I had a locker full of Talisker just waiting to be opened and shared. Being in a boat sailing past the islands of Jura, Colonsay and Iona, in the distance, I could see the small uninhabited island of Staffa coming into view and the tides were good enough for the captain to allow me to have 30 minutes on the island, where i could see something I had only read in books – Fingals Cave.

This amazing cave is composed of basalt pillars surrounding the entrance, with the Atlantic ocean ebbing and flowing into the entrance. I had read that on a rough day the ocean crashed into the cave and created a cathedral of noise. I had read about how the great artist J W Turner had painted it after visiting back in 1832, how Felix Mendelssohn had been moved by the place to compose the Hebridean Overture and how Jules Verne, Wordsworth, Tennyson and Keats had all been visitors there.

This is not somewhere where you can turn up. Mother nature can be unkind sometimes and the Western Isles is notorious for changing its weather pattern on a whim, so, if there was a moment, this was my one chance. Three trips in the dinghy done it. We couldn't land right by the cave as it was too rough, but found a little inlet just to the right and climbed over the rocks up a rough path to the top and sat above the cave with a view across the ocean that was mind blowing.

Strong winds added to the excitement as we got into a group, kneeled down and cracked open a bottle of Talisker 10 year old single malt and poured into our glasses. We looked around the island, grass so green that it seemed we were the only people ever to have walked on it. To our left, there were a group of puffins with their brightly covered orange beaks making strange noises.

The sights and the sounds that afternoon added to the moment when we raised our glasses and then held Talisker in our mouths for around 10 seconds. The burnt bonfire smell, the sweet mouthfeel then the red hot chilli pepper explosion that filled our senses as we all lip smacked with big smiles on our faces and hugged each other

Talisker is a whisky that can shake the senses and we had found the perfect place, alone on the top of a Hebridean island thinking of Turner and what he must have thought of this place back in 1832 and what made Mendelssohn transform from his me-

Colin Dunn giving his audience an emotional moment during a Master Class at Whisky Live London 2011

mory into notes for his Hebrides overture. After a few photos taken we climbed down the island and were back in our boat before the tides changed. For that 30 minutes on Staffa and our whisky tasting experience, time had stood still. Some of the guys still have the picture of that moment as their screensaver.

Now, I realise I can't do this everyday! But, wherever I am in my day job as a whisky ambassador I try to give people the best possible opportunity to fall in love with malt whisky.

Recently at Borough Market in London where some of the best gourmet food can be had, I did a tasting with some stallholders pairing up with six different expressions of Talisker. The stall holders joined me on stage in front of around 80 people and they introduced their different foods and we paired with the single malts;

West coast oysters from Wright Brothers drizzled with a splash of Talisker 57° North

Smoked Hebridean scallops and crème fraiche blini from the Hebridean Smoke House paired with Talisker 18

Montgomery cheddar and Streathdon blue cheese from Neal's Yard with Talisker 175th anniversary bottling

St. Lucian cocoa chocolate from Rabot Estate with Talisker Distillers Edition

A cocktail made from Talisker 10, Lillet Blanc and fresh sage

And finally Talisker 25 tasted neat

This was the whisky from Skye's only distillery coming alive. Talisker in HD. Where the core flavour was able to move in a new dimension.

As malt whisky grows in stature, we in the trade have to look at ways of exciting you, the consumer, and with the interest in food at an all time high, it follows that drink plays a huge part also, in the appreciation.

The same applies in the bars, hotels and clubs scattered around the world, malt whisky is being presented and drunk in many different ways and the bartenders play a hugely important part in this. Their language and presentation has never been more important and tasting notes have to express this. I spend a lot of time with bartenders and encourage them to do their own tasting notes, to show off their individuality, because I too am a customer, and nothing pleases me more than to listen to someone who passes on their "message" just like that tutor did for me back at the start of this article. (I'm still on that journey and long may it continue…).

Express yourself!

The taster has a plethora of ways at their disposal when planning on how /when/ where to taste. The unique flavours of many malt whiskies can be brought to life by introducing the palate to added flavours that work in elevating the spirit to a different or higher definition.

This summer I was tasting strawberries, then dipping them in water and then coating the strawberry in black pepper. This elevated the taste to being fruity and spicy. Then I tasted Talisker which in my opinion, has some of same characteristics.

When I gave the "serve" to the small group of people (who were not whisky drinkers), their palate had been primed by the strawberries and pepper and this accentuated the experience and triggered their taste when drinking the whisky.

Some comments were: "that gave me a warm glow", "that really made my mouth tingle" and "that makes me feel happy". Now these comments are not going to get in a magazine but they are real and that, as a starting point, is the best you can expect – an emotional response that uses words they are using themselves.

The group all agreed that this was a great way "in" to experience whisky on a summer's day and while some would say that Talisker is best neat, I believe that time of day, who you are with, and what is at your disposal to shake the spirit into life, is more important.

Personally, my view on tasting notes is that they are important if you are aware on how to nose and taste. I have been to some tastings, with beginners, where the speaker has said to the audience "What do you get?" And everyone looks to the floor in bewilderment, or are afraid to speak in case their words are laughed at by others.

I tend to focus on people at tastings who I can see are "focused" and are willing to listen and learn a new experience. Their eyes give it away that they want to participate in a whisky experience, whether the whisky is neat, with ice/water or any of the other ways that I am introducing at that time. In fact, I often say to people at tastings that I am joining them on the tasting not talking

to them, because I want the experience too!

Let's be frank here, it is hard to engage everyone when tasting whisky but the challenge is to get as many of the people tasting in using their senses in the surroundings available – verbally or tastefully. I did a small tasting for six people recently where we all had to try our favourite whisky and do the tasting note based on someone we liked in literature, instead of the usual notes. I gave my description based on Hunter S Thompson, father of gonzo journalism, a new form of writing that came out in the 1960's where the writer becomes the focal point of the story. Using the opening lines from the cult classic *Fear and Loathing in Las Vegas*, and metamorphosing it into a tasting note for Port Ellen 10th release:

We were somewhere around Port Ellen, on the edge of the Kildalton shoreline, when the whisky began to take hold. I remember saying something like: I feel a bit light-headed. Maybe you should drive.

Suddenly, there was a terrible roar all around us, and the sky was full of what looked like huge bats, all swooping and screeching and diving around the car, and a voice was screaming
" Liquid history boy, liquid history!"

The freedom of expression when writing a tasting note the way you see it reminds me of Voltaire, who said;
"I disapprove of what you say, but I will defend to the death your right to say it."

Colin Dunn has been in the whisky industry since the last century, initially with Morrison Bowmore where he spread the word on Bowmore, Auchentoshan and Glen Garioch, as well as helping to launch the Suntory Japanese whiskies Yamazaki, Hakushu malts and Hibiki blend in the UK market. At Diageo, Colin is whisky ambassador for their malt portfolio, organising training for bartenders and developing the malt category through presentations at exhibitions and festivals for consumers. Colin has been awarded "Class Magazine" Ambassador of the Year and the United Kingdom Bartenders Guild Ambassador of the Year on two separate occasions .

Emotional Notes

WE ASKED THE AUTHOR of *I Second That Emotion*, Colin Dunn, and four other whisky professionals to write their Emotional Tasting Notes for two single malts – Talisker 10 year old and Aberlour a´bunadh batch 35.

The instructions they were given was to distance themselves from the usual descriptions of flavour and instead try to capture the memories and experiences they were reminded of when tasting the whiskies.

Talisker 10yo

The nose evokes childhood memories of doctor's surgeries, Sunday walks in autumn on the coast of Ireland and my father's well-worn tweed jacket.
The palate's combination of warmth and sweet austerity make me think of windy summer excursions on granite cliffs and the honeyed tones call to mind the beehives on a family friend's farm. The finish is the peat fire in a Donegal cottage in winter. The abiding impression is of reassuring comfort in cold conditions.

TIM FORBES
WEB CONTENT EDITOR
THE WHISKY EXCHANGE

Aberlour a'bunadh

Running into a sweetshop; lurking in the kitchen while my mum makes a chocolate cake; my grandmother letting me have a nip of her sherry at Christmas; late summer apple pies in the garden; picnics and parties; church pews and bake sales. The palate is slightly more serious, bringing memories of sweeping leaves in autumn; yet the tingling spices retain a capricious sense of fun.

Talisker 10yo

Takes me back to walking in the winter. Cold crisp morning when you leave can often evolve into harsh icy reality. A hip flask can become freezing quickly but the liquid always warms and soothes damp joints. In the hills you can almost feel the sweet pepperyness working through your body, the salt tang on your lips demanding another wetting from the flask.

ROB ALLANSON
EDITOR
WHISKY MAGAZINE

Aberlour a´bunadh

A few years ago I took a trip to Cuba to look at the tobacco growing process. I walked into one of the rolling halls and was hit with this sweet, earthy smell from the matured leaves. Abunadh takes me there every time. The room filled with chattering and the constant drone of the foreman reading from the daily newspapers; and of course the heady smell of tobacco.

Talisker 10yo

Nickname Auntie Seaside. Sitting on my steps after a long evening. Waves rolling up the beach, glittering in the light of the full moon. A sip at full strength tingles over the tongue. Waves of orange zest and spice. A peaceful promenade. Glowing street lights sparkle from the heavy glass. Salty tang from the sea and the glass. My mood ebbs. A harmonious moment.

ANNABEL MEIKLE
VENUE MANAGER AT THE VAULTS
THE SCOTCH MALT WHISKY SOCIETY

Aberlour a'bunadh

Curled up by the fireside and my dram shines like a burnished chestnut. I think of polished cedar and dark chocolate. Mohair wrapped around my shoulders and velvet on my tongue. Swirls tangle and dance in the glass with water. Thoughts drift to old churches, burning incense, wax candles. Firelight shimmers through the whisky. My own religious experience. A balm.

Talisker 10yo

Growing up in Speyside I never experienced or appreciated west coast whiskies until I met my husband. Talisker reminds me of my in-laws; the long drive which hugs the coastline, walking along the deserted beaches and sharing coastal/maritime drams with friends watching the sun go down.

SUSAN COLVILLE
REGIONAL SALES MANAGER
WEMYSS MALTS

Aberlour a´bunadh

The rolling hills of Speyside and the view of the River Spey meandering through the village of Aberlour remind me that I'm almost home. Abunadh always transports me back to that place, and the rich lushness of Abunadh reminds me of the rich Speyside landscape. It always makes me smile, makes me happy, and gives me a sense of belonging, of being home.

Talisker 10yo

Cornwall. Winter 1961. My father gives me the task of cleaning the fireplace every morning. As I dust up the burnt charcoal ashes and re-start the fire for the coming day, the invisible smoke impacts on my nostrils and registers in my 9 year old head. Cornwall. Winter 2011. I give my father a glass of Talisker and tell him that the smell reminds me of that

COLIN DUNN
MALT WHISKY AMBASSADOR
DIAGEO

time 50 years ago except, this time, it is in a glass, golden and visible and in liquid form, and we smile and toast the past and present.

Aberlour a´bunadh

When I think about A'bunadh I remember the first time tasting it on the banks of the River Spey. There were 6 of us there and it was our first trip to Speyside to learn about this area, known by some as the cradle of Single Malt Whisky distillation One of my colleagues had a hip flask filled with A'bunadh, and handed it around in tiny plastic cups and the taste, aided by a sharp intake of breath, took us all by surprise and we all giggled as if talking in foreign tongues. Tasting this expression again at my desk brings it all back, and I can write down my thoughts in English!

The New Wave of Blenders

*The old masters are retiring
and a new generation of whisky makers
and blenders is emerging. Will the traditions of the
industry be safe in their hands or will Scoth as we
know it change? Dominic Roskrow reports.*

It was one of those glorious whisky moments. One of those snapshots in time which would almost certainly never be repeated, a whisky awards dinner at which virtually all the great and the good of the industry had gathered together under one roof.

Or perhaps that should read 'the grey and the good'. For just about every great distiller or master blender was present, and the ballroom was packed with every bald head, grey hair and male paunch the whisky industry could serve up. To whisky lovers it was a wall to wall champions league of skilled whisky makers. To an outsider, a boozy bunch of old boys at a senior citizens' reunion.

"If the Temperance movement wanted to give the drinks industry a kicking, a well placed bomb under this building would put the whisky business back years," I muttered to a colleague.

"Or you could just wait a few years for the industry to die of natural causes," my colleague replied wryly.

He had a point. On that evening it looked to all intents and purposes as if the Scotch whisky industry had collectively grown old. Not Kentucky old, admittedly, where it's not uncommon for distillers to work in to their 90s. But nevertheless, no doubt bolstered by years of success, it appeared that the industry had allowed itself to pass its natural 'sell by' date. A bit like a successful sports team reluctant to break up a winning team until age forces it to make wholesale changes and replace a large number of players at the same time, so it was that the world of whisky seemed to be heading for mass retirement.

The question on everyone's lips was would the Scotch malt whisky lose valuable ground if it lost a whole generation of whisky makers at the same time? Would the giants of whisky who had worked their way up from the still room be able to successfully pass their legacy on to a new generation who quite possibly learned their trade on a different road – through university lecture rooms and not among the barrels and the barley at the heart of every distillery?

And most importantly, would it ever be possible to replace a generation of whisky makers which includes among others Colin Scott, John Ramsay, David Stewart, Jim Beveridge, Frank McHardy, Jim McEwan, Iain McCallum and Richard Paterson?

The doomsayers thought not. For some time now there have been dark mutterings about the loss of great whisky characters and the emergence of a new generation of potentially geeky and characterless whisky makers who would create increasingly homogeneous and bland styles of whisky. The fear? A general dumbing down in whiskyproduction.

So do the figures add up? Since that dinner some of the old school have retired to the porch, and several more are set to join them. In their place a new wave of younger whisky makers are at the helm. So has it made a difference? Perhaps now is as good a time as any to take stock and see where the kids are taking whisky next.

If you're a traditionalist and one of those people who prefer to look back with nostalgia rather than embrace the future, look away now, because the bad news for you is that whisky is changing.

That, though, might well be where the bad news ends. For even a cursory glance at the resumes of the debutantes suggests that not only are they holding their own in a buoyant innovative and rapidly evolving industry, but they're instrumental to the speed and quality of that evolution. Whisky's changing all right – but for the better. And arguably it's not despite an influx of new faces, it's because of it.

More women become blenders

These are big statements, broad brush strokes covering the entire industry in a liberal coat of optimistic gloss, so let's look more closely at the evidence. Even at a superficial level you don't have to look very deeply. For a starter, a healthy percentage of the new whisky makers and blenders are women.

And then there are the qualifications. University degrees, true, but just look at the subjects covered. Sure Burn Stewart's Kirstie McCallum and Penderyn's Gillian MacDonald have chemistry degrees, but Edrington's Gordon Motion has a post graduate diploma in brewing and distilling and his colleague Kirsteen Campbell, master blender for The Cutty Sark, has a degree in nutrition and food science.

On the face of it, the emphasis on the theoretical aspect of training does little to reassure those that fear that the romance and art of making whisky is being replaced with the science and theory. Talk to any of the new breed of whisky makers, however, and they'll kick that view in to touch straight-away.

On the contrary, they say – a wider education opened several doors but they found their way to distilling, often by chance. While some clearly sought a career in whisky distilling others stumbled upon it, and while distilling is the core skill set for a good proportion, the likes of Jeremy Stephens at Morrison Bowmore, David Fitt at St George's in Norfolk, England, and Gordon Motion come from a beer brewing, and particularly English beer brewing, background.

In fact David Fitt is a classic example of the new generation of distillers who have steered their skills towards distilling rather than pursuing it as a vocational career.

"After working in education and the media in the mid to late 1980s, I went into the wine trade and eventually became a manager of a busy bar in the City of London," he says.

"In 1990 I left London and came to live near Bury St Edmunds in East Anglia where I worked for the Civil Service for 11 years in a variety of management roles. In 2001, I joined the Greene King brewery in Bury St Edmunds and began to learn about bre-

David Fitt, Distillery Manager at St George's Distillery in Norfolk

Photo: English Whisky Company

wing. After six years there I ended up as a Shift Brewer – basically responsible for all brewing and output from the brewery whilst on shift.

"I learned about brewing both in the classroom and on the job. I have to say the on the job experience was invaluable if only for the opportunity to learn from other people who had more experience than me. When I came to St George's, I worked with Iain Henderson for about three months. He taught me about running the stills, what I should and shouldn't do etc. Being totally new to the world of whisky I had the opportunity to question about why certain things were done in particular ways. I don't have a scientific background at all. However, I did have to re-learn some organic chemistry and brewing theory whilst at Greene King."

Gordon Motion at Edrington argues that, if anything, the whisky industry has done more to preserve the traditional apprenticeship of the job than most professions.

"I spent 18 months shadowing the previous assistant when I originally joined the company and then a further two year handover period before John Ramsay retired," he says.

"These periods of handover for a job are probably unheard of in most other industries, which gives a clue to the importance of passing on the knowledge. The science behind production and maturation can be taught but the blending side is still very much hands on and experience."

Cutty Sark's Kirsteen Campbell agrees: "You can learn to an extent the theory in the classroom and from textbooks but there is no better way to learn than from on the job training," she says.

"For me I still am, and I'm enjoying every minute of it. I have been extremely privileged to work alongside very experienced blenders – John Ramsay, Gordon Motion, and Max McFarlane – and to learn from them. It's not a job where you can simply be handed a procedure and told to get on with it."

"Also when I get the chance I enjoy going to the distilleries to appreciate and understand how they produce their own unique spirit. Although making malt whisky follows generally the same process and can be learned from a textbook, no two distilleries are the same and you really need to understand the complexities."

A break with traditions

One of the key differences between the whisky industry when compared to the one that existed a few years ago, is the way it is diversifying and evolving. Whisky companies are prepared to break out from traditional distillery styles and top provide a 'portfolio' of whiskies from one site. Traditional barriers are being broken down and distillers are happy to explore at the very margins of the world of malt. Technological advances have a part top play in this, but so too do a greater understanding of the science of whisky making, particularly in maturation. In this sense, then, a greater understanding of the theory as well as a continued need for the practice, has equipped the new whisky makers for an increasingly complex approach to making whisky.

"Science certainly gives us more opportunity to develop a deeper understanding of the whole distillery and maturation process, but there is still a lot going on in the cask which we don't fully understand," says Brian Kinsman, who is master blender for William Grant & Sons.

"That said, though, while it's true that most blenders today have a scientific background, they still have to work their way through the ranks to gain the necessary experience and sensory skills. The science helps to explain what we smell and aids our understanding of how the maturation process works but there is no substitute for nosing thousands of samples and building up a knowledge bank of the maturing inventory."

Burn Stewart's Kirstie McCallum agrees: "Technological advances add and compliment the existing techniques and knowledge that we already have and can give us more in-depth knowledge of our product," she says. It might help with understanding the analytical or chemical nature of distillation and flavour formation but experience is still vital. Having a scientific background didn't mean I knew any more than the next person about Scotch whisky when I first joined the industry."

The more things change, though, the more they stay the same. As whisky has evolved so have the jobs of whisky maker, master distiller and master blender, and the jobs can mean different things to different distilleries. In some cases the jobs overlap, in others they are separated out. Talk to the new whisky makers and blenders for any length of time and three things become clear – one, that the heart of the job remains sensory evaluation; two, that no two jobs and no two days within the job are the same; and three, that each whisky maker has found a slightly different way of doing the job to suit them.

Photo: © Burn Stewart Distillers

Kirstie McCallum has worked with producers like Diageo, Chivas Bros and Allied Distillers and is now a blender at Burn Stewart Distillers

Suffice to say, if variety's what you're after, you've come to the right place. Here's Kirsteen Campbell's stab at what a day might entail when working on Cutty Sark:

"Whilst my job is now primarily sensory based, previous experience in chemical analysis and knowledge of the production process helps in understanding quality, how to maintain it and how to manipulate and change it when required," she says.

"My role is primarily based in the sample room, where I'm involved in the new make spirit assessment, and mature spirit checks – single casks to be used in blends as well as checks on liquid which has been marrying, and pre and post filtration samples ready for bottling. The role is very varied and has encompassed new product development, work in the still house on flavour quality, training people in sensory assessment, hosting visits to the sample room, and speaking at events about our whiskies and how we produce them."

At the heart of most whisky companies, there are two sides to whisky making – putting together the distillery malts, and mixing those malts with the product of other distilleries and with grain whiskies to create blends. Making a blend and a single malt are two sides of the same coin. Because a single malt requires putting together whiskies from several different cask types the whisky maker is creating a blend with the qualification that only malts are used, all from the home distillery.

"We apply the same principles to whichever whisky we are making," says Gordon Motion. "Malts are more difficult to maintain the consistency as we only have one ingredient to play with. It's all down to the cask selection. Blends, having more ingredients, and usually being on a bigger scale, are more straightforward to keep consistent from batch to batch."

"I like to think my job is to keep blends consistent. The whiskies available to us are ever changing. My job is to make any change in blend make-up as unnoticeable as possible. 'Consistency in an age of change' is a quote from Matthew Gloag, founder of The Famous Grouse, and I'd like to think we stick by that."

Kirsteen Campbell holds a similar view. "The quality elements we consider are the same," she says. "Is the whisky good enough to use? Can we refill the cask with confidence that it will provide maturity to the next batch of spirit? These parameters are equally important in blends and malts."

In many ways the heart of the job of blending is unchanged, but there has been adjustment over the years in the way it is performed now. That said, though, the variations aren't just generational. The

Gordon Motion, Master Blender for The Edrington Group, has lined up a full days work in the lab

Gillian Macdonald, head distiller at Penderyn, carefully selects the next cask to be bottled

evolving nature of the job means that there are anomalies – for instance, there is the somewhat contradictory role reversal where a traditional and supposedly 'old school' master blender such as Richard Paterson has become a larger than life brand ambassador and industry showman, while Sandy Hyslop, the genial and self-effacing master blender at Ballantine's and very much part of the new generation, prefers to tuck himself away deep in his warehouses and do some old fashioned nosing and evaluating.

For the likes of William Grant's Brian Kinsman and Edrington's Gordon Motion, it's not about a trade off between old-fashioned practical skills and newer classroom taught ones, but about time management and meeting the demands of an employer wanting great whisky to sell and the whisky enthusiast who has a thirst for knowledge and wants to find out more from the masters.

"People want the story behind their favourite whisky these days," says Brian Kinsman. "They want to know more about where their Scotch comes from and how it's made, so part of my job now is to be a spokesman and ambassador for Grant's as I travel the world to public speaking events and conduct nosings and tastings with whisky enthusiasts."

Edrington's Gordon Motion says that there is a lot of pressure these days in time spent in the sampling room.

"I've seen a huge amount of innovation since I joined 13 years ago" he says. "And the innovation is no longer confined to the Scotch whisky category and involves gaining knowledge from outside my comfort zone. There's also an increased demand placed on master blenders for brand ambassadorial work. Thirteen years ago it was rare for a master blender to travel and present to the public. Now it's expected."

Consistency and quality

Despite all the changes there are definitely broad principles which all the new blenders most certainly share with their predecessors. They are all adamant that they will not compromise on quality or corners. No matter what their background or their route to their position, they have all learned from the previous generation and acutely aware that their primary role is as caretakers for the future integrity of their brands.

"I don't feel under pressure to maintain company traditions and act as the custodian of a brand because I feel very passionate about maintaining the traditions of both our brands and our industry," says Burn Stewart's Kirstie McCallum.

"The fact that we have a completely natural product that has been produced using the same methods for hundreds of years and is still produced today using the skills and

Kirsteen Campbell was appointed Cutty Sark Master Blender in autumn 2010

Brian Kinsman succeeded his mentor David Stewart in 2009 to become William Grant's sixth Master Blender since 1887

knowledge handed down from generation to generation makes me feel very proud and very privileged to be part of the Scotch whisky industry."

Kirsteen Campbell agrees. "I feel proud to work for Edrington because we have strong brands and good values, so for me there isn't pressure," she says. "I believe in them fully, and so it comes naturally. I enjoy the fact that I am part of the brands, and in particular Cutty Sark."

Even Gillian MacDonald at Penderyn in Wales, the first whisky maker at a fledgling company, feels the weight of history."I think the consistency of quality is ultimately the priority of the blender," she says. "Of course there is an element of pressure in that high standard. But it is also very important. We are integral to the process of making whisky and the success it has."

Perhaps the sense of tradition is even more pronounced in a family firm such as William Grant & Sons, but like the others Brian Kinsman enjoys the challenge rather than feeling pressurised by it. What William Grant & Sons and other whisky producers understand, however, is that tradition counts for so much but there's a need for evolution and progress, too.

"I am given a huge amount of freedom, carefully balanced with respect for the generations that came before me," Brian Kinsman says. "Being a family owned company the shareholders totally understand the value of innovation and the need to push to develop new processes and flavours.

"Tradition is very much part of our heritage. However, we try to bring new ideas and flavours to Scotch whisky drinkers."

You can almost see generations of previous whisky makers nodding approvingly at his words. You know the likes of Colin Scott, David Stewart and John Ramsay would approve. Eggheads, geeks and boffins they may be. But the future looks well and truly safe in their hands.

Dominic Roskrow is a freelance whisky writer. He edits Whiskeria and The Spirits Business and writes for The Malt Advocate, spcialising in World Whisky. He is the business development director for The Whisky Shop chain. He has been writing about drinks for 20 years and has just completed his fifth book on whisky with a sixth due to be published in September 2012. He lives in Norfolk, home of England's first malt whisky distillery, and is married with three children and is one of the few people in the world to be both a Keeper of the Quaich and a Kentucky Colonel.

Around the World in Eighty Drams

Although the product itself is the same in China and Japan as it is in France and the UK, the way Scotch whisky is enjoyed and perceived is very different. This was witnessed by Neil Ridley when he travelled to some of these countries.

Whichever way you look at it, the world is getting smaller. We have entered an age where everything can be done from the comfort of our living rooms, be it shopping, dating or downloading our viewing and listening pleasures, all realised with a couple of clicks on a mouse.

Whisky too, has entered this brand new digital age. The blogs, forums and websites dedicated to the coverage of whisky have helped create a truly international portal for the enthusiast's appreciation of the spirit. But the stark reality is that only a fraction of the online whisky traffic is focussed on what people are actually drinking internationally and how they are drinking it.

Blended whisky accounts for around 93% of global consumption, with single malts registering a token showing of just 7%. Bizarrely, these percentages are undoubtedly reversed when it comes to the attention and column inches lavished on both types of spirit. What it has highlighted is the growth of blended whiskies in new and emerging markets around the world and the growing enthusiasm to consume them in ways that are perhaps perceived as 'unusual' to traditional whisky enthusiasts.

As a whisky drinker and writer living in the UK but frequently travelling internationally, it always strikes me that even though our understanding of the whisky category in Europe is perhaps more acute, we are much more conservative in our approach to consuming and enjoying the spirit.

"If I was to travel somewhere to look for a vibrant Scotch whisky culture, I wouldn't visit the UK," offers Dr Nick Morgan, Scotch Knowledge & Heritage Director at Diageo Malts.

"For reasons that wouldn't surprise anyone, the blended whisky culture here is pretty moribund, with little aspirational sense about it. Plus, a lot of the malt whisky world is over-reverential in the way it views modes of consumption," he continues.

"The perception of whisky around the world has so many different views that the list is almost endless," highlights George Grant, Director of Sales at the Glenfarclas distillery.

"In Scotland it is the national drink, whereas in India it is almost a right or a 'must have' entitlement. In the USA it is seen as something elusive and the drink that signifies that yes… you have 'made it'. But whisky generally around the world is seen as something to aspire to. The image of it as a drink my father used to drink has almost gone."

So with the exception of some of the UK's first-class cocktail bars serving innovative whisky cocktails or reinvigorating timeless classics, it seems we need to look overseas for new ways to enjoy whisky, where it is becoming a thriving – and an unquestionably aspirational drink.

The victory march of the Highball

Despite a reputation for being a deeply conservative nation, Japan perhaps best highlights how whisky has become a highly versatile drink in the Far East and one, which is enjoyed by a diverse demographic. Since the early 1950's, it has been commonplace for the Japanese to enjoy whisky during meal times, in the form of the Mizuwari, (mixed with crystal clear still mineral water) or with soda water and a twist of lemon zest as a Highball. Recent sales of Kakubin, Suntory's highly popular blended whisky noted for its square bottle, confirm the success of this way of serving whisky, with the

Hakushu Highball

brand now selling an astonishing 3 million, 12 bottle cases annually in Japan alone.

"For the past few years, the popularity of the Highball is continuing to contribute to the expansion of the whisky market by a large amount," explains Kazuyuki Takayama, Suntory Whiskies UK Marketing Manager.

"Because the drinker gets the whisky flavour, as well as refreshment from the soda and zest, it is often enjoyed as a first drink instead of beer in Japan. It is not only a way for previous whisky drinkers to renew their love of the drink, it also allows newcomers such as young people and women to have their first experience of drinking whisky."

Dr Nick Morgan highlights the fact that the Highball serve is not just limited to Japanese blended whiskies either.

"On my last visit to Japan, Talisker and Old Parr Highballs were being served, which worked incredibly well, alongside I.W. Harper bourbon Highballs, although the character of the bourbon was a little lost in such a long drink."

This unquenchable thirst for the serve has given rise to 'Highball Towers' being installed in a number of bars across the country, effectively allowing a bartender to serve pints of pre-mixed Highball to customers in the same way as pulling a pint of lager.

To experience this first hand is a strange, if not slightly disconcerting sight. But with Japan's warmer, more humid climate, a freshly served mug of whisky and soda is about as refreshing and enlightening as it gets. Whilst the thought of 'convenience whisky' may not be to everyone's tastes, the Highball Tower serves as a significant development in how whisky is viewed by a country as culturally diverse as Japan.

Another consumer phenomenon in the off-trade sector has been the vast rise in popularity of pre-mixed cans of whisky and soda sold from street-side vending machines and convenience stores. In 2010, over six million, six litre cases were sold and Suntory's Kazuyuki Takayama estimates that this figure will rise to around 10 million cases in the near future.

By way of a stark contrast, Japanese bar culture harks back to a deep-rooted artisanal flair in its approach to the perfect serve of whisky. Learning the art of ice carving is a skill, which takes years to perfect and presents the apprentice bartender with the

Highball Tower in a Japanese bar (top) and the tools required to make the perfect ice ball (bottom)

possibility of easily losing their fingertips, if the strict rules aren't followed.

Takayuki Suzuki, Bar Director at Bar à Vins, based on the 25th floor of the imposing Shiodome Park Hotel in Tokyo has achieved an almost legendary status in Japan for popularising the ice ball, a perfectly spherical piece of ice, hand carved at lightning speed from a large irregular block, using only an razor sharp knife or ice pick. Suzuki-san, or 'Mr Ice' as he is now known in the bar trade has been honing his craft for over 20 years and now one ice ball takes him just over a minute to carve, yet will keep a whisky or cocktail chilled and undiluted for over half an hour, far longer than cubed ice.

"Traditionally, ice was seen as a symbol of power and luxury" explains Suzuki-san "and it is the quality of ice used in Japan, which makes our drinks so unique."

To eliminate the possibility of any cloudiness, the water is first boiled and then frozen over a long period of time. The result is a dazzling crystal clear block, which, by western standards, is hugely expensive. A classic handmade highball in one of Tokyo's many boutique whisky bars won't be cheap, but the sheer effort in carving an ice ball or in some cases, a perfect ice diamond makes the experience something to truly savour.

It is perhaps ironic that the simple whisky/soda mix of a Highball served with premium hand carved ice is now beginning to develop a cult following in the more 'progressive' bars across Europe. But some of Tokyo's more dedicated boutique bars are lightyears ahead still, when it comes to pushing the boundaries of serving whisky.

Bar Hibiya Whisky–S, nestled in the narrow side streets in Tokyo's vibrant Ginza district offers customers a number of hugely entertaining ways to enjoy a whisky – including in a large brandy snifter with a ball of high quality ice cream ('Whiskream') as well as the chance to blend your own unique creation using a rack of different sample test tubes, including light/medium grain whiskies and 3 distinct flavours of malt labelled 'Sherrywood', 'Estery' and 'Malty'. Once the core of your blend is complete, you can add a dash of 'seasoning' from a small decanter of heavily peated whisky or Sugi, an aromatic, cedary influenced whisky.

The experience of creating a personalised blend in front of a skilled Japanese barman is daunting, but one, which is unquestionably adding huge value to the blended whisky category for a new generation of Japanese whisky drinkers.

Enjoy the pleasures of being your own blender

Diageo's Nick Morgan believes there is a lot more to be done to increase the understanding of malt whisky in China

An aspirational drink in China

Japan may well be the Far East's leading light concerning innovative ways of serving whisky, but one only needs to look to China and Korea to see just how the spirit is beginning to grow in stature as an aspirational drink. In South Korea a recent free trade agreement has seen a huge reduction in the taxation levied on imports of Scotch and sales of mainly aged whisky over 12 years old, (such as Diageo's Windsor Premium Blended, usually drink neat or with ice) have seen a significant rise of 43% in a market currently worth £140 million. In China, sales are forecast to double over the next 5 years, with 1.6 million nine-litre cases sold in 2009.

It is undoubtedly a buoyant time for whisky in the Far East but what do consumers actually make of it?

"Although there are some fantastic single malt whisky bars in some of the major cities in China, understanding of the malt whisky category is still fairly non-existent in general," explains Diageo's Dr Nick Morgan.

Sales of blended Scotch whisky in China have risen sharply over the past several years, but there is a wariness from some distillers, as the rapid spikes of growth can often be attributed to periods of intense advertising for certain key brands. The long-term future of whisky in China may well depend on engendering a deeper sense of aspiration into the spirit, which was the key to the success of its biggest rival, Cognac.

"In a number of less mature whisky markets, it is the higher price of Scotch compared to other spirits that make it aspirational," explains Darren Hosie, Asia Pacific Brand Ambassador for Chivas Brothers.

"This would be the case in China, for example where the ability of being able to afford more expensive Scotch whiskies to show-off is very important. This is also the case when it comes to gift giving within business circles."

One of the most common ways to enjoy a blended whisky in China is again as a long drink, but using chilled green tea as the mixer. More often than not, pre-sweetened, bottled green tea is the preferred option and it is a trend, which has also caught on in neighbouring Hong Kong.

Mark Jenner, manager of the Connaught Hotel's Coburg Bar in Mayfair experienced this unique way of drinking whisky on a recent training visit to the former British colony. "Whisky is served with green tea to produce a longer, more fragrant drink, purely because of the debilitating heat and humidity that exists there. In that environment, it is refreshing and restorative. Perhaps it is slightly depressing, but the upside is that at least people are drinking whisky."

So does he feel that more traditional ways of serving whisky will eventually be adopted by the average Chinese drinker?

"It's difficult to tell as whisky is very much still in its infancy there," he explains. "The term 'strong' is often used – perhaps not just in relation to the % ABV, but more from a flavour profile perspective. The conundrum that no one has really been able to answer yet is what Chinese drinkers find unapproachable about whisky. With a recent single malt tasting I was involved with, most people were drinking it neat and were there to 'learn' about the complexities of single malt, but there's definitely a 'Domino Effect' – people need to be pushed a little."

Dr Morgan feels that perhaps exploring the similarities between blended whisky and tea could provide more of an insight into this cultural phenomenon.

"I'm a green tea drinker so the idea of pairing it with whisky is not really that preposterous," he points out. "Given that there are so many synergies between tea and whisky, certainly in the context of blending, it would be an interesting experiment to take single teas of a certain character and either match them to blends that have a particular signature character, or indeed single malts of a certain signature style."

Will this catch on as a favoured way to enjoy whisky in Europe? Unlikely, but it does highlight how whisky has again become an adaptable and versatile spirit. Like the Highball, this unusual serve has caught the attention of a few of London's more adventurous mixologists, including Albert Dule, who recently created a whisky-based cocktail called the 'Tea Clipper' for the Just Oriental restaurant in Mayfair. Using Cutty Sark Original blended whisky, fresh lemon juice, green tea syrup and muddled pears, the fruity notes, combine with the slightly herbal notes of the sweetened green tea, complimenting the light, vanilla/floral notes of the Cutty Sark.

In India, the climate ultimately dictates how and when people consume whisky, but the searing heat hasn't been prohibitive to its popularity. India currently stands as the largest whisky drinking nation in the world, although sales of domestically produced whisky such as McDowell's No.1, Bagpiper and 8pm (made using a high proportion of fermented molasses) far outstrip imports of Scotch. With a younger, more affluent consumer now trading up to premium Scotch brands such as Johnnie Walker Black Label and single malts such as The Macallan, the future looks hugely promising with sales of premium whisky growing by nearly 20% in 2010.

Sandeep Arora, Director of Spiritual Luxury Living Ltd, India's premier luxury spirits company highlights the drinking habits of this upwardly mobile set of new whisky drinkers.

"Scotch blends (drunk with ice and soda) are mostly enjoyed pre-dinner, though some aged blends are also well appreciated post-dinner. Indian dining starts a lot later than Europe and the timings could be at 8pm to midnight depending on the day or occasion, place, etc. Single malts are considered more premium and hence accorded a higher degree of respect, enjoyed with chilled water."

Glenfarclas' George Grant also highlights the nature of the climate in relation to how whisky is enjoyed. "In India, whisky is almost 100% drunk with soda and lots of Ice," he points out. "There is a big educational drive certainly to change this but the weather dictates that drinks like this should be enjoyed as a long drink."

New whisky bars are cropping up, offering pairings with Indian cuisine and more in-depth tastings, highlighting the distinct regionality of Scotch single malts. The popular Highland Nectar bar at the ITC Gardenia hotel in Bengaluru is helping to establish the more traditional ways of appreciating single malt, as well as developing the Indian palate in the direction of whisky cocktails, both of which are very much still in their infancy.

A growing interest in the Baltic

From the warmer climes of India to the Baltic and an altogether different environment. According to the S.W.A, Russia is the world's largest overall spirits market, consuming 275 million nine-litre cases in 2009, of which, domestically produced vodka accounted for 229 million cases. Whilst whisky accounts for only a fraction of this incredible volume, it is widely viewed as an alternative drink to savour, rather than knock back like vodka.

Studies by the Russian Regional and Federal Alcohol Markets Centre, suggest that the female palate might have something to do with the rise in popularity of whisky, strongly indicating that the characterful fla-

Mixing whisky with chilled green tea is a popular drink in China

The Bar W1640 in Kaunas, Lithuania (top) and their favourite whisky drink with ginger beer (bottom)

vour of whisky appealed to women drinkers who dislike the neutrality of domestically produced vodka.

"Whenever we have held tastings in Russia, we experience a higher level of female attendees than anywhere else," points out Gerry Tosh, Head of Brand Ambassador for Highland Park. "They also really know their stuff too."

So does this signify a development in Russian drinking habits?

"I did see whisky in Russia being drunk like tequila shooters with a wedge of Lemon," recalls George Grant, "but thankfully I have never seen that catch on."

Lithuania is perhaps the Baltic's newest whisky market and is already making considerable headway with the country's very first dedicated whisky bar opening its doors late last year. Bar W1640 is a basement-style bar in the heart of the old town area of Kaunas, about an hour's drive from the capital city, Vilnius. The menu, which easily rivals far more established Scottish or London-based whisky bars has been painstakingly researched by the bar's founders, local dance music duo Lauris Lee and Sarunas Karalius, stocking over 150 whiskies from 60 different Scottish & international distilleries, including a range of rare Japanese, American and other European releases.

The bar prides itself on educating its young, affluent drinkers on the hugely varied flavour profile of world whiskies, as well as introducing regular tasting nights and food matching events to the local clientele.

"Whisky drinking is a new culture and trend here," explains Sarunas "which involves quite a young generation. Sometimes it is surprising to see a girl in her mid-twenties enjoying solid Islay malts!"

As well as drinking most of the malts either neat, or with the addition of water, blended whisky is mostly consumed with ice, "but definitely not with soda," Lauris points out. Instead, both the bar's owners are fans of mixing their blends with a firey, highly flavoursome ginger beer, with a dash of Angostura Bitters and a slice of lime.

This particularly warming but refreshing serve is beginning to be one of the most requested ways to enjoy blends such as Cutty Sark, Ballantine's and Black Bottle, especially during the winter months, when the city's temperatures can reach as low as -20°C.

So with all these emerging markets adopting their own new ways to enjoy whisky, does the future look bleak in terms of stimulating our mature and well-seasoned palates in continental Europe? Perhaps not bleak, but certainly one could argue that whisky is in need of a well-earned makeover. Whereas the single malt category has proven itself worthy to attract newer drinkers in their mid-late 20's, looking to 'drink less, but drink better' the future for blended whisky almost certainly needs some critical attention.

The tide is beginning to turn. Progressive blenders like Compass Box's John Glaser are helping to spark the interest of a new, younger generation of drinker, who feel the need to reclaim blended whisky from the stuffy domains of their fathers or grandfathers. Forward thinking retailers Master Of Malt are turning the art of blending over to the consumer, by selling home blending kits, similar to the one I sampled in that wonderful Japanese bar.

And finally, innovative bartenders are starting to push the 'fun button' with blends again.

On a recent visit to Madrid I was served a blended whisky chilled down with frozen coal, the premise being that traditionally at Christmas, the naughtiest children were given lumps of the black stuff instead of a treat. The treat of course, lies in an overly large measure of whisky and you can't help but smile, whilst feeling like a very good (but slightly naughty) boy at the same time.

Now where's that green tea?

Neil Ridley is a regular contributor to Whisky Magazine *and* Imbibe, *and he is also the co-editor of irreverent whisky blog* www.caskstrength.net, *recently nominated for several online awards. As well as being Drinks Editor for* The Chap, *Neil has written articles on whisky and other spirits for* Aston Martin Magazine *and* The Evening Standard, *as well as providing his opinion on tasting panels for the likes of* The Spirits Business *and the* World Whisky Awards.

Irish Whiskey

– a distinctive spirit about to conquer the world

Although the roots of whisky distillation can be traced back to Ireland, the whiskey produced has played second fiddle to Scotch for centuries. Things are changing though as evidenced by Iorwerth Griffiths when he draws the picture of an industry on the move.

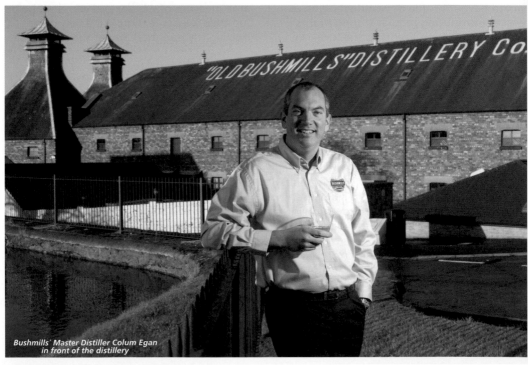

Bushmills' Master Distiller Colum Egan in front of the distillery

In the last few years Irish whiskey has gone from a small niche and largely stagnant category to one of growth and diversity and is now very much a category on the move.

A historic agreement reached in 1966 between the families of the remaining distillers in the Republic of Ireland effectively started the recovery. They put competition aside and amalgamated to form what would become Irish Distillers Group. The only other remaining distiller on the island of Ireland was Northern Ireland's Bushmills and they joined the group in 1972.

To reap the possible rewards of economies of scale, a super distillery was built adjacent to the old Midleton Distillery in County Cork. The New Midleton Distillery would be so versatile that it could make all the different styles that were previously made at the Group's various distilleries. When it opened in 1975, one by one, the remaining distilleries, excepting Bushmills were closed. Other key developments in recent history have been the emergence of the independent Cooley Distillery who burst onto the scene in the late 1980s and redefined Irish whiskey. Also of note is the emergence of the world's largest spirit company, Diageo, into Irish whiskey as the now owners of Bushmills and Wm Grant's purchase of the Tullamore Dew brand.

Irish whiskey sells over 4.5 million cases and overall sales grew by 11% in 2009-2010 making it the most dynamic segment of the global spirits market. Jameson continues to lead the way with double digit growth in five out of the last six years taking the brand beyond the three million case mark. The world's number two Irish whiskey, Tullamore Dew, also grew but only by a third of that achieved by Jameson. It will be interesting to see how William Grant's purchase of the brand will affect such figures in the future. Just behind Jameson in growth terms, if not in absolute sales was an impressive performance by Bushmills – Diageo's work clearly beginning to bear fruit.

There are four main styles of Irish whiskey providing the drinker with a breadth of flavours. Single malt and single grain whiskey would be familiar to the non-Irish whiskey drinker.

A style unique to Ireland is single pot still whiskey with its key feature being a mash-bill of malted and unmalted barley. This developed due to historical reasons – a malt tax was levied on the use of malted barley, therefore some unmalted barley was substituted for malt and a style was born. Other grains can also be used. Pot Still whiskey must be distilled, as one might surmise, in pot stills and is therefore akin to malt whiskey but the difference is in the mashbill.

Finally there is blended whiskey. However, due to the diversity of styles of Irish whiskey there are more permutations to blended whiskey than simply malt and grain. There are also blends of Pot Still and grain as well as Pot Still, malt and grain and even Pot Still and malt.

These styles provide the Irish whiskey drinker with a breadth of flavours from which to choose.

Midleton Distillery

The Pernod Ricard owned Irish Distillers' Midleton Distillery is a necessarily complex place as it was designed to replicate the distillates and whiskey styles of all of the distilleries it was replacing.

The output is triple distilled pot still whiskey and grain whiskey. Malt whiskey can be made but reciprocal agreements with Bushmills mean that very little is actually distilled. Total output is 30 million litres per annum

Pot Still whiskey is made with a proportion of unmalted barley in the region of 50-60% in the mash varying in relation to the quality of the barley rather than the style of whiskey being distilled.

The still house contains four pot stills along one side and two sets of column stills along the other. Different styles of pot still whiskey are made by altering each stage of production.

The wash is typically stronger than an all-malt wash entering the two wash stills at around 10% alcohol. To make light pot still only the stronger portion of the run from the first distillation is collected as low wines, the weaker tails recycled to join incoming wash. For heavy pot still all of the wash is collected and therefore heavier flavour compounds remain in the weaker low wines.

The second distillation takes place in the feints still. For both types of pot still a cut is made to separate off weak feints which are recycled to join a future batch of low wines from the strong feints. The difference at this stage is that the cut for the heavy style will

Midleton stills and Dave Quinn - Master of Whiskey Science at Irish Distillers

be lower. Again, this results in the light pot still being a more refined spirit with fusel oils removed.

The strong feints then go to the spirit still. Here the heads, or strong feints are removed and recycled for a future charge. The cut for light pot still is at a higher strength and narrower than that for heavy pot still. The weak feints from this distillation join future low wines.

Light pot still is characterised by having a delicate, estery and apple fruit aroma, whilst heavy pot still will be more pungent and robustly flavoured.

By altering the parameters at each stage, different types of distillates along the spectrum between light and heavy can be produced as required.

A further complication is that the pot and column stills are linked. This is sometimes used for weak low wines from the first distillation and weak feints from the second and third distillations. They are put through the column stills to produce a small quantity of strong feints for further use in the pot stills.

Triple distillation at Midleton also extends to grain whiskey from the column stills. The wash enters the beer column meeting steam which strips the alcohol from the wash.

Before going to the usual rectifying column there is an extractive column. Boiling water makes its way down this column whilst the high wines flow in the opposite direction. Higher alcohols that are less soluble in water rise upwards and are collected as heads. The other alcohols that are soluble in water drift downwards and are trapped at about 20-25% alcohol.

These proceed to a conventional rectifying column and collected as spirit at 94.5% alcohol. The result is a grain whiskey with a low flavour intensity. Although this is the mainstay of grain whiskey distillation at Midleton, a medium flavoured style is made by altering conditions in the extractive and rectifying columns so that more of the higher alcohols are retained in the final spirit. They also put grain through the pot stills to get yet another style in this most complex of distilleries.

Irish Distillers' wood management regime is one of the best in the industry. Bourbon barrels are the mainstay but Sherry butts make up a significant minority. Such is the importance of Sherry seasoned casks for Midleton whiskeys that bespoke casks are commissioned, air dried and seasoned with Oloroso Sherry at bodegas in Jerez.

Jameson will continue to be the standard bearer for Irish Distillers and, indeed, for Irish whiskey more generally. In 1988 it sold less than half a million cases, most of that in Ireland, it has now broken the three million barrier with a third of sales in the US, the target is an ambitious 10 million. However, the success of Jameson has seen increased attention lavished on their other brands.

Powers, a predominantly domestic brand and single pot still whiskey, a style unique to Irish whiskey and, currently, unique to Irish Distillers, is set to make a big comeback. In 2011 the range was given a makeover and extended, signalling a long awaited reinvigoration of the category.

The first of two new releases is Power's John's Lane 12 Year Old. Slightly confusing in sharing the same age statement as the blended Power's but featuring the name of the original Power's Distillery in Dublin. This is quite a heavy pot still style and very much in the Power's style and is mainly aged in first fill Bourbon wood. The other is Barry Crockett Legacy, named after the current Master Distiller. Although a somewhat lighter pot still whiskey there is a definite wood

presence adding to the character. This has also been aged in first-fill Bourbon wood and rages in age from 10 to 22 years. The aim is that two new single pot still whiskeys will be released annually for the next ten years.

Investment continues apace. A new fermentation plant has been installed and as a result of building a new warehouse each year for the past number of years, they have now run out of space at Midleton. A new site has been commissioned close by for further expansion of warehousing capacity. And they will need it as distillation capacity is being doubled with a second plant, mirroring the current set up, being commissioned that will bring capacity up to 60 million litres per annum.

As well as using Sherry and Bourbon barrels for aging their whiskeys they also use Port pipes, Madeira drums, rum and Marsala casks. It is possible that the whiskeys maturing in them will emerge on to the market is some form in the next few years as might the other whiskey styles they make – malt and grain.

Photo: Irish Distillers

With the huge capacity of Midleton Distillery, it is now wonder the warehouses are filled

Bushmills Distillery

The Bushmills Distillery of today was first registered in 1784 despite the constant references to 1608. In fact that date refers to a license to distil given to Sir Thomas Phillipps covering an area that includes present-day Bushmills. These licenses to distil were sold to local landowners by the Crown in the early seventeenth century for revenue and this gave them a monopoly over making aqua vitae in the area covered by the licence. There is no proof of any connection between Sir Thomas and the present-day Bushmills Distillery.

Bushmills Distillery is owned by Diageo and makes only one kind of whiskey, triple distilled single malt and has a capacity of 4.5 million litres.

Bushmills has four wash stills, noted by the maroon labels on their necks, and six smaller stills with blue labels that are used flexibly for the second and third distillations.

The wash enters the stills and the whole charge is distilled and collected in the weak feints receiver. In the second distillation the first run goes to the strong feints receiver and when the strength drops to about 66%

alcohol the liquid is diverted to the weak feints receiver and awaits the next batch from the wash stills.

The strong feints are distilled a third time with the heads going back to the strong feints receiver and the tails to the weak feints receiver. A narrow cut is taken and becomes Bushmills whiskey in due course.

Due to their heating system the spirit stills cannot be allowed to run dry. When the levels fall to around half capacity they are charged from the weak feints receiver and the result distilled into strong and weak feints. This means that although that particular spirit still may have been doing the third distillation, the drop in the volume of liquid in the still means that a second distillation starts before the third is complete.

Since its takeover by Diageo over £10 million has been spent. This investment has included a new mash tun, a tenth pot still and a new bottling line. On the product front things have been quieter with only re-packaging having happened but 2012 could see some really exciting innovations from Bushmills. The other major plans revolve around maintaining the trend of strong growth in Eastern European markets.

Five of Bushmill Distillery's ten stills

Noel Sweeney - Cooley's Master Blender

Cooley Distillery

The founding of the Cooley Distillery in 1988 has become the stuff of legend. Entrepreneur John Teeling bought an old state potato alcohol distilling plant without ever seeing the site knowing that scrap value alone was worth more than the price. The early years were tough and the fledgling company nearly went out of business and was nearly swallowed whole by Irish Distillers.

From this difficult start the company has flourished and its whiskeys have come to be highly regarded. Finding a route to market remains an issue but the independent Cooley Distillery has managed to find a space for itself between the two giants of Diageo and Pernod Ricard.

Cooley has a grain and malt distillery at Riverstown in County Louth, just south of the border with Northern Ireland.

There are two pot stills on site and most of their work is conventional double distillation. Recently some triple distillation has taken place by collecting low wines from successive distillations and charging the wash still again. The strong feints are then run through the spirit still with the heads and tails being sent back to join the strong feints from the second distillation.

The final spirit is around 72% alcohol as opposed to Cooley's double distilled malt which is weaker at 65-67%.

Grain distillation takes place in a conventional two column Coffey still but as it is made largely of copper it provides a final spirit with more flavour than most grain whiskeys.

A recent innovation has been the Connemara Small Batch Collection featuring limited releases of Connemara, Cooley's peated malt. The first edition was a Sherry finish, currently a heavily peated version – Turf Mor – is available. The next release will be a Belgian Trappist Ale finish. A very limited release Connemara – around three casks – will be Connemara finished in casks with heads made out of Bog Oak, wood preserved in peat bogs.

A big part of the Cooley business plan is the retail own label, or supermarket own brand, trade and Cooley supplies many supermarkets with their own brands.

Cooley have long looked for a business partner to increase their market reach and recently Wm Grant, the Scottish independent whisky distiller were known to be interested but it would seem that things will go no further in this regard.

Currently Cooley are going well with the

The old still at Kilbeggan distillery

distillery running at full capacity. This has created the need for more capital investment to ready the plant for increased production including increased warehousing.

As well as distilling malt and grain whiskey, a recent innovation has been triple distilled pot still whiskey. This will be released as an unaged Poitin at first to provide a glimpse as to the character of the first non-Midleton pot still whiskey since the 1970s.

Kilbeggan Distillery

Cooley also own and operate a second distillery at Kilbeggan in the centre of Ireland. The distillery closed in the 1950s but, luckily, most of the equipment remained in situ until it came into the ownership of the village who operated it as a museum.

From quite early on Cooley matured its whiskey there but, in 2007 an old pot still from the defunct Tullamore Distillery was brought back to life and Kilbeggan distilled again with low wines tankered from their Riverstown plant. A second still, slightly larger was installed in 2009 with the low wines now being triple distilled. Then in 2010 four Oregon pine washbacks and a wooden mash tun were installed making Kilbeggan a fully functioning distillery once again.

Kilbeggan now double distil their own wash with a very slow distillation rate and worm tub condensers. Initially this was single malt. More recently it has been pot still whiskey using the old mash recipe from the Kilbeggan of John Locke's day – malt, unmalted spring barley and oats.

The only whiskey available so far is Kilbeggan Distillery Reserve which was the original double distilled malt and was aged in quarter casks.

Kilbeggan operates as a boutique distillery with innovation as its key focus and the man tasked with this is Alex Chasko from the US and a former brewer bringing a unique perspective. A current experiment is a whiskey made of malted barley and malted rye with Alex tweaking the mash bill aiming for 50:50 if it works.

Rum casks have recently been sourced from Barbados and have malt and grain in them. Also on the cards is unpeated malt finished in Irish stout casks. Brewing malts will feature in future experiments as possibly will beachwood smoked malt.

There is clearly a robust programme of innovation taking place creating much excitement for the future of Irish whiskey.

Tullamore Dew

Until the 1950s Tullamore Dew was distilled at the Daly's Distillery in Tullamore but, as sales of their Irish Mist liqueur grew they contracted whiskey production to the Power's Distillery in Dublin which moved to the Midleton Distillery after its creation by Irish Distillers.

Tullamore Dew is the second biggest selling Irish whiskey in the world. The brand is now owned by William Grants who bought it seeing its undoubted potential and has been immediately earmarked as one of their key brands. Two key pieces of investment are a big advertising campaign and, by summer 2012 the Heritage Centre in Tullamore will have been upgraded to focus on the whiskey.

The brand's main strength is in central and eastern Europe. With Grant's involved, significant growth will be the aim and key potential markets are Asia, South Africa and the US. With things seemingly gone cold in relation to any hook up with Cooley Distillery, earlier medium to long term plans to build their own distillery may well come back on the agenda.

New possibilities

The rejuvenation of Kilbeggan to a fully functional distillery brought the total number of distilleries in Ireland to four. This could be increased again if plans afoot are realised.

In the southwest of Ireland at Dingle in County Kerry there are plans for not one but two distilleries. The Dingle Brewing Company have recently started brewing and are planning to also distil on site.

The other distillers in Dingle are the Porterhouse Brewing Company, owners of a brewery in Dublin and several bars, they are the largest of Ireland's independent craft brewers. They have started by distilling organic gin and vodka with whiskey distilling to start by early 2012. Their plan is to distill Pot Still and single malt whiskeys.

The re-emergence of Belfast on the distilling map is the goal of the Titanic Distillery project. This project is headed by former bus driver turned lottery winner and shrewd investor, Peter Lavery. He already has a whiskey made by Cooley under the Danny Boy label together with the recently launched Titanic whiskey. Currently they are finalising a site for the distillery.

With growth continuing, major investment by all the main players and the possibility of craft distilling, the future of Irish whiskey is looking bright indeed.

Dr Iorwerth Griffiths is a freelance whiskey writer and consultant specialising in Irish whiskey. He has written on the subject for a number of publications including Whisky Magazine *and* Malt Advocate *and hosted tasting events for consumers and the industry. His interests do not stop at whiskey as he has also authored the first ever guide to Irish beer and cider –* Beer and Cider in Ireland: the complete guide – *proving that there's more to life than Guinness.*

A new expression of Tullamore Dew, introduced in summer 2010

from *Barley to Bottle*

the different stages of Malt Whisky production

Barley

Barley (*Hordeum vulgare*) is the fourth most important cereal crop in the world after wheat, maize and rice and it is one of three raw materials needed to produce malt whisky. The other two are water and yeast. Barley is grown all over the world and is mainly used for feeding animals or for producing beer and spirits. The total barley production in Scotland in 2010 was 1.66 million tonnes (of which more than 80% was spring barley and the rest winter barley). The Scottish whisky industry uses about 500,000 tonnes of barley per year and the major part comes from Scottish farms. In 2005, the share grown in Scotland was 90% but it has decreased since then and an increasing share is imported from, e. g. Denmark, Germany, France and Australia not to mention England.

There are two forms of barley that are of interest to producers of beer and whisky: *two-row* and *six-row barley*, with the names alluding to how the kernels are arranged on the plant.

Furthermore, barley can be divided into *spring barley* (planted in spring and harvested in late summer or early autumn) and *winter barley* (planted in autumn and harvested the following autumn).

Finally, through continuous improvement, there are probably over 100,000 different varieties of barley today.

The most common barley for distilling malt whisky is two-row spring barley. This form can be divided into many different varieties, each more or less suitable for whisky production. Until the early 1800s, the traditional *Bere barley*, a six-row variety, was used for making whisky in

Scotland but through plant refinement new kinds with better characteristics were developed. Despite that, both Bruichladdich and Springbank have tried Bere barley for whisky production recently, albeit with mixed results.

In modern times, new varieties were introduced such as Golden Promise in 1966. It was replaced by Prisma and Chariot in the early nineties. The dominating barley strain today is Optic which was introduced in 1995. At its peak it was responsible for two thirds of all distilling barley used in Scotland but is now down to 40%. Recent new varieties include Oxbridge, Belgravia and Publican.

Research is ongoing to find new and better varieties by hybridising and refining existent varieties. The key factors to take into consideration when searching for new varieties are:

• Low percentage of protein content, which is inversely related to the percentage of starch which will be transformed into sugar and finally alcohol. This is measured as *spirit yield* (litres of alcohol/tonne of barley).
A good yield, by today's standards, will be considered to be around 405-420 litres per tonne compared to older varieties with a spirit yield of 380 litres. It depends, however, whether peated or unpeated whisky is produced. Figures will be slightly lower with peated whiskies, as they will when using floor malted barley rather than malt from commercial maltsters.

• Resistance to diseases like mildew, brown rust and leaf spotting.

 • A good capability to germinate, which is a prerequisite for malting.

 • A high yield (from the farmer's point of view) from the fields. The yield of the old variety, Golden Promise, was about two tonnes per acre, whereas Optic produces a yield of three tonnes.

Quite recently experiments have been made using *hull-less barley*, a genetically improved type. Normally the grain is surrounded by a husk, which makes up about 10% of the whole grain, and contains mostly cellulose and lignin. The husk is glumellae which disappear after threshing of hull-less varieties.

By modifying the malting regime for hull-less barley, one does not only shorten the steeping time during the malting, but also reduces germination time, thus saving both time and money. Furthermore, the spirit yield (the amount of spirit obtainable from one ton of barley) increases slightly compared to the traditional barley varieties.

The harvested grain is laboratory-tested when it arrives at the maltings and before the consignment is accepted and brought to the barley store. Thereafter, it is dried by warm air and screened which also functions as purification. It is then cooled to ca 150°C and can subsequently be stored for months before use. The barley is now dormant and it will take several weeks before it wakes up and can germinate.

Malting

Malting is the process during which the barleycorn is modified so that it is possible to extract the sugar in the next step – the *mashing*. This process is used for producing both beer and whisky but when making malt for whisky, low protein barley with a high, starch content is chosen which can be turned into sugar and then alcohol. The largest part of the malt produced in the world is used to make beer while only 3% is used for whisky production.

The barleycorn consists of three parts – the *husk* which is wrapped around a piece of *starch* to which the *embryo* (or germ) is attached. By consuming the starch the embryo will, if not controlled, develop into the roots and shoots of a new barley plant. Malting is all about controlling the germination process.

The harvested barley is dormant between six to sixteen weeks before germination can begin. To determine if the barley is ready a viability test is performed. When the barley has rejuvenated, it is sent to the *steepings* where the barley is immersed in water in order to raise moisture content, so that the germination can begin. Dry barley has a water content of less than 12%. The first steeping water has a temperature of 14-17 degrees and after eight hours the barley has absorbed and contains 32-35% water. At that time the water is drained off and the barley rests in air for 12 hours. Water is, once again, added and finally after another 16 hours the water content has reached the optimal 46% threshold.

During the steeping, a variety of enzymes have become active. *Cytase* starts breaking down the cell walls exposing the starch and *amylase* invades the starch itself, breaking it down into smaller parts. The moist malt is left to germinate either on traditional malting floors or in modern vessels (but more about that later).

The germination process will take about 7-10 days on a malting floor and 2-4 days at modern, commercial maltings. Germination produces heat so at this stage it is vital to turn the barley, so that air is allowed to pass through the grains in order to control temperature. Also, if it is left unturned, the roots tend to grow into each other leaving a rug of entangled grain that can weigh up to 500 tonnes.

During the germination process the enzymes that have been awoken by the steeping continue to do their job, but the germ also starts feeding on the modified starch. In order not to "lose" too much starch, which will then be converted into sugar and in the end alcohol, the maltster needs to terminate the germination at the correct time. This process, known as *kilning*, entails drying the green malt

(as it is now called) with the help of heat.

At this stage, we can take a look at the different types of maltings. The traditional way is *floor malting* where, after steeping, the grain is spread out on a floor made of stone or concrete in a layer 30 cm thick. Two to three times a day for about a week, the green malt has to be turned with shiels (wooden shovels). Thereafter the malt is brought to the kiln where it is spread out on a perforated metal floor. Here it is dried, either directly fired when the smoke from the furnace below passes through the malt bed, or indirectly when heated air passes from a radiator through the malt. The whole process takes between 24 and 48 hours, depending on the size of the kiln and the amount of malt. There are only a handful of distilleries that use this traditional method and when they do, it is generally only for a small part of their requirements.

A peated malt obtains its peaty character during the kilning. *Peat* consists of acidic and decayed vegetation and the place where it has been sourced is important for the character it adds to the finished whisky. Some peat bogs can be up to 10,000 years old and up to 10 metres deep. In the old days, peat was the predominant fuel source of the Highlands. Today it is used to complement other fuels and only to impart flavour to certain whiskies. The smoke from the peat contains *phenols*, of which there are many different kinds; some of the most important are isomeric cresols, xylenols and guaiacol.

The peat is used during the first part of kilning when the green malt has a moisture content of 40-45% and usually stops when the content has reached 18-20%. The kilning then continues until reaching 4% moisture. The content of phenols in malt (or the finished whisky for that matter) is measured in *ppm* (parts per million) of phenols. Commercial maltsters divide their different kinds of peated malt into lightly peated (1-5ppm), medium peated (5-15ppm) and heavily peated (15-50+ppm). The big malting companies actually do not use solid peat at all for their peated malt. Instead, a solution of water and phenols is sprayed on to the barley.

Commercial maltsters use any of three techniques - *Saladin box, Drums* or *SGKV* (Steeping, Germination and Kilning Vessel).

The SGKV, which was developed in the seventies, is the most recent and can process up to 500 tonnes in one batch, performing all the steps in one process.

Saladin boxes can be found at Tamdhu distillery, at Baird's in Inverness, as well as at Crisp in Alloa. They were invented by the Frenchman Charles Saladin in the late 19th century and can handle up to 200 tonnes.

The third method is drum maltings which came into use in the late 1960s. The drums are reliable and easy to use, but have a disadvantage in that only 30 to 50 tonnes of barley can be loaded at a time.

Apart from different varieties of peated and unpeated malt, some distilleries have recently started experimenting with malt types usually developed for the brewing industry - *chocolate malt, roasted malt* and *crystal malt* - adding new flavours to the whisky. From 100 kilos of barley, 80 kilos of malt is produced, and when the malting process is finished, the malt is taken to the mill and then to the mash tun.

Mashing

Before it is possible to start extracting soluble sugars from the malted barley during the mashing, it has to be crushed in a *mill*. The passage from the malt bin leads through a dressing machine where unwanted parts (rootlets etc.) are removed and put into the mill. There are different types of mills but the basic concept is that rollers crack the husks of the barleycorn and grind them to grist.

The most common type is the Porteus two or four roll mill, but some distilleries use a more modern version called Bühler-Miag with up to seven rolls. A few distilleries still use an old but reliable mill called Boby mill. During the milling it is vital that the size of the particles is perfect in order to have an as efficient as possible mashing process.

The requirement depends on the type of mash tun in use and varies between different distilleries. The optimum distribution if one is using a traditional mash tun is 10% *flour*, 70% *grits* and 20% *husk*. With too much flour, the filter in the mash tun can become clogged and with too much husk the water will flow through too quickly. If a lauter mash tun is used, the mash is more shallow (perhaps 0.5-1 metres deep) which gives a quicker drainage and therefore makes it possible to use a finer grind.

The *grist* (as the milled barley malt is called) flows from the mill to the grist hopper where it is stored before taken to the *mash tun*. The latter is a large circular vessel made either of stainless steel or (more uncommon) cast iron. Just one distillery (Glenturret) still uses a wooden mash tun. Most mash tuns are covered with a dome but some that are open are still operated. The sizes vary a great deal, from Glenturret where the mash tun holds 1 tonne of grist, to the giants at

The whole mashing procedure will take about three hours in a modern lauter mash tun and, in the case of Glenfarclas, a batch of 15 tonnes of grist will produce around 75,000 litres of wort. One thing which is important to measure before the fermentation starts is the *Original Gravity (OG)* of the wort, i. e. how rich the wort is in sugars. This will determine the amount of yeast that can be used during the next phase – namely *fermentation*. The density of water at 20 degrees is 1000 and when whisky is produced the OG of the wort will be around 1050.

Glenfarclas;
10 metres in diameter and loaded with 15 tonnes of grist per mash.

The grist is then mashed with hot water in order to extract sugars from the barley. The enzymes, amylase, that were awoken during the malting process, but deactivated during the kilning, now start to transform starch to sugars. Two to five (but usually three) waters are used in the mashing.

The *first water* (which is actually the third water from the previous mashing) is heated to about 65 degrees. The temperature is crucial – if the water is too warm then the enzymes are killed. During the process it is important to keep in mind that certain enzymes are most active at 50 degrees while others are active at higher temperatures.

After the water has been mixed with the grist it is stirred to increase the extraction of sugars. In the olden days this was done manually with large wooden spades. The only distillery which practices that method today is Glenturret.

Today, when talking about *traditional mash tuns*, it refers to the ones where revolving mechanical rakes stir the mash. Many distilleries have switched to the more modern lauter mash tuns commonly used in breweries. In this newer version, a rotating arm is equipped with blades that cut through the mash. Two varieties exist: *semi-lauter* and *full lauter*. In the latter, the knives can be moved not only horizontally, but also vertically. After about 30 minutes the first batch of *wort*, as the mash is now called, is drained off through the perforated floor into the underback or wort receiver.

The *second water* is now filled into the mash tun, this time heated to anywhere between 70 and 85 degrees, depending on the distillery's different preferences. The same procedure follows and the wort is drained off after 30 minutes. By this time, 90% of the starches have been converted into fermentable sugars, but there is still some soluble starch left in the mash and, in order to make use of it, a *third water* is added. The temperature of this water will typically vary between 80 and 95 degrees and after 15 minutes it is drained off. Since this water only contains about 1% sugar, it should not be mixed with the wort already collected, so it is pumped to the hot water tank to be used as part of the first water in the next mashing.

The resulting residue in the mash tun is now called *draff*, consisting of husks and spent grains, which is collected, processed and used for cattle feed. Sometimes it is mixed with the *pot ale* from the distillation and transformed into pellets, so called *dark grains*. Before the collected wort in the wort receiver goes into the washbacks for fermentation, the temperature has to be reduced to 18-20 degrees, otherwise the yeast would be destroyed.

Fermentation

The part of the whisky production when sugar is transformed into alcohol is called the *fermentation*. From the mash tun, where the enzyme amylase breaks down the starch into maltose sugar (almost 50% of the wort), the wort is pumped through a heat exchanger to the *washbacks*. Reducing the heat of the wort to around 20 degrees is essential. If the wort is too hot, the yeast will be destroyed in the next step.

The washbacks, where the fermentation takes place, are large vats, traditionally made of wood but nowadays often made of stainless steel. Wooden washbacks, usually made of larch or Oregon pine, are more difficult to clean, but supporters claim that the wood has a positive effect on the wash. Others say that the material of the washbacks is irrelevant and prefer the efficiency of the stainless steel washbacks. One thing is true though: few distilleries today dare change the material of their washbacks for fear of changing the established character of their whisky. The size of the washbacks can vary between 1,000 and 70,000 litres and they are usually filled two-thirds full.

Now the yeast goes into the wort to start transforming the sugar into alcohol. The process is often described as yeast cells feeding frantically on sugar, which is not entirely correct. During the first (aerobic) phase, the yeast cells reproduce and, in order to do so, they assimilate free, dissolved oxygen from the wort. As the oxygen is reduced and the carbon dioxide increased, the environment becomes anaerobic and hostile to the yeast cells. They need more oxygen and now get this from the sugar molecules. The resultant by-products contain even more carbon dioxide, alcohol and various congeners.

Unlike beer production, the making of malt whisky is not a sterile process. In the mash there will be a variety of wild yeast and bacteria, which will influence the flavour of the spirit. The magnitude of this influence depends on the fermentation time, what kind of distiller's yeast is used and if the washbacks are made of wood or stainless steel. The wooden washbacks are virtually impossible to rid 100% of the bacteria.

All sugar has been utilised after roughly 48 hours and the yeast cells sink to the bottom. The third fermentation then takes place caused by the different bacteria, mainly lactic acid ones, in the wort which no longer face competition from the yeast. The pH decreases and many new congeners are created and the ones present are enhanced. This is called a *malolactic fermentation*. If allowed to ferment for too long, the pH can become too low and the wash destroyed.

So the final result after 48 to 120 hours of fermentation is actually an ale without hops and with an alcohol content between 5 and 8%. Approximately 85% of the solids in the wash have been converted into alcohol and the remaining 15% goes with the wash to the wash still for the first distillation.

Until the early seventies, there was only one type of yeast available, namely *Brewer's Yeast*. Not only did this yeast transform sugar into alcohol, but by being less efficient than modern yeast strains, it also left some sugar and esters in the wash, thus contributing to the flavour of the whisky.

In search of a more efficient yeast strain which could give a higher alcohol content, some producers came up with the cultivated *Distiller's Yeast*. It gave a better financial yield, but there were worries that it would affect the taste of the whisky too much. Since 2005, Brewer's Yeast has not been available outside the brewing industry, so even if the distilling industry would have wanted to, there was no turning back. This is the reason why a lot of research has gone into finding a substitute for Brewer's Yeast that can be used, if not by itself, then in combination with Distiller's Yeast. Yeast is used either in a dried or compressed state or as a liquid (slurry) and the major part of yeast for distilling today comes from two large food companies, Kerry Group and AB Mauri (an affiliate of Associated British Foods).

A great deal of the final character of the new make spirit is determined during fermentation. Some say that 60% is due to fermentation and 40% to distillation. Please note that this is the character of the new make spirit and not the matured whisky. For the latter, the wood and the casks are of the utmost importance. Factors to take into consideration are fermentation time, temperature and alcohol strength of the finished wash. Some distilleries have practised short fermentation times for years, but to suddenly cut down on the fermentation time in order to produce more spirit could easily backfire. The malolactic fermentation, important to create certain congeners, will be shorter and this could also have an impact on the character of the spirit. Some advocates are of the opinion that a fermentation time of at least 60 hours is necessary in order to achieve complexity.

Wash Still

With the exception of Auchentoshan and Hazelburn which both are *triple distilled* and Springbank, Benrinnes and Mortlach, all of which are partially triple distilled, Scottish malt distilleries all practise *double distillation*. This means there are two stills usually working in pairs: a *wash still* and a *spirit still*.

The stills are made of copper which is of the utmost importance. The reaction between the copper and the spirit will reduce any unwanted impurities in the spirit and the more copper contact there is the cleaner the spirit will be. Therefore one could argue that distillers always aim for as much copper contact as possible in order to get as pure spirit as possible. This, however, is not true. In these impurities are also congeners that give each whisky its distinctive taste, so if you are known to produce a full-bodied, powerful spirit you will want to keep more congeners, as opposed to a distillery known for its light and clean whisky.

From the washbacks, where the fermentation has taken place, the (often pre-heated) wash is pumped into the wash still. Thereafter the wash starts to warm up and the first of two distillations commences.

There are different ways of heating the still. The commonest method today is through indirect heating by steam. The steam, which has been heated by either oil or gas, is transported into the bottom of the still by steam coils. The steam coils are, in their turn, connected to round steam kettles, rectangular steam pans or steam plates which heat the wash.

A few distilleries still use the old way of heating the stills by burning an open flame under the still. Glenfiddich has 28 stills, some of them direct-fired by a gas flame, at Glenfarclas all six stills are directly fired by gas and, finally, at Springbank, the wash still is directly fired using oil but also has steam coils installed.

One disadvantage with direct firing is that solids will have a tendency to stick to the bottom and burn, thus affecting the taste of the spirit. To deal with that, a *rummager* is installed at the inside bottom of the kettle. Basically it is a copper chain that revolves, scraping off solids before they burn.

When the temperature in the still has reached 95 degrees, the alcohol will rise as vapours to the top of the still, but before we go into what happens next, let's have a look at the different shapes of the pot stills.

71

There are three main types:

Onion still (traditional still) - as the name indicates, shaped like an onion

Boiling ball still (reflux bulge still) - with a bulb fitted between the pot and the neck

Lantern still - with a narrow "waist" between pot and neck

Within these three groups there is a plethora of variations with wide or narrow necks, long or short necks and with the lyne arm (the copper pipe leading from the top of the neck to the condenser) inclined at various angles.

The reason for having different shapes as well as sizes, is that the shape decides how much copper contact the spirit will have and also how much reflux is obtained when distilling. *Reflux* is the term used for re-distillation of the spirit vapours. If there are tall or narrow necks or a lyne arm that is angled upwards, the result will be that a large portion of the heavier spirit vapours will not make it to the condenser in the first try, but will instead go down to the bottom of the still to be distilled once more. This process will give a lighter spirit.

The boiling ball still will add more copper contact to the spirit and often results in a less heavy spirit than the onion still. The lantern still also adds more copper contact due to its often wide neck and the narrow waist also reduces the risk of the wash frothing and rising up the neck. If the wash cannot be stopped from frothing (or "boiling over") and reaches the condenser, the distillation will be wasted. To avoid frothing (which only appears in the wash still during the first distillation) anywhere between 60 and 80% of the full capacity of the still should be charged. There is a sight glass on the side of the neck to monitor

if the level is rising and then the temperature has to be lowered.

Once the spirit vapours have made their way through the neck and down the lyne arm, they are condensed into liquid and gathered in the low wines and feints receiver. Low wines collected correspond to one third of the wash still charge and the strength is slightly over 20%. When it is pumped to the low wines & feints receiver it is mixed with the foreshots and feints (read more about that under spirit still, below) from the previous distillation in the spirits still. This will raise the alcohol strength to 28% which is extremely important for the next distillation. If the spirit still would have been charged with just the low wines at 20%, the alcohol strength would never reach more than 60% from the spirit still which is too low for the spirit to fractionate, i. e. it would not be possible to collect all the congeners needed to create whisky. When the strength is raised to 28%, it means the distillate from the spirit still will reach the desired 70% in its turn.

Spirit Still

After the spirit from the wash still has been collected in the *low wines & feints receiver*, it is pumped through the low wines charger into the *spirit still*.

At the beginning of the second distillation, the strength of the spirit is around 28%. After a while, when the temperature of the still has increased, the strength will have reached 82%. The risk of frothing that prevails during the first distillation is minimal during the second distillation due to the fact that no carbon dioxide is left in the low wines. On the other hand, it is more important during the second distillation to keep a close watch on the temperature. A high temperature will lessen the reflux and bring heavy congeners through the neck and the lyne arm to the condenser. Depending on the desired character of the spirit, this can result in an unwanted taste.

Traditionally the spirit vapours were condensed using a *worm tub*. This is a large tub, 3 to 5 metres deep, made of wood or cast iron and placed outside the still house. Inside the tub, which is filled with water, is a copper spiral which sometimes measures up to 120 metres long.

The spirit flows through it and is cooled by the surrounding water. Worm tubs are still in use at 13 distilleries.

A more modern cooling device, placed at the end of the lyne arm, is called a *shell and tube condenser*. This is a wide copper tube with a number of smaller copper pipes on the inside, through which cold water flows condensing the surrounding vapours.

The *spirit safe* is divided into two parts - the wash safe and the spirit safe. All of the low wines, distilled in the wash still, are collected into one glass bowl with a hole in the bottom. The spirit from the spirit still, on the other hand, is divided into three fractions - *foreshot, middle cut* and *feints*. The stream of these three parts of the spirit run is directed by a pipe that can be moved to any of two glass containers with openings at the bottom. Traditionally it was the stillman's job to switch the handle but, nowadays, it is often done by computers.

The first part of the run, called the fore-shots and which takes 15-30 minutes, has a high percentage of impurities and unwanted congeners and would have damaged the final spirit if collected. So this part, with an alcoholic strength of 75-80%, goes back to the low wines & feints receiver to be re-distilled.

The next fraction, the middle cut, is the part which will be saved for maturation. This part of the run, which goes into the intermediate spirit receiver, contains up to 100 different aromatic esters that will give the spirit its fruity and fragrant character. After a while, the esters start to decrease and the feints increase.

The feints (the third part) are pleasant to start with and necessary in the spirit. After a while, though, the feints change into a variety of unpleasant aromas and this is where the stillman (or the computer) stops the middle cut and turns the pipe to the first glass container in the spirit safe. Just like the foreshots, the feints are directed to the low wines & feints receiver to become a part of the next distillation.

So, it is obvious that determining the start and end of the middle cut is crucial. To ascertain this, hydrometers are used to measure alcohol strength. Depending on what character one is aiming for in the final whisky, the length of the middle cut differs from distillery to distillery. If a fruity and flowery whisky is desired, the stillman will start collecting the middle cut at around 75% and stop at perhaps 68%. Others, looking for a heavier, more pungent spirit, will start at 70% and will not stop until 60% or even lower. During the middle cut, it is important to run the still as slowly as possible in order to increase the reflux and this will typically take somewhere between two and three hours.

The middle cut is often called the *new make* (the proper term is BPS, British Plain Spirit) and has an alcohol strength of around 70%. The new make is finally pumped from the intermediate spirit receiver to the spirit vat, where the spirit from several distillations is mixed to even out the differences. The spirit vat is placed in the filling store which is the last step before the spirit goes into casks.

Before we go on to Maturation, just a few words on another type of still frequently mentioned in the "*Distilleries around the globe*" section of this book. It is often called *Holstein still*, after one of the biggest manufacturers, but there are other companies producing the same type of still; Christian Carl and Vendome for example. Basically it is a copper pot with a *rectification column* attached to the top. The column is equipped with a number of different plates which, by creating reflux, force parts of the spirit vapours to be re-distilled before entering up the column again and finally cooled into liquid. Normally this type of still is used for distilling eaux de vie and similar spirits but it is, in central Europe and in the US in particular, also used for whisky production. This type of still comes in many shapes and sizes and with a number of plates ranging from two up to over 40.

Maturation

Prior to being filled into the casks for maturation, the new make spirit is diluted and, until recently, the majority of the industry followed the rule that 63.5% was the optimal strength. One argument was that at a higher alcohol strength, maturation would take longer and the formation of certain congeners which would give the final whisky its character, was made difficult. However, this routine has started to change and several producers now fill at a higher strength or even without diluting. The main reason for this is a saving in the number of casks and, thus, warehouse space.

Also, many producers have not followed this routine for all of their production during the years. That is why one can sometimes find cask strength bottlings that are more than 20 years old, but still have an alcohol strength of more than 60%. If it had been filled at 63.5%, two decades of evaporation would have brought the strength down

to somewhere below 50% at the least.

The evaporation we are talking about here is what is generally called the *Angel's Share*. The yearly evaporation in Scotland is around 1.5-2%. Oak is a semi-porous material and alcohol, as well as water, will evaporate during maturation. The rate depends very much on the temperature of the warehouse. Higher temperature means a higher degree of evaporation. The air humidity also plays an important role. High humidity surrounding the cask means that water evaporation is less, which in its turn means that the alcohol is reduced in relation to the amount of water, thus creating a lower alcohol content from year to year. This is the case in Scotland with its high humidity, especially in the winter.

In other places, for example southern

USA, temperature is high and humidity low, so more water than alcohol will be lost from evaporation and this may result in the alcohol strength growing higher during maturation.

Oak & Casks

The importance of the wood for the final character of the whisky cannot be underestimated! It is often claimed that up to 60-80% of the whisky's flavour depends on the cask.

After diluting, the spirit is filled into wooden casks and, according to the Scotch Whisky Act of 1988, it has to be oak to be allowed to be called Scotch whisky. Sometimes different types of wood are used in other parts of the world and there have been occasional experiments in Scotland in the old days with casks made of for example chestnut.

There are more than 400 different kinds of oak in the genus *Quercus* (200 in the USA alone) but only three that are of major interest to the distilleries, all of them belonging to the category white oak:

Pedunculate Oak or English Oak (*Quercus robur*)

Sessile Oak or Durmast Oak (*Quercus petraea*)

American White Oak (*Quercus alba*)

The first two grow in Europe and the last, obviously, in North America, particularly in Arkansas, Kentucky, Missouri and Tennessee. American White Oak is often preferred because it brings in better revenue.

The trees grow faster and it is tighter grained which means it can be sawn rather than split by an axe. This also re-sults in less wasted wood. The European Oak on the other hand, is more porous which means that whisky is lost at a higher speed, but the increased oxidization can often be of benefit during the maturation. European Oak also contains more tannin whereas American Oak has a higher content of vanillin, both contributing to the flavour of the whisky.

A fourth variety of oak which has become increasingly interesting is Japanese Oak (*Quercus mongolica*) or Mizunara Oak as it is also known. Sherry casks were difficult to get hold of just after the second World War and several Japanese distilleries filled whisky into casks of this indigenous oak. They were not fully satisfied with the wood's ability to hold the spirit, so when sherry casks once again became available, these were preferred. Decades later, however, it was discovered that the whisky that had matured in Japanese Oak had a unique sandal or cedar flavour and now most of the distilleries in Japan have started using Japanese Oak again, at least to some extent.

Scotland. The other alternative was to import empty bourbon barrels from the USA. By law, bourbon has to be matured in new, charred oak casks so there was always a good supply to be had from across the Atlantic.

There are about 18 million casks of whisky maturing in Scotland and 95% of these are made of American Oak with 300,000 new casks being shipped every year from the USA to Scotland.

It is important to understand that it really is not the sherry or bourbon itself that affects the oak when speaking of sherry versus bourbon casks and the impact the various type have on the flavour of the whisky.

With just a few exceptions, the spirit destined to become whisky is always filled into a cask that has once held spirit or wine. If it was to be filled into new or virgin oak casks, one needs to be very careful that the wood does not overpower the whisky.

Bourbon, sherry or any other previous filling will soften the oak and help degrade the polymers in the wood into flavour compounds. Basically, it can be said that it conditions the wood. Obviously, a bourbon with its high alcohol content will affect the oak differently than a lower-alcohol sherry or wine. The different levels of alcohol will simply extract or transform different kinds of compounds. If comparing an American Oak cask and a European Oak cask, both having been previously filled with sherry, it will be noticed that the two casks contribute very different flavours to the whisky.

American Oak will, for example, provide a vanilla and coconut flavour while European oak contributes with rich fruits and tannins. This being said, with very short maturations or so called finishes (see more about that below), the character of sherry, bourbon or any other previous wine and spirit will influence the flavour of the final product

The oak's importance for the maturation of whisky can be divided into three parts: subtractive, additive and interactive.

The *subtractive* part is about breaking down and removing especially sulphury compounds in the spirit. Actually, it is not the oak itself doing this job but rather carbon derived from the toasting or charring of the inside of the cask. In order to put the cask together, the oak staves are heated to the point where they obtain a toasted character. For a bourbon cask, however, that is not enough. After the cask has been put together, the inside is exposed to an open flame and the walls are charred to a depth of about one to three millimetres. An American bourbon cask will therefore be more efficient in reducing the sulphur in the spirit.

The *additive* mechanism is about lending both flavour and colour to the spirit. From the wood oils, acids, sugar and esters are extracted which all, to a varying degree, affect the flavour. Another addition to the flavour, at least for shorter maturations or finishes, comes not from the oak itself, but from whichever wine or spirit was in the cask previously (sherry, bourbon, Port etc). Depending on how many times a cask has been used, the effect on the colour will differ. The tannin in the wood also influences the colour and European Oak, being more tannic than American Oak, results in a darker colour.

The *interactive* process is yet the least understood of the three maturation elements. Evaporation and oxidation (when oxygen replaces the evaporated water and alcohol) is one part and this eliminates harshness

and adds complexity to the spirit. But interaction also means oak and spirit together creating compounds that were not present from the beginning. While the first of the two maturation processes are active during the first couple of years, the interactive part will continue during the entire time of maturation and is also very dependent on how the cask is stored (temperature, humidity, atmospheric pressure).

In the olden days, the distilleries would fill their spirit into any wooden cask that they could find because the cask was merely seen as a transport vessel. In the late 1800s, a new regime came into being when distillers started using empty sherry casks from Spain. Huge amounts of sherry were imported to England and casks were cheap. In the mid 1900s, though, the demand for sherry, at least in the UK, had diminished substantially and the producers had to look for other solutions. One was to make their own casks in Spain and lend them to the sherry bodegas for a few years and then bring them to

Blending & Bottling

If we disregard single cask bottlings, which is what the name indicates; one single cask of whisky bottled and almost always at cask strength, all Scotch whisky can be considered blended - also single malts. Blended in this case means two or more casks vatted together before bottling. The process varies considerably among producers and whether it is blended Scotch or single malt, but the basics remain as follows;

Different casks are blended together in big vats where filtered air passes through the whisky to make the blending proper. This is called *rousing*. The whisky is then diluted using de-mineralised water to the appropriate bottling strength, but never below the legal minimum of 40%. Before the next step, which is colouring, the vatted whisky is sometimes left to "marry". The time varies but can sometimes take up to 12 weeks.

Colouring of the whisky is obtained by using caramel (E150). At least among whisky aficionados this step is controversial. Some producers will perform it while others don't, and sometimes the one and the same producer chooses to colour parts of the range and not interfere with others. The reason for colouring is to obtain a consistency between batches and, as opponents to the procedure emphasize, to make the whisky look older. Those against this process state that the caramel will affect the taste.

After the caramel has been added, the whisky is again roused for 10-15 minutes. The next step is *filtering*. Any solids derived from the cask are filtered away using mechanical filters. *Chill filtration* is an extended type of filtering, which is as debated as colouring. This means that the whisky is chilled to anywhere between -4°C and 2°C which will make it turbid. The cloudiness consists of, among other things, various fatty acids, which get caught in the different filters that the whisky will pass through afterwards.

The reason for chill filtering whisky is to avoid the liquid (when the strength is brought down below 46%) becoming less clear if the consumer adds water to it or drinks it with ice, i. e. purely out of a cosmetical regard.

The controversy over chill filtration is due to the fact that during the process, various congeners and esters that might add to the flavour of the whisky, will get caught in the filters as well. To what degree this happens, depends on the temperature of the chilling and also of the filters' sizes and the speed with which the whisky flows through the filters. Independent bottlers rarely chill filter their whisky and several producers have also decided to go for unchill filtered whisky for all, or parts of their production.

After chill filtration the whisky is finally bottled. As previously mentioned, this is the standard procedure when blending and bottling, but the details will vary hugely from producer to producer and from product to product. In recent years, the lack of colouring and chill filtration, have become strong marketing arguments, at least for those producers aiming for the dedicated whisky drinkers.

During the last two decades, new types of casks have entered the scene, besides bourbon and sherry. Today, it is quite common to find whisky that has matured in Port pipes, Madeira casks, rum casks or casks that have held different kinds of wine. In some cases the spirit has been in the same cask for the whole period of maturation, but more frequent is that the whisky is re-racked from a bourbon or sherry cask to obtain a final maturation of a few months or a couple of years in a second cask. There are different terms for this procedure - finishing, enhancing, acing - which aims to give the whisky an added flavour profile.

Casks are also categorised depending on how many times they have been used. The first time a cask is used for maturing whisky, it is called *first-fill*, then comes *second-fill* and from the third filling it is often simply called *re-fill*. A first-fill cask has to be handled with great care when blending the whisky, as the oak and/or previous spirit or wine will sometimes dominate the whisky character. Second-fill and third-fill contribute less and are therefore easier to use in a blend or to sell as a single cask whisky (with no blending). After each filling, most bourbon casks are rejuvenated, which means that a thin layer is shaved off on the inside and then the wood is re-charred, i. e. burnt with a flame to create a carbon surface. Sherry casks are often toasted and sometimes seasoned with new sherry.

Malt distilleries
of Scotland and Ireland

On the following pages, 128 Scottish and Irish distilleries are described in detail. Most are active, while some are mothballed, decommissioned or demolished.

Long since closed distilleries from which whisky is very rare or practically unobtainable are described at the end together with four new and upcoming distilleries.

Japanese malt whisky distilleries are covered on pp. 218-225 and distilleries in other countries on pp. 226-257.

Distilleries that are about to be built or have not left the planning phase yet are treated in the part The Whisky Year That Was (pp. 258-271).

Explanations

Owner:
Name of the owning company, sometimes with the parent company within brackets.

Region/district:
There are four formal malt whisky regions in Scotland today; the Highlands, the Lowlands, Islay and Campbeltown. Where useful we mention a location within a region e.g. Speyside, Orkney, Northern Highlands etc.

Founded:
The year in which the distillery was founded is usually considered as when construction began. The year is rarely the same year in which the distillery was licensed.

Status:
The status of the distillery's production. Active, mothballed (temporarily closed), closed (but most of the equipment still present), dismantled (the equipment is gone but part of or all of the buildings remain even if they are used for other purposes) and demolished.

Visitor centre:
The letters (vc) after status indicate that the distillery has a visitor centre. Many distilleries accept visitors despite not having a visitor centre. It can be worthwhile making an enquiry.

Address:
The distillery´s address.

Tel:
This is generally to the visitor centre, but can also be to the main office.

website:
The distillery's (or in some cases the owner's) website.

Capacity:
The current production capacity expressed in litres of pure alcohol (LPA).

History:
The chronology focuses on the official history of the distillery and independent bottlings are only listed in exceptional cases. They can be found in the text bodies instead.

Tasting notes:
For all the Scottish and Irish distilleries that are not permanently closed we present tasting notes of what, in most cases, can be called the core expression (mainly their best selling 10 or 12 year old).

We have tried to provide notes for official bottlings but in those cases where we have not been able to obtain them, we have turned to independent bottlers.

The whiskies have been tasted by *Gavin D Smith* (GS) and *Dominic Roskrow* (DR), well-known and eperienced whisky profiles who, i.a., where assigned to write the 6th edition of Michael Jackson´s Malt Whisky Companion.

There are also tasting notes for japanese malts and these have been prepared by Chris Bunting.

All notes have been prepared especially for Malt Whisky Yearbook 2011.

Brief distillery glossary

A number of terms occur throughout the distillery directory and are briefly explained here. We can recommend for example *A to Z of Whisky* by Gavin D Smith for more detailed explanations.

Blended malt
A type of whisky where two or more single malts are blended together. The term was introduced a few years ago by SWA to replace the previous term vatted malt. The term is controversial as those who oppose the use of it are of the opinion that it can be confused with 'blended whisky' where malt and grain is blended.

Cask strength
It has become increasingly common in recent times to bottle malt whisky straight from the cask without reducing the alcohol contents to 40, 43 or 46%. A cask strength can be anything between 40 to 65% depending on how long the cask has been matured.

Chill-filtering
A method used for removing unwanted particles and, especially used to prevent the whisky from appearing turbid when water is added. Some producers believe that flavour is affected and therefore avoid chill-filtering.

Continuous still
A type of still used when making grain whisky. The still allows for continuous distillation and re-distillation. Can also be called column still, patent still or Coffey still.

Cooling
The spirit vapours from the stills are cooled into liquids usually by a shell and tube condenser, but an older method (worm tubs) is still in use at some distilleries.

Dark grains
The draff and pot ale from the distillation process is used for making fodder pellets, so-called dark grains.

Drum maltings
The malting method used on all major malting sites today.

Dunnage warehouse
Also called traditional warehouse. The walls are made of stone and the floors of earth. The casks (up to three) are piled on top of each other.

Floor maltings
The traditional method of malting the barley on large wooden floors. This method is only used by a handful of distilleries today.

Lyne arm
The lyne arm leads the spirit vapours from the wash or spirit still to the condenser. The angle of the lyne arm has great significance for reflux and the final character of the whisky.

Mash tun
The procedure after the malt has been milled into grist is called the mashing. The mash tun is usually made of cast iron or stainless steel, but can sometimes be made of wood. The grist is mixed with hot water in order to release the sugars in the barley. The result is the wort which is drawn off through a perforated floor into the underback. The mashed grains in the mash tun are called draff and are then used for making animal feed.

Pagoda roof
A roof shaped as a pagoda which was built over the kiln to lead the smoke away from the drying peat. The pagoda roof was invented by the famous architect Charles Doig. These days pagoda roofs provide mainly aesthetical value as the majority of distilleries usually buy their malt elsewhere.

Peat
A soil layer consisting of plants which have mouldered. Used as fuel in drying the green malts when a more or less peaty whisky is to be produced. In other cases the kiln is usually heated by oil or gas.

PPM
Abbreviation for Parts Per Million. This is used to show the amount of phenols in the peated malt. Peated Islay whisky usually uses malt with 40-60 ppm, which is reduced to 10-20 ppm in the new make spirit.

Purifier
A device used in conjunction with the lyne arm which cools heavier alcohols and lead them back to the still. A handful of distilleries use this technique to make a lighter and cleaner spirit.

Racked warehouse
A modern warehouse with temperature control and built-in shelves. Casks can be stored up to a height of 12.

Reflux
When the heavier vapours in the still are cooled and fall back into the still as liquids. The amount of reflux obtained depends on the shape of the still and the angle of the lyne arm. A distillation process with high reflux gives a lighter, more delicate spirit while a small amount of reflux gives a more robust and flavour-rich whisky.

Saladin box
A method of malting barley which replaced floor maltings. It was invented by the Frenchman Charles Saladin in the late 19th century and was introduced in Scottish distilleries in the 1950s. The only distillery using the method today is Tamdhu.

Shell and tube condenser
The most common method for cooling the spirit vapours. It is a wide copper tube attached to the lyne arm of the still. Cold water is led through a number of smaller copper pipes and cools the surrounding vapours.

Spirit still
The second still, usually a little smaller that the wash still. The low wines are collected in the spirit still for redistilling. Alcohol increases to 64-68% and unwanted impurities disappear. It is only the middle fraction of the distillate (the cut or the heart) which is utilized.

Vatted malt
See blended malt.

Washback
Large tubs of stainless steel or wood in which fermentation takes place. Yeast is added to the worts and the sugars change into alcohol. The result is a wash with an alcoholic content of 6-8% which is then used for distillation.

Wash still
The first and usually largest of the stills. The wash is heated to the boiling point and the alcohol is vaporized. The spirit vapours are cooled in a condenser and the result is low wines with an alcohol content of c 21%.

Worm tub
An older method for cooling the spirit vapours in connection with distilling. This method is still used in approximately ten distilleries. The worm tub consists of a long, spiral-shaped copper pipe which is submerged in water in a large wooden tub, usually outdoors. The spirit vapours are led through the copper spiral so they can condense.

Aberlour

Owner: **Region/district:**
Chivas Brothers Ltd   Speyside
(Pernod Ricard)

Founded: **Status:**   **Capacity:**
1826   Active (vc)   3 700 000 litres

Address: Aberlour, Banffshire AB38 9PJ

Tel: **website:**
01340 881249   www.aberlour.com

History:
1826 – James Gordon and Peter Weir found the first Aberlour Distillery.

1827 – Peter Weir withdraws and James Gordon continues alone.

1879 – A fire devastates most of the distillery. The local banker James Fleming constructs a new distillery a few kilometres upstream the Spey river.

1892 – The distillery is sold to Robert Thorne & Sons Ltd who expands it.

1898 – Another fire rages and almost totally destroys the distillery. The architect Charles Doig is called in to design the new facilities.

1921 – Robert Thorne & Sons Ltd sells Aberlour to a brewery, W. H. Holt & Sons.

1945 – S. Campbell & Sons Ltd buys the distillery.

1962 – Aberlour terminates floor malting.

1973 – Number of stills are increased from two to four.

1975 – Pernod Ricard buys Campbell Distilleries.

2000 – Aberlour a'bunadh is launched. A limited 30 year old cask strength is released.

2001 – Pernod Ricard buys Chivas Brothers from Seagrams and merges Chivas Brothers and Campbell Distilleries under the brand Chivas Brothers.

2002 – A new, modernized visitor centre is inaugurated in August.

2008 – The 18 year old is also introduced outside France.

Aberlour 12 year old

GS – The nose offers brown sugar, honey and sherry, with a hint of grapefruit citrus. The palate is sweet, with buttery caramel, maple syrup and eating apples. Liquorice, peppery oak and mild smoke in the finish.

DR – The nose combines horse chestnut casing then sweet melon and fresh spearmint, the taste is beautifully fresh and clean, with mint and gentle fruit.

There is always a risk in having the greater part of sales on a single market. Glen Grant, number one single malt in Italy, noticed this when the Italian market dipped. In the same way, sales of Aberlour went down 20% during 2009 when the recession hit their biggest market, France. The French turned to the cheaper blended whiskies instead. Only a year later, however, things turned around and the single malt sector in France went up by an incredible 130% and Aberlour was back on track with more than 60% of the volumes going to France.

Aberlour distillery lies on the outskirts of the town with the same name and the first building you see from the road is the 5-star visitor centre. Only around 6,000 visitors come every year, but Aberlour was one of the first distilleries to start concentrating on exclusive quality tours instead of catering to the masses.

The distillery is equipped with one 12 tonnes semi-lauter mash tun, six stainless steel washbacks (painted white) and two pairs of stills. One of the wash stills was replaced in June 2011. There are five warehouses on site (three racked and two dunnage) but only two racked, holding a total of 27,000 casks, are used for maturation. About half of the production is used for single malts. The packaging of the whole range was upgraded in 2010 to achieve a more consistent look and also to include more information on production and maturation of the different expressions.

The core range of Aberlour includes a *10 year old* (sherry/bourbon), a *12 year old Double Cask* matured, a *16 year old Double Cask* matured, an *18 year old* and *a'bunadh*, of which there are 35 batches launched up to and including spring of 2011. In France, a *10 year old Sherry Cask Finish* and the *15 year Cuvée Marie d'Ecosse* are available. Two 'exclusives' are available for the duty free market – *12 year old sherry matured* and *15 year old Double Cask matured*.

12 years old

Meet the Manager

STUART PIRIE
OPERATIONS MANAGER, ABERLOUR, GLENALLACHIE
AND SCAPA DISTILLERIES

When did you start working in the whisky business and when did you start at Aberlour?

I started work in the whisky industry at Glenburgie Distillery in 1974 and I started at Aberlour in 2009.

Had you been working in other lines of business before whisky?

After I left school I worked in a bank for a couple of years.

What kind of education or training do you have?

After leaving school with a number of Highers and a handful of "O" grades I joined a local bank. I then started work in the whisky industry as a "trainee" which was a hands-on training in all aspects of the malt whisky production process and the supervision of those processes.

Describe your career in the whisky business.

I started work in the whisky industry with Hiram Walker & Sons at Glenburgie Distillery in 1974. I moved to be assistant brewer at Miltonduff Distillery and then to Scapa Distillery as brewer and eventually manager. Hiram Walker were taken over by the company that eventually became Allied Distillers and I moved to be manager at Imperial Distillery and then manager at Miltonduff Distillery. I also had several years working as planning manager and business support manager for the malt distillery group. I then became Operations Manager with responsibility for all production and warehousing operations for the Allied Distillers Malt distillery group. Following the Chivas takeover of Allied Distillers I have the role of Operations manager for three distilleries – Aberlour, Glenallachie and Scapa.

What are your main tasks as a manager?

To ensure that the required quantity and quality of new make spirit is produced while meeting or exceeding the standards / targets set by the company and regulatory bodies.

What are the biggest challenges of being a distillery manager?

Achieving the above.

What would be the worst that could go wrong in the production process?

Fire is probably a distillers worst nightmare.

How would you describe the character of Aberlour single malt?

To me Aberlour is everything you would expect from a Speyside single malt – light, fruity and sweet with a complex finish.

What are the main features in the process at Aberlour, contributing to this character?

The malt and yeast are the same used at several distilleries. The excellent quality of the process spring water is only used at Aberlour and the stills are unique to Aberlour all of which will impact the character of the whisky. In maturation the quality of the casks is of great importance weather it be 1st fill ex bourbon casks or ex sherry butts, only the best quality casks are used for Aberlour.

What is your favourite expression of Aberlour and why?

My favourite expression of Aberlour is the 16 year old. The mix of whisky from 1st fill bourbon casks and quality ex sherry casks produces a dram of superb distinction which retains the light sweetness from the bourbon cask and adds the heavier fruit flavours with a hint of spice from the sherry casks.

If it were your decision alone – what new expression of Aberlour would you like to see released?

I would like to see Aberlour matured in a 1st fill peated cask for 16 years.

If you had to choose a favourite dram other than Aberlour, what would that be?

The one I would drink at home is Scapa.

What are the biggest changes you have seen the past 10 years in your profession?

There have been a number of changes but probably the biggest change I have seen is the numbers of audits, both internal company audits and external regulatory audits.

Do you see any major changes in the next 10 years to come?

I see even greater regulation, particularly regarding environmental issues.

Do you have any special interests/hobbies that you pursue?

My ever increasing family seem to take up more and more of my time, however I love going for long walks with the dog and squeezing in the odd game of golf.

Your are not only responsible for Aberlour distillery but also Scapa on Orkney and Glenallachie. What are the main differences between the distillation process at the different distilleries and the character of the spirit?

Aberlour and Glenallachie are less than a mile apart "as the crow flies". Although the processes and raw materials are similar at both sites the new make spirits are quite different. Aberlour is light, sweet, fruity with a hint of blackcurrant. Glenallachie is less sweet and fruity with more robust flavours. The distilleries have different process water supplies and different size stills and condensers which impact on flavour.

Scapa Distillery on Orkney produces a very non typical island malt whisky, it is light, sweet, fruity with a slightly dry salty finish. The fermentation time at Scapa is very long, up to 160 hours. The Lomond type wash still and purifier at Scapa encourage greater reflux in the distillation process which translates in the lightness of the final product.

Aberfeldy

Owner:
John Dewar & Sons
(Bacardi)

Region/district:
Eastern Highlands

Founded: **Status:**
1896   Active (vc)

Capacity:
3 500 000 litres

Address: Aberfeldy, Perthshire PH15 2EB

Tel:
01887 822010 (vc)

website:
www.dewarswow.com

History:
1896 – John and Tommy Dewar embark on the construction of the distillery, a stone's throw from the old Pitilie distillery which was active from 1825 to 1867. Their objective is to produce a single malt for their blended whisky - White Label.

1898 – Production starts in November.

1917-19 – The distillery closes.

1925 – Distillers Company Limited (DCL) takes over.

1972 – Reconstruction takes place, the floor maltings is closed and the two stills are increased to four.

1991 – The first official bottling is a 15 year old in the Flora & Fauna series.

1998 – Bacardi buys John Dewar & Sons from Diageo at a price of £1,150 million.

2000 – A visitor centre opens and a 25 year old is released.

2005 – A 21 year old is launched in October, replacing the 25 year old.

2009 – Two 18 year old single casks are released.

2010 – A 19 year old single cask, exclusive to France, is released.

2011 – A 14 year old single cask is released.

Aberfeldy 12 year old
GS – Sweet, with honeycombs, breakfast cereal and stewed fruits on the nose. Inviting and warming. Mouth-coating and full-bodied on the palate. Sweet, malty, balanced and elegant. The finish is long and complex, becoming progressively more spicy and drying.

DR – The nose is a mix of fresh and clean barley, honey and a hint of smoke. The honey carries through to the palate and the pleasant finish is shaped by a touch of smoke and peppery spice.

The owners of Aberfeldy, Dewar's, belong to the big five whisky producers in Scotland and are also the ones who have invested the most in terms of volume in blended whisky. For Diageo and Chivas Bros single malts constitute 4%, for W Grants 10% and for Edrington as much as 17%. For Dewar's on the other hand, single malt makes up less than 1% of total sales – most of which are Aberfeldy and Glen Deveron. But Aberfeldy distillery is not just an essential part of the Dewar's blend. It illustrates the heritage back to the Dewar brothers who built the distillery. This heritage is also emphasized by Dewar's World of Whiskies, an excellent visitor centre which opened at the distillery in 2000.

In the 70s and 80s Dewar's didn't get that much attention from the owners at the time, Diageo. It wasn't until 1998 when Bacardi took over and increased the product range that the company found its way back to its former glory. Today, Dewar's is the blended Scotch category leader in USA and sales of Aberfeldy single malt has increased by 400% in the last seven years and now sells around 25,000 cases per year.

The equipment at Aberfeldy consists of a stainless steel mash tun, eight washbacks made of Siberian larch, two stainless steel washbacks placed outdoors and two pairs of stills. There are six warehouses on site, though they are no longer used for storage. In 2011 the distillery will be working a 7-day week producing 2.5 million litres of alcohol.

The core range consists of 12 and 21 year old. Two 18 year old single casks were released in 2009, one of them to commemorate Chris Anderson, the Distilleries Manager's retirement. The next single cask was a 19 year old released exclusively for La Maison du Whisky in 2010. In July 2011, a 14 year old single bourbon cask with the final three years in a sherry hogshead was released.

12 years old

Allt-a-Bhainne

Owner: **Region/district:**
Chivas Brothers Ltd   Speyside
(Pernod Ricard)

Founded: **Status:**   **Capacity:**
1975   Active   4 000 000 litres

Address: Glenrinnes, Dufftown,
Banffshire AB55 4DB

Tel: **website:**
01542 783200   -

History:
1975 – The distillery is founded by Chivas Brothers, a subsidiary of Seagrams, in order to secure malt whisky for its blended whiskies. The total cost amounts to £2.7 million.

1989 – Production has doubled.

2001 – Pernod Ricard takes over Chivas Brothers from Seagrams.

2002 – Mothballed in October.

2005 – Production restarts in May.

Deerstalker 12 year old

GS – Cereal and toffee on the sherbety nose, with mildly metallic notes. The palate is light, with fresh fruits. Medium length and warming in the finish.

DR – Autumn fields and damp hay on the nose, a richer, sweeter earth and heathery taste on the palate and a gentle rounded finish.

Halfway between Glenlivet and Dufftown, on the B9009, lies Allt-a-Bhainne distillery. Built around the same time in the mid 1970s as its sister distillery a few miles to the south, Braeval, this is one of Chivas Brothers' workhorses. It means that its purpose is to produce whisky for the owners' different brands of blended Scotch. Allt-a-Bhainne is a signature malt in 100 Pipers and there are also large banderoles showing this in the stillroom. The brand peaked in 2005 with a 340% increase in six years to 3.5 million cases. It has been going downhill since and in 2009, 100 Pipers 'only' sold 2,3 million cases which, after all, gives it a place in the top ten list. The main market is Thailand and the general decrease in whisky sales there and the competition from local whiskies, has affected the brand.

The modern distillery is, surprisingly, equipped with a traditional mash tun with rakes and ploughs, despite the novelty called the lauter mash tun being introduced for whisky production already a decade prior to Allt-a-Bhainne's commissioning. The rest of the equipment consists of eight stainless steel washbacks and two pairs of stills. The distillery is a busy place working 7 days a week with 25 mashes resulting in 4 million litres of alcohol per year. In 2010, 50% of the production was peated spirit with a phenol content in the malted barley of 10ppm and the same amount will be produced during 2011. The whisky is not filled in casks on site but transported by lorry to a facility in Keith. In order to make the distillery more energy efficient, thermal compressors will be installed during 2011, similar to the other distilleries in the Chivas group.

There are no official bottlings of Allt-a-Bhainne and according to Chivas Brothers there are no plans for any either. Independent bottlings can be found, though, in the form of Deerstalker 12 year old from Aberko.

Deerstalker 12 year old

Ardbeg

Owner:
The Glenmorangie Co
(Moët Hennessy)

Region/district:
Islay

Founded:
1815

Status:
Active (vc)

Capacity:
1 150 000 litres

Address: Port Ellen, Islay, Argyll PA42 7EA

Tel:
01496 302244 (vc)

website:
www.ardbeg.com

History:
1794 – First record of a distillery at Ardbeg. It was founded by Alexander Stewart.

1798 – The MacDougalls, later to become licensees of Ardbeg, are active on the site through Duncan MacDougall.

1815 – The current distillery is founded by John MacDougall, son of Duncan MacDougall.

1853 – Alexander MacDougall, John's son, dies and sisters Margaret and Flora MacDougall, assisted by Colin Hay, continue the running of the distillery. Colin Hay takes over the licence when the sisters die.

1888 – Colin Elliot Hay and Alexander Wilson Gray Buchanan renew their license.

1900 – Colin Hay's son takes over the license.

1959 – Ardbeg Distillery Ltd is founded.

1973 – Hiram Walker and Distillers Company Ltd jointly purchase the distillery for £300,000 through Ardbeg Distillery Trust.

1974 – Widely considered as the last vintage of 'old, peaty' Ardbeg. Malt which has not been produced in the distillery's own maltings is used in increasingly larger shares after this year.

1977 – Hiram Walker assumes single control of the distillery. Ardbeg closes its maltings.

1979 – Kildalton, a less peated malt, is produced over a number of years.

1981 – The distillery closes in March.

1987 – Allied Lyons takes over Hiram Walker and thereby Ardbeg.

1989 – Production is restored. All malt is taken from Port Ellen.

1996 – The distillery closes in July and Allied Distillers decides to put it up for sale.

Judging from the cult status that Ardbeg has with whisky aficionados around the world, it may seem odd that it is only the 6th best selling Islay malt with just Bunnahabhain and Kilchoman behind. However, one must keep in mind that for the past decade or so since Glenmorangie took over they have been busy building up stock. The maturing whisky which was part of the deal was very inconsistent in terms of quality and since there was no production 1982-1989 and only sporadic production between 1989 and 1996, large gaps exist in terms of age. The whole production today is used for their own needs and they haven't sold anything to independent bottlers since 1997.

There have been some refurbishing to the distillery during 2011; the old boiler from 1966 was replaced with a new one and one of the washbacks was also replaced, as well as some of the rake gear in the mash tun. The distillery is equipped with a stainless steel semilauter mash tun, six washbacks made of Oregon pine and one pair of stills. The single malt from Ardbeg is by all definitions heavily peated, but compared to the other two Kildalton distilleries, Lagavulin and Laphroaig, it doesn't come off as smoky. One of the reasons is that the purifier which is connected to the spirit still increases the reflux and adds a fruity note and also that the spirit run is already cut at 62,5% to avoid the most pungent types of phenols. During 2011, the distillery will be running a 5-day week with 12 mashes and around 1 million litres in the year.

The core range consists of the *10 year old, Uiegedail, Blasda* and *Corryvreckan*. Blasda, which is lightly peated (8ppm), was first released in 2008. The peatiest ever release from Ardbeg, is *Supernova* and was released for the first time in early 2009. Its phenol level was well in excess of 100ppm. The second edition, *Supernova 2010*, was released in May 2010 with the same phenols level but slightly higher alcohol strength. A couple of months earlier, *Rollercoaster* was released to celebrate the 10th anniversary of the Ardbeg Committee. The Rollercoaster was a vatting of one cask from each year between 1997 and 2006 and, although most casks were ex bourbon, there were also a couple of ex sherry butts included. In June 2011, *Ardbeg Alligator*, another Committee bottling, was released (with a general release in September). The name derives from the fact that some of the whisky was matured in heavily charred barrels. In connection with Feis Isle 2011, there was also a limited release of an Ardbeg distilled *1998* that had been fully matured in *PX sherry* butts.

History (continued):

1997 – Glenmorangie plc buys the distillery for £7 million (whereof £5.5 million is for whisky in storage). On stream from 25th June. Ardbeg 17 years old and Provenance are launched

1998 – A new visitor centre opens.

2000 – Ardbeg 10 years is introduced. The Ardbeg Committee is launched and has 30 000 members after a few years.

2001 – Lord of the Isles 25 years and Ardbeg 1977 are launched.

2002 – Ardbeg Committee Reserve and Ardbeg 1974 are launched.

2003 – Uigeadail is launched.

2004 – Very Young Ardbeg (6 years) and a limited edition of Ardbeg Kildalton (1300 bottles) are launched. The latter is an un-peated cask strength from 1980.

2005 – Serendipity is launched.

2006 – Ardbeg 1965 and Still Young are launched. Distillery Manager Stuart Thomson leaves Ardbeg after nine years. Almost There (9 years old) and Airigh Nam Beist are released.

2007 – Ardbeg Mor, a 10 year old in 4.5 litre bottles is released.

2008 – The new 10 year old, Corryvreckan, Rennaissance, Blasda and Mor II are released.

2009 – Supernova is released, the peatiest expression from Ardbeg ever.

2010 – Rollercoaster and Supernova 2010 are released.

2011 – Ardbeg Alligator is released.

Uigeadail

Blasda

Alligator

Ardbeg 10 year old

GS – Quite sweet on the nose, with soft peat, carbolic soap and Arbroath smokies. Burning peats and dried fruit, followed by sweeter notes of malt and a touch of liquorice in the mouth. Extremely long and smoky in the finish, with a fine balance of cereal sweetness and dry peat notes.

DR – Intense smoke and tar on the nose but with some distinctive sweet lemon notes, a mouth-coating palate with honeyed but firey peat, completely balanced and impressive, and a long smoke tail at the finish.

10 years old

Corryvreckan

Ardmore

Owner:
Beam Global
Spirits & Wine

Region/district:
Highland

Founded: 1898   **Status:** Active   **Capacity:** 5 200 000 litres

Address: Kennethmont,
Aberdeenshire AB54 4NH

Tel: 01464 831213   **website:** www.ardmorewhisky.com

History:
1898 – Adam Teacher, son of William Teacher, starts the construction of Ardmore Distillery which eventually becomes William Teacher & Sons´ first distillery. Adam Teacher passes away before it is completed.

1955 – Stills are increased from two to four.

1973 – A visitor centre is constructed.

1974 – Another four stills are added, increasing the total to eight.

1976 – Allied Breweries takes over William Teacher & Sons and thereby also Ardmore. The own maltings (Saladin box) is terminated.

1999 – A 12 year old is released to commemorate the distillery's 100th anniversary. A 21 year old is launched in a limited edition.

2002 – Ardmore is one of the last distilleries to abandon direct heating (by coal) of the stills in favour of indirect heating through steam.

2005 – Jim Beam Brands becomes new owner when it takes over some 20 spirits and wine brands from Allied Domecq for five billion dollars.

2007 – Ardmore Traditional Cask is launched.

2008 – A 25 and a 30 year old are launched.

Ardmore Traditional

GS – A nose of smoked haddock and butter, plus sweet, fruity malt and spices. Sweet and initially creamy on the palate, spices, peat smoke, tobacco and vanilla emerge and blend together. The finish is long and mellow.

DR – Unique and remarkable mix of burnt meat savouriness on the nose, and a delicatessen of flavours on the palate, smoked vanilla, burnt fruit and a distinctive and highly addictive sweet and savoury mix towards the peated finish.

This distillery was founded by a member of the Teacher´s family in the late 1800s and for many years, the purpose of Ardmore was to produce malt whisky to become a vital part of the Teacher´s blends. It would take almost a century and a change in ownership before the first official bottlings of the single malt reached the market. Apparently there was a demand to be met because only three years later it was selling almost 20,000 cases per year.

Ardmore has always been known to use peated malt (12-14 ppm), a common practice throughout Speyside in the 19th century but abandoned by the vast majority many years ago. There is also an unpeated version beeing produced called Ardlair, which is used by other companies as a blending malt. For 2011 the share of Ardlair will equate to about 30% of the total amount.

The distillery is equipped with a large (12.5 tonnes charge) cast iron mash tun with a copper dome, 14 Douglas fir washbacks (with four of them holding 90,000 litres and the other ten 45,000 litres) and four pairs of stills equipped with sub-coolers to give more copper contact. At the moment, Ardmore is doing 24 mashes per week resulting in 4.9 million litres. Mostly ex bourbon barrels are filled, but also a few Pedro Ximenez sherry, port and cognac casks can be found in the warehouses. Plenty of smaller quarter casks are also in use as a result from the trials that former owner, Allied Domecq, started years ago. A total of 34,000 casks are maturing on site and during 2011 £1m will be invested to replace the roofs of the warehouses.

The core expression is the *Traditional* with no age statement but it is generally made up using a range of ex-bourbon casks from six to thirteen years old. After vatting it is filled into quarter casks where it is allowed to mature for another year before bottling. In 2008 a *25 year old* was launched for UK and duty free, while a *30 year old* was released for the American market and in 2010 the first single cask (exclusive for a retailer in the USA) was released - a *12 year old* first fill bourbon barrel.

Ardmore Traditional Cask

Arran

Owner:
Isle of Arran Distillers

Region/district:
Islands (Arran)

Founded: **Status:** **Capacity:**
1993 Active (vc) 750 000 litres

Address: Lochranza, Isle of Arran KA27 8HJ

Tel: **website:**
01770 830264 www.arranwhisky.com

History:
1993 – Harold Currie founds the distillery.

1995 – Production starts in full on 17th August.

1996 – A one year old spirit is released.

1997 – A visitor centre is opened by the Queen.

1998 – The first release is a 3 year old.

1999 – The Arran 4 years old is released.

2002 – Single Cask 1995 is launched.

2003 – Single Cask 1997, non-chill filtered and Calvados finish is launched.

2004 – Cognac finish, Marsala finish, Port finish and Arran First Distillation 1995 are launched.

2005 – Arran 1996 is launched (6,000 bottles). Two more finishes are launched - Chateau Margaux and Grand Cru Champagne.

2006 – After an unofficial launch in 2005, Arran 10 years old is released as well as a couple of new wood finishes.

2007 – Arran is named Scottish Distiller of the Year by Whisky Magazine. Four new wood finishes and Gordon´s Dram are released.

2008 – The first 12 year old is released as well as four new wood finishes.

2009 – Peated single casks, two wood finishes and 1996 Vintage are released.

2010 – A 14 year old, Rowan Tree, three cask finishes and Machrie Moor (peated) are released.

2011 – The Westie, Sleeping Warrior and a 12 year old cask strength are released.

Arran 14 year old

GS – Very fragrant and perfumed on the nose, with peaches, brandy and ginger snaps. Smooth and creamy on the palate, with spicy summer fruits, apricots and nuts. The lingering finish is nutty and slowly drying.

DR – The precocious ten year old becomes a testy teenager. If the 12 year old was a diversion this is right on track - with sweet, fresh and zesty nose, and rich creamy and rounded palate defined by vanilla, lemon and cream soda. The finish is long and full.

Right from the start in 1993, when the distillery opened as the first legal distillery on Arran since 1837, the company has been run in a professional and goal orientated way. An interesting range of bottlings has been created and sales have increased slowly but steadily. In May 2011, Arran Distillers could report their biggest profit ever, £117,000, compared to a loss of £16,000 the year before. At the same time volumes increased to 13,500 cases sold in 2010.

The semi-lauter mash tun, the four Oregon pine washbacks and the two stills all stand in one room, which allows the production to be easily viewed by the 60,000 annual visitors to the distillery. One dunnage warehouse holds 3,000 casks and a racked warehouse is of a similar capacity. Total production capacity is 750,000 litres and the plan for 2011 is to do 350,000 litres. Of that, 20,000 litres is a peated version with a phenol level of 20ppm (which used to be 12-14ppm before 2009).

The owners´ goal is to have a core range of 10, 14 and 18 year olds by 2014. So far the first two have been released and core expressions are also Robert Burns Malt (5 years old) and The Arran Malt Original - a non-aged version. This was initially created for the French market, targeted at chain stores like CarreFour, but is now being rolled out to other markets in Germany and Holland. Limited releases for 2011 are the third edition of Icons of Arran, The Westie, distilled in 1998, the second edition of the peated Machrie Moor, The Sleeping Warrior (11 year old) bottled in association with The National Trust for Scotland and 12 year old cask strength. The last will be a yearly recurrence replacement for the many single casks that used to be released. There will however, still be a few older, premium single casks every year from both bourbon and sherry casks. Finally, the single malt range is completed with three different cask finishes - Amarone, Port and Sauternes. The distillery also produces two blends (Robert Burns and Lochranza) and a cream liqueur called Arran Gold.

14 years old

Auchroisk

Owner:
Diageo

Region/district:
Speyside

Founded: Status:
1974 Active

Capacity:
3 800 000 litres

Address: Mulben, Banffshire AB55 6XS

Tel:
01542 885000

website:
www.malts.com

History:
1972 – Building of the distillery commences by Justerini & Brooks (which, together with W. A. Gilbey, make up the group IDV) in order to produce blending whisky. In February the same year IDV is purchased by the brewery Watney Mann which, in July, merges into Grand Metropolitan.

1974 – The distillery is completed and, despite the intention of producing malt for blending, the first year's production is sold 12 years later as single malt thanks to the high quality.

1986 – The first whisky is marketed under the name Singleton.

1997 – Grand Metropolitan and Guinness merge into the conglomerate Diageo. Simultaneously, the subsidiaries United Distillers (to Guinness) and International Distillers & Vintners (to Grand Metropolitan) form the new company United Distillers & Vintners (UDV).

2001 – The name Singleton is abandoned and the whisky is now marketed under the name of Auchroisk in the Flora & Fauna series.

2003 – Apart from the 10 year old in the Flora & Fauna series, a 28 year old from 1974, the distillery's first year, is launched in the Rare Malt series.

2010 – A Manager's Choice single cask and a limited 20 year old are released.

Auchroisk 10 year old
GS – Malt and spice on the light nose, with developing nuts and floral notes. Quite voluptuous on the palate, with fresh fruit and milk chocolate. Raisins in the finish.

DR – Young and zesty and citrusy on the nose, warming tangerine and citrus fruits and a touch of salt on the palate, medium long malty finish.

If you drive on the A95 from Keith towards Craigellachie and turn right just after Mulben, you will, after a few miles, discover a huge site on the right hand side of the road. This is Auchroisk, a distillery unknown to most and the impact of the site is really not due to the distillery (which is medium sized) but the ten huge, racked warehouses with the capacity of storing 250,000 casks. Many of the Diageo distilleries in the Speyside area (for example Knockando, Glen Spey and Strathmill) are maturing their whisky at Auchroisk. But that's not all. In due course, the matured malt whisky is then blended at Auchroisk and shipped to any of the bottling plants where the final blending with grain spirit, as well as bottling, takes place. This blend of malt whiskies is called part blend.

The distillery itself, is equipped with one stainless steel semilauter mash tun, eight stainless steel washbacks and four pairs of stills. The spacious stillhouse with four stills on each side was a role modell for the stillhouse at the latest of Diageo's distilleries, Roseisle, built in 2009. The character of Auchroisk new make is nutty and, to achieve that, they produce a cloudy wort and ferment for only 45 hours, except during the weekends when the fermentation is extended to 130 hours. Auchroisk is currently on full production which means 18 12-tonnes mashes per week and almost 4 million litres in the year. Apart from producing whisky, mainly for the J&B blend, Auchroisk is also a backup for production of Gordon's gin should any problems occur at Cameronbridge distillery. Trials have been performed but any commercial distilling has of yet not needed to be implemented.

The core range from Auchroisk is simply the *10 year old Flora & Fauna* bottling. In 2010, the distillery became better known when two new, limited, releases appeared. The first was a *single sherry cask* distilled in *1999* and released as part of the Manager's Choice series. Six months later a *20 year old* from *1990* was launched in connection with the traditional Special Release. It was, again, a cask strength but was a mix of American and European oak.

10 years old

Meet the Manager

PAUL HOOPER
SITE OPERATIONS MANAGER, AUCHROISK DISTILLERY

When did you start working in the whisky business and when did you start at Auchroisk?

I started in the Whisky Industry in 2006, as a Student Project Scientist, working at the Diageo European Technical centre in Menstrie. My role included being involved in a wide range of Distillation and Maturation projects, as well as Sensory Trials. I started as Site Operations Manager at Auchroisk in May 2011.

Had you been working in other lines of business before whisky?

Whisky was the first part of the business that I have worked in. I have had some experience in Brewing, spending 6 months at Uganda Breweries Limited (part of Diageo) as part of my Graduate Scheme rotation.

What kind of education or training do you have?

I studied for four years at Cardiff University to obtain a BSc (Hons) in Biotechnology, including a Professional Training Year at Diageo. I have subsequently achieved a Diploma in Distilling from Heriot Watt University through distance learning. I have received on the job training as part of the Graduate Scheme, whereby I shadowed other Managers and Operators.

Describe your career in the whisky business.

As mentioned I started as Project Scientist. After completing my degree I was successful in obtaining a place on the Diageo Scotland Graduate Scheme. My first placement involved working on the expansion project of Cameronbridge Distillery in Fife. My 2nd placement was as Trainee Site Operations Manager at Mortlach and then on to Africa to be involved with a Supply Chain based role as an Implementation Manager.

What are your main tasks as a manager?

My main roles as a manager are: ensuring the Health and Safety standards of the site and its operations are maintained. Making sure the Key Performance Indicators (KPI's) are achieved. Being a People Manager to the operators at the Distillery. Overseeing any maintenance or Capital Expenditure work on the site. Ensuring the site complies with HMRC and Environmental rules and regulations. Plus much more!

What are the biggest challenges of being a distillery manager?

The biggest challenge, but also the best thing about the job is that every day is different and there is always something that pops up that you didn't expect!

What would be the worst that could go wrong in the production process?

Power cuts in the snow!

How would you describe the character of Auchroisk single malt?

I would say that the Auchroisk 10 year old from the Flora and Fauna range has zesty notes with a big bold palate.

What are the main features in the process at Auchroisk, contributing to this character?

A mixture of long and short fermentation run times using cloudy worts coupled with a balanced distillation using high necked stills with nearly horizontal Lyne Arms. The wood type used for the Flora and Fauna edition is predominantly American Oak, which allows for the distillery character to shine.

What is your favourite expression of Auchroisk and why?

The Singleton of Auchroisk – for its smooth, sweet malty and sherry notes.

If it were your decision alone – what new expression of Auchroisk would you like to see released?

I would like to see the use of European Oak used more to give a predominantly sherry finish.

If you had to choose a favourite dram other than Auchroisk, what would that be?

Mortlach Flora and Fauna edition for its deep Sherry Cask colour and meaty/sulphury notes.

Do you see any major changes in the next 10 years to come?

Major changes I foresee are in relation to the move to zero carbon emissions from the industry. We are bringing in new technology to reduce emission levels, particularly green technology to turn the by-products of distillation into power which can then be used to power our distilleries.

Do you have any special interests or hobbies that you pursue?

Currently pursuing to be a Special Constable in Grampian Police.

You mentioned you spent a year working at Cameronbridge grain distillery with an expansion project. Please tell us some more.

During my time at Cameronbridge Grain Distillery in Fife – I worked on a large expansion project, whereby the pre-distillation capacity of the site was significantly increased. My role primarily involved the management of contractors that were carrying out the work and ensuring that they carried it out in a safe manner through a range of Safe Systems of Work. I was also involved with the commissioning of the new equipment and software, as well as training others on how to use it. With the expansion, Cameronbridge is now the biggest distillery in Scotland and the sheer scale of Grain Distilling makes it a fascinating part of the business to be part of.

The vast majority of distillery managers in Scotland were born here. How has it been coming from Cornwall to manage a Scottish distillery?

Cornwall and Scotland are very similar. The people are very friendly, the scenery beautiful and the seasons unpredictable! Scotland is my 2nd home and it is the people that I have to thank for making me feel so welcome.

Auchentoshan

Owner:
Morrison Bowmore
(Suntory)

Region/district:
Lowlands

Founded: 1823
Status: Active (vc)
Capacity: 1 750 000 litres

Address: Dalmuir, Clydebank, Glasgow G81 4SJ

Tel: 01389 878561
website: www.auchentoshan.com

History:

1800 – First mention of the distillery Duntocher, which may be identical to Auchentoshan.

1823 – An official license is obtained by the owner, Mr. Thorne.

1903 – The distillery is purchased by John Maclachlan.

1923 – G. & J. Maclachlan goes bankrupt and a new company, Maclachlans Ltd, is formed.

1941 – The distillery is severely damaged by a German bomb raid and reconstruction does not commence until 1948.

1960 – Maclachlans Ltd is purchased by the brewery J. & R. Tennant Brewers.

1969 – Auchentoshan is bought by Eadie Cairns Ltd who starts major modernizations.

1984 – Stanley P. Morrison, eventually becoming Morrison Bowmore, becomes new owner.

1994 – Suntory buys Morrison Bowmore.

2002 – Auchentoshan Three Wood is launched.

2004 – More than a £1 million is spent on a new, refurbished visitor centre. The oldest Auchentoshan ever, 42 years, is released.

2006 – Auchentoshan 18 year old is released.

2007 – A 40 year old and a 1976 30 year old are released.

2008 – New packaging as well as new expressions - Classic, 18 year old and 1988.

2010 – Two vintages, 1977 and 1998, are released.

2011 – Two vintages, 1975 and 1999, and Valinch are released.

Auchentoshan 12 year old

GS – The nose features fruit & nut chocolate, cinnamon and oak. Smooth and sweet in the mouth, with citrus fruits and cloves. Drying gently in a gingery finish.

DR – Toffee, rose water and Milk Chocolate Crisp on the nose, grape and crisp apple on the palate before a spicy fruity interplay in a lengthy finish.

There are only five distilleries in the Lowlands today and it is only Auchentoshan that practices what this part of Scotland is famous for, namely triple distillation. Perhaps this unique selling point is one of the reasons for the distillery's impressive increase in sales during the last four years when volumes increased with over 60% to 50,000 cases sold in 2010. Taiwan, the UK, Scandinavia and USA are the biggest markets. The success is also reflected by the increased speed of production. For many years they distilled 500,000 litres per year but the prognoses for 2011 is at 1,2 million litres. The distillery lies embedded in a valley just outside Glasgow near the busy A82. It is equipped with a semi-lauter mash tun, four Oregon pine washbacks and three stills. There are another three washbacks which are not in use at the moment. The spirit matures in three dunnage and two racked warehouses. In 2011, the distillery manager, Jeremy Stephens, moved on to become Senior Blender for Morrison Bowmore (owners of Auchentoshan, as well as Bowmore and Glen Garioch) while his predecessor on that job, Iain McCallum, took an ambassadorial role for the company.

Auchentoshan has an exquisite visitor centre which was inaugurated in 2005 and it is now attracting 20,000 visitors per year. The style is very contemporary which includes a wooden bar, shaped like a circle, where the distillery tour ends. The core range consists of *Classic, 12 years, Three Wood, 18 years* and *21 years*. *Select* (no age statement) has been moved to the duty free range. Limited releases for 2009/2010 included a *Vintage 1978* bourbon matured, a *Vintage 1977* and a *Vintage 1998* matured in a fino sherry cask. In 2011 these were followed up by a *1975 bourbon maturation*, a *1999 Bourdeaux wine maturation* and the *Valinch*. The last one will from now on be released in small batches every Father's Day in June and it is basically a cask strength, unchillfiltered version of the Classic.

12 years old

Aultmore

Owner:
John Dewar & Sons
(Bacardi)

Region/district:
Speyside

Founded: 1896 **Status:** Active **Capacity:** 3 030 000 litres

Address: Keith, Banffshire AB55 6QY

Tel: 01542 881800 **website:** -

History:

1896 – Alexander Edward, owner of Benrinnes and co-founder of Craigellachie Distillery, builds Aultmore.

1897 – Production starts.

1898 – Production is doubled; the company Oban & Aultmore Glenlivet Distilleries Ltd manages Aultmore.

1923 – Alexander Edward sells Aultmore for £20,000 to John Dewar & Sons.

1925 – Dewar's becomes part of Distillers Company Limited (DCL).

1930 – The administration is transferred to Scottish Malt Distillers (SMD).

1971 – The stills are increased from two to four.

1991 – UDV launches a 12-year old Aultmore in the Flora & Fauna series.

1996 – A 21 year old cask strength is marketed as a Rare Malt.

1998 – Diageo sells Dewar's and Bombay Gin to Bacardi for £1,150 million.

2004 – A new official bottling is launched (12 years old).

Aultmore 12 year old

GS – Gentle spice and fudge notes on the fragrant nose. Fresh fruits and restrained vanilla in the mouth. Nutty and drying in a medium-length finish.

DR – Orange blossom and flowers on the nose, lemon and lime Starburst on the palate, with late sherbet spicy and drying and more-ish finish. Altogether, zesty and very pleasant.

Aultmore distillery was built as early as 1896 but when you travel the A96 and look to your left, a mile before you reach Keith, you see a very modern, shining white complex of buildings. The distillery was completely rebuilt at the beginning of the 1970s and nothing is left of the old buildings. The distillery is part of the Dewar's group, a company which attracted a lot of potential buyers in 1998. Diageo, the owners at the time, had, through the merger of Guinness and Grand Metropolitan, grown too big and due to competition concerns from the Federal Trade Commission, were forced to sell both Dewar's and Bombay Sapphire gin. The two were expected to bring in £800m but after frantic bidding from Bacardi, Pernod Ricard, Allied Domecq and Seagram's, Bacardi stood out as the winner, but at a price of £1150m. This was the company's second acquisition in Scotland, six years earlier they bought Macduff distillery.

Since 2008 production has been running seven days a week which, for 2011, means 2.6 million litres of alcohol. A Steinecker full lauter mash tun, six washbacks made of larch and two pairs of stills are operated. The stillhouse control system was modernised in 2008. All the warehouses were demolished in 1996; in fact, Dewar's no longer has any maturation capacity at any of its distilleries. Instead, the company has redeveloped its headquarters at Westthorn in Glasgow, where another five warehouses have been constructed. A new site at Poniel has been bought where the first two, of 18 planned, warehouses with a total capacity of 140,000 casks were opened in 2009 followed by another four in 2010. Aultmore was one of the first distilleries to build a dark grains plant in order to process pot ale and draff into cattle feed. It became operational in 1977 but closed in 1985. It then reopened in 1989 but was finally taken out of production in 1993. Most of the output is used in Dewar's blended whiskies, but a *12 year old* official bottling has been for sale since 2004.

12 years old

Balblair

Owner:
Inver House Distillers
(Thai Beverages plc)

Region/district:
Northern Highlands

Founded: **Status:** **Capacity:**
1790 Active (vc) 1 400 000 litres

Address: Edderton, Tain, Ross-shire IV19 1LB

Tel:
01862 821273

website:
www.balblair.com

History:
1790 – The distillery is founded by John Ross.

1836 – John Ross dies and his son Andrew Ross takes over with the help of his sons.

1872 – New buildings replace the old.

1873 – Andrew Ross dies and his son James takes over.

1894 – Balnagowan Estate signs a new lease for 60 years with Alexander Cowan. He builds a new distillery, a few kilometres from the old.

1911 – Cowan is forced to cease payments and the distillery closes.

1941 – Balnagowan Estate goes bankrupt and the distillery is put up for sale.

1948 – The lawyer Robert Cumming from Keith buys Balblair for £48,000.

1949 – Production restarts.

1970 – Cumming sells Balblair to Hiram Walker.

1988 – Allied Distillers becomes the new owner through the merger between Hiram Walker and Allied Vintners.

1996 – Allied Domecq sells the distillery to Inver House Distillers.

2000 – Balblair Elements and the first version of Balblair 33 years are launched.

2001 – Thai company Pacific Spirits (part of the Great Oriole Group) takes over Inver House.

2004 – Balblair 38 years is launched.

2005 – 12 year old Peaty Cask, 1979 (26 years) and 1970 (35 years) are launched.

2006 – International Beverage Holdings acquires Pacific Spirits UK.

2007 – Three new vintages replace the entire former range.

2008 – Vintage 1975 and 1965 are released.

2009 – Vintage 1991 and 1990 are released.

2010 – Vintage 1978 and 2000 are released.

2011 – Vintage 1995 and 1993 are released

Balblair 2000

GS – Peach and pineapple on the nose, with coconut and honeyed vanilla. Toasted marshmallows with time. Relatively light-bodied, sweet, with lively spice, ginger and youthful oak on the palate. Fudge in the finish, and a contrasting hint of dark chocolate at the last.

DR – Exotic sweet tinned fruits on the nose, syrupy sweet pear, apple and peach on the palate and a dollop of sweet spice towards the end. The finish is sweet, spicy and fruity.

The sight of a railway track just outside the distillery is not an unusual one in Scotland. The importance of the railway for transporting goods to and from the site was of such a magnitude, that the owner of Balblair distillery in the 1890s did not hesitate to move the distillery (originally founded in 1790) a couple of miles to Edderton to have a railway station at the front gates. However, of even more importance was the water source, which to this day is piped from the original well more than 4 miles away. Edderton railway station closed in 1960.

The equipment consists of a stainless steel mash tun, six Oregon pine washbacks and one pair of stills. There is actually a third still but it has not been used since 1969. The spirit is matured in eight dunnage warehouses with a capacity of 26,000 casks. Currently, a six-day week is in place with 17 mashes, and the target for 2011 is to produce 1.4 million litres of alcohol. For the first time, at least in modern days, the owners will be producing 200,000 litres of peated spirit during 2011 with a phenol specification of no less than 80ppm in the barley (circa 30-40ppm in the new make). During 2010 more than 5,000 9-litre cases of Balblair single malt were sold. So far, only one of the five distilleries in the InverHouse group has been able to boast with a visitor's centre (at Pulteney distillery) but now the time has come for yet another one. Balblair will start accepting visitors as from autumn 2011.

The current core range consists of three vintages – *1978, 1989* and *2000*. In 2009, Balblair *1990* was released as a duty free exclusive and early 2010 saw the launch of the bourbon-matured Balblair *1991* for the American market. In 2011 the *1995* Vintage was released as an exclusive for the Swedish market but the same vintage will also replace the 1990 as the duty free expression. A limited release of *1993* Vintage was also presented to the French and Russian markets.

Balblair 2000

90

Balmenach

Owner:
Inver House Distillers
(Thai Beverages plc)

Region/district:
Speyside

Founded: **Status:**
1824 Active

Capacity:
2 000 000 litres

Address: Cromdale, Moray PH26 3PF

Tel:
01479 872569

website:
www.inverhouse.com

History:

1824 – The distillery is licensed to James MacGregor who operated a small farm distillery by the name of Balminoch.

1897 – Balmenach Glenlivet Distillery Company is founded.

1922 – The MacGregor family sells to a consortium consisting of MacDonald Green, Peter Dawson and James Watson.

1925 – The consortium becomes part of Distillers Company Limited (DCL).

1930 – Production is transferred to Scottish Malt Distillers (SMD).

1962 – The number of stills is increased to six.

1964 – Floor maltings replaced with Saladin box.

1992 – The first official bottling is a 12 year old.

1993 – The distillery is mothballed in May.

1997 – Inver House Distillers buys Balmenach from United Distillers.

1998 – Production recommences.

2001 – Thai company Pacific Spirits takes over Inver House at the price of £56 million. The new owner launches a 27 and a 28 year old.

2002 – To commemorate the Queen's Golden Jubilee a 25-year old Balmenach is launched.

2006 – International Beverage Holdings acquires Pacific Spirits UK.

2009 – Gin production commences.

Deerstalker 18 year old

GS – An intriguing and inviting nose, with herbal notes, eucalyptus, heather and hints of sherry. Rich and warming on the palate, big-bodied, with well harmonised malt and sherry flavours prevailing. The finish is long and sophisticated.

DR – Pine needles, lemon and grapefruit and flu powder on the nose, rich sherry and a trace of sulphur on the palate, with savoury lemon and a traces of peat. A medium and citrusy finish.

The last distillery you encounter travelling west in the Speyside area, is Balmenach. This is the only distillery belonging to the Inver House group who can't flaunt with an official bottling. No stocks of mature whisky were included in the deal when the distillery was bought in 1997 from United Distillers and even though the whisky from their own production is now well over ten years, there is no sign of any change in their bottling strategy. Some 30% of the production is sold to other companies and the rest goes into their own blends, such as MacArthur's, Catto's and Hankey Bannister.

A semilauter gear was fitted into the old cast iron mash tun in 2006 and there are also six washbacks made of Douglas fir and three pairs of stills connected to worm tubs for cooling the spirit vapours. The distillery is currently doing 16 mashes per week which is slightly below the maximum capacity. The three dunnage warehouses hold 9,500 casks at the moment.

In 2009 the business at Balmenach took an interesting turn. At the same time as they continued to produce whiskey, a gin still from the 1920s was installed in the old filling room. Purchased neutral spirit is pumped through a vaporiser and then to the berry chamber where the vapours travel upwards passing five trays with 11 different kinds of botanicals (among others heather, rowan berry, apples and coriander) and finally end up in the condenser. In the first year, 6,000 litres of Caorunn gin were made increasing to 15,000 litres in 2011 which means just 15 days of production.

The only "official" bottling of the whisky so far is the 12 year old Flora & Fauna from the previous owner and this is now becoming increasingly difficult to find. There are, however, other Balmenach on the market. One is produced by an independent company called Aberko in Glasgow under the name Deerstalker 18 years.

Deerstalker 18 years

Balvenie

Owner:
William Grant & Sons

Region/district:
Speyside

Founded: 1892　**Status:** Active (vc)　**Capacity:** 5 600 000 litres

Address: Dufftown, Keith, Banffshire AB55 4DH

Tel: 01340 820373　**website:** www.thebalvenie.com

History:
1892 – William Grant rebuilds Balvenie New House to Balvenie Distillery (Glen Gordon was the name originally intended). Part of the equipment is brought in from Lagavulin and Glen Albyn.

1893 – The first distillation takes place in May.

1957 – The two stills are increased by another two.

1965 – Two new stills are installed.

1971 – Another two stills are installed and eight stills are now running.

1973 – The first official bottling appears.

1982 – Founder's Reserve, in an eye-catching Cognac-reminiscent bottle, is launched.

1990 – A new distillery, Kininvie, is opened on the premises.

1996 – Two vintage bottlings and a Port wood finish are launched.

2001 – The Balvenie Islay Cask, with 17 years in bourbon casks and six months in Islay casks, is released.

2002 – Balvenie releases 83 bottles of a 50 year old that has been in sherry casks since January 1952. Recommended price £6,000 a bottle.

2004 – The Balvenie Thirty is released to commemorate Malt Master David Stewart's 30th anniversary at Balvenie.

2005 – The Balvenie Rum Wood Finish 14 years old is released.

2006 – The Balvenie New Wood 17 years old, Roasted Malt 14 years old and Portwood 1993 are released.

2007 – Vintage Cask 1974 and Sherry Oak 17 years old are released.

2008 – Signature, Vintage 1976, Balvenie Rose and Rum Cask 17 year old are released.

2009 – Vintage 1978, 17 year old Madeira finish, 14 year old rum finish and Golden Cask 14 years old are released.

2010 – A 40 year old, Peated Cask and Carribean Cask are released.

2011 – The second batch of Tun 1401 is released.

The Balvenie Doublewood 12 year old

GS – Nuts and spicy malt on the nose, full-bodied, with soft fruit, vanilla, sherry and a hint of peat. Dry and spicy in a luxurious, lengthy finish.

DR – Red fruits and berries, a hint of smoke on the nose, on the palate mouth filling, rich and fruity and, surprisingly, with a peat presence. Lots of sherry and some toffee in the finish.

Balvenie is one of few distilleries still doing some of their own maltings. Around five percent of requirements, are produced every week and the owners are actually looking to increase the share. For the first six hours the malt is dried using peat and for the remaining 42 hours it is dried with coal. The phenol content is around 5ppm. Until recently their own malted barley was always mixed with purchased barley but experiments distilling spirit from just their own malt have been made. Except for their own maltings the distillery also has its own coppersmith and cooperage. The distillery has a full lauter mash tun, nine wooden and five stainless steel washbacks. The number of wash stills was increased to five and spirit stills to six, divided into two still rooms in 2008, when the facilities were expanded. For 2011, the production plan is 22 mashes per week, which means 80% of full capacity. Both bourbon (80%) and sherry casks (20%) are used, stored in a total of 44 dunnage, racked or palletised warehouses shared with Kininvie and Glenfiddich.

A total of 182,000 cases were sold in 2010 and the core range consists of *Doublewood 12 years old, Signature 12 years, Single Barrel 15 years, Portwood 21 years, 30 year old* and the *40 year old*. The Signature 12 years (now in its fourth edition) is a marriage between first fill bourbon barrels, refill bourbon and Oloroso sherry butts and replaced the 10 year old Founder's Reserve a couple of years ago. Recent limited bottlings include *The Balvenie Peated cask 17 year old*, the US exclusive rum finish *Carribean Cask, 14 year old Cuban Selection* for the French and Taiwanese markets and *Tun 1401*. The last one was first released in autumn 2010 and was made up of six different barrels (both sherry and bourbon) from 1966 to 1988. A *second batch* was released in summer 2011 and this time it was 10 barrels from 1969 to 1989. The Duty Free range consists of *Peated Cask* and *21 year old port wood* bottled at higher strength and the *14 year old Golden cask*.

The Balvenie Signature

Meet the Manager

STUART WATTS
DISTILLERY MANAGER, BALVENIE, GLENFIDDICH
AND KININVIE DISTILLERIES

When did you start working in the whisky business and when did you start at Balvenie distillery?

I've been working in the whisky business for 11 years, having become the Balvenie distillery manager in 2009.

Had you been working in other lines of business before whisky?

Before working in whisky, I was a research scientist.

What kind of education or training do you have?

Originally I completed a degree (BSc (Hons)) in Biochemistry. I then went on to do a PhD, which was sponsored by Suntory, looking at flavour formation during Scotch Whisky distillation.

Describe your career in the whisky business.

Since completing my PhD, I've worked for William Grant & Sons Ltd. Initially I worked in the Technical Support team, supporting our distilleries and liquid development projects. I then moved on to be a production team leader at our grain distillery. At that time, I also supported the development of our gin distillery to meet the growing demand for our Hendrick's gin brand. Following this, I became Production manager at the Girvan site, responsible for our grain distillery and newest malt Ailsa Bay. Most recently I moved to Dufftown to manage the Balvenie distillery.

What are your main tasks as a manager?

A lot of my focus is on future development, making sure we have everything in place for our future needs. As many of the distillery building are now quite old, there is a lot of work to co-ordinate with our engineering teams to ensure we keep the operation in good working order. Of course, our people are a major focus of my role as we strive to ensure our teams are well supported and trained.

What are the biggest challenges of being a distillery manager?

With such a large team on the Dufftown site, the task of ensuring everyone understands our priorities and is working toward them takes up a lot of time.

What would be the worst that could go wrong in the production process?

I've probably faced one of my worst nightmares during my first winter in Dufftown when 10 of our warehouses were severely damaged by snow. We ended up removing a quarter of our stock from the site to let us carry out repairs. A year and half later we're almost back to normal.

How would you describe the character of The Balvenie single malt?

The Balvenie has quite a rich quality, with a distinctive honeyness that comes through in all the variants.

What are the main features in the process at Balvenie distillery, contributing to this character?

I would say undoubtedly that the distinctive The Balvenie stills are a major contributor to the character. The larger size and relatively slow distillation rates are certainly contributing factors, allowing the wash to interact with the copper still, developing the richer qualities of the new make. The quality of wood is so important to the final product. Sherry wood and ex bourbons feature so highly in the Balvenie variants that we are careful to ensure we specify exactly what type of casks we are looking for.

What is your favourite expression of The Balvenie and why?

Without question, my favourite is the Balvenie Doublewood. It has the rich qualities synonymous with Balvenie as well as the sweet vanilla qualities of first fill bourbons.

If it were your decision alone – what new expression of The Balvenie would you like to see released?

In my role it´s more about producing the different styles of spirit that will ultimately end up in the finished variants. I'm happy to leave the final decision to David Stewart, the longest serving malt master in the industry.

If you had to choose a favourite dram other than The Balvenie, what would that be?

I have fairly eclectic tastes when it comes to Whisky. There are some Speysides, such as Glenrothes and Glendronach that I'm very fond of, but I have also grown to love the Islays, especially those that have had a longer time in cask, such as Lagavulin 17 or Ardbeg 30.

What are the biggest changes you have seen the past 10 years in your profession?

We try hard to ensure we keep making the same quality of spirit from the distillery so that The Balvenie retains its distinctive character. So many of the supporting processes have, however, radically changed. Certainly computers play a much bigger part in how we run our distilleries these days from how we manage our maintenance systems to how we measure the strength of our whisky.

Do you see any major changes in the next 10 years to come?

I think the environmental impact of our distilleries will be a big focus for the future, continuing to reduce the energy needed to make our product and looking at ways to gain benefits from our distillery by-products.

Do you have any special interests or hobbies that you pursue?

I have always been keen on hill walking, but haven't managed to do as much as I used to, so more recently, I have been making an effort to get back out and enjoy the fantastic countryside.

How important is it for Balvenie to have your own maltings, coppersmith and cooperage on site?

We believe these are really important elements for the Balvenie distillery. The Maltings may not be the most efficient way to produce malt whisky, but there is a quality perspective that we don't want to lose. It gives us the ability to malt our own barley direct from the Balvenie home farm to our own specification. It's a similar story with the coppersmith and coopers; it means we are able to retain these skills at the distillery.

Ben Nevis

Owner:
Ben Nevis Distillery Ltd
(Nikka, Asahi Breweries)

Region/district:
Western Highlands

Founded: 1825
Status: Active (vc)
Capacity: 1 800 000 litres

Address: Lochy Bridge, Fort William PH33 6TJ

Tel: 01397 702476
website: www.bennevisdistillery.com

History:
1825 – The distillery is founded by 'Long' John McDonald.

1856 – Long John dies and his son Donald P. McDonald takes over.

1878 – Demand is so great that another distillery, Nevis Distillery, is built nearby.

1908 – Both distilleries merge into one.

1941 – D. P. McDonald & Sons sells the distillery to Ben Nevis Distillery Ltd headed by the Canadian millionaire Joseph W. Hobbs.

1955 – Hobbs installs a Coffey still which makes it possible to produce both grain and malt whisky.

1964 – Joseph Hobbs dies.

1978 – Production is stopped.

1981 – Joseph Hobbs Jr sells the distillery back to Long John Distillers and Whitbread.

1984 – After restoration and reconstruction totalling £2 million, Ben Nevis opens up again.

1986 – The distillery closes again.

1989 – Whitbread sells the distillery to Nikka Whisky Distilling Company Ltd.

1990 – The distillery opens up again.

1991 – A visitor centre is inaugurated.

1996 – Ben Nevis 10 years old is launched.

2006 – A 13 year old port finish is released.

2007 – 1992 single cask is released.

2010 – A 25 year old is released.

Ben Nevis 10 year old

GS – The nose is initially quite green, with developing nutty, orange notes. Coffee, brittle toffee and peat are present on the slightly oily palate, along with chewy oak, which persists to the finish, together with more coffee and a hint of dark chocolate.

DR – Grape skins, over-ripe pear on the nose, baked apple and liquorice roots on the palate, pleasant malty finish.

Ben Nevis has had a long and colourful history under the ownership of the eccentric Joseph Hobbs since it was founded by "Long" John MacDonald in 1825. He was, among other things, responsible for introducing the Coffey still so the distillery could produce both malt and grain spirit. A period of melancholy followed during the eighties when the distillery was under the ownership of Whitbread. Despite some investments it was primarily used during most of the decade for warehousing and trial production and it was only during 1984-1986 that there was production. Japan with Nikka Whisky Distilling was the saviour when it acquired Ben Nevis, installed a new mash tun and replaced the concrete washbacks Joseph Hobbs had installed.

Ben Nevis is currently equipped with one lauter mash tun, six stainless steel washbacks and two made of Oregon pine and two pairs of stills. Two distinctive spirits are distilled at Ben Nevis. Fermentation is 48 hours in the steel washbacks and the spirit is destined to become either single malt or part of the Dew of Ben Nevis blend. In the wooden washbacks, fermentation time is 96 hours and this version is sent as newmake directly to the owners, Nikka, in Japan. It is used there at a very young age in the popular blend Nikka Black (or just Black as it was renamed in 2009). At the moment, the distillery is doing nine mashes per week, which equals 800,000 litres per year.

Ben Nevis had produced peated whisky for some time but stopped five years ago. No peated bottlings have yet been released though. Since 1996 the core of the range has been a *10 year old*. Some one-off bottlings have appeared at regular intervals, such as the *13 year old Port finish* released in 2006 and the *1992 single cask* released in 2007. In early 2010, a limited release was made of a *25 year old* which sold out quickly. Another batch was released again in June 2010. It has spent the first 12 years in a fresh bourbon cask that was then re-racked to a fresh sherry cask.

10 years old

BenRiach

Owner:
Benriach Distillery Co

Region/district:
Speyside

Founded: **Status:** **Capacity:**
1897 Active 2 800 000 litres

Address:
Longmorn, Elgin, Morayshire IV30 8SJ

Tel: **website:**
01343 862888 www.benriachdistillery.co.uk

History:
1897 – John Duff & Co founds the distillery.

1899 – Longmorn Distilleries Co. buys the distillery.

1903 – The distillery is mothballed.

1965 – The distillery is reopened by the new owner, The Glenlivet Distillers Ltd.

1978 – Seagram Distillers takes over.

1983 – Seagrams starts producing a peated Benriach.

1985 – The number of stills is increased to four.

1994 – The first official bottling is 10 years old.

1999 – The maltings is decommissioned.

2002 – The distillery is mothballed in October.

2004 – Intra Trading, buys Benriach together with the former Director at Burn Stewart, Billy Walker. The price is £5.4 million.

2004 – Standard, Curiositas and 12, 16 and 20 year olds are released.

2005 – Four different vintages are released in limited editions - 1966, 1970, 1978 och 1984.

2006 – Sixteen new releases, i.a. a 25 year old, a 30 year old and 8 different vintages.

2007 – A 40 year old and three new heavily peated expressions are released.

2008 – New expressions include a peated Madeira finish, a 15 year old Sauternes finish and nine single casks.

2009 – Two wood finishes (Moscatel and Gaja Barolo) and nine single casks are released.

2010 – Triple distilled Solstice and heavily peated Horizons are released.

2011 – A 45 year old and 12 vintages are released.

BenRiach Curiositas

GS – The nose is medicinal, with tarmac and a balancing heathery fragrance. Sweet fruits and beeswax in the mouth merge with major peat smoke flavours. Iodine and black pepper. Spicy, phenolic and tar-like in the finish.

DR – Complex nose with sooty smoke, cocoa powder and lemon. Lots of charcoal smoke and heavy peat on the palate, but melon and peach too. A long finish mixing sweet fruit with an acerbic wood fire smokiness.

BenRiach 12 year old

GS – Malt, orange and pineapple on the nose, floral with vanilla notes. Soft fruits, brittle toffee and honey on the smooth palate, with a finish of spicy milk chocolate.

DR – Classic Speyside nose, with a rich blend of fruits, vanilla and honey. On the palate ripe fruits are balanced by crisp barley and sweet honey, and the finish is balanced, rounded and pleasant.

The traditional way of producing malted barley for whisky production, was for every distillery to have its own malting floors. Currently there are only six distilleries left in Scotland practising this method, but in 2012 this group will be expanding with yet another one – BenRiach. Their floor malting stopped in 1999 having run for 101 years but now the owners have decided to start producing a part of their requirement "in-house".

Since 2004, when BenRiach was acquired, the owners have made huge investments – in 2008, when GlenDronach distillery was bought and in 2010 when they took over Chivas Brothers´ Newbridge bottling plant on the ouskirts of Edinburgh. The company now has the possibility of doing all their own bottling, as well as bottling for other companies. The distillery is equipped with a traditional cast iron mash tun, eight washbacks made of stainless steel and two pairs of stills. One of the old stills was replaced by a new one in January 2010 and there are plans to install a fifth still. The production for 2011 will be 1.85 million litres of alcohol (which includes 200,000 litres of peated spirit) with 60% being sold to Chivas Brothers for their blends. A small amount of triple distilled spirit has been produced every year since 2005, and for 2011 this amounts to 20,000 litres. In 2010, 12,600 cases of BenRiach were sold.

The core range of BenRiach is *Heart of Speyside* (no age), *12, 16, 20, 25* and *30 years old* in what the distillery calls Classic Speyside style and *Birnie Moss, Curiositas 10 year old, Authenticus 21 year old* and the four *12 year olds* named *Fumosus* (heavily peated whiskies with different finishes) as the peated varieties. There are six different *wood finishes (12-16 years)* and in 2010 two specials were released – *Solstice*, a 12 year old triple distilled and *Horizons*, 15 years old, heavily peated and with a Tawny port finish. In July 2011, *12 vintages* from 1971 to 1993 were released and late autumn saw the launch of a *45 year old* single cask from 1966 and *The Firkin Cask* which has matured for 32 years in a 45 litre firkin cask.

Curiositas 10 year old

Benrinnes

Owner: Diageo

Region/district: Speyside

Founded: 1826

Status: Active

Capacity: 2 500 000 litres

Address: Aberlour, Banffshire AB38 9NN

Tel: 01340 872600

website: www.malts.com

History:

1826 – The first Benrinnes distillery is built at Whitehouse Farm by Peter McKenzie.

1829 – A flood destroys the distillery.

1834 – A new distillery, Lyne of Ruthrie, is constructed a few kilometres from the first one. The owner, John Innes files for bankruptcy and William Smith & Company takes over.

1864 – William Smith & Company goes bankrupt and David Edward becomes the new owner.

1896 – Benrinnes is ravaged by fire which prompts major refurbishment. David Edward dies and his son Alexander Edward takes over.

1922 – John Dewar & Sons takes over ownership.

1925 – John Dewar & Sons becomes part of Distillers Company Limited (DCL).

1955/56 – The distillery is completely rebuilt.

1964 – Floor maltings is replaced by a Saladin box.

1966 – The number of stills doubles to six.

1984 – The Saladin box is taken out of service and the malt is purchased centrally.

1991 – The first official bottling from Benrinnes is a 15 year old in the Flora & Fauna series.

1996 – United Distillers releases a 21 year old cask strength in their Rare Malts series.

2009 – A 23 year old (6,000 bottles) is launched as a part of this year's Special Releases.

2010 – A Manager's Choice 1996 is released.

Benrinnes 15 year old

GS – A brief flash of caramel shortcake on the initial nose, soon becoming more peppery and leathery, with some sherry. Ultimately savoury and burnt rubber notes. Big-bodied, viscous, with gravy, dark chocolate and more pepper. A medium-length finish features mild smoke and lively spices.

DR – Cucumber, water melon and some caramel on the nose, sherried and full palate with some figs and harsher notes. The finish is medium long and complex.

To whisky lovers, Benrinnes is probably the most well known mountain in Scotland. Whenever you travel the southern parts of the Speyside area, you will see it rise 840 metres above sealevel, and with it's location, right at the foot of the mountain, it is also appropriate that this distillery has taken the same name. Benrinnes distillery draws its process water from wells on Benrinnes in the same way as four other distilleries located a little bit further away – Aberlour, All-a-Bhainne, Dailuaine and Glenfarclas. Nothing remains of the first Benrinnes distillery that they began building in 1826, in fact it was situated a few kilometres from where it is now. Neither is the second distillery left to view, instead you will see a creation from the 1950's. The distillery is equipped with a stainless steel lauter mash tun, eight washbacks made of Oregon pine and six stills. They use both short (65 hours) and long (100-105 hours) fermentations. For a long time the stills have been run three and three instead of in pairs. This technique is reminiscent of Springbank's partial triple distillation and was probably adopted in connection with rebuilding the distillery in 1955. For the last couple of years, though, this has changed and two wash stills are now feeding four spirit stills; two of which were originally the intermediate stills. Worm tubs are used for condensation. During 2011, Benrinnes is producing at full capacity, which means 16 mashes of 8.5 tonnes, amounting to 2.5 million litres of alcohol.

The lion's share of Benrinnes' production is used in blended whiskies – J&B, Johnnie Walker and Crawford's 3 Star – and there is only one official single malt, the Flora & Fauna *15 years old*. In autumn 2009, a *23 year old* from 1985 was released as part of Diageo's annual Special Releases and in May 2010 came another new release, a *Manager's Choice* from *1996*, drawn from a refill bourbon cask.

Flora & Fauna 15 years old

Benromach

Owner:
Gordon & MacPhail

Region/district:
Speyside

Founded: **Status:**
1898   Active (vc)

Capacity:
500 000 litres

Address: Invererne Road, Forres,
Morayshire IV36 3EB

Tel:
01309 675968

website:
www.benromach.com

History:
1898 – Benromach Distillery Company starts the distillery.

1911 – Harvey McNair & Co buys the distillery.

1919 – John Joseph Calder buys Benromach and sells it to recently founded Benromach Distillery Ltd owned by several breweries.

1931 – Benromach is mothballed.

1937 – The distillery reopens.

1938 – Joseph Hobbs buys Benromach through Associated Scottish Distillers and sells it on to National Distillers of America (NDA).

1953 – NDA sells Benromach to Distillers Company Limited (DCL).

1966 – The distillery is refurbished.

1968 – Floor maltings is abolished.

1983 – Benromach is mothballed in March.

1993 – Gordon & McPhail buys Benromach from United Distillers.

1998 – The distillery is once again in operation. A 17 year old is released to commemorate this and the distillery's 100th anniversary.

1999 – A visitor centre is opened.

2004 – The first bottle distilled by the new owner is released under the name 'Benromach Traditional' in May. Other novelties (although distilled in UD times) include a 21 year Tokaji finish and a Vintage 1969.

2005 – A Port Wood finish (22 years old) and a Vintage 1968 are released together with the Benromach Classic 55 years.

2006 – Benromach Organic is released.

2007 – Peat Smoke, the first heavily peated whisky from the distillery, is released.

2008 – Benromach Origins Golden Promise is released.

2009 – Benromach 10 years old is released.

2010 – New batches of Peatsmoke and Origins are released.

2011 – New edition of Peatsmoke, a 2001 Hermitage finish and a 30 year old are released.

Benromach 10 year old

GS – A nose that is initially quite smoky, with wet grass, butter, ginger and brittle toffee. Mouth-coating, spicy, malty and nutty on the palate, with developing citrus fruits, raisins and soft wood smoke. The finish is warming, with lingering barbecue notes.

DR – Lemon custard creams, apricots and then pine table polish on the nose, spicy virgin oak, refreshing sharp barley and pine needles on the palate, and a complex and intriguing spicy and wood shaving finish.

Benromach distillery had a tough start. After the completion of the building it remained silent for ten years due to the Pattison crash in the late 1800s. A few years of production was interrupted by the first world war and then the distillery was closed 1925-37 and again 1983-98. By then it had come into the hands of the renowned independent bottler Gordon & MacPhail who decided to equip the distillery from scratch with the aim to produce a whisky in the style of Speysiders from the first part of the 20th century. Benromach is the smallest working distillery in Speyside and is equipped with a very small (1.5 tonnes) semi-lauter mash tun with a copper dome. There are four washbacks made of larchwood from the old washbacks and resized to accomodate 11,000 litres with a long fermentation time that varies between 72 and 120 hours. Finally, there is one pair of stills that were custom made when they took over the distillery. Only two people are employed in the production and, although it has the capacity to produce 500,000 litres per annum, the output for 2011 is approximately 130,000 litres of alcohol with small batches being peated. Almost the entire production is destined to be sold as single malt and only a very small amount is used for Gordon & MacPhail blends.

The core range consists of *Traditional* (around 6 years old), *10 year old* (released in 2010), *25 year old, Vintage 1968* and *Classic 55 years old*. There are also special editions; *Organic* – the first single malt to be fully certified organic by the Soil Association, *Peatsmoke* – produced using peated barley with the fourth batch (35ppm) relased in 2011 and *Origins* – three batches highlighting how differences in the process produces different whiskies. New, limited editions released in 2011 are a *2001 Hermitage wood finish*, a *cask strength*, also from *2001*, matured in first fill bourbon casks and a *30 year old* matured in sherry butts. Older limited releases include an *8 year old* with a finish in *PX sherry* casks.

10 year old

Bladnoch

Owner:
Co-ordinated
Development Services

Region/district:
Lowlands

Founded: 1817
Status: Active (vc)
Capacity: 250 000 litres

Address: Bladnoch, Wigtown,
Wigtonshire DG8 9AB

Tel: 01988 402605
website: www.bladnoch.co.uk

History:
1817 – Brothers Thomas and John McClelland found the distillery.

1825 – The McClelland brothers obtain a licence.

1878 – John McClelland's son Charlie reconstructs and refurbishes the distillery.

1905 – Production stops.

1911 – Dunville & Co. from Ireland buys T. & A. McClelland Ltd for £10,775. Production is intermittent until 1936.

1937 – Dunville & Co. is liquidated and Bladnoch is wound up. Ross & Coulter from Glasgow buys the distillery after the war. The equipment is dismantled and shipped to Sweden.

1956 – A. B. Grant (Bladnoch Distillery Ltd.) takes over and restarts production with four new stills.

1964 – McGown and Cameron becomes new owners.

1966 – The number of stills is increased from two to four.

1973 – Inver House Distillers buys Bladnoch.

1983 – Arthur Bell and Sons take over.

1985 – Guiness Group buys Arthur Bell & Sons which, from 1989, are included in United Distillers.

1988 – A visitor centre is built.

1993 – United Distillers mothballs Bladnoch in June.

1994 – Raymond Armstrong from Northern Ireland buys Bladnoch in October.

2000 – Production commences in December.

2003 – The first bottles from Raymond Armstrong are launched, a 15 year old cask strength from UD casks.

2004 – New varieties follow suit: e. g. 13 year olds 40% and 55%.

2008 – First release of whisky produced after the take-over in 2000 - three 6 year olds.

2009 – An 8 year old of own production and a 19 year old are released.

2011 – Distiller's Choice is released.

Bladnoch is the southernmost of the Scottish distilleries, situated a mile outside Wigtown. The distillery's fate appeared to be sealed when it was mothballed by United Distillers (later Diageo) in 1993 together with Rosebank, Pittyvaich and Balmenach. However, along came Raymond Armstrong, a builder from Northern Ireland, who bought it with the reservation from Diageo that it should not be used for whisky production. In 2000, after lobbying from Armstrong and the local community, Diageo gave permission for Bladnoch to start producing again.

When Armstrong took over, the distillery had been absolutely stripped from equipment, with exception of the stills and washbacks. Also, there was not a single cask of maturing whisky included in the deal. Armstrong commenced the resurrection and in December 2000 the first distillation was made. The distillery is equipped with a stainless steel semi-lauter mash tun, six washbacks made of Oregon pine (of which only three are in use) and one pair of stills. Due to the increase in production costs (barley, casks and fuel), the owners took a decision in 2009 to seize production for the time being. Normally they do four mashes per working week with a fermentation time of just under three days and the highest annual volume produced was 250,000 litres in 2007. Of the 11 warehouses on site, Bladnoch uses only one for their own purposes while the others are rented to other distilleries.

Until recently, all official bottlings have come from the previous owner's production. These included *13 to 19 year olds* but, in spring of 2010, a couple of *20 year olds* were also released. In 2008 the first release from stock distilled under the current ownership appeared. Three *6 year old cask strengths* were released – a bourbon matured, a sherry matured and one lightly peated from a bourbon barrel. During 2009/2010 a range of *8 year olds* were released with similar maturation and recently a *9 year old* peated version was released. A *Distiller's Choice* with no age statement was launched in 2011.

8 year old

Bladnoch 8 year old

GS – Bright, fresh and citric, with lemon, cereal, soft toffee and nuts on the nose. Medium in body, the palate is gingery and very lively, with vanilla, hot spices and hazelnuts. The finish offers persistently fruity spice.

Blair Athol

Owner: **Region/district:**
Diageo   Eastern Highlands

Founded: **Status:**   **Capacity:**
1798   Active (vc)   2 500 000 litres

Address: Perth Road, Pitlochry,
Perthshire PH16 5LY

Tel: **website:**
01796 482003   www.malts.com

History:
1798 – John Stewart and Robert Robertson found Aldour Distillery, the predecessor to Blair Athol. The name is taken from the adjacent river Allt Dour.

1825 – The distillery is expanded by Robert Robertson and takes the name Blair Athol Distillery.

1826 – The Duke of Atholl leases the distillery to Alexander Connacher & Co.

1832 – The distillery closes.

1860 – Elizabeth Connacher runs the distillery.

1882 – Peter Mackenzie & Company Distillers Ltd of Edinburgh (future founder of Dufftown Distillery) buys Blair Athol and expands it.

1932 – The distillery is mothballed.

1933 – Arthur Bell & Sons takes over by acquiring Peter Mackenzie & Company.

1949 – Production restarts.

1973 – Stills are expanded from two to four.

1985 – Guinness Group buys Arthur Bell & Sons.

1987 – A visitor centre is built.

2003 – A 27 year old cask strength from 1975 is launched in Diageo's Rare Malts series.

2010 – A distillery exclusive with no age statement and a single cask from 1995 are released.

For the greater part of the summer in 2010 Blair Athol distillery was closed for refurbishing. Four washbacks made of steel and four made of wood were exchanged for six stainless steel washbacks. This may seem odd for two reasons; first of all, Diageo tend to have wooden washbacks at distilleries with visitor centres because they look more "authentic". The second reason is that most producers are unwilling to change anything in the equipment and going from wood to steel during fermentation might change the character of the spirit, although no conclusive evidence supports that theory.

Blair Athol distillery is the spiritual home of Bell's blended Scotch and it was actually bought by Arthur Bell & Sons in 1933. Today Bell's is the third biggest blended whisky in the Diageo stable (after Johnnie Walker and J&B) and sold around 2.4 million cases in 2010 which gives it spot number 8 on the top ten list. In the UK however, it is the number one Scotch whisky. It has been a neck to neck struggle the past few years with Famous Grouse, but in 2009 Bell's took a giant leap and now has 20% of the UK market. The range of Bell's was expanded in 1993 from Original to also include an 8 year old and then in 2003 when the blended malt Special Reserve was launched.

Blair Athol is one of the oldest distilleries in Scotland and is equipped with a semi-lauter mash tun, six washbacks made of stainless steel and two pairs of stills. The distillery is running seven days a week giving a production of 2.5 million litres of spirit.

The distillery has an excellent visitor centre and it is Diageo's third busiest after Talisker and Oban, attracting almost 40,000 visitors per year.

The only official bottling used to be the *12 year old Flora & Fauna*. In 2010, a *first fill sherry* bottled at *cask strength* and without age statement was released as a distillery exclusive. A couple of months earlier, a *single cask* distilled in *1995* was released as part of the Manager's Choice series.

Blair Athol 12 year old

GS – The nose is mellow and sherried, with brittle toffee. Sweet and fragrant. Relatively rich on the palate, with malt, raisins, sultanas and sherry. The finish is lengthy, elegant and slowly drying.

DR – The nose is rich and full, with orange and citrus fruit. The palate, too, is big and chunky, with some tannin and spice in the mix, and with water, parma violet notes.

Distillery Exclusive no age

Bowmore

Owner:
Morrison Bowmore
Distillers (Suntory)

Region/district:
Islay

Founded: **Status:** **Capacity:**
1779 Active (vc) 2 000 000 litres

Address: School Street, Bowmore, Islay,
Argyll PA43 7GS

Tel: **website:**
01496 810441 www.bowmore.com

History:
1779 – Bowmore Distillery is founded by
John Simpson and becomes the oldest Islay
distillery.

1837 – The distillery is sold to James and
William Mutter of Glasgow.

1892 – After additional construction, the
distillery is sold to Bowmore Distillery
Company Ltd, a consortium of English
businessmen.

1925 – J. B. Sheriff and Company takes over.

1929 – Distillers Company Limited (DCL) takes
over.

1950 – William Grigor & Son takes over.

1963 – Stanley P. Morrison buys the distillery
for £117,000 and forms Morrison Bowmore
Distillers Ltd.

1989 – Japanese Suntory buys a 35% stake in
Morrison Bowmore.

1993 – The legendary Black Bowmore is
launched. The recommended price is £100
(today it is at least ten times that if it can be
found). Another two versions are released
1994 and 1995.

1994 – Suntory now controls all of Morrison
Bowmore.

1995 – Bowmore is nominated 'Distiller of the
Year' in the International Wine and Spirits
competition.

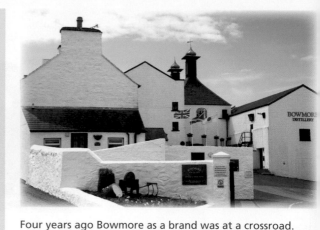

Four years ago Bowmore as a brand was at a crossroad.
Sales had certainly increased by 16% since 2002, but in
times when peated whiskies were in high demand and
competitors as Laphroaig, Ardbeg and Talisker increased
35-50%, this was mainly seen as a failure. Consumer confidence, at least amongst the whisky aficionados, was also
low and for them, Bowmore was seldom the first choice.
All the more gratifying for the owners, Morrison Bowmore,
to see that a complete change of scene has happened since
then. Sales volumes have increased by 26% to 175,000
cases sold in 2010 (whereof 85% is exported) in spite of the
disastrous economic downturn that started in 2008. The recent limited bottlings like Tempest, Laimrig and a few vintages have furthermore got the whisky enthusiasts to start
talking about Bowmore with newly gained respect. What
started this whole scene change was the complete overhaul
of the range in 2007 and the new focus on the Duty Free
market in favour of selling through supermarkets.
Bowmore is one of few Scottish distilleries with its own
malting floor (three in fact), with as much as 40% of the
malt requirement produced in-house. The remaining part
is bought from Simpsons in Berwick-upon-Tweed. Both
parts have a phenol specification of 25ppm and are always
mixed before mashing. The distillery has a stainless steel
semi-lauter mash tun, six washbacks of Oregon pine and
two pairs of stills. 27,000 casks are stored in two dunnage
and one racked warehouse. The building closest to the sea
and dating back to the 1700s, is probably the oldest whisky
warehouse still in use in Scotland. In 2011 they will be speeding up production compared to last year and will be doing
12-13 mashes per week and 1,7 million litres in the year.
The core range for domestic markets includes *Legend* (no
age), *12 years, Darkest 15 years, 18 years* and *25 years*. The
duty free line-up contains *Surf, Enigma, Mariner (15 years
old), 17 year old* and *Cask Strength*. Limited releases for
2011 are *Vintage 1982* (501 bottles), the third edition of
Tempest from first fill American oak bourbon casks and
bottled at cask strength and, finally, batch two of *Laimrig*.
The latter, was released for the first time in 2009 as an
exclusive for the Swedish market, but this year it will also
be launched in Switzerland, Canada and Taiwan. It has matured in ex-bourbon casks with an added finish in Oloroso
sherry butts. Limited releases from 2010 include a *40 year
old* and *Vintage 1981* and during 2007-2009, a handful of
extremely rare bottlings distilled in 1964 were released;
Black Bowmore, White Bowmore and *Gold Bowmore*.

History (continued):

1996 – A Bowmore 1957 (38 years) is bottled at 40.1% but is not released until 2000.

1999 – Bowmore Darkest with three years finish on Oloroso barrels is launched. A Claret cask strength is also released in 12,000 bottles.

2000 – Bowmore Dusk with two years finish in Bordeaux barrels is launched.

2001 – Bowmore Dawn with two years finish on Port pipes is launched. A bottle from 1890 is sold at an auction in Glasgow and brings in £14,300 which is a new world record.

2002 – A 37 year old Bowmore from 1964 and matured in fino casks is launched in a limited edition of 300 bottles (recommended price £1,500).

2003 – Another two expressions complete the wood trilogy which started with 1964 Fino - 1964 Bourbon and 1964 Oloroso.

2004 – Morrison Bowmore buys one of the most outstanding collections of Bowmore Single Malt from the private collector Hans Sommer. It totals more than 200 bottles and includes a number of Black Bowmore.

2005 – Bowmore 1989 Bourbon (16 years) and 1971 (34 years) are launched.

2006 – Bowmore 1990 Oloroso (16 years) and 1968 (37 years) are launched. A new and upgraded visitor centre is opened.

2007 – Dusk and Dawn disappear from the range and an 18 year old is introduced. New packaging for the whole range. 1991 (16yo) Port and Black Bowmore are released.

2008 – White Bowmore and a 1992 Vintage with Bourdeaux finish are launched.

2009 – Gold Bowmore, Maltmen´s Selection, Laimrig and Bowmore Tempest are released.

2010 – A 40 year old and Vintage 1981 are released.

2011– Vintage 1982 and new batches of Tempest and Laimrig are released.

Bowmore 12 year old

GS – An enticing nose of lemon and gentle brine leads into a smoky, citric palate, with notes of cocoa and boiled sweets appearing in the lengthy, complex finish.

DR – Rich peat and seaweed and the merest hint of characteristic palma violets on the nose, smoked fish in butter, menthol cough sweets and lemon on the palate, sweet peat in the finish.

Vintage 1982

Laimrig
2nd edition

Bowmore Tempest
3rd edition

12 years old

15 years old Darkest

18 years old

Braeval

Owner:
Chivas Brothers Ltd
(Pernod Ricard)

Region/district:
Speyside

Founded: **Status:** **Capacity:**
1973   Active   4 000 000 litres

Address: Chapeltown of Glenlivet,
Ballindalloch, Banffshire AB37 9JS

Tel: **website:**
01542 783042   -

History:
1973 – The Chivas and Glenlivet Group founds Braes of Glenlivet, the name which will be used for the first 20 years. The Glenlivet, Tomintoul and Tamnavulin are the only other distilleries situated in the Livet Glen valley. Production starts in October.

1975 – Three stills are increased to five.

1978 – Five stills are further expanded to six.

1994 – The distillery changes name to Braeval.

2001 – Pernod Ricard takes over Chivas Brothers.

2002 – Braeval is mothballed in October.

2008 – The distillery starts producing again in July.

Deerstalker 10 year old

DR – Grass and violin bow on the nose, zippy sherbet and citrus fruit on the palate, with a clean and refreshing finish.

Braeval (or Braes of Glenlivet as it is sometimes called) is situated in a very remote part of the Highlands south of Glenlivet and with Tamnavulin as its closest distillery neighbour. The isolated Braes was a haven for illicit distillers from the 1780s to the early 1800s and the whisky was smuggled out of the valley along narrow paths. But the secluded area also proved to be a foot-hold for persecuted Catholics during most part of the 18th century. It was also here that they established a school for priests, Scalan – the forbidden college. The ruins are still there to be seen.
The distillery is both impressive and surprisingly handsome, despite that it was built to function as a typical working distillery. It is also the highest situated distillery in Scotland at 1665 feet above sea level, beating Dalwhinnie with almost 100 feet.
When Braeval was built in the mid 1970s, a new type of efficient mash tun (the lauter tun) had already been introduced at other distilleries. It was therefore surprising that the new distillery (as well as its sister distillery Allt-a-Bhainne) was equipped with the old fashioned type of mash tun with rakes. In 2012, however, a new mash tun will be installed of the same highly efficient type as Glenlivet, only slightly smaller. The rest of the equipment consists of thirteen washbacks made of stainless steel (there used to be 15 but two of them have recently been converted into hot water storage tanks) and six stills. There used to be four pairs but now each of the two wash stills serve two spirit stills. The capacity is 25 mashes per week and since there are no warehouses on site, the spirit is tankered away for filling and storage. The whole production is used for blended Scotch and there are no official bottlings.
Independent bottler, Aberko Ltd., have two versions from the distillery in their range of Deerstalker single malts – a 10 year old and a 15 year old.

Deerstalker 10 year old

New Websites To Watch

www.connosr.com
This whisky social networking community is a virtual smorgasbord for any whisky lover! Pierre and Jean-Luc bring you (apart from a community where you, yourself, can contribute), reviews, news, features and from autumn 2011, Dominic Roskrow´s new on-line magazine – World Whisky Review!

www.jewishsinglemaltwhiskysociety.com
A blog filled mainly by whisky reviews (accompanied by lots of great images) but also interviews and field trips. The beauty of the site is the way Joshua "Yossi" Hatton writes – captivating and with good humour. He has also linked his reviews with different moods to give you a hint when to drink that particular whisky.

www.canadianwhisky.org
Finally – a website about Canadian whisky! Certified Malt Maniac and Canadian, Davin de Kergommeaux, presents reviews, news and views on the subject. The design is highly professional as is the quality of the content.

www.whiskyisrael.co.il
Gal Granov has hosted this blog for two years now and one thing that impresses me is that almost every day, there is something new to read. And it´s high quality stuff! It is mostly whisky reviews but recently Gal has added reports from his trips around the whisky world. More of that, please!

www.thebalvenie.com
Few websites from the producers deserve to be in this list. There´s simply to much marketing to cope with! The Balvenie is an exception and mainly for one thing – The Whisky Academy. This is a series of 34 short films covering every angle of the whisky subject and starring the likes of Charles Maclean, Sukhinder Singh, David Stewart etc.

www.thewhiskywire.com
Steve Rush mixes great reviews of the very latest bottlings with presentations of some classic expressions. No scores – "just" well-written comments! Add to that whisky news and, not least, interviews with lots of whisky insiders.

Some Old Favourites

www.maltmadness.com
Our all-time favourite with something for everyone. Managed by malt maniac Johannes van den Heuvel.

www.maltmaniacs.org
A bunch of knowledgeable whisky lovers dissect, debate, attack and praise the phenomena of the whisky world.

blog.maltadvocate.com
John Hansell is well situated with his contacts in the business to write a first class blog on every aspect of whisky.

www.whiskyfun.com
Serge Valentin, one of the Malt Maniacs, is almost always first with well written tasting notes on new releases.

www.nonjatta.blogspot.com
A blog by Chris Bunting with a wealth of interesting information on Japanese whisky as well as Japanese culture.

www.whiskyreviews.blogspot.com
Ralfy does this video blog with tastings and field reports in an educational yet easy-going and entertaining way.

www.caskstrength.net
Joel and Neil won a Drammie Award for this blog and deservedly so. Initiated, entertaining and well written.

www.edinburghwhiskyblog.com
Lucas and Chris review new releases, interview industry people and cover various news from the whisky world.

www.whiskycast.com
The best whisky-related podcast on the internet and one that sets the standard for podcasts in other genres as well.

www.whiskywhiskywhisky.com
An active forum for whisky friends with lots of daily comments on new whiskies, industry news, whisky events etc.

www.whiskyintelligence.com
The best site on all kinds of whisky news. The first whisky website you should log into every morning!

www.whisky-news.com
Apart from daily news, this site contains tasting notes, distillery portraits, lists of retailers, events etc.

www.dramming.com
Takes a wide-angle view of the whisky world including trip reports, whisky ratings, whisky business, articles etc.

www.guidscotchdrink.com
Tasting notes is one part of this site but the highlights are the many comments on current events and trends.

www.whiskyforum.se
Swedish whisky forum with more than 1,800 enthusiasts. Excellent debate as well as more than 2,000 tasting notes.

www.whisky-pages.com
Top class whisky site with features, directories, tasting notes, book reviews, whisky news, glossary and a forum.

www.whiskynotes.be
This blog is almost entirely about tasting notes (and lots of them, not least independent bottlings) plus some news.

www.whiskyforeveryone.com
Educational site, perfect for beginners, with a blog where both new releases and affordable standards are reviewed.

blog.thewhiskyexchange.com
Tim Forbes from The Whisky Exchange writes about new bottlings as well as the whisky industry in general.

www.ardbegproject.com
A temple for those of you who want to know everything about Ardbeg distillery and, especially, all the bottlings.

www.whiskymag.com
The official website of the printed 'Whisky Magazine'. A very active whisky forum with over 3000 members.

www.whisky-distilleries.info
A great site that is absolutely packed with information about distilleries as well as history and recent bottlings.

Bruichladdich

Owner: **Region/district:**
Bruichladdich Distillery Co Islay

Founded: **Status:**   **Capacity:**
1881   Active (vc)   1 500 000 litres

Address: Bruichladdich, Islay, Argyll PA49 7UN

Tel: **website:**
01496 850221   www.bruichladdich.com

History:
1881 – Barnett Harvey builds the distillery with money left by his brother William III to his three sons William IV, Robert and John Gourlay. The Harvey family already owns the distilleries Yoker and Dundashill.

1886 – Bruichladdich Distillery Company Ltd is founded and reconstruction commences.

1889 – William Harvey becomes Manager and remains on that post until his death in 1937.

1929 – Temporary closure.

1936 – The distillery reopens.

1938 – Joseph Hobbs, Hatim Attari and Alexander Tolmie purchase the distillery for £23 000 through the company Train & McIntyre.

1938 – Operations are moved to Associated Scottish Distillers.

1952 – The distillery is sold to Ross & Coulter from Glasgow.

1960 – A. B. Grant buys Ross & Coulter.

1961 – Own maltings ceases and malt is brought in from Port Ellen.

1968 – Invergordon Distillers take over.

1975 – The number of stills increases to four.

1983 – Temporary closure.

1993 – Whyte & Mackay buys Invergordon Distillers.

1995 – The distillery is mothballed in January.

1998 – In production again for a few months, and then mothballed.

During 2011, the owners of Bruichladdich could celebrate the 10th anniversary of the first distillation since they took over in 2000. Part of the celebration was the release of their first won 10 year old but they also laucnhed a complete new website. The future looks bright for the company as they are now selling no less than 40,000 cases per year. The profit before tax (£905,000) was up by 61% compared to 2009 and they had a turnover of £7m. The plans to build a new distillery on the old Port Charlotte site still exist. They have the planning permission but for finacial resons they have decided to put the start of the building on hold.

Last year, the only functioning Lomond still in the industry, was installed. It was brought to Bruichladdich in 2004 just before Inverleven distillery (where it had been working until 1985) was to be demolished. Contrary to ordinary pot stills, Lomond stills have a rectifying column attached with plates that can be adjusted to achieve the desired amount of reflux. So far, the still has been used for the production of Botanist Gin, a new addition to Bruichladdich´s range. The distillery is also equipped with a cast iron, open mash tun from 1881, six washbacks of Oregon pine and two pairs of stills. The yearly production at Bruichladdich has now increased to 800,000 litres of alcohol and all whisky produced is based on Scottish barley.

There are three main lines in Bruichladdich's production; lightly peated Bruichladdich, moderately peated Port Charlotte and the heavily peated Octomore. A traditional core range has become increasingly difficult to identify as many of the first bottlings with an age statement are sold out. *Rocks, Laddie Classic, Organic, Islay Grown, 18 year old, Black Art, Infinity, PC* and *Octomore*. The biggest news in 2011, was the addition of the first *10 year old* from the new owner´s production, which was released in September. A new expression of Port Charlotte was released in autumn 2011, *PC9*, and this will be the last limited release of PC. From 2012 it will have reached the age of 10 and be a part of the core range. Two new releases of Octomore also saw the light of day during 2011 – *Octomore 4_167* and *Octomore 4.2*. During Islay Festival in May, two bourbon matured expressions were launched, *The Ancien Regime* (12 years) was among the very last spirit to be distilled under the previous owners and *Rennaisance* (9 years) is from the first batches produced under the new regime. Included in limited releases during 2011 were also new versions of the *40 year old* and *Islay Barley 2004* as well as a *10 year old Micro Provenance*.

History (continued):

2000 – Murray McDavid buys the distillery from JBB Greater Europe for £6.5 million.

2001 – Jim McEwan from Bowmore becomes Production Director. The first distillation (Port Charlotte) is on 29th May and the first distillation of Bruichladdich starts in July. In September the owners' first bottlings from the old casks are released, 10, 15 and 20 years old.

2002 – The world's most heavily peated whisky is produced on 23rd October when Octomore (80ppm) is distilled.

2003 – Bruichladdich becomes the only distillery on Islay bottling on-site. It is awarded Distillery of the Year for the second time and launches the golf series, Links, 14 years old.

2004 – Second edition of the 20 year old (nicknamed Flirtation) and 3D, also called The Peat Proposal, are launched.

2005 – Several new expressions are launched - the second edition of 3D, Infinity (a mix of 1989, 1990, 1991 and Port Charlotte), Rocks, Legacy Series IV, The Yellow Submarine and The Twenty 'Islands'.

2006 – Included in a number of new releases in autumn is the first official bottling of Port Charlotte; PC5.

2007 – New releases include Redder Still, Legacy 6, two new Links, PC6 and an 18 year old.

2008 – More than 20 new expressions including the first Octomore, Bruichladdich 2001, PC7, Golder Still and two sherry matured from 1998.

2009 – New releases include Classic, Organic, Black Art, Infinity 3, PC8, Octomore 2 and X4+3 - the first quadruple distilled single malt.

2010 – PC Multi Vintage, Organic MV, Octomore/3_152, Bruichladdich 40 year old are released.

2011 – The first 10 year old from own production is released as well as PC9, Octomore 4_167, Ancien Regime and Rennaisance.

PC 9

Octomore/3_152

Organic

Rennaisance

Rocks

The Laddie Ten

Bruichladdich 12 year old

GS – A light, elegant nose of fresh fruit and vanilla fudge. Medium-bodied, smooth, and malty. Becoming nuttier. Spicy oak in the finish.

DR – Very welcoming mix of melon, grape and pear on the nose, and over-ripe peach, soft melon and other sweet fruits on the palate, with a delightful clean and fresh finish.

Port Charlotte PC8

GS – A big hit of sweet peat and malt on the nose. Liquorice and a hint of rubber when water is added. Quite dry on the slightly peppery palate; sweeter and fruitier when diluted. Lingering ash notes in the lengthy, plain chocolate finish.

DR – Classic Port Charlotte peaty smoky nose, but a maturer note on the palate. It's big and bold with citrus fruits, but with sweet honeycomb and Horlicks malt drink in the mix. The peat coats the mouth and lingers on.

Bunnahabhain

Owner: **Region/district:**
Burn Stewart Distillers   Islay
(CL Financial)

Founded: **Status:**   **Capacity:**
1881   Active (vc)   2 500 000 litres

Address: Port Askaig, Islay, Argyll PA46 7RP

Tel: **website:**
01496 840646   www.bunnahabhain.com

History:
1881 – William Robertson of Robertson & Baxter, founds the distillery together with the brothers William and James Greenless, owners of Islay Distillers Company Ltd.

1883 – Production starts in earnest in January.

1887 – Islay Distillers Company Ltd merges with William Grant & Co. in order to form Highland Distilleries Company Limited.

1963 – The two stills are augmented by two more.

1982 – The distillery closes.

1984 – The distillery reopens. A 21 year old is released to commemorate the 100th anniversary of Bunnahabhain.

1999 – Edrington takes over Highland Distillers and mothballs Bunnahabhain but allows for a few weeks of production a year.

2001 – A 35 year old from 1965 is released in a limited edition of 594 bottles during Islay Whisky Festival.

2002 – As in the previous year, Islay Whisky Festival features another Bunnahabhain – 1966, a 35 year old in sherry casks. Auld Acquaintance 1968 is launched at the Islay Jazz Festival.

2003 – In April Edrington sells Bunnahabhain and Black Bottle to Burn Stewart Distilleries (C. L. World Brands) at the princely sum of £10 million. A 40 year old from 1963 is launched.

2004 – The first limited edition of the peated version is a 6 year old called Moine.

2005 – Three limited editions are released - 34 years old, 18 years old and 25 years old.

2006 – 14 year old Pedro Ximenez and 35 years old are launched.

2008 – Darach Ur is released for the travel retail market and Toiteach (a peated 10 year old) is launched on a few selected markets.

2009 – Moine Cask Strength is released during Feis Isle.

2010 – The peated Cruach-Mhòna and a limited 30 year old are released.

When Burn Stewart took over Bunnahabhain distillery from Edrington in 2003, they also got the famous blend Black Bottle. The idea with that brand is that it should contain malt whisky from all the distilleries on Islay. For quite a few years now, it has been hard for the owners to acquire whisky from some of the Islay neighbours, so they have to rely more and more on Bunnahabhain malt. That is one reason why the owners have increased the production of peated Bunnahabhain (which at least since the 1960s has been unpeated) and it now stands at 20% of the total. Black Bottle is selling around 40,000 cases per year while Bunnahabhain single malt sells 16,000 cases.

The distillery is equipped with a traditional stainless steel mash tun, six washbacks made of Oregon Pine and two pairs of stills. The washbacks are huge (110,000 litres) but are only filled with 66,000 litres of wort for the 70-80 hours of fermentation. The stills are also quite big but only filled to 47% which gives more copper contact for the spirit and a lighter whisky. The spirit destined for single malt bottling and for the Black Bottle blend is stored on site in six dunnage and one racked warehouse, (totalling 21,000 casks) while the rest is shipped to other sites for maturation. The production for 2011 will be 1.3 million litres.

The core range consists of *12, 18* and *25 years old*, as well as a *10 year old* version of the peated Bunnahabhain called *Toiteach*. There are also two travel retail exclusives. The first, released in 2008, is *Darach Ur* with no age statement and in 2010, *Cruach-Mhòna* was released. The latter is a peatier version of Toiteach made up from young, heavily peated Bunnahabhain matured in ex bourbon and refill casks along with 20-21 years old matured in ex sherry butts. For Islay Festival 2011, a *14 year old* with a 3 year finish in Cognac casks was launched. Previous limited bottlings include a *30 year old* released in 2010.

12 years old

Bunnahabhain 12 year old

GS – The nose is fresh, with light peat and discreet smoke. More overt peat on the nutty and fruity palate, but still restrained for an Islay. The finish is full-bodied and lingering, with a hint of vanilla and some smoke.

DR – Ginger and barley candy on the nose, then sweet and sour mix on the palate, lots of sweetness but with a distinctive savoury and earthy undertow.

Bushmills

Owner:
Diageo

Region/district:
N Ireland (Co. Antrim)

Founded: **Status:** **Capacity:**
1784 Active (vc) 4 500 000 litres

Address: 2 Distillery Road, Bushmills,
Co. Antrim BT57 8XH

Tel: **website:**
028 20731521 www.bushmills.com

History:
1608 – James I issues Sir Thomas Philips a licence for whiskey distilling.

1784 – The distillery is formally registered.

1885 – Fire destroys part of the distillery.

1890 – S.S. Bushmills, the distillery's own steamship, makes its maiden voyage across the Atlantic to deliver whiskey to America and then heads on to Singapore, China and Japan.

1923 – The distillery is acquired by Belfast wine and spirit merchant Samuel Wilson Boyd. Anticipating the end of US prohibition, he gears Bushmills up for expansion and increases production.

1939-1945 – No distilling during the war. The distillery is partly converted to accommodate American servicemen.

1972 – Bushmills joins Irish Distillers Group which was formed in 1966. Floor maltings ceases.

1987 – Pernod Ricard acquires Irish Distillers.

1996 – Bushmills 16 years old is launched.

2005 – Bushmills is sold to Diageo at a price tag of €295.5 million as a result of Pernod Ricard's acquisition of Allied Domecq.

2007 – The 40 year old cast iron mash tun is replaced by a new one of stainless steel at a cost of £1.4m.

2008 – Celebrations commemorate the 400th anniversary of the original license to distil, granted to the area in 1608.

Bushmills 10 year old
DR – Autumn orchard of over-ripe apples on the nose, soft red apples and pear on the palate, soft sweetie finish.

In the late 1980s the picture of Irish whiskey was painted a completely different way than today. All production in the country laid in the hands of Pernod Ricard, as did the ownership of two of the biggest brands. Irish whiskey was furthermore as a category, outside the whisky consumers' thirst for new and exciting brands. Today we have three companies producing the whiskey and three big companies owning one each of the top brands (Jameson/PernodRicard, Tullamore Dew/W Grant & Sons and Bushmills/Diageo) with a new kid on the block climbing fast in the shape of Cooley's. What's even more important – there is a buzz surrounding whiskey from Ireland and not just in the old markets but around the world.

Diageo have clearly shown that Bushmills is a brand to invest in, even if the plans may seem somewhat unrealistic. Since the take-over in 2005, no less than £10 million has flowed into the distillery, resulting in a new mash tun, new stills, more warehouses and a new bottle design. Bushmill's now has ten stills and since 2008, the production runs seven days a week which means 4.5 million litres a year. Two kinds of malt are used, one unpeated and one slightly peated. The distillery uses triple distillation, which is the traditional Irish method.

A few years ago Diageo set the goal to sell 1 million cases of Bushmills by 2012 but in 2009 they had only managed to sell 500,000 cases which gives them place number three in the rankings after Jameson (3 million) and Tullamore Dew (650,000 cases).

Bushmills' core range of single malts consists of a 10 year old, a 10 year old *Triple Wood* with a finish in Port pipes for 6-9 months and a *21 year old* finished in Madeira casks for two years. There is also a *12 year old Distillery Reserve* which is sold exclusively at the distillery and the *1608 Anniversary Edition*. Black Bush and Bushmills Original are the two main blended whiskeys in the range. Bushmills is open to the public and the visitor centre receives more than 100,000 visitors per year.

10 years old

Caol Ila

Owner:
Diageo

Region/district:
Islay

Founded: **Status:** **Capacity:**
1846 Active (vc) 6 400 000 litres

Address: Port Askaig, Islay, Argyll PA46 7RL

Tel: **website:**
01496 302760 www.malts.com

History:
1846 – Hector Henderson founds Caol Ila.

1852 – Henderson, Lamont & Co. is subjected to financial difficulties and Henderson is forced to sell Caol Ila to Norman Buchanan.

1863 – Norman Buchanan encounters financial troubles and sells to the blending company Bulloch, Lade & Co. from Glasgow.

1879 – The distillery is rebuilt and expanded.

1920 – Bulloch, Lade & Co. is liquidated and the distillery is taken over by Caol Ila Distillery.

1927 – DCL becomes sole owners.

1972 – All the buildings, except for the warehouses, are demolished and rebuilt.

1974 – The renovation, which totals £1 million, is complete and six new stills are installed.

1999 – Experiments with a completely unpeated malt are performed.

2002 – The first official bottlings since Flora & Fauna/Rare Malt appear; 12 years, 18 years and Cask Strength (c. 10 years).

2003 – A 25 year old cask strength is released.

2005 – A 25 year old Special Release is launched.

2006 – Unpeated 8 year old and 1993 Moscatel finish are released.

2007 – The second edition of the unpeated 8 year old is released.

2008 – The third edition of unpeated 8 year old is released.

2009 – The fourth edition of the unpeated version (10 year old) is released.

2010 – A 25 year old, a 1999 Feis Isle bottling and a 1997 Manager's Choice are released.

2011 – An unpeated 12 year old and the unaged Moch are released.

Caol Ila 12 year old
GS – Iodine, fresh fish and smoked bacon feature on the nose, along with more delicate, floral notes. Smoke, malt, lemon and peat on the slightly oily palate. Peppery peat in the drying finish.

DR – Barbecued fish and seaweed on the nose, oily bacon-fat, squeezed lemon and sweet smoke on the palate, immensely satisfying citrusy seaside barbecue of a finish.

Peated single malt from Islay is constantly sought-after by the whisky buffs around the world. To Diageo it is also a vital part of their major blended whiskies, not least Johnnie Walker and, with an increasing demand for that brand, comes a need for more production capacity. Caol Ila is by far the biggest distillery on Islay and already in 2010, the owners went from a 5-day production week to a 7-day but that wasn't enough. A decision was made to increase the capacity from 5.7 million litres per year to 6.4 million. In June 2011 the distillery closed for six months for a major upgrading. The cast iron mash tun from 1989 was replaced by a full lauter mash tun with a 13 tonnes capacity and two new wooden washbacks were installed, giving a total number of 10 washbacks. A new control system was installed in the stillhouse but the number of stills (eight) remained the same. The whole investment amounted to £3.5m and it makes Caol Ila the fifth biggest malt whisky distillery in Scotland. The whisky from Caol Ila is peated but production runs of unpeated spirit has at least occurred up until 2005. The outcome is destined for blended whisky but limited editions of unpeated Caol Ila have been released.

Sales of Caol Ila single malt have seen an impressive increase in the last few years and the brand currently sells around 50,000 cases per year. The core range consists of *12* and *18 years old*, *Distiller's Edition* Moscatel finish and *Cask Strength*, but was extended with a *25 year old* in summer 2010. At the beginning of 2011, *Caol Ila Moch*, the first official bottling from the distillery without an age statement or distillation year, was released for select European markets and in conjunction with the 2011 Islay Festival, a *2000 sherry-matured* from European oak was released. The sixth edition of the *unpeated Caol Ila*, a *12 year old*, was released in autumn 2011.

Caol Ila Moch

Cardhu

Cardhu

Owner:		Region/district:
Diageo		Speyside
Founded:	Status:	Capacity:
1824	Active (vc)	3 200 000 litres

Address:
Knockando, Aberlour, Moray AB38 7RY

Tel:
01479 874635 (vc)

website:
www.discovering-distilleries.com

History:
1824 – John Cumming applies for and obtains a licence for Cardhu Distillery.

1846 – John Cumming dies and his son Lewis takes over.

1872 – Lewis dies and his wife Elizabeth takes over.

1884 – A new distillery is built to replace the old.

1893 – John Walker & Sons purchases Cardhu for £20,500 but the Cumming family continues operations. The whisky changes name from Cardow to Cardhu.

1908 – The name reverts to Cardow.

1960-61 – Reconstruction and expansion of stills from four to six.

1981 – The name changes to Cardhu.

1998 – A visitor centre is constructed.

2002 – Diageo changes Cardhu single malt to a vatted malt with contributions from other distilleries in it.

2003 – The whisky industry protests sharply against Diageo's plans.

2004 – Diageo withdraws Cardhu Pure Malt.

2005 – The 12 year old Cardhu Single Malt is relaunched and a 22 year old is released.

2009 – Cardhu 1997, a single cask in the new Manager's Choice range is released.

Cardhu 12 year old

GS – The nose is relatively light and floral, quite sweet, with pears, nuts and a whiff of distant peat. Medium-bodied, malty and sweet in the mouth. Medium-length in the finish, with sweet smoke, malt and a hint of peat.

DR – Honeycomb and chocolate Crunchie bar on the nose, fluffy over-ripe apples, toffee, boiled sweets on the palate, delightful clean and crisp finish.

When you drive on the B9102 from Macallan you come to a small cluster of five distilleries cluttered around River Spey. Four of them (two closed and two producing) are hidden down in the glen but the fifth, Cardhu, lies proudly on a small hill just by the road. It is an exceptionally beautiful distillery and with that location it is a bit surprising that only 5,000 visitors a year find their way here when ten times as many go to the more remote Talisker on Skye. Cardhu is without comparison the best selling of the Diageo single malts (with Talisker in second place) and the main market is Spain where it is number one. The troublesome Iberian market has, however, decreased Cardhu's sales the last eight years. The sales of Scotch single malt has decreased by 40% in the country since 2004 and that is exactly the same figure as Cardhu shows.

The distillery is equipped with one stainless steel full lauter mash tun, ten washbacks (six made of Scottish larch, two of stainless steel and two newlymade of Douglas fir) and all with a fermentation time of 64 hours and three pairs of stills. During 2011, Cardhu will be working a seven-day week with a production of a little more than three million litres of alcohol. On site are five dunnage warehouses with 7,500 casks maturing, mainly American hogsheads and a few European sherry butts.

Cardhu is a signature malt for Johnnie Walker and the distillery is also the spiritual home for the world famous blend. The core range consists of the *12 year old only*. In October 2006, a *Special Cask Reserve* with no age statement was released in Spain. A *single cask from 1997* was released in autumn 2009 as part of the new series Manager's Choice.

12 years old

Clynelish

Owner:
Diageo

Region/district:
Northern Highlands

Founded:
1967

Status:
Active (vc)

Capacity:
4 200 000 litres

Address: Brora, Sutherland KW9 6LR

Tel:
01408 623003 (vc)

website:
www.malts.com

History:
1819 – The 1st Duke of Sutherland founds a distillery called Clynelish Distillery.

1827 – The first licensed distiller, James Harper, files for bankruptcy and John Matheson takes over.

1846 – George Lawson & Sons become new licensees.

1896 – James Ainslie & Heilbron takes over.

1912 – James Ainslie & Co. narrowly escapes bankruptcy and Distillers Company Limited (DCL) takes over together with James Risk.

1916 – John Walker & Sons buys a stake of James Risk's stocks.

1931 – The distillery is mothballed.

1939 – Production restarts.

1960 – The distillery becomes electrified.

1967 – A new distillery, also named Clynelish, is built adjacent to the first one.

1968 – 'Old' Clynelish is mothballed in August.

1969 – 'Old' Clynelish is reopened as Brora and starts using a very peaty malt.

1983 – Brora is closed in March.

2002 – A 14 year old is released.

2006 – A Distiller´s Edition 1991 finished in Oloroso casks is released.

2009 – A 12 year old is released for Friends of the Classic Malts.

2010 – A 1997 Manager´s Choice single cask is released.

Clynelish distillery was founded by the 1st Duke of Sutherland, one of the most controversial persons in Scottish history. At the beginning of the 19th century he had the largest private estate in Europe (1.5 million acres) and was also the wealthiest man in the United Kingdom. He was of the opinion that the land where farmers had lived for centuries could better be used for sheep farming and from1811-1820 he forced thousands of tenants from their homes. This has become known as The Highland Clearances. But the distillery that we call Clynelish today is a modern one, yet lies on the same site as the old distillery which ended its days under the name Brora (see page 207). Clynelish and Brora were operating together for 14 years but the character of the single malts are completely different, with Brora being much more peated (at least some of the bottlings). Clynelish distillery, with its beautiful still house with one wall glazed, is equipped with a cast iron full lauter mash tun, eight wooden washbacks, two stainless steel washbacks installed in 2008 and three pairs of stills (with the spirit stills being larger than the wash stills). One distinct character in the Clynelish spirit is a degree of waxiness and it is assumed that it comes from the cast iron low wines and feints receivers that they use. In these vessels a layer of oily residue is created quickly which most distilleries clean out regularly. At Clynelish they don´t and this probably adds to the flavour, as do the long fermentations (80 hours). Since 2008, the distillery has been running at full capacity every year doing 18 mashes per week, producing 4.2 million litres of alcohol.

The Clynelish single malt sells around 8,000 cases per year. Official bottlings include a *14 year old* and a *Distiller´s Edition* with an Oloroso Seco finish. The first distillery shop exclusive, a *cask strength*, was released in 2008. In 2009 another addition was made to the range, a *12 year old* for Friends of the Classic Malts and in 2010 a *single cask* (first fill bourbon) distilled in 1997 was released as part of the Manager´s Choice series.

Clynelish 14 year old
GS – A nose that is fragrant, spicy and complex, with candle wax, malt and a whiff of smoke. Notably smooth in the mouth, with honey and contrasting citric notes, plus spicy peat, before a brine and tropical fruit finish.

DR – Fresh green fruit and unripe melon on the nose, sweet almost fizzy lemon sherbet on the palate, a wispy hint of peat and pepper, and satisfying and balanced finish.

14 years old

Cooley

Owner:
Cooley Distillery plc

Region/district:
Ireland (County Louth)

Founded: 1987
Status: Active
Capacity: 3 250 000 litres

Address: Riverstown, Cooley, Co. Louth

Tel: +353 (0)42 9376102
website: www.cooleywhiskey.com

History:

1987 – John Teeling purchases Ceimici Teo Distillery in Dundalk. Previously it has produced spirits in column stills (e. g. vodka) and is now renamed Cooley Distillery.

1988 – Willie McCarter acquires part of A. A. Watt Distillery and the brand Tyrconnell and merges with Teeling. Teeling simultaneously buys decommissioned Locke's Kilbeggan Distillery.

1989 – A pair of pot stills is installed for production of both malt and grain whiskey.

1992 – Locke's Single Malt, without age statement, is launched as the first single malt from the distillery. Cooley encounters financial troubles and and stops production.

1995 – Finances improve and production resumes.

1996 – Connemara is launched.

2000 – Locke's 8 year old single malt is launched.

2003 – The Connemara 12 year old is launched.

2006 – Five Connemara Single Casks from 1992 are released.

2007 – Kilbeggan distillery is reopened.

2009 – New packaging for the Connemara range and release of the first in The Small Batch Collection.

2010 – The heavily peated Connemara Turf Mor is released.

2011 – Connemara Bog Oak is released.

Connemara 12 year old

DR – Soft fruit and tarry peat on the nose, then fluffy red apples, toffee and smoke intriguingly mixed into an unusual and very enticing whole. Smoke in the finish.

The success for Cooley Distillery continues. Apart from scooping awards for ther whiskies, turnover in 2010 increased by 12% to €16m and the US market was a particulkar reason for rejoyce, with sales doubling last year. But the success doesn't come cheap. No less than €7.5m has been spent the last two years in new bottling equipment at Cooley, a new warehouse (with another one potentially being added) and maintenance work on both the grain and malt distilleries.

Operating both pot stills and column stills at Cooley, means they can produce both malt and grain whiskey. The equipment consists of a mash tun and washbacks made of stainless steel, two copper pot stills and two column stills. During 2011 they will be distilling more or less at full capacity which equals 650,000 litres of malt spirit and 2.6 million litres of grain spirit. They have already started experimenting with triple distillation and are looking into production of pure pot still as well. There are more than 60,000 casks in the warehouses and apart from producing for their own needs, Cooley also sells a large quantity to other companies and supemarkets.

The Cooley range of whiskies consists of several brands. *Connemara* single malts, which are all more or less peated, consist of a no age, a *12 year old*, a *cask strength*, *sherry finish* and the heavily peated *Turf Mor*. The two latter are part of a series of limited expressions called The Small Batch Collection. A new member of this range for 2011 is *Bog Oak* with the whiskey maturing in 3000 year old oak found in the Irish bog. The rest of Cooley's single malt range includes *Tyrconnel no age*, *Tyrconnel 15 year old single cask* and *Tyrconnel wood finishes* as well as *Lucke's 8 years old*.

A number of blended whiskeys are also produced as is a single grain, *Greenore 8 years old*. An *18 year old* version of the latter was recently released.

Connemara 12 years old

Cragganmore

Diageo

Region/district:
Speyside

Founded: 1869
Status: Active (vc)
Capacity: 2 000 000 litres

Address: Ballindalloch, Moray AB37 9AB

Tel: 01479 874700
website: www.malts.com

History:
1869 – John Smith, who already runs Ballindalloch and Glenfarclas Distilleries, founds Cragganmore.

1886 – John Smith dies and his brother George takes over operations.

1893 – John's son Gordon, at 21, is old enough to assume responsibility for operations.

1901 – The distillery is refurbished and modernized with help of the famous architect Charles Doig.

1912 – Gordon Smith dies and his widow Mary Jane supervises operations.

1917 – The distillery closes.

1918 – The distillery reopens and Mary Jane installs electric lighting.

1923 – The distillery is sold to the newly formed Cragganmore Distillery Co. where Mackie & Co. and Sir George Macpherson-Grant of Ballindalloch Estate share ownership.

1927 – White Horse Distillers is bought by DCL which thus obtains 50% of Cragganmore.

1964 – The number of stills is increased from two to four.

1965 – DCL buys the remainder of Cragganmore.

1988 – Cragganmore 12 years becomes one of six selected for United Distillers´ Classic Malts.

1998 – Cragganmore Distillers Edition Double Matured (port) is launched for the first time.

2002 – A visitor centre opens in May.

2006 – A 17 year old from 1988 is released.

2010 – Manager´s Choice single cask 1997 and a limited 21 year old are released.

Cragganmore 12 year old
GS – A nose of sherry, brittle toffee, nuts, mild wood smoke, angelica and mixed peel. Elegant on the malty palate, with herbal and fruit notes, notably orange. Medium in length, with a drying, slightly smoky finish.

DR – The nose has honey, soft fruits and sweet spring meadow notes and is very inviting, and on the palate soft barley, summer fruits and a sweetness lead up to an almost tangy finish.

Cragganmore distillery was built in the same year (1869) that the Strathspey Railway was inaugurated and was one of the first distilleries in the Speyside area that started using the more modern way of transporting raw material, as well as mature whisky.

The distillery is equipped with a stainless steel full lauter mash tun which was installed in 1997. There are also six washbacks made of Oregon pine and two pairs of stills. The two spirit stills are peculiar with flat tops, which had already been introduced in the times of the founder, John Smith. As if that was not enough, the unusually T-shaped lyne arms increase the reflux which, together with the long fermentation time, sets the character of the spirit. The stills are attached to cast iron worm tubs on the outside for cooling the spirit vapours. Part of the production matures in three dunnage warehouses on site. Parts of the stills were replaced in 2011 and two of the washbacks are due for replacement in 2012. The distillery is currently doing 16 mashes per week, i. e. 1.6 million litres in the year.

For the past decade the sales of Cragganmore single malt has been stable at around 350,000 bottles per year and it also plays an important part in two blended whiskies; Old Parr and White Horse. The distillery lies a bit tucked away by a side road from the busy A95, but the number of visitors is increasing steadily and 2-3,000 people find their way to the visitor centre every year. The core range is made up of a *12 year old* and a *Distiller's Edition* with a finish in Port pipes. Two new limited bottlings appeared in 2010; a single *sherry cask* distilled in *1997* released as part of the Manager´s Choice series and a *21 year old* launched as a part of the yearly Special Releases. Older limited bottlings include a *14 year old*, a *29 year old* distilled in 1973 and a *17 year old* 2006.

12 years old

Craigellachie

Owner:
John Dewar & Sons
(Bacardi)

Region/district:
Speyside

Founded: **Status:** **Capacity:**
1891 Active 4 000 000 litres

Address: Aberlour, Banffshire AB38 9ST

Tel:
01340 872971

website:
-

History:

1891 – The distillery is built by Craigellachie–Glenlivet Distillery Company which has Alexander Edward and Peter Mackie as part-owners. The famous Charles Doig is the architect.

1898 – Production does not start until this year.

1916 – Mackie & Company Distillers Ltd takes over.

1924 – Peter Mackie dies and Mackie & Company changes name to White Horse Distillers.

1927 – White Horse Distillers are bought by Distillers Company Limited (DCL).

1930 – Administration is transferred to Scottish Malt Distillers (SMD), a subsidiary of DCL.

1964 – Refurbishing takes place and two new stills are bought, increasing the number to four.

1998 – United Distillers & Vintners (UDV) sells Craigellachie together with Aberfeldy, Brackla and Aultmore and the blending company John Dewar & Sons to Bacardi Martini.

2004 – The first bottlings from the new owners are a new 14 year old which replaces UDV's Flora & Fauna and a 21 year old cask strength from 1982 produced for Craigellachie Hotel.

Craigellachie 14 year old

GS – Citrus fruits, cereal and even a whiff of smoke on the nose. Comparatively full-bodied, with sweet fruits, malt and spice on the palate, plus earthy notes and a touch of liquorice in the slightly smoky and quite lengthy finish.

DR – Intriguing and deep mix of light fruits on the nose, a spicy bite then clean and smooth mouth feel, and a soft finish.

The Craigellachie distillery and the surrounding village takes its name from the huge cliff which dominates the landscape and actually means "rocky hill". The village dates back to the mid 18th century with the distillery being built around a century and a half later. This is right in the heart of the whisky country and while Craigellachie itself is a rather anonymous distillery, it is surrounded by famous neighbours – Macallan to the west, Glenfiddich to the south and Glen Grant to the north.

Malted barley is bought from Glenesk Maltings and the distillery has a modern Steinecker full lauter mash tun, installed in 2001, which replaced the old open cast iron mash tun. With its six revolving arms, the mash tun is an important reason for the distilleries effictiveness. Not only is the mashing time decreased severely, but a well implemented mashing also increases the spirit yield. At Craigellachie they constantly yield around 420 litres of spirit per tonne of barley. There are also eight washbacks made of larch with a fermentation time of 56-60 hours and two pairs of stills. The spirit vapours from the stills are condensed through worm tubs. The tub itself (in Craigellachies case made out of cast iron) can last for many years but the worms (the copper pipes where the spirit is condensed) need to be replaced every 5 to 10 years. In 2010/2011, a heat recovery system was installed to improve the energy efficiency. At the same time a new cooling tower was built to help cool the water that goes back into Spey river so as not to interfere with the fish population in the river. Without that, the distillery might have been forced to close down during the hottest period of the summer. Production during 2011 will be 21 mashes per week – the equivalent of 3.6 million litres of alcohol.

Most of the production goes into Dewar's blends but a *14 year old* was launched in 2004 and this is, so far, the only official bottling.

14 years old

Dailuaine

Owner:		Region/district:
Diageo		Speyside

Founded:	Status:	Capacity:
1852	Active	3 400 000 litres

Address: Carron, Banffshire AB38 7RE

Tel:	website:
01340 872500	www.malts.com

History:

1852 – The distillery is founded by William Mackenzie.

1865 – William Mackenzie dies and his widow leases the distillery to James Fleming, a banker from Aberlour.

1879 – William Mackenzie's son forms Mackenzie and Company with Fleming.

1891 – Dailuaine-Glenlivet Distillery Ltd is founded.

1898 – Dailuaine-Glenlivet Distillery Ltd merges with Talisker Distillery Ltd and forms Dailuaine-Talisker Distilleries Ltd.

1915 – Thomas Mackenzie dies without heirs.

1916 – Dailuaine-Talisker Company Ltd is bought by the previous customers John Dewar & Sons, John Walker & Sons and James Buchanan & Co.

1917 – A fire rages and the pagoda roof collapses. The distillery is forced to close.

1920 – The distillery reopens.

1925 – Distillers Company Limited (DCL) takes over.

1960 – Refurbishing. The stills increase from four to six and a Saladin box replaces the floor maltings.

1965 – Indirect still heating through steam is installed.

1983 – On site maltings is closed down and malt is purchased centrally.

1991 – The first official bottling, a 16 year old, is launched in the Flora & Fauna series.

1996 – A 22 year old cask strength from 1973 is launched as a Rare Malt.

1997 – A cask strength version of the 16 year old is launched.

2000 – A 17 year old Manager's Dram matured in sherry casks is launched.

2010 – A single cask from 1997 is released.

Dailuaine is one of many distilleries whose main task is to produce malt whisky to become part of a blended Scotch. Usually, the whisky from a certain distillery has its character set since decades back and the most important thing is to see that this character remains the same. Dailuaine is quite unique, however, because during the last five years, the owners (Diageo) have deliberately produced three different types of malt whisky here to ensure that supplies of certain flavour profiles are available for their blends. Until 2006, the newmake from the distillery was sulphury, to some extent thanks two a couple of steel condensers that have now been removed. From 2006 to 2010 a green and grassy type of spirit was distilled and from 2011 the newmake has a nutty character. This last flavour has been achieved through a more intense stirring of the mash tun to produce a cloudy wort and through shortened fermentation times.

The distillery, nicely tucked away by the Spey River, is equipped with a stainless steel full lauter mash tun, eight washbacks made of larch and three pairs of stills. The stills are nowadays equipped with copper condensers. There are also eight magnificent granite warehouses but the last time they were used for storing whisky was in 1989. Instead, the spirit is tankered away to Cambus for filling and then to the Diageo warehouses in Blackrange. In 2011 they will be doing 16 mashes per week during a 5-day week which is pretty much full production (3.4 million litres).

On the site lies a dark grains plants processing draff and pot ale into cattle feed and a bioplant which treats spent lees and wastewater. A decision has recently been made by the owners to upgrade the bioplant at a cost of £9.5m.

The core range is only the *16 year old* in the Flora & Fauna series. In April 2010 a limited ex-sherry *single cask* from *1997* was released as part of the Manager's Choice series.

Flora & Fauna 16 years old

Dailuaine 16 year old

GS – Barley, sherry and nuts on the substantial nose, developing into maple syrup. Medium-bodied, rich and malty in the mouth, with more sherry and nuts, plus ripe oranges, fruitcake, spice and a little smoke. The finish is lengthy and slightly oily, with almonds, cedar and slightly smoky oak.

DR – Rich and full nose, with plum, apricot jam and some treacle toffee. The palate is very full, rich, rounded and sweet with apricot and red berries. The finish is medium, fruity and sweet.

Dalmore

Owner:
Whyte & Mackay Ltd
(United Spirits)

Region/district:
Northern Highlands

Founded:
1839

Status:
Active (vc)

Capacity:
3 700 000 litres

Address: Alness, Ross-shire IV17 0UT

Tel:
01349 882362

website:
www.thedalmore.com

History:

1839 – Alexander Matheson founds the distillery.

1867 – Three Mackenzie brothers run the distillery.

1886 – Alexander Matheson dies.

1891 – Sir Kenneth Matheson sells the distillery for £14,500 to the Mackenzie brothers.

1917 – The Royal Navy moves in to start manufacturing American mines.

1920 – The Royal Navy moves out and leaves behind a distillery damaged by an explosion.

1922 – The distillery is in production again.

1956 – Floor malting replaced by a Saladin box.

1960 – Mackenzie Brothers (Dalmore) Ltd merges with Whyte & Mackay and forms the company Dalmore-Whyte & Mackay Ltd.

1966 – The number of stills is increased to eight.

1982 – The Saladin box is abandoned.

1990 – American Brands buys Whyte & Mackay.

1996 – Whyte & Mackay changes name to JBB (Greater Europe).

2001 – Through management buy-out, JBB (Greater Europe) is bought from Fortune Brands and changes name to Kyndal Spirits.

2002 – Kyndal Spirits changes name to Whyte & Mackay.

2004 – A new visitor centre opens.

2007 – United Spirits buys Whyte & Mackay. 15 year old, 1973 Cabernet Sauvignon and a 40 year old are released.

2008 – 1263 King Alexander III and Vintage 1974 are released.

2009 – New releases include an 18 year old, a 58 year old and a Vintage 1951.

2010 – The Dalmore Mackenzie 1992 Vintage is released.

2011 – More expressions in the River Collection and 1995 Castle Leod are released.

Dalmore 12 year old

GS – The attractively perfumed nose offers sweet malt, thick cut orange marmalade, sherry and a hint of leather. Full-bodied, with an initially quite dry sherry taste, though sweeter sherry develops in the mouth, along with spice and balancing, delicate, citrus notes. The finish is lengthy, with more spices, ginger, lingering Seville oranges and vanilla.

DR – Orange jelly and squidgy fruit on the nose, an impressive full confectionery and fruit salad taste on the softest of peat beds, and a wonderful and warming finish.

Under the guidance of Master Blender Richard Patterson, Dalmore single malt has slowly but surely been established as one of the most respected malt whiskies of Scotland. Therefore the owners, Whyte & Mackay, felt it necessary that the rather small visitor centre which opened in 2004, was upgraded. No less than £1m was invested and the new centre and shop opened during the summer of 2011.
The distillery is equipped with a semi-lauter mash tun, eight washbacks made of Oregon pine and four pairs of stills. The spirit stills have water jackets, a peculiar device that cannot be seen anywhere else. This allows cold water to circulate between the reflux bowl and the neck of the stills, thus increasing the reflux. Two weeks per year, a heavily pea-ted spirit is produced using a total of 800 tonnes of malt peated at 50 ppm. The owners expect to do 22 mashes per week during 2011 which amounts to 3.7 million litres.
In later years Dalmore has become known for its limited releases of rare and expensive whiskies. In last year's edition of the Yearbook we could report on *Candela, Sirius* and the most expensive, *Selene* at £12,500. In the autumn of 2010 this was matched by the 45 year old *Au-rora*, the 59 year old *Eos* and, in particular, the three decanters of *Dalmore Trinitas 64 year old*, sold for £100,000 each! In January 2011 *Astrum*, distil-led in 1966 with an 18 months finish in Gonzalez Byass casks, was released. The core range consists of *12, 15, 18 year old, Gran Reserva* and *1263 King Alexander III*. Limited releases in 2011 include *The Rivers Collection* where a part of the profit is donated to support the conservation of the rivers in Scotland. The concept was introduced in 2010 with the release of the *Dee Dram* and was expan-ded in 2011 to include the rivers *Spey, Tay* and *Tweed*. All expressions contain a 12 year old Dalmore. A *Dalmore 1995 Castle Leod* with an 18 months Bordeaux finish was also released.

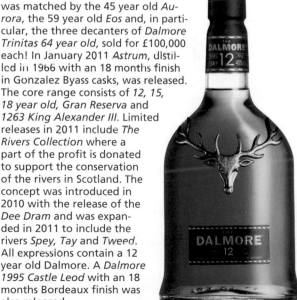

12 years old

Dalwhinnie

Owner:
Diageo

Region/district:
Northern Highlands

Founded: 1897

Status: Active (vc)

Capacity: 2 200 000 litres

Address: Dalwhinnie, Inverness-shire PH19 1AB

Tel: 01540 672219 (vc)

website: www.malts.com

History:
1897 – John Grant, George Sellar and Alexander Mackenzie from Kingussie commence building the facilities. The first name is Strathspey and the construction work amounts to £10,000.

1898 – Production starts in February. The owner encounters financial troubles after a few months and John Somerville & Co and A P Blyth & Sons take over in November and change the name to Dalwhinnie.

1905 – America's largest distillers, Cook & Bernheimer in New York, buys Dalwhinnie for £1,250 at an auction. The administration of Dalwhinnie is placed in the newly formed company James Munro & Sons.

1919 – Macdonald Greenlees & Willliams Ltd headed by Sir James Calder buys Dalwhinnie.

1926 – Macdonald Greenlees & Williams Ltd is bought by Distillers Company Ltd (DCL) which licences Dalwhinnie to James Buchanan & Co.

1930 – Operations are transferred to Scottish Malt Distilleries (SMD).

1934 – The distillery is closed after a fire in February.

1938 – The distillery opens again.

1968 – The maltings is decommissioned.

1986 – A complete refurbishing takes place.

1987 – Dalwhinnie 15 years becomes one of the selected six in United Distillers' Classic Malts.

1991 – A visitor centre is constructed.

1992 – The distillery closes and goes through a major refurbishment costing £3.2 million.

1995 – The distillery opens in March.

1998 – Dalwhinnie Distillers Edition 1980 (oloroso) is introduced for the first time. The other five in The Classic Malts, each with a different finish, are also introduced as Distillers Editions for the first time.

2002 – A 36 year old is released.

2003 – A 29 year old is released.

2006 – A 20 year old is released.

2010 – A Manager's Choice 1992 is released.

Dalwhinnie 15 year old

GS – The nose is fresh, with pine needles, heather and vanilla. Sweet and balanced on the fruity palate, with honey, malt and a very subtle note of peat. The medium length finish dries elegantly.

DR – Full honey and sweet peat on the nose, a rich creamy mouthfeel and a delicious honey and exotic fruits mix all layered on soft peat foundations.

It is virtually impossible to miss Dalwhinnie distillery when you travel the A9 between Perth and Inverness. There it is, on the outskirts of the Cairngorm wilderness, and not tucked away in a glen but exposed to wind and not least the cold. This is, in fact, the coldest place in Scotland. But not everyone passes the distillery – some 20,000 people stop by every year at the visitor centre.

Dalwhinnie is an important part of the Buchanan blend (as evidenced by the sign on the wall) which is incredibly popular in Mexico and Venezuela. In 2010 sales volumes of the brand increased by 10% which means a total of around 1.5 million cases. But as one of the original six Classic Malts, the single malt from the distillery also sells well, more than 70,000 cases last year.

Dalwhinnie distillery is equipped with a full lauter mash tun, six wooden washbacks (with a fermentation time of 60 hours) and just the one pair of stills. From the stills, the lyne arms lead out through the roofs to the wooden worm-tubs outside. During the eighties, the owners replaced the existing worm tubs with tube condensers but, after a while, discovered that the spirit's character changed and the worms were reinstalled.

The owners put up a target recently that they had to increase the total production of malt whisky within the company to 20 million litres. Ten of them would come from the new distillery Roseisle and the rest by squeezing out more from the other 27 distilleries. Dalwhinnie's contribution is to increase the number of working weeks during 2011 to 50 instead of the regular 46 and with 15 mashes per week they will manage to do 2.2 million litres this year. The core range is made up of a *15 year old* and a *Distiller's Edition*. In January 2010, a *1992 Dalwhinnie single cask* from re-fill American Oak was released as part of the Manager's Choice series.

15 years old

Deanston

Owner:
Burn Stewart Distillers
(C L Financial)

Region/district:
Eastern Highlands

Founded:
1965

Status:
Active (vc)

Capacity:
3 000 000 litres

Address: Deanston, Perthshire FK16 6AG

Tel:
01786 841422

website:
www.burnstewartdistillers.com

History:

1965 – A weavery from 1785 is transformed into Deanston Distillery by James Finlay & Co. and Brodie Hepburn Ltd (Deanston Distillery Co.). Brodie Hepburn also runs Tullibardine Distillery.

1966 – Production commences in October.

1971 – The first single malt is named Old Bannockburn.

1972 – Invergordon Distillers takes over.

1974 – The first single malt bearing the name Deanston is produced.

1982 – The distillery closes.

1990 – Burn Stewart Distillers from Glasgow buys the distillery for £2.1 million.

1991 – The distillery resumes production.

1999 – C L Financial buys an 18% stake of Burn Stewart.

2002 – C L Financial acquires the remaining stake.

2006 – Deanston 30 years old is released.

2009 – A new version of the 12 year old is released.

2010 – Virgin Oak is released.

Deanston distillery was Burn Stewart Distillers first acquisition (in 1990), followed by Tobermory (1993) and Bunnahabhain (2003). The master blender (and director for all three distilleries) Ian MacMillan, a traditionalist at heart, soon found that the character of all three single malts had changed over the years and decided to make an attempt to bring them back to their respective roots. For Tobermory and Bunnahabhain it meant adding peated versions to the range but for Deanston it meant recreating a fruity, estery style. To achieve this, he introduced low gravity worts, longer fermentations and slower distillation.

The equipment consists of a traditional open top cast iron mash tun, eight stainless steel washbacks and two pairs of stills. During 2011, the distillery will be running at two thirds of its capacity, producing 2 million litres of alcohol. Every August since 2000 a small part of organic spirit has been produced. It is estimated to be 16,000 litres in 2011. There are two warehouses, one modern racked and one listed building from the old mill.

Apart from being a brand in its own right, Deanston single malt constitutes an important part of Burn Stewart's own blend Scottish Leader, a popular whisky not least in Taiwan.

From July 2010, all single malts from Burn Stewart are uncoloured, unchillfiltered and bottled at 46,3%. This plan to increase the quality of the whole range already started with Deanston in 2009 and Bunnahabhain and Tobermory followed in 2010. The new core range is small, just a *12 year old* and *Virgin Oak*. The latter is a non-age statement malt with a finish in Virgin Oak casks. There is also a *30 year old* exclusive to the US market as well as a special *12 year old* bottling for Marks & Spencer. The *Organic Deanston 10 year old*, announced last year, is due for release in 2012.

Deanston 12 year old

GS – A fresh, fruity nose with malt and honey. The palate displays cloves, ginger, honey and malt, while the finish is long, quite dry and pleasantly herbal.

DR – Fresh and young crystallized barley on the nose with some cut hay and grass. On the palate it's a fruit sandwich, with orange and yellow fruits at first, then a cough candy honey and aniseed centre, and orange marmalade late on. The finish is intensely fruity with some spice.

12 years old

Dufftown

Owner:
Diageo

Region/district:
Speyside

Founded: 1896
Status: Active
Capacity: 5 800 000 litres

Address: Dufftown, Keith, Banffshire AB55 4BR

Tel: 01340 822100
website: www.malts.com

History:
1895 – Peter Mackenzie, Richard Stackpole, John Symon and Charles MacPherson build the distillery Dufftown-Glenlivet in an old mill.

1896 – Production starts in November.

1897 – The distillery is owned by P. Mackenzie & Co., who also owns Blair Athol in Pitlochry.

1933 – P. Mackenzie & Co. is bought by Arthur Bell & Sons for £56,000.

1968 – The floor maltings is discontinued and malt is bought from outside suppliers. The number of stills is increased from two to four.

1974 – The number of stills is increased from four to six.

1979 – The stills are increased by a further two to eight.

1985 – Guinness buys Arthur Bell & Sons.

1997 – Guinness and Grand Metropolitan merge to form Diageo.

2006 – The Singleton of Dufftown 12 year old is launched as a special duty free bottling.

2008 – The Singleton of Dufftown is made available also in the UK.

2010 – A Manager's Choice 1997 is released.

Singleton of Dufftown 12 year old

GS – The nose is sweet, almost violet-like, with underlying malt. Big and bold on the palate, this is an upfront yet very drinkable whisky. The finish is medium to long, warming, spicy, with slowly fading notes of sherry and fudge.

DR – Honeycomb and tinned peach and apricot in syrup on the nose, sharp and spicy clean barley on the palate, with some bitter orange notes towards the finish.

There's no doubt about it – with six active distilleries, Dufftown is the whisky capital of Scotland or maybe even of the world. Four of the distilleries lie on the outskirts of town, while two of them, Mortlach and Dufftown, are situated within the community. Unlike its closest neighbour, Mortlach, which has become something of a cult whisky, Dufftown has lived a quiet life producing malt whisky for the blends. Exactly 100 years after the start this has all changed. In 2006 the single malt was launched with all earnesty for the first time when it was released as a duty free exclusive under the name Singleton of Dufftown. Today the brand is available also in the UK and rest of Europe.

Dufftown distillery is Diageo's third largest after Roseisle and Caol Ila and working 7 days per week, which is the current production, it produces almost 6 million litres of alcohol per year. The distillery is equipped with one of the biggest mash tuns in the industry, with a capacity of no less than 13 tonnes. It is a full lauter model and was installed in 1979. There are twelve stainless steel washbacks which replaced old wooden ones in 1998 and the fermentation time is quite long, 72-80 hours. Throughout the years, stills have been added and it is a bit of a mystery how all of them have managed to fit into such small premises. Today there are three pairs of stills with the usual tube condensers but also equipped with subcoolers. Eight racked warehouses on site at present hold approximately 90,000 casks. About 97% of the production goes into blended whiskies, especially Bell's. The core range consists of *Singleton of Dufftown 12 year old* and *15 year old*. A higher proportion of European oak has been used for the Singleton version compared to the old *Flora & Fauna 15 year old* which can still be found. In January 2010, a *1997 Dufftown* was released as a part of the Manager's Choice range.

The Singleton of Dufftown

Edradour

Owner:
Signatory Vintage
Scotch Whisky Co. Ltd

Region/district:
Eastern Highlands

Founded: 1825
Status: Active (vc)
Capacity: 90 000 litres

Address: Pitlochry, Perthshire PH16 5JP

Tel: 01796 472095
website: www.edradour.com

History:

1825 – Probably the year when a distillery called Glenforres is founded by farmers in Perthshire.

1837 – The first year Edradour is mentioned.

1841 – The farmers form a proprietary company, John MacGlashan & Co.

1886 – J. G. Turney & Sons acquires Edradour through its subsidiary William Whitely & Co.

1922 – William Whiteley buys the distillery. The distillery is renamed Glenforres-Glenlivet.

1975 – Pernod Ricard buys Campbell Distilleries.

1982 – Campbell Distilleries (Pernod Ricard) buys Edradour and builds a visitor centre.

1986 – The first single malt is released.

2002 – Edradour is bought by Andrew Symington from Signatory for £5.4 million. The product range is expanded with a 10 year old and a 13 year old cask strength.

2003 – A 30 year old and a 10 year old are released. A heavily peated variety is also distilled.

2004 – A number of wood finishes are launched as cask strength.

2006 – The first bottling of peated Ballechin is released.

2007 – A Madeira matured Ballechin is released.

2008 – A Ballechin matured in Port pipes and a 10 year old Edradour with a Sauternes finish are released.

2009 – Fourth edition of Ballechin (Oloroso) is released.

2010 – Ballechin #5 Marsala is released.

2011 – Ballechin #6 Bourbon and a 26 year old PX sherry finish are relased.

Edradour 10 year old

GS – Cider apples, malt, almonds, vanilla and honey ar present on the nose, along with a hint of smoke and sherry. The palate is rich, creamy and malty, with a persistent nuttiness and quite a pronounced kick of slightly leathery sherry. Spices and sherry dominate the medium to long finish.

DR – Lemon and lime, rich fruits and some mint on the nose, sharp grape, herring and honey on the palate, and a lingering and pleasant fruity finish with hints of smoke.

Ballechin No 4 Oloroso Sherry

GS – A nose of profound, yet polished, notes of peat and sherry, which merge nicely. The palate is luxurious and smooth, with warm leather and stewed fruit notes to the fore, while insistent, spicy peat develops and lasts through a long, warming finish.

Edradour distillery is one of the smallest in the business and, at the same time, one of the most picturesque. No wonder then that almost 100,000 visitors find their way to this distillery near Pitlochry in Perthshire. Ever since the independent bottler, Andrew Symington, bought the distillery 15 years ago, they have continued doing things on a very small scale and in a traditional way.

They have an open, traditional cast iron mash tun from 1910 with a mash size of only 1.15 tonnes. To cool the worts, they are unique in using a Morton refrigerator. The two washbacks are made of Oregon pine and the two stills are connected to a more than 100 year old wormtub. In 2011 they will be doing 6 mashes per week and 110,000 litres of alcohol in the year. During the last few years, 25% of the production has been heavily peated. New warehouses were completed in 2010 and now all of the production is stored on site, as well as casks from the Signatory range. The major part of the spirit is filled into sherry butts, except for the peated spirit which goes into first fill bourbon casks.

The core expression is the *10 year old* and *Caledonia Selection*. This last one is a new series with a *12 year old Oloroso* maturation being the first. A large number of single casks, vintages and wood finishes have been released in addition to this. A series of wood finishes was commenced in 2004. The most recent ones have been *Chateau Neuf du Pape, Sauternes, Moscatel, Sassicaia, Port, Madeira* and *Rum*. In 2011 the last of the 1985 stock was released in the form of *26 year old PX sherry finish* and there were also two expressions from 2003 – a *Chardonnay matured* and a *Sauternes matured*, both bottled at 46%. Another side of the range from Edradour are the peated whiskies under the name *Ballechin*. The first release was in 2006 and edition number 6, a bourbon cask matured, appeared in summer 2011. The phenol specification for the malt used for Ballechin is 50ppm.

Caledonia 12 years old

Fettercairn

Owner:
Whyte & Mackay Ltd
(United Spirits)

Region/district:
Eastern Highlands

Founded:
1824

Status:
Active (vc)

Capacity:
2 300 000 litres

Address: Fettercairn, Laurencekirk,
Kincardineshire AB30 1YB

Tel:
01561 340205

website:
www.whyteandmackay.co.uk

History:
1824 – Sir Alexander Ramsay founds the distillery.

1830 – Sir John Gladstone buys the distillery.

1887 – A fire erupts and the distillery is forced to close for repairs.

1890 – Thomas Gladstone dies and his son John Robert takes over. The distillery reopens.

1912 – The company is close to liquidation and John Gladstone buys out the other investors.

1926 –The distillery is mothballed.

1939 – The distillery is bought by Associated Scottish Distillers Ltd. Production restarts.

1960 – The maltings discontinues.

1966 – The stills are increased from two to four.

1971 – The distillery is bought by Tomintoul-Glenlivet Distillery Co. Ltd.

1973 – Tomintoul-Glenlivet Distillery Co. Ltd is bought by Whyte & Mackay Distillers Ltd.

1974 – The mega group of companies Lonrho buys Whyte & Mackay.

1988 – Lonrho sells to Brent Walker Group plc.

1989 – A visitor centre opens.

1990 – American Brands Inc. buys Whyte & Mackay for £160 million.

1996 – Whyte & Mackay and Jim Beam Brands merge to become JBB Worldwide.

2001 – Kyndal Spirits, a company formed by managers at Whyte & Mackay, buys Whyte & Mackay from JBB Worldwide.

2002 – The whisky changes name to Fettercairn 1824.

2003 – Kyndal Spirits changes name to Whyte & Mackay.

2007 – United Spirits buys Whyte & Mackay. A 23 year old single cask is released.

2009 – 24, 30 and 40 year olds are released.

2010 – Fettercairn Fior is launched.

Fettercairn Fior

GS – A complex, weighty nose of toffee, sherry, ginger, orange and smoke. More orange and smoke on the palate, with a sherried nuttiness and hints of treacle toffee. Mild, spicy oak and a touch of liquorice in the lengthy finish.

DR – A big whisky from the off, earthy and rustic on the nose, with bitter orange, cocoa, nuts and burnt toffee on the nose, full mouth feel with toasty orange marmalade, chocolate and peat. The finish includes wood, burnt toffee and spice.

Whyte & Mackay have their four distilleries nicely spread out, not only geographically but also in terms of character, from the rich and complex Dalmore in the north, through the dry and malty (peated or non-peated) Jura in the west via the light, perfect blending malt Tamnavulin smack in the middle of Speyside to the fruity Fettercairn in Howe of Mearns in the Eastern Highlands. Fettercairn distillery is equipped with a traditional mash tun with rakes made of cast iron, eight washbacks made of Douglas fir and two pairs of stills. One feature makes it unique among Scottish distilleries; cooling water is allowed to trickle along the spirit still necks and is collected at the base for circulation towards the top again, in order to increase reflux and thereby produce a lighter and cleaner spirit. The stills are connected to copper condensers where the spirit vapours turn to liquid. This is the common way of doing it, but until 1995, at Fettercairn these condensers were made of stainless steel (in similar with Dailuaine) which, no doubt, resulted in a heavier, more sulphury spirit. There are 14 dunnage warehouses on site holding 32,000 casks with the oldest from 1962. For 2011 the production is moving up to a 7-day week with 25 mashes, reaching 2 million litres of alcohol for the year. For five of these weeks, the spirit will be heavily peated (55ppm in the barley).

Since 2002 when the bottle, name and packaging of the whisky was changed, nothing much happened to the range of Fettercairn. The core range simply consisted of a *12 year old*. The suddenly things changed; in autumn 2009, a range of very old and limited bott-lings (*24, 30* and *40 year olds*) saw the light of day. An *18 year old single cask* bottled at 50% was launched for sale at the distillery only and in spring 2010 the old 12 year old was scrapped in favour of the new *Fettercairn Fior* - bottled at 42% and containing a portion of peated Fettercairn as well. A new single cask, replacing the 18 year old, was released in 2011 in the shape of a *13 year old* bottled at 58%.

Fettercairn Fior

Glenallachie

Owner:
Chivas Brothers
(Pernod Ricard)

Region/district:
Speyside

Founded: 1967

Status: Active

Capacity: 3 200 000 litres

Address: Aberlour, Banffshire AB38 9LR

Tel: 01542 783042

website: -

History:
1967 – The distillery is founded by Mackinlay, McPherson & Co., a subsidiary of Scottish & Newcastle Breweries Ltd. William Delmé Evans is architect.

1985 – Scottish & Newcastle Breweries Ltd sells Charles Mackinlay Ltd to Invergordon Distillers which acquires both Glenallachie and Isle of Jura.

1987 – The distillery is decommissioned.

1989 – Campbell Distillers (Pernod Ricard) buys the distillery, increases the number of stills from two to four and takes up production again.

2005 – The first official bottling for many years becomes a Cask Strength Edition from 1989.

In more recent years Scotch whisky producers have been heavily engaged in two areas unrelated to the quality of the spirit, namely energy efficiency and waste water treatment. The latter has become more vital since the streams surrounding the distilleries supply the water needed for the production. Three years ago, after several trials, a Membrane Bioreactor was installed at Glenallachie to make all the distillery's waste water suitable for discharging into the local watercourse. The procedure is a mix of biological treatment and adding kalic to increase the pH, thus reducing the impact of influent copper.

The distillery, just outside Aberlour and in the shadow of Ben Rinnes, is equipped with a semi-lauter mash tun, six stainless steel lined washbacks and two pairs of stills. The wash stills are lantern-shaped while the spirit stills are of the onion model. All four stills are unusually connected to horizontal tube condensers, rather than vertical ones and the capacity is 18 mashes per week. The spirit is filled into bourbon casks and matured in 12 racked and two palletised warehouses. The distillery is currently running at full capacity, which entails 3.2 million litres of alcohol.

The most important role for the whisky from Glenallachie is to be the backbone of one of the best selling blends in the world, Clan Campbell. The brand has remained fairly unaffected by the economic turbulence of the last few years and with sales of 1.75 million cases per year, is placed just below the top ten list.

Currently, the only official bottling from Glenallachie is a *16 year old cask strength* matured in first fill Oloroso casks and released in 2005. This is for sale at Chivas' visitor centres together with the other releases in the cask strength range.

Glenallachie 16 year old 56,7%

GS – Major Sherry influence right through this expression, starting with warm leather and a hint of cloves on the fragrant nose, progressing through a Christmas pudding palate, featuring sultanas, dates and lots of spice, to a lengthy, sherried, leathery finish.

· CHIVAS BROTHERS ·
CASK STRENGTH EDITION
NON CHILL-FILTERED
Single Speyside Malt Scotch Whisky
Glenallachie
16 YEARS   GA 16 002
Bottled straight from the cask at   56.7 %vol
1989   2005   50cl.
PRODUCT OF SCOTLAND

1989 16 years old

Glenburgie

Owner:
Chivas Brothers
(Pernod Ricard)

Region/district:
Speyside

Founded: 1810 **Status:** Active **Capacity:** 4 200 000 litres

Address: Glenburgie, Forres,
Morayshire IV36 2QY

Tel: 01343 850258

website: -

History:
1810 – William Paul founds Kilnflat Distillery. Official production starts in 1829.

1870 – Kilnflat distillery closes.

1878 – The distillery reopens under the name Glenburgie-Glenlivet, Charles Hay is licensee.

1884 – Alexander Fraser & Co. takes over.

1925 – Alexander Fraser & Co. files for bankruptcy and the receiver Donald Mustad assumes control of operations.

1927 – James & George Stodart Ltd buys the distillery which by this time is inactive.

1930 – Hiram Walker buys 60% of James & George Stodart Ltd.

1936 – Hiram Walker buys Glenburgie Distillery in October. Production restarts.

1958 – Lomond stills are installed producing a single malt, Glencraig. Floor malting ceases.

1981 – The Lomond stills are replaced by conventional stills.

1987 – Allied Lyons buys Hiram Walker.

2002 – A 15 year old is released.

2004 – A £4.3 million refurbishment and reconstruction takes place.

2005 – Chivas Brothers (Pernod Ricard) becomes the new owner through the acquisition of Allied Domecq.

2006 – The number of stills are increased from four to six in May.

A decision was made in 2003 by the owners at the time, Allied Domecq, to refurbish Glenburgie distillery, but it didn´t stop at that. The old distillery was simply knocked down and a new one was built on the same site. The design of the new, highly efficient distillery was so succesful that when the current owners, Pernod Ricard, were building a new stillhouse for Glenlivet two years ago, they decided to do a replica of the one at Glenburgie.

Glenburgie´s significance is due to the fact that it is one of the signature malts of Ballantine´s blended Scotch. This is today the second best selling Scotch after Johnnie Walker with a particularly strong position in Europe and Asia. The strength of the brand, celebrating its 100th anniversary in 2010, relies on the standard expression, Ballantine´s Finest without age statement, which constitutes 95% of the total sales – 6.2 million cases in 2010.

All the equipment at Glenburgie distillery fits on one level in one gigantic room. Most of it is new but four stills, the mill and the boiler were brought in from the old distillery. The only remaining building of the original distillery is the custom´s house which is now used as a tasting room. A huge lawn fills up the rest of the view. The distillery is equipped with a full lauter mash tun, 12 stainless steel washbacks and three pairs of stills. The majority of the production is filled into bourbon casks and part thereof are matured in four dunnage, two racked and two palletised warehouses.

A single malt from Glenburgie named Glencraig can still be found on the market. It came into being by Hiram Walker's experimenting with Lomond stills in the fifties. Glenburgie's first Lomond still was a small model, originating in Dumbarton. It was replaced in 1958 by a pair of full-size Lomond stills and it is the make from these stills that received the name Glencraig.

The only official bottling is a *15 year old cask strength*.

Glenburgie 10 year old G&M

GS – Fresh and fruity on the nose, with toasted malt and a mildly herbal note. Soft fruits and mild oak on the palate, while the finish is subtly drying, with a touch of ginger.

DR – Classic sherry, barley and prickly wood on the nose, sweet and gentle red berry on the palate, and a warming mouth-filling soft and pleasant finish.

15 years old cask strength

Glencadam

Owner:
Angus Dundee Distillers

Region/district:
Eastern Highlands

Founded: 1825
Status: Active
Capacity: 1 300 000 litres

Address: Brechin, Angus DD9 7PA

Tel: 01356 622217
website: www.glencadamdistillery.co.uk

History:

1825 – George Cooper founds the distillery.

1827 – David Scott takes over.

1837 – The distillery is sold by David Scott.

1852 – Alexander Miln Thompson becomes the owner.

1857 – Glencadam Distillery Company is formed.

1891 – Gilmour, Thompson & Co Ltd takes over.

1954 – Hiram Walker takes over.

1959 – Refurbishing and modernization of the distillery.

1987 – Allied Lyons buys Hiram Walker Gooderham & Worts.

1994 – Allied Lyons changes name to Allied Domecq.

2000 – The distillery is mothballed.

2003 – Allied Domecq sells the distillery to Angus Dundee Distillers.

2005 – The new owner releases a 15 year old.

2008 – A re-designed 15 year old and a new 10 year old are introduced.

2009 – A 25 and a 30 year old are released in limited numbers.

2010 – A 12 year old port finish, a 14 year old sherry finish, a 21 year old and a 32 year old are released.

Glencadam 10 year old

GS – A light and delicate, floral nose, with tinned pears and fondant cream. Medium-bodied, smooth, with citrus fruits and gently-spiced oak on the palate. The finish is quite long and fruity, with a hint of barley.

DR – Fruity and treacle toffee nose, sweet, fruity and with uncluttered malt on the palate, and a clean medium long fruity finish.

Tables turn quickly in the Scotch whisky business as witnessed by the rise and fall of Glencadam´s previous owner, Allied Domecq. The origin of the company was based on three English breweries all founded in the 18th and 19th century. Through many mergers the company was at the end of the 1990's the third largest drinks company in the world but they had their eyes set on becoming even bigger. In 2000, they approached the industry leader Diageo, with a proposal that they should jointly buy Seagram Spirits & Wine. Diageo declined, only to perform the same operation the year thereafter, but this time together with Pernod Ricard. After that it was downhill for Allied Domecq and in 2005 the company was bought buy Pernod Ricard. A couple of years before, Glencadam had been sold to a considerably smaller player, Angus Dundee who admirably has taken care of both the distillery and the product.

Today, Glencadam is not only a busy distillery, but also hosts a huge filling and bottling plant with 16 large tanks for blending malt and grain whisky. Angus Dundee, is responsible for 4-5% of the total export of Scotch and 3.8 million litres per year can be blended at Glencadam.

The distillery is equipped with a traditional cast iron mash tun from the eighties and the mashing time is quite long – nine hours. There are six stainless steel washbacks and one pair of stills. The external heat exchanger on the wash still is from the fifties and perhaps the first in the business. The distillery is currently working seven days a week, which enables 16 mashes per week and 1.3 million litres of alcohol per year. On site are two dunnage warehouses from 1825, three from the 1950s and one racked.

The core range consists of a *10 year old*, a *15 year old* and the recently introduced *21 year old*. Two limited editions were released In 2009 (*25* and *30 year old*) and they were followed up by two finishes (a *12 year old port* and a *14 year old Oloroso sherry*) and a *32 year old single cask* in late 2010.

10 years old

Glendronach

Owner:
Benriach Distillery Co

Region/district:
Speyside

Founded:
1826

Status:
Active (vc)

Capacity:
1 400 000 litres

Address: Forgue, Aberdeenshire AB54 6DB

Tel:
01466 730202

website:
www.glendronachdistillery.com

History:

1826 – The distillery is founded by a consortium. James Allardes is one of the owners.

1837 – The major part of the distillery is destroyed in a fire.

1852 – Walter Scott (from Teaninich) takes over.

1887 – Walter Scott dies and Glendronach is taken over by a consortium from Leith.

1920 – Charles Grant buys Glendronach for £9,000 and starts production three months later.

1960 – William Teacher & Sons buys the distillery.

1966-67 – The number of stills is increased to four.

1976 – A visitor centre is opened.

1976 – Allied Breweries takes over William Teacher & Sons.

1996 – The distillery is mothballed.

2002 – Production is resumed on 14th May.

2005 – Glendronach 33 years old is launched. The distillery closes to rebuild from coal to indirect firing by steam. Reopens in September. Chivas Brothers (Pernod Ricard) becomes new owner through the acquisition of Allied Domecq.

2008 – Pernod Ricard sells the distillery to the owners of BenRiach distillery.

2009 – Relaunch of the whole range - 12, 15 and 18 year old including limited editions of a 33 year old and five single casks.

2010 – A 31 year old, a 1996 single cask and a total of 11 vintages and four wood finishes are released. A visitor centre is opened.

2011 – The 21 year old Parliament and 11 vintages are released.

For many years, GlenDronach single malt was the backbone of Teacher's blended Scotch (not anymore though) together with the neighbouring Ardmore. But unlike Ardmore, GlenDronach also succeeded in building a reputation as a single malt as well. A lot of people came to enjoy this powerful, sherried malt and the solid customer base was probably one of the reasons for Billy Walker to buy the distillery in 2008 in clear view of other suitors. In 2010, the brand sold 13,000 cases thereby surpassing its sister BenRiach which didn't have the same historical reputation to count on. The distillery equipment consists of a cast iron mash tun with rakes, nine Oregon pine washbacks, two wash stills with heat exchangers and two spirit stills. By the end of 2011, six of the old washbacks will have been replaced by six new ones, this time made of Scottish larch. Glendronach was the last Scottish distillery to fire the stills with coal. This old, traditional process continued until September 2005 when indirect heating using steam coils replaced it.

The new owners took over 9,000 casks of maturing whisky when they bought the distillery which is now maturing in three dunnage and three racked warehouses. This year there will be an average of 17 mashes a week resulting in 1.1 million litres of alcohol. Some 50% is aimed for its own releases and the rest will be sold to Pernod Ricard for their blended whiskies.

The core range is the *8 (Octarine),12 (Original), 15 (Revival), 18 (Allardice)* and *31 year old (Grandeur)*. In September 2011 the range was expanded with a *21 year old (Parliament)* as well. There are four wood finishes (*Virgin Oak, Sauternes, Moscatel* and *Tawny Port*) all 14 or 15 years old. In line with the last couple of years, several single casks (all sherry) were also released; in July *six vintages from 1971 to 1994* and then in October another *five vintages, 1972 to 1993*. Around the same time, a *1968 single cask* was released – the oldest stocked at the distillery. A *single cask from 1996* was released in 2010 to celebrate the opening of the new visitor centre.

Revival 15 years old

Glendronach Original 12 year old

GS – A sweet nose of Christmas cake fresh from the oven. Smooth on the palate, with sherry, soft oak, fruit, almonds and spices. The finish is comparatively dry and nutty, ending with bitter chocolate.

DR – Sherry, red berries, vanilla and traces of mint-flavoured toffee on the nose, an intriguing palate of cranberry and blueberry, a peaty carpet and some pepper, and a medium savoury and peaty finish.

Glendullan

Owner:
Diageo

Region/district:
Speyside

Founded: 1897 **Status:** Active **Capacity:** 3 700 000 litres

Address: Dufftown, Keith, Banffshire AB55 4DJ

Tel: 01340 822100 **website:** www.malts.com

History:
1896-97 – William Williams & Sons, a blending company with Three Stars and Strahdon among its brands, founds the distillery.

1902 – Glendullan is delivered to the Royal Court and becomes the favourite whisky of Edward VII.

1919 – Macdonald Greenlees buys a share of the company and Macdonald Greenlees & Williams Distillers is formed.

1926 – Distillers Company Limited (DCL) buys Glendullan.

1930 – Glendullan is transferred to Scottish Malt Distillers (SMD).

1962 – Major refurbishing and reconstruction.

1972 – A brand new distillery, accommodating six stills, is constructed next to the old one and both operate simultaneously during a few years.

1985 – The oldest of the two distilleries is mothballed.

1995 – The first launch of Glendullan in the Rare Malts series becomes a 22 year old from 1972.

2005 – A 26 year old from 1978 is launched in the Rare Malts series.

2007 – Singleton of Glendullan is launched in the USA.

Singleton of Glendullan 12 year old

GS – The nose is spicy, with brittle toffee, vanilla, new leather and hazelnuts. Spicy and sweet on the smooth palate, with citrus fruits, more vanilla and fresh oak. Drying and pleasingly peppery in the finish.

DR – The nose has a mix of fruits including grapefruit melon and even banana, the taste is moreish, with the citrus and melon notes coming through. Warm and pleasant finish.

Glendullan was the last of the famous Dufftown distilleries to be built, at least in the 19th century. During the 20th century a few more would be added. The distillery is situated just one minute's drive east of Glenfiddich at a river which, in spite of the distillery's name, isn't Dullan but Fiddich. The confluence of the two rivers lies just a mile to the south of Glendullan. If you drive from Glenfiddich, the first distillery you will spot (on your left side) is the closed Parkmore, while Glendullan can be found a little further on, on your right side. The distillery that opened in 1896 is not the one distilling today; a new Glendullan was built in 1972 next to the old one. The two were operated in parallel for a few years until 1985 when the old distillery closed. It is now used as a workshop for Diageo's distillery engineering team. The old distillery was equipped with one pair of stills with a capacity of one million litres a year.

A major upgrade of the distillery was completed in 2010 which included new control systems for both mash house and stillhouse, as well as a new full lauter stainless steel mash tun from Abercrombies. The equipment also consists of 8 washbacks made of larch and three pairs of stills. The distillery is working a five day week so there will be both short fermentations (65 hours) and long fermentations during the weekends (100 hours). The plan for 2011 is to do 15 mashes per week which means 3.7 million litres of alcohol in the year.

Glendullan is an important part of the blend Old Parr, already launched in 1909, and a big seller in Japan and South America today. The core range consists of *Singleton of Glendullan 12 year old*, aimed at the American market. Previously there has also been a *12 year old* in the Flora & Fauna series which can still be found. In 2010, a *single cask from 1995* was released as part of the Manager's Choice series.

The old distillery

The Singleton of Glendullan

125

Glen Elgin

Owner:		Region/district:
Diageo		Speyside

Founded:	Status:	Capacity:
1898	Active	1 700 000 litres

Address: Longmorn, Morayshire IV30 3SL

Tel:	website:
01343 862100	www.malts.com

History:

1898 – The bankers William Simpson and James Carle found Glen Elgin.

1900 – Production starts in May but the distillery closes just five months later.

1901 – The distillery is auctioned for £4,000 to the Glen Elgin-Glenlivet Distillery Co. and is mothballed.

1906 – The wine producer J. J. Blanche & Co. buys the distillery for £7,000 and production resumes.

1929 – J. J. Blanche dies and the distillery is put up for sale again.

1930 – Scottish Malt Distillers (SMD) buys it and the license goes to White Horse Distillers.

1964 – Expansion from two to six stills plus other refurbishing takes place.

1992 – The distillery closes for refurbishing and installation of new stills.

1995 – Production resumes in September.

2001 – A 12 year old is launched in the Flora & Fauna series.

2002 – The Flora & Fauna series malt is replaced by Hidden Malt 12 years.

2003 – A 32 year old cask strength from 1971 is released.

2008 – A 16 year old is launched as a Special Release.

2009 – Glen Elgin 1998, a single cask in the new Manager's Choice range is released.

Glen Elgin 12 year old

GS – A nose of rich, fruity sherry, figs and fragrant spice. Full-bodied, soft, malty and honeyed in the mouth. The finish is lengthy, slightly perfumed, with spicy oak.

DR – Ginger, crystallised barley sweet and a complex array of fruit on the nose, a beautiful balanced taste with light fruit, sweet spice and a zesty freshness and mouth filling finish.

Glen Elgin distillery doesn't have a visitor centre but if you fancy taking a look at the exteriors, you'd better keep your eyes open in order to find it. Once you've reached the small hamlet of Fogwatt on the A941 from Elgin to Rothes, drive slowly or you will miss it in the 15 seconds it takes to drive through the village. Look out for two small roads turning left. Take either one and look for the distillery's chimney. The whisky from Glen Elgin is not widely known as a single malt, but the spirit has for a long time been an essential part of the blended whisky White Horse.

The distillery is equipped with a 8.2 tonnes Steinecker full lauter mash tun from 2001, six washbacks made of larch and six small stills that stand in line in the stillhouse. The stills, with their slightly descending lyne arms, are connected to six wooden worm tubs placed in the yard. They were installed in 2004 replacing six old worm tubs. Spirit from the new production is stored at Glenlossie and Auchroisk, while the older production is stored in two dunnage warehouses on site. In 2011, the distillery will be doing 11 mashes per week (four short fermentations and seven long). The wormtubs and the small stills would suggest that the spirit from Glen Elgin is heavy and robust while, in fact, it is light and fruity. This is due to the long fermentation (56 hours and 120 hours over the weekend) of a clear wort and, not least, the slow distillation.

In 2001, Glen Elgin was launched as a part of the Flora & Fauna series, but was replaced the year thereafter by a new *12 year old* in what was then called "Hidden Malts". Three limited editions have also been released: a *19 year old* in 2000, a *32 year old* in 2003 and, finally, a *16 year old* was launched in 2008. In autumn of 2009, a *single cask* from *1998* was released as part of the new series Manager's Choice.

12 years old

Meet the Manager

JOANNE REAVLEY
SITE OPERATIONS MANAGER, GLEN ELGIN DISTILLERY

When did you start working in the whisky business and when did you start at Glen Elgin?

I started work with Diageo in November 2000 in our packaging plant in Glasgow. After several years in packaging I moved into a continuous improvement role which gave me a wider insight into the business, this in turn influenced my decision to move to malt distilling in May 2009.

Had you been working in other lines of business before whisky?

I started to work in the biochemical industry, from there I moved into the cosmetics industry, in both cases I was involved in the manufacturing sector.

What kind of education or training do you have?

I left University with an Honours Degree in Biochemistry and Pharmacology.

Describe your career in the whisky business.

I have spent the last eleven years in the Whisky industry, initially managing high speed packaging lines. The packaging side of the business is intense, technology is constantly moving on as the requirements of our customers evolve with the markets and I witnessed many changes in equipment on the lines over the years and had to manage the operator capability through these times. I then moved into a continuous improvement role, looking at Lean Manufacturing within the packaging sites to improve the efficiency of the processes. Lean Manufacturing is now a Global phenomenon within Diageo and I am proud to have been one of the first team members to have embarked on the journey towards Manufacturing Excellence. With this experience under my belt I decided to make the move to Malt Distilling.

What are your main tasks as a manager?

Firstly, we look after the people who drive the process, we ensure that as a business we are compliant in all aspects of Health & Safety & HMRC. We have high standards and an impeccable reputation to maintain. But we must also strive to deliver a spirit that is of the highest quality and consistent with the traditional character of the distillery, so that our blenders can rely on us to give them what they need.

What are the biggest challenges of being a distillery manager?

The Process! It can be a challenge when Mother Nature interferes, we need a plentiful supply of water for our process, so we need the rain, when the temperatures outside fluctuate we have to react quickly to get the best out of our fermentations and we are of course using live products, yeast, malt etc so these can challenge us.

What would be the worst that could go wrong in the production process?

Safety is the biggest priority for any Diageo Manager and I would hate for anyone to get hurt when they were at work

How would you describe the character of Glen Elgin single malt?

We have a light fruity character at this site, which is unusual as we have worm tub condensers which would generally be associated with heavier characters.

What are the main features in the process at Glen Elgin, contributing to this character?

We look for a long fermentation to generate our fruity character, and a relatively long distillation to give the spirit plenty of copper contact.

What is your favourite expression of Glen Elgin and why?

I have a bottle of Glen Elgin 32 year old locked away in the cupboard of my office, I would love to get my hands on one of my own.

If it were your decision alone – what new expression of Glen Elgin would you like to see released?

In general Glen Elgin is quite hard to come by in different expressions, so it would be nice to see a version in a different cask finish.

If you had to choose a favourite dram other than Glen Elgin, what would that be?

I do enjoy a glass of Cragganmore.

What are the biggest changes you have seen the past 5-10 years in your profession?

Technology has kept our business growing and moving forward. We have gleaned an expert knowledge of what makes our products great and managers, like myself, are trained to ensure consistent quality standards of our products are met.

Do you see any major changes in the next 10 years to come?

There will always be change for the business as it continues to grow, but what this will look like for Glen Elgin, who knows?

Do you have any special interests or hobbies that you pursue?

I own two horses and like nothing better than enjoying the glorious Speyside countryside on horseback.

Glen Elgin belongs to a group of Diageo distilleries called Speyside West. Is there any cooperation (or competition for that matter) between the distilleries on a regular basis?

Speyside West managers meet regularly to discuss issues, share best practices and learnings. My fellow managers in this group are part of my team and we all pull together and help each other. Even as a larger group of managers across all Diageo Malt Distilleries, we all know one another and meet up throughout the year. Although we are spread across the length and breadth of Scotland, technology makes it possible for us to communicate face to face at the touch of a button.

Glenfarclas

Owner: J. & G. Grant

Region/district: Speyside

Founded: 1836

Status: Active (vc)

Capacity: 3 000 000 litres

Address: Ballindalloch, Banffshire AB37 9BD

Tel: 01807 500257

website: www.glenfarclas.co.uk

History:

1836 – Robert Hay founds the distillery on the original site since 1797.

1865 – Robert Hay passes away and John Grant and his son George buy the distillery for £511.19s on 8th June. They lease it to John Smith at The Glenlivet Distillery.

1870 – John Smith resigns in order to start Cragganmore and J. & G. Grant Ltd takes over.

1889 – John Grant dies and George Grant takes over.

1890 – George Grant dies and his widow Barbara takes over the license while sons John and George control operations.

1895 – John and George Grant take over and form The Glenfarclas-Glenlivet Distillery Co. Ltd with the infamous Pattison, Elder & Co.

1898 – Pattison becomes bankrupt. Glenfarclas encounters financial problems after a major overhaul of the distillery but survives by mortgaging and selling stored whisky to R. I. Cameron, a whisky broker from Elgin.

1914 – John Grant leaves due to ill health and George continues alone.

1948 – The Grant family celebrates the distillery's 100th anniversary, a century of active licensing. It is 9 years late, as the actual anniversary coincided with WW2.

Many years ago, the stills in all of Scotlands distilleries would have been directly fired, i. e. with a flame beneath the bottom of the still, using either peat, coal, oil or gas as fuel. In time this regime was replaced by steam coils and pans being built into the stills and only Macallan, Glenfiddich, Glenfarclas and Springbank (one of the stills) continued in the traditional manner. For a little more than a year now, Macallan has heated all their stills with steam and Glenfiddich has moved to indirect firing in one of their still houses (with the other probably following soon). The chances of Glenfarclas following are highly unlikely. They tried doing it in 1981 but stopped when it changed the character of the whisky. This says a lot about the family-owned distillery where traditions mean a lot simply because it works.

The distillery is equipped with a very large semi-lauter mash tun, which measures ten metres in diameter and holds 16.5 tonnes of grist. There are twelve stainless steel washbacks where the wort is fermented for 48 hours. The three pairs of stills are some of the biggest in Scotland and the wash stills are equipped with rummagers. This is a copper chain rotating at the bottom of the still to prevent solids from sticking to the copper. In summer 2011, a new control system was installed for the milling, mashing and fermentation.

There are 30 dunnage warehouses on-site which hold more than 50,000 casks. Glenfarclas uses an unusually large share of sherry butts, mainly Oloroso. For the single malts, first and second fill casks are used and for blends, refill casks. When bourbon barrels are used they are never first fill. The Glenfarclas core range consists of *10, 12, 15, 21, 25, 30* and *40 years old* as well as the *105 Cask Strength*. There is also a *17 year old* targeted towards USA, Japan and the Duty Free market. Limited releases during 2011 are *175th Anniversary* containing whiskies from six decades dating back to the 1950s and *Chairman's Reserve*, made up of four casks that have matured for 175 years. A special bottling, lightly sherried and without age statement, called *Glenfarclas Heritage* was originally launched for the French hypermarket trade but is now also available in Germany, Luxemburg, Switzerland and Austria. There have also been bottlings of *Heritage at 60%* and limited vintage versions. The owners also continue to release bottlings in their *Family Casks* series with vintages from *1952 to 1994*. So far 84 casks have been released.

History (continued):

1949 – George Grant senior dies and sons George Scott and John Peter inherit the distillery.

1960 – Stills are increased from two to four.

1968 – Glenfarclas is first to launch a cask-strength single malt. It is later named Glenfarclas 105.

1972 – Floor maltings is abandoned and malt is purchased centrally.

1973 – A visitor centre is opened.

1976 – Enlargement from four stills to six.

2001 – Glenfarclas launches its first Flower of Scotland gift tin which becomes a great success and increases sales by 30%.

2002 – George S Grant dies and is succeeded as company chairman by his son John L S Grant

2003 – Two new gift tins are released (10 years old and 105 cask strength).

2005 – A 50 year old is released to commemorate the bi-centenary of John Grant´s birth.

2006 – Ten new vintages are released.

2007 – Family Casks, a series of single cask bottlings from 43 consecutive years, is released.

2008 – New releases in the Family Cask range. Glenfarclas 105 40 years old is released.

2009 – A third release in the Family Casks series.

2010 – A 40 year old and new vintages from Family Casks are released.

2011 – Chairman´s Reserve and 175th Anniversary are released.

105 Cask Strength
(Duty Free version)   40 years old   175th Anniversary

Glenfarclas 10 year old

GS – Full and richly sherried on the nose, with nuts, fruit cake and a hint of citrus fruit. The palate is big, with ripe fruit, brittle toffee, some peat and oak. Medium length and gingery in the finish.

DR – Creamy sherry and bitter oranges on the nose, rich fruit cake and red berries on the palate with a pleasant spice and barley interplay and long and warming finish.

10 years old   12 years old   The Family Casks 1959

Glenfiddich

Owner:
William Grant & Sons

Region/district:
Speyside

Founded: **Status:**
1886   Active (vc)

Capacity:
12 000 000 litres

Address: Dufftown, Keith, Banffshire AB55 4DH

Tel: **website:**
01340 820373 (vc)   www.glenfiddich.com

History:

1886 – The distillery is founded by William Grant, 47 years old, who had learned the trade at Mortlach Distillery. The equipment is bought from Mrs. Cummings of Cardow Distillery. The construction totals £800.

1887 – The first distilling takes place on Christmas Day.

1892 – William Grant builds Balvenie.

1898 – The blending company Pattisons, largest customer of Glenfiddich, files for bankruptcy and Grant decides to blend their own whisky. Standfast becomes one of their major brands.

1903 – William Grant & Sons is formed.

1957 – The famous, three-cornered bottle is introduced.

1958 – The floor maltings is closed.

1963 – Glennfiddich becomes the first whisky to be marketed as single malt in the UK and the rest of the world.

1964 – A version of Standfast's three-cornered bottle is launched for Glenfiddich in green glass.

1969 – Glenfiddich becomes the first distillery in Scotland to open a visitor centre.

1974 – 16 new stills are installed.

2001 – 1965 Vintage Reserve is launched in a limited edition of 480 bottles. Glenfiddich 1937 is bottled (61 bottles).

The owners of Glenfiddich can look back on an excellent year for their flagship malt. Volumes increased by no less than 9% to 954,000 cases sold. This further cements Glenfiddich's position as the best selling single malt in the world, a position it has held for decades now. Four years ago they were hoping to reach the one million mark as the first single malt brand ever in just a couple of years but the global recession put a stop to that. Now, however, it seems that the goal could be within reach already next year. Glenfiddich distillery is equipped with two big, stainless steel, full lauter mash tuns (11.2 tonnes) and 24 Douglas fir washbacks with a fermentation time of 66 hours. One still room holds 5 wash and 10 spirit stills and the other 5 and 8 respectively. The wash stills are all onion-shaped while half of the spirit stills are of the lantern model and the rest have a boiling ball. A lot of money has been invested in the distillery recently in order to make it more energy efficient. One of the measures taken was to switch to internally fired stills in stillhouse No. 1, using steam coils. The stills in stillhouse No. 2, however, are still directly fired using gas. Fortyfour warehouses on site are shared with Balvenie and Kininvie. Due to heavy snowfall in January 2010, several of the warehouses collapsed and 230,000 casks had to be relocated to other premises. By summer 2011, all the damaged buildings had either been repaired or replaced. The production was increased last year and they now make 12 million litres of alcohol in a year.

Glenfiddich's core range consists of *12, 15, 18, 21, 30 years old* and the newest member, *Rich Oak 14 year old*. The latter, released in February 2010, was matured in second fill Bourbon barrels for 14 years and then received a finish of 12 weeks in new European Oak and another six in new American Oak. *Caoran Reserve*, the peated version of Glenfiddich introduced in 2002, has disappeared from the range. The *15 year old cask strength* (Distillery Edition), previously a duty free exclusive, can now be found in key markets worldwide. Recent limited bottlings include the *40* and the *50 year old*. Another limited edition from last year, and one that sold out quickly, was *Snow Phoenix* which was released to commemorate the fall and rise of the damaged warehouses. A new expression, earmarked for Duty Free was released in spring 2011. The *19 year old Madeira finish* was the first in a completely new range called *Age of Discovery*. This year's *Vintage Reserve* (from 1974) was chosen by a number of Glenfiddich Brand Ambassadors and for the first time it was a vatting and not a single cask.

History (continued):

2002 – Glenfiddich Gran Reserva 21 years old, finished in Cuban rum casks is launched. Caoran Reserve 12 years, an attempt to recreate the peaty Glenfiddich produced during the war years, is launched. Glenfiddich Rare Collection 1937 (61 bottles) is launched and becomes the oldest Scotch whisky on the market.

2003 – 1973 Vintage Reserve (440 bottles) is launched.

2004 – 1991 Vintage Reserve (13 years) and 1972 Vintage Reserve (519 bottles) are launched.

2005 – Circa £1.7 million is invested in a new visitor centre.

2006 – 1973 Vintage Reserve, 33 years (861 bottles) and 12 year old Toasted Oak are released.

2007 – 1976 Vintage Reserve, 31 years is released in September.

2008 – 1977 Vintage Reserve is released.

2009 – A 50 year old and 1975 Vintage Reserve are released.

2010 – Rich Oak, 1978 Vintage Reserve, the 6th edition of 40 year old and Snow Phoenix are released.

2011 – 1974 Vintage Reserve and a 19 year old Madeira finish are released.

Glenfiddich 12 year old

GS – Delicate, floral and slightly fruity on the nose. Well mannered in the mouth, malty, elegant and soft. Rich, fruit flavours dominate the palate, with a developing nuttiness and an elusive whiff of peat smoke in the fragrant finish.

DR – Classic rich fruit and peerless clean barley nose, fruit bowl and sharp malt palate and pleasant and warming lengthy finish.

Snow Phoenix   1978 Vintage Reserve   Age of Discovery 19 years old

12 years old   Rich Oak   18 years old

131

Glen Garioch

Owner:
Morrison Bowmore
(Suntory)

Region/district:
Eastern Highlands

Founded: 1797
Status: Active (vc)
Capacity: 1 000 000 litres

Address: Oldmeldrum, Inverurie,
Aberdeenshire AB51 0ES

Tel: 01651 873450
website: www.glengarioch.com

History:

1797 – Thomas Simpson founds Glen Garioch.

1837 – The distillery is bought by John Manson & Co., owner of Strathmeldrum Distillery.

1908 – Glengarioch Distillery Company, owned by William Sanderson, buys the distillery.

1933 – Sanderson & Son merges with the gin maker Booth's Distilleries Ltd.

1937 – Booth's Distilleries Ltd is acquired by Distillers Company Limited (DCL).

1968 – Glen Garioch is decommissioned.

1970 – It is sold to Stanley P. Morrison Ltd.

1973 – Production starts again.

1978 – Stills are increased from two to three.

1982 – Becomes the first distillery to use gas from the North Sea for heating.

1994 – Suntory controls all of Morrison Bowmore Distilleries Ltd.

1995 – The distillery is mothballed in October.

1997 – The distillery reopens in August.

2004 – Glen Garioch 46 year old is released.

2005 – 15 year old Bordeaux Cask Finish is launched. A visitor centre opens in October.

2006 – An 8 year old is released.

2009 – Complete revamp of the range - 1979 Founders Reserve (unaged), 12 year old, Vintage 1978 and 1990 are released.

2010 – 1991 vintage is released.

2011 – Two vintages, 1986 and 1994, are released.

Glen Garioch 12 years old

GS – Luscious and sweet on the nose, focusing on fresh fruits: peaches and pineapple, plus vanilla, malt and a hint of sherry. Full-bodied and nicely textured, with more fresh fruit on the palate, along with spice, brittle toffee and finally quite dry oak notes.

DR – Surprisingly floral and light on the nose, with fruity sweetness. The taste includes tinned sweet pear, vanilla and caramel with some earthiness as an undercarpet. There is some spice in the finale.

Glen Garioch is one of the few distilleries in Scotland where you can drive by in the street and look right onto the stills just a couple of metres away. Located in the middle of the small town of Oldmeldrum, west of Aberdeen, appropriately placed on Distillery Road, Glen Garioch is one of the oldest distilleries in Scotland.

The distillery is equipped with a 4.4 tonne full lauter mash tun, eight stainless steel washbacks and one pair of stills. There is also a third still which has not been in use for a long time. The spirit is tankered to Glasgow, filled into casks and returned to be stored in the distillery's four warehouses. The current capacity is one million litres but in 2011, Glen Garioch will be aiming for 570,000 litres (10 mashes per week).

The entire range from Glen Garioch was revamped two years ago and if you pay attention you will find two different traces in the character of the different expressions. The core bottlings (Founder's Reserve and the 12 year old) are unpeated, while phenols are easily detected in the range of vintages. The reason for this is that when the distillery was using their own floor maltings (until 1994) the malt was peated with a specification of 8-10 ppm.

Glen Garioch single malt was at its peak in terms of sales volumes around 2005 when 250,000 bottles were sold in a year. In 2010, after the relaunch, total volumes were down to 110,000 bottles which only shows that it takes time to establish a new range with the customers.

The new core range is *1797 Founder's Reserve* (without age statement) and a *12 year old*, both of them bottled at the rather unusual strength of 48% and non-chill-filtered. There will also be a number of limited cask strength vintages released every year. The first three were *1978, 1990* and *1991*. In 2011 two new ones were launched – *1986* and *1994*.

12 years old

Meet the Manager

KENNY GRANT
DISTILLERY MANAGER, GLEN GARIOCH DISTILLERY

When did you start working in the whisky business and when did you start at Glen Garioch?

I started at the distillery in November 1987 in the malt barns.

Had you been working in other lines of business before whisky?

I left school at 16 did painting and decorating for 2 years then joined the army from 1982 -1985. After that I was putting up fences for 2 years before joining the distillery.

What kind of education or training do you have?

Training on the job for all production I have also done management training for the job I am in now.

Describe your career in the whisky business.

I have been with the company since 1987 apart from 2 years 1995-1997 when the distillery was shut down.

What are your main tasks as a manager?

Main tasks are making sure the plant is running ok, ordering stock materials, making sure all health and safety is up to scratch. Doing vip tours when needed.

What are the biggest challenges of being a distillery manager?

Making sure everything is going to plan even when you are dealing with breakdowns and all the other problems that come along.

What would be the worst that could go wrong in the production process?

Big loss of spirit or wash, a fire or an explosion on site.

How would you describe the character of Glen Garioch single malt?

Glengarioch is a sweet vanilla, malty whisky with floral, heathery notes.

What are the main features in the process at Glen Garioch, contributing to this character?

The main features being the spring water we use mixed with dried yeast and the shape of the stills.

What is your favourite expression of Glen Garioch and why?

The old 15 year old in the tartan tubes was probably one of the best drams we had, very popular in the shop also. It was a dram you could

have sitting at home with your feet up and really enjoy.

If it were your decision alone – what new expression of Glen Garioch would you like to see released?

Probably another 21 year old – at the time in the distillery it would have been the oldest bottle we had and was very popular with a presentation box that was pretty smart also.

If you had to choose a favourite dram other than Glen Garioch, what would that be?

I would say the old Auchentoshan 10 year old.

What are the biggest changes you have seen the past 10 years in your profession?

In the last 10 years at Glengarioch the opening of a visitor centre in 2006 was a good thing for the distillery. As for the distillery itself updating the plant with modern equipment valves and such that can be opened and shut by computers. Having the computers in place also lets the process operator know what stage every thing is at.

Do you see any major changes in the next 10 years to come?

Being a small distillery there is not much you can change, if we did go up in production we probably would need a new washstill and more washbacks. Other changes are anything to do with climate change, recycling, water abstraction and minimizing fuel usage, gas and electricity.

Do you have any special interests or hobbies that you pursue?

For the last four years I started to do Triathlons having giving up trying to play football. It´s a big change from just doing one sport, now I have to swim, bike and run. When you go to events the atmosphere is good and the people are really friendly. Some people take their kids as well so it can be a bit of a family thing.

You still have the floor maltings intact although they haven´t been used since 1994. Are there any plans to start malting again?

No plans yet to do anything with the malt barns floor.

You are the manager of one of the few urban distilleries left in Scotland. Does that have any implications, for example when it comes to transports, waste treatment, expansion etc?

If we were to expand we have some ground around the distillery to use, waste treatment is not a problem, transport is not too bad but if tankers and CLV,s picking new spirit or casks, come up from head office, it´s about 300 miles round trip.

During the 70s and 80s, the operations at Glen Garioch included a rather unusual side-track, not related to whisky. Please tell me a little about that.

In the 1970s we had the tomatoes at the distillery as well. We had one big plastic covered greenhouse and one big glass greenhouse and these were heated by the waste heat from the distillery. We employed 3 or 4 people to work there as well and they were under the watchful eye of Jim Mccoll and his wife.

Glen Garioch has sometimes been called the oldest working distillery in Scotland. What is the company´s official opinion and when was it actually founded?

The distillery was founded in 1797 but there was word that someone had been looking somewhere and found that the dates could make the distillery older but nothing has come of the news yet. It would be a great thing for the distillery if it was said to be older than it is.

Glenglassaugh

Owner:
Glenglassaugh Distillery Co
(Scaent Group)

Region/district:
Speyside

Founded: | **Status:** | **Capacity:**
1875 | Active | 1 100 000 litres

Address: Portsoy, Banffshire AB45 2SQ

Tel:
01261 842367

website:
www.glenglassaugh.com

History:
1873-75 – The distillery is founded by Glenglassaugh Distillery Company.

1887 – Alexander Morrison embarks on renovation work.

1892 – Alexander Morrison, the sole survivor of the original founders, sells the distillery to Robertson & Baxter. They in turn sell it on to Highland Distilleries Company for £15,000.

1908 – The distillery closes.

1931 – The distillery reopens.

1936 – The distillery closes.

1957-59 – Substantial reconstruction, including acquisition of new stills, takes place. Own maltings are abandoned.

1960 – The distillery reopens.

1986 – Glenglassaugh is mothballed.

2005 – A 22 year old is released.

2006 – Three limited editions are released - 19 years old, 38 years old and 44 years old.

2008 – The distillery is bought by the Scaent Group for £5m. Three bottlings are released - 21, 30 and 40 year old.

2009 – New make spirit and 6 months old are released.

2010 – A 26 year old replaces the 21 year old.

2011 – A 35 year old and the first bottling from the new owners production, a 3 year old, are released.

Glenglassaugh distillery, re-opened in 2008, has already gained a large amount of devoted followers and before the end of 2011, they will have their own visitor centre. The equipment of the distillery consists of a Porteus cast iron mash tun with rakes, four wooden washbacks and two stainless steel ones (although the last two are not being used) and one pair of stills. In 2011 the plan is to do four mashes per week, which corresponds to just over 200,000 litres of alcohol. The first peated production was done in 2009 and for 2011 around 10% of the production will be peated. It is vital to build up stock because only 400 casks of maturing Glenglassaugh (from 1963 to 1986) were included when Scaent bought the distillery. The whisky is matured in a combination of dunnage and racked warehouses and there is a lot of experimenting going on regarding which type of cask is filled. Recent trials include using sweet wine casks from Masandra on the Black Sea coast in Crimea, a winery famous for producing wine for the Tsars. The core range is *26 year old* (a vatting of several casks), *aged over 30 years* and *aged over 40 years*. The last two are single casks. Part of the

---

Glenglassaugh 26 year old

GS – Initially, aromas of of marshmallow, then mossy and herbal, with cracked pepper and ginger. Refined and balanced on the palate, with malt, summer berries and a hint of milk chocolate. Medium to long in the finish, with citrus fruit notes.

DR – Rich red berries, sweet vanilla and apple crumble on the nose, toasted almonds, honeyed oats and breakfast bar on the palate and a pleasant sweet and fruity conclusion.

core range are also four spirit drinks (either new make or spirit aged six to twelve months); *Clearac, Blushes, Fledgling XB* and *Peated*. Limited releases include a *37* and a *43 year old* which can only be bought as a trio in combination with the 26 year old. In 2010/2011 a series of four single casks named after previous distillery managers was launched; *Dod Cameron (1986), Jim Cryle (1974), Bert Forsyth (1968)* and *Walter Grant (1967)*. A new limited series called *The Chosen Few* was introduced in 2011 with the first release, a *35 year old*, in August and end of 2011 also saw the first *3 year old* bottling from the new owner´s poduction.

26 years old

Glengoyne

Owner:
Ian Macleod Distillers

Region/district:
Southern Highlands

Founded: 1833
Status: Active (vc)
Capacity: 1 100 000 litres

Address: Dumgoyne by Killearn, Glasgow G63 9LB

Tel: 01360 550254 (vc)
website: www.glengoyne.com

History:

1833 – The distillery is licensed under the name Burnfoot Distilleries by the Edmonstone family.

1876 – Lang Brothers buys the distillery and changes the name to Glenguin.

1905 – The name changes to Glengoyne.

1910 – Own floor maltings ceases.

1965-66 – Robertson & Baxter takes over Lang Brothers and the distillery is refurbished. The stills are increased from two to three.

2001 – Glengoyne Scottish Oak Finish (16 years old) is launched.

2003 – Ian MacLeod Distillers Ltd buys the distillery plus the brand Langs from the Edrington Group for £7.2 million.

2004 – A 12 year old cask strength is released.

2005 – Limited editions of a 19 year old, a 32 year old and a 37 year old cask strength are launched.

2006 – Nine "choices" from Stillmen, Mashmen and Manager are released.

2007 – A new version of the 21 year old, two Warehousemen's Choice, Vintage 1972 and two single casks are released.

2008 – A 16 year old Shiraz cask finish, three single casks and Heritage Gold are released.

2009 – A 40 year old, two single casks and a new 12 year old are launched.

2010 – Two single casks, 1987 and 1997, released.

2011 – A 24 year old single cask is released.

Glengoyne 12 year old

GS – Fresh and well-rounded on the nose, with medium sweet aromas suggesting malt, oak, and a hint of sherry. Smooth and delicate on the palate, slightly oaky, with a suggestion of cooking apples. The finish is pleasingly long, with buttery, vanilla notes.

DR – Tinned pear and peach on the nose, crystallised barley, lemon and grapefruit on the palate, and a fruity and peppery finish.

Family owned producers of Scotch whisky had a tendency to do better during the economic downturn that started in 2008, compared to the big companies and the owners of Glengoyne distillery, Ian MacLeod Distillers, is the best example of this. The last two years' turnover has increased by 45% and profit during this time is up no less than 170%! The biggest contributor to this success is sales of their flagship brand Glengoyne single malt, with an increase of 40% during last year to 55,000 cases sold. The biggest brand in the portfolio is the Scotch blend, King Robert II, selling more than 500,000 cases per year, especially in Asia and Middle East.

Glengoyne distillery is equipped with a traditional mash tun with rakes, six Oregon pine washbacks, one wash still and two spirit stills. In 2011, 13 mashes per week are made which entails 820,000 litres of alcohol. Both short (56 hours) and long (110) fermentations are practised which, together with the exceptionally slow distillation, contributes to a subtle and complex character of Glengoyne single malt. All produce destined for single malt sales is stored in two dunnage warehouses, while the part that goes for blending, is stored in four newly constructed palletised warehouses with a capacity of 40,000 casks. Glengoyne are dedicated to filling sherry casks (with exception of the new 12 year old) and except for a few casks of the 40 year old saved for future bottlings, the oldest cask in the warehouse is from 1983. The high quality visitor centre receives 40,000 visitors annually and on offer are no less than five different distillery tours.

The core range consists of *10, 12, 12 (cask strength), 17, 21 years old* and the newly introduced *13 year old port finish* released in September 2010. The line-up for duty free consists of the unaged *Burnfoot* and *14 year old Heritage Gold*. One limited *single cask* was released in autumn 2011 – a *24 year old* sherry matured. Older limited editions include a *40 year old* released in 2009 and two *single casks* (*13* and *23 years old*) launched in 2010.

12 years old

Glen Grant

Owner: Campari Group
Region/district: Speyside

Founded: 1840
Status: Active (vc)
Capacity: 5 900 000 litres

Address: Elgin Road, Rothes, Banffshire AB38 7BS

Tel: 01340 832118
website: www.glengrant.com

History:

1840 – The brothers James and John Grant, managers of Dandelaith Distillery, found the distillery.

1861 – The distillery becomes the first to install electric lighting.

1864 – John Grant dies.

1872 – James Grant passes away and the distillery is inherited by his son, James junior (Major James Grant).

1897 – James Grant decides to build another distillery across the road; it is named Glen Grant No. 2.

1902 – Glen Grant No. 2 is mothballed.

1931 – Major Grant dies and is succeeded by his grandson Major Douglas Mackessack.

1953 – J. & J. Grant merges with George & J. G. Smith who runs Glenlivet distillery, forming The Glenlivet & Glen Grant Distillers Ltd.

1961 – Armando Giovinetti and Douglas Mackessak found a friendship that eventually leads to Glen Grant becoming the most sold malt whisky in Italy.

1965 – Glen Grant No. 2 is back in production, but renamed Caperdonich.

During the last decades, Glen Grant has always been among the top five single malts in the world saleswise (at some time even number two), but for some reason it has never achieved the same recognition as Glenfiddich, Glenlivet and Macallan. There have been no spectacular crystal decanters and no vintage releases (except from Gordon & MacPhail). Their focus has been on young malts with Italy as the main market and when sales started decreasing there, the distillery hit a downward spiral in terms of sales. Things started to change in 2006 when Campari bought the distillery and Dennis Malcolm was hired as a manager. New, interesting bottlings saw the light of day and last year, sales figures showed that Glen Grant is back on track. Volumes increased by 32% to 328,000 cases, performance was good in the three main markets – Italy (which is the biggest market by far), France and Germany – and the brand has been re-launched in USA. The next big market for Glen Grant, according to the owners, could be China. The distillery is equipped with a semi-lauter mash tun, ten Oregon pine washbacks and four pairs of stills. The wash stills are peculiar in that they have vertical sides at the base of the neck and all eight stills are fitted with purifiers. This gives an increased reflux and creates a light and delicate whisky. There have been discussions of a possible capacity expansion by adding another four pairs of stills, but these plans have been put on hold. Production has slowed down recently and for 2011 it is expected to be 2.5 million litres. Bourbon casks are used for maturation and the share of sherry butts is less than 10% (mainly used for the 10 year old). The previous owner, Chivas Brothers, still owns most of the warehouses but, in 2008, Glen Grant bought eleven warehouses in Rothes. A reconstruction of the visitor centre took place in late 2008 at a cost of £500,000 with The Major's Coachmans House being converted into a new and very elegant visitor centre. Some 10,000 visitors come here every year, not least to visit the unique garden landscaped by John Grant, known as the Major, in the late 1800s. Some 50% of the production goes into blended whisky, especially Chivas Regal. The Glen Grant core range of single malts consists of *Major's Reserve* with no age statement but probably around 7 years old, a *5 year old* sold in Italy only, a *10 year old* and the recently introduced *16 year old*. Recent limited editions include the *170th Anniversary Edition* from 2010 and in summer 2011, 732 bottles of a *25 year old* from sherry butts.

History (continued):

1972 – The Glenlivet & Glen Grant Distillers merges with Hill Thompson & Co. and Longmorn-Glenlivet Ltd to form The Glenlivet Distillers. The drum maltings ceases.

1973 – Stills are increased from four to six.

1977 – The Chivas & Glenlivet Group (Seagrams) buys Glen Grant Distillery. Stills are increased from six to ten.

2001 – Pernod Ricard and Diageo buy Seagrams Spirits and Wine, with Pernod acquiring the Chivas Group.

2006 – Campari buys Glen Grant for €115 million in a deal that includes the acquisition of Old Smuggler and Braemar for another €15 million.

2007 – The entire range is re-packaged and re-launched and a 15 year old single cask is released. Reconstruction of the visitor centre.

2008 – Two limited cask strengths - a 16 year old and a 27 year old - are released.

2009 – Cellar Reserve 1992 is released.

2010 – A 170th Anniversary bottling is released.

2011 – A 25 year old is released.

Glen Grant 10 year old

GS – Relatively dry on the nose, with cooking apples. Fresh and fruity on the palate, with a comparatively lengthy, malty finish, which features almonds and hazelnuts.

DR – Sweet banana and toffee, vanilla and pear on the nose, sweet barley, crystallised pineapple on the palate with a touch of honey and finally a cinnamon and spice note at the finish.

16 years old	25 years old	Cellar Reserve 1992

10 years old	The Major's Reserve

Glengyle

Owner:
Mitchell´s Glengyle Ltd

Region/district:
Campbeltown

Founded:
2004

Status:
Active

Capacity:
750 000 litres

Address: 85 Longrow, Campbeltown, Argyll PA28 6EX

Tel:
01586 552009

website:
www.kilkerran.com

History:

1872 – The original Glengyle Distillery is built by William Mitchell.

1919 – The distillery is bought by West Highland Malt Distilleries Ltd.

1925 – The distillery is closed.

1929 – The warehouses (but no stock) are purchased by the Craig Brothers and rebuilt into a petrol station and garage.

1941 – The distillery is acquired by the Bloch Brothers.

1957 – Campbell Henderson applies for planning permission with the intention of reopening the distillery.

2000 – Hedley Wright, owner of Springbank Distillery and related to founder William Mitchell, acquires the distillery.

2004 – The first distillation after reconstruction takes place in March.

2007 – The first limited release - a 3 year old.

2009 – Kilkerran "Work in progress" is released.

2010 – Kilkerran "Work in progress 2" is released.

2011 – Kilkerran "Work in progress 3" is released.

Kilkerran Work in Progress 2

GS – A fresh and fruity nose, with tinned pears and fragrant spice. More fruit in the mouth, with quite lively oak and a hint of ginger. Steadily drying in a medium-length finish.

DR – Full, rich and fruity on the nose, oily, intense and savoury on the palate, but with a bewitching and very different fruity heart. Earthy,oily and savoury but blossoming nicely.

When J & A Mitchell bought the closed Glengyle distillery in 2000, they took care to retain as many of the original facilities as possible. The boiler house was the only building that had to be constructed. The equipment, however, was gone ever since the distillery had closed way back in 1925, so stills (as well as spirit safe and spirit receivers) had to be bought from another closed distillery, Ben Wyvis. To increase the reflux the body of the stills were reshaped and the lye pipes made slightly ascending. The Boby mill was acquired from Craigellachie and the 4 tonnes semi lauter mash tun was made by Forsyth´s in Rothes. The four washbacks, with a capacity of 30,000 litres each, are also newly made, from boat skin larch. The fermentation time is at least 72 hours, sometimes longer. Malt is brought over from neighbouring Springbank whose staff also run operations. Although the capacity is 750,000 litres, the plan for the period August 2011 to July 2012 is to produce only 33,000 litres.

One of the previous owners of Glengyle was the whisky broker Bloch Brothers with Sir Maurice Bloch at the helm. When they took over in 1940, they already owned Scapa (1936) and Glen Scotia (1933). They never managed to start up production at Glengyle and in 1954, Sir Maurice sold his entire business to Hiram Walker for a sum that today values to £40m. Shortly after that he set up a charitable trust which funded several organisations as well as Glasgow University. Sir Maurice died in 1964.

The name Kilkerran is used for the whisky as Glengyle was already in use for a vatted malt produced by Loch Lomond Distillers. The first, widely available bottling was a 5 year old, named *Kilkerran Work in Progress*, released in summer 2009. In June 2010, *the second edition of Kilkerran Work in Progress* appeared as a 6 year old and in June 2011, *Kilkerran WIP 3* was released with a majority of the casks being ex-bourbon with an addition of ex-sherry butts. A total of 9,000 bottles were released.

*Kilkerran
- Work in Progress III*

Glenkinchie

Glenlivet

Owner: Diageo   **Region/district:** Lowlands

Founded: 1837   **Status:** Active (vc)   **Capacity:** 2 350 000 litres

Address: Pencaitland, Trenent, East Lothian EH34 5ET

Tel: 01875 342004   **website:** www.malts.com

History:

1825 – A distillery known as Milton is founded by John and George Rate.

1837 – The Rate brothers are registered as licensees of a distillery named Glenkinchie.

1853 – John Rate sells the distillery to a farmer by the name of Christie who converts it to a sawmill.

1881 – The buildings are bought by a consortium from Edinburgh.

1890 – Glenkinchie Distillery Company is founded. Reconstruction and refurbishment is on-going for the next few years.

1914 – Glenkinchie forms Scottish Malt Distillers (SMD) with four other lowland distilleries.

1939-45 – Glenkinchie is one of few distilleries allowed to maintain production during the war.

1968 – Floor maltings is decommissioned.

1969 – The maltings is converted into a museum.

1988 – Glenkinchie 10 years becomes one of selected six in the Classic Malt series.

1998 – A Distiller's Edition with Amontillado finish is launched.

2007 – A 12 year old and a 20 year old cask strength are released.

2010 – A cask strength exclusive for the visitor centre, a 1992 single cask and a 20 year old are released.

Glenkinchie 12 year old

GS – The nose is fresh and floral, with spices and citrus fruits, plus a hint of marshmallow. Notably elegant. Water releases cut grass and lemon notes. Medium-bodied, smooth, sweet and fruity, with malt, butter and cheesecake. The finish is comparatively long and drying, initially rather herbal.

DR – The nose is light and flowery, with wet meadow notes and cucumber, the palate is pure barley with a touch of star anise spice and an earthy note.

Only five distilleries produce malt whisky in the Lowlands today (Glenkinchie, Auchentoshan, Bladnoch and the two newly constructed Daftmill and Ailsa Bay) but in the second half of the 18th century, the area was more or less the birthplace of commercial whisky distilling in Scotland. As time passed, legislative decisions and a change in consumers' preferences worked in the favour of malt whiskies produced in the Highlands and a majority of the Lowland malt distilleries were closed before the second World War. The only one (except for the five mentioned) to survive into the 1990s was Rosebank.

Glenkinchie is equipped with a full lauter mash tun (9.5 tonnes) and to achieve the desired character, the operators aim for a clear wort with as little solids as possible being carried over into the washbacks. There are six of them, all wooden, and because of the clear wort the wash gets very lively during the 63 hour fermentation and switchers are working constantly to keep the froth down. There is only one pair of stills but they are, on the other hand, very big - in fact, the wash still (30,963 litres) is the biggest in Scotland. Steeply descending lyne arms give very little reflux and condensation of the spirit vapours take place in a cast irom worm tub. The distillery is currently working 7 days and 14 mashes per week which amounts to 2.5 million litres of alcohol per year. Three dunnage warehouses on site have 10,000 casks maturing, the oldest from 1952.

Glenkinchie is one of the six original Classic Malts and the proximity to Edinburgh is one reason why more than 40,000 visitors find their way to the distillery and its excellent visitor centre each year.

The core range consists of a *12 year old* and a *Distiller's Edition 14 years old* since 2007. There is also a *cask strength without age statement* sold exclusively at the visitor centre. Recent limited editions include a *Manager's Choice 1992 single cask* and a *20 year old cask strength* distilled in 1990, both released in 2010.

12 years old

139

Glenlivet

Owner:
Chivas Brothers
(Pernod Ricard)

Region/district:
Speyside

Founded: 1824
Status: Active (vc)
Capacity: 10 500 000 litres

Address: Ballindalloch, Banffshire AB37 9DB

Tel: 01340 821720 (vc)
website: www.theglenlivet.com

History:
1817 – George Smith inherits the farm distillery Upper Drummin from his father Andrew Smith who has been distilling on the site since 1774.

1840 – George Smith buys Delnabo farm near Tomintoul and leases Cairngorm Distillery. His son William takes over operations at Upper Drummin.

1845 – George Smith leases three other farms, one of which is situated on the river Livet and is called Minmore.

1846 – William Smith develops tuberculosis and his brother John Gordon moves back home to assist his father. Sales of Smith's Glenlivet increases steadily and neither Upper Drummin nor Cairngorm Distillery can meet demand.

1858 – George Smith buys Minmore farm, which he has leased for some time, and obtains permission from the Duke of Gordon to build a distillery.

1859 – Upper Drummin and Cairngorm close and all equipment is brought to Minmore which is renamed The Glenlivet Distillery.

1864 – George Smith cooperates with the whisky agent Andrew P. Usher and exports the whisky with great success.

1871 – George Smith dies and his son John Gordon takes over.

The overall goal for the owners of Glenlivet is to establish it as the number one single malt in the world in terms of sales. Currently in a very close fight with Macallan (both brands sold around 700,000 cases in 2010) over second place, this means that the brand must dethrone Glenfiddich which has been at the very top for decades now. It also means that they have to plan for bigger volumes and the most important step towards that was taken in 2009 when a £10m expansion took place, increasing capacity by 80%. New stills, new mashtun and new washbacks were fitted into a new stillhouse adjacent to the visitor centre.

In order for the extension to blend in with the older buildings stones from the old malt barn were used and the result was stunning. This must be one of the most beautiful still rooms in Scotland, not least for the magnificent view of the Livet valley.

After the expansion, the equipment was divided into two still rooms. In the old, there are eight stills where three of the stills were replaced in June 2011 while two others had their heads replaced. There are also eight wooden washbacks and the old mash tun (which has been mothballed). The new still house (which resembles the Glenburgie still house) has a new, Briggs mash tun with six arms (12.6 tonnes capacity) which is highly efficient, bringing the mashing time down from 6 hours to just over 3 hours. There are also eight new Oregon pine washbacks made in Dufftown and three pairs of stills with subcoolers. The wash stills are heated using heat exchangers while the spirit stills all have kettles inside. The fermentation time is 50 hours and they try to get as clear worts as possible to achieve the Glenlivet character of the spirit. The maximum capacity is 42 mashes per week but during 2011 they will be doing 38 mashes – almost 10 million litres of alcohol in the year.

Glenlivet's core range (or Classic Range as they call it themselves) is the *12 year old, French Oak 15 years, 18 year old, 21 year old Archive* and *Glenlivet XXV*. Four expressions are earmarked for the Duty Free market: *First Fill Sherry Cask 12 years old, 15 years old, Nadurra* (16 years old and non-chill filtered) and (from July 2011) *Glenlivet Master Distiller's Reserve*. Recent limited releases include *1973 Cellar Collection* (released in 2009), the 21 year old *Glenlivet Founder's Reserve*, released to celebrate the expansion of the distillery and two more expressions of the *Nadurra* - a *cask strength* version released in the USA and *Nadurra Triumph 1991* which is an 18 year old distilled solely from the Triumph barley variety. There is also a *16 year old cask strength* sold exclusively at the distillery.

History (continued):

1880 – John Gordon Smith applies for and is granted sole rights to the name The Glenlivet. All distilleries wishing to use Glenlivet in their names must from now hyphenate it with their brand names.

1890 – A fire breaks out and some of the buildings are replaced.

1896 – Another two stills are installed.

1901 – John Gordon Smith dies.

1904 – John Gordon's nephew George Smith Grant takes over.

1921 – Captain Bill Smith Grant, son of George Smith Grant, takes over.

1953 – George & J. G. Smith Ltd merges with J. & J. Grant of Glen Grant Distillery and forms the company Glenlivet & Glen Grant Distillers.

1966 – Floor maltings closes.

1970 – Glenlivet & Glen Grant Distillers Ltd merges with Longmorn-Glenlivet Distilleries Ltd and Hill Thomson & Co. Ltd to form The Glenlivet Distillers Ltd.

1978 – Seagrams buys The Glenlivet Distillers Ltd. A visitor centre opens.

1996/97 – The visitor centre is expanded, and a multimedia facility installed.

2000 – French Oak 12 years and American Oak 12 years are launched

2001 – Pernod Ricard and Diageo buy Seagram Spirits & Wine. Pernod Ricard thereby gains control of the Chivas group.

2004 – This year sees a lavish relaunch of Glenlivet. French Oak 15 years replaces the previous 12 year old.

2005 – Two new duty-free versions are introduced – The Glenlivet 12 year old First Fill and Nadurra. The 1972 Cellar Collection (2,015 bottles) is launched.

2006 – Nadurra 16 year old cask strength and 1969 Cellar Collection are released. Glenlivet sells more than 500,000 cases for the first time in one year.

2007 – Glenlivet XXV is released.

2009 – Four more stills are installed and the capacity increases to 8.5 million litres. Nadurra Triumph 1991 is released.

2010 – Another two stills are commissioned and capacity increases to 10.5 million litres. Glenlivet Founder's Reserve is released.

2011 – Glenlivet Master Distiller's Reserve is released for the duty free market.

Glenlivet 12 year old

GS – A lovely, honeyed, floral, fragrant nose. Medium-bodied, smooth and malty on the palate, with vanilla sweetness. Not as sweet, however, as the nose might suggest. The finish is pleasantly lengthy and sophisticated.

DR – Freshly chopped apple, rhubarb and crisp barley on the nose, soft rounded and beautiful mouth feel with green fruit and gooseberries and a delicate, rounded and medium long finish.

18 years old

21 Archive

The Glenlivet XXV

12 years old

15 years old

Master Distiller's Reserve

Glenlossie

Owner:
Diageo

Region/district:
Speyside

Founded: **Status:** **Capacity:**
1876 Active 1 800 000 litres

Address: Birnie, Elgin, Morayshire IV30 8SS

Tel: **website:**
01343 862000 www.malts.com

History:
1876 – John Duff, former manager at Glendronach Distillery, founds the distillery. Alexander Grigor Allan (to become part-owner of Talisker Distillery), the whisky trader George Thomson and Charles Shirres (both will co-found Longmorn Distillery some 20 years later with John Duff) and H. Mackay are also involved in the company.

1895 – The company Glenlossie-Glenlivet Distillery Co. is formed. Alexander Grigor Allan passes away.

1896 – John Duff becomes more involved in Longmorn and Mackay takes over management of Glenlossie.

1919 – Distillers Company Limited (DCL) takes over the company.

1929 – A fire breaks out and causes considerable damage.

1930 – DCL transfers operations to Scottish Malt Distillers (SMD).

1962 – Stills are increased from four to six.

1971 – Another distillery, Mannochmore, is constructed by SMD on the premises. A dark grains plant is installed.

1990 – A 10 year old is launched in the Flora & Fauna series.

2010 – A Manager's Choice single cask from 1999 is released.

Glenlossie 10 year old

GS – Cereal, silage and vanilla notes on the relatively light nose, with a voluptuous, sweet palate, offering plums, ginger and barley sugar, plus a hint of oak. The finish is medium in length, with grist and slightly peppery oak.

DR – Powdery and light, with salt and pepper on the nose, big, earthy and spicy palate; savoury and full, with a long and mouth-coating finish.

Two distilleries share the same site a few miles southwest of Elgin. The older brother, Glenlossie, was founded in 1876 and its younger sister, Mannochmore, almost 100 years later. To make the place even busier, a dark grains plant to take care of the residues from whisky making, was also built. But it does not stop there; in August 2011, Diageo submitted a planning application to build a bioenergy plant which will produce energy from 30,000 tonnes of draff per year. The cost for the facility will be £6m.

In the old days, all distilleries would have had washbacks made of wood for the fermentation. Today, many distilleries have changed them to stainless steel ones. They are easier to clean and facilitate the control of the fermentation process. However, the change from wood to steel often happened in the 1970s and 1980s due to a chase for efficiency. Today whisky producers are much more reluctant to make drastic changes in equipment for fear of altering the character of the whisky and they often prefer to exchange like for like. This is also what they are doing at Glenlossie at the moment. Three of the washbacks made of larch were replaced with replicas last year, another three were replaced in summer 2011 and another two are due for replacement next summer – all of them made of larch!

The complete equipment setup of the distillery is one stainless steel full lauter mash tun (8.2 tonnes) installed in 1992, eight washbacks and three pairs of stills. The spirit stills are also equipped with purifiers between the lyne arms and the condensers to increase the reflux which gives a light and clean spirit. The workforce used to alternate between Glenlossie and its sister distillery, Mannochmore but since 2007 both distilleries are producing simultaneously. During 2011 the the distillery will be working a five-day week with 12 mashes, resulting in 1.8 million litres of alcohol.

The whisky is mainly used for blends, especially Haig, and the only official bottling available today is a *10 year old*. In 2010 a *first fill bourbon cask* distilled in 1999 was released as a part of the Manager's Choice range.

Flora & Fauna 10 years old

New Books We Enjoyed

Hans Offringa has written several excellent books on the whisky subject and a few years ago he published *Whisky & Jazz*. This year he continues on the whisky and music track. In *Bourbon & Blues* Offringa combines two American icons, the drink and the music, and how they reflect themselves in one another.

The combination of whisky and food has become a hot topic lately and here is a new, fresh addition to the range of books on the subject – *Whisky & Food*. Jan Groth, a global Scotch ambassador, brings you his detailed knowledge on whisky and how to enjoy whisky with food. Lots of recipes, anecdotes and travel accounts and, not least, stunning photos by Arne Adler.

Ten years ago, David Wishart wrote what would become a classic on how to enjoy and describe malt whisky according to different flavour dimensions. Here is the recently updated version of *Whisky Classified* including everything that happened in the last decade.

Ian Buxton has become more or less the expert on portraying whisky brands and companies. This year he has been involved in no less than tree books on that theme; *Cutty Sark: The Making of a Whisky Brand*, *The Famous Grouse Whisky Companion* and *Glenfarclas 175*.

Finally, let´s look at a new book coming in May 2012 with the ambitious title *1001 Whiskies You Must Taste Before You Die*. Edited by Dominic Roskrow and with contributions from 20 whisky experts, this tome (960 pages!) gives you facts and tasting notes of whiskies from all over the world.

The Famous Grouse Whisky Companion ISBN 978-0091944742	**Glenfarclas 175** ISBN 978-1906476755	**Bourbon & Blues** ISBN 978-9078668008
Cutty Sark: The Making of a Whisky Brand ISBN 978-1780270265	**Whisky Classified** ISBN 978-1862059139	**Whisky & Food** ISBN 978-1908233042

1001 Whiskies You Must Taste Before You Die
ISBN 978-0789324870

Recommended Magazines

Malt Advocate
www.maltadvocate.com

Whisky Magazine
www.whiskymag.com

Whisky Time
www.whiskytime-magazin.com

Der Whisky-Botschafter
www.whiskybotschafter.com

Whisky Passion
www.whiskypassion.nl

Allt om Whisky
www.alltomwhisky.se

Glenmorangie

Owner:
The Glenmorangie Co
(Moët Hennessy)

Region/district:
Northern Highlands

Founded:
1843

Status:
Active (vc)

Capacity:
6 000 000 litres

Address: Tain, Ross-shire IV19 1BR

Tel:
01862 892477 (vc)

website:
www.glenmorangie.com

History:
1843 – William Mathesen applies for a license for a farm distillery called Morangie, which is rebuilt by them. Production took place here in 1738, and possibly since 1703.

1849 – Production starts in November.

1880 – Exports to foreign destinations such as Rome and San Francisco commence.

1887 – The distillery is rebuilt and Glenmorangie Distillery Company Ltd is formed.

1918 – 40% of the distillery is sold to Macdonald & Muir Ltd and 60 % to the whisky dealer Durham. Macdonald & Muir takes over Durham's share by the late thirties.

1931 – The distillery closes.

1936 – Production restarts in November.

1980 – Number of stills increases from two to four and own maltings ceases.

1990 – The number of stills is doubled to eight.

1994 – A visitor centre opens. September sees the launch of Glenmorangie Port Wood Finish which marks the start of a number of different wood finishes.

1995 – Glenmorangie´s Tain l´Hermitage (Rhone wine) is launched.

1996 – Two different wood finishes are launched, Madeira and Sherry. Glenmorangie plc is formed.

Glenmorangie single malt has not been able to keep up with the three leading brands on the market. The sales volumes have been reduced to that of 2002 whilst Glenlivet has increased with 75% for the same period and Macallan with no less than 130%. But perhaps a change is on the horizon. On the very important American market, where Glenmorangie previously have not been very active, the brand now holds sixth place with 52,000 cases sold in 2010. In fact, they showed the biggest increase (40%) of all brands between the years 2008-2010. The brands's strong-hold is still the home market (UK) where Glenmorangie holds second place behind Glenfiddich.

In a big expansion during 2009, the distillery had a new, full lauter mash tun with a 13 tonnes capacity, four new, stainless steel washbacks added to the existing eight, a new boiler and, last but not least, four new stills which makes the total number of stills now ten. They are the tallest in Scotland and replicas of old gin type of stills. The whole investment, estimating to £4.5m, increased the capacity from 4 million to 6 million litres per year.

Glenmorangie has always been very particular with the casks that are used. American oak is preferred and a part of them, known as designer casks, come from slow growth woods in the Ozarks, Missouri. They are air-dried for a mini-mum of two years and then dried further through mecha-nical means.

In September 2011, the visitor centre was re-launched after an extensive redesign and expansion and now includes new galleries, dramming room and a VIP area.

The core range consists of *Original* (the former 10 year old), *18 year old* and *25 year old*. There are three wood finishes: *Quinta Ruban* (port), *Nectar D´Or* (Sauternes) and *Lasanta* (sherry). Added to the core range are *Astar* and *Signet*. Astar has matured in designer casks while Signet is an unusual piece of work which has been crafted by the distillery's two whisky creators, Bill Lumsden and Rachel Barrie. A portion of the whisky (20%) has been made using chocolate malt, which is normally used to produce porter and stout. A series of bottlings, called Private Collection, started in 2009 with the release of *Sonnalta PX* and was followed up a year later with lightly peated *Finealta*. In July 2011, *Glenmorangie Pride* was released. This is a 28 year old whisky discovered in the casks in 1999 by Bill Lumsden. He decided to re-rack the whisky into Sauternes barriques for another ten years – the longest extra maturation for any Glenmorangie whisky.

History (continued):

1997 – A museum opens.

2001 – A limited edition of a cask strength port wood finish is released in July, Cote de Beaune Wood Finish is launched in September and Three Cask (ex-Bourbon, charred oak and ex-Rioja) is launched in October for Sainsbury's.

2002 – A Sauternes finish, a 20 year Glenmorangie with two and a half years in Sauternes casks, is launched.

2003 – Burgundy Wood Finish is launched in July and a limited edition of cask strength Madeira-matured (i. e. not just finished) in August.

2004 – Glenmorangie buys the Scotch Malt Whisky Society. The Macdonald family decides to sell Glenmorangie plc (including the distilleries Glenmorangie, Glen Moray and Ardbeg) to Moët Hennessy at £300 million. A new version of Glenmorangie Tain l´Hermitage (28 years) is released and Glenmorangie Artisan Cask is launched in November.

2005 – A 30 year old is launched.

2007 – The entire range gets a complete makeover with 15 and 30 year olds being discontinued and the rest given new names as well as new packaging.

2008 – An expansion of production capacity is started. Astar and Signet are launched.

2009 – The expansion is finished and Sonnalta PX is released for duty free.

2010 – Finealta is released.

2011 – 28 year old Glenmorangie Pride is released.

Glenmorangie Original

GS – The nose offers fresh fruits, butterscotch and toffee. Silky smooth in the mouth, mild spice, vanilla, and well-defined toffee. The fruity finish has a final flourish of ginger.

DR – Rounded honey and light tangerine on the nose, much weightier on the palate, with vanilla, honey, oranges and lemons nudging alongside some tannins and soft peat, all coming together in a rich and warming finish.

Signet · Astar · Finealta

Glenmorangie Pride

Original (10 years old) · 18 years old · Nectar D´Or

145

Glen Moray

Owner:
La Martiniquaise

Region/district:
Speyside

Founded: **Status:** **Capacity:**
1897 Active (vc) 2 300 000 litres

Address: Bruceland Road, Elgin,
Morayshire IV30 1YE

Tel: **website:**
01343 542577 www.glenmoray.com

History:
1897 – West Brewery, dated 1828, is reconstructed as Glen Moray Distillery.

1910 – The distillery closes.

1920 – Financial troubles force the distillery to be put up for sale. Buyer is Macdonald & Muir.

1923 – Production restarts.

1958 – A reconstruction takes place and the floor maltings are replaced by a Saladin box.

1978 – Own maltings are terminated.

1979 – Number of stills is increased to four.

1992 – Two old stills are replaced by new.

1996 – Macdonald & Muir Ltd changes name to Glenmorangie plc.

1999 – Three wood finishes are introduced - Chardonnay (no age) and Chenin Blanc (12 and 16 years respectively).

2004 – Louis Vuitton Moët Hennessy buys Glenmorangie plc for £300 million. A new visitor centre is inaugurated and a 1986 cask strength, a 20 and a 30 year old are released. Wood finishing ceases.

2005 – The Fifth Chapter (Manager's Choice from Graham Coull) is released.

2006 – Two vintages, 1963 and 1964, and a new Manager's Choice are released.

2007 – The second edition of Mountain Oak is released.

2008 – The distillery is sold to La Martiniquaise.

2009 – A 14 year old Port finish and an 8 year old matured in red wines casks are released.

2011 – Two cask finishes and a 10 year old Chardonnay maturation are released.

Saleswise Glen Moray single malt was on top in 2004 when it was one of the four best selling malts in the UK domestic market. Total sales at that time were 50,000 cases per year, and thanks to the interest of the new owners, La Martiniquaise, taking over in 2009 the numbers are moving in that direction again. The French spirits company, already established in 1934, has had a presence in Scotland since 2004, with its huge plant called Glen Turner near Bathgate – an investment of £15m. Here, several brands (Glen Turner, Label 5 and Sir Edwards) are matured, blended and bottled for the French market. A decision then taken to expand the site to also include a production unit. In autumn 2010 a grain distillery by the name Starlaw with the capacity of producing 25 million litres was commissioned at a cost of £30m. There are also plans to expand into distilling 5 million litres of malt whisky.

Glen Moray distillery is equipped with a stainless steel mash tun, five stainless steel washbacks and two pairs of stills. Last year 2.3 million litres were distilled, a record for the distillery, and they expect to do the same for 2011. Apparently this is not enough and the owner is looking into various options to increase the capacity. In 2009, the distillery, for the first time, produced a share of whisky from peated malt with around 40ppm phenols. The volume of the first batch amounted to 300,000 litres and for 2011 they will be doing 220,000 litres. It will mainly be used in the owner's Label 5 blended whisky.

The core range consists of *Classic, 12* and *16 years old*. The Classic used to be an 8 year old but is now a mix of 3, 5 and 7 year old whiskies. Limited editions released in 2011 are a *10 year old Chardonnay matured* expression and two *cask finishes – port* and *madeira*. There is also talk of releasing a *40 year old* at the end of 2011 or beginning of 2012 from one of the remaining casks from 1971. Older limited editions include *Signature*, a *30 year old*, a *14 year old port finish* and an 8 year old matured in red wine casks.

12 years old

Glen Moray 12 year old

GS – Mellow on the nose, with vanilla, pear drops and some oak. Smooth in the mouth, with spicy malt, vanilla and summer fruits. The finish is relatively short, with spicy fruit.

DR – Maltesers and soft vanilla ice cream on the nose, full and rich sweet malt, a touch of vanilla and hints of tannin on the palate and a pleasant and pleasing finish.

Glen Ord

Owner:
Diageo

Region/district:
Northern Highlands

Founded: **Status:** **Capacity:**
1838   Active (vc)   5 000 000 litres

Address: Muir of Ord, Ross-shire IV6 7UJ

Tel: **website:**
01463 872004 (vc)   www.malts.com

History:

1838 – Thomas Mackenzie founds the distillery and licenses it to Ord Distillery Co. (Robert Johnstone and Donald MacLennan).

1847 – The distillery is put up for sale.

1855 – Alexander MacLennan and Thomas McGregor buy the distillery.

1870 – Alexander MacLennan dies and the distillery is taken over by his widow who even-tually marries the banker Alexander Mackenzie.

1877 – Alexander Mackenzie leases the distillery.

1878 – Alexander Mackenzie builds a new still house and barely manages to start production before a fire destroys it.

1882 – Mackenzie registers the name Glenoran to be used for whisky from Glen Ord.

1896 – Alexander Mackenzie dies and the distillery is sold to the blending company James Watson & Co. for £15,800.

1923 – John Jabez Watson, James Watson's son, dies and the distillery is sold to John Dewar & Sons. The name is changed from Glen Oran to Glen Ord.

1925 – Dewar's joins Distillers Company Limited.

1961 – Floor maltings is abandoned in favour of a Saladin box.

1966 – The two stills are increased to six.

1968 – To augment the Saladin box a drum maltings is built.

1983 – Malting in the Saladin box ceases.

1988 – A visitor centre is opened.

2002 – A 12 year old is launched.

2003 – A limited-edition cask strength, 28 years, is launched.

2004 – A 25 year old is launched.

2005 – A 30 year old is launched as a Special Release from Diageo.

2006 – A 12 year old Singleton of Glen Ord is launched.

2010 – A Singleton of Glen Ord 15 year old is released in Taiwan.

2011 – Two more washbacks are installed, increasing the capacity by 25%.

Singleton of Glen Ord 12 year old

GS – Honeyed malt and milk chocolate on the nose, with a hint of orange. These characte-ristics carry over onto the sweet, easy-drinking palate, along with a biscuity note. Subtly drying, with a medium-length, spicy finish.

DR – Red fruits and blackcurrant, mince pies, red apple and sherry on the nose, enjoyable taste of apple, prune and cinnamon, and a delightful and more-ish finish.

Glen Ord distillery is situated 15 miles west of Inverness in the fertile Black Isle. These surroundings were also the home of Ferintosh distillery (actually the name for several distilleries under the same ownership) in the 18th century. The success for Ferintosh was so great that at one time, two thirds of the whisky sold in Scotland came from the distillery and sometimes Ferintosh was used as a synonym for whisky. Today, Glen Ord hasn´t achieved the same dominant position as Ferintosh, but this fairly anonymous brand (at least in Europe) can brag about being the fastest expanding Scotch single malt in terms of volumes sold in the last few years. It all started in 2006 when it was relaun-ched under the name Singleton of Glen Ord and targeted at the Far East markets and especially Taiwan. In just a few years it went from nothing to 100,000 cases sold!

The equipment consists of a new 12.5 tonnes stainless steel full lauter mash tun which in 2010 replaced the old one made of cast iron, ten washbacks made of Oregon pine (two of them installed in October 2011, increasing the capacity by 25%) and three pairs of stills. The distillery was closed between July 2010 and January 2011 to do the upgrade of the mash house, but is now back on 7-day production with 21 mashes per week (5 million litres in the year). The total cost for the recent upgrade was £3.2m.

A major part of the site is occupied by the Glen Ord Maltings built in 1968. Equipped with 18 drums and with a capa-city of 38,000 tonnes per year it produces malt for several other Diageo distilleries.

The core expression is the Single-ton of Glen Ord 12 year old, with a 50/50 mix of sherry and bour-bon casks. Other expressions in the range are the 15 year old, the 18 year old and two extremely limited ones – 32 and 35 year old.

The Singleton of Glen Ord

Glenrothes

Owner: The Edrington Group
(the brand is owned by Berry Bros)

Region/district: Speyside

Founded: 1878

Status: Active

Capacity: 5 600 000 litres

Address: Rothes, Morayshire AB38 7AA

Tel: 01340 872300

website: www.theglenrothes.com

History:
1878 – James Stuart & Co., licensees of Macallan since 1868, begins planning a new distillery in Rothes. Robert Dick, William Grant and John Cruickshank are partners in the company. Stuart has financial problems so Dick, Grant and Cruickshank terminate the partnership, form William Grant & Co. and continue the building of the distillery in Rothes.

1879 – Production starts in May.

1884 – The distillery changes name to Glenrothes-Glenlivet.

1887 – William Grant & Co. joins forces with Islay Distillery Co. (owners of Bunnahabhain Distillery) and forms Highland Distillers Company.

1897 – A fire ravages the distillery in December.

1898 – Capacity doubles.

1903 – An explosion causes substantial damage.

1963 – Expansion from four to six stills.

1980 – Expansion from six to eight stills.

1989 – Expansion from eight to ten stills.

1999 – Edrington and William Grant & Sons buy Highland Distillers.

2002 – Four single cask malts from 1966 and 1967 are launched.

2005 – A 30 year old is launched together with Select Reserve and Vintage 1985.

2006 – 1994 and 1975 Vintage are launched.

2007 – A 25 year old is released as a duty free item.

2008 – 1978 Vintage and Robur Reserve are launched.

2009 – The Glenrothes John Ramsay, two vintages (1988 and 1998), Alba Reserve and Three Decades are released.

2010 – Berry Brothers takes over the brand while Edrington remains owner of the distillery.

Glenrothes Select Reserve

GS – The nose offers ripe fruits, spice and toffee, with a whiff of Golden Syrup. Faint wood polish in the mouth, vanilla, spicy and slightly citric. Creamy and complex. Slightly nutty, with some orange, in the drying finish.

DR – On the nose, oranges dominating a fruit bowl of flavours that includes berries among the citrus. The palate is wonderfully rounded and complete, a masterclass in fruit, wood and spice balance, and the finish is a total joy, perfectly weighted and balanced.

The ownership situation at Glenrothes is like nothing else in the industry. The distillery itself is owned and operated by Edrington (who also owns Macallan and Highland Park) but the single malt brand itself is in the hands of Berry Bros & Rudd (BBR). This arrangement was finalised in 2010 when BBR took over the Glenrothes brand and they handed over the responsibility for the blended whisky Cutty Sark to Edrington. Glenrothes is no stranger to BBR as they have long been the marketeers and distributors of the brand. The distillery is equipped with a stainless steel full lauter mash tun from the 1970s – probably one of the first in the business. Ten washbacks made of Oregon pine are in one room, whilst an adjacent modern tun room houses eight new stainless steel washbacks. The wash from the different types of washbacks are always mixed before distillation. The magnificent, cathedral like still house has five pairs of stills performing a very slow distillation. The middle cut of the spirit run takes no less than five hours. The distillery has its own cooperage and there is also blending of mature spirit for Famous Grouse taking place on site.

For 2011 they will be doing 28 mashes per week which amounts to slightly less than 50% of the capacity. Around 2% of the production is bottled as single malt, 40% is sold to other companies and the rest goes into Famous Grouse and Cutty Sark.

The core expression of Glenrothes is the *Select Reserve* without age statement, while it is the vintages that have brought fame to Glenrothes. The most recent vintages are *1988, 1995* and *1998*. In 2009, *Alba Reserve*, matured solely in American Oak refill bourbon casks, was added to the core range. The duty free range include a *25 year old*, *Robur Reserve* and *Three Decades* (with whiskies from the seventies, eighties and nineties). In 2010 a limited edition was released, *The Glenrothes John Ramsay*, the last vatting from the now retired Master Blender, John Ramsay.

1995 Vintage

Meet the Manager

ALASDAIR ANDERSON
DISTILLERY MANAGER, GLENROTHES DISTILLERY

When did you start working in the whisky business and when did you start at Glenrothes?

On leaving high school in 1980 I was fortunate to obtain a summer job in the Maltings at Tamdhu. It didn't take long to discover that the whisky business with its mix of people, locations and not forgetting the end result was something I would love to be part of. My first experience of working at Glenrothes was in 1999.

Had you been working in other lines of business before whisky?

The usual summer jobs for this area, peat cutting, forestry and farming.

What kind of education or training do you have?

Formally I've completed the General Certificate in Distilling, the Certificate in Malting Competence and the Diploma in Distilling. I have also been fortunate to work with very knowledgeable colleagues who greatly furthered my knowledge of the process and life in general.

Describe your career in the whisky business.

Since 1980 I have worked my way through each department of the malting and whisky production both at The Glenrothes and Tamdhu. 1998-1999 I had the role of assistant to our innovations manager where I had the privilege of working in the industry in Orkney, Islay, Perthshire and various sites on Speyside. 2000-2007; Production supervisor for both The Glenrothes and Tamdhu. 2007-2010; Production manager for Tamdhu Distillery, maltings and warehousing. 2010-present day; Production manager for Glenrothes Distillery and warehousing

What are your main tasks as a manager?

To ensure the smooth operation of Glenrothes distillery ensuring the production of the highest quality spirit is done safely, legally and all of this whilst protecting our environment for the future.

What are the biggest challenges of being a distillery manager?

Protecting and improving the work started by my predecessors with the every tightening noose of compliance issues.

What would be the worst that could go wrong in the production process?

If we were half way through a production week in winter and the boiler went down, the thought of -10°C and no steam would be high on my list of worst nightmares.

How would you describe the character of Glenrothes single malt?

Elegant, balanced, complex, fruity, citrus, vanilla and spicy. Delicious!

What are the main features in the process at Glenrothes, contributing to this character?

Combining wash from both wooden and stainless steel washbacks; tall copper pot stills; very slow second distillation delivering a clean fruity spirit.

What is your favourite expression of Glenrothes and why?

Vintage 1998 "pure heaven in a glass" is the epitome of all that we do at Glenrothes. Soft round and with a creamy texture it prolongs the elegance balance and full flavour of Glenrothes.

If it were your decision alone – what new expression of Glenrothes would you like to see released?

I've never been a great fan of the sometimes overpowering effects off first fill casks so for me it would be 2nd fill casks be it Spanish or American or preferably both. The ethereal character which shows itself after about 20 years in these casks would definitely be on my list of last drams before I die.

If you had to choose a favourite dram other than Glenrothes, what would that be?

That's a hard question but if I was pushed a Knockando 18 year old wouldn't be far from the top of my list however if I was marooned on a desert island a mixed vintage case of The Famous Grouse malts would be my wish.

What are the biggest changes you have seen the past 10 years in your profession?

The downsizing of the workforce at each distillery through the increasing use of improved control systems has seen many small rural communities being affected. An increasing drain on my time all be it for very valid reasons is the increasing requirement to comply with ever constraining legislation whether it be for Health & Safety, Food/Feed safety or Environmental reasons

Do you see any major changes in the next 10 years to come?

Being merely a custodian of a part of the whisky industry I will continue evolving my area however the main challenges on the horizon are the future supply of our raw materials be it high quality malting barley or energy. The pursuit of particularly the reduction in energy consumption will have to be carefully introduced mainly due to the possible effect of, if we are not careful, removing the unique character from each distillery.

Do you have any special interests or hobbies that you pursue?

Anything with two wheels has been my way of relaxing away from the distilleries. Prior to marriage, broken bones and my body not keeping up, Moto-X was my weekend pursuit. Now road cycling is my passion and with living in one of the most scenic areas of the world it's a great way to explore the area.

How important is it to have your own cooperage on site?

We place a great emphasis on the quality of wood we use, so for us it is very important to control the quality of casks from the beginning and to retain the skills required within the group.

Glen Scotia

Owner: **Region/district:**
Loch Lomond Distillery Co   Campbeltown

Founded: **Status:**   **Capacity:**
1832   Active   750 000 litres

Address: High Street, Campbeltown,
Argyll PA28 6DS

Tel: **website:**
01586 552288   www.glenscotia-distillery.co.uk

History:
1832 – The family Galbraith founds Scotia Distillery (the year 1835 is mentioned by the distillery itself on labels).

1895 – The distillery is sold to Stewart Galbraith.

1919 – Sold to West Highland Malt Distillers.

1924 – West Highland Malt Distillers goes bankrupt and one of its directors, Duncan MacCallum, buys the distillery.

1928 – The distillery closes.

1930 – Duncan MacCallum commits suicide and the Bloch brothers take over.

1933 – Production restarts.

1954 – Hiram Walker takes over.

1955 – A. Gillies & Co. becomes new owner.

1970 – A. Gillies & Co. becomes part of Amalgated Distillers Products.

1979–82 – Reconstruction takes place.

1984 – The distillery closes.

1989 – Amalgated Distillers Products is taken over by Gibson International and production restarts.

1994 – Glen Catrine Bonded Warehouse Ltd takes over and the distillery is mothballed.

1999 – Production restarts 5th May through J. A. Mitchell & Co., owner of Springbank.

2000 – Loch Lomond Distillers runs operations with its own staff from May onwards.

2005 – A 12 year old is released.

2006 – A peated version from 1999 is released.

Glen Scotia 12 year old

GS – Initially floral on the nose, then gummy, with spice, citrus fruit and a faintly phenolic note. Quite full-bodied, peaty and nutty on the palate. Lengthy in the mildly herbal finish, with a whiff of smoke.

DR – The nose is of rich fudge and butter, the palate sliced apricot, walnut and fudge, with a medium finish touched with sweet spice.

Glen Scotia´s part in the whisky world of Campbeltown, has been that of the little brother of Springbank. Founded in 1832, the story told after 1928 is one of constant change of ownership, closures and even suicides. The latter, concerning an owner at the time, Duncan MacCallum, also founded the rumour that Glen Scotia would have its own ghost. Glen Catrine Bonded Warehouse (owners of Loch Lomond distillery) took over in 1994 and showed the same lack of interest as previous owners, at least for a while. But finally there has been a turn of the tide! At present, Glen Scotia is having its biggest upgrade since the 1970s. All six washbacks made of Corten steel are being replaced by stainless steel ones, an effluent system to take care of spent lees and pot ale is being installed and there are also plans to start using the second warehouse which has been redundant for years! The addition of a newly constructed website (to be launched in the near future) clearly shows that the owners have started noticing "the little brother".

Glen Scotia lies hidden away between modern high-rise buildings and it is only the sign at the gate that reveals malt whisky production. The equipment consists of a traditional cast iron mash tun, six new washbacks made of stainless steel and one pair of stills. Fermentation time is usually 48 hours but can be as long as up to five days.

During 2011, there will be three mashes per week which will give 130,000 litres of alcohol in the year. Medium peated barley (15ppm) has been used for two periods per year since 1999. The core range consists of a *12 year old* but there are now plans of also introducing a *10 year old*. Peated expressions (*6* and *7 year old*) were released in 2006 and 2007 in the owner´s Distillery Select range and some single casks of the unpeated version have also been bottled. Older expressions include a *17 year old* and the occasional *vintage*.

12 years old

Glen Spey

Owner: **Region/district:**
Diageo   Speyside

Founded: **Status:**   **Capacity:**
1878   Active   1 400 000 litres

Address: Rothes, Morayshire AB38 7AU

Tel: **website:**
01340 831215   www.malts.com

History:
1878 – James Stuart & Co. founds the distillery which becomes known by the name Mill of Rothes.

1886 – James Stuart buys Macallan.

1887 – W. & A. Gilbey buys the distillery for £11,000 thus becoming the first English company to buy a Scottish malt distillery.

1920 – A fire breaks out.

1962 – W. & A. Gilbey combines forces with United Wine Traders and forms International Distillers & Vintners (IDV).

1970 – The stills are increased from two to four.

1972 – IDV is bought by Watney Mann who is then acquired by Grand Metropolitan.

1997 – Guiness and Grand Metropolitan merge to form Diageo.

2001 – A 12 year old is launched in the Flora & Fauna series.

2010 – A 21 year old is released as part of the Special Releases and a 1996 Manager's Choice single cask is launched.

Since the mothballed Caperdonich was sold to Forsyth's coppersmiths in 2010, there are four distilleries remaining in Rothes. Coming into the town from the north, the first two distilleries are easily spotted with Speyburn on the left hand side of the A941 and with large signs in the round-about showing the way to Glen Grant. The other two on the other hand, Glenrothes and Glen Spey, are easy to miss both hidden away in streets of their own just before leaving Rothes. Glen Spey is the least known. Behind the gates lies a distillery that has spent most of its existence producing malt for blended Scotch, in particular for J&B. Glen Spey was the first distillery in Scotland to have English owners when W. & A. Gilbey bought it in 1887. At that time the Gilbey brothers were not known for their gin. That production did not start until 1895. They actually started as wine traders but the ravaging of the vine-louse in France in the 1860s led them to the whiskey business. The following years, they purchased another two distilleries, namely Strathmill and Knockando.

The distillery is equipped with a semi lauter mash tun, eight stainless steel mash tuns and two pairs of stills where the spirit stills are equipped with purifiers to obtain a lighter character of the spirit. The distillery is producing on a 5-day week basis and this means that they practise short fermentations (just 46 hours) during the weekdays and long fermentations (100 hours) over the weekend. To even out differences in the character, the two versions are always mixed before distillation. For 2011 a production of 1.4 million litres is planned (18 mashes per week).

The core expresion is the *12 year old Flora & Fauna* bottling. In 2010, two limited releases were made – a *single cask* from new American Oak, distilled in *1996*, was released as a part of the Manager's Choice series and as part of the yearly Special Releases, a *21 year old* with a maturation in ex-sherry American oak was launched.

12 years old

Glen Spey 12 year old

GS – Tropical fruits and malt on the comparatively delicate nose. Medium-bodied with fresh fruits and vanilla toffee on the palate, becoming steadily nuttier and drier in a gently oaky, mildly smoky finish.

DR – Delicate and floral on the nose, a complex mix of flavours on the palate with orange, citrus fruits, honey, vanilla and cinnamon in the mix.

151

Glentauchers

Owner:
Chivas Brothers
(Pernod Ricard)

Region/district:
Speyside

Founded: 1897
Status: Active
Capacity: 4 500 000 litres

Address: Glentauchers, Keith,
Banffshire AB55 6YL

Tel: 01542 860272
website: -

History:
1897 – James Buchanan and W. P. Lowrie, a whisky merchant from Glasgow, found the distillery.

1898 – Production starts.

1906 – James Buchanan & Co. takes over the whole distillery and acquires an 80% share in W. P. Lowrie & Co.

1915 – James Buchanan & Co. merges with Dewars.

1923-25 – Mashing house and maltings are rebuilt.

1925 – Buchanan-Dewars joins Distillers Company Limited (DCL).

1930 – Glentauchers is transferred to Scottish Malt Distillers (SMD).

1965 – The number of stills is increased from two to six.

1969 – Floor maltings is decommissioned.

1985 – DCL mothballs the distillery.

1989 – United Distillers (formerly DCL) sells the distillery to Caledonian Malt Whisky Distillers, a subsidiary of Allied Distillers.

1992 – Production recommences in August.

2000 – A 15 year old Glentauchers is released.

2005 – Chivas Brothers (Pernod Ricard) become the new owner through the acquisition of Allied Domecq.

Glentauchers 1991 Gordon & MacPhail

GS – Fresh and floral aromas, with sweet fruits and peppery peaches. Medium to full-bodied in the mouth, with cereal and sweet spice. The finish is medium to long.

DR – Deep plum and sherry on the nose, then cocoa and blackcurrant. The palate is soft, with plum, raisin and green banana, and the finish is banana and date cake.

If you drive the A95 between Keith and Craigellachie, you find this fairly anonymous distillery sitting just by the road. What you see, however, is not the original front of the site. If you continue just a little bit and turn right you'll discover that the distillery was built right next to the railway. In early days this would have been the front as evidenced by the remains of a large and beautiful, but, today, faded sign directly painted on the distillery wall saying: Glentauchers Distillery. Unfortunately, the owners have decided to cover part of the name with a blue and white plastic banner with the distillery name instead.

From the first days until today, Glentauchers role has been to produce malt whisky for blends. Founded by whisky baron, James Buchanan, Black & White was obviously the first to rely on Glentauchers for its character. As owners changed hands over the years it became a signature malt for Teacher's and today it is an integral part of Ballantine's.

The distillery is equipped with a 12 tonnes stainless steel full lauter mash tun installed in 2007 with the copperdome from the old mash tun fitted on top. There are six washbacks made of European larch and tree pairs of stills. Since 2006 the distillation is what you would call balanced, i. e. one wash still and one spirit still work together and they have their own designated low wines and feints receiver.

The spirit is filled in bourbon casks and part of them will mature in the two racked warehouses on site holding a total of 6,000 casks, while the rest is taken to Chivas' central warehouses in Keith. The capacity of Glentauchers is generally considered to be 3.4 million litres but that is with a six-day production cycle. With 19 mashes, the full capacity is more in the range of 4.5 million litres.

An official 15 year old was released by Allied Domecq some years ago but the current owners have not yet released any bottlings of Glentauchers.

Gordon & MacPhail Glentauchers 1990

Glenturret

Owner:
The Edrington Group

Region/district:
Eastern Highlands

Founded: 1775
Status: Active (vc)
Capacity: 340 000 litres

Address: The Hosh, Crieff, Perthshire PH7 4HA

Tel: 01764 656565
website: www.thefamousgrouse.com

History:

1775 – Whisky smugglers establish a small illicit farm distillery named Hosh Distillery.

1818 – John Drummond is licensee until 1837.

1826 – A distillery in the vicinity is named Glenturret, but is decommissioned before 1852.

1852 – John McCallum is licensee until 1874.

1875 – Hosh Distillery takes over the name Glenturret Distillery and is managed by Thomas Stewart.

1903 – Mitchell Bros Ltd takes over.

1921 – Production ceases and the buildings are used for whisky storage only.

1929 – Mitchell Bros Ltd is liquidated, the distillery dismantled and the facilities are used as storage for agricultural needs.

1957 – James Fairlie buys the distillery and re-equips it.

1959 – Production restarts.

1981 – Remy-Cointreau buys the distillery and invests in a visitor centre.

1990 – Highland Distillers takes over.

1999 – Edrington and William Grant & Sons buy Highland Distillers for £601 million. The purchasing company, 1887 Company, is a joint venture between Edrington (70%) and William Grant (30%).

2002 – The Famous Grouse Experience, a visitor centre costing £2.5 million, is inaugurated.

2003 – A 10 year old Glenturret replaces the 12 year old as the distillery's standard release.

2007 – Three new single casks are released.

Glenturret 10 year old

GS – Nutty and slightly oily on the nose, with barley and citrus fruits. Sweet and honeyed on the full, fruity palate, with a balancing note of oak. Medium length in the sweet finish.

DR – Full and rich honeyed nose, oily and fruity palate with some appealing rootsy savouriness. Something of the farmyard about it. Charming finish.

Glenturret is one of the oldest (perhaps the oldest) working distillery in Scotland but, first and foremost, it is the spiritual home of the Famous Grouse blended Scotch – the best selling whisky in Scotland since 1980. The range of the brand, which sells just under 3 million cases per year, has been extended recently by the introduction of the peated Black Grouse (2007), the blended grain whisky Snow Grouse (2008) and the de luxe version Naked Grouse (2009). Another extension of the range came in 2000 with Famous Grouse blended malt with sales increasing remarkably after it was launched in Taiwan in 2004. Since then, sales have gone down by 80% due to heavy competition, not least from local brands like Matisse and Prime Blue – both of which are made of imported Scotch.

Glenturret distillery is equipped with an open stainless steel mash tun dressed in wood and it is perhaps the only one in Scotland where the mash is still turned manually by large wooden spades. There are also eight Douglas fir washbacks, one pair of stills and 10,500 casks maturing in six warehouses on site. Eight mashes a week result in 156,000 litres of spirit per year. Peated whisky, destined for the Black Grouse blend, has been distilled since 2009.

"The Famous Grouse Experience" is the distillery's visitor centre. Opened in 2002, it has since been expanded continuously and now receives no less than 100,000 visitors per year. In addition to the fixed activities at the centre, a Whisky & Music Festival was held for the first time in August 2011.

It is often claimed that Glenturret single malt is an important part of Famous Grouse blend, but even if the whole output from the distillery went into the Famous Grouse, it would only constitute 1% of the content. There is only one official bottling in the core range, the *10 year old*. A limited edition of three *single casks* was released in 2007.

10 years old

Highland Park

Owner:
The Edrington Group

Region/district:
Highlands (Orkney)

Founded: **Status:** **Capacity:**
1798 Active (vc) 2 500 000 litres

Address: Holm Road, Kirkwall, Orkney KW15 1SU

Tel: **website:**
01856 874619 www.highlandpark.co.uk

History:
1798 – David Robertson founds the distillery. The local smuggler and businessman Magnus Eunson previously operated an illicit whisky production on the site.

1816 – John Robertson, an Excise Officer who arrested Magnus Eunson, takes over production.

1826 – Highland Park obtains a license and the distillery is taken over by Robert Borwick.

1840 – Robert´s son George Borwick takes over but the distillery deteriorates.

1869 – The younger brother James Borwick inherits Highland Park and attempts to sell it as he does not consider the distillation of spirits as compatible with his priesthood.

1876 – Stuart & Mackay becomes involved and improves the business by exporting to Norway and India.

1895 – James Grant (of Glenlivet Distillery) buys Highland Park.

1898 – James Grant expands capacity from two to four stills.

1937 – Highland Distilleries buys Highland Park.

1979 – Highland Distilleries invests considerably in marketing Highland Park as single malt which increases sales markedly.

The last decade has been a success for Highland Park single malt with sales increasing by 175% since 2000 to almost 120,000 cases in 2010. It is one of Scotland´s oldest distilleries and lies beautifully situated on the outskirts of Kirkwall, overlooking both the town and Scapa Bay. It is also one of few distilleries malting part of their barley (20%) themselves, with the balance coming from Simpson´s in Berwick-upon-Tweed. There are five malting floors with a capacity of almost 36 tonnes of barley. The malt is dried for 18 hours using peat and the final 18 hours using coke. The phenol content is 20-40 ppm in own malt, while the externally sourced malt is unpeated. The local peat used for their own maltings is crucial to the character of Highland Park. Trees haven´t grown on Orkney since Neolithic times and most of the peat used is younger than that and will therefore create a different flavour compared to peat from other parts of Scotland. The peat is cut on Hobbister Moor, seven miles from the distillery.

The distillery equipment consists of one semilauter mash tun, twelve Oregon pine washbacks and two pairs of stills. The whisky matures in 19 dunnage and four racked warehouses, holding a total of 44,000 casks. The part that is sold as single malt has always matured in sherry casks while the whisky destined for blending (Famous Grouse and Cutty Sark) has been filled into bourbon barrels. The plan for 2011 is to produce 1.7 million litres of alcohol.

At Highland Park they are extremely particular about the wood that they use and the owners spend £10m every year on casks alone.

The core range of Highland Park consists of *12, 15, 18, 25, 30* and *40 years old*. Travel retail exclusives since 2010 are four different vintages – *1973, 1990, 1994* and *1998*. Added to that range in 2011, was a *Vintage 1978*, bottled at a higher strength (47.8%) than the rest. Another duty free expression was released in spring 2011 – *Leif Eriksson* – which has matured in American oak (both ex-bourbon and ex-sherry). A trilogy of limited releases started in 2009 with *15 year old Earl Magnus*, continued in 2010 with *12 year old Saint Magnus* and ended with the *18 year old Earl Haakon* in 2011. They are all bottled at cask strength and the names celebrate the Viking heritage of Orkney. Another limited range, *Orcadian Vintages*, started in 2008 with *1968*, followed by *1964* and *1970* and, in autumn 2011, *1971 and 1976*. In autumn 2010 a *50 year old*, the oldest ever bottling from Highland Park, was released. A total of 275 bottles which will be released over four years.

History (continued):

1986 – A visitor centre, considered one of Scotland's finest, is opened.

1997 – Two new Highland Park are launched, an 18 year old and a 25 year old.

1999 – Highland Distillers are acquired by Edrington Group and William Grant & Sons.

2000 – Visit Scotland awards Highland Park "Five Star Visitor Attraction". The distillery has spent over £2 million on the visitor centre and distillery.

2005 – Highland Park 30 years old is released. A 16 year old for the Duty Free market and Ambassador´s Cask 1984 are released.

2006 – The second edition of Ambassador´s Cask, a 10 year old from 1996, is released. New packaging is introduced.

2007 – The Rebus 20, a 21 year old duty free exclusive, a 38 year old and a 39 year old are released.

2008 – A 40 year old and the third and fourth editions of Ambassador´s Cask are released.

2009 – Two vintages and Earl Magnus 15 year are released.

2010 – A 50 year old, Saint Magnus 12 year old, Orcadian Vintage 1970 and four duty free vintages are released.

2011 – Vintage 1978, Leif Eriksson and 18 year old Earl Haakon are released.

Highland Park 12 year old

GS – The nose is fragrant and floral, with hints of heather and some spice. Smooth and honeyed on the palate, with citric fruits, malt and distinctive tones of wood smoke in the warm, lengthy, slightly peaty finish.

DR – Honey, peat and marmalade fruit in balance on the nose, then on the palate a big mouth feel with dark chocolate, chilli, sharp barley and honey, concluding with a monster pot pouri of a finish.

Leif Eriksson *Earl Haakon* *Vintage 1978*

18 years old

12 years old *25 years old*

155

Inchgower

Owner: **Region/district:**
Diageo   Speyside

Founded: **Status:**   **Capacity:**
1871   Active   2 900 000 litres

Address: Buckie, Banffshire AB56 5AB

Tel: **website:**
01542 836700   www.malts.com

History:
1871 – Alexander Wilson & Co. founds the distillery. Equipment from the disused Tochieneal Distillery, also owned by Alexander Wilson, is installed.

1936 – Alexander Wilson & Co. becomes bankrupt and Buckie Town Council buys the distillery and the family's home for £1,600.

1938 – The distillery is sold on to Arthur Bell & Sons for £3,000.

1966 – Capacity doubles to four stills.

1985 – Guinness acquires Arthur Bell & Sons.

1987 – United Distillers is formed by a merger between Arthur Bell & Sons and DCL.

1997 – Inchgower 1974 (22 years) is released as a Rare Malt.

2004 – Inchgower 1976 (27 years) is released as a Rare Malt.

2010 – A single cask from 1993 is released.

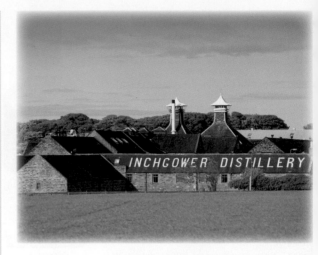

The single malt from Inchgower distillery is an excellent example of how a malt is tailormade to complement the full taste in a blended Scotch, in this case Bell´s. When you do the second distillation in the spirit still you only collect the middle cut for maturation and the length of time in this process depends on the desired taste. Usually you stop collecting when the alcohol strength is around 62-64% unless you are making a peated whisky like Lagavulin where the lower cut point is 59% in order to get all the phenols coming in late. At Inchgower (which is unpeated) you don´t stop until 55% which gives an unusual character adding to the Bell´s flavour profile.

The distillery belongs to a small group of three coastal distilleries (the other two being Glenglassaugh and Macduff) all situated on the south side of Moray Firth.

It is difficult to miss as it is situated just at the A98 near the small fishing port of Buckie. If one is driving from Elgin towards Banff it is even easier to spot as the name appears on the roof.

The distillery is equipped with a stainless steel semi-lauter mash tun, six washbacks made from Oregon pine and two pairs of stills. Two of the washbacks were replaced in summer 2011. Most of the production is matured elsewhere, but there are also five dunnage and four racked warehouses on site with room for 60,000 casks. For 2011 they will be doing 18 mashes per week which means 2.9 million litres of alcohol in the year. Since they are operating on a 7-day week, they only do short fermentations, 46-54 hours.

As mentioned, the absolutely greater part of production is used for Bell´s blended whisky. Besides the official Flora & Fauna *14 years old* there have been a few limited releases. In 2010 a *single sherry cask* distilled in *1993* appeared in the Manager´s Choice series.

Inchgower 14 year old
GS – Ripe pears and a hint of brine on the light nose. Grassy and gingery in the mouth, with some acidity. The finish is spicy, dry and relatively short.

DR – Rootsy, fresh cut grass and hay nose, light grassy and hay-like palate, and incredibly delicate barley-like nose, with a very delicate dusting of spice.

*Flora & Fauna
14 years old*

156

Jura

Owner: **Region/district:**
Whyte & Mackay   Highlands (Jura)
(United Spirits)

Founded: **Status:**   **Capacity:**
1810   Active (vc)   2 200 000 litres

Address: Craighouse, Isle of Jura PA60 7XT

Tel: **website:**
01496 820240   www.isleofjura.com

History:
1810 – Archibald Campbell founds a distillery named Small Isles Distillery.

1853 – Richard Campbell leases the distillery to Norman Buchanan from Glasgow.

1867 – Buchanan files for bankruptcy and J. & K. Orr takes over the distillery.

1876 – The licence is transferred to James Ferguson & Sons.

1901 – The distillery closes and Ferguson dismantles the distillery.

1960 – Charles Mackinlay & Co. embarks on reconstruction and extension of the distillery. Newly formed Scottish & Newcastle Breweries acquires Charles Mackinlay & Co.

1962 – Scottish & Newcastle forms Mackinlay-McPherson for the operation of Isle of Jura.

1963 – The first distilling takes place.

1978 – Stills are doubled from two to four.

1985 – Invergordon Distilleries acquires Charles Mackinlay & Co., Isle of Jura and Glenallachie from Scottish & Newcastle Breweries.

1993 – Whyte & Mackay (Fortune Brands) buys Invergordon Distillers.

1996 – Whyte & Mackay changes name to JBB (Greater Europe).

2001 – The management of JBB (Greater Europe) buys out the company from the owners Fortune Brands and changes the name to Kyndal.

2002 – Isle of Jura Superstition is launched.

2003 – Kyndal reverts back to its old name, Whyte & Mackay. Isle of Jura 1984 is launched.

2004 – Two cask strengths (15 and 30 years old) are released in limited numbers.

2006 – The 40 year old Jura is released.

2007 – United Spirits buys Whyte & Mackay. The 18 year old Delmé-Evans and an 8 year old heavily peated expression are released.

2008 – A series of four different vintages, called Elements, is released.

2009 – The peated Prophecy and three new vintages called Paps of Jura are released.

2010 – Boutique Barrels and a 21 year old Anniversary bottling are released.

Jura 10 year old

GS – Resin, oil and pine notes on the delicate nose. Light-bodied in the mouth, with malt and drying saltiness. The finish is malty, nutty, with more salt, plus just a wisp of smoke.

DR – The nose is sweet condensed milk, the palate an intriguing mix of earthy malt and tangy spice, with a medium sweet and spice finish.

The journey that Jura Distillery has undertaken the last few years is nothing but impressive. From only selling 30,000 cases annually the sales numbers have gone through the roof. During 2010 they increased by 50% with 92,000 cases sold worldwide. According to the owners, this means that Jura single malt is now the third best selling in the UK after Glenfiddich and Glenmorangie. The number of visitors to the distillery has also increased and in summer of 2011 a new visitor centre was opened at an estimated cost of £100,000. The reasons for Jura's success are intensified marketing, but more importantly more exciting range of whiskies and, not least, improved quality. An important part of the latter commenced in 1999 when thousands of maturing casks were re-racked into oak of a higher quality.

Jura distillery is equipped with one semi-lauter mash tun, six stainless steel washbacks and two pairs of stills. During 2011 the distillery is working a five-day week producing 1,750,000 litres of alcohol. Almost 40% of that is destined to become single malt and is matured in the five racked warehouses on site with the oldest cask being from 1973. Since the restart of the distillery in 1963, Jura single malt has been unpeated, but in 2002 the first expression containing peated whisky was introduced and today they produce peated spirit for four weeks per year.

The core range consists of *Origin* (10 years), *Diurach's Own* (16 years), *Superstition* (13% peated Jura and various casks from 13 to 21 years of age) as well as the peated *Prophecy* which was released in 2009 and is the only unchillfiltered of the four. This year's special bottling for the Islay Whisky Festival was distilled in 1996 and matured in French Limousine oak. Limited releases from 2010 include the three *Boutique Barrels* and, to celebrate the 200th anniversary of the distillery, a *21 year old* which had matured in a Vintage 1963 Gonzales Byass cask.

10 years old

Kilbeggan

Owner:
Cooley Distillery plc

Region/district:
Ireland

Founded: **Status:** **Capacity:**
1757 Active (vc) 80 000 litres

Address: Kilbeggan, Co. Westmeath

Tel:
+353 (0)57 933 2183

website: www.kilbegganwhiskey.com

History:
1757 – The distillery is founded by the McManus family.

1794 – The Codd family takes over and capacity is doubled.

1843 – John Locke & Sons buy the distillery.

1954 – Production stops.

1957 – The distillery is officially closed.

1988 – Cooley Distillery plc buys the brand Kilbeggan as well as the old distillery to use it for warehousing.

2007 – The first distillation in the refurbished distillery takes place on 19 March.

2010 – The first single malt since the resurrection is released.

2011 – Kilbeggan 18 year old, a blended whiskey, is released.

Kilbeggan distillery has now been producing for four years since the sensational re-birth as the oldest, producing whiskey distillery in the world. The owners (who also have Cooley distillery under their wings) could also celebrate one million visitors to The Old Kilbeggan Distillery Experience in September 2011.

The distillery, which lies in the town Kilbeggan on the N6 and just an hour's drive west of Dublin, was bought by John Teeling and his Cooley Distillery way back in 1988. The distillery and its equipment was in fairly good condition, however, thanks to some locals who had maintained it and even ascertained that its distilling licence was still valid. Eventually, the new owner decided to reinstate the distillery to its former glory and to start distilling again. Meanwhile, a blended Kilbeggan whiskey, a brand taken over simultaneously with the distillery, was selling with great success. In March 2007, 250 years after Kilbeggan was built, the first spirit ran from the still under supervision of descendants of the four families that had been involved with the distillery.

At first, the mashing, fermentation and first distillation were made at Cooley distillery while the final distillation took place at Kilbeggan. Today, however, the distillery is equipped with a wooden mash tun, four Oregon pine washbacks and two stills with one of them being 180 years old. There is no triple distillation at Kilbeggan but they produce both pure pot still whiskey (unmalted and malted barley mixed) and malt whiskey. There is also talk of bringing an old Coffey still, last used by Tullamore, back to life.

The first, and so far the only, single malt whiskey release (a *3 year old* bottled at 40%) from the new production came in June 2010 and it will probably be a while before the next expression is launched. The blended range of Kilbeggan includes a *no age statement*, a *15 year old* and, since early 2011, an *18 year old* and the owners are now investigating using the malt whiskey produced at Kilbeggan in the Kilbeggan blend.

Kilbeggan Distillery Reserve
GS – Highly individualistic on the nose. Oily and herbal, with tarragon, warm leather, paper gum, and even violets. The palate is quite delicate, yet far from fragile, with gentle leather and developing fruity spices. Drying in a medium-length finish.

Kilbeggan Distillery Reserve

Kilchoman

Owner:
Kilchoman Distillery Co.

Region/district:
Islay

Founded: 2005
Status: Active (vc)
Capacity: 110 000 litres

Address: Rockside farm, Bruichladdich, Islay PA49 7UT

Tel: 01496 850011
website: www.kilchomandistillery.com

History:
2002 – Plans are formed for a new distillery at Rockside Farm on western Islay.

2005 – Production starts in June.

2006 – A fire breaks out in the kiln causing a few weeks´ production stop but malting has to cease for the rest of the year.

2007 – The distillery is expanded with two new washbacks.

2009 – The first single malt, a 3 year old, is released on 9th September followed by a second release.

2010 – Three new releases and an introduction to the US market. John Maclellan from Bunnahabhain joins the team as General Manager.

2011 – Kilchoman 100% Islay is released as well as a 4 year old and a 5 year old.

Kilchoman Third Release

GS – The nose offers sweet smoke, buttery fish, toasted oats and berries. Sweet on the palate, with spicy, youthful oak notes, more berries and vanilla fudge. Medium length in the warming, gently spiced, finish.

DR – Amazingly integrated for one so young, with the peat and sweet toffee nose reflected on the palate by steam train smoke and rich berried fruits. The finish is long and balanced. This is pioneering modern malt travelling in to unchartered territory.

The latest distillery to open up on Islay, Kilchoman lies on the western part of the island, a few miles from Bruichladdich. The man behind it, Anthony Wills, moved to Scotland in 1995 having 25 years of experience as wine trader and an independent bottler of whisky before he took a faithful leap and started the distillery construction on the estates of Rockside Farm. Less than 10 years later Kilchoman single malt has made a name for itself both amongst consumers and within the trade. In 2010, 50,000 bottles were sold and Anthony expects to increase that to 70,000 in 2011, not least through recent efforts to break in to the American market.

Kilchoman has its own floor maltings with a third of barley requirements coming from fields surrounding the distillery. The malt is peated to 20 to 25 ppm and the remaining malt (50 ppm) is bought from Port Ellen. Other equipment include a stainless steel semi-lauter mash tun, four stainless steel washbacks and one pair of stills. The distillery is currently running at full capacity. The spirit is filled into fresh and refill bourbon casks (80%) and fresh oloroso sherry butts (20%). Maturation takes place in a dunnage warehouse and another warehouse with space for 9,000 casks will be completed by the end of 2011. The *Inaugural Release*, bourbonmatured for 3 years with a six months Oloroso finish, was launched in September 2009. This was followed up by *Winter 2009* with 2.5 months sherry finish. This in turn was followed by *Spring 2010* with a 3 months Oloroso finish, *Summer 2010*, the first all-bourbon expression and the first to be sold in the US, *Winter 2010*, a 3 year old matured in fresh bourbon barrels and *Spring 2011*, the first where both 3 and 4 year old whiskies are vatted. In June 2011 it was time for the first *Kilchoman 100% Islay* where the barley used all comes from their own farm and has been malted at the distillery. This was followed up by a *4 year old* from sherry casks in September and a *5 year old* in November.

Kilchoman 100% Islay

Kininvie

Owner:
William Grant & Sons

Region/district:
Speyside

Founded: **Status:**
1990   Active

Capacity:
4 800 000 litres

Address: Dufftown, Keith,
Banffshire AB55 4DH

Tel:
01340 820373

website:
-

History:
1990 – Kininvie distillery is inaugurated on 26th June and the first distillation takes place 18th July.

2001 – A bottling of blended whisky containing Kininvie malt is released under the name Hazelwood Centennial Reserve 20 years old.

2006 – The first expression of a Kininvie single malt is released as a 15 year old under the name Hazelwood.

2008 – In February a 17 year old Hazelwood Reserve is launched at Heathrow's Terminal 5.

Kininvie distillery only consists of one still house constructed in white, corrugated metal tucked away behind Balvenie. The owners, William Grant & Sons, built it as a working distillery producing malt whisky for the increasingly popular Grant's blended whiskies. The still house, visible from the Balvenie tun room, was erected in 1990 and the distillery came on stream in July of the same year.

Kininvie is equipped with a stainless steel full lauter mash tun which is placed next to Balvenie's in the Balvenie distillery. The tun is filled with 10.8 tonnes of malted barley and can run 28 mashes per week. Ten Douglas fir washbacks (six large and four small) can be found in two separate rooms next to the Balvenie washbacks. Three wash stills and six spirit stills are all heated by steam coils. The only piece of equipment that Kininvie shares with Balvenie is the mill.

Kininvie malt whisky is frequently sold to other companies for blending purposes under the name Aldundee. To protect it from being sold as Kininvie single malt, the whisky is always "teaspooned", i. e. a small percentage of Balvenie whisky is blended with the make.

Kininvie malt is mainly used for the Grant's blend but is also a major part of the blended malt Monkey Shoulder. The first time that Kininvie appeared as an official single malt bottling was in August 2006, when a *Hazelwood 15 year old* was launched to celebrate the 105th birthday of Janet Sheed Roberts (who turned 110 on 13th August 2011), the last surviving grandchild of the founder of the company, William Grant, and who opened the distillery in 1990. Since 1933 she had lived at Hazelwood House, close to the distillery. In February 2008 it was time for a *17 year old* to celebrate her 107th birthday. This expression had aged in ex sherry casks and was actually the first to become publicly available as it was sold at Heathrow's Terminal 5.

A bottling under the name Hazelwood had already been released in 2001 to celebrate miss Roberts' one hundredth birthday, but this was not a single malt.

Hazelwood Reserve 17 year old

GS – New leather and creamy nougat on the nose. Developing molasses notes with time. Rich, leathery and spicy on the palate, with oranges and milk chocolate. Lengthy and elegant in the finish.

*Hazelwood Reserve
17 years old*

Knockando

Owner:
Diageo.

Region/district:
Speyside

Founded: **Status:** **Capacity:**
1898 Active 1 300 000 litres

Address: Knockando, Morayshire AB38 7RT

Tel: **website:**
01340 882000 www.malts.com

History:
1898 – John Thompson founds the distillery. The architect is Charles Doig.

1899 – Production starts in May.

1900 – The distillery closes in March and J. Thompson & Co. takes over administration.

1904 – W. & A. Gilbey purchases the distillery for £3,500 and production restarts in October.

1962 – W. & A. Gilbey merges with United Wine Traders (including Justerini & Brooks) and forms International Distillers & Vintners (IDV).

1968 – Floor maltings is decommissioned.

1969 – The number of stills is increased to four.

1972 – IDV is acquired by Watney Mann who, in its turn, is taken over by Grand Metropolitan.

1978 – Justerini & Brooks launches a 12 year old Knockando.

1997 – Grand Metropolitan and Guinness merge and form Diageo; simultaneously IDV and United Distillers merge to United Distillers & Vintners.

2010 – A Manager's Choice 1996 is released.

Knockando 12 year old

GS – Delicate and fragrant on the nose, with hints of malt, worn leather, and hay. Quite full in the mouth, smooth and honeyed, with gingery malt and a suggestion of white rum. Medium length in the finish, with cereal and more ginger.

DR – Beeswax, honey and gentle peat on the nose, the palate is altogether bolder, with pepper and earthy peat in evidence mixing it with very sweet crystallised barley and a sweet and rounded finish.

Knockando has never been one of those distilleries that you can easily spot driving through the Strathspey area. It is nestled down in the Spey valley just by the river itself at the end of a road. Quite contrary to one of its nearest neighbours, Cardhu which sits on the top of a small hill just by the B9102 road. There used to be a visitor centre at Knockando but it closed more than a decade ago. Still, in terms of sales, it is fairly well-known, especially in Spain and France and it sells around 50,000 cases per year which makes it Diageo's 7th best selling single malt.

The distillery is equipped with a semi-lauter mash tun, eight Douglas fir washbacks and two pairs of stills. Knockando's heavy, nutty character, a result of the cloudy worts coming from the mash tun, has given it its fame. However, in order to balance the taste, the distillers also wish to create the typical Speyside floral notes by using boiling balls on the spirit stills to increase reflux.

Knockando has always worked a five-day week with 16 mashes per week, 8 short fermentations (48 hours) and 8 long (104 hours). They stopped filling casks at the distillery eight years ago. Instead it is tankered away to Auchroisk and Glenlossie and some of the casks are returned to the distillery for maturation in two dunnage and two racked warehouses. There is a fifth warehouse called Ultima after the legendary J&B Ultima blend released in 1994, where whiskies from 128 distilleries (116 malts and 12 grains) were blended together. One cask from each distillery is still kept in this warehouse.

Since the 1970s, Knockando single malt has been bottled according to vintage and without any age state-ment, but lately bottles on all markets show both vintage and age on the label. The core range consists of a *12 year old* (90% bourbon and 10% sherry), an *18 year old Slow Matured* (20% sherry), mainly reserved for the French market and a *21 year old Master Reserve* (30% sherry casks). In autumn 2011 a *25 year old* matured in European oak was released as part of the Special Releases range.

25 years old

Knockdhu

Owner:
Inver House Distillers
(Thai Beverages plc)

Region/district:
Speyside

Founded: 1893
Status: Active
Capacity: 1 650 000 litres

Address: Knock, By Huntly,
Aberdeenshire AB54 7LJ

Tel: 01466 771223
website: www.ancnoc.com

History:
1893 – Distillers Company Limited (DCL) starts construction of the distillery.

1894 – Production starts in October.

1930 – Scottish Malt Distillers (SMD) takes over production.

1983 – The distillery closes in March.

1988 – Inver House buys the distillery from United Distillers.

1989 – Production restarts on 6th February.

1990 – First official bottling of Knockdhu.

1993 – First official bottling of An Cnoc, the new name to avoid confusion with Knockando.

2001 – Pacific Spirits (Great Oriole Group) purchases Inver House Distillers at a price of $85 million.

2003 – Reintroduction of An Cnoc 12 years, with new, contemporary packaging.

2004 – A 14 year old from 1990 is launched.

2005 – Two limited editions, a 30 year old from 1975 and a 14 year old from 1991 are launched.

2006 – International Beverage Holdings acquires Pacific Spirits UK.

2007 – anCnoc 1993 is released.

2008 – anCnoc 16 year old is released.

2011 – A Vintage 1996 is released.

An Cnoc 12 year old

GS – A pretty, sweet, floral nose, with barley notes. Medium bodied, with a whiff of delicate smoke, spices and boiled sweets on the palate. Drier in the mouth than the nose suggests. The finish is quite short and drying.

DR – Complex and layered nose, with delicate peat, green fruits and pear. On the palate there's a full savoury peatiness then tingling yellow fruity follow through and fairydust finale.

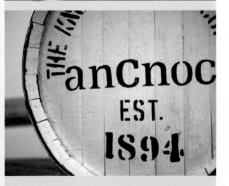

The demand for peated single malts has increased year by year and the producers, particularly on Islay, have become more and more reluctant to sell any of their stock to others. The problem is for those who need peated whisky for their blends and don´t have any distilleries of their own. InverHouse is in a much better position. Around 90% of their sales are blended Scotch and some of them require an amount of peated whisky. At the same time they are the owners of five distilleries and, although none of them have been known for peated whisky, two of them (Knochdhu and Balblair) are now producing it, at least for part of the year. Knockdhu's production has increased during 2011 with a 25% peated production with a phenol content of 15-20ppm in the newmake.

The distillery is equipped with a stainless steel lauter mash tun installed (but retaining the old copper canopy) in 2009, six washbacks made of Oregon pine and one pair of stills. The spirit is condensed using a cast iron worm tub. The owners made a smart move when they replaced the old cast iron mash tun. The new tun has the same diameter, but is deeper than the previous one, which made it possible to increase the capacity by 100,000 litres per year. In 2011 they increased production even further by shortening the shut down period over Christmas and they will be able to get 1.65 million litres of alcohol this year. In general, a mix of bourbon and sherry casks are used and in 2010 they made a big investment in high quality Oloroso casks. The casks used to be stored in one racked and four dunnage warehouses. Two of the warehouses were damaged in the heavy snowfall in January 2010 and had to be knocked down. One of them was rebuilt in 2011.

The biggest markets for AnCnoc are UK, USA, Sweden and Germany and 150,000 bottles were sold in 2010. The core range consists of *12* and *16 year old*. A *1996 Vintage* was released in 2011 and due in early 2012, is a *35 year old*, the oldest expression yet to be released by the owner.

Vintage 1996

Lagavulin

Owner: Diageo

Region/district: Islay

Founded: 1816

Status: Active (vc)

Capacity: 2 250 000 litres

Address: Port Ellen, Islay, Argyll PA42 7DZ

Tel: 01496 302749 (vc)

website: www.malts.com

History:

1816 – John Johnston founds the distillery.

1825 – John Johnston takes over the adjacent distillery Ardmore founded in 1817 by Archibald Campbell and closed in 1821.

1835 – Production at Ardmore ceases.

1837 – Both distilleries are merged and operated under the name Lagavulin by Donald Johnston.

1852 – The brother of the wine and spirits dealer Alexander Graham, John Crawford Graham, purchases the distillery.

1867 – The distillery is acquired by James Logan Mackie & Co. and refurbishment starts.

1878 – Peter Mackie is employed.

1889 – James Logan Mackie passes away and nephew Peter Mackie inherits the distillery.

1890 – J. L. Mackie & Co. changes name to Mackie & Co. Peter Mackie launches White Horse onto the export market with Lagavulin included in the blend. White Horse blended is not available on the domestic market until 1901.

1908 – Peter Mackie uses the old distillery buildings to build a new distillery, Malt Mill, on the site.

When peated whisky had its big consumer breakthrough, Lagavulin single malt was in the lead. Due to limited supplies, caused by a temporary, lower production pace in the mid-eighties, the brand fell from the number one position among Islay malts to third behind Laphroaig and Bowmore. Things have started to shape up though, the sales volumes are back over the 100,000 cases level and stock of the popular 16 year old are increasing. Operations have run 24 hours a day, seven days a week, for some time now to avoid getting into the same troublesome situation again. This means 28 mashes per week and 2.25 million litres of spirit.

In spring 2011, the distillery got a new manager when Georgie Crawford moved from Skye where she had been working as the Talisker visitor centre manager, to replace Peter Campbell who went to Speyside where he will be responsible for Cardhu distillery. For Georgie it was like returning home, since she grew up on Islay. Another homecoming took place in June 2011, when a 130-year old bottle of Lagavulin was returned to the distillery after having been bough at an auction. The whisky had been maturing for 30 years in a cask before being bottled in 1911. The bottle can now be seen in the distillery visitor centre.

The distillery is equipped with a stainless steel full lauter mash tun, ten washbacks made of larch and two pairs of stills. The spirit stills are filled to 95% of its capacity during distillation which is very unconventional. The result is that the spirit vapour's diminished contact with the copper, produces a more robust spirit. The tough production scheme causes wear and tear on the stills and in 2009, the body of No. 1 wash still and the head of No. 2 had to be replaced. Bourbon hogsheads are used almost without exception for maturation and all of the new production is stored on the mainland. There are only around 16,000 casks on Islay, split between warehouses at Lagavulin, Port Ellen and Caol Ila. The core range of Lagavulin consists of *12 year old cask strength*, *16 year old* and the *Distiller's Edition*, a Pedro Ximenez sherry finish. In 2010 a *distillery exclusive bottling*, available only at the distillery, was added to the range which basically is a slightly older, cask strength version of the Distiller's Edition. The Islay Festival special release for 2011 was a *single cask* distilled in *1998* and bottled at cask strength. As in recent years, a new *12 year old* was released in autumn 2011 as a Special Release. This was the tenth edition.

History (continued):

1924 – Peter Mackie passes away and Mackie & Co. changes name to White Horse Distillers.

1927 – White Horse Distillers becomes part of Distillers Company Limited (DCL).

1930 – The distillery is administered under Scottish Malt Distillers (SMD).

1952 – An explosive fire breaks out and causes considerable damage.

1960 – Malt Mills distillery closes and today it houses Lagavulin's visitor centre.

1974 – Floor maltings are decommisioned and malt is bought from Port Ellen instead.

1988 – Lagavulin 16 years becomes one of six Classic Malts.

1998 – A Pedro Ximenez sherry finish is launched as a Distillers Edition.

2002 – Two cask strengths (12 years and 25 years) are launched.

2006 – A 30 year old is released.

2007 – A 21 year old from 1985 and the sixth edition of the 12 year old are released.

2008 – A new 12 year old is released.

2009 – A new 12 year old appears as a Special Release.

2010 – A new edition of the 12 year old, a single cask exclusive for the distillery and a Manager's Choice single cask are released.

2011 – The 10th edition of the 12 year old cask strength is released.

The 130 year old bottling of Lagavulin accompanied by four managers - Peter Campbell, John Thomson, Donald Renwick and Georgie Crawford

Lagavulin 12 year old

GS – Soft and buttery on the nose, with dominant, fruily, peat smoke, grilled fish and a hint of vanilla sweetness. More fresh fruit notes develop with the addition of water. Medium-bodied, quite oily in texture, heavily smoked, sweet malt and nuts. The finish is very long and ashy, with lingering sweet peat.

DR – A monster truck nose with rich smoke, lychee and unripe pear, with prickly smoke and banana skin notes on the palate, and a superb long dark chocolate and smoky finish.

30 years old

Distiller's Edition

16 years old   12 years old (10th ed.)   Distillery Exclusive no age

Laphroaig

Owner:
Beam Global
Spirits & Wine

Region/district:
Islay

Founded: **Status:**   **Capacity:**
1810   Active (vc)   2 900 000 litres

Address: Port Ellen, Islay, Argyll PA42 7DU

Tel: **website:**
01496 302418   www.laphroaig.com

History:
1810 – Brothers Alexander and Donald Johnston found Laphroaig.

1815 – Official year of starting.

1836 – Donald buys out Alexander and takes over operations.

1837 – James and Andrew Gairdner found Ardenistiel a stone's throw from Laphroaig.

1847 – Donald Johnston is killed in an accident in the distillery when he falls into a kettle of boiling hot burnt ale. The Manager of neighbouring Lagavulin, Walter Graham, takes over.

1857 – Operation is back in the hands of the Johnston family when Donald's son Dugald takes over.

circa 1860 – Ardenistiel Distillery merges with Laphroaig.

1877 – Dugald, being without heirs, passes away and his sister Isabella, married to their cousin Alexander takes over.

1907 – Alexander Johnston dies and the distillery is inherited by his two sisters Catherine Johnston and Mrs. William Hunter (Isabella Johnston).

1908 – Ian Hunter arrives in Islay to assist his mother and aunt with the distillery.

1924 – The two stills are increased to four.

In 2001, Laphroaig took over from Lagavulin as the number one selling Islay single malt and has not moved since. In fact, 2009 was the first year sales decreased, but with an 8% increase during 2010, they were back to the same levels as 2008, namely 185,000 cases. Having the biggest fan club in the business also helps. Friends of Laphroaig have 430,000 registered members from 150 countries!

Laphroaig is one of very few distilleries with its own maltings. Four malting floors hold 7 tonnes each and together account for 15% of its requirements, another 70% comes from Port Ellen maltings on Islay, while 15% are imported from the mainland. Malt from different suppliers is always blended before mashing. Only on one occasion (at least in modern times), in 2003, was there a batch made just from the floor maltings. There is a stainless steel full lauter mash tun and six washbacks that are also made of stainless steel. The distillery uses an unusual combination of three wash stills and four spirit stills. The first part of the spirit run contains a lot of sweet esters and to avoid these (as they are not in line with the Laphroaig character), the longest foreshots in the industry (45 minutes) are practised. During 2011, they will be working full time producing 2.85 million litres of alcohol. The spirit is matured in three dunnage and five racked warehouses.

The owners of Laphroaig have spent lots of effort creating unique experiences for their visitors. The visitor centre includes a shop, tasting bar, lounge and museum and apart from the more traditional tours ending up in a tasting, you can book a Hunter's Hike. This includes a walk to the water source, cutting peat at Glen Machrie and working the malt floors. Every activity is rewarded by a dram!

The core range consists of *10 year old, 10 year old cask strength, Quarter Cask, 18 year old* and *25 year old*. A new addition to the core range from September 2011 was *Triple Wood*, a combination of ex-bourbon, quarter casks and oloroso sherry casks, previously only available as a duty free item. To replace Triple Wood in travel retail came another triple matured expression, *Laphroaig PX*, without age statement but made up of whiskies between 5 and 10 years old. In conjunction with Feis Isle, a new limited version of *Cairdeas* called *The Ileach Edition* was released, considerably younger than previous editions, only 8 years old. Later in the year it was released in Sweden and in USA to name but a few. Previous Cairdeas bottlings have been *12 year old, 30 year old* and *Master Edition*.

History (continued):

1927 – Catherine Johnston dies and Ian Hunter takes over.

1928 – Isabella Johnston dies and Ian Hunter becomes sole owner.

1950 – Ian Hunter forms D. Johnston & Company

1954 – Ian Hunter passes away and management of the distillery is taken over by Elisabeth "Bessie" Williamson, who was previously Ian Hunters PA and secretary. She becomes Director of the Board and Managing Director.

1967 – Seager Evans & Company buys the distillery through Long John Distillery, having already acquired part of Laphroaig in 1962. The number of stills is increased from four to five.

1972 – Bessie Williamson retires. Another two stills are installed bringing the total to seven.

1975 – Whitbread & Co. buys Seager Evans (now renamed Long John International) from Schenley International.

1989 – The spirits division of Whitbread is sold to Allied Distillers.

1991 – Allied Distillers launches Caledonian Malts. Laphroaig is one of the four malts included.

1994 – HRH Prince Charles gives his Royal Warrant to Laphroaig. Friends of Laphroaig is founded.

1995 – A 10 year old cask strength is launched.

2001 – 4,000 bottles of a 40 year old, the oldest-ever Laphroaig, are released.

2004 – Quarter Cask, a mix of different ages with a finish in quarter casks (i. e. 125 litres) is launched.

2005 – Fortune Brands becomes new owner.

2007 – A vintage 1980 (27 years old) and a 25 year old are released.

2008 – Cairdeas, Cairdeas 30 year old and Triple Wood are released.

2009 – An 18 year old is released.

2010 – A 20 year old for French Duty Free and Cairdeas Master Edition are launched.

2011 – Laphroaig PX and Cairdeas - The Ileach Edition are released.

Laphroaig 10 year old

GS – Old-fashioned sticking plaster, peat smoke and seaweed leap off the nose, followed by something a little sweeter and fruitier. Massive on the palate, with fish oil, salt and plankton, though the finish is quite tight and increasingly drying.

DR – Salt, peat, seawood and tar in a glorious and absorbing nose, then structured and rock like barley with waves of tarry peat washing over them, then a long phenolic and peaty finish.

18 years old

Cairdeas Master Edition   Triple Wood

10 years old   10 years old cask strength   Quarter Cask

167

Linkwood

Owner:
Diageo

Region/district:
Speyside

Founded: **Status:**   **Capacity:**
1821   Active   3 500 000 litres

Address: Elgin, Morayshire IV30 3RD

Tel: **website:**
01343 862000   www.malts.com

History:
1821 – Peter Brown founds the distillery.

1868 – Peter Brown passes away and his son William inherits the distillery.

1872 – William demolishes the distillery and builds a new one.

1897 – Linkwood Glenlivet Distillery Company Ltd takes over operations.

1902 – Innes Cameron, a whisky trader from Elgin, joins the Board and eventually becomes the major shareholder and Director.

1932 – Innes Cameron dies and Scottish Malt Distillers takes over in 1933.

1962 – Major refurbishment takes place.

1971 – The two stills are increased by four. Technically, the four new stills belong to a new distillery sometimes referred to as Linkwood B.

1985 – Linkwood A (the two original stills) closes.

1990 – Linkwood A is in production again for a few months each year.

2002 – A 26 year old from 1975 is launched as a Rare Malt.

2005 – A 30 year old from 1974 is launched as a Rare Malt.

2008 – Three different wood finishes (all 26 year old) are released.

2009 – A Manager's Choice 1996 is released.

Linkwood 12 year old

GS – Floral, grassy and fragrant on the nutty nose, while the slightly oily palate becomes increasingly sweet, ending up at marzipan and almonds. The relatively lengthy finish is quite dry and citric.

DR – Sweet and squidgy with over-ripe melon and soft pear on the nose, and a delightful palate of marzipan, vanilla, green apples and a touch of spice. The finish is balanced, pleasant and very enticing.

The production stopped at Linkwood end of February 2011 and only re-commenced 4 months later. The reason for the closure was some major refurbishing and replacement of equipment; a new stainless steel lauter mash tun is replacing the old cast iron tun, parts of both wash stills are being replaced, as well as the intermediate spirit receiver, mash house and still house are having new control systems put in place. Five of the washbacks are also being rehooped, a new dust handling system is being installed and the draff handling equipment and the caustic cleaning system are being upgraded. This just goes to show the complexity of producing whisky – it's not just about distilling, putting into casks and selling after ten years!

Linkwood has been renovated and expanded several times over the years and is divided into one old and one new still house, the latter having been built in 1971. The old still house has not been used since 1996. When it was operational, a cast iron worm tub was used to cool the spirit vapours. After this year's refurbishing the distillery will be equipped with a stainless steel full lauter mash tun, five wooden washbacks (plus six smaller ones in the old building) with a fermentation time of 75 hours, and two pairs of stills. In 2010 they were producing at full capacity (3.5 million litres) but due to this year's standstill the 2011 volume will be more in the region of 1.7 million litres. The beautiful dam at the distillery is used for condensing only; the processed water comes from springs near Millbuies Loch.

Linkwood has always played an important role in major blends such as Johnnie Walker and White Horse but around a million litres are sold to other companies as well each year. The core expression is a *12 year old* Flora & Fauna. In 2008 a limited edition of three *26 year old* bottlings were released, all of them finished for the last 14 years in three different types of casks - port, rum and sweet red wine. The most recent expression was a *Manager's Choice from 1996*, released in autumn 2009.

12 years old

Loch Lomond

Owner:
Loch Lomond
Distillery Co.

Region/district:
Western Highlands

Founded: **Status:**   **Capacity:**
1965   Active   4 000 000 litres

Address: Lomond Estate, Alexandria G83 0TL

Tel: **website:**
01389 752781   www.lochlomonddistillery.com

History:

1965 – The distillery is built by Littlemill Distillery Company Ltd owned by Duncan Thomas and American Barton Brands.

1966 – Production commences.

1971 – Duncan Thomas is bought out and Barton Brands reforms as Barton Distilling (Scotland) Ltd.

1984 – The distillery closes.

1985 – Glen Catrine Bonded Warehouse Ltd buys Loch Lomond Distillery.

1987 – The distillery resumes production.

1993 – Grain spirits are also distilled.

1997 – A fire destroys 300,000 litres of maturing whisky.

1999 – Two more stills are installed.

2005 – Inchmoan and Craiglodge are officially launched for the first time. Both are 4 years old from 2001. Inchmurrin 12 years is launched.

2006 – Inchmurrin 4 years, Croftengea 1996 (9 years), Glen Douglas 2001 (4 years) and Inchfad 2002 (5 years) are launched.

2010 – A peated Loch Lomond with no age statement is released as well as a Vintage 1966.

Inchmurrin 12 year old

GS – Malt and spicy oranges on the nose; newly-opened glossy magazines. The palate is lively and spicy with notes of caramel, fudge and honey. Fudge and spice persist in the medium-length finish.

Loch Lomond distillery doesn't have a visitor centre but for a whisky freak it is pure heaven to come here. The sheer size of the site, the diversity of the production techniques and the love of experimenting, all add to giving this distillery a special position in Scotland.

The former dye factory in Alexandria, which was converted into a distillery in 1965, has a most unusual set-up of equipment. One full lauter mash tun complemented by ten 25,000 litres and eight 50,000 litres washbacks, are all made of stainless steel. Going on to the stills it becomes fascinating; first of all, there are two traditional copper pot stills. Then there are four copper stills where the swan necks have been exchanged with rectifying columns which enables making different types of spirit in the same stills. Furthermore, there is one Coffey still for continuous distillation where, for example, the Rhosdhu single malt is produced. As this was not enough, an additional distillery with continuous stills producing grain whisky is housed in the same building. For the grain side of production there are twelve 100,000 litres and eight 200,000 litres washbacks. The total capacity is 4 million litres of malt spirit and 18 million litres of grain. On site is also a cooperage and 30 palletised and racked warehouses.

Peated malt is produced one month every year. Half of the production is intended for own bottlings and the rest is sold to other companies. The company also includes the largest independent bottler of spirit in Scotland, Glen Catrine Bonded Warehouse.

Loch Lomond produces a broad range of whiskies. The core range of malts is *Loch Lomond Blue Label* (no age statement), *Black Label* (18 year old), *Green Label* (peated) and *Loch Lomond 1966*. From time to time, they also release other expressions in their Distillery Select range; *Inchmurrin, Rhosdhu, Inchmoan, Craiglodge, Croftengea, Glen Douglas* and *Inchfad*. The range is completed by *Red Label* which is a single blended whisky (i. e. malt and grain whisky from the same distillery).

Inchmurrin 12 years old

Longmorn

Owner:
Chivas Brothers
(Pernod Ricard)

Region/district:
Speyside

Founded: **Status:**   **Capacity:**
1894   Active   3 500 000 litres

Address: Longmorn, Morayshire IV30 8SJ

Tel: **website:**
01343 554139   -

History:

1893 – John Duff & Company, which founded Glenlossie already in 1876, starts construction. John Duff, George Thomson and Charles Shirres are involved in the company. The total cost amounts to £20,000.

1894 – First production in December.

1897 – John Duff buys out the others and founds Longmorn Distillery.

1898 – John Duff builds another distillery next to Longmorn which is called Benriach (at times aka Longmorn no. 2). Duff declares bankruptcy and the shares are sold by the bank to James R. Grant.

1970 – The distillery company is merged with The Glenlivet & Glen Grant Distilleries and Hill Thomson & Co. Ltd. Own floor maltings ceases.

1972 – The number of stills is increased from four to six. Spirit stills are converted to steam firing.

1974 – Another two stills are added.

1978 – Seagrams takes over through The Chivas & Glenlivet Group.

1994 – Wash stills are converted to steam firing.

2001 – Pernod Ricard buys Seagram Spirits & Wine together with Diageo and Pernod Ricard takes over the Chivas group.

2004 – A 17 year old cask strength is released.

2007 – A 16 year old is released replacing the 15 year old.

Longmorn 16 year old

GS – The nose offers cream, spice, toffee apples and honey. Medium bodied in the mouth, with fudge, butter and lots of spice. The finish is quite long, with oak and late-lingering dry spices.

DR – Cut flowers and mixed fruit on the nose, rounded and full fruit and honey with some wood and spice adding complexity, long and rich finish.

Longmorn is one of five single malt brands the owners Pernod Ricard are investing in. They have nine additional malt distilleries whose main purpose is to serve the company's blended whiskies. Pernod Ricard is the third largest producer of wine and spirits in the world but their commitment to the whisky business is of latter days. The first step was taken in 1975 when Campbell Distillers (including Aberlour) was bought. Followed by the acquisition of Irish Distillers and Jameson in 1988, part of Segrams (including Chivas Regal and Glenlivet) in 2001 and finally the take-over of Allied Domecq in 2005 where Ballantine´s was included.

Longmorn distillery is equipped with an 8 tonnes stainless steel traditional mash tun with rakes and the wooden washbacks were replaced some years ago by eight stainless steel ones. The four wash stills and the four spirit stills are separated in their own still houses, actually the same building, but with a sliding door in-between. On site there are six dunnage and six palletised warehouses, of which three are placed with neighbouring BenRiach distillery. Longmorn has always had a symbiotic relation to BenRiach and the last one was actually named Longmorn 2 when it was built. Even today, Longmorn supplies BenRiach with water from boreholes and also takes care of the effluent.

At the beginning of the 21st century, Longmorn single malt sold around 6,000 cases per year. With the relaunch of the brand in 2007, when the 16 year old was released, the owners hoped to increase that figure substantially. Marketwise, the idea is to follow in the footsteps of Glenlivet which means Taiwan, France and the USA.

The core range is the *16 year old* and there is also a *17 year old cask strength* for sale at Chivas´ visitor centres.

16 years old

Macallan

Owner:
Edrington Group

Region/district:
Speyside

Founded: **Status:**   **Capacity:**
1824   Active (vc)   8 750 000 litres

Address: Easter Elchies, Craigellachie,
Morayshire AB38 9RX

Tel: **website:**
01340 871471   www.themacallan.com

History:
1824 – The distillery is licensed to Alexander Reid under the name Elchies Distillery.

1847 – Alexander Reid passes away and James Shearer Priest and James Davidson take over.

1868 – James Stuart takes over the licence. He founds Glen Spey distillery a decade later.

1886 – James Stuart buys the distillery.

1892 – Stuart sells the distillery to Roderick Kemp from Elgin. Kemp expands the distillery and names it Macallan-Glenlivet.

1909 – Roderick Kemp passes away and the Roderick Kemp Trust is established to secure the family's future ownership.

1965 – The number of stills is increased from six to twelve.

1966 – The trust is reformed as a private limited company.

1968 – The company is introduced on the London Stock Exchange.

1974 – The number of stills is increased to 18.

1975 – Another three stills are added, now making the total 21.

1979 – Allan Schiach, descendant of Roderick Kemp, becomes the new chairman of the board after Peter Schiach.

1984 – The first official 18 year old single malt is launched.

1986 – Japanese Suntory buys 25% of Macallan-Glenlivet plc stocks.

To challenge Glenfiddich single malt for the top spot in terms of sales is a tough task, but for the second place, the battle between Glenlivet and Macallan has been fierce since 2004. At the moment Macallan is in the lead, thanks to a remarkable growth during 2010. For the first time ever, the brand managed to sell over 700,000 cases which can be attributed to a 14% increase compared to 2009. The key to this success lies in Asia where Macallan is the category leader and more than 50% of the sales of Macallan is in that region. Already in 2003, the owners opened an office in Shanghai and today they have their own distribution companies in Taiwan, South Korea, China and Singapore. It is therefore no coincidence that the most recent addition to the duty free range was first launched at selected Asian airports.

Since 2008, when the old still room was re-commissioned, the production takes place in two separate plants. The number one plant holds one full lauter mash tun, 16 stainless steel washbacks, five wash stills and ten spirit stills. The recommissioned number two plant is comprised of one semi-lauter mash tun, six new wooden washbacks, two wash stills and four spirit stills. Macallan was one of very few distilleries in Scotland that was still heating some of their stills by direct fire (using gas). However, after the summer closure in 2010, all stills are indirectly fired using steam. Warehouse capacity has increased substantially over the last couple of years and there are now 16 dunnage and 21 racked warehouses in place, with another four (holding 80,000 casks) being planned for. The distillery is currently working at full capacity.

For several years, Macallan was one of few distilleries still using the old barley type, Golden Promise, for part of their production. Golden Promise has now been replaced for good by Minstrel which makes up 20% of the production. Since 2004, the Macallan core range is divided into *Sherry Oak* (exclusively matured in ex-sherry casks) and *Fine Oak* (a combination of ex-sherry and ex-bourbon) – both ranges represented by a variety of ages. The new duty free range, named *The Macallan 1824 Collection*, holds six expressions; *Select Oak, Whisky Maker´s Edition, Estate Reserve, 1824 Limited Release, Oscuro* and *Macallan MMIX* the last one released in June 2011. There is also a number of bottlings available at the distillery only, as well as *The Fine & Rare* – vintages from *1926* to *1976*. A cooperation with crystal maker Lalique, has so far resulted in three very rare bottlings, the last one a *57 year old* released in 2010.

History (continued):

1996 – Highland Distilleries buys the remaining stocks and terminate the Kemp family's influence on Macallan. 1874 Replica is launched.

1999 – Edrington and William Grant & Sons buys Highland Distilleries (where Edrington, Suntory and Remy-Cointreau already are shareholders) for £601 million. They form the 1887 Company which owns Highland Distilleries with 70% held by Edrington and 30% by William Grant & Sons (excepting the 25% share held by Suntory).

2000 – The first single cask from Macallan (1981) is named Exceptional 1.

2001 – A new visitor centre is opened.

2002 – Elegancia replaces 12 year old in the duty-free range. 1841 Replica, Exceptional II and Exceptional III, from 1980, are also launched.

2003 – 1876 Replica and Exceptional IV, single cask from 1990 are released.

2004 – Exceptional V, single cask from 1989 is released as well as Exceptional VI, single cask from 1990. The Fine Oak series is launched.

2005 – New expressions are Macallan Woodland Estate, Winter Edition and the 50 year old.

2006 – Fine Oak 17 years old and Vintage 1975 are launched.

2007 – 1851 Inspiration and Whisky Maker's Selection are released as a part of the Travel Retail range. 12 year old Gran Reserva is launched in Taiwan and Japan.

2008 – Estate Oak and 55 year old Lalique are released.

2009 – Capacity increased by another six stills. The Macallan 1824 Collection, a range of four duty free expressions, is launched. A 57 year old Lalique bottling is released.

2010 – Oscuro is released for Duty Free.

2011 – Macallan MMIX is released for duty free.

Oscuro   Whisky Maker's Edition   Select Oak

Fine Oak 17 yo   1949 vintage   Cask Strength

Macallan 12 year old Sherry Oak

GS – The nose is luscious, with buttery sherry and Christmas cake characteristics. Rich and firm on the palate, with sherry, elegant oak and Jaffa oranges. The finish is long and malty, with slightly smoky spice.

DR – Unmistakenly the sherried version of The Macallan, with a classic red berry and orange mix. The palate is plummy, with intense sherry and some toffee and cocoa notes. The finish is medium long sweet and fruity.

Macallan 12 year old Fine Oak

GS – The nose is perfumed and quite complex, with marzipan and malty toffee. Expansive on the palate, with oranges, marmalade, milk chocolate and oak. Medium in length, balanced and comparatively sweet.

DR – Vanilla, butterscotch, satsumas and orange candy on the nose, mixed grapefruit, orange and other fruits on the palate and then a big dash of spice, and a reasonably long and balanced mix of fruit and spice in the finish.

12 years old   18 years old   25 years old   Elegancia

Macduff

Owner:
John Dewar & Sons Ltd
(Bacardi)

Region/district:
Highlands

Founded: 1962
Status: Active
Capacity: 3 340 000 litres

Address: Banff, Aberdeenshire AB45 3JT

Tel: 01261 812612
website: -

History:
1962 – The distillery is founded by Marty Dyke, George Crawford and Brodie Hepburn (who is also involved in Tullibardine and Deanston). Macduff Distillers Ltd is the name of the company.

1963 – Production starts.

1965 – The number of stills is increased from two to three.

1967 – Stills now total four.

1972 – William Lawson Distillers buys the distillery from Glendeveron Distilleries.

1980 – William Lawson is bought by Martini Rossi through the subsidiary General Beverage Corporation.

1990 – A fifth still is installed.

1992 – Bacardi buys Martini Rossi (including William Lawson) and transfers Macduff to the subsidiary John Dewar & Sons.

Glen Deveron 10 year old

GS – Sherry, malt and a slightly earthy note on the nose. Smooth and sweet in the mouth, with vanilla, spice and a hint of smoke. Sweet right to the finish.

DR – The nose is a mix of crisp barley, orange, hay and a trace of smoke, and on the palate an oily and fruity combination beautifully coats the mouth before giving way to a pepper, savoury and astringent finish.

Macduff distillery has a very nice location on the eastern outskirts of Banff on the Moray Firth coast. The best view of the distillery, set opposite a golf course surrounded by green moors, is from the bridge where the River Deveron flows into the North Sea. This is a distillery whose whisky is almost entirely destined to become a part of Dewar's own blend, William Lawson. The tiny fraction (around 26,000 cases in 2010) that is bottled as a single malt is sold under the name Glen Deveron, unless it is an indpendent bottling, when the distillery name is used instead. The William Lawson blend is just below the top ten in terms of volumes (they sold 1.6 million cases last year) and has its biggest market in France but with Russia expanding quickly.

Macduff distillery is equipped with a very efficient 6-roller Bühler Miag mill from 2007, a stainless steel semi-lauter mash tun, nine washbacks made of stainless steel and the rather unusual set-up of five stills (two wash stills and three spirit stills). The fifth still was installed in 1990. In order to fit the stills into the still room, the lyne arms on four of the stills are bent in a peculiar way and on one of the wash stills it is U-shaped. Because of limited space, they have chosen to have vertical condensers on the wash stills but horizontal on the spirit stills. For maturation, a mix of sherry and bourbon casks is used but nothing is maturing on site, even though they have seven large warehouses. In 2011 the distillery is working a 7-day week but only for 40 weeks. This means 26 mashes/week and 2.8 million litres in the year.

The most common official bottling of Glen Deveron is the *10 year old* but there is also a *15 year old* to be found. Older versions of *8* and *12 year olds* are also available.

10 years old

Mannochmore

Owner: Diageo

Region/district: Speyside

Founded: 1971

Status: Active

Capacity: 3 450 000 litres

Address: Elgin, Morayshire IV30 8SS

Tel: 01343 862000

website: www.malts.com

History:
1971 – Scottish Malt Distillers (SMD) founds the distillery on the site of their sister distillery Glenlossie. It is managed by John Haig & Co. Ltd.

1985 – The distillery is mothballed.

1989 – In production again.

1992 – A Flora & Fauna series 12 years old becomes the first official bottling.

1997 – United Distillers launches Loch Dhu – The Black Whisky which is a 10 year old Mannochmore. A 22 year old Rare Malt from 1974 and a sherry-matured Manager's Dram 18 years are also launched.

2009 – An 18 year old is released.

2010 – A Manager's Choice 1998 is released.

Mannochmore 12 year old
GS – Perfumed and fresh on the light, citric nose, with a sweet, floral, fragrant palate, featuring vanilla, ginger and even a hint of mint. Medium length in the finish, with a note of lingering almonds.

DR – Buttery, with lemon, sweet dough and floral notes on the nose, oily, malty and floral on the palate and with a relatively short finish.

Two miles south of Elgin, in the small hamlet of Thomshill, lies a site with two distilleries – one (Glenlossie) built in the 1870s and the other (Mannochmore) a hundred years later. In addition to this they also have no less than 14 warehouses with space for 250,000 casks and a huge dark grains plant which processes draff and pot ale from 21 different distilleries. Draff is the residue from the mashing of the malt and the pot ale is the left over from the wash stills after distillation. The pot ale is processed into a heavy syrup using evaporators, while moisture is extracted from the draff. The two are then mixed together, dried, formed into pellets and sold as animal feed. Diageo operates another, slightly smaller, dark grains plant at Dailuaine distillery. In 2012 the site will be busier than normal. Mannochmore will be closed for a period of time when the old mash tun is replaced and during the year, a new biomass burner will be completed. This is not the first time the owners, Diageo, invest in this type of energy-saving equipment. The new distillery at Roseisle, six miles to the north, has a similar construction which produces more than 70% of the steam required to operate the distillery.

Mannochmore is equipped with a large cast iron lauter mash tun (11.1 tonnes), eight washbacks made of larch and three pairs of stills, with the spirit stills being larger than the wash stills.

Mannochmore has never been widely known as a single malt but in 1996, a famous (or rather infamous) bottling from the distillery appeared under the name Loch Dhu – the black whisky. This was an unsuccessful event and the brand was taken off the market in 2000.

The core range of Mannochmore is just a *12 year old Flora & Fauna*. In 2009, a limited *18 year old* matured in re-charred sherry casks, bourbon casks and new American Oak casks was released and in 2010 it was time for a sherry matured *single cask from 1998* in the Manager's Choice range.

Flora & Fauna 12 years old

Miltonduff

Owner: **Region/district:**
Chivas Brothers   Speyside
(Pernod Ricard)

Founded: **Status:**   **Capacity:**
1824   Active   5 500 000 litres

Address: Miltonduff, Elgin,
Morayshire IV30 8TQ

Tel: **website:**
01343 547433   -

History:
1824 – Andrew Peary and Robert Bain obtain a licence for Miltonduff Distillery. It has previously operated as an illicit farm distillery called Milton Distillery but changes name when the Duff family buys the site it is operating on.

1866 – William Stuart buys the distillery.

1895 – Thomas Yool & Co. becomes new part-owner.

1936 – Thomas Yool & Co. sells the distillery to Hiram Walker Gooderham & Worts. The latter transfers administration to the newly acquired subsidiary George Ballantine & Son.

1964 – A pair of Lomond stills is installed to produce the rare Mosstowie.

1974-75 – Major reconstruction of the distillery.

1981 – The Lomond stills are decommissioned and replaced by two ordinary pot stills, the number of stills now totalling six.

1986 – Allied Lyons buys 51% of Hiram Walker.

1987 – Allied Lyons acquires the rest of Hiram Walker.

1991 – Allied Distillers follow United Distillers' example of Classic Malts and introduce Caledonian Malts in which Tormore, Glendronach and Laphroaig are included in addition to Miltonduff. Tormore is later replaced by Scapa.

2005 – Chivas Brothers (Pernod Ricard) becomes the new owner through the acquisition of Allied Domecq.

Miltonduff 10 year old (Gordon & MacPhail)

GS – Fresh and fruity on the nose, with toasted malt and a mildly herbal note. Soft fruits and mild oak on the palate, while the finish is subtly drying, with a touch of ginger.

DR – Clean, honeyed and deceptively gentle on the nose, chunky malt and clean vanilla on the plate, pleasant and warming finish.

Energy efficiency is the name of the game for whisky producers these days. Not only to lessen the impact on the environment but also for economic reasons. Fuel is one of the biggest expenses in whisky production, and capital outlay made to keep these costs down are normally assured to see a return on the investment. Over the past year, a heat recovery project has been carried out at Miltonduff. Thermo compressors have been installed to the external heaters on the wash stills and this will develop 40% of the steam required to heat the stills. This makes it one of the most energy efficient distilleries in the industry.

Together with Glenburgie, Miltonduff is considered the most important single malt in the Ballantine's blended whisky. It is the second most sold Scotch blend in the world (after Johnnie Walker) and has kept this position since 2007 passing J&B. Sales figures for 2010 showed a recovery of 7% compared to the disastrous year of 2009 and 6.2 million cases were sold.

The distillery is equipped with a full lauter mash tun which, when producing at full capacity, performs 40 mashes a week. There are no less than 16 stainless steel washbacks and three pairs of stills. A balanced distillation similar to that of, for example, Glenburgie, incorporating one wash and one spirit still working in tandem and served by a designated feints and low wines receiver, was introduced in autumn 2009. Several racked warehouses on the site hold a total of 54,000 casks.

From 1964 to 1981 Lomond stills were also used at Miltonduff. The malt from these stills was named Mosstowie and is still available. An official *Miltonduff 1991, 18 years old*, was recently released in Chivas Brothers cask strength series. Otherwise, Gordon & MacPhail are more or less responsible for "official" bottlings from Miltonduff.

18 years old cask strength

Mortlach

Owner:		Region/district:
Diageo		Speyside

Founded:	Status:	Capacity:
1823	Active	3 800 000 litres

Address: Dufftown, Keith, Banffshire AB55 4AQ

Tel:	website:
01340 822100	www.malts.com

History:
1823 – The distillery is founded by James Findlater.

1824 – Donald Macintosh and Alexander Gordon become part-owners.

1831 – The distillery is sold to John Robertson for £270.

1832 – A. & T. Gregory buys Mortlach.

1837 – James and John Grant of Aberlour become part-owners. No production takes place.

1842 – The distillery is now owned by John Alexander Gordon and the Grant brothers.

1851 – Mortlach is producing again after having been used as a church and a brewery for some years.

1853 – George Cowie joins and becomes part-owner.

1867 – John Alexander Gordon dies and Cowie becomes sole owner.

1895 – George Cowie Jr. joins the company.

1897 – The number of stills is increased from three to six.

1923 – Alexander Cowie sells the distillery to John Walker & Sons.

1925 – John Walker becomes part of Distillers Company Limited (DCL).

1930 – The administration is transferred to Scottish Malt Distillers (SMD).

1964 – Major refurbishment.

1968 – Floor maltings ceases.

1996 – Mortlach 1972 (23 years) is released as a Rare Malt. The distillery is renovated at a cost of £1.5 million.

1998 – Mortlach 1978 (20 years) is released as a Rare Malt.

2004 – Mortlach 1971, a 32 year old cask strength is released.

2009 – Mortlach 1997, a single cask in the new Manager's Choice range is released.

Mortlach 16 year old

GS – A rich, confident and spicy, sherried nose, with sweet treacle and pepper. Complex, elegant, yet masterful. Sherry, Christmas cake, gunpowder, black pepper on the palate. A long, relatively dry, and slightly smoky, gingery finish.

DR – Christmas cake and rich sherry nose, and a rich full plum-fruit and soft summer fruit palate. The finish is rich, full and long, with the wood making its presence felt.

On the slopes leading down to River Dullan lies Mortlach, the oldest of many distilleries in Dufftown. Regional character in the sense that all whiskies produced in the Speyside area taste alike is a concept that people are slowly moving away from. Just take a look at Mortlach single malt that has nothing to do with the preconception of Speyside malt being fragrant and floral. Instead, this is perhaps the heaviest, most robust whisky from the area and one which takes time to mature.

The distillery is equipped with a 12 tonnes full lauter mash tun and six washbacks made of larch which each holds 90,000 litres but are charged with 55,000 litres of wort. In the stillhouse are six stills in various sizes with slightly descending lyne arms. The distillation process at Mortlach, sometimes called partial triple distillation, is unique in Scotland. There are three wash stills and three spirit stills where the No. 3 pair act as a traditional double distillation. The low wines from wash stills No. 1 and 2 are directed to the remaining two spirit stills according to a certain distribution. In one of the spirit stills, called Wee Witchie, the charge is redistilled twice and with all the various distillations taken into account, it can be said that Mortlach is distilled 2.8 times. All spirit is condensed using five worm tubs made of larch and one made of stainless steel, which adds to the powerful character. The whole process is very efficient and it takes just one operator on each shift to control it. The plans for 2011 are to do 16 mashes per week and 3.8 million litres of alcohol in the year. On the site are six beautiful dunnage warehouses holding 9,000 casks. Mortlach is important to the Johnnie Walker blends and especially Black Label. A few years ago, when demand for Black Label was increasing rapidly, it was almost impossible to obtain any official bottling of Mortlach but production has increased since. The only official core bottling of Mortlach is the *16 year old Flora & Fauna*. In 2009, a Mortlach *1997 single cask* was released in the new range Manager's Choice.

Flora & Fauna 16 years of

Meet the Manager

SEAN PHILLIPS
SITE OPERATIONS MANAGER, MORTLACH DISTILLERY

When did you start working in the whisky business and when did you start at Mortlach?

I started in the whisky business and at Mortlach 30th May 2005. Then in 2006 I moved to Dufftown distillery and in October 2010 I moved back to Mortlach. I joined Diageo on 3rd November 1986 therefore I'm in my 25th Year with the company.

Had you been working in other lines of business before whisky?

When I joined the company in1986 at the age of 18, I was employed as a bottling line operator and within a year I became a training instructor on the bottling lines making Gordon's Gin. In 1989 I moved into the Gordon's Gin distillery as a Distillery Technician and then after about 6 years I got made up to a Gin Distiller and I was 1 of about 10 people at that time to be given the Gordon's Gin recipe – a very proud moment. In 2000 I relocated to Scotland with the gin stills where I became the Tanqueray & Tanqueray No.10 Master Distiller.

What kind of education or training do you have?

I left school at the age of 16 with just my standard grades, and between the ages of 16 – 18 I did various jobs. With regards to my training in the drinks industry I've gained my knowledge and expertise from some of the best distillers and managers that have worked for the company therefore it's been on the job training.

Describe your career in the whisky business.

My career has been with Diageo. In 2005 I became a Site Operations Manager at Mortlach distillery which is part of the Speyside Fast Group. Prior to that I worked as a gin & vodka distiller where I gained a huge amount of knowledge with regards to the distillation process.

What are your main tasks as a manager?

The main task for me is safety first (Zero Harm) and to ensure everyone goes home safely every day. Ensuring as a business we are fully compliant in all aspects of Health and Safety & HMR&C.

What are the biggest challenges of being a distillery manager?

Making sure that we produce precisely the right spirit, at the right time, cost-effectively, safely and consistently

What would be the worst that could go wrong in the production process?

Someone being injured on site and anything that could affect the quality of our spirit

How would you describe the character of Mortlach single malt?

Strong meaty Bovril nose, long lasting on the palate.

What are the main features in the process at Mortlach, contributing to this character?

The main feature is our complex distillation process and the way we control the temperatures of our cooling water in the worm tubs.

What is your favourite expression of Mortlach and why?

It is difficult to get your hands on different expressions of Mortlach. I do enjoy the 16 year old Flora and Fauna bottling.

If you had to choose a favourite dram other than Mortlach, what would that be?

Pittyvaich.

What are the biggest changes you have seen the past 10-15 years in your profession?

For me it's been around governance and improving our carbon footprint.

Do you see any major changes in the next 10 years to come?

Yes – protecting and improving the environment, achieving zero waste to landfill, reducing energy costs and having more bio-energy plants.

Do you have any special interests or hobbies that you pursue?

Yes – I'm a very keen golfer I play at least twice a week. I love to cook and I'll try different ingredients to impress. One of my own dishes is to marinate a fillet steak in Lagavulin which gives the steak a great smoky flavour, the marinate makes a great sauce to go with the fillet steak.

Besides being distillery manager, you are also part of the nosing team. Please tell me some more about that.

Twice a week I go into Moray House and I nose all the new make spirit samples for all the Malt Distilling sites in Diageo. There are a number of different characters that your nose needs to be tuned, therefore training your nose takes a long time to achieve and you must nose on a regular basis to ensure your nose stays tuned. As a nosing panellist you are checking to make sure each site is consistently achieving its desired new make spirit character.

Could you tell me a little more about the distillation process at Mortlach and how that affects the spirit?

The unique distillation process at Mortlach is down to "The Wee Witchie". The story about the Wee Witchie came from the late John Winton who was the manager at Mortlach for some years and then went on to become a Distillery Inspector. John was somewhat of a notoriety on distilling. During a site visit he was heard to say "Aye! That's the Wee Witchie in the corner."

You need to have one run of spirit from No.1 spirit still in every filling at Mortlach to give Mortlach its true character. The difference in No.1 Spirit Still is that it only produces spirit every 3rd charge, the other two charges are made up of low wines from itself and tails from nos. 1 & 2 wash stills, "tails" being the weaker distillate at the end of each run. The weaker charges – or dud runs as they are called – are distilled off without removing spirit from them, thus building up the strength for the spirit charge.

Oban

Owner: **Region/district:**
Diageo   Western Highlands

Founded: **Status:**   **Capacity:**
1794   Active (vc)   670 000 litres

Address: Stafford Street, Oban, Argyll PA34 5NH

Tel: **website:**
01631 572004 (vc)   www.malts.com

History:
1793 – John and Hugh Stevenson found the distillery on premises previously used for brewing.

1794 – Start of operations.

1820 – Hugh Stevenson dies.

1821 – Hugh Stevenson's son Thomas takes over.

1829 – Bad investments force Thomas Stevenson into bankruptcy. His eldest son John takes over operations at the distillery.

1830 – John buys the distillery from his father's creditors for £1,500.

1866 – Peter Cumstie buys the distillery.

1883 – Cumstie sells Oban to James Walter Higgins who refurbishes and modernizes it.

1898 – The Oban & Aultmore-Glenlivet Co. takes over with Alexander Edwards at the helm.

1923 – The Oban Distillery Co. owned by Buchanan-Dewar takes over.

1925 – Buchanan-Dewar becomes part of Distillers Company Limited (DCL).

1930 – Administration is transferred to Scottish Malt Distillers (SMD).

1931 – Production ceases.

1937 – In production again.

1968 – Floor maltings ceases and the distillery closes for reconstruction.

1972 – Reopening of the distillery.

1979 – Oban 12 years is on sale.

1988 – United Distillers launches Classic Malts. Oban 14 year is selected to represent Western Highlands.

1989 – A visitor centre is built.

1998 – A Distillers' Edition is launched.

2002– The oldest Oban (32 years) so far is launched in a limited edition of 6,000 bottles.

2004 – A 20 year old cask strength from 1984 (1,260 bottles) is released.

2009 – Oban 2000, a single cask in the new Manager's Choice range is released.

2010 – A no age distillery exclusive is released.

Oban 14 year old

GS – Lightly smoky on the honeyed, floral nose. Toffee, cereal and a hint of peat. The palate offers initial cooked fruits, becoming spicier. Complex, bittersweet, malt, oak and more gentle smoke. The finish is quite lengthy, with spicy oak, toffee and discreet, new leather.

DR – A mixed nose of heather, honey, pineapple and nuts, a perfectly balanced mix of grapey fruit, pineapple chunks, roast nuts and smoky undertow, and a rounded and fruity finish, drying and more-ish.

Oban is the biggest town in Western Scotland and it is also on the way to popular tourist destinations such as Skye if you come from the south. No wonder then that Oban distillery is the second most visited of all Diageo's distilleries. No less than 32,000 visitors during 2010 found their way to the excellent visitor centre and very well-stocked shop. The town itself, which today stands at 9,000 inhabitants, was a mere fishing village when John and Hugh Stevenson arrived in the late 1700s. Apart from building the distillery they also established a boat building yard and a tannery. Their activities set the base for the continuous growth of this town.

Oban is one of the original six Classic Malts and it sells around 65,000 cases per year, which makes it the fifth best selling single malt in the company and the biggest seller in the USA of all the Diageo malts.

The distillery, which is the second smallest in the Diageo group after Royal Lochnagar, is equipped with a traditional stainless steel mash tun with rakes, four washbacks made of European larch and one pair of stills. Attached to the stills is a rectangular, stainless steel double worm tub to condensate the spirit vapours. The distillery is running at full capacity, i.e. 700,000 litres. The size of the stills could allow for more, but the bottleneck is the washbacks. One washback will fill the wash still twice, however, the character of Oban single malt is dependent on long fermentations (110 hours), hence they can only manage six mashes per week. All of the production is used for single malts.

The core range consists of two expressions – a *14 year old* and a *Distiller's Edition* with a montilla fino sherry finish. In 2010 a *distillery exclusive* bottling, available only at the distillery, was released. It is finished in fino sherry casks and has no age statement. Older limited editions include a *32 year old*, a *20 year old* and, exclusive to the American market (8,700 bottles), an *18 year old* released in 2008.

14 years old

Pulteney

History:

1826 – James Henderson founds the distillery.

1920 – The distillery is bought by James Watson.

1923 – Buchanan-Dewar takes over.

1925 – Buchanan-Dewar becomes part of Distillers Company Limited (DCL).

1930 – Production ceases.

1951 – In production again after being acquired by the solicitor Robert Cumming.

1955 – Cumming sells to James & George Stodart, a subsidiary to Hiram Walker & Sons.

1958 – The distillery is rebuilt.

1959 – The floor maltings close.

1961 – Allied Breweries buys James & George Stodart Ltd.

1981 – Allied Breweries changes name to Allied Lyons after the acquisition of J Lyons in 1978.

1995 – Allied Domecq sells Pulteney to Inver House Distillers.

1997 – Old Pulteney 12 years is launched.

2001 – Pacific Spirits (Great Oriole Group) buys Inver House at a price of $85 million.

2004 – A 17 year old is launched.

2005 – A 21 year old is launched.

2006 – International Beverage Holdings acquires Pacific Spirits UK.

2009 – A 30 year old is released.

2010 – WK499 Isabella Fortuna is released.

2011 – A 40 year old is released.

Old Pulteney 12 year old

GS – The nose presents pleasingly fresh malt and floral notes, with a touch of pine. The palate is comparatively sweet, with malt, spices, fresh fruit and a suggestion of salt. The finish is medium in length, drying and decidedly nutty.

DR – Honey and lemon lozenges on the nose, sweet citrus fruits, chunky malt and some traces of sea brine on the palate, an amusing sweet and sour two step at the finish.

Pulteney is the most northerly distillery on the Scottish mainland and is situated in the small town of Wick (c 7,000 inhabitants). This was once the busiest herring port in Europe. Old Pulteney (as the whisky from Pulteney distillery is called) is, together with Speyburn, the best-selling of Inver House´s single malts.

The semi-lauter mash tun is made of cast iron and due for replacement in 2012. There are six washbacks, five made of Corten steel and one of stainless steel and the fermentation time varies from 52 hours to 100 hours. The Corten steel washbacks go back to early 1920 and will probably be exchanged in a couple of years. Dry yeast is used for the fermentation which is quite unusual these days. Pulteney has one pair of stills. The wash still is equipped with a huge ball creating added reflux. Its top is quaintly chopped off as the still was apparently too tall for the stillroom when it was installed. The spirit still is equipped with a purifier (which hasn´t been used for years) and both stills use stainless steel worm tubs with 110 metre long copper worms for condensing the spirit. The capacity is 1.8 million litres but for 2011, there will be 16 mashes per week, which is the equivalent of 1.4 million litres of alcohol. New roofs were laid on the five warehouses (three dunnage and two racked) in 2008/2009, which can hold 24,000 casks. Around 40% of the production is sold to other companies. The core range is made up of *12, 17* and *21 years old*. In 2009, a *30 year old*, the oldest Old Pulteney at the time, was released. Three years later (in 2012) it is time for an even older expression – a *40 year old*. Filled in 1968, the three sherry butts and one bourbon barrel yielded 363 bottles. 2010 saw the first release of a Duty Free exclusive from Pulteney, the non-aged *WK499 Isabella Fortuna*, named after one of Wick´s two remaining herring drifters. In 2011 a general release of the Isabella Fortuna was made.

12 years old

Royal Brackla

Owner:		Region/district:
John Dewar & Sons (Bacardi)		Highlands

Founded:	Status:	Capacity:
1812	Active	4 000 000 litres

Address: Cawdor, Nairn, Nairnshire IV12 5QY

Tel:	website:
01667 402002	-

History:
1812 – The distillery is founded by Captain William Fraser.

1835 – Brackla becomes the first of three distilleries allowed to use 'Royal' in the name.

1852 – Robert Fraser & Co. takes over the distillery.

1898 – The distillery is rebuilt and Royal Brackla Distillery Company Limited is founded.

1919 – John Mitchell and James Leict from Aberdeen purchase Royal Brackla.

1926 – John Bisset & Company Ltd takes over.

1943 – Scottish Malt Distillers (SMD) buys John Bisset & Company Ltd and thereby acquires Royal Brackla.

1966 – The maltings closes.

1970 – Two stills are increased to four.

1985 – The distillery is mothballed.

1991 – Production resumes.

1993 – A 10 year old Royal Brackla is launched in United Distillers' Flora & Fauna series.

1997 – UDV spends more than £2 million on improvements and refurbishing.

1998 – Bacardi–Martini buys Dewar's from Diageo.

2004 – A new 10 year old is launched.

Royal Brackla 10 year old

GS – An attractive malty, fruity, floral nose, with peaches and apricots. Quite full-bodied, the creamy palate exhibits sweet malt, spice and fresh fruit. The finish is medium to long, with vanilla and gently-spiced oak.

DR – Pineapple and citrus fruits on the nose, candy barley, melon and pleasant sweet spice on the palate, medium sweet finish with a trace of green melon.

Soon to celebrate its 200th anniversary (in 2012), this distillery can reflect on a first century where it was considerably more in the limelight than during the second. When it was founded in Nairnshire by Captain William Fraser, whisky smuggling was at its peak in the area. It would be another 11 years before the Excise Act of 1823 was passed in order to suppress illicit distilling and Captain Fraser used to complain that "he was surrounded by people who drank nothing but whisky, yet he could not sell 100 gallons in a year." He was considerably happier in 1835 when the distillery was the first to be given a royal warrant by King William IV and the whisky became known as "The King's Own Whisky". More success followed in 1860 when Andrew Usher, whose company was also a partner in the distillery, used Royal Brackla malt in his (and Scotland's) first blended whisky. This was made possible through another law, the Spirit Act of 1860, which allowed mixing of grain whisky with malt whisky.

For most of the 20th century though, the whisky from Royal Brackla has been a part of various blended brands, since 1998, when Bacardi took over, especially Dewar's. The distillery, beautifully situated just south of Nairn and Moray Firth, is equipped with a big (12 tonnes) full lauter mash tun from 1997. There are six wooden washbacks (but with stainless steel tops) and another two made of stainless steel which are insulated because they are placed outside and the fermentation time is quite long (72 hours). Finally, there are two pairs of stills. At the moment the distillery is running at full capacity, which means 17 mashes per week and 4 million litres of alcohol per year. This makes it the biggest distillery in the Dewar's group.

Today's core range consists of a *10 year old* and a limited edition of a *25 year old*. The range is about to be expanded though. It has already been announced that one (and perhaps two) new expressions of Royal Brackla will be released in 2012.

10 years old

182

Royal Lochnagar

Owner: **Region/district:**
Diageo   Eastern Highlands

Founded: **Status:**   **Capacity:**
1845   Active (vc)   450 000 litres

Address: Crathie, Ballater,
Aberdeenshire AB35 5TB

Tel: **website:**
01339 742700   www.malts.com

History:
1823 – James Robertson founds a distillery in Glen Feardan on the north bank of River Dee.

1826 – The distillery is burnt down by competitors but Robertson decides to establish a new distillery near the mountain Lochnagar.

1841 – This distillery is also burnt down.

1845 – A new distillery is built by John Begg, this time on the south bank of River Dee. It is named New Lochnagar.

1848 – Lochnagar obtains a Royal Warrant.

1882 – John Begg passes away and his son Henry Farquharson Begg inherits the distillery.

1896 – Henry Farquharson Begg dies.

1906 – The children of Henry Begg rebuild the distillery.

1916 – The distillery is sold to John Dewar & Sons.

1925 – John Dewar & Sons becomes part of Distillers Company Limited (DCL).

1963 – A major reconstruction takes place.

2004 – A 30 year old cask strength from 1974 is launched in the Rare Malts series (6,000 bottles).

2008 – A Distiller's Edition with a Moscatel finish is released.

2010 – A Manager's Choice 1994 is released.

Royal Lochnagar 12 year old

GS – Light toffee on the nose, along with some green notes of freshly-sawn timber. The palate offers a pleasing and quite complex blend of caramel, dry sherry and spice, followed by a hint of liquorice before the slightly scented finish develops.

DR – Rich fruit and honey on the nose, sophisticated mix of crystal barley, chunky fruit and delicious peat base and a warming and rounded finish.

Royal Lochnagar, Diageo's smallest distillery, lies in beautiful surroundings with Royal Deeside and the imposing Lochnagar mountain to the south and Balmoral, the Queen's summer residence, just a stone's throw to the north. Royal Lochnagar is one of the most traditional distilleries in all of Scotland. The nine hour mashing is done in batches of 5.4 tonnes in an open, traditional cast iron mash tun using rakes. Fermentation takes place in two wooden washbacks, with short fermentations of 75 hours and long of 126 hours. The long fermentation helps create the light character the owners are looking for. There is one pair of stills with the wash still holding 7,000 litres and the spirit still 5,500 litres. The heart of the spirit run starts at 75% and they cut at 61% before heavier compounds starts to affect the spirit. The lyne arms are slightly descending and the cooling of the spirit vapours takes place in cast iron worm tubs. The whole production is filled on site with around 1,000 casks stored in the only warehouse (which previously was used for the maltings) and the rest is sent to Glenlossie for maturation.

For 2011 four mashes per week will be made, resulting in 375,000 litres of alcohol per year, which is close to the maximum capacity. The pretty visitor centre attracts 10,000 visitors a year, a figure that could easily be quadrupled if it had been more accessible by way of one of the main roads. In June 2011 Donald Renwick, one of the veterans amongst Diageo distillery managers, retired. He was responsible for Royal Lochnagar and previously the manager at Lagavulin distillery.

Part of the production is reserved for more exclusive Johnnie Walker expressions like Blue Label while the rest is sold as single malt. The core range consists of the *12 year old* and the more unusual expression *Selected Reserve*. The latter is a vatting of selected casks, usually around 18-20 years of age. There is also a *Distiller's Edition* with a second maturation in Muscat casks. In 2010 a *single cask* distilled in *1994* was released as part of the Manager's Choice series.

12 years old

Scapa

Owner:		Region/district:
Chivas Brothers (Pernod Ricard)		Highlands (Orkney)

Founded:	Status:	Capacity:
1885	Active	1 500 000 litres

Address: Scapa, St Ola, Kirkwall, Orkney KW15 1SE

Tel:	website:
01856 876585	www.scapamalt.com

History:
1885 – Macfarlane & Townsend founds the distillery with John Townsend at the helm.
1919 – Scapa Distillery Company Ltd takes over.
1934 – Scapa Distillery Company goes into voluntary liquidation and production ceases.
1936 – Production resumes.
1936 – Bloch Brothers Ltd (John and Sir Maurice) takes over.
1954 – Hiram Walker & Sons takes over.
1959 – A Lomond still is installed.
1978 – The distillery is modernized.
1994 – The distillery is mothballed.
1997 – Production takes place a few months each year using staff from Highland Park.
2004 – Extensive refurbishing takes place at a cost of £2.1 million. Scapa 14 years is launched.
2005 – Production ceases in April and phase two of the refurbishment programme starts. Chivas Brothers becomes the new owner.
2006 – Scapa 1992 (14 years) is launched.
2008 – Scapa 16 years is launched.

Scapa 16 year old

GS – The nose offers apricots and peaches, nougat and mixed spices. Pretty, yet profound. Medium-bodied, with caramel and spice notes in the mouth. The finish is medium in length and gingery, with fat, buttery notes emerging at the end.

DR – Sweet baked banana in cream with shortbread on the nose. The taste is a delightful mix of sweet and sour, with sugar and salt sparring but kept apart by green and orange fruit. There's a late sharper note towards lengthy fruit finish.

Just a year or two before Allied Domecq was taken over by Pernod Ricard in 2005, they started to invest heavily in some of their distilleries. Glendronach was brought back to life in 2002 and £4.3 m were invested in a complete reconstruction of Glenburgie. The most unexpected move, however, was their commitment to refurbish and reopen Scapa distillery at Orkney. To invest £2.1 m in a remote distillery with a small production capacity and a brand that had never had any extensive marketing came as a surprise to many.

Today the distillery continues to flourish under its new owners and bottles of the 16 year old are now easy to come by. Scapa Distillery is magnificently situated by the sandy beach at the interior of Scapa Bay. The equipment consists of a new semi-lauter mash tun installed in 2004 and eight washbacks. Four of them (installed in 1968) are made of stainless steel, while the old ones (1955) are made of Corten steel. Scapa probably has the longest fermentation time of any distillery in Scotland. All the washbacks are filled and left for up to 160 hours before distillation begins. A long fermentation may positively contribute to the final character of the spirit, creating esters which give a fruity character. The downside of too long fermentations is that it may create a bacteria known as acrolein which will add a pungent and burnt taste to the end product. The wash still is of Lomond type with the rectification plates removed, while the spirit still is of a traditional onion design. Both stills are equipped with purifiers. Distillation takes place from Monday to Wednesday, resulting in a production of circa 400,000 litres of alcohol and the entire output is destined for single malts. There are three dunnage and three racked warehouses, but only the latter are in use today.

The Scapa core range is just the *16 year old*, while limited editions include a *25 year old* from 1980 and a *Vintage 1992*. There is also a *16 year old cask strength* sold exclusively at Chivas' visitor centres.

16 years old

Speyburn

Owner:
Inver House Distillers
(Thai Beverages plc)

Region/district:
Speyside

Founded: 1897
Status: Active
Capacity: 2 000 000 litres

Address: Rothes, Aberlour,
Morayshire AB38 7AG

Tel: 01340 831213
website: www.speyburn.com

History:
1897 – Brothers John and Edward Hopkin and their cousin Edward Broughton found the distillery through John Hopkin & Co. They already own Tobermory. The architect is Charles Doig. Building the distillery costs £17,000 and the distillery is transferred to Speyburn-Glenlivet Distillery Company.

1916 – Distillers Company Limited (DCL) acquires John Hopkin & Co. and the distillery.

1930 – Production stops.

1934 – Productions restarts.

1962 – Speyburn is transferred to Scottish Malt Distillers (SMD).

1968 – Drum maltings closes.

1991 – Inver House Distillers buys Speyburn.

1992 – A 10 year old is launched as a replacement for the 12 year old in the Flora & Fauna series.

2001 – Pacific Spirits (Great Oriole Group) buys Inver House for $85 million.

2005 – A 25 year old Solera is released.

2006 – Inver House changes owner when International Beverage Holdings acquires Pacific Spirits UK.

2009 – The un-aged Bradan Orach is introduced for the American market.

Speyburn 10 year old

GS – Soft and elegant on the spicy, nutty nose. Smooth in the mouth, with vanilla, spice and more nuts. The finish is medium, spicy and drying.

DR – Sweet malt nose, then one of the sweetest and most easy-drinking of all malts, with the faintest touch of smoke in the mix. Like eating a bag of sugar.

Speyburn single malt may be unknown to most whisky lovers in Europe but has shown to be successful in the American market. During its peak in USA it was the sixth most sold single malt with 35,000 cases per year. Sales have slowed down since and today sales lie around 20,000 cases and time will tell if the new extension of the range, Bradan Orach, will increase sales to its former levels.

Since 2001, Speyburn (like the rest of the Inver House distilleries) have had Thai owners. The names of the companies have changed but one man has always been around, Charoen Sirivadhanabhakdi, today the third richest man in Thailand. The son of a Bangkok street vendor, he now controls most of the Thai beer and spirits market and at 66 years of age, his five children run the daily business which also includes hotels, shopping malls and real estate.

The drinks part of the business comprises of 18 distilleries and three breweries in Thailand and five distilleries in Scotland. Speyburn distillery is equipped with a stainless steel mash tun which replaced the old cast iron tun in 2008. There are six washbacks of which two were changed to Oregon pine during in 2010, while the others are made of larch. Finally, there is one wash still (17,300 litres) and one spirit still (13,200 litres) using stainless steel worm tubs with 104 metre long copper tubes for cooling.

There are three dunnage warehouses with 5,000 casks where the spirit intended for bottling as single malt is maturing. In 1900, Speyburn was the first distillery to abandon floor malting in favour of a new method – drum malting. In the late sixties, the maltings closed and ready malt was bought instead, but the drum maltings are still there to see, protected by Historic Scotland.

The core range of Speyburn single malt is the *10 year old* and *Bradan Orach* without age statement. Previous limited releases include *21, 25* and *25 year old Solera*.

10 years old

Speyside

Speyburn

Owner:		Region/district:
Speyside Distillers Co.		Speyside

Founded:	Status:	Capacity:
1976	Active	600 000 litres

Address: Glen Tromie, Kingussie
Inverness-shire PH21 1NS

Tel:	website:
01540 661060	www.speysidedistillery.co.uk

History:
1956 – George Christie buys a piece of land at Drumguish near Kingussie.

1957 – George Christie starts a grain distillery near Alloa.

1962 – George Christie (founder of Speyside Distillery Group in the fifties) commissions the drystone dyker Alex Fairlie to build a distillery in Drumguish.

1986 – Scowis assumes ownership.

1987 – The distillery is completed.

1990 – The distillery is on stream in December.

1993 – The first single malt, Drumguish, is launched.

1999 – Speyside 8 years is launched.

2000 – Speyside Distilleries is sold to a group of private investors including Ricky Christie, Ian Jerman and Sir James Ackroyd.

2001 – Speyside 10 years is launched.

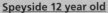

Speyside 12 year old

GS – A nicely-balanced nose of herbs and toasted barley. Medium-bodied, with a suggestion of peat, plus hazelnuts and oak. Toffee and orange notes in the lingering finish.

DR – Rootsy damp straw nose, a sharp and clean barley delivery on the palate with an earthy, peaty undertow, and a willowy, nutty savoury finish.

Speyside is one of the newest distilleries in Scotland with the building commencing in 1962 and the first distillation taking place 28 years later, in 1990. When the first 10 year old was launched in 2001, the former blender, grain whisky distiller and founder of the distillery, Georg Christie, was no longer one of the owners. His son Ricky had at that time, alongside a group of investors, taken over. However, George Christie, who is now in his mid nineties, still lives up the road from the distillery.

The distillery is equipped with a semi-lauter mash tun, four stainless steel washbacks and one pair of stills. There are no warehouses on site. Instead, the spirit is tankered away to the company's bonded warehouses in Glasgow. The total production for 2011 will be around 400,000 litres of alcohol and they will also do three weeks of peated production with a malt specification of 50ppm. The owners are also discussing the possibility of putting in a small grain still as well, but nothing has yet been decided. Speyside produces three brands of single malt; *Speyside* with the core range of *12* and *15 year old*, *Drumguish* and the quaint and almost black *Cu Dubh*. Apart from the distillery at Drumguish, there is a diverse range of activities at the company's base in Rutherglen, Glasgow. Cask warehousing, a bottling plant and a blending operation are all found here. A range of 20 brands of blended whiskies are produced as well as two ranges of single malts from other distilleries – Scott's Selection and Private Cellar. The total number of staff is 80 and exports go to more than 100 countries with the US and the Far East as top markets. A lot of effort has recently been put into expanding the range of Scott's Selection single cask bottlings. Among other things, a series of old grain whiskies going back to the early 1960s, has been launched.

12 years old

Whisky Chronology

continued on page 191

1644 The Scottish parliament instates a new law on Excise Duty to be paid for each pint of aqua vitae that is produced.

1698 Berry Bros. is founded.

1756 Arthur Guinness Son & Co. is established.

1774 A law prohibiting wash stills less than 400 gallons and spirit stills less than 100 gallons is passed.

1784 The Wash Act is introduced to encourage legal distilling in the Highlands.

1805 Seager Evans (producer of gin) is formed.

1814 Matthew Gloag embarks on a career as a whisky merchant in Perth.

1814 The Excise Act states that the smallest size of a Highland still is to be 500 gallons.

1816 The Small Stills Act states that the smallest allowed size of a still is 40 gallons in all of Scotland.

1820 John Walker establishes himself as a grocer and wine and spirits merchant in Kilmarnock.

1823 An Excise Act states that a licence is required to suppress illicit distilling.

1826 Robert Stein invents a patent still for continuous distilling.

1827 George Ballantine becomes established as a grocer and wine merchant in Edinburgh.

1828 J. & A. Mitchell & Co. (Springbank) is founded.

1830 Aenas Coffey patents an improved version of Robert Steins patent still which is named Coffey still.

1830 William Teacher obtains a liquor licence for a shop in Glasgow.

1831 Justerini & Brooks is formed.

1841 James Chivas forms a company in Aberdeen.

1842 William Cadenhead Ltd is formed.

1846 John Dewar is established as a wholesale wine and spirit merchant in Perth.

1853 Andrew Usher & Co. starts to produce blended whisky.

1857 Walter and Alfred Gilbey start their career as wine merchants in London.

1857 Joseph Seagram & Sons is founded.

1857 William and Robert Hill join forces with William Thomson and found Hill Thomson & Co.

1858 James and John Chivas found Chivas Brothers.

1860 Roberston & Baxter is established.

1865 Eight Lowland grain distilleries form Scotch Distillers Association.

1865 The passing of The Blending Act allows for malt and grain whisky being blended.

1869 W. P. Lowrie & Co. is founded.

1870 Greenlees Brothers is established.

1874 The North of Scotland Malt Distillers Association is founded.

1875 William Teacher founds William Teacher & Sons.

1877 Distillers Company Limited (DCL) is founded by six grain distilleries.

1882 James Whyte and Charles Mackay found Whyte & Mackay.

1885 The North British Distillery Co. is formed.

1886 Alexander Walker brings in his sons to the company and founds John Walker & Sons Ltd.

1886 William Grant and Sons is founded.

1887 Highland Distillers is founded.

1888 John Alicius Haig founds Haig & Haig Ltd.

1890 Mackie & Co. is established.

1893 McDonald & Muir is founded.

1895 Gordon & MacPhail is founded.

1895 Arthur Bell & Sons is founded.

1896 Matthew Gloag & Son establish The Grouse.

1898 The Pattison crash.

1906 Buchanan takes over W. P. Lowrie.

1907 Robertson & Baxter buys Haig & Haig.

1914 Scottish Malt Distillers is founded.

1915 Buchanan and Dewars merge into Scotch Whisky Brands.

1915 Immature spirits act requires that whisky must be bonded for two years prior to bottling.

1916 The bonding time is increased to three years.

1917 The Whisky Association, a predecessor to SWA, is formed.

1919 James Barclay and R. A. McKinlay acquire Ballantines.

1919 Scotch Whisky Brands becomes Buchanan & Dewar.

1919 John Haig & Co. and Andrew Usher & Co. join DCL.

1920 Prohibition is introduced in the United States.

1922 Roberston & Baxter is acquired by DCL, Walker and Buchanan-Dewar.

1924 Sir Peter Mackie dies and the company changes name to White Horse Distillers.

1925 The Big Amalgamation – DCL merges with Buchanan-Dewar and Walker.

1925 DCL acquires W. P. Lowrie & Co.

1925 DCL buys Scottish Malt Distillers.

1926 Pot-Still Malt Distillers replaces North of Scotland Malt Distillers Association.

1927 DCL acquires White Horse Distillers.

1928 Distillers Corporation of Canada buys Joseph E. Seagram & Sons.

1933 The Prohibition ends in USA.

1934 Arthur Bell & Sons buys P. Mackenzie & Co.

1935 William Sanderson & Son merges with Booth's Distillers.

1935 Hiram Walker acquires George Ballantine & Son.

1936 Seager Evans buys W. H. Chaplin and the brand Long John.

1936 Lundy & Morrison buys Chivas Bros.

1937 Hiram Walker (Scotland) is formed.

1942 Scotch Whisky Association (SWA) is formed.

1949 Lundie & Morrison sells Chivas Bros to Robert Brown & Co. (subsidiary of Seagrams).

1950 Seagrams buys Strathisla and transfers administration to Chivas Brothers.

1950 Douglas Laing & Co. is founded.

1951 Morrison Bowmore Distillers Ltd is founded.

1952 George & G. J. Smith Ltd and J. & J. Grant form The Glenlivet & Glen Grant Distillers Ltd.

1952 Justerini & Brooks merges with Twiss, Browning & Hallowes and form United Wine Traders.

1956 Inver House is founded.

1956 Seager Evans is acquired by Schenley Industries Inc.

1958 Watney Mann is formed through merger between Watney, Coombe Reid & Co. and Mann, Crossman & Paulin Ltd.

1960 Edrington Holdings is formed.

1960 Whyte & Mackay merges with Mackenzie Brothers and takes over Dalmore Distillery.

1961 Ind Coope, Tetley Walker and Ansells form Ind Coope Tetley Ansell (later to become Allied Breweries).

Springbank

Owner:
Springbank Distillers
(J & A Mitchell)

Region/district:
Campbeltown

Founded:
1828

Status:
Active (vc)

Capacity:
750 000 litres

Address: Well Close, Campbeltown,
Argyll PA28 6ET

Tel:
01586 552085

website:
www.springbankdistillers.com

History:
1828 – The Reid family, in-laws of the Mitchells (see below), founds the distillery.

1837 – The Reid family encounters financial difficulties and John and William Mitchell buy the distillery.

1897 – J. & A. Mitchell Co Ltd is founded.

1926 – The depression forces the distillery to close.

1933 – The distillery is back in production.

1960 – Own maltings ceases.

1969 – J. & A. Mitchell buys the independent bottler Cadenhead.

1979 – The distillery closes.

1985 – A 10 year old Longrow is launched.

1987 – Limited production restarts.

1989 – Production restarts.

1992 – Springbank takes up its maltings again.

1997 – First distillation of Hazelburn.

1998 – Springbank 12 years is launched.

1999 – Dha Mhile (7 years), the world's first organic single malt, is released.

2000 – A 10 year old is launched.

2001 – Springbank 1965 'Local barley' (36 years), 741 bottles, is launched.

2002 – Number one in the series Wood Expressions is a 12 year old with five years on Demerara rum casks. Next is a Longrow sherry cask (13 years). A relaunch of the 15 year old replaces the 21 year old.

Springbank is just one of three surving distilleries in Campbeltown – a town which, in its glory days in the late 1800s, had more than 25 distilleries operating at the same time. The end came as a result of World War I, the prohibition in the USA and the closing of coal mines in the area and in the 1930s there were only three distilleries left. Through all these years, Springbank has retained its reputation and today it is considered by many as one of the stars of Scotch single malts.

At one time, Springbank distillery was described as "an old eccentric" of the whisky world. The owners probably take that as a compliment because no other distillery is so determined to walk their own way and not looking to others for inspiration. During production for example, the people at Springbank prefer low gravity worts from the mashing (with an OG of 1046) compared to most distilleries where 1060 or sometimes higher is used to increase efficiency. This, together with a low-strength wash (5% compared to the normal 8%) and long fermentation are key factors contributing to the Springbank flavour character.

Springbank produces three distinctive single malts with different phenol contents in the malted barley. Springbank is distilled two and a half times (12-15ppm), Longrow is distilled twice (50-55 ppm) and Hazelburn is distilled three times (unpeated). Currently, Springbank makes up 60% of production, while the remaining part is split between Longrow and Hazelburn. Currently around 100,000 litres are produced in a year at Springbank.

The distillery is equipped with an open cast iron mash tun, six washbacks made of Scandinavian larch, one wash still and two spirit stills. The wash still is unique in Scotland, as it is fired by both an open oil-fire and internal steam coils. Ordinary condensers are used to cool the spirit vapours, except in the first of the two spirit stills, where a worm tub is used. Springbank is unique in Scotland as they malt their whole need of barley using own floor maltings.

The core range of Springbank distillery is *Springbank 10, 15* and *18 years, Springbank 12 year old cask strength* (new for 2010), *Springbank CV, Longrow 14 year old, Longrow 18 year old* (new for 2011), *Longrow CV, Hazelburn 8* and *12 years old* and *Hazelburn CV* (new for 2010). Limited release for 2010 was a *Springbank 12 year old claret wood* expression and 2011 saw the launch of *Hazelburn 8 year old Sauternes* wood expression and an *11 year old Springbank* produced from local barley (for Springbank Society members only). In 2012 we may also see the return of the once famous 21 year old Springbank as a very limited release.

History (continued):

2004 – J. & A. Mitchell's main owner, Hedley Wright, reopens Glengyle Distillery. Springbank 10 years 100 proof is launched as well as Springbank Wood Expression bourbon, Longrow 14 years old, Springbank 32 years old and Springbank 14 years Port Wood.

2005 – 2 400 bottles of Springbank 21 years old are released in March. The first version of Hazel-burn (8 years old) is released. Longrow Tokaji Wood Expression is launched.

2006 – Longrow 10 years 100 proof, Spring-bank 25 years (1,200 bottles), Springbank 9 years Marsala finish, Springbank 11 years Madeira finish and a new Hazelburn 8 year old are released.

2007 – Springbank Vintage 1997 and a 16 year old rum wood are released.

2008 – The distillery closes temporarily. Three new releases of Longrow - CV, 18 year old and 7 year old Gaja Barolo.

2009 – Springbank Madeira 11 year old, Springbank 18 year old, Springbank Vintage 2001 and Hazelburn 12 year old are released.

2010 – Springbank 12 year old cask strentgh and a 12 year old claret expression together with new editions of the CV and 18 year old are released. Longrow 10 year old cask strength and Hazelburn CV are also new.

2011 – Longrow 18 year old and Hazelburn 8 year old Sauternes wood expression are released.

Longrow
18 years old

Hazelburn 12 years old

Springbank
18 years old

Springbank 10 year old 100 proof

GS – Fresh and briny on the nose, with toffee and fruit notes following through. Sweet and smooth on the palate, with developing brine, wood smoke and vanilla toffee. The finish is lengthy, with more salt and a suggestion of coconut oil.

DR – The nose is full, sweet and full of barley but with some oak and spice, the palate is rich full and savoury, with a long, full and spicy finish.

Longrow 10 year old 100 proof

DR – Subtle lemon and daffodil nose with traces of phenols, sweet, fruity and oily palate covered in a smattering of charcoal dust, lengthy, subtle and fragrant finish.

Hazelburn 12 year old

GS – A highly aromatic nose, featuring nutty toffee, sherry, dried fruits and dark chocolate. The palate is rich and spicy, with cocoa, coffee, ginger and sweeter notes of caramel and orange marmalade. Long and spicy in the finish, with more caramel, coffee, chocolate and oak notes.

DR – Rich and fruity nose of nectarine, peach, plums and some nuttiness. On the palate rich plums, red berries, dry sherry and drying tannins, with an intense rich and fruity finish.

Springbank CV

Longrow CV

189

Strathisla

Owner: Chivas Brothers (Pernod Ricard)

Region/district: Speyside

Founded: 1786
Status: Active (vc)
Capacity: 2 400 000 litres

Address: Seafield Avenue, Keith, Banffshire AB55 5BS

Tel: 01542 783044
website: www.maltwhiskydistilleries.com

History:

1786 – Alexander Milne and George Taylor found the distillery under the name Milltown, but soon change it to Milton.

1825 – MacDonald Ingram & Co. purchases the distillery.

1830 – William Longmore acquires the distillery.

1870 – The distillery name changes to Strathisla.

1880 – William Longmore retires and hands operations to his son-in-law John Geddes-Brown. William Longmore & Co. is formed.

1890 – The distillery changes name to Milton.

1940 – Jay (George) Pomeroy acquires majority shares in William Longmore & Co. Pomeroy is jailed as a result of dubious business transactions and the distillery goes bankrupt in 1949.

1950 – Chivas Brothers buys the run-down distillery at a compulsory auction for £71,000 and starts restoration.

1951 – The name reverts to Strathisla.

1965 – The number of stills is increased from two to four.

1970 – A heavily peated whisky, Craigduff, is produced but production stops later.

2001 – The Chivas Group is acquired by Pernod Ricard.

Strathisla 12 year old

GS – Rich on the nose, with sherry, stewed fruits, spices and lots of malt. Full-bodied and almost syrupy on the palate. Toffee, honey, nuts, a whiff of peat and a suggestion of oak. The finish is medium in length, slightly smoky and a with a final flash of ginger.

DR – Rich, full and fruity nose with lots of barley, then barley, currants and a touch of oak, peat and pepper, concluding with a complex and intriguing finish.

Strathisla distillery is one of the most picturesque distilleries in Scotland with an excellent visitor centre. At the same time, this is the spiritual home of Chivas Regal where Strathisla malt plays an important part so focus is more on the world famous blend. Chivas Regal was number five on the 2010 global sales list for Scotch blends, a place they have held since 2005. With a 16% increase in sales from 2009 to 2010, translating to 4.5 million cases, it was the superior climber of all the top brands. On the other hand Chivas Regal lost the most during the last financial crisis and have just managed to pull themselves back up. However, Chivas Regal is still the number one premium whisky in the important Chinese and Indian markets. Strathisla may be one of the oldest distilleries in Scotland but the close connection to the Chivas Regal brand doesn't reach further back than 1950 (even though Strathisla malt had been used in the blend before that) when the Canadian company Seagram's bought the distillery and transferred it to the, also newly bought, Chivas Brothers. Strathisla distillery is equipped with a traditional stainless steel mash tun with a raised copper canopy, ten washbacks of Oregon pine (formerly eleven, but one has been remade into a pot ale tank) and two pairs of stills. The spirit produced at Strathisla is piped to nearby Glen Keith distillery (mothballed since 2000 but according to rumours due for re-opening before 2013) for filling or to be tankered away. A small amount is stored on site in two racked and one dunnage warehouse. Chivas Brothers also hold large warehousing, filling and blending facilities in Keith and nearby Mulben.

Pernod Ricard has only released two official bottlings of Strathisla - the *12 year old* and a *16 year old cask strength* sold at the distillery.

12 years old

Whisky Chronology
continued from page 187

1962 United Wine Traders merges with W. A Gilbey and forms United Distillers & Vintners.

1963 Ind Coope Tetley Ansell changes name to Allied Breweries.

1964 Inver House Distillers becomes a subsidiary to Publicker Industries.

1965 Invergordon Distillers is formed.

1969 Allied Breweries buys Alexander Stewart & Son.

1969 Seager Evans changes name to Long John International.

1970 Highland Distilleries Co. buys Matthew Gloag & Son Ltd.

1970 Hill Thomson merges with Glenlivet & Glen Grant Distilleries and form The Glenlivet Distilleries.

1972 International Distillers & Vintners (IDV) is bought by Watney Mann.

1972 Watney Mann is bought by Grand Metropolitan.

1973 House of Fraser buys Whyte & Mackay.

1974 Lonhro buys Whyte & Mackay.

1975 Pernod Ricard buys Campbell Distillers.

1975 Schenley sells Long John International to Whitbread & Company.

1976 Allied Brewers takes over William Teacher & Sons.

1978 Seagram buys the Glenlivet Distillers Limited.

1978 Allied Breweries buys J. Lyons.

1981 Allied Breweries changes name to Allied-Lyons.

1983 Grand Met buys International Distillers & Vintners (IDV).

1985 Scottish & Newcastle Breweries sells their whisky division to Invergordon Distillers.

1985 Guinness Group buys Bell's for £356 million.

1986 DCL sells A. & A. Crawford to Whyte & Mackay.

1986 Allied Lyons buys 51% of Hiram Walker Gooderham & Worts.

1987 Guinness buys DCL, who merges with Arthur Bell to become United Distillers, for £2,35bn.

1987 Louis Vuitton and Moët Hennessy merge into LVMH.

1988 Andrew Symington and his brother Brian found Signatory Vintage Scotch Whisky.

1987 Allied Lyons buys the remaining 49% of Hiram Walker Gooderham & Worts.

1988 Allied Distillers becomes a new subsidiary to Allied Lyons and is made up of Ballantine, Long John International, Stewarts of Dundee and William Teacher.

1988 United Distillers launches 'The Classic Malts'.

1988 Management buy-out of Inver House from Publicker Industries.

1989 Lonhro sells Whyte & Mackay to Brent Walker.

1989 Whitbread's wine & spirits division is acquired by Allied Lyons for £545 million.

1989 Management buys out Invergordon Distillers from Hawker Siddely.

1990 Fortune Brands (then called American Brands) buys Whyte & Mackay from Brent Walker for £165 million.

1990 Guinness and LVMH in 12% cross-shareholding.

1991 Allied Lyons buys Long John from Whitbread.

1993 United Distillers sells Benromach to Gordon & MacPhail.

1993 Whyte & Mackay (Fortune Brands) buys Invergordon Distillers for £382 million.

1994 Allied Lyons acquires Pedro Domecq and changes name to Allied Domecq plc.

1995 Blackadder International is founded by Robin Tucek and John Lamond.

1996 Highland Distilleries buys Macallan-Glenlivet plc.

1996 Whyte & Mackay changes name to JBB (Greater Europe).

1997 Guinness and Grand Metropolitan form Diageo. United Distillers and International Distillers & Vintners (IDV), merge and form United Distillers & Vintners (UDV).

1997 Fortune Brands transfers administration of Whyte & Mackay to Jim Beam Brands.

1997 Glenmorangie plc buys Ardbeg distillery for £7 million.

1998 Diageo sells Dewars and Bombay to Bacardi for £1 150 million.

1998 Highland Distilleries changes name to Highland Distillers Ltd.

1999 Edrington Group and William Grant & Sons buy Highland Distillers for £601 million. Grant and Edrington form 1887 Company, owned 70% by Edrington and 30% by Grant.

1999 Gordon & MacPhail introduces their 'Rare Old Series'.

2000 Allied Domecq suggests Diageo that they jointly acquire Seagram Spirits & Wine, but Diageo declines.

2001 Pernod Ricard and Diageo buy Seagram Spirits & Wine from Vivendi Universal for £5 710 million (5,7 billion) on 21st December.

2001 Pacific Spirits, owned by Great Oriole Group, buys Inver House Distillers at a price tag of £56 million.

2001 West LB bank and management buy out the Fortune Brands subsidiary JBB (Greater Europe) for £208 million in October. The new company is called Kyndal.

2001 Chivas Brothers and Campbell Distillers form Chivas Brothers.

2001 Murray McDavid buys Bruichladdich from Whyte & Mackay.

2002 Trinidad-based venture capitalists CL Financial buys Burn Stewart Distillers for £50 million.

2003 Kyndal changes name to Whyte & Mackay.

2003 Robert Tchenguiz owns 35% of Whyte & Mackay while West LB holds 21%.

2004 Glenmorangie plc buys Scotch Malt Whisky Society.

2004 Ian Bankier, formerly Burn Stewart Distillers, buys Whisky Shop retail chain for £1,5 million.

2004 Moët Hennessy (owned by Diageo and LVMH) buys Glenmorangie plc for £300 million.

2005 Pernod Ricard buys Allied Domecq.

2005 Pernod Ricard sells Bushmills to Diageo.

2006 Pernod Ricard sells Glen Grant distillery to Campari.

2007 United Spirits buys Whyte & Mackay.

2008 Glenmorangie sells Glen Moray distillery to La Martiniquaise, Pernod Ricard sells Glendronach distillery to BenRiach and Glenglassaugh distillery is sold to Sceant Group for £5m.

2010 William Grant & Sons buys the spirit and liqueur part of C&C Group (with i. a. Tullamore Dew and Carolans). Berry Bros sells Cutty Sark to Edrington who, in turn, sells Glenrothes single malt to Berry Bros.

2011 Edrington sells Tamdhu distillery to Ian Macleod Distillers.

Strathmill

Owner:
Diageo

Region/district:
Speyside

Founded: 1891
Status: Active
Capacity: 2 300 000 litres

Address: Keith, Banffshire AB55 5DQ

Tel: 01542 883000
website: www.malts.com

History:
1891 – The distillery is founded in an old mill from 1823 and is named Glenisla-Glenlivet Distillery.

1892 – The inauguration takes place in June.

1895 – The gin company W. & A. Gilbey buys the distillery for £9,500 and names it Strathmill.

1962 – W. & A. Gilbey merges with United Wine Traders (including Justerini & Brooks) and forms International Distillers & Vintners (IDV).

1968 – The number of stills is increased from two to four and purifiers are added.

1972 – IDV is bought by Watney Mann which later the same year is acquired by Grand Metropolitan.

1993 – Strathmill becomes available as a single malt for the first time since 1909 as a result of a bottling (1980) from Oddbins.

1997 – Guinness and Grand Metropolitan merge and form Diageo.

2001 – The first official bottling is a 12 year old in the Flora & Fauna series.

2010 – A Manager´s Choice single cask from 1996 is released.

Strathmill 12 year old
GS – Quite reticent on the nose, with nuts, grass and a hint of ginger. Spicy vanilla and nuts dominate the palate. The finish is drying, with peppery oak.

DR – Butterscotch and summer flowers mixed with lemon flu powder, and some powdery, talc-like notes on the nose, the palate has some apricot and peach fruits before a wave of salt and pepper and a spicy conclusion.

Once a corn mill, Strathmill was converted into a distillery in the late 1800s. Together with Strathisla it is one of two distilleries operating in Keith, although rumours has it that the nearby, mothballed Glen Keith is about to be opened again soon by the owners, Chivas Brothers. Strathmill is neatly tucked away right next to the River Isla flowing through Keith. The whisky produced is a key part of the J&B blended Scotch and very little reaches the market as single malt. J&B is currently in third place on the sales list with almost 5 million cases sold in a year. Unlike Johnnie Walker, which is enjoying stellar growth in the whisky booming Far East, J&B has to struggle in Europe with Spain being the biggest market for a long time. Sales volumes for J&B have dropped by 20% during the last decade, not least because of the troubled economy.

The distillery is equipped with a stainless steel semi-lauter mash tun, six stainless steel washbacks and two pairs of stills. Strathmill is one of a select few distilleries using a facility called purifier on the spirit stills. This device is mounted between the lyne arm and the condenser and acts as a mini-condenser, allowing the lighter alcohols to travel towards the condenser and forcing the heavier alcohols to go back into the still for another distillation. The result is a lighter and fruitier spirit. One mash (9 tonnes) will fill one washback with 44,000 litres of wort and one washback will fill the two wash stills twice. During 2011 the distillery will be operational on a 5-day week basis producing around 1.8 million litres of alcohol. The spirit is tankered away to Auchroisk for filling and some of the casks find their way back for storage in two racked and five dunnage warehouses on-site.

The only official bottling was a *12 year old* in the Flora & Fauna series until January 2010, when a new, American oak, *single cask* distilled in *1996* was released as part of the Manager's Choice series.

Flora & Fauna 12 years

Meet the Manager

ALISTAIR ABBOTT
SITE OPERATIONS MANAGER, STRATHMILL DISTILLERY

When did you start working in the whisky business and when did you start at Strathmill?

Strathmill was my first experience of the whisky business and I started in July 2009.

Had you been working in other lines of business before whisky?

Previously I worked in the brewing industry for nine years. I started as an operator in a regional brewery in Henley-upon-Thames for a year, then worked in logistics for two years, four years on high speed bottling lines and canning lines for Scottish and Newcastle and then another two years working for Anheuser Busch within brewing.

What kind of education or training do you have?

I have a brewing and distilling degree from Herriot Watt University, but have found that the best education is a combination of experience on site, learning from your colleagues, and the training supplied by Diageo, every day is a school day.

Describe your career in the whisky business.

My career within distilling to date is still relatively short with two years under my belt at Strathmill and now for the last eight months I have been responsible for Glendullan Distillery too.

What are your main tasks as a manager and what are the biggest challenges of being a distillery manager?

Maintaining the quality and consistency of the spirit we produce, true to the distillery character, is obviously a very high priority. Alongside that, a manager's main task is to ensure the safety of all the employees and visitors to site.
A lot of time is spent working with the team at site to continuously review the working environment to ensure that everybody goes home every day without harm.
Other tasks include insuring that the high standards of spirit quality and process efficiency are maintained and a big challenge for the business at the moment is the cost of energy, so we are looking at ways of minimising fuel and electricity use, for both the benefit of the environment and from a cost perspective.

What would be the worst that could go wrong in the production process?

The worst that could go wrong would be any serious harm coming to somebody on site. To have to tell a family that there has been a serious accident would be one of the most difficult things to ever have to do.

How would you describe the character of Strathmill single malt?

Light, fruity with slight oily on the nose, smooth sweet and malty on the palate with a slight spice.

What are the main features in the process at Strathmill, contributing to this character?

The main difference that sets Strathmill apart from other distilleries is the use of the purifiers on the spirit stills. This is where the vapours are cooled prior to the condenser to maximise reflux back into the still. It is critical that the temperature of the cooling water that supplies these is monitored closely to ensure that the new make spirit character is maintained.

What is your favourite expression of Strathmill and why?

It is difficult to get your hands on different expressions of Strathmill. I do enjoy the Flora and Fauna bottling 12 year old – now officially called Distillery Malts.

If it were your decision alone – what new expression of Strathmill would you like to see released?

If it were my decision alone I would like to see some more variety including limited editions or some different cask finishes.

If you had to choose a favourite dram other than Strathmill, what would that be?

My favourites at the minute are Mortlach, Oban and Talisker. I like a bit of variety.

Do you see any major changes in your profession in the next 10 years to come?

With volumes set to increase significantly in the next few years, there will be even more focus on ensuring the production targets are met whilst ensuring that the spirit quality is maintained. This means that we will be working the distilleries harder than ever before.

Do you have any special interests or hobbies that you pursue?

I enjoy taking advantage of the fact that with living in Speyside there are lots of outdoor activities right on your doorstep. I enjoy canoeing and mountain biking and a bit of hill walking.

You are also responsible for Glendullan distillery. What are the main differences between the distillation process and the character of the spirit?

Distilling processes and the new make spirit character are similar, the main aspect that sets them apart would be the use of the purifiers at Strathmill.

What did you learn from your career in the brewing industry that you are now able to use at a whisky distillery?

What I have learnt most from my experience in both industries is that quality is of the utmost importance. A high level of consistency in operation is required and your team need to be focused on ensuring that process parameters are adhered to. If this is all in place then you will produce either good beer or good spirit time after time.

Talisker

Owner:
Diageo

Region/district:
Highlands (Skye)

Founded: 1830

Status: Active (vc)

Visitor centre: 2 600 000 litres

Address: Carbost, Isle of Skye, Inverness-shire IV47 8SR

Tel: 01478 614308 (vc)

website: www.taliskerwhisky.com

History:

1830 – Hugh and Kenneth MacAskill, sons of the local doctor, found the distillery.

1848 – The brothers transfer the lease to North of Scotland Bank and Jack Westland from the bank runs the operations.

1854 – Kenneth MacAskill dies.

1857 – North of Scotland Bank sells the distillery to Donald MacLennan for £500.

1863 – MacLennan experiences difficulties in making operations viable and puts the distillery up for sale.

1865 – MacLennan, still working at the distillery, nominates John Anderson as agent in Glasgow.

1867 – Anderson & Co. from Glasgow takes over.

1879 – John Anderson is imprisoned after having sold non-existing casks of whisky.

1880 – New owners are now Alexander Grigor Allan and Roderick Kemp.

1892 – Kemp sells his share and buys Macallan Distillery instead.

1894 – The Talisker Distillery Ltd is founded.

1895 – Allan dies and Thomas Mackenzie, who has been his partner, takes over.

1898 – Talisker Distillery merges with Dailuaine-Glenlivet Distillers and Imperial Distillers to form Dailuaine-Talisker Distillers Company.

1916 – Thomas Mackenzie dies and the distillery is taken over by a consortium consisting of, among others, John Walker, John Dewar, W. P. Lowrie and Distillers Company Limited (DCL).

Five years ago it looked like the days of Talisker being the only distillery on Skye were numbered. Pràban na Linne (or as it is sometimes called, Gaelic Whiskies) announced that they had plans to build a distillery near Torabhaig. Nothing much has happened since and at the end of December 2010, the founder and owner of the company, Sir Iain Noble passed away at the age of 75, which could mean that the plans have now been shelved indefinitely.

With the exception of the rapidly increasing sales figures for the Singleton brand, there is no doubt that Diageo's biggest malt whisky success over the last years is Talisker. An increase of 120% to 110,000 cases in ten years and the ever-growing number of visitors speak for themselves. Although isolated and an hour's drive after passing the bridge from the mainland, it is Diageo's most visited distillery.

The malt comes from Glen Ord maltings peated at 18-20 ppm which gives a phenol content of 5-7 ppm in the new make. The distillery is equipped with a stainless steel lauter mash tun with a capacity of 8 tonnes, eight washbacks (two of which were installed in 2008 for capacity increase) and five stills – two wash stills and three spirit stills, all of them connected to wooden wormtubs. The odd number of stills is a leftover from the time when Talisker was triple distilled, a practice which stopped in 1928. The wash stills are equipped with a special type of purifiers, using the colder outside air and a u-bend in the lyne arm, instead of a water jacket. The purifiers increase the reflux during distillation. The fermentation time is quite long (65-75 hours) and the middle cut from the spirit still is collected between 76% and 65% which gives a medium peated spirit. A large part of the phenol compounds occur late in the middle cut and distilleries known for heavily peated malts won't cut until much later (55-60%). Only a small part of the produce (mostly refill bourbon) is matured on the island while the rest is tankered and taken to the mainland for storage. The distillery is currently running at full capacity.

Talisker's core range consists of 10 year old, 18 year old, a Distiller's Edition with an Amoroso sherry finish and Talisker 57° North. A 12 year old cask strength is sold at the distillery only. Limited releases in autumn 2011 were new editions of 25 and 30 year old and a very rare 34 year old. Only 50 bottles of the last one were allocated to the UK market.

History (continued):

1928 – The distillery abandons triple distillation.

1930 – Administration of the distillery is transferred to Scottish Malt Distillers (SMD).

1960 – On 22nd November the distillery catches fire and substantial damage occurs.

1962 – The distillery reopens after the fire with five new identical copies of the destroyed stills.

1972 – Malting ceases and malt is now purchased from Glen Ord Central Maltings.

1988 – United Distillers introduce Classic Malts, Talisker 10 years included. A visitor centre is opened.

1998 – A new stainless steel/copper mash tun and five new worm tubs are installed. Talisker is launched as a Distillers Edition with an amoroso sherry finish.

2004 – Two new bottlings appear, an 18 year old and a 25 year old.

2005 – To celebrate the 175th birthday of the distillery, Talisker 175th Anniversary is released. The third edition of the 25 year old cask strength is released.

2006 – A 30 year old and the fourth edition of the 25 year old are released.

2007 – The second edition of the 30 year old and the fifth edition of the 25 year old are released.

2008 – Talisker 57º North, sixth edition of the 25 year old and third edition of the 30 year old are launched.

2009 – New editions of the 25 and 30 year old are released.

2010 – A 1994 Manager´s Choice single cask and a new edition of the 30 year old are released.

2011 – Three limited releases - 25, 30 and 34 year old.

Talisker 10 year old
GS – Quite dense and smoky on the nose, with smoked fish, bladderwrack, sweet fruit and peat. Full-bodied and peaty in the mouthy; complex, with ginger, ozone, dark chocolate, black pepper and a kick of chilli in the long, smoky tail.

DR – Grilled oily fish in lemon oil, on the nose, dry salt and pepper on the palate, peat and pepper in a tastebud treat of a finish.

57º North   *25 years old 7th edition*   *30 years old 5th edition*

10 years old   *18 years old*   *Distiller´s Edition 1992*

Tamnavulin

Owner:
Whyte & Mackay
(United Spirits)

Region/district:
Speyside

Founded: 1966
Status: Active
Capacity: 4 000 000 litres

Address: Tomnavoulin, Ballindalloch,
Banffshire AB3 9JA

Tel: 01807 590285
website: -

History:
1966 – Tamnavulin-Glenlivet Distillery Company, a subsidiary of Invergordon Distillers Ltd, founds Tamnavulin.

1993 – Whyte & Mackay buys Invergordon Distillers.

1995 – The distillery closes in May.

1996 – Whyte & Mackay changes name to JBB (Greater Europe).

2000 – Distillation takes place for six weeks.

2001 – Company management buy out operations for £208 million and rename the company Kyndal.

2003 – Kyndal changes name to Whyte & Mackay.

2007 – United Spirits buys Whyte & Mackay. Tamnavulin is opened again in July after having been mothballed for 12 years.

Tamnavulin 12 year old

GS – Delicate and floral on the nose, with light malt and fruit gums. Light to medium bodied, fresh, malty and spicy on the palate, with a whiff of background smoke. The finish is medium in length, with lingering spice, smoke, and notes of caramel.

DR – Wet hay, celery and cucumber on the nose and a delightful exotic fruit and citrus taste and a satisfying and pleasant finish.

The pace of production at Tamnavulin distillery has increased annually since its re-opening in 2007. The whisky from the distillery is badly needed by the owners, Whyte & Mackay, for their blends especially now that the brand is being launched throughout India. They also don't possess any great volumes of mature Tamnavulin malt to rely on. The first owners, Invergordon Distillers, never produced any greater amounts and then it was mothballed for 12 years with the exception of 2000 when it was temporarily opened and 400,000 litres were produced. In 2011, for the first time since re-opening, the distillery will be running at full production, producing 23 mashes per week and 4 million litres in the year.

The distillery is equipped with a full lauter mash tun with 10.5 tonnes capacity, eight washbacks (four of them made of stainless steel and the rest of Corten steel) with a maturation time of 48 hours and three pairs of stills. The wash stills were all replaced in summer 2008, and in 2010 three new spirit stills were fitted. Two racked warehouses (10 casks high) on site have a capacity of 34,250 casks with the oldest ones dating back to 1967, but several of the caks are from other distilleries. Two hundred casks are filled every week on site, while the rest of the production is tankered to Invergordon for filling.

Tamnavulin is situated in a very scenic part of the Highlands with Glenlivet, Tomintoul and Braeval as its closest neighbours. There used to be a visitor centre run by the local community, but it closed at the end of the nineties.

The only standard release of Tamnavulin, for quite some time now, has been a *12 year old*. A number of aged *Stillman's Dram* have also been launched, the most recent being a *30 year old*.

12 years old

Teaninich

Owner:
Diageo

Region/district:
Northern Highlands

Founded: **Status:** **Capacity:**
1817 Active 4 400 000 litres

Address: Alness, Ross-shire IV17 0XB

Tel: **website:**
01349 885001 www.malts.com

History:

1817 – Captain Hugh Monro, owner of the estate Teaninich, founds the distillery.

1831 – Captain Munro sells the estate to his younger brother John.

1850 – John Munro, who spends most of his time in India, leases Teaninich to the infamous Robert Pattison from Leith.

1869 – John McGilchrist Ross takes over the licence.

1895 – Munro & Cameron takes over the licence.

1898 – Munro & Cameron buys the distillery.

1904 – Robert Innes Cameron becomes sole owner of Teaninich.

1932 – Robert Innes Cameron dies.

1933 – The estate of Robert Innes Cameron sells the distillery to Distillers Company Limited.

1970 – A new distillation unit with six stills is commissioned and becomes known as the A side.

1975 – A dark grains plant is built.

1984 – The B side of the distillery is mothballed.

1985 – The A side is also mothballed.

1991 – The A side is in production again.

1992 – United Distillers launches a 10 year old Teaninich in the Flora & Fauna series.

1999 – The B side is decommissioned.

2000 – A mash filter is installed.

2009 – Teaninich 1996, a single cask in the new Manager´s Choice range is released.

Teaninich 10 year old

GS – The nose is initially fresh and grassy, quite light, with vanilla and hints of tinned pineapple. Mediumbodied, smooth, slightly oily, with cereal and spice in the mouth. Nutty and slowly drying in the finish, with pepper and a suggestion of cocoa powder notes.

DR – All about the barley this one, with clean, sweet ginger barley on the nose, and a clean and crealy palate with some orange and other citrus notes. Pleasant, clean and impressive with a wave of spices late on.

There are three whisky distilleries in the vicinity of the town of Alness on The Cromarty Firth. Two of them belong to Whyte & Mackay – Dalmore, producer of premium single malts and Invergordon, a grain distillery producing 36 million litres of alcohol per year. The third distillery, Teaninich, lies in an industrial estate on the outskirts of the town and has a fairly unknown existence. This has not always been the case though. At one time, back in the seventies, Teaninich was one of the largest distilleries in Scotland with a capacity of 6 million litres.

Two elements in the production process of Teaninich differ from that of other distilleries. The malt is ground into a very fine flour without husks in an Asnong hammer mill. Once the grist has been mixed with water, the mash passes through a Meura 2001 mash filter and the wort is collected. Water is added a second time in the filter and a second run of mash is obtained. The procedure is repeated three times until a washback is filled. Using a mash filter is common practice at many beer breweries, but Teaninich is the only Scottish distillery using the technique. According to the Site Operations Manager, Willie MacDougall, the advantages with the mash filter is that you can deal with a wide range of malt specifications and you get very clear worts. The mash filter was installed in 2000.

Besides the mash filter the distillery is equipped with 10 washbacks – eight made of larch and two of stainless steel – and six stills. The fermentation time in the washbacks is 75 hours. There are no warehouses on site; instead 4-5 tankers leave the distillery each week for filling elsewhere. Twenty mashes are done per week, corresponding to 4.4 million litres which is more or less at capacity. Teaninich is mainly produced to be a component of Johnnie Walker blended whiskies. The only official bottling used to be a *10 year old* in the Flora & Fauna series until autumn of 2009, when a *Teaninich 1996* single cask was released in the new range Manager´s Choice.

Flora & Fauna 10 years old

Tobermory

Owner:
Burn Stewart Distillers
(C L Financial)

Region/district:
Highland (Mull)

Founded: **Status:**   **Capacity:**
1798   Active (vc)   1 000 000 litres

Address: Tobermory, Isle of Mull,
Argyllshire PA75 6NR

Tel: **website:**
01688 302647   www.burnstewartdistillers.com

History:
1798 – John Sinclair founds the distillery.

1837 – The distillery closes.

1878 – The distillery reopens.

1890 – John Hopkins & Company buys the
distillery.

1916 – Distillers Company Limited (DCL) takes
over John Hopkins & Company.

1930 – The distillery closes.

1972 – A shipping company in Liverpool and
the sherrymaker Domecq buy the buildings
and embark on refurbishment. When work is
completed it is named Ledaig Distillery Ltd.

1975 – Ledaig Distillery Ltd files for bankruptcy
and the distillery closes again.

1979 – The estate agent Kirkleavington
Property buys the distillery, forms a new
company, Tobermory Distillers Ltd and starts
production.

1982 – No production. Some of the buildings
are converted into flats and some are rented
to a dairy company for cheese storage.

1989 – Production resumes.

1993 – Burn Stewart Distillers buys Tobermory
for £600,000 and pays an additional £200,000
for the whisky supply.

2002 – Trinidad-based venture capitalists CL
Financial buys Burn Stewart Distillers for £50m.

2005 – A 32 year old from 1972 is launched.

2007 – A Ledaig 10 year old is released.

2008 – A limited edition Tobermory 15 year
old is released.

Tobermory 10 year old

GS – Fresh and nutty on the nose, with citrus
fruit and brittle toffee. A whiff of peat.
Medium-bodied, quite dry on the palate
with delicate peat, malt and nuts. The finish
is medium to long, with a hint of mint and a
slight citric tang.

DR – Barley and crystal ginger on the nose,
but the palate carries this, with a nice oily
mouth feel, and creamed fruits giving way to
a sharper spicier conclusion.

Ledaig 10 year old

GS – The nose is profoundly peaty, sweet and
full, with notes of butter and smoked fish.
Bold, yet sweet on the palate, with iodine,
soft peat and heather. Developing spices. The
finish is medium to long, with pepper, ginger,
liquorice and peat.

DR – Peat and smoke on the nose, more fruity
and malty on the palate but with a definite
tarry heart, and then gristly smoke in the
finish.

The only distillery on the island of Mull was working under
the name Tobermory from when it was built until its
closure in 1930. When it re-opened in 1972, the name
was changed to Ledaig and then again back to Tobermory when Burn Stewart took over in 1993. Single malt is
released under both names with Ledaig being reserved for
the peated versions with a phenol content of 30-40ppm.
Peat was used in the old days but was re-introuced in 1996
when Master Blender, Ian Macmillan, decided to recreate
the old style of Tobermory single malt. The first intentions
were to use it only for blending but, after a few years, they
decided to release it as a single malt as well and the first
Ledaig 10 year old was launched in 2007.

The distillery is equipped with a traditional cast iron mash
tun, four wooden washbacks and two pairs of stills with
unusual S-shaped lyne arms to increase the reflux. Storage
space is small and most produce is sent
to Deanston distillery for maturation.
However, in 2007 a part of the old tun
room was converted into a small warehouse. During 2011 there will be five to
six mashes per week resulting in almost
700,000 litres of alcohol. There is a 50/50
split in total production between peated
Ledaig and unpeated Tobermory and to
ensure there is no cross contamination
of distillates, additional feints vessels have been installed. Mashing
and fermentation of Ledaig is
similar to Tobermory's, but the
spirit run has a lower cut off point
(59% compared to Tobermory's
63%) in order to collect the peaty
flavours.

The core range from Tobermory
distillery is 10 and 15 year old
Tobermory and 10 year old
Ledaig – all of them unchillfiltered and bottled at 46,3%.
Previously there have been plenty
of limited releases of Ledaig and
also a 32 year old Tobermory
from 2005. The next limited
releases will probably be 40 year
olds of both Tobermory and
Ledaig, due for release in 2012.

10 years old

Tomatin

Owner: **Region/district:**
Tomatin Distillery Co   Highland
(Takara Shuzo Co. Ltd., Kokubu & Co., The
Marubeni Corporation)

Founded: **Status:**   **Capacity:**
1897   Active (vc)   5 000 000 litres

Address: Tomatin, Inverness-shire IV13 7YT

Tel: **website:**
01463 248144 (vc)   www.tomatin.com

History:
1897 – The Inverness businessmen behind Tomatin Spey Distillery Company found Tomatin.

1906 – Production ceases.

1909 – Production resumes through Tomatin Distillers Co. Ltd.

1956 – Stills are increased from two to four.

1958 – Another two stills are added.

1961 – The six stills are increased to ten.

1964 – One more still is installed.

1974 – The stills now total 23 and the maltings closes.

1985 – The distillery company goes into liquidation.

1986 – Two long-time customers, Takara Shuzo Co. and Okara & Co., buy Tomatin through Tomatin Distillery Co. Tomatin thus becomes the first distillery to be acquired by Japanese interests.

1997 – Tomatin Distillery Co buys J. W. Hardie and the brand Antiquary.

1998 – Okura & Co, owners of 20% of Tomatin Distillery, is liquidated and Marubeni buys out part of their shareholding.

2004 – Tomatin 12 years is launched.

2005 – A 25 year old and a 1973 Vintage are released.

2006 – An 18 year old and a 1962 Vintage are launched.

2008 – A 30 and a 40 year old as well as several vintages from 1975 and 1995 are released.

2009 – A 15 year old, a 21 year old and four single casks (1973, 1982, 1997 and 1999) are released.

2010 – The first peated release - a 4 year old exclusive for Japan.

2011 – A 30 year old and Tomatin Decades are released.

Tomatin 12 year old

GS – Barley, spice, buttery oak and a floral note on the nose. Sweet and medium-bodied, with toffee apples, spice and herbs in the mouth. Medium-length in the finish, with sweet fruitiness.

DR – Strawberry cream and raspberry ripple ice cream and pecan on the nose, delicate zesty barley on the palate, with a sweet citrus and powdery spice mix contributing to a very welcoming finish. More-ish.

Sales of Tomatin single malts is increasing steadily while at the same time the range is expanding. In 2010, 17,000 cases were sold with USA taking almost 40% of the total and with Sweden and Japan as the other top markets. At the moment the owners are expanding into new markets such as Eastern Europe and Africa, but have also started to show an interest in the Far East. The distillery got a new manager in August 2011 when Graham Eunson, who had been managing Glenglassaugh for three years, joined the team. The previous manager, Douglas Campbell, continues his work as brand ambassador and master distiller.

Tomatin was Scotland's largest distillery from 1975-1980 with a production of 12 million litres of alcohol and equipped with no less than 23 stills. Today, the capacity is 5 million litres (actual production in 2011 is 1,7 million) as 11 of the original stills were dismantled in 2002.

The distillery is equipped with two stainless steel mash tuns (one is not being used), 12 stainless steel washbacks and six pairs of stills. There are 12 racked and two dunnage warehouses (where whisky destined to be bottled as single malts are maturing) holding 170,000 casks. The distillery also has a cooperage with two coopers working. Until now, the production at Tomatin has been very much a hands-on experience, but during 2010 the stillhouse was completely re-wired and computerised.

Normally the whisky produced by Tomatin is unpeated, but since 2005 a peated spirit (15ppm) has been produced during the last week of every year.

The core range of single malts consists of *12, 15, 18* and *30 year old*. The last one recently replaced the 25 year old. Limited editions in 2009/2010 included a *21 year old*, a *1999 single cask* with a Tempranillo finish, as well as *single casks from 1973, 1982* and *1997*. In 2011, *Tomatin Decades* was released to celebrate Douglas Campbell's 50th year at Tomatin and the whisky contains single malt from each decade Douglas has worked at the distillery.

12 years old

Tomintoul

Owner:		Region/district:
Angus Dundee Distillers		Speyside

Founded:	Status:	Capacity:
1964	Active	3 300 000 litres

Address: Ballindalloch, Banffshire AB37 9AQ

Tel: 01807 590274 **website:** www.tomintouldistillery.co.uk

History:

1964 –The distillery is founded by Tomintoul Distillery Ltd, which is owned by Hay & MacLeod & Co. and W. & S. Strong & Co.

1965 – On stream in July.

1973 – Scottish & Universal Investment Trust, owned by the Fraser family, buys the distillery. It buys Whyte & Mackay the same year and transfers Tomintoul to that company.

1974 – The two stills are increased to four and Tomintoul 12 years is launched.

1978 – Lonhro buys Scottish & Universal Investment Trust.

1989 – Lonhro sells Whyte & Mackay to Brent Walker.

1990 – American Brands buys Whyte & Mackay.

1996 – Whyte & Mackay changes name to JBB (Greater Europe).

2000 – Angus Dundee plc buys Tomintoul.

2002 – Tomintoul 10 year is launched as the first bottling after the change of ownership.

2003 – Tomintoul 16 years is launched.

2004 – Tomintoul 27 years is launched.

2005 – A young, peated version called Old Ballantruan is launched.

2008 – 1976 Vintage and Peaty Tang are released.

2009 – A 14 year old and a 33 year old are released.

2010 – A 12 year old Port wood finish is released.

2011 – A 21 year old, a 10 year old Ballantruan and Vintage 1966 are released.

Tomintoul 10 year old

GS – A light, fresh and fruity nose, with ripe peaches and pineapple cheesecake, delicate spice and background malt. Medium-bodied, fruity and fudgy on the palate. The finish offers wine gums, mild, gently spiced oak, malt and a suggestion of smoke.

DR – Toffee and fruit on the nose then an easy, pleasant rounded and sweet barley taste before a gently fading finish.

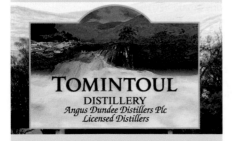

Founded by Terry Hillman more than 50 years ago, Angus Dundee Distillers is today run by his two children, Tania and Aaron, among others. The core of the business is to produce and sell blended Scotch and without having made too much of a fuss, they are now responsible for 5% of all Scotch that is exported. Amongst their brands, Angus Dundee, Scottish Royal, Big Ben, Pipers Clan and Parkers should be mentioned. Their UK offices are in Glasgow and London and since 2006 they also have an operation in Shanghai for the important Chinese market. In the year 2000 they bought Tomintoul distillery and three years later Glencadam.

Tomintoul distillery lies in beautiful surroundings a few miles southeast of Glenlivet. The equipment consists of one mash tun and six washbacks, all made of stainless steel, and two pairs of stills heated by steam kettles. There are currently 15 mashes per week, which means that capacity is used to the full, and the six racked warehouses have a storage capacity of 116,000 casks. The malt used for mashing is lightly peated, but for three weeks this year, heavily peated (55 ppm) malt will be used for the peated range. A blend centre was built in 2003 with ten blending vats varying in size from 10,000 litres to 100,000 litres.

A major part of the production is used in different blended whiskies, but the last five years have seen the range of single malts expand considerably. The core range consists of *10 year old*, *14 year old* (released in 2009), *16 year old* and *Old Ballantruan*, a peaty expression. In spring 2011, the core range was further complimented with a *21 year old*. Limited expressions, expected to be released towards the end of 2011, are a *10 year old Ballantruan* and a *Vintage 1966* – the oldest bottling from the distillery so far. Recent limited editions have included a *12 year old portwood finish*, the *1976 Vintage*, a *12 year old Oloroso finish* and *Peaty Tang*, a vatting of 4-5 year old peated Tomintoul and 8 year old unpeated Tomintoul.

21 years old

Tormore

Owner:
Chivas Brothers
(Pernod Ricard)

Region/district:
Speyside

Founded:
1958

Status:
Active

Capacity:
4 100 000 litres

Address: Tormore, Advie, Grantown-on-Spey, Morayshire PH26 3LR

Tel:
01807 510244

website:
-

History:
1958 – Schenley International, owners of Long John, founds the distillery.

1960 – The distillery is ready for production.

1972 – The number of stills is increased from four to eight.

1975 – Schenley sells Long John and its distilleries (including Tormore) to Whitbread.

1989 – Allied Lyons (to become Allied Domecq) buys the spirits division of Whitbread.

1991 – Allied Distillers introduce Caledonian Malts where Miltonduff, Glendronach and Laphroaig are represented besides Tormore. Tormore is later replaced by Scapa.

2004 – Tormore 12 year old is launched as an official bottling.

2005 – Chivas Brothers (Pernod Ricard) becomes new owners through the acquisition of Allied Domecq.

A few years ago, the owners of Tormore registered a website for the brand. Apparently plans had been made to pull the distillery out of its anonymity but nothing came of it. The website has been discontinued and the distillery is back to doing what it was originally constructed for – producing malt whisky for blends. There is something very contradictory about Tormore; a grand building sitting next to the traffic of the A95 in the middle of Speyside and, yet, almost completely unknown as a single malt brand. When it was planned in the early 1950s, it was the owners (Schenley Industries) decision that it should become a showpiece distillery and the famous architect, Sir Albert Richardson, was called in and no expenses were saved. The roof of the building (made of copper) alone cost £40,000 (today's value is £650,000), whilst the entire building cost £600,000 (more than £10 million today).

The equipment at Tormore is made up of one stainless steel lauter mash tun from Newmill Ironworks in Elgin with a charge of 10 tonnes and eight stainless steel washbacks with 50 hours of fermentation serving four pairs of stills. All the stills are fitted with purifiers resulting in a lighter spirit. From the very beginning, it was decided that the character of Tormore malt should be quite light which suited both the American taste at that time and also made it suitable as a packer in various blends. The spirit is tankered away to Keith Bonds or another Chivas Bros facility for filling in ex-bourbon casks. Part of it returns to the distillery for maturation in a combination of six palletised and racked warehouses.

There is only one official bottling, a *12 year old* introduced in 2004/5. A 15 year old was released several years ago but has been difficult to obtain lately.

Tormore 12 year old

GS – Caramel on the nose, with hints of lemon and mint, mildly spicy, gentle and enticing. Good weight of body, and a creamy, honeyed mouth feel. Fudge and mixed spices, notably ginger, dry in the increasingly complex finish.

DR – A perfumey and delicate smell on the nose and soft but pleasant palate with macaroni cake and toasted almond in the mix, and a soft fading finish.

12 years old

Tullibardine

Owner:
Tullibardine Distillery Ltd

Region/district:
Highlands

Founded: 1949

Status: Active (vc)

Capacity: 2 700 000 litres

Address: Blackford, Perthshire PH4 1QG

Tel: 01764 682252

website: www.tullibardine.com

History:

1949 – The architect William Delmé-Evans founds the distillery.

1953 – The distillery is sold to Brodie Hepburn.

1971 – Invergordon Distillers buys Brodie Hepburn Ltd.

1973 – The number of stills increases to four.

1993 – Whyte & Mackay (owned by Fortune Brands) buys Invergordon Distillers.

1994 – Tullibardine is mothballed.

1996 – Whyte & Mackay changes name to JBB (Greater Europe).

2001 – JBB (Greater Europe) is bought out from Fortune Brands by management and changes name to Kyndal (Whyte & Mackay from 2003).

2003 – A consortium including Michael Beamish buys Tullibardine in June for £1.1 million. The distillery is in production again by December. The first official bottling from the new owner is a 10 year old from 1993.

2004 – Three new vintage malts, from 1964, 1973 and 1988 respectively, are launched.

2005 – Three wood finishes from 1993, Port, Moscatel and Marsala, are launched together with a 1986 John Black selection.

2006 – Vintage 1966, Sherry Wood 1993 and a new John Black selection are launched.

2007 – Five different wood finishes are released as well as a couple of single cask vintages.

2008 – A Vintage 1968 40 year old is released.

2009 – Aged Oak is released.

2011 – Three vintages (1962, 1964 and 1976) and a wood finish are released.

Tullibardine Aged Oak

GS – The nose exhibits barley, light citrus fruits, pear drops, marzipan and cocoa. Oily in the mouth, slightly earthy, with Brazil nuts and developing vanilla and lemon on the palate. The finish is drying and slightly woody, with lingering spices.

DR – Syrupy fruit and honey-filled lemon lozenges on the nose, a light and creamy ginger barley core on the palate, with some wood. Oak and fruit dominate a medium finish.

A couple of years ago it was reported that Tullibardine distillery was up for sale and a pricetag of £15m was mentioned. Since then, the company has presented its biggest profit ever (£515,000 for the year ending 31 May 2010) and more exciting bottlings have been released so it looks like the current owners are quite happy with the way things are at the moment. The distillery is situated in the village of Blackford on the A9 between Perth and Stirling, with a large commercial outlet next door. Together they attract no less than 130,000 visitors every year. The equipment consists of a stainless steel mash tun, nine stainless steel washbacks and two pairs of stills. In 2011 the owners expect to run at full capacity, which means 24 mashes per week resulting in 2,7 million litres of alcohol in the year.

By the end of 2011 all single malts (except single casks) will be bottled at 46% and un-chillfiltered. Since the change of ownership in 2003, caramel has never been used for colouring the whisky and they have also increased the amount of first fill casks being used to 90%.

During the first couple of years, the core range from Tullibardine was a little tricky to identify. The range has been refined since last year and, for the first time, the owners could release a bottling containing whisky distilled after the take-over – Aged Oak. The first year, Aged Oak was a mix of young spirit with a 10% addition of whisky distilled in 1992, but now it consists of whisky from 2004 and 2005. Apart from *Aged Oak*, the current range consists of *vintages from 1988 and 1993*, as well as five different *cask finishes* (sherry, port, rum, banyuls and sauternes with the latter being re-introduced in late 2011). The cask finishes are all non-aged. Recent limited releases include *1965* and *1992 vintages* from late 2010 and *1962, 1964* and *1976* launched in summer 2011, together with a *1992 wood finish from Chateau Lafite casks*. The oldest whisky in the warehouse (one quarter cask from 1952) will be bottled in 2012 as a 60 year old to celebrate the Coronation of the Queen.

Aged Oak

The really new ones!

Daftmill

Owner:	Region/district:	Founded:
Cuthbert family	Lowlands	2005
Status:	Capacity:	website:
Active	c 65 000 litres	www.daftmill.com
Address:		Tel:
By Cupar, Fife KY15 5RF		01337 830303

Permission was granted in 2003 for a steading at Daftmill Farmhouse in Fife, dating back to 1655, to be converted into a distillery. Contrary to most other new distilleries selling shares in their enterprise, Hazel and Francis Cuthbert, together with Francis' brother Ian, have funded the entire operation themselves. The first distillation was on 16th December 2005 and around 20,000 litres are produced in a year.

It is run as a typical farmhouse distillery. The barley, which recently changed from Optic to Publican, is grown on the farm and they also supply other distilleries, such as Macallan to mention but one. The malting is done without peat at Crisp's in Alloa. The equipment consists of a one tonne semi-lauter mash tun with a copper dome, two stainless steel washbacks with a 90 hour fermentation and one pair of stills with slightly ascending lyne arms. The wash still has a capacity of 3,000

litres and the spirit still 1,600 litres. The Cuthbert's aim is to do a light, Lowland style whisky similar to Rosebank. In order to achieve this they have very short foreshots (7 minutes) and the spirit run starts at 78% to capture all of the fruity esters and already comes off at 73%. The spirit is filled mainly into ex-bourbon casks but there are also a few sherry butts in the two dunnage warehouses.

It could have been possible to launch a 3 year old whisky already in December 2008, but Francis Cuthbert himself says that the first release is still a good few years away.

Abhainn Dearg

Owner:	Region/district:	
Mark Tayburn	Islands (Isle of Lewis)	
Founded:	Status:	Capacity:
2008	Active	c 20 000 litres
Address:		
Carnish, Isle of Lewis, Outer Hebrides HS2 9EX		
Tel:	website:	
01851 672429	www.abhainndearg.co.uk	

When Kilchoman Distillery opened on Islay in 2005 it became the westernmost distillery in Scotland. This did not last for long though, three years later, in September 2008, spirit flowed from a newly constructed distillery in Uig on the island of Lewis in the Outer Hebrides. The Gaelic name of this distillery is Abhainn Dearg which means Red River, and the founder and owner is Mark "Marko" Tayburn who was born and raised on the island. Very little was known about Abhain Dearg until it was suddenly ready and producing.

Part of the distillery was converted from an old fish farm while some of the buildings are new. There are two 500 kg mash tuns made of stainless steel and two 7,500 litre washbacks made of Douglas fir with a fermentation time of 4 days. The two stills are modelled after an old, illicit still which is now on display at the distillery. The wash still has a capacity of 2,112 litres and the spirit still 2,057 litres. Both have very long necks and steeply

descending lye pipes leading out into two wooden worm tubs. To start with Marko is using ex-bourbon barrels for maturation but is planning for ex-sherry butts as well. Some 50 tonnes of malted barley is imported while 5 tonnes is grown locally and slightly peated. This year over ten acres of the Golden Promise variety were planted. In 2010, 10,000 litres of spirit was distilled.

The first limited release, in October 2011, was a 3 year old unpeated whisky. However, already in 2010, an 18 months old spirit was bottled at 65% .

Roseisle

Owner:	Region/district:	
Diageo	Highlands	
Founded:	Status:	Capacity:
2009	Active	12 500 000 litres
Address:		Tel:
Roseisle, Morayshire IV30 5YP		01343 832100

The planning for a new mega distillery at Roseisle, a few miles west of Elgin, commenced in early 2006, and in October 2007 it was approved by Moray Council. The first test run from one pair of stills was in February 2009 and from August that year it was more or less in full production. The distillery is located on the same site as the already existing Roseisle maltings.

Due to the large capacity, the distillery has three malt bins each holding 115 tonnes of malted barley. The distillery is equipped with two stainless steel mash tuns with 13 tonnes capacity each. There are 14 huge (116,000 litres) stainless steel washbacks and two full mashes feed one washback which feeds all seven wash stills. There is a total of 14 stills with the wash stills being heated by external heat exchangers while the spirit stills are heated using steam coils. The spirit vapours are cooled through copper condensers but on three spirit stills and three wash stills there are also stainless steel condensers attached, that you an switch to for a more sulphury spirit. All stills are equipped with flanges in four places for easier maintenance. The stills were manufactured by Diageo´s own coppersmiths at Abercrombies, Alloa. The whole distillery can work with just two

operators but in spite of hi tech and computers, one operator opens up the man doors on the stills after each run, in order for the copper to rejuvenate for 30 minutes. At the moment they are doing 42 mashes per week which means 10 million litres of alcohol, but there is a possibility of increasing it to 12.5 million litres.

The total cost for the distillery was £40m and how to use the hot water in an efficient way was very much a focal point from the beginning. For example, Roseisle is connected by means of two long pipes with Burghead maltings, 3 km north of the distillery. Hot water is pumped from Roseisle and then used in the seven kilns at Burghead and cold water is then pumped back to Roseisle. The pot ale from the distillation will be piped into anaerobic fermenters to be transformed into biogas and the dried solids will act as a biomass fuel source. The biomass burner on the site, producing steam for the distillery, covers 72% of the total requirement. Furthermore, green technology has reduced the emission of carbon dioxide to only 15% of an ordinary, same-sized distillery. At the moment they are producing two styles of spirit at Roseisle – heavy Speyside and light Speyside. So far no peated spirit has been distilled. For the heavy style a fermentation time of 50-60 hours is used and for the lighter style, 75 hours. Twelve road tankers per week transport the spirit to Cambus for filling and maturation.

Ailsa Bay

Owner:	Region/district:
William Grant & Sons	Lowlands

Founded:	Status:	Capacity:
2007	Active	6 250 000 litres

Address:	Tel:
Girvan, Ayrshire KA26 9PT	01465 713091

It was not haphazardly that William Grant constructed its new, large malt distillery at Girvan near Ayr on Scotland's west coast. Girvan Distillery, one of seven Scottish grain distilleries with a capacity of 75 million litres, was already located there and the site also holds a giant warehousing (39 warehouses to be exact) and blending complex. It was the perfect place bearing in mind that the produce from Ailsa Bay is destined for blended whisky. There has been malt whisky distillation at Girvan before by the much smaller Ladyburn Distillery (from 1968 to 1975).

It only took nine months to build the distillery which was commissioned in September 2007. It is equipped with a 12.5 tonne full lauter mash tun and 12 washbacks made of stainless steel. Each washback will hold 50,000 litres and fermentation time is between 72 and 78 hours. There are eight stills, made according to the same standards as Balvenie's, with one pair having stainless steel condensers instead of copper. That way, they have the possibility of making batches of a more sulphury spirit if desired. A unique feature is the octangular spirit safe which sits between the two rows of stills. Each side corresponds to one specific still. Another feature is the preheater for the wash. This is quite common in Cognac where wine heaters let steam pass through the wine tank for the next distillation in order to save heat and speed up the distillation. By using this technique at Ailsa Bay, the wash enters the still preheated at 60° C. To increase efficiency and to get more alcohol, high gravity distillation is used. The wash stills are heated using external heat exchangers but they also have interior steam coils. The spirit stills are heated by steam coils. The distillery is currently working at full capacity which means 25 mashes per week and 6.25 million litres of alcohol in the year.

Four different types of spirit are produced; one lighter and sweeter, one heavier and two peated with the peatiest having a malt specification of 50ppm. A majority of the casks (60-70%) used for maturation, are refill bourbon casks and the rest is made up of first fill bourbon and sherry casks.

Photo: © Erkin Tuzmuhamedov

Closed Distilleries

Port Ellen Distillery

To a whisky enthusiast, the closing of a distillery is always a sad thing. Perhaps not as dramatic as the extinction of wildlife species but the whisky industry needs its biodiversity just as nature does. As a whisky drinker you don´t want to end up seeing the same handful of "species" when you roam the shelves but you want to experience that tingling feeling of excitement when you twitch your first record of an almost extinct Glenury or Banff.

One big difference to nature is that when the distillery is gone, it does not necessarily mean that the whisky is gone. Some of the 29 distilleries on the following pages have been closed (or even demolished) for nearly thirty years but new bottlings keep popping up all the same.

However, for some of them time is running out as there will soon be no more whisky left in stock to bottle. And even if there was, the quality in some cases would be below par, to say the least, due to the prolonged time in oak wood. So if you happen to come across some of these whiskies (and you have the money because they seldom come cheap), grab the chance because "they are the last of the Mohicans".

And if you wish to be able to spend money on other things in life as well, visit one of the many whisky shows or attend a tasting because once in a blue moon the rarest of the rare will end up there and you´ll be able to get a small dram of liquid history. Another way would be to visit *www.masterofmalt.com*, an excellent whisky shop on the internet which came up with the brilliant idea some time ago to sell small 3 cl samples of many of their whiskies. Last time I had a look you could order for example Brora, Imperial, Glenisla and Linlithgow.

The distilleries on the following pages is not a homogeneous group though. Whereas most of them are closed and stripped of the equipment (and some even demolished without a trace of its former glory), there are a few that we label with the term mothballed, i. e. most of the equipment is still there with the possibility of resuming production. One obvious example of this is, of course, Tamdhu – mothballed by Edrington in 2009 and bought by Ian Macleod Distillers in summer 2011. The new owners will start distilling again in 2012 which will move the distillery back to the section of the living distilleries in next year´s Malt Whisky Yearbook.

There are only two more distilleries that stand a chance of coming back to life – Glen Keith and Imperial. Chances are slim for the latter. Some of the equipment is still there but the owners, Chivas Bros, have shown no signs of starting up the production and the only chance would probably be if a buyer turned up, in similar with Glenglassaugh – closed for 22 years only to be re-surrected under new regime in 2008. Glen Keith, on the other hand, may well see the stills running again in the near future. Rumour has it that Chivas Bros are looking to re-start production there within the next year or so.

Brora

Owner:		Region/district:
Diageo		Northern Highlands
Founded:	Status:	Capacity:
1819	Closed	

History:

1819 – The Marquis of Stafford, 1st Duke of Sutherland, founds the distillery as Clynelish Distillery.

1827 – The first licensed distiller, James Harper, files for bankruptcy and John Matheson takes over.

1828 – James Harper is back as licensee.

1834 – Andrew Ross takes over the license.

1846 – George Lawson & Sons takes over.

1896 – James Ainslie & Heilbron takes over and rebuilds the facilities.

1912 – James Ainslie & Co. narrowly escapes bankruptcy and Distillers Company Limited (DCL) takes over together with James Risk.

1916 – John Walker & Sons buys a stake of James Risk's stocks.

1925 – DCL buys out Risk.

1930 – Scottish Malt Distillers (SMD) takes over.

1931 – The distillery is mothballed.

1939 – Production restarts.

1960 – The distillery becomes electrified (until now it has been using locally mined coal from Brora).

1967 – A new distillery is built adjacent to the first one, it is also named Clynelish and both operate in parallel from August.

1968 – 'Old' Clynelish is mothballed in August.

1969 – 'Old' Clynelish is reopened as Brora and starts using a very peaty malt over the next couple of years

1983 – Brora is closed in March.

1995 – Brora 1972 (20 years) and Brora 1972 (22 years) are launched as Rare Malts.

1996 – Brora 1975 (20 years) is launched as a Rare Malt.

1998 – Brora 1977 (21 years) is launched as a Rare Malt.

2001 – Brora 1977 (24 years) is launched as a Rare Malt.

2002 – A 30 year old cask strength is released in a limited edition.

2003 – Brora 1982 (20 years) is launched as a Rare Malt.

2011 – The tenth release of Brora – a 32 year old.

Although founded under the name Clynelish distillery in 1819, it is under the name Brora that the single malt has enjoyed its newfound fame during the past two decades. The whisky has mostly appealed to peat freaks around the world but, for the first 140 years, it actually wasn't that peated. In 1967 DCL decided to build a new, modern distillery on the same site. This was given the name Clynelish and it was decided the old distillery should be closed. Shortly after, the demand for peated whisky, especially for the blend Johnnie Walker, increased and the old site re-opened but now under the name Brora and the "recipe" for the whisky was changed to a heavily peated malt. This continued from 1969 to 1973 and after that the peatiness was reduced, even if single peated batches turned up until the late seventies.

Brora closed permanently in 1983 but the buildings still stand next to the new Clynelish. The two stills, the feints receiver, the spirit receiver and the brass safe remain, while the warehouses are used for storage of spirit from Clynelish. The first distillery was built in the time referred to as the Highland Clearances. Many land-owners wished to increase the yield of their lands and consequently went into large-scale sheep farming. Thousands of families were ruthlessly forced away and the most infamous of the large land-owners was the Marquis of Stafford who founded Clynelish (Brora) in 1819.

Since 1995 Diageo has regularly released different expressions of Brora in the *Rare Malts* series. The latest, which also became the last, appeared in 2003. In 2002 a new range was created, called *Special Releases* and bottlings of Brora have appeared ever since. In autumn 2010 it was a *30 year old* and by autumn 2011 the time had come for the tenth expression, a *32 year old* and the oldest ever distillery bottling of Brora. Very few independent bottlings of Brora turn up nowadays. The latest was a 28 year old from Douglas Laing in 2009.

32 years old

Banff

Owner: Diageo *Region:* Speyside *Founded:* 1824 *Status:* Demolished

Banff's tragic history of numerous fires, explosions and bombings have contributed to its fame. The most spectacular incident was when a lone Junkers Ju-88 bombed one of the warehouses in 1941. Hundreds of casks exploded and several thousand litres of whisky were destroyed. The distillery was closed in 1983 and the buildings were destroyed in a fire in 1991. The distillery was owned for 80 years by the Simpson family but when their company filed for bankruptcy in 1932, it was sold to Scottish Malt Distillers which later would be a part of Diageo. When the distillery was at its largest it produced 1 million litres per year in three pairs of stills.

Recent bottlings:
There has only been one official Rare Malts bottling from 2004. A number of expressions from the seventies have been released recently; Dewar Rattray 1975, Douglas Laing 1971, Duncan Taylor 1975 and a 34 year old from The Whisky Agency.

Caperdonich

Owner: Chivas Bros *Region:* Speyside *Founded:* 1897 *Status:* Closed

The distillery was founded by James Grant, owner of Glen Grant which was located in Rothes just a few hundred metres away. Five years after the opening, the distillery was shut down and was re-opened again in 1965 under the name Caperdonich. In 2002 it was mothballed yet again, never to be re-opened. Parts of the equipment were dismantled to be used in other distilleries within the company. In 2010 the distillery was sold to the manufacturer of copper pot stills, Forsyth´s in Rothes, who already had business adjacent to it. In the old days a pipe connected Caperdonich and Glen Grant for easy transport of spirit, ready to be filled.

Recent bottlings:
An official cask strength was released in 2005. Recent bottlings from independents are a 14 year old distilled in 1996 from Cadenheads, a 15 year old (1995) from Dewar Rattray and a 28 year old (1982) released by Douglas Laing.

Coleburn

Owner: Diageo *Region:* Speyside *Founded:* 1897 *Status:* Dismantled

Like so many other distilleries, Coleburn was taken over by DCL (the predecessor of Diageo) in the 1930s. Although the single malt never became well known, Coleburn was used as an experimental workshop where new production techniques were tested. In 1985 the distillery was mothballed and never opened again. Two brothers, Dale and Mark Winchester, bought the buildings in 2004 with the intention of transforming the site into an entertainment centre. After a lengthy process, they were granted planning permission in 2010 and the reconstruction work, transforming it into a 60-bedroom hotel and a spa, has commenced.

Recent bottlings:
There has only been one official Rare Malts bottling from 2000, while Independent bottlings are also rare. One of the latest was a 36 year old released in 2006 by Signatory.

Convalmore

Owner: *Region:*   *Founded:*   *Status:*
Diageo   Speyside   1894   Dismantled

This distillery is still intact and can be seen in Dufftown next to Balvenie distillery. The buildings were sold to William Grant´s in 1990 and they now use it for storage. Diageo, however, still holds the rights to the brand. In the early 20th century, experimental distilling of malt whisky in continuous stills (the same method used for producing grain whisky) took place at Convalmore. The distillery closed in 1985. One of the more famous owners of this distillery was James Buchanan who used Convalmore single malt as a part of his famous blend Black & White. He later sold the distillery to DCL (later Diageo).

Recent bottlings:
The latest bottling from the owners was a 28 year old released in 2005. The latest independent bottling was a 32 year old from 1975 released by Douglas Laing in 2007.

Dallas Dhu

Owner: *Region:*   *Founded:*   *Status:*
Diageo   Speyside   1898   Closed

Dallas Dhu distillery is located along the A96 between Elgin and Inverness and is still intact, equipment and all, but hasn´t produced since 1983. Three years later, Diageo sold the distillery to Historic Scotland and it became a museum which is open all year round. One of the founders of the distillery, Alexander Edwards, belonged to the more energetic men in the 19th century Scotch whisky business. Not only did he start Dallas Dhu but also established Aultmore, Benromach and Craigellachie and owned Benrinnes and Oban. For a period, the malt whisky from Dallas Dhu, was a part of the immensely popular blended Scotch, Roderick Dhu.

Recent bottlings:
There are two Rare Malts bottlings from Diageo, the latest in 1997. The latest from independents is a 31 year old released by Signatory in 2010 and there have also been a few releases for Historic Scotland – the current owners.

Glen Albyn

Owner: *Region:*   *Founded:*   *Status:*
Diageo   N Highlands   1844   Demolished

Glen Albyn was one of three Inverness distilleries surviving into the 1980s. Today, there is no whisky production left in the city. The first forty years were not very productive for Glen Albyn. Fire and bankruptcy prevented the success and in 1866 the buildings were transformed into a flour mill. In 1884 it was converted back to a distillery and continued producing whisky until 1983 when it was closed by the owners at the time, Diageo. Three years later the distillery was demolished.

Recent bottlings:
Glen Albyn has been released as a Rare Malt by the owners on one occasion. It is rarely seen from independents as well - a 28 year old released in 2009 by Signatory was the latest.

Glenesk

Owner: Diageo   **Region:** E Highlands   **Founded:** 1897   **Status:** Demolished

Few distilleries, if any, have operated under as many names as Glenesk; Highland Esk, North Esk, Montrose and Hillside. The distillery was one of four operating close to Montrose between Aberdeen and Dundee. Today only Glencadam remains. At one stage the distillery was re-built for grain production but reverted to malt distilling. In 1968 a large drum maltings was built adjacent to the distillery and the Glenesk maltings still operate today under the ownership of Boortmalt, the fifth largest producer of malt in the world. The distillery building was demolished in 1996.

Recent bottlings:
The single malt from Glen Esk has been bottled on three occasions as a Rare Malts, the latest in 1997. It is also very rare with the independent bottlers. Last time it appeared was in 2007 when Duncan Taylor released a 26 year old distilled in 1981.

Glen Keith

Owner: Chivas Bros   **Region:** Speyside   **Founded:** 1957   **Status:** Mothballed

Unlike many of the closed distilleries on these pages, Glen Keith was mothballed rather late, in 2000. Rumour has it that the owners have plans to revive the distillery within the next year or so. Although no whisky production is taking place, Glen Keith still plays an important role as it accommodates a technical centre and a laboratory for the owners. The boiler at Glen Keith is used for nearby Strathisla´s production and the spirit from Strathisla is pumped to Glen Keith for filling. The distillery has an exciting history with triple distillation, production of heavily peated whisky, malt whisky produced in column stills and trials with new yeast strains.

Recent bottlings:
The official 10 year old is now very hard to find. Instead, independents have started to take an interest. A very old (40 years) was released by The Whisky Agency in 2010 and in 2011 came a 16 year old Barolo finish from Ian Macleod.

Glenlochy

Owner: Diageo   **Region:** W Highlands   **Founded:** 1898   **Status:** Demolished

Glenlochy was one of three distilleries in Fort William at the beginning of the 1900s. In 1908 Nevis merged with Ben Nevis distillery (which exists to this day) and in 1983 (a disastrous year for Scotch whisky industry when eight distilleries were closed), the time had come for Glenlochy to close for good. Today, all the buildings have been demolished, with the exception of the kiln with its pagoda roof and the malt barn which both have been turned into flats. For a period of time, the distillery was owned by an energetic and somewhat eccentric Canadian gentleman by the name of Joseph Hobbs who, after having sold the distillery to DCL, bought the second distillery in town, Ben Nevis.

Recent bottlings:
Glenlochy has occurred twice in the Rare Malts series. Recent independent bottlings are rare; a 49 year old from 2003 by Douglas Laing and a 24 year old released by Duncan Taylor in 2005.

Glen Mhor

Owner: *Region:* *Founded:* *Status:*
Diageo N Highlands 1892 Demolished

Glen Mhor is one of the last three Inverness distilleries and probably the one with the best reputation when it comes to the whisky that it produced. When the manager of nearby Glen Albyn, John Birnie, was refused to buy shares in the distillery he was managing, he decided to build his own and founded Glen Mhor. Almost thirty years later he also bought Glen Albyn and both distilleries were owned by the Birnie family until 1972 when they were sold to DCL. Glen Mhor was closed in 1983 and three years later the buildings were demolished. Today there is a supermarket on the site.

Recent bottlings:
Glen Mhor has appeared on two ocasions as Rare Malts. A couple of years ago three 27 year olds all distilled in 1982 were released by Signatory, Berry Brothers, Cadenheads and Douglas Laing and from the latter also a 32 year old distilled in 1975

Glenury Royal

Owner: *Region:* *Founded:* *Status:*
Diageo E Highlands 1825 Demolished

Glenury Royal did not have a lucky start. Already a few weeks after inception in 1825, a fire destroyed the whole kiln, the greater part of the grain lofts and the malting barn, as well as the stock of barley and malt. Just two weeks later, distillery worker James Clark, fell into the boiler and died after a few hours. The founder of Glenury was the eccentric Captain Robert Barclay Allardyce, the first to walk 1000 miles in 1000 hours in 1809 and also an excellent middle-distance runner and boxer. The distillery closed in 1983 and part of the building was demolished a decade later with the rest converted into flats.

Recent bottlings:
Bottled as a Rare Malt on three occasions. Even more spectacular were three Diageo bottlings released 2003-2007; two 36 year olds and a 50 year old. In autumn 2011 a 40 year old was released. There are few independent bottlings, the latest being a 32 year old released in 2008 by Douglas Laing.

Imperial

Owner: *Region:* *Founded:* *Status:*
Chivas Bros Speyside 1897 Closed

Rumours of the resurrection of this closed distillery have flourished from time to time during the last decade. Six years ago, the owner commissioned an estate agent to sell the buildings and convert them into flats. Shortly after that, Chivas Bros withdrew it from the market. Most of the equipment is still there, even though there was an attempt in 2009, which failed, to loot the distillery. In over a century, Imperial distillery was out of production for 60% of the time, but when it produced it had a capacity of 1.6 million litres per year. If rumours have it right and Chivas Bros restart Glen Keith, it will mean that Imperial is the last of their distilleries to remain closed.

Recent bottlings:
The 15 year old official bottling is hard to find these days but independents are more frequent. Gordon & MacPhail and Duncan Taylor both made releases in 2010 of Imperial distilled in 1997 and Douglas Laing released a 16 year old in 2011.

Littlemill

Owner: Loch Lomond Distillery Co. *Region:* Lowlands *Founded:* 1772 *Status:* Demolished

Until 1992 when production stopped, Littlemill was Scotland's oldest working distillery and could trace its roots back to 1772, possibly even back to the 1750s! Triple distillation was practised at Littlemill until 1930 and after that some new equipment was installed, for example, stills with rectifying columns. The stills were also isolated with aluminium. The goal was to create whiskies that would mature faster. Two such experimental releases were Dunglas and Dumbuck. In 1996 the distillery was dismantled and part of the buildings demolished and in 2004 much of the remaining buildings were destroyed in a fire.

Recent bottlings:
This is one of the few closed distilleries where official bottlings are released regularly. The official 12 year old is now closer to 19 years! A 20 year old was released in April 2011 by Hart Brothers to celebrate the wedding of Prince William and Kate Middleton.

Lochside

Owner: Chivas Bros *Region:* E Highlands *Founded:* 1957 *Status:* Demolished

Originally a brewery for two centuries, In the last 35 years of production Lochside was a whisky distillery. The Canadian, Joseph Hobbs, started distilling grain whisky and then added malt whisky production in the same way as he had done at Ben Nevis and Lochside. Most of the output was made for the blended whisky Sandy MacNab's. In the early 1970s, the Spanish company DYC became the owner and the output was destined for Spanish blended whisky. In 1992 the distillery was mothballed and five years later all the equipment and stock were removed. All the distillery buildings were demolished in 2005.

Recent bottlings:
There are no recent official bottlings. A handful of independent bottlings, however, have appeared in 2010/2011; a 21 year old (1989) from Douglas Laing, a 29 year old (1981) from The Whisky Agency and a 29 year old (1981) was released by The Whisky Exchange.

Millburn

Owner: Diageo *Region:* N Highlands *Founded:* 1807 *Status:* Dismantled

The distillery is the oldest of those Inverness distilleries that made it into modern times and it is also the only one where the buildings are still standing. It is now a hotel and restaurant owned by Premier Inn. With one pair of stills, the capacity was no more than 300,000 litres. The problem with Millburn distillery was that it could never be expanded due to its location, sandwiched in between the river, a hill and the surrounding streets. It was bought by the London-based gin producer Booth's in the 1920s and shortly after that absorbed into the giant DCL. In 1985 it was closed and three years later all the equipment was removed.

Recent bottlings:
Three bottlings of Millburn have appeared as Rare Malts, the latest in 2005. Other bottlings are scarce. The most recent was a 33 year old distilled in 1974, released by Blackadder.

North Port

Owner: *Region:* *Founded:* *Status:*
Diageo E Highlands 1820 Demolished

The names North Port and Brechin are used interchangeably on the labels of this single malt. Brechin is the name of the city and North Port comes from a gate in the wall which surrounded the city. The distillery was run by members of the Guthrie family for more than a century until 1922 when DCL took over. Diageo then closed 21 of their 45 distilleries between 1983 and 1985 of which North Port was one. It was dismantled piece by piece and was finally demolished in 1994 to make room for a supermarket.The distillery had one pair of stills and produced 500,000 litres per year.

Recent bottlings:
North Port was released as a Rare Malt by Diageo twice and in 2005 also as part of the Special Releases (a 28 year old). Independent bottlings are very rare - the latest (distilled in 1981) was released by Duncan Taylor in 2008.

Pittyvaich

Owner: *Region:* *Founded:* *Status:*
Diageo Speyside 1974 Demolished

The life span for this relatively modern distillery was short. It was built by Arthur Bell & Sons on the same ground as Dufftown distillery which also belonged to them and the four stills were exact replicas of the Dufftown stills. Bells was bought by Guinness in 1985 and the distillery was eventually absorbed into DCL (later Diageo). For a few years in the 1990s, Pittyvaich was also a back up plant for gin distillation (in the same way that Auchroisk is today) in connection with the production of Gordon´s gin having moved from Essex till Cameronbridge. The distillery was mothballed in 1993 and has now been demolished.

Recent bottlings:
An official 12 year old Flora & Fauna can still be obtained and in 2009 a 20 year old was released by the owners. Recent independents include an 18 year old from Douglas Laing and a 23 year old rum finish by Cadenheads, both released in 2008.

Rosebank

Owner: *Region:* *Founded:* *Status:*
Diageo Lowlands 1798 Dismantled

When Rosebank in Falkirk was mothballed in 1993, there were only two working malt distilleries left in the Lowlands – Glenkinchie and Auchentoshan. The whisky from the distillery has always had a great amount of supporters and there was a glimmer of hope that a new company would start up the distillery again. At the beginning of 2010 though, most of the equipment was stolen and furthermore, Diageo has indicated that they are not interested in selling the brand. The buildings are still intact and most of them have been turned into restaurants, offices and flats. The whisky from Rosebank is triple distilled.

Recent bottlings:
The official 12 year old Flora & Fauna is still released and in autumn 2011 a 21 year old Special Release appeared. Three independent bottlings, all distilled in 1990, were released in 2011 by Ian Macleod, Cadenheads and Douglas Laing.

Port Ellen

Owner:		Region/district:
Diageo		Islay
Founded:	Status:	Capacity:
1825	Dismantled	

History:
1825 – Alexander Kerr Mackay assisted by Walter Campbell founds the distillery. Mackay runs into financial troubles after a few months and his three relatives John Morrison, Patrick Thomson and George Maclennan take over.

1833 – John Ramsay, a cousin to John Morrison, comes from Glasgow to take over.

1836 – Ramsay is granted a lease on the distillery from the Laird of Islay.

1892 – Ramsay dies and the distillery is inherited by his widow, Lucy.

1906 – Lucy Ramsay dies and her son Captain Iain Ramsay takes over.

1920 – Iain Ramsay sells to Buchanan-Dewar who transfers the administration to the company Port Ellen Distillery Co. Ltd.

1925 – Buchanan-Dewar joins Distillers Company Limited (DCL).

1929 – No production.

1930 – Administration is transferred to Scottish Malt Distillers (SMD) and the distillery is mothballed.

1967 – In production again after reconstruction and doubling of the number of stills from two to four.

1973 – A large drum maltings is installed.

1980 – Queen Elisabeth visits the distillery and a commemorative special bottling is made.

1983 – The distillery is mothballed.

1987 – The distillery closes permanently but the maltings continue to deliver malt to all Islay distilleries.

1998 – Port Ellen 1978 (20 years) is released as a Rare Malt.

2000 – Port Ellen 1978 (22 years) is released as a Rare Malt.

2001 – Port Ellen cask strength first edition is released.

2011 – The 11th release of Port Ellen - a 32 year old from 1979.

When Port Ellen closed in 1983 it was one of three Islay distilleries owned by Diageo (then DCL). The other two were Lagavulin and Caol Ila who had been operating uninterruptedly for many years. Port Ellen, mothballed since 1930, had only been producing for 16 years since re-opening, which made it easy for the owners to single out which Islay distillery was to close when malt whisky demand decreased. It was also the smallest of the three, with an annual output of 1.7 million litres of alcohol. The stills were shipped abroad early in the 1990s, possibly destined for India, and the distillery buildings were destroyed shortly afterwards. The whisky from Port Ellen is so popular, however, that rumours of distilling starting up again, do flourish from time to time.

Today, the site is associated with the huge drum maltings that was built in 1973. It supplies all Islay distilleries and a few others, with a large proportion of their malt. There are seven germination drums with a capacity of handling 51 tonnes of barley each. Three kilns are used to dry the barley and for every batch, an average of 6 tonnes of peat are required which means 2,000 tonnes per year. The peat was taken from Duich Moss until 1993 when conservationists managed to obtain national nature reserve status for the area in order to protect the thousands of Barnacle Geese that make a stop-over there during their migration. Nowadays the peat is taken from nearby Castlehill.

Besides a couple of versions in the *Rare Malts* series, Diageo began releasing one official bottling a year in 2001 and in autumn 2011 it was time for the 11th release – a *32 year old* distilled in 1979. Port Ellen is a favourite with independent bottlers. Two of the most recent ones are a 31 year old released by Douglas Laing and a 1982 from The Whisky Exchange to celebrate the Royal Wedding between Prince William and Kate Middleton.

32 years old

St Magdalene

Owner: *Region:*   *Founded:*   *Status:*
Diageo   Lowlands   1795   Dismantled

At one time, the small town of Linlithgow in East Lothian had no less than five distilleries. St Magdalene was one of them and also the last to close in 1983. The distillery came into ownership of the giant DCL quite early (1912) and was at the time a large distillery with 14 washbacks, five stills and with the possibility of producing more than 1 million litres of alcohol. Ten years after the closure the distillery was carefully re-built into flats, making it possible to still see most of the old buildings, including the pagoda roofs.

Recent bottlings:
These include two official bottlings in the Rare Malts series. In 2008/2009 a handful of independent releases appeared, all of them distilled in 1982 and released by Ian MacLeod, Douglas Laing, Blackadder, Signatory and Berry Brother. The latest was a 28 year old from Douglas Laing released in 2011.

Tamdhu

Owner: *Region:*   *Founded:*   *Status:*
Edrington   Speyside   1896   Mothballed

It came as a surprise when the owners of Tamdhu declared in November 2009 that the distillery would be mothballed because Edrington had to "rebalance their distillation capacity". The whisky has never been big as a single malt but plays an important role in both Famous Grouse and Cutty Sark blends. Adjacent to the distillery is also maltings using Saladin boxes producing 14,000 tonnes of malt per year. The future of the distillery, with a capacity of making 4 million litres per year, was a bit uncertain for a while but in summer 2011, it was announced that Ian Macleod Distillers had bought the distillery with the intention of starting production again in 2012.

Recent bottlings:
Until recently, the owners bottled Tamdu without age statement and also released a couple of older ones (18 and 25 years old). The latest of the independents was a 21 year old from 1989, bottled in early 2011 by Douglas Laing.

To be able to find a bottling from one of the closed distilleries, you would in most cases have to rely on the independent bottlers. Few official bottlings from the owners are released, with the exception of Brora, Port Ellen and Littlemill. On rare occasions, the owners do release some surprises and here are three of the latest – Glenugie 32 year old and Inverleven 36 year old in Chivas Bros new range Deoch an Doras from 2010 and 21 year old Rosebank in Diageo´s Special Releases 2011.

Ben Wyvis

Owner: *Region:*   *Founded:*   *Status:*
Whyte & Mackay   N Highlands   1965   Dismantled

The large grain distillery, Invergordon, today producing 36 million litres of grain whisky per year, was established in 1959 on the Cromarty Firth, east of Alness. Six years later a small malt distillery, Ben Wyvis, was built on the same site with the purpose of producing malt whisky for Invergordon Distiller's blends. The distillery was equipped with one mash tun, six washbacks and one pair of stills. Funnily enough the stills are still in use today at Glengyle distillery. Production at Ben Wyvis stopped in 1976 and in 1977 the distillery was closed and dismantled.

Bottlings:
There have been only a few releases of Ben Wyvis. The first, a 27 year old, was released by Invergordon in 1999, followed by a 31 year old from Signatory in 2000 and finally a 37 year old from Kyndal (later Whyte & Mackay) in 2002. It is highly unlikely that there will be more Ben Wyvis single malt to bottle.

Inverleven

Owner: *Region:*   *Founded:*   *Status:*
Chivas Bros   Lowlands   1938   Demolished

Dumbarton was the largest grain distillery in Scotland when it was built in 1938. It was mothballed in 2002 and finally closed in 2003 when Allied Domecq moved all their grain production to Strathclyde. On the same site, Inverleven malt distillery was built, equipped with one pair of traditional pot stills. In 1956 a Lomond still was added and this still (with the aid of Inverleven's wash still), technically became a second distillery called Lomond. Inverleven was mothballed in 1991 and finally closed. The Lomond still is now working again since 2010 at Bruichladdich distillery.

Bottlings:
The first official bottling of Inverleven came as late as in 2010 when Chivas Bros released a 36 year old in a new range called Deoch an Doras. The latest independent was a 31 year released by Signatory in 2008. The whisky from the Lomond still was bottled in 1992 by the Scotch Malt Whisky Society.

Glen Flagler / Killyloch

Owner: *Region:*   *Founded:*   *Status:*
Inver House   Lowlands   1964   Closed

In 1964 Inver House Distillers was bought by the American company, Publicker Industries, and that same year they decided to expand the production side as well. Moffat Paper Mills in Airdrie was bought and rebuilt into one grain distillery (Garnheath) and two malt distilleries (Glen Flagler and Killyloch). A maltings was also built which, at the time, became the biggest in Europe. The American interest in the Scotch whisky industry faded rapidly and Killyloch was closed in 1975, while Glen Flagler continued to produce for another decade.

Bottlings:
Glen Flagler was bottled as an 8 year old by the owners in the 70s. The next release came in the mid 1990s when Signatory released both Glen Flagler and Killyloch (23 year old) and finally in 2003 when Inver House bottled a Glen Flagler 1973 and a Killyloch 1967. A peated version of Glen Flagler, produced until 1970, was called Islebrae.

Kinclaith

Owner: *Region:*   *Founded:*   *Status:*
Chivas Bros   Lowlands   1957   Demolished

This was the last malt distillery to be built in Glasgow and was constructed on the grounds of Strathclyde grain distillery by Seager Evans (later Long John International). Strathclyde still exists today and produces 40 million litres of grain spirit per year. Kinclaith distillery was equipped with one pair of stills and produced malt whisky to become a part of the Long John blend. In 1975 it was dismantled to make room for an extension of the grain distillery. It was later demolished in 1982.

Bottlings:
There are no official bottlings of Kinclaith. The latest from independents came in 2005 when Duncan Taylor and Signatory both released 35 year old bottlings. Older releases include a 32 year old from Gordon & MacPhail released in 1996 and a 20 year old from Cadenheads in 1985.

Glenugie

Owner: *Region:*   *Founded:*   *Status:*
Chivas Bros   E Highlands   1831   Demolished

Glenugie, positioned in Peterhead, was the most Eastern distillery in Scotland, producing whisky for six years before it was converted into a brewery. In 1875 whisky distillation started again, but production was very intermittent until 1937 when Seager Evans & Co took over. Eventually they expanded the distillery to four stills and the capacity was around 1 million litres per year. After several ownership changes Glenugie became part of the brewery giant, Whitbread, in 1975. The final blow came in 1983 when Glenugie, together with seven other distilleries, was closed never to open again.

Bottlings:
The first official bottling of Glenugie came as late as in 2010 when Chivas Bros (the current owners of the brand) released a 32 year old single sherry cask in a new range called Deoch an Doras. Recent independent bottlings include a 33 year old with 8 years Oloroso finish from Signatory, released in 2011.

Ladyburn

Owner: *Region:*   *Founded:*   *Status:*
W Grant & Sons   Lowlands   1966   Dismantled

In 1963 William Grant & Sons built their huge grain distillery in Girvan in Ayrshire. Three years later they also decided to build a malt distillery on the site which was given the name Ladyburn. The distillery was equipped with two pairs of stills and they also tested a new type of continuous mashing. The whole idea was to produce malt whisky to become a part of Grant's blended whisky. The distillery was closed in 1975 and finally dismantled during the 1980s. In 2008 a new malt distillery opened up at Girvan under the name Ailsa Bay.

Bottlings:
The latest official bottling from the owners was a 27 year old distilled in 1973 and released in 2001. Independent bottlings have appeared occasionally, sometimes under the name Ayrshire. The most recent was a 35 year old, released by Signatory in 2010.

Distilleries per owner

c = closed, d = demolished, mb = mothballed, dm = dismantled

Diageo
Auchroisk
Banff (d)
Benrinnes
Blair Athol
Brora (c)
Bushmills
Caol Ila
Cardhu
Clynelish
Coleburn (dm)
Convalmore (dm)
Cragganmore
Dailuaine
Dallas Dhu (c)
Dalwhinnie
Dufftown
Glen Albyn (d)
Glendullan
Glen Elgin
Glenesk (dm)
Glenkinchie
Glenlochy (d)
Glenlossie
Glen Mhor (d)
Glen Ord
Glen Spey
Glenury Royal (d)
Inchgower
Knockando
Lagavulin
Linkwood
Mannochmore
Millburn (dm)
Mortlach
North Port (d)
Oban
Pittyvaich (d)
Port Ellen (dm)
Rosebank (c)
Roseisle
Royal Lochnagar
St Magdalene (dm)
Strathmill
Talisker
Teaninich

Pernod Ricard
Aberlour
Allt-a-Bhainne
Braeval
Caperdonich (c)
Glenallachie
Glenburgie
Glen Keith (mb)
Glenlivet
Glentauchers
Glenugie (dm)
Imperial (c)
Inverleven (d)
Kinclaith (d)
Lochside (d)
Longmorn

Miltonduff
Scapa
Strathisla
Tormore

Edrington Group
Glenrothes
Glenturret
Highland Park
Macallan

Inver House (Thai Beverage)
Balblair
Balmenach
Glen Flagler (d)
Knockdhu
Pulteney
Speyburn

John Dewar & Sons (Bacardi)
Aberfeldy
Aultmore
Craigellachie
Macduff
Royal Brackla

Whyte & Mackay (United Spirits)
Dalmore
Fettercairn
Jura
Tamnavulin

William Grant & Sons
Ailsa Bay
Balvenie
Glenfiddich
Kininvie
Ladyburn (dm)

Glenmorangie Co. (Moët Hennessy)
Ardbeg
Glenmorangie

Morrison Bowmore (Suntory)
Auchentoshan
Bowmore
Glen Garioch

Burn Stewart Distillers (CL Financial)
Bunnahabhain
Deanston
Tobermory

Loch Lomond Distillers
Glen Scotia
Littlemill (d)
Loch Lomond

Angus Dundee Distillers
Glencadam
Tomintoul

J & A Mitchell
Glengyle
Springbank

Beam
Ardmore
Laphroaig

Benriach Distillery Co.
Benriach
Glendronach

Campari Group
Glen Grant

Isle of Arran Distillers
Arran

Signatory Vintage Scotch Whisky Co.
Edradour

Ian Macleod Distillers
Glengoyne
Tamdhu

Tomatin Distillery Co. (Marubeni Europe plc)
Tomatin

J & G Grant
Glenfarclas

Bruichladdich Distillery Co. (Murray McDavid)
Bruichladdich

Co-ordinated Development Services
Bladnoch

Gordon & MacPhail
Benromach

Glenglassaugh Distillery Co (Scaent Group)
Glenglassaugh

La Martiniquaise
Glen Moray

Ben Nevis Distillery Ltd (Nikka)
Ben Nevis

Tullibardine Distillery Ltd
Tullibardine

Speyside Distillers Co.
Speyside

Cooley Distillery plc
Cooley
Kilbeggan

Kilchoman Distillery Co.
Kilchoman

Cuthbert family
Daftmill

Mark Tayburn
Abhainn Dearg

Single malts from Japan

by Chris Bunting

In Japan, business associates send each other greeting cards in the dog days of summer called "shochu mimai." Literally, "mimai" is the word used for a visit to a sick person or an inquiry after someone's health, and "shochu" means "in the middle of the heat". So, these cards are basically a way to say: "It's hotter than hell's door hinges. How are you surviving?" The messages are usually fairly formulaic, juggling a few set phrases of thanks and looking forward to a profitable relationship over the short sprint to the next greeting card season at New Year.

This year's message from Seichi Koshimizu, chief blender at Suntory Whisky, was altogether more stark and meaningful. He asked what role making whisky could have in the aftermath of the tremendous destruction wrought by the Great East Japan Earthquake, which killed at least 15,000 people. Koshimizu said: "I can only imagine what those who went through the earthquake, tsunami and nuclear accident have suffered. The road of recovery seems to stretch a long way ahead. Watching the news reports every day, I cannot help thinking about the meaning of my job."

Some in Japan's alcohol business do not have that luxury. They have not been watching the news; they have been caught up in it. The tsunami devastated some of the best sake breweries in Japan and caused significant damage to the beer industry, temporarily stopping operations at breweries owned by Kirin, Asahi and Sapporo.

In terms of physical damage, the whisky firms got off relatively lightly. The only distillery in the disaster area is Nikka Whisky's Miyagikyo distil-lery, about 150 kilometers due west of the initial epicenter. Crucially, it is inland and in the hills, so it escaped the huge tsunami that caused most of the damage in Tohoku. After some anxious days in which no news seemed to be coming out of Miyagikyo, production manager Minoru Miake reported that there had only been minor damage to the distillery and its stock. The workers and their families were safe. At Ichiro Akuto's Chichibu distillery in Saitama prefecture, well outside the main disaster area, there was also some very minor damage to a water tank and some fencing.

The elephant in the room, of course, was the Fukushima nuclear plant accident. Masahito Matsushima at Hombo Shuzo, which restarted its Shinshu distillery this year, says: "This earthquake was unprecedented and we cannot yet fathom the impact of it on the whisky business, but we do know at least that the export trade will have difficulties, some of which will be due to the nuclear plant scare stories."

In the first days of the disaster, it was difficult to respond to nuclear fears because the facts were not available. However, there is now a lot more information. Most of Japan's distilleries are a long way from the Fukushima plant and the wind does not appear to have been blowing in their direction at the crucial times, on March 15 and between March 20-23, when an Atomic Energy Society of Japan study now says much of the contamination around Fukushima took place.

Miyagikyo is within the 160 km area around the plant that was the focus of a Japanese government survey of deposited cesium-134 and cesium-137 levels in mid-July and that survey has offered some much needed perspective. A wide area around the Miyagikyo distillery recorded accumulated cesium-134 and cesium-137 of between 0 kilobecquerels and 29 kilobecquerels per square meter as of July 16. While the mere presence of any radioactive substance may be alarming to some, it is worth noting that an International Atomic Energy Agency report reported between 10 and 40 kilobecquerels of cesium-137 per square meter (cesium-134 was not measured) across large areas of Scotland, including some important whisky producing areas, following the Chernobyl accident. Many parts of Western Europe were far worse affected. Radiation levels of between 0.07 and 0.08 microsieverts per hour were being recorded in Sendai city, just to the east of Miyagikyo, by Tohoku University academics in mid-August. That is about the same as average natural background radiation in Norway and marginally more than the average level across the whole of France (0.068), according to figures from a 1993 report from the United Nations Scientific Committee on the Effects of Atomic Radiation.

Of more immediate concern to makers than radiation was the earthquakes impact on the economy and, more particularly, the entertainment industry. Pubs saw a 19% plunge in sales in March, followed by an 11% drop in April.

"Right after the quake, the unstable electricity supply and austere mood hit bar drinking and pushed down whisky consumption", Akuto explains. "But it has recovered a great deal... For a small company like ours, at least, there does not seem to have been too much impact."

Whisky sales continue to grow

Both of the main makers, Nikka and Suntory, are still predicting growth in whisky sales in fiscal 2011 and the fashion for whisky highballs that has been largely responsible for the revival in whisky consumption in Japan since 2009 appears still to be in full swing. Kirin, owner of the Fuji-Gotemba distillery, said whisky sales in the first half of 2011 were up 20 percent, with men and women in their 20s continuing to enter the whisky market. Suntory and Nikka, the other two main makers, are seeing similar figures.

The foreign market for Japanese whisky has been like the curate's egg: good in parts. Aiko Shima, spokeswoman for Nikka whisky, said the company was targeting a 37% increase in sales in Europe in 2011, while Suntory says the difficult-to-crack U.S. market is at last showing signs of yielding, with sales there of Yamazaki single malt up 28% year-on-year.

However, according to Marcin Miller at the independent importer Number One Drinks Company: "This has been a year in which the boom in Japanese whiskies overseas has been able to catch its breath, which is not necessarily a bad thing. Having established a great reputation over recent years, the timing of the natural disasters that befell Japan was unfortunate to say the least.

"As far as Number One is concerned, the effects were tangible; our model is not based on holding stock so, when exports were stopped, we had nothing to sell – pure and simple. I noted that some retailers seemed to be raising their prices as unfounded rumours were rife about distilleries being destroyed. The lasting effect will depend on consumer confidence and currently we're inundated with enquiries from potential importers. We are not in a position where we have endless supply of 10 year old to shift. Therefore, we are dependent on the more knowledgeable whisky enthusiast who, in my experience, tends to be intelligent and well-balanced. It has been a difficult year, but I hope that we can assist the Japanese economy in a small way by continuing to distribute these amazing whiskies around the world."

That excellence was underlined just days before the earthquake, when it was announced that Japanese whiskies had scooped both the best single malt in the world prize (Yamazaki 1984) and the best blended whisky (Hibiki 21) award at the World Whiskies Awards. It was the second time in four years that Japan had achieved the feat.

Hombo Shuzo's restarting of the Shinshu distillery in February was perhaps the most exciting development in the independent sector in 2011 and, in the early summer, the Bordeaux-based company Les Whiskies du Monde announced that it was importing a new range of malts and blends to Europe, including Akashi single malts from Eigashima's White Oak distillery, and Isawa single malts from Monde Shuzo in Fuefuki City, Yamanashi Prefecture.

In August, we learned that Number One Drinks had bought all of the of the remaining inventory of the Karuizawa distillery through an Asian partner. It was both good news and terrible news for Japanese whisky fans, appearing to confirm the demise of the long-established Karuizawa distillery, but also securing a large quantity of quality whisky dating back to 1960 for a company with a proven track record of innovation and high quality.

It has been an extraordinary year for Japan and for its whisky industry. Much of what happened could only be endured, but Suntory's Chief Blender Koshimizu resolved his "shochu mimai" question about the meaning of making whisky in the context of disaster in a positive way.

"Whisky was called the water of life and spirits are supposed to be a source of life and energy," he said. "Alcohol is supposed to help release people from stress. I can only pray that whisky can play its role and bring smiles back onto people's faces."

We can probably all raise a glass to that sentiment.

Chris Bunting has just published a guide to Japanese alcohol culture and drinking establishments called Drinking Japan (www.drinkingjapan. com). He works for a Japanese daily newspaper and writes about Japanese whisky at www.nonjatta.com He has lived in Japan for 6 years.

Chichibu

Owner: Venture Whisky   **Founded**: 2008
Capacity: 90,000 litres/year
Malt whisky range: A range of "newborn" spirit
bottlings, with the first Chichibu whisky due in
October 2011.

Three years after it started distilling in spring 2008, the
Chichibu distillery faced a landmark year in 2011, the first
year it could release proper, 3-year aged whisky. At the
time of writing, that whisky had not yet hit the market.
It was due to be released in Japan on October 10 under
the rather regal name "Ichiro's Malt Chichibu the First"
and was expected to be a 61.8% alcohol, cask strength
bottling from a bourbon barrel. But, if the distillery's
range of new spirit bottlings over the past three years are
anything to go by, we can look forward to high quality
and a fairly wide palette of styles in the coming years.
We have already had intriguing glimpses of a variety of
approaches including mizunara-aged spiciness, heavy
peating and lighter styles.

Ichiro Akuto, the scion of a sake making family that
got into whisky making in the 1980s but had to sell-up in
2000, is working out of a fairly utilitarian building in the
forested hills of Saitama Prefecture. He uses a pair of stills
manufactured by Forsyths in Scotland and five washbacks
made of Japanese oak, a very unusual choice of material.
Perhaps the most distinctive characteristic of Akuto's
operation is a focus on locally produced raw materials.
While most Japanese distillers use mainly imported malt,
the distillery has been growing its own barley and floor
malting is now underway. There was minor damage to
the distillery in the March 11 quake, but Akuto says the
business is doing well with more bars and quality shops
latching on to its Ichiro's Malt brand in 2011.

Tasting note:
*Single Malt Newborn Double Matured (Cask 447;
Distilled April-May 2008. Bottled October 2009)*
Remarkably good for such a young spirit. An intense
and complex nose with floral and lemon and honey
notes. A plummy sweetness on the palate accented
with citrus. Substance is given by an underlying
breadiness. A medium finish with spicy, piney
flavours and a touch of liquorice.

White Oak Distillery

Owner: Eigashima Shuzo   **Founded**: 1919
Capacity: 60,000 litres/year
Malt whisky range: Akashi Single Malt 8 years old,
Akashi Single Malt 5 years old, Akashi single Malt
12 years old

Eigashima Shuzo is moving fast. In 2007, after much chiv-
vying from single malt enthusiasts in Japan, the company
released the first of its Akashi single malts – an 8 year
old bottling that had sold out by September 2009. The
company confirmed its transformation from a producer
of cheaper blends into a premium whisky maker last
year, with the release of 5 year old and 12 year old
single malts and an Akashi blend. In 2011, Akashi piled
into the export market, with an exclusive deal with the
French outfit Les Whiskies du Monde to export the blend
and the 5 and 12 year old single malts. While the blend
available in Japan has until now been an eclectic mix of
Eigashima's own malt, Scotch and molasses-based spirit,
Les Whiskies du Monde says the spirit exported to Europe
is a special export version with only the conventional
malt and grain combination. Meanwhile, Eigashima is
continuing to develop its range. It has relatively limited
old stocks of whisky, but is hoping to release a small
amount of 14 year old single malt, finished either in
sherry or white wine barrels, in the middle of 2012.

The emergence of White Oak as a premium whisky distillery is one of the most captivating stories in Japanese
whisky in recent years. It sits on the Akashi strait, one of
Japan's most famous coastal fishing areas in Japan, and
the old wooden buildings that house its sake brewery are
worthy of a picture postcard.
The whisky operation is housed
in a white building opposite and
houses four stainless steel washbacks, a 4,500 litre wash still and
a 3,000 litre spirit still.
A growing fan base is
eagerly awaiting what
trickles out the stills next.

Tasting note:
*Akashi Single Malt
Whisky 5 year old*
A marked honey smell.
This one, like the 8 year
old before it, is extre-
mely mild on the palate
but there is even more
sweetness here: honey
and butter, cereal and
the memory of treacle
at the finish. Not a
complicated whisky but
very drinkable.

Fuji Gotemba

Owner: Kirin Holdings   **Founded**: 1973
Capacity: 12,000,000 litres (including grain whisky)
Malt whisky range: Fujisanroku Single Malt 18 year old. A range of Fuji-Gotemba single casks and special bottlings are available at the distillery.

The past few years have been a time of great change for Japanese whisky, but Kirin's distillery at Fuji Gotemba has ploughed a remarkably straight furrow. It is set in a forested area at the foot of Mount Fuji and takes its water directly from snow and rain running off the great volcano. The name of Kirin's Fujisanroku 50° blended whisky literally means "At the base of Mount Fuji" and features a dreamy picture of the mountain on its label and has been prospering mightily in the current whisky highball boom.

However, when it comes to developing the distillery's brand in the single malt market, Kirin have been conservative, with just one 18 year old Fujisanroku single malt generally available. It costs about 14,000 yen (126 euros or 183 dollars) a bottle. Kirin says sales of the single malt are "steady" and appears to be cautious about following Suntory and Nikka's drives into the international market.

"We do regard (the export market) as important because it would give us the chance to show Fuji Gotemba's whisky to the world, but we need to have a solid foundation in the Japanese market first," a spokesperson for the company said.

As I wrote last year, Kirin is likely to make an impact if and when it does make a determined move into the single malt and international markets. It is a huge company that competes toe to toe with Suntory and Nikka's owner Asahi in other markets. In the meantime, though, the management's priorities appear to be elsewhere.

Hakushu

Owner: Suntory   **Founded**: 1973
Capacity: 3,000,000 litres
Malt whisky range: Hakushu Single Malt 10, 12, 18 and 25 years old and a wide range of limited bottlings.

Suntory's distillery at Hakushu has continued its success in major competitions. After tasting gold in 2009 at both the International Wine and Spirit Competition and the International Spirits Challenge, it brought back another hat full of prizes over the past year. At the IWSC, the 12 year old Hakushu single malt earned gold, while the 18 year old scooped both a gold medal and the IWSC trophy. The 25 year old earned gold at the International Spirits Challenge. The continual round of such awards can get a bit wearing, but for Hakushu, which is sometimes in the shadow of its sibling distillery at Yamazaki, the recognition is significant.

Hakushu was once the biggest distillery in the world, with 36 stills at both its Hakushu west and east distilleries pumping out huge quantities of whisky at its peak in the 1980s. Now, it is only the 12 stills at Hakushu East that produce malt, but the wide variety of sizes and designs of those remaining stills allow a sometimes surprising range of styles of spirit. The 12 year old official bottling is popular for its light, spicy style, but as you go up the range you can find whiskies of great complexity and depth. It is still much harder to find Hakushu whisky outside Japan than Yamazaki malts. That may be the result of a deliberate decision by Suntory to concentrate its efforts. However, there were signs in 2011 of increased availability of Hakushu whiskies in some foreign markets.

Tasting note:
Hakushu 12 year old
A restrained nose with grapes, caramel and a floral flourish. Light and playful in the mouth with dried apricot sweetness and a well-controlled pepperiness. A very slight medicinal note emerges at the finish.

Hanyu

Owner: Toa Shuzo **Founded**: 1941
Capacity: Dismantled
Malt whisky range: A wide variety of limited Ichiro's Malt "card series" and other bottlings; Full Proof Europe's 1988 and 1990 Hanyu single casks; Toa Shuzo's Golden Horse 8 year old

The drumbeat of new releases from the old Hanyu distillery seemed to slow slightly over the past year. The distillery was closed in 2000 and dismantled in 2004, but continues to hold a powerful grip on the imagination of the premium Japanese whisky market mainly because of the Ichiro's Malt card series range marketed by Ichiro Akuto of Chichibu distillery.

Akuto originally salvaged about 400 casks after his family business was sold to another firm that was not interested in marketing whisky, There is no sign of that supply running out just yet, but Akuto is trying to move away from an over reliance on it as he tries to establish his new distillery.

"The card series (of Hanyu Malts) tend to sell out as soon as they come out. But those whiskies are single casks and are limited," he says. Akuto is trying to develop a supplementary range of blends and vatted malts, of which his Mizunara Wood Reserve pure malts and the Malt and Grain blended whisky released in 2011 are examples. Those whiskies partly draw on the old Hanyu stock but are eking it out by drawing on other distilleries.

Devotees of the Hanyu single malts need not despair yet. The most recent additions to the Ichiro's card series deck were 463 bottles of the 11 year old 10 of Hearts (61% alcohol by volume), matured in a hogshead and then a Madeira cask, and the 11 year old 546 bottles of the Four of Diamonds (59.9% alcohol by volume), a hogshead and sherry butt product. There was also a bottling for Whisky Live Tokyo 2011 of a Hanyu whisky that had been distilled in 2000 and matured in a refill hogshead and a mizunara oak cask.

Tasting note:
Ichiro's Malt 8 of Hearts Bottle 2008. Cask 9303
A fudgy almost cheesy nose. The palate is more austere than many Ichiro's Malt bottlings with dry chewing stick and ginger tastes and a bitter sweetness emerging in a medium-length finish.

Karuizawa

Owner: Kirin Holdings **Founded**: 1956
Capacity: Closed
Malt whisky range: Karuizawa 12 years old, Karuizawa 17 years old, Karuizawa Vintage bottlings, the Noh Series bottlings and other independent bottlings in Europe.

The curtain seems to have come down on Karuizawa. Some of us had entertained slim hopes that it might be revived following its effective mothballing in 2001, but the announcement in August that an Asian firm acting on behalf of the U.K.-based firm Number One Drinks had acquired all of the distillery's remaining inventory seemed to be a final nail in the coffin of this historically important and respected distillery.

A spokesperson for Kirin, the company that owns the distillery, said the museum on its site would be closed from November 6, 2011, raising questions about its future use. Kirin have not been specific about their plans, but they have closed other facilities in northwestern and central Japan, and have a strategy of concentrating their operations on fewer sites and in fewer divisions. The dream of Kirin's Fuji-Gotemba and Karuizawa operating in tandem does appear to be dead.

However, Karuizawa's legacy is very much alive. Marcin Miller, joint director of Number One Drinks, says: "The intention is to bottle as many casks as possible at the Karuizawa distillery, but we will also be transferring some stock to Chichibu, where we will be putting together younger vattings as well as more releases for the Noh series."

A string of bottlings under Number One's Vintage and Noh series brands have really been flying the flag for Karuizawa over the past few years, and the news that an innovative, quality-oriented firm like Number One Drinks has acquired the remaining stock probably means we can look forward to some very interesting bottlings in the near future. The oldest casks date back to the 1960s and run through to 2000.

Tasting note:
Karuizawa Noh 1976, Cask No. 6719
A powerful nose, with loads of sweet sherry. Even with a generous splash of water, this is an uncompromising drink, with delicious fruit jam, prune and faint wood notes developing. A long finish with mustier old wood and tobacco flavours.

Miyagikyo

Owner: Nikka Whisky   **Founded**: 1969
Capacity: 5,000,000 litres
Malt whisky range: Miyagikyo Single Malt (no age statement), Miyagikyo Single Malt 10, 12 and 15 years old and an annual 20 year old limited release named after the year it was distilled.

Despite its proximity to the epicenter March 11 earthquake, the Miyagikyo distillery suffered only minor damage to its buildings and stock in the disaster. None of the workers at the distillery and their families appear to have been hurt and, as discussed in detail in the introduction to this chapter, it is also becoming clear that fears that the distillery would be seriously affected by the nuclear crisis at the Fukushima plant have not materialised. The most serious effect was on transportation, with shipments stopped for many weeks because of the widespread disruption in the region.

Nevertheless, it has been a terrible year for the people at a distillery whose Coffey stills and eight pot stills are the workhorses of Nikka's whisky operation. Judging by some of the correspondence to my website, there is a real determination among many Japanese and foreign whisky fans to do something to support the distillery by enjoying its elegant products.

Miyagikyo, also known as the Sendai distillery, opened in 1969, just before Suntory's Hakushu. Nikka's founder Masataka Taketsuru identified its location, sandwiched between the Hirosegawa and Nikkawagawa rivers and surrounded by mountains, as ideal for making whisky. It has sometimes been overshadowed by Nikka's much older Yoichi distillery in Hokkaido, but in recent years has been making waves of its own, with its 12 year old expression winning the best Japanese single malt category in the 2009 World Whisky Awards and a gold medal at the International Spirits Challenge (ISC) in 2010.

Tasting note:
Miyagikyo 10 year old
A restrained, butter and vanilla nose. Starts out mild and sweet in the mouth but opens out with big oaky, dark chocolate and tobacco gestures. Miyagikyo has a reputation for relatively quiet malts but this young bottling shows the danger of type casting

Shinshu

Owner: Hombo Shuzo   **Founded**: 1960
Capacity: 25,000 litres
Malt whisky range: Mars Maltage Komagatake Single Malt 10 year old; Mars Single Cask Vintage Malt Whisky Komagatake 1988, 1989 and 1992. Maltage Komagatake and "3 plus 25" pure malt.

Things were looking pretty gloomy for Shinshu a year and a half ago, when a visitor to the distillery reported that one of its long disused stills was too damaged to be run and that its warehouse, which had not received new spirit since the early 1990s, was running low. In July of last year, however, Hombo Shuzo , the general brewing and distilling company that owns Shinshu, announced that it had decided to overhaul the distilling room and get back into production.

"We started up again in February and things went smoothly," reports Masahito Matsushima of Hombo. "We produced about 25, 000 liters of spirit by April, the end of this year's distilling run."

For the foreseeable future, production will be intermittent, with the next distilling period scheduled between the end of this year and next April. The 2011 spirit is mainly being matured in bourbon barrels, with a few new casks and sherry barrels also being used.

It is great to have Hombo and its Mars whisky brand back because the company has an important place in Japanese whisky history. Its stills were designed back in 1960 by Kiichiro Iwai, who was one of the men who decided to send Nikka Whisky founder Masataka Taketsuru on his historic journey to Scotland in 1918 and was the manager who received Taketsuru's report on whisky making on his return. Hombo is considering whether to release new spirit bottlings in the way Chichibu did in the three years before it could release proper whisky, but nothing has yet been decided. In the meantime, we can enjoy their Komagatake single cask series, and two new vatted malts released to coincide with the restart of distilling: the 10 year old Maltage Komagatake pure malt and the Mars Maltage "3 plus 25," which includes whisky made from Hombo's two previous distillery sites in Kagoshima and Yamanashi prefectures.

Yamazaki

Owner: Suntory **Founded**: 1924
Capacity: 3,500,000 litres
Malt whisky range: Yamazaki Single Malt 10, 12, 18, 25, 35 and 50 years old and a range of limited edition bottlings.

The Yamazaki distillery, nestled in forested hills between Kyoto and Osaka, was the first malt whisky distillery in Japan when it was set up by Shinjiro Torii and Masataka Taketsuru in 1924, and it is possible that it might establish itself as the first major Japanese distillery with a truly global reach in the 2010s.

This year, sales of Yamazaki in the United States were up 28% year-on-year. While many Japanese whiskies have enjoyed success in Europe, Japanese whisky makers have until now failed to make any serious impact on the U.S. market. While the amounts being sold are still tiny compared with the major Scottish and U.S. distillers, Suntory does seem committed to building a global presence for Yamazaki. The news that the Yamazaki 1984 had won the best single malt award at the World Whiskies Award (while Suntory's Hibiki 21 won the best blend) was overshadowed by the March 11 quake a few days later, but Yamazaki's brand is certainly on the move.

That success is not without its difficulties. In June, Suntory's Global Brand Ambassador and former Yamazaki distillery manager Hiroyoshi Miyamoto warned that Yamazaki supplies might not be able to meet global demand and that the amounts available for export would have to be adjusted.

Basically, Suntory says the problem is that it reduced its distilling because of the Japanese whisky market's substantial contraction over the past 25 years. The sudden increase of demand in Japan over the past two or three years has been putting strain on stocks, particularly for younger single malts dating back to the slump. Despite alarmist reports to the contrary, Yamazaki's stocks of its 10 year old Yamazaki whisky have not run out, but supply is short enough for Suntory to have stopped some shipments of its youngest single malt bottling this year.

Tasting note:
Yamazaki 25 year old
Cereal and rich jammy, port soaked smells. In the mouth: jam, red wine, vanilla and treacle overlaid on woods and tannins. The finish is slightly drying.

Yoichi

Owner: Nikka Whisky **Founded**: 1934
Capacity: 5,000,000 litres
Malt whisky range: Yoichi Single Malt (no age statement); Yoichi Single Malt 10, 12, 15 and 20 years old and an annual 20 year old limited release named after the year it was distilled.

Yoichi distillery was built by the father of Japanese' whisky Masataka Taketsuru when he split from Suntory in 1934 and is Japan's second oldest distillery. Taketsuru chose the location because he felt it was similar to the maritime distilleries in which he worked during his visit to Scotland in 1919 and 1920 and the distillery goes out of its way to preserve the techniques taught by Taketsuru, still using old coal-fired pot stills and tending to favour charred, unused casks for maturing its whiskies.

At the 2010 International Spirits Challenge, the 15 year old Yoichi won a gold medal for the second year running, adding yet another award to the many gongs its spirits have garnered since 2001, when it was a 10 year old Yoichi whisky that won the "Best of the Best" award at Whisky Magazine's World Whiskies Awards, and started to attract global attention to Japanese whisky.

Tasting note:
Yoichi 12 year old
Plump squashy dried apricots on the nose. Sweet and mild on first tasting but then becomes more assertive and complex, with earthy themes developing. Yoichi has a reputation for providing some of the more "masculine" of Japanese malts. This is a good example.

Distilleries
around the globe

James Sedgwick Distillery, South Africa

One of the most important issues for a whisky distiller to address, once he has started his operation, is how to survive the first years economically. In most cases, whisky requires a certain time of maturation before it can be bottled and turned into cash. One way of solving this would be to produce a number of other spirits which don´t require maturation, like, for instance, gin and vodka and let the sales fund the whisky production. Another way is to speed up maturation or sell the whisky at a younger age. For years, the small craft distillers around the world have been celebrated for their ingenuity and their will to challenge the established producers. Reports have been written on how the Scots should beware of the competition and whisky aficionados have tried to find ways of getting hold of bottlings from those new kids on the whisky block.

Lately, a new discussion about craft distillers has started, mainly in the USA. Some people argue that cutting corners when it comes to maturation will only result in an inferior product, while others maintain the view that we should not compare the whisky from some of these new producers with the products from the established distilleries. It is a different drink altogether albeit made from the same ingredients - barley, water and yeast. The reason why this discussion has started in USA is that, in contrast with many other whisky producing countries, there is no law stipulating a minimum time of maturation in order to call the final product whisky. One day in a cask is enough for you to be able to sell it as whisky. In order to put the prefix "straight" to the name though, it has to be matured for a minimum time of two years.

But even if you don´t have the benefit of a lenient legislation, there are other ways of (at least supposedly) speeding up the maturation and that is by using smaller casks. In accordance with those who advocate this method, smaller casks will increase the wood to whisky ratio, which means the wood will have a more intense impact on the maturing spirit and the whisky will be ready to drink in a shorter time. On the opposite side are the people saying that it is not just about getting as much impact from the oak as possible but to allow this to happen under perfect conditions, including a long period of time. Otherwise the result will be a lack of complexity and balance.

In spite of these discussions, the number of enthusiastic and competent craftsmen continue to make their way into the world of whisky making. A number of new entries from USA are included in this year´s edition, bringing the total up to 31, and we have now reached a point where it is almost impossible to keep track of all the newcomers, especially since we are looking only for those who have malt whisky on their agenda.

Sweden is another country where the interest is booming. The three distilleries from last year have been supplemented by another three and there are more in the pipeline, for example Lappland Destilleri in Arvidsjaur (at the same latitude as Alaska) which will become the world´s most northerly whisky distillery when finished.

Meanwhile, the distilleries outside Scotland, Ireland and Japan, are not only about small operations. In Taiwan, Kavalan distillery (with a capacity to produce 4 million litres in a year) are preparing to start exporting their whiskies to other countries. Amrut in India is already established in Europe and USA and continue to astonish with exciting bottlings. Mackmyra in Sweden is also getting a foothold on the American market and is working on yet another distillery to be ready in late 2011.

These three producers have already released single malts that can compete with many of their Scottish equals, yet at the same time are both unique and distinctive in character.

EUROPE

Austria _____

DISTILLERY: Waldviertler Roggenhof,
Roggenreith
FOUNDED: 1995
OWNER/MANAGER: Johann & Monika Haider
www.roggenhof.at

In the small village of Roggenreith in northern Austria, Johann and Monika Haider have been distilling whisky since 1995. In 2005, they opened up a Whisky Experience World with guided tours, a video show, whisky tasting and exhibitions. Six years later, more than 75,000 visitors find their way to the distillery every year. Roggenhof was the first whisky distillery in Austria and over the years production has increased to currently reach 30,000 litres. The capacity is 100,000 litres annually.

The wash is allowed to ferment for 72 hours before it reaches either of the two 450 litre Christian Carl copper stills. The desired strength is reached in one single distillation, thanks to the attached column.

The new make is filled in casks made of the local Manhartsberger Oak adding a slight vanilla flavour and left to mature for three years. When the casks are used a second time, the whisky matures for five years. The casks are used a third time, but only after dismantling, shaving and charring before filling. Spirit on third fill casks is expected to mature for 12-18 years. A new warehouse was commissioned in June 2009 so there is now storage capacity for almost 3,000 barrels. Two single malts made of barley are available: Gersten Malzwhisky J. H. (light malt) and Gersten Malzwhisky J. H. Karamell (dark, roasted malt). There are also three different rye whiskies. Two new expressions were released in autumn 2011 – one single malt and one from dark, malted rye and both of them peated.

Johann Haider from Waldviertler Roggenhof

DISTILLERY: Wolfram Ortner Destillerie,
Bad Kleinkirchheim
FOUNDED: 1990
OWNER/MANAGER: Wolfram Ortner
www.wob.at

Fruit brandies of all kinds make up the bulk of Wolfram Ortner´s produce, as well as cigars, coffee and other luxuries. For the last years he has also been producing malt whisky. New oak of different kinds (Limousin, Alolier, Nevers, Vosges and American) is used for the maturation process. His first single malt, WOB DÖ MALT Vergin, began selling in 2001 and an additional product line, in which Ortner mixes his whisky with other distillates such as orange/moscatel, is called WOB Marriage.

DISTILLERY: Reisetbauer, Kirchberg-Thening
FOUNDED: 1994 (whisky since 1995)
OWNER/MANAGER: Julia & Hans Resisetbauer
www.reisetbauer.at

This is a family-owned farm distillery near Linz in northern Austria specialising in brandies and fruit schnapps. Since 1995, a range of malt whiskies are also produced. The distillery is equipped with five 350 litre stills. All stills are heated, using hot water rather than steam, which, according to Hans Reisetbauer, allows for a more delicate and gentle distillation. The 70 hour-long fermentation takes place in stainless steel washbacks. Approximately 20,000 litres of pure alcohol destined for whisky making are produced annually, using local barley to make the unpeated malt. Casks are sourced locally from the best Austrian wine producers.

In 2002, the first whisky was released as a 6 year old. The current range includes a 7 year old single malt which consists of a vatting of whiskies aged in casks that have previously contained Chardonnay and Trockenbeerenauslese. There is also a 10 year old cask strength aged exclusively in Trockenbeerenauslese and a 12 year old (the first for Austria) which has also undergone maturation in Trockenbeerenauslese barrels. The whisky is currently exported to Germany, Switzerland, France, the Netherlands, Denmark, Russia, the United Kingdom and the USA.

DISTILLERY: Destillerie Weutz,
St. Nikolai im Sausal
FOUNDED: 2002
OWNER/MANAGER: Michael & Brigitte Weutz
www.weutz.at

This family distillery, initially producing schnapps and liqueur from fruits and berries, is situated in Steiermark in the south of Austria. In 2004 Michael Weutz started cooperation with the brewer Michael Löscher and since then Weutz has added whisky to its produce based on the wash from the brewery. The business grew quickly and in 2006 the distillery moved to a bigger location. Since 2004, 14 different malt whiskies have been produced. Some of them are produced in the traditional Scottish style: Hot Stone, St. Nikolaus and the peated Black Peat. Others are more unorthodox, for example Green Panther, in which 5% pumpkin seeds are added to the mash, and Franziska based on elderflower. Apart from barley wheat, corn and spelt are also used for some expressions. Annual production is currently at approximately 14,000 litres and for maturation casks made of French Limousin and Alliere oak are used.

DISTILLERY: Old Raven, Neustift
FOUNDED: 2004
OWNER/MANAGER: Andreas Schmidt
www.oldraven.at

In 1999, Andreas Schmidt opened up his Rabenbräu brewery on their family estate. Five years later a distillery was added, located in what used to be a Hungarian customs house before 1914. More than 250,000 litres of beer are produced yearly and the wash from the brewery is used for distillation of the 2,000 litres of single malt whisky every year. Old Raven, which is triple distilled, comes in three expressions – Old Raven, Old Raven Smoky and Old Raven R1 Smoky. The last one was filled into a PX sherry cask which had been used to mature Islay whisky. The first whisky was released in 2009 as a 5 year old.

Belgium _____

DISTILLERY: The Owl Distillery, Grâce Hollogne
FOUNDED: 1997
OWNER/MANAGER: Etienne Bouillon (manager),
                 Luc Foubert and Pierre Roberti
www.belgianwhisky.com
www.thebelgianowl.com

In October 2007, Belgium's first single malt 'The Belgian Owl', was released. The next bottling came in June 2008 but was exclusively reserved for private customers. The first commercial bottling was introduced in November 2008, and in February 2009 another 2,766 bottles were released. Bouillon expects to produce around 24,000 bottles annually with five releases per year. A limited cask strength expression, 44 months old, was released end of 2009.

The distillery is equipped with a mash tun holding 4.1 tonnes per mash, one washback where the wash is fermented for 60-100 hours and finally one wash still (550 litres) and one spirit still (450 litres). Every step of production (including malting) is carried out at the distillery near Liege and maturation takes place in first fill bourbon casks from Kentucky. The whisky is neither coloured nor chill-filtered. At the moment, The Belgian Owl is sold in Belgium, The Netherlands and France.

DISTILLERY: Het Anker Distillery, Blaasfeld
FOUNDED: 1369 (whisky since 2003)
OWNER/MANAGER: Charles Leclef (owner)
www.hetanker.be

Seven years ago the producer of the quality beer Gouden Carolus, Brouwerij Het Anker, and its owner, Charles Leclef, decided to find out how whisky, distilled from the brewery's wash, would taste. Distillation of the spirits

was tasked to nearby genever distiller, Filliers, and was done in a genever column still. The result was Gouden Carolus Single Malt – the third Belgian malt whisky to reach the market after Belgian Owl and Goldlys. The first 3,000 bottles were released in January 2008.

No new releases were made in 2009. Instead, Leclef concentrated on the next step in the project, namely, building a distillery of his own with pot stills. The location chosen was not at the brewery in Mechelen, but at Leclef's family estate, Molenberg, at Blaasfeld. Leclef is the fifth generation of a family that long since has been involved in distilling genever and brewing beer. The distillery started producing in October 2010 and they hope to be open for visitors as well by April 2012. The stills have been made by Forsyth's in Scotland with a wash still of 3,000 litre capacity and a spirit still of 2,000 litres. The wash for the distillation is made at the brewery in Mechelen and it is basically a Gouden Carolus Tripel beer without hops and spices and with a fermentation time of four to five days. To get the character the owners are looking for, the middle cut during the spirit run is quite small with the collection of the spirit starting at 74% and a cut off point at 68%. It will be possible to make 100,000 litres of alcohol per year and the first release will be in December 2013.

Czech Rebublic _____

DISTILLERY: Gold Cock Distillery
FOUNDED: 1877
OWNER/MANAGER: Rudolf Jelinek a.s
www.rjelinek.cz

The distilling of Gold Cock whisky started already in 1877. Gold Cock was originally a malt whisky made from abundunt local barley. Now it is produced in two versions – a 3 year old blended whisky and a 12 year old malt. Production was stopped for a while but after the brand and distillery were acquired by R. Jelinek a.s., the leading Czech producer of plum brandy, the whisky began life anew. The malt whisky is double distilled in 500 litre traditional pot stills. The new owner has created a small whisky museum which is also home to the club Friends of Gold Cock Whisky with private vaults, where any enthusiast can store his bottlings of Gold Cock.

The location for Het Anker's new distillery

Gold Cock 12 year old single malt

Denmark _____

DISTILLERY: Stauning Whisky, Stauning
FOUNDED: 2006
OWNER/MANAGER: Stauning Whisky A/S
www.stauningwhisky.dk

The first Danish purpose-built malt whisky distillery entered a more adolescent phase in May 2009, after having experimented with two small pilot stills bought from Spain. Two new, Portugese-made stills of 1,000 and 600 litres respectively were installed and the distillery could try its wings. Only the new stills are currently used, but it is possible that the smaller stills will be used for special distillations in the future.

The aim has always been to be self-sustaining and Danish barley is bought and turned into malt on an own malting floor. The germinating barley usually has to be turned 6-8 times a day, but Stauning has constructed an automatic "grain turner" to do the job. Two core expressions were decided on – Peated Reserve and Traditional Reserve – and the peat for the first one is acquired from one of few remaining peat bogs in Denmark. A further variety, a rye whisky, has also entered production. The whisky is made from 100% malted rye, like e. g. Old Potrero Single Malt from USA. Most of production is stored in first fill ex-bourbon barrels from Makers Mark. The first release of a rye was made in spring 2011 and the second (called Stauning Rye - Second Opinion) was bottled at 48% and released in August 2011.

A first, limited edition of 750 bottles each of the two single malt expressions will be released in May 2012. The annual production is roughly 7,000 litres, but is expected to be increased.

DISTILLERY: Braunstein, Køge
FOUNDED: 2005 (whisky since 2007)
OWNER/MANAGER: Michael & Claus Braunstein
www.braunstein.dk

Denmark's first micro-distillery was built in an already existing brewery in Køge, just south of Copenhagen. Unlike many other brewery/whisky distillery enterprises around

the world, the owners consider the whisky production to be on equal terms with beer production, even in financial terms.

The wash, of course, comes from the own brewery. A Holstein type of still, with four plates in the rectification column, is used for distillation and the spirit is distilled once. For five winter months, peated whisky (+60ppm) is produced, while the rest of the year is devoted to unpeated varieties. Peated malt is bought from Port Ellen, unpeated from Simpsons, but as much as 40% is from ecologically grown Danish barley. The lion's share of the whisky is stored on ex-bourbon (peated version) and first fill Oloroso casks (unpeated) from 190 up to 500 litres. The long-term aspirations are to produce a 100% Danish whisky.

The Braunstein brothers filled their first spirit casks in March 2007 and have produced 50,000 litres annually since then. Their first release and the first release of a malt whisky produced in Denmark was on 22nd March 2010 – a 3 year old single Oloroso sherry cask called Edition No. 1. In May the same year, Library Collection 10:1, bottled at 46% was released followed by Library Collection 10:2, the first Braunstein to be peated. In December 2010, Library Collection 10:3 (sherry cask and unpeated) was released together with Edition No. 2, a cask strength ex-bourbon barrel. April 2011 saw the release of Library Collection 11:1 (unpeated sherry cask) followed by Library Collection 11:2 in September and finally, the first Braunstein whisky from 100% ecologically grown barley, was released as Edition No. 3.

DISTILLERY: Ørbæk Bryggeri, Ørbæk
FOUNDED: 1997 (whisky since 2007)
OWNER/MANAGER: Niels and Nicolai Rømer
www.oerbaek-bryggeri.nu

Niels Rømer and his son, Nicolai, have run Ørbæk Brewery since 1997 on the Danish island of Fyn. It is now one of many combinations of a micro-brewery and a micro-distillery where the wash from the brewery is used to produce whisky. Aspirations to start distilling whisky already appeared in 2007, but it took another two years to get the final approvals from Health and Safety authorities. In June 2009 the first barrels of Isle of Fionia single malt were filled and the first release is planned for 2012. The whisky, in common with Ørbæk's beer, will be ecological and two different expressions are planned

The still room of Braunstein Distillery

The first release of a rye whisky from Stauning

– Isle of Fionia and the peated Fionia Smoked Whisky. It is matured in ex-bourbon barrels from Jack Daniels and ex-sherry casks. Within five years the estimated yearly production will amount to 10-20,000 bottles. In April 2011, the Römer family announced that they had plans to open yet another distillery in Nyborg, some 10 miles from the existing plant. An old railway workshop was bought and if everything goes according to plan, the new distillery could open in 2013.

DISTILLERY: Fary Lochan Destilleri, Give
FOUNDED: 2009
OWNER/MANAGER: Jens Erik Jørgensen
www.farylochan.dk

This is the second, purpose-built whisky distillery in Denmark to come on stream and, just like the first, Stauning, it is situated in Jutland. The first cask was filled on 31st of December 2009 and the owner has recently increased the production from 3,000 bottles per year to 6,000. The actual capacity of the distillery is 12,000 bottles.

Jørgensen imports most of the malted barley from the UK, but he also malts some Danish barley by himself. A part of his own malted barley is dried using nettles instead of peat to create a special flavour. This is a well-known technique used in Denmark to produce smoked cheese. After mashing, it is fermented for five days in a 600 litre stainless steel washback. Distillation is performed in two traditional copper pot stills from Forsyth's in Scotland – a 300 litre wash still and a 200 litre spirit still. The spirit is matured in ex-bourbon barrels, some of which have been remade into quarter casks. Jørgensen is aiming for a soft and mellow character of the whisky, but some of it will also be lightly or medium smoked. The first release (750 bottles very lightly smoked) is expected to take place in autumn 2013.

England _____

DISTILLERY: St. George's Distillery,
Roudham, Norfolk
FOUNDED: 2006
OWNER/MANAGER: The English Whisky Co.
www.englishwhisky.co.uk

St. George's Distillery near Thetford in Norfolk was started by father and son, James and Andrew Nelstrop, and came on stream on12th December 2006. This made it the first English malt whisky distillery for over a hundred years. Customers, both in the UK and abroad, have had the opportunity to follow the development of the whisky

via releases of new make, as well as 18 months old spirit, both peated and unpeated. These were called Chapters 1 to 4. Finally, in December 2009, it was time for the release of the first legal whisky called Chapter 5 – unpeated and without chill filtering or colouring. This was a limited release but, soon afterwards, Chapter 6 was released in larger quantities. The next expression (Chapter 8) was a limited release of a lightly peated 3 year old, followed in June 2010 by Chapter 9 (with the same style but more widely available). Chapter 7, a 3 year old with 6 months finish in a rum cask, was planned for a launch in spring 2010, but was not released until autumn 2010 together with Chapter 10, which has a sherry cask finish. The next bottling, Chapter 11, appeared in July 2011. This is the heaviest peated expression so far (50ppm) while Chapters 8 and 9 had a phenol content of 32ppm. Chapter 11 is between 3 and 4 years old and has matured in bourbon casks. It will be on allocation until May 2012 when a possible general release could be due. In between the Chapter releases there are also very limited bottlings of the so called Founder's Private Cellar.

Nearly 50,000 bottles were sold in 2010 and the owners hope to increase that to 60,000 bottles for 2011. Important markets are Benelux, France, Scotland, Japan, Singapore and England.

The distillery is equipped with a stainless steel semi-lauter mash tun with a copper top and three stainless steel washbacks with a fermentation time of 85 hours. There is one pair of stills, the wash still with a capacity of 2,800 litres and the spirit still of 1,800 litre capacity. First fill bourbon barrels are mainly used for maturation but the odd Sherry, Madeira and Port casks have also been filled. The casks are stored in a dunnage warehouse on site which is now slowly filling up, but the construction of another warehouse will start in August 2010. Non-peated malt is bought from Crisp Malting Group and peated malt from Simpson's Malt in Berwick-upon-Tweed. Around 60% of production is unpeated and the rest is peated.

Recently, a bottling line was installed, giving St. George's the possibility to bottle using its own water source. The capacity is 800 bottles per day. Around 150,000 bottles will be produced during 2011.

St George's Distillery and a bottle of Chapter 11

Finland

DISTILLERY: Teerenpeli, Lahti
FOUNDED: 2002
OWNER/MANAGER: Anssi Pyysing
www.teerenpeli.com

The first Teerenpeli Single Malt was sold as a 3 year old in late 2005, though solely at the owner's restaurant in Lahti. Four years later, the first bottles of a 6 year old were sold in the Teerenpeli Restaurants and later that year also in the state owned ALKO-shops. In spring 2011, it was time for an 8 year old, which was introduced at Whisky Live in London. This is a mix of whisky from both bourbon and sherry casks. A limited edition, a vatted expression with Teerenpeli and an undisclosed Speyside malt for sale only at the restaurants, was released at the end of 2010.

Teerenpeli is equipped with one wash still (1,500 litres) and one spirit still (900 litres) and the average fermentation time in the washback is 70 hours. Lightly peated malt obtained locally is used and the whisky matures in ex-sherry and ex-bourbon casks from Speyside Cooperage. 7,500 bottles are produced annually. In August 2010 a new mash tun was installed and later that month a new visitor centre was opened.

France

DISTILLERY: Glann ar Mor, Pleubian, Bretagne
FOUNDED: 1999
OWNER/MANAGER: Jean Donnay
www.glannarmor.com

Glann ar Mor Distillery in Brittany ("Glann ar Mor" literally means "By the Sea" in Breton language) reached one of its goals in 2008: the first official bottling was launched – a 3 year old unpeated version. The next release came in September 2009, this time a peated version under the name Kornog ("West Wind") and bottled from a bourbon barrel at cask strength. February 2010 saw the second editions of both versions (which sold out in a fortnight) and this time bottled at 46%. The next bottling was in November and from 2011, larger quantities became available.

The owner of Glann ar Mor Distillery in Brittany, Jean Donnay, already started his first trials back in 1999. He then made some changes to the distillery and the process and regular production commenced on 12th June 2005. The distillery is very much about celebrating the traditional way of distilling malt whisky. The two small stills are directly fired and Donnay uses worm tubs for condensing the spirit. He practises a long fermentation in wooden washbacks and the distillation is very slow. For maturation, first fill bourbon barrels and ex-Sauternes casks are used and when the whisky is bottled, there is neither chill filtration nor caramel colouring. The full capacity is 50,000 bottles per year. In 2008 the company opened its new premises, including a larger warehouse and a visitor centre, a couple of miles away from the distillery's location, still by the seaside.

There are two versions of the whisky from Glann ar Mor – the unpeated Glann ar Mor matured in bourbon barrels and the peated Kornog matured in either bourbon barrels or Sauternes casks. The first release, in 2008, was a 3 year old Glann ar Mor followed in 2009 by a Kornog bottled at cask strength. The most recent expressions are the bourbon matured Kornog Taouarc'h Eilvet 11 BC, Glann ar Mor - 2eil Gwech 11 and Kornog Saint Ivy 2011, the last one bottled at cask strength.

Currently available in Europe only, Jean has plans to sell his whisky in the USA as well, however the introduction has been delayed due to the costs involved producing special 75 cl bottles for the American market.

Apart from the Glann ar Mor venture, Jean Donnay has also specialised in double maturation Single Malts. The "Celtique Connexion" range includes whiskies originally distilled and matured in Scotland, then further matured at the company's seaside warehouse. The casks used for this are from Sauternes, Vin de Paille du Jura, Armagnac, Champagne and Coteau du Layon, amongst others.

The whiskies can be found at www.tregorwhisky.com

The worm tub at Glann ar Mor distillery and Kornog Saint Ivy, one of the most recent bottlings

DISTILLERY: Distillerie Guillon,
Louvois, Champagne
FOUNDED: 1997
OWNER/MANAGER: Thierry Guillon
www.whisky-guillon.com

Thierry Guillon, originally a wine man, decided in 1997 to begin distilling whisky. Not perhaps a novel idea if it was not for the fact that the distillery is located in the heart of the Champagne district. But besides champagne this area is also known as a major barley producer in France. In fact, several Scottish maltsters buy barley from this region. Guillon has increased his production steadily and now makes 140,000 bottles a year and has 1,200 casks maturing on site.

The range of single malts is quite large and vary in age between 4 and 10 years. Guillon No. 1, has a particularly interesting maturation process. It is a 5 year old matured in a new oak cask the first year, a whisky barrel the second year, then white wine, red wine and finally the last year in a Port pipe. Apart from single malts there is also a blend in the range, Le Premium Blend, consisting of 50% malt and 50% grain whisky and a whisky liqueur. The whisky is exported to several European countries, as well as to China. There is also a visitor centre, which attracts 15,000 visitors per year.

DISTILLERY: Distillerie Bertrand,
Uberach, Alsace
FOUNDED: 1874 (whisky since 2002)
OWNER/MANAGER: Affiliate of Wolfberger
www.distillerie-bertrand.com

Distillerie Bertrand is an independent affiliate of Wolfberger, the large wine and eaux-de-vie producer. The manager, Jean Metzger, gets his malt from a local brewer and then distils it in Holstein type stills. Two different types of whisky are produced. One is a single malt at 42.2%, non-chill filtered and with maturation in both new barrels and barrels which have previously contained the fortified wine Banyuls. The other is a single cask at 43.8% matured only in Banyuls barrels. The first bottles, aged 4 years, were released in late 2006 and the annual production is around 7,000 bottles with currently 5,000 bottles being sold per year. In late 2008 Jean Metzger released a limited Single Cask Collection from six different Banyuls barrels. In June 2009 the next expression came – a double matured whisky with a 12 months finish in a Vin Jaune barrel. New releases for 2010 included a 6 year old with three months´ finish in a Pinot Gris vendange tardive cask from Alsace and a 7 year old matured in a Banyuls cask. There are also plans for future releases of whisky matured in cognac and champagne barrels.

At the moment, Uberach Single Malt Alsace, a name taken from the village, is only sold in France, Germany, Switzerland, Luxembourg and Andorra.

DISTILLERY: Distillerie Warenghem,
Lannion, Bretagne
FOUNDED: 1900 (whisky since 1994)
OWNER/MANAGER: Warenghem
www.distillerie-warenghem.com

Leon Warenghem founded the distillery at the beginning of the 20th century but Armorik, the first malt whisky, was not distilled until 1994 and released in 1999. Since 1983 Gilles Leîzour has run the distillery. The Armorik single malt now exists in two versions; a 4 year old that is bottled at 40%, matured in bourbon barrels and finished in sherry casks, and a 7 year old (42%) with a double maturation in fresh oak and sherry butts. Three blended whiskies supplement the range; Whisky Breton W. B., a 3 year old with 25% share of malt, Breizh matured in fresh oak and with a 50% malt content, as well as Galleg, matured in both sherry and bourbon casks and also with a 50% malt content.

Germany

DISTILLERY: Slyrs Destillerie, Schliersee
FOUNDED: 1928 (whisky since 1999)
OWNER/MANAGER: Florian Stetter
www.slyrs.de

Lantenhammer Destillerie in Schliersee, Bavaria was founded in 1928 and was producing mainly brandy until 1999 when whisky came into the picture, and in 2003 Slyrs Destillerie was founded. The malt, smoked with beech, comes from locally grown grain, and the spirit is distilled twice at low temperatures in the 1,500 litre stills. Maturation takes place in charred 225-litre casks of new American White Oak from Missouri. Recently the owner decided to double the capacity of the distillery. Investments in three new fermentation tanks (washbacks) and a malt silo during 2009/2010 increased the capacity to 60,000 bottles.

The non chill-filtered whisky is called Slyrs after the original name of the surrounding area, Schliers. Around 30,000 bottles were released in 2008 and every year 3,000-5,000 bottles are kept for later release. A cask strength version has been bottled a couple of times under the name Raritas Diaboli and a 12 year old is planned for 2015. Slyrs whisky is available in several European countries and is also exported to the USA and Australia.

DISTILLERY: Spreewälder Feinbrand- &
Likörfabrik, Schlepzig
FOUNDED: 2004 (whisky production)
OWNER/MANAGER: Torsten Römer
www.spreewaldbrennerei.de

This distillery with attached brewery lies in Spreewald, circa 100 km south-east of Berlin. The main product range consists of different kinds of beers, eau-de-vie and rum, and since 2004 also malt whisky.

In the beginning, a 100 litre still with an attached column was used, but in late summer of 2010, a new still was installed. This 650 litre still has eight trays in the fractionating column, is fired using gas and has been specially designed by the famous still manufacturer, Christian Carl. The annual production of whisky and rum has now increased to 15,000 litres per year.

French Oak casks, that have previously contained wine made of Sylvaner and Riesling grapes, are used for maturation, as well as new medium toasted Spessart oak casks. Torsten Römer is also looking for other casks in Germany (Sylvaner), France (Sauternes) and Spain (Manzanilla). Before filling into casks the spirit is left for six months in stainless steel tanks. The whisky, which was first released in December 2007 as a 3 year old, is called Sloupisti, which is the ancient Sorbic name of the village Schlepzig. Most of the production is bottled at 40%, but a cask strength bottling was released in autumn 2010. Some barrels are also reserved for a 12 year old to be released in 2016. In 2011, forty barriques (225 litre) of single malt were filled and the next project Torsten is looking at is making rum from molasses from Sudan, India and Equador. He has already tried it in the smaller still and filled into used whisky casks. The rum will eventually be sold under the name Blotha.

DISTILLERY: Whisky-Destillerie Blaue Maus,
Eggolsheim-Neuses
FOUNDED: 1980
OWNER/MANAGER: Robert Fleischmann
www.fleischmann-whisky.de

This is the oldest single malt whisky distillery in Germany and it celebrated its 25th anniversary in February 2008.

The first distillate, never released on the market, was made in 1983. It took 15 years until the first whisky, Glen Mouse 1986, appeared. Fleischmann uses unpeated malt and the whisky matures for approximately eight years in casks of fresh German Oak. All whisky from Blaue Maus are single cask and with the release of two new expressions in 2010, Elbe 1 and Otto´s Uisge Beatha, there are currently eight single malts, the others being Blaue Maus, Spinnaker, Krottentaler, Schwarzer Pirat, Grüner Hund and Old Fahr. Some of them are released at cask strength while others are reduced to 40%. The oldest bottlings are more than 20 years old. A new expression was introduced quite recently; Austrasier is the first grain whisky from the distillery. In 2006 a new distillery was built solely for whisky production while mostly new types of malt are produced in the older distillery.

DISTILLERY: Hammerschmiede, Zorge
FOUNDED: 1984 (whisky since 2002)
OWNER/MANAGER: Karl-Theodor and
Alexander Buchholz
www.hammerschmiede.de

In common with many other small whisky producers on mainland Europe, Hammerschmiede´s main products are liqueurs, bitters and spirits from fruit, berries and herbs. But whisky distilling was embarked on in 2002 and whisky production has now increased to 15% of the total.

Unpeated malt is acquired in Germany and mature the spirit in a variety of casks – German oak, sherry, cognac, port, bordeaux, bergerac, marsala, malaga and madeira casks, as well as Dornfelder barriques (German red wine).

The first 278 bottles were released in early 2006 under the name Glan Iarran. Today, all whisky produced has changed name to Glen Els after the small river Elsbach which flows past the premises. So far, the owners have specialized in single cask releases and this will continue. In autumn 2010, however, the first "distillery edition" of Glen Els was launched – 5,000 bottles mostly from ex-sherry casks.

So far the whisky has been matured for 3-4 years, but older expressions can be expected in the future. The bottlings for 2011 have been their Unique Distillery Edition (2,500 bottles) as well as a number of single casks (Madeira, Marsala, Port, Sherry and German oak).

Hammerschmiede´s new bottle

A special, limited expression (100 bottles) is planned for 2012 to celebrate the distillery´s 10th anniversary. At the moment 8,000 bottles are sold annually.

DISTILLERY: Bayerwald-Bärwurzerei und
Spezialitäten-Brennerei Liebl, Kötzting
FOUNDED: 1970 (whisky since 2006)
OWNER/MANAGER: Gerhard Liebl Jr.
www.bayerischer-whisky.de

In 1970 Gerhard Liebl started spirit distillation from fruits and berries. The distillery was rebuilt and expanded on several occasions until 2006, when his son, Gerhard Liebl Jr., built a completely new whisky distillery nearby. Leibl Jr. uses 100% Bavarian malt and the wash is left to ferment for 3-5 days. It is then double distilled in Holstein stills (wash still 400 litres and spirit still 150 litres). Assisted by the attached rectification columns, completely different levels of alcohol compared to a Scottish distillery are obtained. The low wines from the wash still are at 40% and the middle cut from the spirit still at 85%. Maturation takes place in first or second fill ex-bourbon barrels, except for whisky destined to be bottled as single casks. Sherry, Port, Bordeaux and Cognac casks are used here. The whisky is non chill-filtered and non-coloured. About 10,000 litres of whisky are produced per year and in spring and summer 2009 the first 1,500 bottles bearing the name Coillmór were released in three different expressions – American White Oak, Sherry single cask and Bordeaux single cask. Since then, a number of other expressions have been released such as Port single cask and a peated version. All the single cask releases are bottled at 46%

DISTILLERY: Brennerei Höhler, Aarbergen
FOUNDED: 1895 (whisky since 2001)
OWNER/MANAGER: Holger Höhler
www.brennerei-hoehler.de

The main produce from this distillery in Hessen consists of different distillates from fruit and berries. In November 2000, a new 390 litre still with four rectifying plates from Firma Christian Carl was installed. Whisky production commenced thereafter. The first whisky, a bourbon variety, was distilled in 2001 and released in 2004. Since then, Holger Höhler has experimented with different types of grain (rye, barley, spelt and oat). There was a limited release of a single malt in July 2007 and a very limited amount of whisky has been released since then. Until recently, all casks were made from Sessart oak with a storage capacity of between 30 and 75 litres. In spring 2007 Höhler started filling 225 litres barriques. He aims to increase production and eventually launch older whisky.

DISTILLERY: Preussische Whiskydestillerie,
Mark Landin
FOUNDED: 2009
OWNER/MANAGER: Cornelia Bohn
www.preussischerwhisky.de

Cornelia Bohn, one of few female whisky producers in Germany, transformed an 1850s stable into a whisky distillery in 2009. Thinking whisky production would be her hobby, she has kept her job as a pharmacist at a local drugstore during this process. A 550 litre copper still with a 4-plate rectification column attached was bought from Firma Arnold Holstein and the malt is brought in from a malting in Bamberg. Some of the malt is smoked (not peated) using beechwood. Maturation takes place in casks made of American oak but also the German Spessart oak. Around 2000 litres per year are produced and the first release of a 3 year old whisky is scheduled for December 2012.

Liechtenstein

DISTILLERY: Brennerei Telser, Triesen
FOUNDED: 1880 (whisky production since 2006)
OWNER/MANAGER: Telser family
www.brennerei-telser.com

The first distillery in Liechtenstein to produce whisky is not a new distillery. It has existed since 1880 and is now run by the fourth generation of the family. Traditions are strong and Telser is probably the only distillery in Europe still using a wood fire to heat the small stills (150 and 120 litres). Like so many other distilleries on mainland Europe, Telser produces mainly spirits from fruits and berries, including grappa and vodka. For whisky, the distillery uses a mixture of different malts (some peated) that are also used by local breweries. The first bottling of Telsington was distilled in May 2006 and released in July 2009. After an extremely long fermentation (10 days), the spirit was triple distilled, filled into a Pinot Noir barrique and left to mature for three years in a 500 year old cellar with an earth floor resembling the dunnage warehouses of Scotland. The second release of Telsington (distilled in 2007) consisted of 200 bottles released in June 2010, non chill-filtered and bottled at 42%. In autumn 2011, time had come for the third edition. This time it was a 4 year old whisky with an even longer fermentation than before (two weeks). The first three releases have all been single casks but the owners are now planning for a launch of a new core whisky which will be released in greater numbers. The T4, probably with a launch date around Christmas, will be 3 years old and this time not a single cask.

The stills at Brennerei Telser

The Netherlands

DISTILLERY: Us Heit Distillery, Bolsward
FOUNDED: 2002
OWNER/MANAGER: Aart van der Linde
www.usheitdistillery.nl

This is one of many examples where a beer brewery also contains a whisky distillery. Frysk Hynder, as the whisky is called, was the first Dutch whisky and made its debut in 2005 at 3 years of age. The barley is grown in surrounding Friesland and malted at the distillery. The owner of the brewery and distillery, Aart van der Linde, has even developed a malting technique which he describes on a separate website - *www.mouteryfryslan.nl*. Some 10,000 bottles are produced annually and the whisky is matured in various casks - sherry, bourbon, red wine, port and cognac.

DISTILLERY: Vallei Distilleerderij, Leusden
FOUNDED: 2002 (officially opened 2004)
OWNER/MANAGER: Bert Burger
www.valleibieren.nl

This is the latest addition to Dutch whisky distilleries. Bert Burger buys barley from a local farmer but apart from that he is very much in control of the whole process from malting to bottling. The whisky is double distilled in pot stills and he produces some 2,500 litres per year. The first trials were in 2002 but in 2004 the distillery was officially opened. After a while Burger started bottling his 2 year old spirit as Valley single malt spirit in 40 ml bottles for customers to try. Finally, on 1st December 2007, the first bottles of single malt whisky reached the market as a 3 year old. Other products include whisky liqueur and two kinds of beer.

DISTILLERY: Zuidam Distillers, Baarle Nassau
FOUNDED: 1974 (whisky since 1998)
OWNER/MANAGER: Zuidam family
www.zuidam.eu

Zuidam Distillers was started in 1974 as a traditional family distillery producing liqueurs, genever, gin and vodka. The first attempts to distil malt whisky took place in 1998, but according to one of the owners, Patrick van Zuidam, the result is not fit for bottling. Instead, the first release was from the 2002 production and it was bottled in 2007 as a 5 year old.

In 2009 there were two limited editions of 8 year olds, one matured in new American Oak and one in new French Oak. This year also saw the first bottling of a 5 year old 100% potstill rye whisky. The next release, in 2010, was a peated version of the 5 year old. The malt was imported from Scotland with a phenol specification of 20ppm. Patrick's plans for the next bottlings include a cask strength rye and a cask strength malt matured in French oak.

The whisky is double distilled in two 1,000 litre pot stills made by Kothe & Holstein in Germany. For distillation of other spirits, the distillery is also equipped with two more stills of 500 and 2,000 litres respectively. The malt is sourced both locally and abroad and there are three stainless steel mash tuns. Fermentation is slow (five days) and takes place at a low temperature. The spirit is matured in new barrels made of American White Oak, but ex bourbon and ex Oloroso sherry casks are also used. Fermentation capacity has recently been increased to cope with the rising demand, both for the whisky and genever, and in August 2011 the building of additional warehouses was started.

Russia

DISTILLERY: Kizlyarskoye, Mirny, Kizlyar, Republic of Dagestan
FOUNDED: 2003
OWNER/MANAGER: Nauchno-Proizvodstvenoye Predpriyatie Whisky Rossii

In 1948 a winery called Kizlyarski was founded on the outskirts of Kizlyar in Dagestan. Most of the wines are sold locally but some brandy is produced which has become fairly well-known in other parts of Russia.

In 2003 a group of enthusiasts led by Alibek Irazi-hanov, current CEO and distillery manager, ventured into an experiment in the field of whisky. Today the equipment consists of four copper pot stills (5,000 litres each) and a stainless steel column still. Capacity is 3,000 litres of malt whisky per day and 6,000 litres of grain whisky. The spirit is matured on American oak as well as Russian oak from Maikop.

So far production has been very scarce and most of the time the stills are used for distillation of brandy. No official volumes of maturing whiskies are disclosed, nor is it clear when the company will start a consistent regular whisky distillation. But the company receives state support and is listed in prospective Dagestan state plan of Wine and Vineyards development, so it should be just a matter of time for all bureaucratic issues to be resolved.

Spain

DISTILLERY: Distilerio Molino del Arco, Segovia
FOUNDED: 1959
OWNER/MANAGER: Distilerias y Crianza del Whisky (DYC)
www.dyc.es

Spain's first whisky distillery is definitely not a small artisan distillery like so many others on these pages. Established by Nicomedes Garcia Lopez already in 1959 (with whisky distilling commencing three years later), this is a distillery with capacity for producing eight million litres of grain whisky and two million litres of malt whisky per year. In addition to that, vodka and rum are produced and there are in-house maltings which safe-guard malted barley for the production. The distillery is equipped with six copper pot stills and there are 250,000 casks maturing on site. The blending and bottling plant which used to sit beside the distillery is now relocated to the Anis Castellana plant at Valverde del Majano.

The big seller when it comes to whiskies is a blend simply called DYC which is around 4 years old. It is currently the third most sold whisky in Spain and is supplemented by an 8 year old blend and, since 2007, also by DYC Pure Malt, i. e. a vatted malt consisting of malt from the distillery and from selected Scottish distilleries. It can safely be assumed that two of these Scottish single malts come from Laphroaig and Ardmore, as Beam Global owns both, as well as DYC.

A brand new expression was also launched in 2009 to commemorate the distillery's 50th anniversary – a 10 year old single malt, the first from the distillery. In 2006, Beam Global introduced DYC blended whisky on the Indian market. It was launched as an IMFL brand (Indian Made Foreign Liquor) which means that the variety of DYC sold in India is produced from imported malt and grain whisky produced in India. The goal was to sell 500,000 cases per year. In spring of 2010 the brand was revamped

and positioned with a lower price. Obviously, sales in the premium segment were not as well as expected. Less than a year later, in February 2011, Beam announced that they would be phasing out the brand in India and instead focus completely on growing Teacher's which already has a strong position on the Indian market. Total, worldwide, sales of the brand was 1.2 million cases in 2009.

DYC has an interesting liaison with a Scottish distillery which dates back to the early seventies. It bought Lochside Distillery north of Dundee in 1973 to safeguard malt whisky requirements and retained it until it stopped production in 1992. During that time DYC was acquired by Pedro Domecq, which, in turn, was acquired by Allied Lyons, which eventually changed its name to Allied Domecq. When the latter was bought by Pernod Ricard in 2005, a small share, including DYC, went to Beam Global.

Sweden

DISTILLERY: Mackmyra Svensk Whisky, Valbo
FOUNDED: 1999
OWNER/MANAGER: Mackmyra Svensk Whisky AB
www.mackmyra.se

The first single malt from Sweden has already during its short lifetime been praised both in Sweden and abroad. Inspired by this positive feed-back, the company revealed plans in 2009 to build a brand new facility in Gävle, a few miles from the present distillery at Mackmyra.

The first stage, estimated at almost £5 million, consists of a visitor distillery and storage. Thereafter 'Mackmyra Whiskyby' (Mackmyra Whisky Village) will expand in different phases over the next ten years. The total investments are expected to amount to approximately £50 million and the capacity of the two distilleries will be approximately 2 million bottles per year, which is three times that of today. Building permission was granted in April 2010 and the construction work started in early

Mackmyra´ new distillery

2011. The stills, made by Forsyth´s in Scotland arrived in June of the same year and distillation is expected to start sometime during the second half of 2011. The construction of the distillery is quite extraordinary and with its 37 metre structure it is perhaps one of the tallest distilleries in the world. The reason for the height is that this will be a gravity fed distillery with malt and water coming in at the top of the building and then the entire production process "works itself" downwards to reach the stills at the bottom. The plan is to make a very energy efficient distillery.

Mackmyra whisky is based on two basic recipes, one resulting in a fruity and elegant whisky, the other being more peaty. The peatiness does not stem from peat, but from juniper wood and bog moss. The first release in 2006/2007 was a series of six called Preludium. The first "real" launch was in June 2008 – 'Den Första Utgåvan' (The First Edition). It was still a fairly young whisky and 95% bourbon casks and 5% casks made from Swedish Oak were used. Approximately 45% of the mix is stored in 100 litre casks. In 2009, Special:02 and Special:03 were launched, the second and third in a new series of limited editions. The sixth release in that series, also known as Sommaräng (summer meadow), was released in May 2011.

Another range of limited editions is called Moment which consists of exceptional casks selected by the Master Blender Angela D`Orazio. Four bottlings have so far been released in that series. A core expression has also been launched, Mackmyra Brukswhisky, with a maturation in first fill bourbon casks, spiced up with sherry casks and Swedish oak and bottled at 41.4%. The casks for The First Edition had all matured at a depth of 50 metres in the Archean rock in an abandoned mine in northern Sweden. Mackmyra has another four storage sites: an island in the archipelago of Stockholm, one is found along the west coast, another at a castle in the southernmost part of Sweden and (the latest) on the same site as the new distillery. About 15% of Mackmyra's production is exported and the goal is to increase it to 50%. Apart from the UK, Mackmyra is available in Canada (since autumn 2010) and USA (since April 2011).

DISTILLERY: Spirit of Hven, Ven
FOUNDED: 2007
OWNER/MANAGER: Backafallsbyn AB
www.hven.com

The second Swedish distillery to come on stream, after Mackmyra, was Spirit of Hven, a distillery situated on the island of Ven right between Sweden and Denmark. The first distillation took place in May 2008.

Henric Molin, founder and owner, is a trained chemist but this is not the only similarity with Bill Lumsden, Head of Whisky Creation at Glenmorangie. Henric is equally concerned about choosing the right oak for his casks and, like Lumsden, he sources his oak mainly in Missouri. The oak is left to air dry for three to five years before the casks are loaned to, especially, wine producers in both the USA and Europe. It is mostly sweet wines that are filled in the casks but dry white wines and bourbon could also be used. Around 70% of the casks are made of American White Oak while the rest are of Spanish Red Oak (*Quercus falcata*) and (a few percent) of Japanese Mizunara Oak (*Quercus mongolica*). By 2013, Henric will have built a wood analysis and test centre to be able to examine, not only 300 hunderd different types of oak, but also how spirit matures in other types of wood.

Henric's initial objective was to keep the whole process of whisky-making on the distillery premises. Starting in autumn of 2009 some 10% of the barley is malted on site, but more and more will come from own maltings as time passes. Peat was initially bought from Islay for the peated varieties, but nowadays, he sources his peat from mainland Sweden. During malting, the peat is spiced up with local seaweed and sea-grass. The malt is dried for 48 hours using peat smoke and the final 30 hours in hot air. The distillery is equipped with a 500 kilogram mash tun, six washbacks made of stainless steel and one pair of stills – wash still 2,000 litres and spirit still 1,500 litres. Two years ago, Henric made arrangements in the still house where he can easily divert certain, unwanted parts of the middle cut, hence creating the exact flavour profile he desires. But his ambitions wont stop at that. He is now installing an instrument for performing GCMS (gas chromatography/mass spectrometry) in his laboratory. Using a

Mackmyra Moment Urberg

Henric Molin at work in his Spirit of Hven distillery

new application with an upgraded olfactory port, he will, with great accuracy, be able to determine which flavour compounds will appear during the different stages of production.

A long fermentation time of 90-120 hours is used in order to achieve a more fully flavoured product with high citric notes and a nutty character. The spirit yield at the distillery, 410-420 litres per tonne of malted barley, is quite impressive given the fact that the distillery is small and part of the production is peated whisky. The yield from his own malted barley is 390 litres.

Henric is (to use his own words) obsessed with being able to trace the exact origin of every bottle of whisky down to the field of barley and the specific oak used for the cask. One batch from the spirit still fills exactly one cask and only one cask is made from each oak tree. The plans are to produce four different types of malt whisky – organic, unpeated, lightly peated and heavily peated. The latter has an astonishing level of phenolic compounds in the new make – 94ppm! The first release (without age statement) will be of the lightly peated version in February 2012. Around 15,000 litres of whisky are hoped to be produced during 2011, but also rum made from sugar beet, vodka, gin, aquavit and calvados are expected to be distilled. Much of Henric's time is now spent being a consultant for Swedish and, in particular, foreign distilling companies. For example, he was recently involved in launching a new vodka in Vietnam.

DISTILLERY: Smögen Whisky AB, Hunnebostrand
FOUNDED: 2010
OWNER/MANAGER: Pär Caldenby
www.smogenwhisky.se

In August 2010, Smögen Whisky on the west coast of Sweden, produced their first spirit. This project has quietly progressed since 2009 without any drum banging and thus became Sweden's third whisky distillery, following Mackmyra and Spirit of Hven. Pär Caldenby – lawyer, whisky enthusiast and the author of Enjoying Malt Whisky is behind it all. He has designed the facilities himself and much of the equipment is constructed locally. The three washbacks, for example, carry 1,600 litres each and are rebuilt milk tanks. The wash still (900 litres), spirit still (600 litres), spirit safe and the horizontal condensers have

all been made by Forsyths in Scotland. The maturation will take place in casks made of new, toasted French Oak but some of them will also have held sherry. Ex-bourbon barrels made of American white oak and Sauternes cask are also used. The cask size ranges from 28 to 500 litres. Heavily peated malt is imported from Scotland and the vision is to produce an Islay-type of whisky. Some of the batches produced have had a phenol content of almost 70ppm. In summer 2011, the first production from own barley, grown at the distillery, was made. The current production volume is 10-15,000 litres in a year.

DISTILLERY: Box Destilleri, Bjärtrå
FOUNDED: 2010
OWNER/MANAGER: Ådalen Destilleri AB
www.boxwhisky.se

The company was founded in 2005 by Mats and Per de Vahl who, during their travels to Scotland, had been inspired to start their own distillery in Sweden. Buildings from the 19th century that had previously been used both as a sawmill and a powerplant, were restructured and equipped with an, at least, 100 years old 4-roller Boby mill from a closed English brewery, a semilauter mash tun with a capacity of 1.5 tonnes and three stainless steel washbacks holding 8,000 litres each and with a fermentation time of 2-4 days. The wash still (3,800 litres) and the spirit still (2,500 litres) were both ordered from Forsyth's in Scotland. The first distillation was made in November 2010 and the distillery has a capacity of 100,000 litres.

Box Destilleri will be making two types of whisky – fruity/ unpeated and peated. For the first, the malted barley comes from Sweden whereas the peated malt is imported from Belgium, where it has been dried using peat from Islay. Three different phenol levels have been tested so far – 31, 39 and 45ppm. A majority of the casks are first fill bourbon in a variety of sizes from 200 litres down to 40 litres. A number of Oloroso casks and virgin oak casks have also been filled. The company has imported and bottled single malts from Scotland to keep up the cash flow until its own whisky has matured. Future casks (39 litres) are also being sold and it is also possible to visit the distillery. The first whisky is expected to be bottled towards the end of 2013.

The still house at Box distillery

DISTILLERY: Grythyttan Whisky, Lillkyrka
FOUNDED: 2010
OWNER/MANAGER: Grythyttan Whisky AB
www.grythyttanwhisky.se

The company was founded on Benny Borghs initiative in 2007 at a farm dating back to the 13th century, situated about 180 km west of Stockholm. The company has around 800 share-holders and the distillery came on stream in October 2010. In common with most Swedish distilleries, the stills (900 litres wash still and 600 litres spirit still) were made at Forsyth's in Scotland and the three washbacks are made of Oregon pine. The distillery has its own water source and the water is cleaned using reversed osmosis.

Three different malt varieties are used; unpeated Swedish malt and, imported from Scotland, medium peated (16ppm) and heavily peated (50ppm). For maturation ex-sherry casks are used as a first choice, but ex-bourbon barrels from Maker's Mark, as well as casks which have previously contained sauternes, madeira, cognac and rum, are also used. The capacity of the distillery is 24,000 litres per year. The distillery has a visitor centre and they are also selling new make spirit and future casks. The release date for the first whisky has not yet been decided.

DISTILLERY: Norrtelje Brenneri, Norrtälje
FOUNDED: 2002 (whisky since 2009)
OWNER/MANAGER: Richard Jansson
www.norrteljebrenneri.se

This distillery, situated 70 kilometres north of Stockholm, was founded on a farm which has belonged to the owner's family for five generations. The production consists mainly of spirits from ecologically grown fruits and berries. Since 2009, a single malt whisky from ecologically grown barley is also produced. The whisky is double distilled in copper pot stills (400 and 150 litres respectively) from Christian Carl in Germany. Most of the production is matured in 250 litre Oloroso casks with a finish of 3-6 months in French oak casks which have previously held the distillery's own apple spirit. The character of the whisky will be fruity and lightly peated (6ppm) and the first bottling may appear in 2013.

Switzerland _____

DISTILLERY: Whisky Castle, Elfingen, Aargau
FOUNDED: 2002
OWNER/MANAGER: Ruedi Käser
www.whisky-castle.com

The first whisky from this distillery in Elfingen, in the north of Switzerland, reached the market in 2004. It was a single malt under the name Castle Hill. Since then the range of malt whiskies has been expanded and today include Castle Hill Doublewood (3 years old matured both in casks made of chestnut and oak), Whisky Smoke Barley (at least 3 years old matured in new oak), Fullmoon (matured in casks from Hungary) and Terroir (4 years old made from Swiss barley and matured in Swiss oak). All these are bottled at 43%.

Adding to these are Cask Strength (5 years old and bottled at 58%) and Edition Käser (71% matured in new oak casks from Bordeaux). For a year now, Käser has also made three special single malts for the cruise ship company, Hapag Lloyd. Two new releases were made in October 2010 – Girl's Choice, which is a light 3 year old whisky aged in white wine barrels, and Port Cask, which is 4 years old with a full maturation in port pipes and bottled at 50%. All released whiskies are unpeated, but some of them have a smoky flavour which derives from the beech wood used to dry the malt.

A new distillery was built in 2005 and commissioned in 2006, hence the annual production has increased from 5,000 to 25,000 bottles. Ruedi Käser has also constructed a complete visitor's experience, including a restaurant and a shop. The whisky can be bought in Germany, The Netherlands and Austria apart from Switzerland and has also recently been exported to China.

DISTILLERY: Bauernhofbrennerei Lüthy, Muhen, Aargau
FOUNDED: 1997 (whisky since 2005)
OWNER/MANAGER: Urs Lüthy
www.swiss-single-malt.ch

The farm distillery, Lüthy, in the north of Switzerland, started in 1997 by producing distillates from fruit, as well as grappa, absinthe and schnapps. The range was expanded to include whisky in 2005 which was distilled in a mobile pot still distillery. Lüthy's ambition is to only use grain from Switzerland in his production. Since it was impossible to obtain peated malt from Swiss barley, he decided to build his own floor maltings in autumn 2009.

The first single malt expression to be launched in December 2008, was Insel-Whisky, matured in a Chardonnay cask. It was followed by Wyna-Whisky from a sherry cask in April 2009 and Lenzburg-Whisky, another Chardonnay maturation and bottled in September 2009. The most recent bottling was Swiss Spelt UrDinkel Whisky, made from spelt and matured in a Pinot Noir cask. The selection is so far limited as only 500-1000 bottles are filled per year.

DISTILLERY: Spezialitätenbrennerei Zürcher, Port, Bern
FOUNDED: 1954 (whisky from 2000)
OWNER/MANAGER: Daniel & Ursula Zürcher
www.lakeland-whisky.ch

The first in the Zürcher family to distil whisky was Heinz Zürcher in 2000, who released the first 1,000 bottles of Lakeland single malt in 2003.

Daniel and Ursula Zürcher took over in 2004. They continued their uncle's work with whisky and launched a second release in 2006. The main focus of the distillery is specialising in various distillates of fruit, absinth and liqueur. The latest barrel of Lakeland single malt was released in 2009 as a 3 year old, but the Zürchers are working on the release of older whiskies in the future. The wash for the whisky is bought from Rugenbräu brewery in Interlaken and maturation takes place in Oloroso sherry casks.

Cooperation with the brewery has developed in recent years in that Zürcher sometimes distils the wash and then sends back the new make to the brewery for it to be filled into casks to mature. Two expressions from Rugenbräu exist, both of which have matured in American Oak Oloroso casks – Swiss Highland Single Malt Classic (46% and released for the first time in 2007) and Swiss Highland Single Malt Ice Label (cask strength and released for the first time in 2008). The latter is an interesting novelty; it has matured for almost 4 years at 3,454 metres altitude in the ice of Jungfraujoch with a constant temperature of minus 4 degrees Celsius. In April 2010 a new edition of the Ice Label was released and there are now around 70 casks maturing.

DISTILLERY: Brennerei Stadelmann, Altbüron, Luzern
FOUNDED: 1932 (whisky since 2003)
OWNER/MANAGER: Hans Stadelmann
www.schnapsbrennen.ch

Established in the 1930s this distillery was mobile for its first 70 years. The current owner's grandfather and father would visit farmers and distil local fruits and berries. Hans Stadelmann took over in 1972 and in 2001 decided to build a stationary distillery which would also be suitable for crop distilling. The distillery was equipped with three Holstein-type stills (150-250 litres) and the first whisky was distilled for a local whisky club in 2003. In 2005 the first Luzerner Hinterländer Single Malt was released, although not as a whisky since it was just 1 year old. A year later the first 3 year old was bottled for the whisky club under the name Dorfbachwasser and finally, in 2010, the first official bottling from the distillery in the shape of a 3 year old single malt whisky was released. In autumn 2011, the fourth release was made, a 3 year old matured in a Merlot cask. The distillery has a visitor centre, where groups can tour the distillery and sample the whisky and other spirits from the range. Stadelmann's produce is available both at the distillery, as well as from a webshop.

DISTILLERY: Brauerei Locher, Appenzell, Appenzell Innerrhoden
FOUNDED: 1886 (whisky since 1998)
OWNER/MANAGER: Locher family
www.säntisspirits.ch, www.saentismalt.ch

This old, family-owned brewery started to produce whisky in 1998 when the Swiss government changed laws, which had been applicable since WWII, and allowed spirit to be distilled from grain. The whole production of the whisky takes place in the brewery where there is a Steinecker mash tun holding 10,000 litres. The spirit ferments in stainless steel vats and, for distillation, Holstein stills are used. Brauerei Locher is unique in using old (70 to 100 years) beer casks for the maturation.

The production amounts to a couple of thousand bottles per year and at the moment there are three expressions; Säntis, bottled at 40%, Dreifaltigkeit which is slightly peated having matured in toasted casks and bottled at 52% and, finally, Sigel which has matured in very small casks and is bottled at 40%. A new addition to the range for 2011 was a single malt called Der Whisky ohne Namen (The whisky with no name) with a finish in French oak casks and bottled at 64%. 2011 also saw the opening of a new visitor centre.

DISTILLERY: Whisky Brennerei Hollen, Lauwil, Baselland
FOUNDED: 1999 (for whisky distillation)
OWNER/MANAGER: The Bader family.
www.swiss-whisky.ch, www.single-malt.ch

Since WW1 Switzerland has had a law forbidding the use of staple foods such as potatoes and grain for making alcohol. On 1st July 1999 this was abolished and the spirit streamed through the stills of Holle the very same day making it the first Swiss producer of malt whisky. The whisky is stored on French oak casks, which have been used for white wine (Chardonnay) or red wine (Pinot Noir). There are currently circa 100 casks in the warehouse. Most bottlings are 4 years old and contain 42% alcohol. A 5 year old has also been released, which has had three years in Pinot Noir casks followed by two years in Chardonnay casks. Other expressions include a peated version and a cask strength Chardonnay-matured.

In Spring 2008, an Easter bottling having had six years on two different casks – American Oak bourbon and French Oak which previously had contained Chardonnay – was released. Bader also recently launched what he calls a dessert whisky from a white wine cask as well as his first single grain whisky, and July 2009 saw the release of a 10 year old. Annual production amounts to roughly 30,000 bottles. The main production of the distillery consists of schnapps distilled from a variety of fruit.

DISTILLERY: Etter Distillerie, Zug,
FOUNDED: 1870 (whisky since 2007)
OWNER/MANAGER: Etter family
www.etter-distillerie.ch

The distillery was started in 1870 by Paul Etter and has been in the family ever since. Today it is the third and fourth generations who are running it. Their main produce is eaux de vie from various fruits and berries with cherry as their speciality (Kirsch). A sidetrack to the business was entered in 2007 when they decided to distil their first malt whisky. The malted barley was bought from a brewery (Brauerei Baar), distilled at Etter, filled into wine casks and left to mature in moist caves for a minimum of three years. The first release was made in October 2010 under the name Johnett Single Malt Whisky.

The still room of Etter Distillerie

DISTILLERY: Brennerei Hagen,
　　　　　　 Hüttwilen, Thurgau
FOUNDED: 1999
OWNER/MANAGER: Ueli Hagen
www.distillerie-hagen.ch

A triple distilled malt whisky is, since a few years, produced by Ueli Hagen in the small village of Hüttwilen in the northernmost part of Switzerland. The spirit is matured in bourbon barrels and the first produce was sold in 2002 as a 3 year old. Ueli Hagen produces mainly schnapps and absinth and distills around 300 bottles of malt whisky a year, a number he expects to double. He has recently been experimenting; four years ago when he was building a new cow shed, he found a 1700 year old oak tree in the ground so he put pieces of the oak into a maturing barrel of spirit and he says it gives the whisky a slightly peated touch.

DISTILLERY: Destillatia AG (Olde Deer),
　　　　　　 Langenthal, Bern
FOUNDED: 2005
OWNER/MANAGER: Hans Baumberger
www.olde-deer.ch

The distillery was built in 2005 under the same roof as the brewery Brau AG Langenthal (already established in 2001). The reason for this co-habitation was to access a wash for distillation and thereby avoiding investments in mashing equipment. The wash (in which both peated and unpeated malt is used) is fermented for five days and after that distilled three times, using a Holstein type of still. The casks are all 225 litres and Swiss oak (Chardonnay), French oak (Chardonnay and red wine) and ex sherry casks are used. The first whisky was produced in 2005 and released in 2008 under the name, Olde Deer. Since then a new 3 year old has been released every year. From June 2010, the whisky can be bought using their on-line shop. Apart from whisky, the distillery also produces rum, whisky liqueur and schnapps.

DISTILLERY: Burgdorfer Gasthausbrauerei,
　　　　　　 Burgdorf, Bern
FOUNDED: 1999
OWNER/MANAGER: Thomas Gerber
www.burgdorferbier.ch

The Burgdorfer Single Malt Whisky is an excellent example of the kind of cross-fertilization that more and more breweries are choosing. When a wash is made for beer brewing, it is an excellent opportunity to use the batch (without adding hops) to distil spirit which can be made into whisky. The first whisky from Burgdorfer was released as a five year old in 2006 and it is sold using a kind of subscription system. The customer pays 50 swiss francs for a 50 cl bottle and receives it 5 years later. They produce around 300 bottles annually.

Wales ————————

DISTILLERY: Penderyn Distillery, Penderyn
FOUNDED: 2000
OWNER/MANAGER: Welsh Whisky Company Ltd
www.welsh-whisky.co.uk

In 1998 four private individuals started The Welsh Whisky Company and two years later, the first Welsh distillery in more than a hundred years started distilling.

A new type of still, developed by David Faraday for Penderyn Distillery, differs from the Scottish and Irish procedures in that the whole process from wash to new make takes place in one single still. But that is not the sole difference. Every distillery in Scotland is required by law, to do the mashing and fermenting on site. At Penderyn, though, the wash is bought from a regional beer brewer and transported to the distillery on a weekly basis. The normal procedure at a brewery is to boil the wash to clear it from any lactic acid which can make it appear cloudy. This was a problem for Penderyn as lactic acid creates a second fermentation which is beneficial in a whisky context and adds more taste. Penderyn has solved this by pumping the wash to a heated tank where lactic acid is added before distillation is commenced. The first year 60,000 bottles were produced and now production has increased to 100,000 bottles. The distillery is working 24 hours a day to keep up with the increasing demand and now seems to have reached the capacity ceiling of the current equipment. There are long-term plans for one more still or even another distillery, but the timing for this expansion has not yet been announced

The first single malt was launched in March 2004. The core range consists of Penderyn Madeira Finish, Penderyn Sherrywood and Penderyn Peated. Recent limited releases include Rich Madeira (in 2008) and Portwood Single Cask (2009). Two single casks were released in summer and early autumn 2010 – one was a 2000 Vintage bourbon-matured and the other an Oloroso sherry maturation. A special version selected for La Maison du Whisky and the French market is Penderyn 41, bourbon matured with a light Madeira finish and bottled at 41%.

During 2010, sales increased by almost 20% and 140,000 bottles were sold. The main market is UK with 75% of total sales mainly through supermarkets like Asda, Tesco, Sainsbury´s and Waitrose. Twenty percent goes on export with France as the biggest market. The turnover for the company in 2010 was £3.1m.

A visitor centre was officially opened by HRH, The Prince of Wales, in June 2008 at a total cost of £850,000 and almost 30,000 visitors come here every year.

Penderyn´s head distiller - Gillian Macdonald

NORTH AMERICA

USA _____

DISTILLERY: Stranahans Whiskey Distillery,
Denver, Colorado
FOUNDED: 2003
OWNER/MANAGER: Proximo Spirits
www.stranahans.com

Due to the increased demand for Stranahan´s Colorado Whiskey, the founder, Jess Graber, had to find a solution to keep up with demand. Until 2009, wash had been purchased from a couple of local breweries, but then he wanted to bring it up one step by producing wash in-house. The equipment required was found in the closed Heavenly Daze Brewery in Denver, but instead of just buying the mash tun and fermenters, he ended up buying the entire 60,000 square foot building. The whole operation was moved to the new location in May 2009. The next step was to add more stills and two wash stills and one spirit still were ordered from Vendome Copper Works to be installed in summer 2011.

In December 2010, the distillery was acquired by New York based Proximo Spirits (makers of Hangar 1 Vodka and Kraken Rum among others) but, apparently, Jess Graber is still involved in the production.

Up until now the first distillation has taken place in a 2,800 litre Vendome combined pot still/column still, while the second distillation has been in a 950 litre pot still. The whiskey is filled into heavily charred barrels of new American White Oak and left to mature for a minimum of two years. Up to 20 barrels with ages between 2 and 5 years are married together when bottling.

The first three barrels were bottled in April 2006 and, so far, more than 150,000 bottles have been produced. In spring 2009 different wood finishes named Snowflakes were released. A new expression of Snowflake called Solitude was released in 2011 which had matured first in American white oak, then in port pipes made of European oak and finally in Hungarian oak which had previously held Chardonnay.

STILLERY: Clear Creek Distillery,
Portland, Oregon
FOUNDED: 1985
OWNER/MANAGER: Stephen McCarthy
www.clearcreekdistillery.com

Steve McCarthy in Oregon was one of the first to produce malt whiskey in the USA and his 3 year old single malt has earned a reputation as a high-quality whiskey fully comparable to the best Scotch whiskies. Like many other small distilleries, Clear Creek started by distilling eau-de-vie from fruit, especially pears, and then expanded the product line into whiskey. They began making whiskey in 1996 and the first bottles were on the market three years later.

There is only one expression at the moment, McCarthy´s Oregon Single Malt 3 years old. Steve has for a long time hoped to launch an 8 year old, but so far it has simply not been possible to save adequate quantities due to high demand.

The whiskey is reminiscent of an Islay and, in fact, the malt is purchased directly from Islay with a phenol specification of 30-40 ppm. It is then made into wash at the Widmer Brothers Brewery in Portland and distilled in Holstein pot stills. Steve expanded the number of pot stills to four last year to try and catch up with demand. Maturation takes place in ex-sherry butts with a finish in new Oregon White Oak hogsheads.

Steve has doubled the production of whiskey every year since 2004 which does not, however, seem to be enough to satisfy demand. The procedure used to be one release in March and one in August with both of them selling out quickly and 2008 was no exception. In 2009 he changed it to one release per year, with the August one being the biggest ever – 700 cases. The most recent release was June 2011. Unlike many of the single malts from the USA, McCarthy´s Oregon Single Malt is available in several European countries.

DISTILLERY: Charbay Winery & Distillery,
St. Helena, California
FOUNDED: 1983
OWNER/MANAGER: Miles and Marko Karakasevic
www.charbay.com

Charbay has a wide range of products: vodka, grappa, pastis, rum, port and since 1999 also malt whiskey. That was the year when Miles and Marko decided to take 20,000 gallons of Pilsner and double distil it in their Charentais pot still, normally used for distilling, for example, cognac. From this distillation, a 4 year old called Double-Barrel Release One (two barrels) was launched in 2002. There were 840 bottles at cask strength and non-chill filtered. The whiskey is quite unique since a ready beer, hops and all, rather than wash from a brewery is used.

It took six years before Release II appeared in 2008, this time with 22 barrels. It was matured for six years in heavily charred new American White oak. After six years, five barrels were picked out and the whiskey received another three years of maturation in stainless steel tanks. In January 2010 a different type of whiskey, Charbay´s Doubled & Twisted Light Whiskey, designed by Marko Karakasevic, was launched. It was distilled from bottle-ready IPA beer (India Pale Ale), aged for one day in oak barrels and then for six years in stainless steel tanks. The second release of Doubled & Twisted came in summer 2011 – this time as a 5 year old which had matured in a French oak Chardonnay cask. In October, a 14 month old Charbay IPA Whiskey (the whole maturation in French oak) was released, together with a Charbay IPA Light

Marko Karakasevic of Charbay Distillery

Whiskey (one day on oak and then filled into stainless steel tank). The plan for spring 2012 is to release the first whiskey distilled from stout. It is Marko´s intention to release a 14 months old from each distillation and to save some for release at 6 and 12 years respectively.

DISTILLERY: The Ellensburg Distillery,
Ellensburg, Washington
FOUNDED: 2008
OWNER/MANAGER: Berle Wilson Figgins Jr.
www.theellensburgdistillery.com

Former winemaker Berle "Rusty" Figgins Jr. decided to leave the wine-making business after 10 years to open a distillery instead. The distilled produce includes malt whiskey, rye whiskey, cream liqueur and brandy. The malt whiskey is made from an all-malt mash, incorporating a proprietary blend of pale ale, crystal and chocolate malts, while the wort is fermented with native yeast.

The distillation process is a bit unusual. Rusty uses two alambic pot stills of a design which originates in Armagnac. Both stills, which are united with a T-shaped lyne arm, are simultaneously filled with equal volumes and the spirit is distilled twice. The character is aromatic and full-flavoured from the very beginning and, according to Rusty, this is achieved by the distilling technique where the spirit vapour from each still is manifolded together, to afford a degree of back pressure which increases the degree of reflux. The new make is filled into new American Oak barrels of 112.5 litres and after six months it is re-racked to 225 litre ex sherry casks for another six months. The distillery equipment was recently expanded and they now have four 800-litre washbacks made from French oak.

The first Gold Buckle Club malt whiskey (300 bottles) was bottled in September 2009 and the second release in December 2010. Rusty has now finetuned the mashbill and, for future releases, it will be 85% Washington Select two-row malt and 5% each of crystal, caramel and chocolate malt. Furthermore, maturation will start in an ex sherry cask and finish in new American oak. In late 2011, Washington's first whiskey containing rye, was bottled under the name Emmer & Rye and was made of rye, emmer, spelt, maize and malted barley. Meanwhile, two new types of whiskey have recently been distilled – one with 50% unpeated Washington two-row barley and 50% heavily peated malt from Bairds in Scotland and the other a rye whiskey with 65% rye, 25% wheat and 10% malted barley.

DISTILLERY: Eades Distillery,
Lovingston, Virginia
FOUNDED: 2008
OWNER/MANAGER: The Virginia Distillers Co.
(Chris Allwood, Joe Hungate, Brian Gray)
www.eadeswhisky.com

Chris Allwood and his partners spent the first two years of this project to find funding of around $5m to complete their plans for a distillery in Nelson County, Virginia. The plan was originally to start distilling in spring 2009 but, as is often the case, things do take longer time than expected when building a distillery. As of summer 2011, the building is complete and the stills are in place. Phase two is to install all the piping and mechanicals and the plan now is to have whisky in casks by autumn 2012.

The equipment has been made in Scotland by Northern Fabricators: a 2 tonne mash tun, a 10,000 litre wash still and an 8,000 litre spirit still. The construction is designed and supervised by Harry Cockburn with over 40 years' experience in the business, which includes a past at Morrison Bowmore. The malting of locally grown barley will be done on-site and they are cooperating with Virginia Tech University to test around six strains in order to find the best variety.

Initial production volumes are expected to be around 2,500 barrels of 200 litres each per year and the spirit will mature mainly in bourbon barrels, but port pipes and wine barrels from local wineries will also be used. It will probably take at least four years before the first bottlings of matured whiskey are for sale.

Meanwhile, the owners have created a series of vatted malt whiskies called "Eades Anticipation Series". The idea is to select two different malts aged anything between 10 and 18 years for each bottling, marry them and then let them go through a second maturation in wine barrels. The second edition of the series was released in spring 2010 with the following combinations: Eades Highland, a combination of Ben Nevis and Clynelish, Eades Speyside with Dufftown and Mortlach and, finally, Eades Islay where Bowmore and Caol Ila have been married. They are currently working on a third edition of the series to be released in spring 2012.

DISTILLERY: Triple Eight Distillery,
Nantucket, Massachusetts
FOUNDED: 2000
OWNER/MANAGER: Cisco Brewers
www.ciscobrewers.com

In 1995 Cisco Brewers was established and five years later it was expanded with Triple Eight Distillery. The base of the whiskey production is, of course, wash from the brewery where Maris Otter barley is used. The first distillation took place as early as ten years ago and the first 888 bottles (5 barrels) were released on 8th August 2008 as an 8 year old. To keep in line, the price of these first bottles was $888. The whiskey is named Notch (as in "not Scotch").

Annual production is approximately 5,000 bottles and the storage is on ex-bourbon casks from Brown Forman (Woodford Reserve) and finished in French Oak. The latest release of Notch was a 10 year old in summer 2010.

The Nantucket facility consists of a brewery, winery and distillery. Triple Eight also produces vodka and rum that are already available on the market. Whiskey production was moved to a new distillery in May 2007.

Spirit Still No. 1 at Ellensburg Distillery

DISTILLERY: Prichard´s Distillery, Kelso, Tennessee
FOUNDED: 1999
OWNER/MANAGER: Phil Prichard
www.prichardsdistillery.com

Phil Prichard's original intentions were to construct a distillery in Manchester, Tennessee, but religious-fuel-led opposition became too strong. He turned to an old schoolhouse in Kelso instead. When he started in 1999, it became the first legal distillery for 50 years in Tennessee. Eleven years later, it is the third largest in the state after giants Jack Daniel's and George Dickel.

Prichard produces around 20,000 cases per year with different kinds of rum as the main track. The biggest seller, however, is a bourbon-based liqueur called Sweet Lucy which is responsible for 50% of sales. Bourbon and single malt whisky has recently started to be produced and a double-barrel bourbon has been on the market for some time now. In autumn 2010 it was time for the first single malt. It has been distilled in pot stills and has matured in heavily charred 15-gallon barrels. Technically it isn´t a single malt from 100% barley as it contains 15% rye as well. At the same time a Tennessee whiskey, made from white corn, was released. Prichard's Distillery's range is sold in 44 states and in eight European countries.

DISTILLERY: Lexington Brewing & Distilling Co., Lexington, Kentucky
FOUNDED: 1999
OWNER/MANAGER: Pearse Lyons
www.lyonsspirits.com

Most of the producers of malt whiskey in the USA have a background in brewing, winemaking or distilling other spirits. This also applies to Lexington Brewing & Distilling Company, as whiskey production is derived from their production of Kentucky Ale. Dr Pearse Lyons' background is interesting – being the owner, the founder and a native of Ireland, he used to work for Irish Distillers in the 1970s. In 1980 he changed direction and founded Alltech Inc, a biotechnology company specializing in animal

nutrition and feed supplements. Alltech purchased Lexington Brewing Company in 1999, with the intent to produce an ale that would resemble both an Irish red ale and an English ale. Dr Lyons, holding a PhD in brewing and distilling, obviously knew what he was doing, as the ales became an instant success. In 2008, two traditional copper pot stills from Scotland were installed with the aim to produce Kentucky´s first malt whiskey. North American 2-row malted barley is mashed in a lauter mash tun and fermented using a yeast designed by Alltech. The capacity of the distillery part is 450,000 litres of pure alcohol per year and in autumn 2011 they were breaking ground for a new distillery as well. The first single malt whiskey was released in August 2010 under the name Pearse Lyons Reserve and in autumn 2011 it was time for a release of their Town Branch bourbon.

DISTILLERY: RoughStock Distillery, Bozeman, Montana
FOUNDED: 2008
OWNER/MANAGER: Kari & Bryan Schultz
www.montanawhiskey.com

Unlike many other American micro distilleries relying on obtaining mash from a nearby brewery, RoughStock buys its 100% Montana grown and malted barley and then mill it and mash themselves in a 1,500 gallon mash cooker. The mash is not drained off into a wash, but fermented directly from the mash tun in open top fermenters for 72 hours before double distillation in a 250 gallon Vendome copper still. Maturation is on a mix of quarter casks and 225 litre barrels made from new American oak. Bryan Schultz also has spirit ageing in French oak and in casks that have contained fortified wine.

In September 2009, the first bottles of RoughStock Montana Whiskey, the first legally made whiskey in Montana's history since Prohibition, were released. Since then, another 25 or so batches have been released, with each batch consisting of between 35 and 60 cases. A limited Distiller´s Select Release bottled at 60% has also been launched. Apart from Montana Whiskey made from

Prichard´s Single Malt Whiskey   *Pearse Lyons Reserve*   *RoughStock Montana Whiskey*

100% malted barley, the product range also includes Spring Wheat Whiskey, Sweet Corn Whiskey and Straight Rye Whiskey,

Total capacity is around 35,000 bottles per year. To increase the capacity, Bryan has recently ordered an additional still (750 gallons).

DISTILLERY: Tuthilltown Spirits,
Gardiner, New York
FOUNDED: 2003
OWNER/MANAGER: Ralph Erenzo & Brian Lee
www.tuthilltown.com

This is the first whiskey distillery in the State of New York since Prohibition. Just 80 miles north of New York City, Ralph Erenzo and Brian Lee, with the help of six employees produce bourbon, single malt whiskey, rye whiskey, rum and vodkas distilled from local apples. Erenzo bought the 18th century property in 2001 with the intention of turning it into a rock climbers ranch, but neighbours objected. A change in the law in New York State made it possible to start a micro-distillery. Erenzo thus changed direction and started distilling instead. Erenzo and Lee built the distillery, acquired licences and learned the basic craft over the following two years.

The first products came onto the shelves in 2006 in New York and the range now consists of Hudson Baby Bourbon, made from 100% New York corn and the company's biggest seller by far, Four Grain Bourbon (corn, rye, wheat and malted barley), Single Malt Whiskey (aged in small, new, charred American Oak casks), Manhattan Rye, New York Corn Whiskey, Heart of the Hudson Vodka and Spirit of the Hudson Vodka.

A cooperative venture was announced between Tuthilltown and William Grant & Sons (Grants, Glenfiddich, Balvenie et al) in June 2010, in which W Grants acquired the Hudson Whiskey brand line in order to market and distribute it around the world. Tuthilltown Spirits remains an independent company that will continue to produce the different spirits. The produce from Tuthilltown currently sells in 17 US states, in Europe and in Australia.

In July 2009 the distillery crew hand-harvested the first crop of rye grown at the distillery, and opened for its first public tours. Tuthilltown's new whiskey tasting room and shop are in the barrel room, the first at a distillery in New York since 1919. Private single cask bottling of whiskey is also available to consumers at the distillery.

DISTILLERY: St. George Distillery,
Alameda, California
FOUNDED: 1982
OWNER/MANAGER: Jörg Rupf/Lance Winters
www.stgeorgespirits.com

The distillery is situated in a hangar at Alameda Point, the old naval air station on the San Fransisco Bay. It was founded by Jörg Rupf, a German immigrant who came to California in 1979 and who was to become one of the forerunners when it came to craft distilling in America. In 1996, Lance Winters joined him and today he is Distiller as well as co-owner.

The main produce is based on eau-de-vie from locally grown fruit, and vodka under the brand name Hangar One. Whiskey production was picked up in 1996 and the first single malt appeared on the market in 1999. Like in so many other craft distilleries, the wash is not produced in-house. St George's obtain their from Sierra Nevada Brewery. One advantage of cooperating with a brewery is that brewer's yeast can be used, something Scottish producers had to give up on in 2005 when it became unavailable. Lance Winters, in common with many other distillers, claims that the fruity character of the whiskey is a result of using brewer's yeast rather than distiller's yeast. Some of the malt used has been dried with alder and beech but is non-peated. Maturation is in bourbon barrels (80%), French Oak (15%) or port pipes (5%). St. George Single Malt used to be sold as three years old, but

nowadays comes to the market as a blend of whiskeys aged from 4 to 12 years.

DISTILLERY: Nashoba Valley Winery,
Bolton, Massachusetts
FOUNDED: 1978 (whiskey since 2003)
OWNER/MANAGER: Richard Pelletier
www.nashobawinery.com

Nashoba Valley Winery lies in the heart of Massachusetts' apple country, just 40 minutes from Boston and is owned by Richard Pelletier since 1995. Although mainly about wines, the facilities have in recent years expanded with a brewery (producing ten different kinds of ales and lagers) and Massachusetts' first distillery, which holds a farmer's distiller's license. Here Pelletier produces a wide range of spirits including vodka, brandy and grappa.

Since 2003 malt whiskey is also distilled. The malt is imported from England, France and Canada and the wash is produced in his own brewery. The whiskey is matured in a combination of ex bourbon barrels and American and French Oak casks, which previously have contained wine from the estate. Richard Pelletier produces around 9,000 bottles per year.

In autumn 2009, Stimulus, the first single malt was released. The two casks were distilled in 2004. The second release of a 5 year old came in 2010 and it is Richard's plan to release a 5 year old once a year. At the same time he has also put aside whiskey to be sold as a 10 year old and, eventually, as a 15 year old. The first 10 year old is due in 2014 and during that same year he will also bottle a rye whiskey and a corn whiskey. At the moment they are producing about 20 barrels per year.

DISTILLERY: Edgefield Distillery,
Troutdale, Oregon
FOUNDED: 1998
OWNER/MANAGER: Mike and Brian McMenamin
www.mcmenamins.com

Brothers Mike and Brian McMenamin started their first pub in Portland, Oregon in 1983. It has now expanded to a chain of more than 50 pubs and hotels in Oregon and Washington. More than 20 of the pubs have adjoining microbreweries (the first opened in 1985) and it is now the fourth-largest chain of brewpubs in the United States.

The chain's first distillery opened in 1998 at their huge Edgefield property in Troutdale and their first whiskey, Hogshead Whiskey (46%), was bottled in 2002. Annual production now stands at 10,000 litres, thanks to a newly installed second washback. In the past, ex bourbon casks were used for maturation, but now only charred, new American White Oak barrels are used. A second distillery was opened in September 2011 at the company's Cornelius Pass Roadhouse location in Hillsboro. A 19th century charentais alambic still has been acquired and the initial focus will be on whiskey and then moving on to brandy and gin.

Hogshead Whiskey is the top seller but Head Distiller, James Whelan, envisages producing four to eight barrels of "specialty" whiskies that will differ from the Hogshead. Most of these specialty whiskies are destined to become Devil's Bit, a limited bottling released every year on St. Patrick's Day. In 2010 it was an 8 year old whiskey made of 51% red winter wheat and 49% barley. A peated version produced from 100% barley is designated to become Devil's Bit in the future and in 2010 Whelan also barreled a whiskey from organic, floor-malted Maris Otter pale malt which is imported from Thomas Fawcett in the UK. The latest expression, released in June 2011, was Monkey Puzzle which basically is their Hogshead Whiskey matured for three years but with an infusion of hops and honey added to the fully-matured whiskey.

DISTILLERY: Woodstone Creek Distillery,
Cincinnati, Ohio
FOUNDED: 1999
OWNER/MANAGER: Donald and Linda Outterson
www.woodstonecreek.com

Since the start in 2003, Don and Linda Outterson have
run this winery/distillery part-time, keeping their full-
time jobs. The reason for focussing primarily on the
winery is that Ohio state laws are considerably more
lenient when it comes to wine than whiskey. Still, in 2008
a change came through allowing sales of whiskey to
take place directly from the distillery premises. The next
step the Outtersons (and other distillers in the state) are
lobbying for, is that tastings of the spirit will be allowed
on the site.

The first whiskey, a five grain bourbon (white and yellow corn, malted barley, malted rye, and malted wheat),
was released as Barrel #2 on 4th July 2008 to celebrate
the change in Ohio´s regulations. The second release,
Barrel #1, was launched on 25th November to celebrate
Thanksgiving Day. Both bourbons were made of malted
grains (no enzymes), 51% corn, sweet mash and without
chill-filtering and colouring. In 2010, the Outtersons
released a peated 10 year old single malt from malted
barley which they call "The Murray Cask", named after
Jim Murray who praised it in his Whisky Bible. In 2011
this was followed up by a 12 year old unpeated single
malt whiskey and they are also working on a blended
whiskey which will probably be released in 2012.

Don Outterson opened a farm winery in Lebanon,
Ohio in 1999 and relocated to the present facilities in
2003. The malted barley is imported from Scotland and
port and sherry casks of own production are used for
maturation. The capacity for single malts in the future is
planned to be 10 barrels per year.

DISTILLERY: High Plains Distillery,
Atchison, Kansas
FOUNDED: 2004
OWNER/MANAGER: Seth Fox
www.highplainsinc.com

Former process engineer, Seth Fox, is mainly known for
his Most Wanted Vodka of which he sells over 13,000
cases a year in Kansas, Missouri and Texas. The product
range was expanded in late 2006 also to include a Most
Wanted Kansas Whiskey (reminiscent of a Canadian
whisky) and Kansas Bourbon Mash. Fox continued in
2007 to produce his first single malt whiskey made from
malted barley but it has not been released yet. He also
produces Pioneer Whiskey and a premium vodka called
Fox Vodka which is filtered five extra times. The two
stills were bought second-hand from Surrey in England.
When High Plains opened, it was the first legal distillery
in Kansas since 1880. In 2009 he expanded the facility in
order to accommodate a production of 70-80,000 cases
per year, compared to previous 20,000.

DISTILLERY: Copper Fox Distillery,
Sperryville, Virginia
FOUNDED: 2000
OWNER/MANAGER: Rick Wasmund
www.copperfox.biz

Copper Fox Distillery was founded in 2000 by Rick
Wasmund using the premises and licence of an old,
existing distillery. The first whiskey, Copper Fox Whiskey,
was made in cooperation with the distillery which they
were about to buy, but after a disagreement over the
contract the project came to a halt. In 2005 they moved
to another site, built a new distillery and began distilling
in January 2006.

Rick Wasmund has become one of the most unorthodox producers of single malt. The malted barley is dried
using smoke from selected fruitwood but variations of

that concept are also used in other places, for example
Sweden. It is the maturation process that Rick takes one
step further thereby differing from common practice. In
every barrel of new make spirit, he adds plenty of hand
chipped and toasted chips of apple and cherry trees, as
well as oak wood.

Adding to the flavour, Wasmund also believes that
this procedure drastically speeds up the time necessary
for maturation. In fact, he bottles his Wasmund´s Single
Malt after just four months in the barrel. Every batch
ranging from 250 to 1,500 bottles tastes a little different
and the distillery is now producing around 2,500 bottles
every month. Other expressions in the range are Copper
Fox Rye Whiskey with a mash bill of 2/3 Virginia rye and
1/3 malted barley and two unaged spirits – Rye Spirit and
Single Malt Spirit.

DISTILLERY: Dry Fly Distilling, Spokane,
Washington
FOUNDED: 2007
OWNER/MANAGER: Don Poffenroth
& Kent Fleischmann
www.dryflydistilling.com

Dry Fly Distilling started production in autumn 2007 and
became the first grain distillery to open in Washington
since Prohibition. To ensure a positive cash flow from
the start, in common with many other distilleries, vodka
and gin were produced. The first batch of malt whisky
was distilled on 4th January 2008. The owners expect to
make 200-300 cases of malt whisky annually, but the first
bottling will probably not be released until 2013/2014.
However, there are a couple of other whiskies in production and one of them is quite unusual – Washington
Wheat Whiskey. It was first released in August 2009 and,
at that time, it was only the second of this style following
Heaven Hill's launch of Bernheim Straight Wheat Whiskey in 2005. In July 2011, Dry Fly Distilling launched the
first bourbon ever made in Washington State. It was a 3
year old, the oldest release yet from the owners, made of
corn, wheat and malted barley.

The original equipment consisted of one still, a
Christian Carl manufactured in Germany. In autumn
2008 another still was installed, as well as two additional
fermenters, which raised capacity to 10,000 cases per
annum. Dry Fly Distilling is currently sold in 20 states and
in Canada.

DISTILLERY: St. James Spirits,
Irwindale, California
FOUNDED: 1995
OWNER/MANAGER: Jim Busuttil
www.saintjamesspirits.com

Peregrine Rock is the name of the 3 year old single
malt Jim Busuttil produces in Irwindale, east of Los
Angeles. The malt comes from Baird Malts in the UK and
is medium peated. Heavy charred new American Oak
barrels, but also ex-bourbon barrels from Jim Beam and
Jack Daniels are used.

DISTILLERY: New Holland Brewing Co.,
Holland, Michigan
FOUNDED: 1996 (whiskey since 2005)
OWNER/MANAGER: Brett VanderKamp, David
White, Fred Bueltmann
www.newhollandbrew.com

This company started as a beer brewery, but after a decade, it opened up a micro-distillery as well and the wash
used for the beer is now also used for distilling whiskey.
There is a variety of malts for mashing and the house ale
yeast is used for fermentation. Until August 2011, the
spirit was double distilled in a 225 litre, self-constructed
pot still. At that time, the capacity had increased tenfold

mainly as a result of the installation of a 3,000-litre still. This still had been built in 1932 and hasn´t been used since the early 1940s but was restored.

The first cases of New Holland Artisan Spirits were released in December 2008 and among them were Zeppelin Bend, a 3 year old (minimum) straight-malt whiskey which is now their flagship brand. In autumn 2010, a new series of releases called Brewer´s Whiskey began. They have all aged in small (five and eight gallon) casks and the first bottling was Double Down Barley, 6 months old. This was followed up in summer 2011 by Malthouse (a mix of three different malted barleys and two malted ryes) and Walley Rye. In autumn 2011 came the next two releases; Ichabod´s Flask and a bourbon. Batch number 2 of Double Down Barley is due for release in spring 2012 and for that, some experimentation has been going on. Toasted staves of different wood other than oak (for example hickory) have been integrated into the casks to see what effect this would have on the whiskey. Other new products during 2011 were an orange liqueur called Clockwork and a white whiskey.

DISTILLERY: Corsair Artisan,
            Bowling Green, Kentucky and
            Nashville, Tennessee
FOUNDED: 2008
OWNER/MANAGER: Darek Bell, Andrew Webber
            and Amy Lee Bell
www.corsairartisan.com

The two founders of Corsair Artisan, Darek Bell and Andrew Webber, were based in Nashville when they came up with the idea in 2008 to start up a distillery. At that time Tennessee didn´t allow this, so the first distillery was opened across the border in Bowling Green, Kentucky. Two years later, the legislation in Tennessee had changed and a second distillery and brewery was opened up in Nashville in a building which used to house the Yazoo Brewery. Apart from producing 16 different types of beer, the brewery is also where the wash for all the whisky production takes place. In Nashville, they also have a 240 gallon antique copper pot still. For those whiskies in the range that require a second distillation, the low wines are taken to Bowling Green and the custom made 50 gallon still from Vendome Copper.

Corsair Artisan has a wide range of spirits; gin, vodka, absinthe, rum and whiskey. So far two types of whiskey have been released – Wry Moon, an unaged 100% rye whiskey and Triple Smoke Whiskey. The latter is made from three different types of smoked malt – cherry wood smoked from USA, peat smoked from Scotland and beech wood smoked from Germany. Added to that is 10% chocolate malt for flavour complexity. The spirit then matures in heavily charred barrels (#4) of new American oak for two months. The owners do a lot of experiments smoking the barley, using for example alder and pecan.

DISTILLERY: Bull Run Distillery,
            Portland, Oregon
FOUNDED: 2011
OWNER/MANAGER: Lee Medoff and
            Patrick Bernards
www.bullrundistillery.com

This is one of the newest distilleries in the USA, founded by Lee Medoff, an experienced man in the industry. A former brewer, Lee co-founded House Spirits in 2002 together with Christian Krogstad. Among the spirits produced was Medoyeff Vodka, a brand that Lee took with him when he decided to found a new distillery together with entrepreneur and businessman, Patrick Bernards. The company was formed in 2010 and in early autumn 2011, it was time for the first distillation. The distillery is equipped with two pot stills (800 gallons each) of Lee´s own design and manufactured locally. The plan to start with, is to use local breweries for the production of the wash but already next year, they may be installing their own mashing equipment.

Darek Bell, one of the owners of Corsair Artisan   *Lee Medoff at his new Bull Run Distillery*

Except for Medoyeff Vodka which is already for sale, the distillery will also produce two types of rum from turbinado sugar. The first one, Pacific White Rum will be released in autumn 2011 while the Pacific Dark Rum is scheduled for winter 2011/2012. However, the main mission of the distillery is whiskey based on 100% malted barley. It will be unpeated with a maturation of at least two years in new American oak barrels. The idea is to do an All Oregon Whiskey from Oregon malt, Oregon oak and Oregon water. In five years from now, the goal is to sell 12,000 cases per year.

DISTILLERY: Ballast Point Brewing & Distilling, San Diego, California
FOUNDED: 1996 (whiskey since 2008)
OWNER/MANAGER: Jack White, Yuseff Cherney
www.ballastpointspirits.com

Building on Jack White´s Home Brew Mart, he and Yuseff Cherney started Ballast Point Brewing Company in 1996. The two decided that, when the beer brewing business had increased to 10,000 barrels per year, a distillery would be added to the operation. Distilling started in 2008 and became the first craft distillery in San Diego. The first product to see the light of day was Old Grove gin in August 2009, followed by Three Sheets rum in April 2010. That same month their malt whiskey, Devil´s Share Whiskey, was presented at the American Distilling Institute´s annual conference.

DISTILLERY: Rogue Ales & Spirits, Newport, Oregon
FOUNDED: 2009
OWNER/MANAGER: Jack Joyce
www.rogue.com

The company started in 1988 as a combined pub and brewery. Over the years the business expanded and now consists of one brewery, two combined brewery/pubs, two distillery pubs (Portland and Newport) and five pubs scattered over Oregon, Washington and California. The main business is still producing Rogue Ales, but apart from whiskey, rum and gin are also distilled.

Two malt whiskies have been released so far. The first, Dead Guy Whiskey, was launched in December 2009 and

is based on five different types of barley. Distillers yeast is added to the wort and after fermentation it is distilled twice in a 150 gallon Vendom copper pot still. The spirit is matured for one month in charred barrels made of American Oak. The second expression was released in June 2010 under the name Chatoe Rogue Oregon Single Malt Whiskey. It is made from barley grown on Rogue´s own farm in Tygh Valley. The malt is smoked using Oregon Alder wood chips and the spirit is matured for three months. At the moment 300 cases of Dead Guy Whiskey and 100 cases of Chatoe Rogue are produced monthly. The whiskey can be bought in 30 states in the US and is also exported to Canada, Puerto Rico, Philippines, Japan and Australia.

DISTILLERY: The Solas Distillery, La Vista, Nebraska
FOUNDED: 2009
OWNER/MANAGER: Zac Triemert, Brian McGee, Jason Payne
www.solasdistillery.com

The Solas Distillery, the first licensed distillery in Nebraska since prohibition, can trace its origins back to 2005, when Zac Triemert, at that time master brewer of Upstream Brewing Company in Omaha, persuaded his colleagues, Brian McGee and Jason Payne, to set up their own brewery. At first they brewed out of another Omaha brewery. In 2008 their own Lucky Bucket brewery was ready to roll and a year later, at the same premises, a distillery was built. The two units, which are housed in the same building, are separated by a 12 foot fence for legal reasons. The first product to hit the market in November 2009 was Joss Vodka, with the Cuban-style Chava Rum next to be released (due sometime in 2011). In February 2010 single malt whiskey was distilled but it will not be ready to bottle until February 2013.

Zac Triemert, who has a Master's Degree in distilling from Herriot-Watt University in Edinburgh, lets the wash ferment for seven days and then distills it in two copper pot stills from Forsyth´s in Scotland. The wash still holds 500 gallons, the spirit still 300 gallons and the whiskey is matured in a variety of casks that have previously contained wine or bourbon. A few, charred, new casks are used as well.

The still house at Rogue Ales & Spirits

DISTILLERY: DownSlope Distilling,
Centennial, Colorado
FOUNDED: 2008
OWNER/MANAGER: Mitch Abate,
Matt & Andy Causey
www.downslopedistilling.com

The three founders were brought together by their interest and passion for craft-brewing when they started the distillery in 2008 and in 2009 they finally got their licence to start distilling. The distillery is equipped with two stills – one very elegant, copper pot still made by Copper Moonshine Stills in Arkansas and a vodka still of an in-house design. The first products to be launched in August 2009 were a vodka made from sugar cane and a white rum. More vodkas and rums were to follow and in April 2010 the first whiskey, Double-Diamond Whiskey, was released. It is made from malted barley and a fraction of rye and matured in small, medium-toasted casks. A year later, Double Diamond Whiskey has become a success and is now about 45% of the sales. A whiskey from 100% malted barley (a small percentage of which is peated) has also been produced, but has yet to be released. The barley used was Maris Otter, a strain that has not been used in Scotland for ages due to its low yield. The owners of DownSlope prefer it to others because of the flavour they consider it adds to the spirit.

DISTILLERY: Green Mountain Distillers,
Stowe, Vermont,
FOUNDED: 2001
OWNER/MANAGER: Harold Faircloth III,
Tim Danahy
www.greenmountaindistillers.com

Tim Danahy and Howie Faircloth, previously in the beer brewing business, started Green Mountain Distillers in 2001. It is an unusual distillery in the respect of being Certified Organic. The first product to hit the shelves was Sunshine Vodka in 2004, which became a huge success and was followed in summer 2009 with two new versions – Organic Lemon and Organic Orange. Two years earlier, Green Mountain Distillers had also released Maple Syrup Liqueur. However, a 100% organic malt whiskey has always been on their minds. The first batches were already distilled in September 2004, but unlike many other distillers in the USA, Tim and Howie decided to let it mature for quite a number of years. The first release (less than 1000 bottles) can be expected in autumn 2011 and will by then, probably, be the first certified organic malt whisky produced in USA.

DISTILLERY: House Spirits Distillery,
Portland, Oregon
FOUNDED: 2004
OWNER/MANAGER: Matt Mount,
Christian Krogstad
www.housespirits.com

This distillery was started in Corvallis in 2004 by two former brewers from Portland, Lee Medoff and Christian Krogstad. A year later, operations were moved to its present location in Portland. In 2010, Lee Medoff left the company to start a new distillery also in Portland, Bull Run Distillery (see page 247). In the absolute vicinity of House Spirits another five distilleries have been established, producing vodka, gin, rum and brandy and the area is now called Distillery Row.

The main products for House Spirits are Aviation Gin and Krogstad Aquavit but there are also big plans for whiskey installed. The first three expressions were released in December 2009. Two of them had been matured for 2 years and 8 months with one bottled at 45% and the other a cask strength at 56.8%. The third bottling was a white dog bottled at 50%. White dog is the non-

matured spirit and corresponds roughly to what is called new make in Scotland and poitín in Ireland. More white dog whiskies were released in 2011 and in October 2010 a blended whiskey (40% malted spirits and 60% grain spirits) called Slab Town Whiskey was also released. For the double distillation, a 1,500 litre still is used and the spirit is filled into new charred American oak.

DISTILLERY: Rebecca Creek Distillery,
San Antonio, Texas
FOUNDED: 2010
OWNER/MANAGER: Steve Ison and Mike Cameron
www.rebeccacreekdistillery.com

With a background in the insurance business, Mike Cameron and Steve Ison started Rebecca Creek Distillery in 2010. Fermenters and a mash system were bought from Newland Systems in Canada and the 3,000 litre copper pot still, together with the column, was made by the well-known Christian Carl in Germany. Apparently the still was the largest the company had shipped to USA. The malted barley is sourced from Cargill in Sheboygen, Wisconsin and for maturation charred American oak is used.

The first product to be launched was Enchanted Rock Vodka which is currently sold in Texas. The first year alone, 30,000 cases of vodka were sold. First whiskey to be released was Rebecca Creek Fine Texas Whiskey, a blended whiskey which was launched in autumn 2011. Steve and Mike plan for a release of their Single Malt Whiskey sometime in spring 2012.

At the moment, the production capacity for vodka is 100,000 cases per year and for whiskey 10-20,000 cases, but the owners have even bigger plans, namely, to become the largest craft distillery in North America with a yearly production of 150,000 cases of vodka and 75,000 cases of whiskey.

DISTILLERY: High West Distillery,
Park City, Utah
FOUNDED: 2007
OWNER/MANAGER: David Perkins
www.highwest.com

This is probably Utah´s first legal distillery since 1870. Even though it has not been established for more than

Rebecca Creek Fine Texas Whiskey

four years the owner, David Perkins, has already made a name for himself mainly because of the releases of several rye whiskies. None of these have been distilled at High West distillery though. Perkins has instead bought casks of mature whiskies and blended them himself. The first (released in 2008) was Rendezvous Rye, a mix of two whiskies (16 and 6 years old). Since then, he has also released a 16 year old and a 21 year old rye. The two most recent bottlings (from summer 2011) were a 12 year old rye and Double Rye which is a mix of a 2 year old and a 16 year old whiskey. Meanwhile, Perkins has been distilling vodka from oats and he has also released an unaged oat whiskey from his own production called Western Oat which contains 85% oats and 15% malted barley. A single malt from 100% barley is in the pipeline and will probably be released in autumn 2011 as an unaged whiskey under the name High Country Single Malt.

Perkins has a background as a biochemist and when he opened up his distillery he also added a saloon and a restaurant to the premises.

DISTILLERY: Balcones Distillery,
Waco, Texas
FOUNDED: 2008
OWNER/MANAGER: Chip Tate
www.balconesdistilling.com

When this distillery was established the founder, Chip Tate, did not go the usual way by ordering stills from one of the well-known manufacturers but instead went about and built the stills himself. The creativity in doing this is also reflected in the first whiskies that were produced. Chip Tate was the first to use Hopi blue corn, unique to the southwest America, for distillation. Three different expressions of blue corn whiskey have been released so far – the first was Baby Blue, bottled at 46%, followed by True Blue which is a cask strength version. The third variety is called Brimstone Smoked Whiskey but the smoky flavours do not derive from drying the grain using smoke but it is, instead, the whisky itself that is treated with smoke from Texas scrub oak. Chip Tate has also distilled single malt whiskey from 100% malted barley, both unpeated and peated, but neither has yet been released. The demand for Balcones whiskies has grown rapidly and Chip Tate will be moving the production to a bigger site nearby.

DISTILLERY: Cedar Ridge Vineyards,
Swisher, Iowa
FOUNDED: 2003
OWNER/MANAGER: Jeff Quint
www.crwine.com

Jeff Quint and his wife Laurie started Cedar Ridge Vineyards in downtown Cedar Rapids in 2003 and expanded the business soon afterwards to also include a distillery. After a while they moved to the present location in Swisher, between Cedar Rapids and Iowa City where they now have two stills in the distillery part. The first spirit produced was Clearheart Vodka that later was complemented with gin, rum and grappa. The first whiskey, being a bourbon, was released on 1 July 2011 and they have also distilled malt whiskey from 100% malted barley which is expected to be released later in 2011. Cedar Ridge was the first distillery to open in Iowa since the end of Prohibition

Canada _____

DISTILLERY: Glenora Distillery,
Glenville, Nova Scotia
FOUNDED: 1990
OWNER/MANAGER: Lauchie MacLean
www.glenoradistillery.com

Situated in Nova Scotia, Glenora was the first malt whisky distillery in Canada. The first launch of in-house produce came in 2000 but a whisky called Kenloch had been sold before that. This was a 5 year old vatting of some of Glenora's own malt whisky and whisky from Bowmore Distillery on Islay. The first expression, a 10 year old, came in September 2000 and was named Glen Breton. Since then several expressions have been launched, among them single casks and sometimes under the name Glenora. A new expression, Glen Breton Ice (10 years old), the world's first single malt aged in an ice wine barrel, was launched in November 2006. Interest was massive and another release came onto the market in spring of 2007. In 2008 a 15 year old version was available from the distillery only. A 15 year old version of Glen Breton single malt was released under the name Battle of the Glen in June 2010. The release commemorated the distillery's victorious outcome of the ten year-long struggle with Scotch Whisky Association (see below).

Glenora's whisky has not been easy to obtain outside Canada, but exports currently go to countries such as the USA, Poland, Sweden, Switzerland, Spain and Singapore.

Since 2001 Glenora was been locked in a legal fight with Scotch Whisky Association (SWA) over the name of Glen Breton. The opinion of SWA is that the use of the word Glen is misleading and confusing for the customer and will make many believe that they are actually buying a Scotch whisky. The distillery, on the other hand, states that Glen is an established geographical name in this part of Canada. In 2007 the Trademarks Opposition Board in Ottawa ruled in favour of the distillery's right to continue to sell the whisky under the name Glen Breton. SWA appealed and won in April 2008 when a Federal Court reversed the previous ruling. The next step was Glenora's appeal to Canada's Federal Court of Appeal in December 2008 which ruled in favour of the distillery by January 2009. SWA decided not to give up but to petition the Supreme Court of Canada to overturn the Court of Appeal's decision. Finally, on 11 June 2009, the Supreme Court dismissed the application for a third appeal filed by SWA and, in November 2009, Glen Breton was entered as a registered mark on the Trademarks Register of Canada.

DISTILLERY: Victoria Spirits, Victoria (Vancouver Island), British Columbia
FOUNDED: 2008 (whisky since 2009)
OWNER/MANAGER: Bryan Murray
www.victoriaspirits.com

This family-run distillery actually has its roots in a winery called Winchester Cellars, founded by Ken Winchester back in 2002. Bryan Murray, the owner of Victoria Spirits, came in as an investor, but soon started to work with Ken on the distilling part of the business. Before Ken left the business in 2008, he took part in introducing Victoria Gin, which currently is the big-selling product with 10,000 bottles a year.

The Murray family left the wine part of the business in order to increase the spirits role and the next product on the list was a single malt whisky. The first batch was distilled in late 2009 by Bryan's son, Peter Hunt, using wash from a local brewery owned by Matt Phillips. The still is a 120 litre German-made copper pot-still fired by wood. The whisky will initially be matured in small casks (octaves) made of new American Oak, but old Bourbon barrels will also be used. Peter Hunt hopes to use Garry Oak (a.k.a. Oregon White Oak whih is abundant on Vancouver Island) for maturation in the future. The first release is expected sometime in 2013 and the working name of the whisky is Craigdarroch.

DISTILLERY: Shelter Point Distillery, Vancouver Island, British Columbia
FOUNDED: 2009
OWNER/MANAGER: Andrew Currie, Jay Oddleifson, Patrick Evans
www.shelterpointdistillery.com

Andrew Currie, who co-founded Arran Distillery in Scotland 18 years ago, and Jay Oddleifson, a former accountant who was the CFO of Mount Washington Alpine Resort, are the men behind Shelter Point Distillery, just north of Comox on Vancouver Island. The buildings were completed in 2009 and in May 2010 all the equipment was in place. That means a one ton mash tun, five washbacks made of stainless steel and one pair of stills (a 5,000 litre wash still and a 4,000 litre spirit still). Both stills and the spirit safe were made by Forsyth´s in Scotland. The idea was to start distillation in September 2010 but federal, provincial and local licensing requirements, multiple inspections and one mechanical complication after another delayed the startup with eight months. Since June 2011 however, they have produced four bathces of whisky every week under the supervision of distillery manager Mike Nicholson. The yearly capacity is 92,000 litres of pure alcohol. Barley is grown on the estate and is expected to be used in the whisky production.

DISTILLERY: Pemberton Distillery, Pemberton, British Columbia
FOUNDED: 2009 (whisky since 2010)
OWNER/MANAGER: Tyler Schramm
www.pembertondistillery.ca

This is one of the most recently established distilleries in Canada. Distilling started in July 2009, with vodka from potatoes being their first product. Almost 98% of all the vodkas of the world are made from grain and Tyler came up with the idea to use potatoes while studying brewing and distilling at the renowned Heriot-Watt University in Edinburgh. The organically grown potatoes are sourced locally, and the distillery itself, is a Certified Organic processing facility. Tyler uses a copper pot still from Arnold Holstein and the first vodka, Schramm Vodka, was launched in August 2009. In June 2010, Tyler started his first trials, distilling a single malt whisky using organic malted barley from the Okanagan Valley. He filled four ex-bourbon barrels with unpeated spirit and another five were filled in 2011. At that time he also produced five barrels of lightly peated new make. The first release of this whisky will probably not take place for another four years.

DISTILLERY: Still Waters Distillery, Concord, Ontario
FOUNDED: 2009
OWNER/MANAGER: Barry Bernstein, Barry Stein
www.stillwatersdistillery.com

Barry Bernstein and Barry Stein started their carrier in the whisky business as Canada´s first independent bottler, importing casks from Scottish distilleries and selling the whisky across Canada.The next step came in January 2009 when they opened their Still Waters distillery in Concord, on the northern outskirts of Toronto. A pot still and two columns, all from Christian Carl in Germany, were installed. Even though whisky is their main interest, their first success was with triple distilled, charcoal filtered, single malt vodka. They have at the moment a dozen barrels of maturing malt whisky in stock, some of it nearly two years old.

AUSTRALIA & NEW ZEALAND

Australia

DISTILLERY: Bakery Hill Distillery, North Balwyn, Victoria
FOUNDED: 1998
OWNER/MANAGER: David Baker
www.bakeryhilldistillery.com.au

In 2008 Bakery Hill Distillery, situated at the base of Mt Dandenong northeast of Melbourne, completed the installation of a 2,000 litre brewery and now has total control of all the processes from milling the grain to bottling the matured spirit. During 2009 the brewing part of the production was fine-tuned and Baker's evaluation was that the results were stunning. This, according to Baker, led to 2010 becoming a year of consolidation, to allow for focussing on making larger volumes and targeting more markets. The whisky has recently been introduced in France, Germany and Sweden. Apart from distillation, environmental adjustments and engineering were in focus last year. The distillery waste, spent grain and pot ale used to be disposed of, but are now sent to Yarra Valley to be used as stock feed and fertiliser. The next step on the green agenda will be using rainwater.

The first spirit at Bakery Hill Distillery was produced in 2000 and the first single malt was launched in autumn 2003. Three different versions are available - Classic and Peated (both matured in ex-bourbon casks) and Double Wood (ex-bourbon and a finish in French Oak). As Classic and Peated are also available as cask strength bottlings, they can be considered two more varieties. The whisky is double-distilled in a copper pot still. All unpeated malt comes from an Australian maltster, while the malt for

Bakery Hill Cask Strength

the peated version is imported from the UK. With the Bakery Hill Distillery being situated in the southern part of Australia, the climate is very different to that of Scotland. The overall ambient temperatures are much higher while the air mass is much drier. These factors influence the rate of flavour development and whisky character, and David Baker is constantly experimenting with a wide variety of oak to find the optimal path.

DISTILLERY: Lark Distillery, Hobart, Tasmania
FOUNDED: 1992
OWNER/MANAGER: Bill Lark
www.larkdistillery.com.au

One can consider Bill Lark the father of the modern whisky distilling we see today in Australia. In 1992 he was the first person for 153 years to take out a distillation license in Tasmania. Since then he has not just established himself as a producer of malt whiskies of high quality but has also helped several new distilleries to start up. Recently he co-founded the Tasmanian Distillers Group together with the five other whisky distilleries on the island.

Bill Lark´s original establishment in Kingston was moved to Hobart in 2001. In 2006 a new distillery was constructed on a farm at Mt Pleasant, 15 minutes from Hobart. The farm grows barley for Cascade Brewery and at the moment that is where Lark Distillery gets its malt from. However, the intention is to set up own floor maltings within two years thereby enabling them to produce everything in-house, from barley field to bottle, at one site. Not only that – in 2004 they secured their own peat bog at Brown Marsh and in January 2007 they also purchased the cooperage that makes the barrels. All in all, they are now very much in control of the whole chain. The "old site" down in Hobart by the waterfront is now a showcase for the Lark whisky with a shop, café and whisky bar with over 100 different single malts.

The core product in the whisky range is the Single Cask Malt Whisky at 43% but Bill Lark has also released a Distillers Selection at 46% and a Cask Strength at 58%, both of which are also single cask. The range is completed by a malt whisky liqueur called Slainte and a Pure Malt Spirit at 45%. The whisky is double-distilled in an 1,800 litre wash still and a 600 litre spirit still and then matured in 100 litre "quarter casks". An important achievement for Lark distillery in 2011, was when they secured access to high quality port barrels from Seppeltsfield Wine in Barossa Valley. The barrels are cut down by a cooper, shaved and re-charred, and put back together as 100 litre casks.

The demand for Lark single malt has grown rapidly in recent years, also outside Australia. Through La Maison du Whisky it is selling well in Europe and was also introduced to the American market during 2011. Bill Lark now has his eyes set on China and expects to sell the first cases there before the end of 2011.

DISTILLERY: Hellyers Road Distillery, Burnie, Tasmania
FOUNDED: 1999
OWNER/MANAGER: Betta Milk Co-op
www.hellyersroaddistillery.com.au

Hellyer´s Road Distillery is the largest single malt whisky distillery in Australia. The capacity allows for 500 casks per year to be produced but there are also 2,500 200-litre casks in bond. The Tasmanian barley is malted at Cascade Brewery in Hobart and peat from Scotland is used for the peated expressions. Batches of 6.5 tonnes of grist are loaded into the mash tun and then the wash is fermented for 65 hours. There is only one pair of stills but they compensate for numbers by size. The wash still has a capacity of 60,000 litres which is twice that of the largest wash still in Scotland at Glenkinchie Distillery. The spirit still's capacity is 30,000 litres and the interesting part here is the really slow distillation. The foreshots take around 4-5 hours and the middle cut will last for 24 hours, which is six to seven times longer compared to practice in Scotland. Maturation takes place in ex-bourbon casks but they also use Tasmanian red wine barrels for part of it.

There are four varieties of Hellyers Road Single Malt Whisky in the range: Original, Slightly Peated, Peated and (the most recent one) Pinot Noir finish with an additional three months maturation in Pinot Noir casks from a Tasmanian winery. The produce has, so far, only been sold in Australia but the vodka exports to the USA started in autumn 2009 and the first batches of whisky reached France in autumn 2010.

Bill Lark (right) with his friends at Seppeltsfield Cooperage

DISTILLERY: Nant Distillery, Bothwell, Tasmania
FOUNDED: 2007
OWNER/MANAGER: Keith Batt
www.nantdistillery.com.au

Nant distillery, in Bothwell in the Central Highlands of Tasmania, started when Queensland businessman, Keith Batt, bought the property in 2004. He embarked on refurbishing the Historic Sandstone Water Mill on the Estate that was built in 1823 and converted it into a whisky distillery. The first distillation took place on 5th April 2008. Keith's idea is to manage the whole production process on site. Barley has been grown on the estate since 1821 and continues to this day. On the Estate there was also a 180 year old water-driven flour mill which is now used for grinding the barley into grist. Keith plans to start with floor malting on the site close to the end of 2012 and peat from the original Nant summer highland grazing property, Lake Echo, will be used in the malting process. The distillery is equipped with a 1,800 litre wash still and a 600 litre spirit still and wooden washbacks are used for the fermentation. Keith uses quarter casks of 100 litres, previously used for port, sherry and bourbon, for maturation. Production is approximately 200 100-litres barrels per year.

In June 2010 the first bottlings from the distillery saw the light of day. The release was split into two different styles – the Blood Tub series with five individual bottlings at 43% from five different 20 litre casks that had previously contained port and a Double Wood bottling, with maturation both in French Oak port casks and American Oak sherry. A further two releases followed with whisky matured in French oak port and American oak port. The fourth release was made in August 2011 (American oak port).

DISTILLERY: Old Hobart Distillery
Blackmans Bay, Tasmania
FOUNDED: 2005
OWNER/MANAGER: Casey Overeem
www.oldhobartdistillery.com

Even though Casey Overeem did not start his distillery until 2007, he had spent several years experimenting with different types of distillation which were inspired by travels to Norway and Scotland. The distillery (previously known as Overeem Distillery) came on stream in 2007 with assistance from the omnipresent Bill Lark (see Lark distillery) and others. The mashing is done at Lark distillery where Overeem also has his own washbacks and the wash is made to his specific requirement, i. a. with his own yeast. The wash is then transported to Old Hobart Distillery where the distillation takes place in two stills (wash still of 1,800 litres and spirit still of 600 litres) made by the Hobart still maker, Knapp-Lewer. The spirit is matured in casks that have previously contained either port, bourbon or sherry. Most of the production is slightly peated and during 2011 Overeem plans to make 5,000 litres with production increasing every year. The first release is due in November 2011 and will consist of four different expressions, all single casks and distilled in 2007; two cask strengths from port and sherry casks and two bottled at 43%, also from port and sherry. The first bottling of the bourbon matured will take place in a few years' time.

DISTILLERY: Great Southern Distilling Company,
Albany, Western Australia
FOUNDED: 2004
OWNER/MANAGER: Great Southern Distilling
Company Pty Ltd/Cameron Syme
www.distillery.com.au

This is the only whisky distillery in the western part of Australia. It was built in Albany on the south-western tip of Australia in 2004 with whisky production commencing in late 2005. Throughout the initial years, production of whisky, brandy, vodka and gin took place in a set of sheds on the outskirts of Albany. A move was made in October 2007 to a new, custom-built distillery with a visitor centre on Princess Royal Harbour.

Production takes place in pot stills (one wash still of 1,900 litres and one spirit still of 580 litres) and a 600 litre copper pot antique gin still has also been installed. The fermentation time is unusually long – 7 to 10 days and for maturation a mix of ex-bourbon, ex-house brandy and ex-sherry barrels are used, as well as new and reshaved/charred American Oak and French Oak casks. Great Southern Vodkas and Gin have been available for sale since October 2006.

The first expression of the whisky, called Limeburners, was released in April 2008 with the second appearing a couple of months later. Both releases are single casks and non-chill filtered. Limeburner single malt whisky releases are named M for malt with a unique barrel number. The latest release was M68. In autumn 2010, the first peated version of Limeburners (M59) was released. The peat that has been used, is sourced from the nearby Porongurup ranges. The whiskies are bottled either at barrel strength (63%) or diluted to 43%.

DISTILLERY: Victoria Valley Distillery, Essendon
Fields, Melbourne, Victoria
FOUNDED: 2008
OWNER/MANAGER: David Vitale,
Lark Distillery m fl
www.victoriavalley.com.au

This is the very latest distillery to come on stream in Australia. Co-founder, Managing Director and Head Distiller is David Vitale who previously worked with sales and marketing at Lark Distilleries in Tasmania. Bill Lark from the aforementioned distillery has also taken part in the start-up of Victoria Valley. The owner is still looking for a final location for the production but settled for an interim site at Essendon Fields, Melbourne's original airport. The distillery is actually fitted into an old Qantas maintenance hangar. The stills (an 1,800 litre wash still and a 600 litre spirit still) were bought from Joadja Creek Distillery in Mittagong and contribute to an initial capacity of 20,000 cases of whisky in a year. The target is to

The stills of Old Hobart Distillery

253

increase to 50,000 cases in the future. Until summer 2011, they had produced around 500 barrels of various sizes.

David produces three types of whisky – a single malt, an American-style bourbon and an Australian-style whisky that will provide a clear point of difference. Part of the whisky matures in Pedro Ximenez sherry butts and the first whisky will be ready to launch in October 2011.

DISTILLERY: Tasmania Distillery,
Cambridge, Tasmania
FOUNDED: 1996
OWNER/MANAGER: Patrick Maguire
www.tasmaniadistillery.com

Three generations of whisky can trace its origin from Tasmania Distillery. The first was distilled between 1996 and 1998 and, according to the current owner, Patrick Maguire, the quality is so poor that he does not want to bottle it. The second generation was distilled from November 1999 to July 2001 and is bottled today under the name Sullivan's Cove. The third generation is the whisky distilled from 2003, until now under Patrick and his three partners' ownership, and will not be bottled until it has reached 12 years of age.

The range used to be made up of three different 7 year old whiskies - Sullivan's Cove Single Cask (used to be bottled at 60% but has changed to around 50%) matured in either bourbon casks or port casks and Sullivan's Cove Double Cask (40%) which is a marriage of port and bourbon casks. In May 2010, the distillery launched its first 10 year old versions of both the bourbon and the port matured.

Tasmania distillery obtains wash from Cascade Brewery located in Hobart, near to the distillery. The whisky is then double distilled, although there is only one still at the distillery. The model is of a French brandy design with a worm condenser attached. 12,000 litres of wash from Cascade make up one production run and it takes five wash runs and two spirit runs to complete the process. There is generally one production run every two weeks. Annual production amounts to 120 casks of 200 litres each of non chill-filtered whisky, which is matured in American Oak bourbon casks and French Oak port barrels.

In 2010, Patrick bought a disused train tunnel, a few kilometres from the distillery, in which he plans to stock all whisky from autumn 2011 and, perhaps, in a few years' time build a new distillery. The tunnel provides a cooler and more even temperature, not to be taken on lightly in this part of the world, where great differences in temperature occur during the year.

Apart from Australia, the whisky is available in Scandinavia, France, Belgium, Holland, Korea, Singapore, Taiwan, Hong-Kong, China and Canada. It was also recently introduced at Harrods in London and Maguire hopes to be able to launch Sullivan's Cove in USA before Christmas 2011.

DISTILLERY: Timboon Railway Shed Distillery,
Timboon, Victoria
FOUNDED: 2007
OWNER/MANAGER: Tim Marwood
www.timboondistillery.com

The small town of Timboon lies 200 kilometres southwest of Melbourne. Here Tim Marwood established his combination of a distillery and a restaurant in 2007 in a renovated railway goods shed. Using a pilsner malted barley, Marwood obtains the wash (1,000 litres) from the local Red Duck microbrewery. The wash is then distilled twice in a 600 litre pot still. For maturation, resized (20 litres) and retoasted ex-port, tokay and bourbon barrels are used. In June 2010 the first release was made and in June 2011, the distillery came up for sale. Tim and his family had decided to concentrate on what was the main business in the very beginning, namely making ice cream.

New Zealand _____

DISTILLERY: New Zealand Malt Whisky Co,
Oamaru, South Island
FOUNDED: 2000
OWNER/MANAGER: Extra Eight
www.thenzwhisky.com
www.milfordwhisky.co.nz

In 2001, Warren Preston bought the entire stock of single malt and blended whisky from decommissioned Wilsons Willowbank Distillery in Dunedin. The supplies that Preston acquired consisted of, among other things, 400 casks of single malt whisky including production dating back to 1987. Before he bought it, the whisky was sold under the name Lammerlaw, but Preston renamed it Milford. There have been 10, 12, 15, 18 and 20 year old bottlings. Preston also had plans to build a distillery in Oamaru. He was granted a five year consent in 2007 from the local authorities to build a boutique distillery at a highland property near Queenstown at Nevis Bluff on the Kawaru River. In August 2009, however, the site was offered for sale at an auction. Preston decided it would make more sense to build the distillery adjacent to the existing warehouses in Oamaru with a plan to start distilling in 2009

In February 2010, however, the company was evicted from its premises and one month later the company was placed in receivership with a debt of NZ$3 million. In October 2010, rescue came in the form of a syndicate of nine international investors led by Interglobal Brands Pty. Their capital injection revived the company and the founder, Warren Preston, will also continue to work in the business. Plans to build a distillery still exist although it may be at another location.

With the new ownership, exports of Milford whisky took off again in 2011 and, for example, 56 cases were exported to The Netherlands in April 2011 with more international orders in the pipeline.

ASIA

India _____

DISTILLERY: Amrut Distilleries Ltd., Bangalore
FOUNDED: 1948
OWNER/MANAGER: Jagdale Group
www.amrutdistilleries.com
www.amrutwhisky.co.uk

The family-owned distillery, based in Bangalore, south India, started to distil malt whisky in the mid-eighties. More than 6 million litres of spirits (including rum, gin and vodka) is manufactured a year, of which 1 million litres is whisky. Most of the whisky goes to blended brands, but Amrut single malt was introduced in 2004. It was first introduced in Scotland, can now be found in more than 20 countries and has recently been introduced to the American market. Funnily enough, it took until 2010 before it was launched in India. In 2009 total sales on the export market were 5,000 cases, an increase of more than 40% compared to the previous year.

The distillery is equipped with two pairs of stills, each with a capacity of 5,000 litres. The barley is sourced from the north of India, malted in Jaipur and Delhi and finally distilled in Bangalore. The small amount of peated malt that is used, comes from Inverness. Ex bourbon casks are most commonly used for maturation, but sherry casks and casks made of new oak can also be found in the warehouse. The whisky is bottled without chill-filtering or colouring. The conditions for maturation differ much from the Scottish environment. The temperature in the summer is close to 40° C and it rarely falls below 20° C in winter. Hence the much larger evaporation, between 10-16% per year. This, in turn, means that it is not cost efficient to mature the whisky for more than four years.

The Amrut family of single malts has grown considerably in recent years and ingenuity is great when it comes to new limited releases. The core range consists of unpeated and peated versions bottled at 46%, a cask strength and a peated cask strength. Special releases include Amrut Fusion which is based on 25% peated malt from Scotland and 75% unpeated Indian malt, Amrut Two Continents, where maturing casks have been brought from India to Scotland for their final period of maturation and, finally, Intermediate Sherry Matured, which means that the new spirit has matured in ex-bourbon or virgin oak, then re-racked to sherry butts and with a third, and final, maturation in ex-bourbon casks. Recent additions to the range are Kadhambam (released in autumn 2010) which is a peated Amrut which has matured in ex Oloroso butts, ex Bangalore Blue Brandy casks and then finally in ex rum casks. In summer 2011 Amrut Herald, with four years bourbon maturation in India and a final 18 months on the German island of Helgoland, was launched followed in the autumn by the second edition of both Kadhambam (this time unpeated) and Two Continents and, finally, Amrut Portonova with a maturation in bourbon casks, then 9 months in port pipes and back to bourbon casks for the last 8 months.

DISTILLERY: McDowell's, Ponda, Goa
FOUNDED: 1988 (malt whisky)
OWNER/MANAGER: UB Group
www.unitedspirits.in

In 1826 the Scotsman, Angus McDowell, established himself as an importer of wines, spirits and cigars in Madras (Chennai) and the firm was incorporated in 1898. In the same town another Scotsman, Thomas Leishman, founded United Breweries in 1915. Both companies were bought by Vital Mallya around 1950 and today United

Breweries (in which the spirits division consists of United Spirits) is the second largest producer of alcohol in the world after Diageo. Vijay Mallya, the son of Vital, is acting as chairman since 1983.

United Spirits dominates the Indian spirits market of which it has a share of 60%. In the fiscal year ending March 2011, sales of 114 million cases of spirit could be reported, which makes the company the world's largest spirits producer in the world in terms of volume. United Spirits has 21 brands in the so-called Millionaire's Club to which brands that sell more than 1 million nine-litre cases per year belong.

The aboslute majority of United Spirits' whiskies are Indian whisky, i. e. made of molasses. The major brands in the group are huge sales-wise. Bagpiper blended whisky is the world's best-selling whisky with more than 16.4 million cases sold in 2010/2011. McDowell's No 1 is one of the fastest growing whiskies in the world. It sold almost 15 million cases in 2010/2011 compared to 2.5 million 10 years ago. Seven of the top 25 best selling whiskies of the world belong to United Spirits and they also have some of the fastest growing whisky brands in their range showing double digit growth during 2010; Director's Special Black (+42%), Old Tavern (+33%) and McDowell's Green Label (+27%). Single malt sales are, of course, negligible compared to these figures. McDowell's Single Malt is made at the distillery in Ponda (Goa) and sells some 20,000 cases each year. It has matured for 3-4 years in ex-bourbon casks.

McDowell's launched the world's first diet whisky, McDowell's No.1 Diet Mate, in 2006. It is a blend of whisky and the herb, garcinia, which increases the rate of metabolism. In 2007 United Spirits Limited acquired the Scottish whisky-maker, Whyte & Mackay, (with Whyte & Mackay blends and Dalmore, Jura and Fettercairn distilleries) for £595m.

Pakistan _____

DISTILLERY: Murree Brewery Ltd., Rawalpindi
FOUNDED: 1860
OWNER/MANAGER: Bhandara family
www.murreebrewery.com

Murree Brewery in Rawalpindi started as a beer brewery supplying the British Army. The assortment was completed with whisky, gin, rum, vodka and brandy. Three single malts have been available for some time; 3, 8 and 12 years respectively. In 2005 an 18 year old single malt was launched and the following year their oldest expression so far, a 20 year old, reached the market. There are also a number of blended whiskies such as Vat No. 1, Lion and Dew of Himalaya.

Company sources mention a supply of half a million litres of whisky in underground storage. The brewery makes its own malt (using both floor maltings and Saladin box) and produces 2.6 million litres of beer every year and approximately 440,000 litres of whisky. Total annual sales in 2008/2009 amounted to Rs. 2,3 billion ($28 million).

Murree Brewery consists of three divisions – the liquor division (responsible for 70% of income and almost 100% of the profit), Tops division (mainly fruit juices) and a glass division (which manufactures glass containers for the company and other customers).

Muslims are prohibited by their religion to drink alcohol, so it is not surprising that in a country where 97% are Muslims, the whisky market is quite small. Only about 3 million litres per year are sold, mainly to the Christian, Hindu and Parsee minorities. Murree Brewery is the market leader with a 36% share.

Amrut Kadhambam and Intermediate Sherry

Taiwan

DISTILLERY: Yuan Shan Distillery, Yuanshan,
Yilan County
FOUNDED: 2005
OWNER/MANAGER: King Car Food Industrial Co.
www.kavalanwhisky.com

The first whisky distillery in Taiwan lies in the north-
eastern part of the country, in Yilan County, just one
hour from Taipei. The area is flat between two mountain
ranges and it was built in record time with construction
lasting just eight months. The first distillation took place
on 11th March 2006.

The distillery is divided into two units, with the first
completed in 2006. It is equipped with a semi-lauter
stainless steel mash tun with copper top and eight closed
stainless steel washbacks with a 60 hour fermentation
time. The malted barley is imported with Baird´s of
Inverness as the main supplier. There are two pairs of
lantern-shaped copper stills with descending lye pipes.
The capacity of the wash stills is 12,000 litres and of the
spirit stills 7,000 litres. After 10-15 minutes of foreshots,
the heart of the spirit run takes 2-3 hours. The cut points
differ from what is common in Scotland. To capture the
sweetness (important to the Chinese consumers), collecting starts at 78% and stops already at 72%. The extreme
cut points are also determined by the climate and the
quick maturation. The spirit vapours are cooled using
tube condensers but due to the hot climate, subcoolers
are also used. The total capacity of this unit is 1.3 million
litres per year.

The second unit of the distillery was completed in 2008
and consists of a full lauter Steinecker mash tun, 12 stainless steel washbacks and eight Holstein stills. The stills
function, unusually enough, in pairs and two pairs have
rectification columns with four plates, while the other
two pairs have seven plates. This unit, with a 2.6 million
litre capacity, is used for spirits other than whisky.

The warehouse is five stories high with the first four
floors palletised and the top floor more of a traditional
dunnage warehouse. The casks are tied together four
and four due to the earthquake risk. The climate in
Taiwan is very hot and humid and on the top floors of
the warehouse the temperature can reach 42° C. Hence
the angel´s share is quite dramatic – no less than 15% is
lost every year. The warehouse harbours 30,000 casks and
there is a need for more warehousing capacity within the
near future. The ideal solution would be to build up in
the cooler mountains, but in order to do that, the legislation must be changed, as warehousing must currently
be in close proximity to the production plant. The whisky
matures mainly in ex bourbon barrels and ex sherry casks
with a few other types used for experimentation.

There is also an impressive visitor centre on site. No less
than one million visitors come here per annum, which is
roughly the same number as all Scottish distilleries' visitor
centres together.

The first release of Kavalan (as the whisky from the
distillery is called) was in December 2008 and this is now
one of the core expressions. In July 2009, a port finish
version called Concertmaster appeared and then in
August, two different single casks were launched – one
ex-bourbon and one ex-Oloroso sherry, both bottled at
cask strength under the name Solist. A third single cask,
this time from a Fino cask, was released just in time for
Chinese New Year in 2010. In 2011 the release of single
casks continued with another version of Solist Fino
bottled at 58%, Solist Vinho, bottled at 59% and with a
maturation in Portuguese wine barriques, and finally a
new core expression – King Car Conductor. This was the
first whisky from Kavalan to be bottled under the company name and is a mix of eight different types of casks,
unchillfiltered and bottled at 46%.

The recipe of the Classic Kavalan is quite complex and
includes six different types of casks - fresh bourbon, fresh
sherry, refill bourbon, red wine casks from Spain and
two different white wine casks from Portugal. The most
important market is mainland China, but the whisky is
also exported to Macau, Hong Kong, Malaysia, Japan
and Cyprus. The owners are currently working on having
Kavalan available to American and European consumers.

The owning company, King Car Group, with 2,000 employees, was already founded in 1956 and runs businesses
in several fields; biotechnology and aquaculture, among
others. It is also famous for its canned coffee, Mr. Brown,
which is also exported to Europe.

Yuan Shan Distillery in Taiwan - home of Kavalan Single Malt and one of the latest bottlings, King Car Whisky

Turkey

DISTILLERY: Tekel (Mey Icki), Ankara
FOUNDED: 1930 (whisky since 1963)
OWNER/MANAGER: Diageo
www.mey.com.tr

Tekel, owned by the Turkish state, was sold to four companies, Nurol, Limak, Özaltin and Tütsab, in 2004 for $292 million. They formed a holding company, Mey Icki, to market and distribute the products but kept the company name Tekel. In 2006 Mey Icki was sold to the American Texas Pacific Group for $900 million. In February 2011 the company was sold again, to Diageo for $2.1bn.

Mey Icki has a large range of beverages, mainly consisting of wine and raki, but vodka, gin, 'cognac' and whisky are also included. The main product is raki which accounts for 77% of the sales and 60% of the total revenues. A total of 6 million cases (all products included) were sold in 2010 at a total value of £300m. Tekel has produced a whisky named Ankara Turk Viskisi since 1963. It can probably not be called a single malt as it is reported to contain a portion of malted rye and rice mixed with malted barley. The whisky is aged for three years in oak casks.

AFRICA

South Africa

DISTILLERY: James Sedgwick Distillery, Wellington, Western Cape
FOUNDED: 1886 (whisky production since 1990)
OWNER/MANAGER: Distell Group Ltd.
www.threeshipswhisky.co.za

Distell Group Ltd. was formed in 2000 by a merger between Stellenbosch Farmers' Winery (founded in 1925) and Distillers Corporation (founded in 1945) although the James Sedgwick Distillery was already established in 1886. The company produces a huge range of wines and spirits. One of the most successful brands was introduced in 1989 – Amarula Cream, today the second best-selling cream liqueur in the world.

James Sedgwick Distillery has been the home to South African whisky since 1990. The distillery is currently under major expansion and will, when finished, be equipped with one still with two columns for production of grain whisky, two pot stills for malt whisky and one still with six columns designated for neutral spirit. There are also two mash tuns and 23 washbacks. Grain whisky is distilled for nine months of the year, malt whisky for two (always during the winter months July/August) and one month is devoted to maintenance. The barley for the malt whisky is imported from UK maltsters.

In Distell's whisky portfolio, it is the Three Ships brand, introduced in 1977, that makes up for most of the sales. The range consists of Select and 5 year old Premium Select, both of which are a blend of South African and Scotch whiskies. Furthermore, there is Bourbon Cask Finish, the first 100% South African blended whisky and the 10 year old single malt. The latter was launched for the first time in 2003 and it wasn't until autumn 2010 that the next batch was released. It sold out quickly and another 8,000 bottles were launched in October 2011. Apart from the Three Ships range, Distell also produces two 3 year old blended whiskies – Harrier and Knight.

James Sedgwick distillery has the capability of producing both malt and grain whisky and two years ago produced yet another first for South Africa. A "single grain" whisky was released under the name Bain's Cape Mountain Whisky. It is double matured in the same style of cask and, although it has no age statement, it is matured for a minimum of five years.

DISTILLERY: Drayman's Distillery, Silverton, Pretoria
FOUNDED: 2006
OWNER/MANAGER: Moritz Kallmeyer
www.draymans.com

Being a full-time beer brewer since 1997, Moritz Kallmeyer began distilling malt whisky in July 2006. Until last year, production was small, but operations have now been expanded to two pot stills. The new wash still has a capacity of 1,500 litres with the old spirit still holding 800 litres. The spirit still was reconstructed from a stainless steel tank in which perfume was imported. He also believes in letting the wash spend up to ten days in the washback, to allow the malolactic fermentation to transfer its character to the spirit. The whisky matures in French oak casks which have previously held red wine from the Cape area.

Kallmeyer's first whisky was released as a 4 year old in autumn 2010 under the name Drayman's Highveld Single Malt. The next batch is due early 2012. Kallmeyer also works with other distillates such as Mampoer, which is a local brandy, a honey liqueur and fruit schnapps. The main source of income, however, does not come from the distillery but from production of craft beers.

Kallmeyer is also, together with property lawyer, As Botha, involved in a new whisky venture. The concept consists of a whisky distillery and boutique beer house on a working farm and the early thought was to establish it on Hatherley Agri Estate in Mpumalanga province, 80 km northeast of Pretoria. Plans have changed and they are now hoping to build the complex on an African game farm in the Cradle of Humankind – a World Heritage site in Gauteng

Three Ships Single Malt and Drayman's Highveld Single Malt

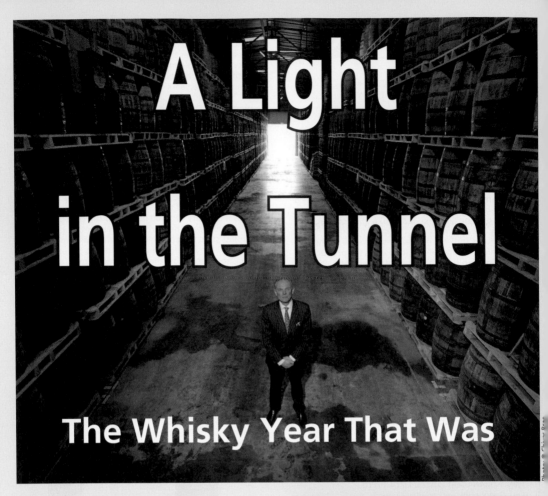

A Light in the Tunnel

The Whisky Year That Was

Scotch whisky industry – heading for new records!

There is no doubt – the Scotch whisky industry has seen the light in the tunnel. It looks like the effects of the global recession from late 2008 only affected the companies during the first half of 2009. When the year came to an end, the figures showed yet another record year for Scotch whisky. Focus had shifted from the more expensive single malts to more affordable blended whiskies. Then came 2010 with single malts bouncing back big time and premium blends getting more attention from customers. The total value of exported Scotch increased by 10% to £3.45bn – a new record! The volume on the other hand, decreased by 2,3% to the equivalent of 1061 million 70 cl bottles, which is close to the volume exported in 2006. So, it is pretty obvious that less bottles are sold but at a higher price. In fact, the producers´ revenue for an average bottle of Scotch whisky in 2006 was £2.38, while the same ratio in 2010 was £3.25, an increase of 36%!

The picture for 2010, if broken down into malt and blends, is as follows (note that bulk shipments are not included, except in the total figure for Scotch):

BOTTLED SINGLE MALT - EXPORT
Value: +18% to £577m
Volume: +31.2% to 84.6m bottles

BOTTLED BLENDED SCOTCH - EXPORT
Value: +5% to £2.60bn
Volume: -8.4% to 776m bottles

TOTAL SCOTCH - EXPORT
Value: +10% to £3.45bn
Volume: -2.3% to 1061m bottles

If we look at the top ten export markets, only two of them have decreased by value during 2010, while five have decreased by volume. The most important market in terms of value is still the USA. During 2010 exports increased by 19% and the total value is now at £499m. Especially Scotch single malt showed strong performance and the only spirits category with a bigger increase was Irish whiskey. While still in North America, Mexico is now Scotch whisky´s 15th largest market, thanks to an increase in value by 41%. In South America, traditionally a strong market for Scotch blended whiskies, Brazil has increased and is now the 11th largest market in the world. Venezuela, which was in sixth place last year, fell by 46% to £63m. On the other hand, this only means that it is back to the figures of 2008. It is a volatile market where political and economic changes have a very rapid effect going both ways.

Asia, the second biggest market for Scotch after Europe, was a disappointment in 2009 with a decrease of 9% in terms of value. On the other hand, the region came back in full force during 2010. There are currently three countries amongst the top ten – Singapore (+32%), South Korea (+36%) and Taiwan (+26%). The situation in Taiwan is particularly impressive as sales increased also during 2009 (+21%) when export to most of the others countries in the region declined. More and more companies have set up their own distribution companies in Asia and from being focused on blended whiskies, consumers now to a greater extent, seem ready to embrace also single malts. Two countries that are not in the top ten list are India and China, but these are potentially huge markets for the future. A recent forecast predicts a 200% growth in malt whisky sales in India until 2015 and 115% in China.

In Africa the figures by value were up 41% to a total of £213m. It is also in Africa where we find one of last year's biggest gainers, South Africa, increasing by no less than 56% in terms of value and which brings it to fifth place on the global list, both in terms of value and volume. As much as 80% of the exports to Africa, go to South Africa. In the Australasian region (read Australia, which accounts for 90% of the total) export by value increased by 3% to £72m.

The biggest region, with a share of 36% is still Europe with a total value of £1.26bn (excl.UK). This is the same figure as last year, but if we look in detail at different countries, there have been many changes, mainly due to the economic turbulence especially in the Mediterranean countries. Greece, for example, fell from 5th place to 9th, due to a decrease in value by 26%. This mainly affected single malts and only 300,000 bottles were exported to the country during 2010. Of more importance is Spain, the third biggest market for Scotch, both in terms of value and volume. The decrease during 2009 continued with the same magnitude in 2010 (-15%) and the biggest category, blended Scotch, has now gone down by 40% since 2007 to 66 million bottles.

The situation in France, the biggest market in the world in terms of volumes, is more stable. Although volumes decreased by 8%, value increased by 4% which can be attributed to the sales of single malts where volumes have increased by a staggering 127% during the year. The fourth European country on the top ten list, Germany, performed well with an increase of 22% in value. For some years now, Eastern Europe has been a market in the focus of many producers, and, although sales to a handful of countries declined during 2010 (Bulgaria and Hungary), most of them showed a healthy increase; Estonia (+42%), Latvia (+83%), Poland (+18%) and Russia (+63%).

First months of 2011

The first figures for 2011 (January to June), confirmed most of the observations noted during 2010. The increase in USA continued (up by 14%) while South America virtually exploded with a 49% increase for the first six months with exports to Brazil rising by 56%. In Asia, where shipments of Scotch increased by 33%, it was countries such as India, China, Thailand and Taiwan leading the way. Taiwan is now a top five market for Scotch whisky. In Europe, France and Germany continued to do well, as did several countries in Eastern Europe, especially Estonia, Latvia, Poland and Russia. In the Mediterranean area however, due to the troubled economies, the outlook was still gloomy.

The big players

Diageo
Diageo is the world's largest drinks company with mega brands like Johnnie Walker, Smirnoff, Captain Morgan, Bailey's, Crown Royal and J&B in the portfolio. For the fiscal year ending 30th June 2011, the CEO of the company, Paul Walsh, could report an organic growth in net sales by 5% to £9.94bn. With exchange rate movements, acquisitions and disposals taken into consideration, net sales increased by 2%. Operating profit before exceptional items increased by 5% to £2.88bn. Net profit increased by 17% to £1.9bn but a substantial part of that was due to a significantly lower tax rate (14.5%) compared to last year (21.3%). If we look at net sales for the different markets, North America increased by a mere 1% but is by far the biggest market for Diageo, both in terms of sales and profit. International (which comprises South America, Africa, Middle East, Australia and Duty Free) is now the second biggest market and net sales increased by 16%, driven by double digit growth in most of the South American markets. Europe has fallen to third place and showed a

Paul Walsh - Diageo's optimistic CEO

Americas grew by 8% but USA only by 2%, mainly thanks to Absolut and Jameson. Europe, excluding France, showed a mix of directions with Spain (-5%) and Greece (-33%) declining while Eastern and Central Europe increased (+9%). France, finally, grew by 4% and amongst the whiskies it was above all Ballantine's and Jameson that increased.

The best selling brands within Pernod Ricard are known as the Top 14 and this category represents 58% of the total sales for the group. Four of these brands are whiskies; Chivas Regal (+7%), Ballantine's (+7%), Jameson (+17%) and Glenlivet (+13%).

During the year, Pernod Ricard has worked hard on reducing their debt caused in particular by the acquisition of Absolut Vodka, and managed to reduce it by €1,546m but a staggering €9,038 still remains.

United Spirits

The most important goal for United Spirits and its owner Vijay Mallya, was to sell more cases by 31 March 2011 than its arch rival Diageo and thus would become the largest spirits company in the world by volume. They succeeded by selling 114 million cases. But they will not stop there. The next target is to sell 200 million cases within 5 years!

United Spirits Limited, part of the Indian UB Group, could report a net profit after tax of Rs. 4.03 billion, which was an increase of 7% compared to the previous year. Total turnover rose even more (+29%) to Rs. 64.02 billion. Part of the increase was due to the incorporation of Balaji Distilleries earlier in the year which makes comparison with last year's figures a bit misleading. United Spirits have more than 140 brands in their portfolio including Scotch whisky, Indian whisky, vodka, rum, brandy and wine. Since last year, 21 of the brands are so called "millionaire brands, i.e. a brand selling more than one million cases in a year. The latest brand to enter the list was McDowell's No 1 Platinum. What is even more remarkable is that the brand was introduced to the market as

Photo: Pernod Ricard

Patrick Ricard - Pernod Ricard's chairman of the board

decrease in net sales by 5%. Not surprisingly, it was three countries in particular which recorded negative figures – Ireland (-11%), Spain/Portugal (-21%) and Greece (-39%). On the other side of the scale were Russia, Eastern Europe and Germany which all showed double digit net sales growth. Finally, Asia is still a market where Diageo haven't yet explored all the possibilities (at least compared to some of their competitors). Net sales grew by 16% but it is still the smallest of Diageo's markets.

With the exception of J&B, all whisk(e)y brands performed well with Johnnie Walker increasing 11%, both in volume and net sales and the brand sold around 16 million cases. Other whisky brands which performed well were Buchanan's, Windsor and Bushmills.

Paul Walsh, commenting on the results, said that emerging markets are expected to provide 50% of the company's annual net sales by 2015 compared to 40% today. He also declared that total net sales are expected to rise by an average of 6% per year for the next three years.

Pernod Ricard

When the world's third largest drinks company by volume and second largest by value, announced their results for the year ending 30 June 2011, it became obvious that not only Diageo of the big companies had experienced a good year. Net sales were up by 8% to €7,643m while net profit increased even more, +10% to €1,045m, exceeding for the first time €1,000m.

Not surprisingly the best market was Asia/Rest of the World with a growth of +19%. In particular it was increased sales in China, India, Vietnam, Taiwan and Duty Free that was the driving force.

McDowell's Signature - one of United Spirits' biggest brands

late as March 2010 and has already managed to reach 2.5 million cases!

United Spirits' biggest brand is Bagpiper whisky which sold 16.4 million cases during 2010, a total of 500,000 cases more than Johnnie Walker, the most sold Scotch whisky. It should be noted that while the volumes are bigger, in terms of global revenue, Johnnie Walker is still six to seven times bigger than Bagpiper.

In 2007, United Spirits entered the Scotch whisky market for the first time when Whyte & Mackay was acquired for £595m. Four malt distilleries (Dalmore, Isle of Jura, Fettercairn and Tamnavulin), a bottling-plant and stocks of 115 million litres were included in the deal.

Morrison Bowmore

When Morrison Bowmore (owner of Bowmore, Auchentoshan and Glen Garioch distilleries), published their report for the fiscal year 2010, they could look back on two years with increased pre-tax profits – 2008 (+13%) and 2009 (+7%). For 2010, the success continued with an increase of 11% to £4.2m. Net profits, however, dropped by 12% to £2.1m. The reason was said to be higher costs, including one-off charges for roof repairs at the Springburn site.

Net sales during 2010 rose by 5.5% to £41.5m, driven by strong performances, especially by Bowmore (volumes up 7% to 175,000 cases) and Auchentoshan (+ 22% to 50,000 cases). The McClelland range of single malts also performed well.

The result was also boosted by the agreement that was concluded with Drambuie Liqueur Company in early 2010 to provide Drambuie with supply chain services covering whisky procurement, blending, bottling, warehousing and logistics at the plant in Springburn. The same services had previously been supplied by Glenmorangie at their Broxburn facility.

Edrington

Like few other companies, Edrington, the world's fourth largest producer of single malt Scotch whisky, has managed to get through the recession without major issues. For the year ending March 2011, the turnover reached £553m, an increase of 18% compared to last year. The profit before taxes also increased (by 19%) to £142m. One should keep in mind that the purchase of Cutty Sark blend from Berry Brothers was completed in April 2010, so sales of 1 million bottles of the brand has affected the figures but the existing portfolio also performed very well.

The volume of Macallan grew by 14% to over 700,000 cases and it is now the number two single malt in the world, both in terms of volume and value behind Glenfiddich, but just ahead of Glenlivet. Sales of Highland Park have also increased, by 9%. The Famous Grouse blend showed a positive but modest increase of 4%. Within that range, Black Grouse showed strength, increasing sales figures by 21%.

Asia is one of the biggest markets, not least for Macallan that has 50% of its sales there. Hence the strategic importance of buying the Maxxium distribution companies in China and Hong Kong in 2010.

Fifty percent of all Macallan that is sold goes to Asia

LVMH

LVMH Moët Hennessy Louis Vuitton SA is the world's leading luxury goods vendor. It provides products ranging from champagne and perfumes, to designer handbags and jewellery. The Wines & Spirits business group includes brands such as Moët & Chandon Champagne and Hennessy Cognac, with Glenmorangie and Ardbeg representing Scotch whisky.

For 2010, the company could report a staggering 73% rise in profit with a rapid growth in demand for luxury goods in Asian markets being the main driver. An important part of the profit leap, however, was the company´s purchase of a stake in Hermes International. Profits from recurring operations were still an impressive €4.32 billion (+29%).

Wine & Spirits is the second largest division in the company with a turnover of €3261 million (+19%) and profit of €930 million (+22%). Champagne and cognac are by far the most important segments of the division and there have been speculations for a couple of years now whether or not LVMH will keep the Scotch whiskies or sell them. On the other hand there have also been rumours discussing the possibility of the entire Wine & Spirits division being sold in order to concentrate on fashion and jewellery.

Glenmorangie Company

Glenmorangie Company, owner of Glenmorangie and Ardbeg and a subsidiary to LVMH, is still going through a transition from a company of single malts, blended whisky and bulk- and third party sales to a solely single malt Scotch company. This already started in 2008 and the results for 2010 still indicates a negative impact of this transition. Net sales were certainly up 3.2% to £75.55m but restructuring costs impacted the net profits which fell by 1.4% to £8.6m. On the other hand,

if one just looks at the part of the business now in focus and exclude business cut in the restructuring, net sales increased by almost 18% and operating profits by 7%.

Special subjects for rejoicing in 2010 have been a number of limited releases, for example Glenmorangie Sonnalta PX and Ardbeg Supernova.

Ian Macleod Distillers

Founded in 1933, this is one of the largest family-owned companies in the UK spirits industry, acting both as an independent bottler, blender and owner of two distilleries – Glengoyne and Tamdhu. The latter was acquired in summer 2011 from Edrington who mothballed the distillery in 2009. Eight years earlier, Glengoyne was also bought from Edrington.

For the financial year ending 30 September 2010, the turnover increased by no less than 22% to £31.9m, while the profit grew even more, +41% to £3.1m. The main momentum behind these encouraging numbers was the increase of sales of Glengoyne single malt (+40% in volumes and +49% in value). The biggest markets for Glengoyne are France, Germany and Scandinavia. Ian Macleod Distillers are also well established in the Indian market, not least through their blended whisky, King Robert II, selling 500,000 cases per year. To get a better stronghold on the Indian market, a subsidiary was established in 2010, by way of Ian Macleod Distillers India Private Ltd.

Gruppo Campari

The company managed to top the results of the fiscal year for 2009 and now seems to be on its way to more solid ground after the recession. Sales have increased by 15% to €1163m with net profits reaching €156m – up 14% compared to the previous year. Spirits account for 75% of the group´s sales, with Campari, Aperol, SKYY Vodka, Wild Turkey and Glen Grant as the big brands. In terms of regions, Campari Group concentrates on Italy (one third of the sales), the rest of Europe and the Americas. Only 7% of the sales are in the rest of the world and compared to the competitors, there is more work to be done on the important and growing Asian market. In 2009 the sales figures for Glen Grant slowed down by 4%, so an increase by 9% for 2010 was a good sign that the single malt had started finding its way back. Campari Group has spent quite a lot of money these past two years on acquisitions. In May 2009 they bought Wild Turkey bourbon at a cost of $581m and in October 2010

The distillers of the Campari-owned Wild Turkey Bourbon - Jimmy and Eddie Russel

Photo: Campari Group

they paid €128,5m to get Frangelico, Carolans and Irish Mist from William Grant & Sons. It has also been decided to more than double the capacity at Wild Turkey distillery in Kentucky at a cost of $50m.

Fortune Brands

The American company with its headquarter in Deerfield, Illinois, is active in three different business areas; Home & Security, Golf and Spirits. The latter is contained within subsidiary Beam Global Spirits & Wine, which has major spirits brands such as Jim Beam, Maker's Mark, Canadian Club, Courvoisier and, in Scotch, Teacher's and Laphroaig. A recent addition to the line-up is Cruzan rum.

The diversity of the company's business activities has made it difficult to maintain a decent growth in recent years. Even though total sales increased in 2010 by 7% to $7,141m, this is substantially lower than sales in 2007 ($8,563). Profits grew by 51% compared to 2009, but the actual figure ($764m) is also much lower than 2007 ($1,376m). Home & Security and Golf have been two segments proven hard to become profitable and, therefore, a decision was made to sell off everything by the end of 2011, except Beam Global Spirits, which is responsible for 70% of last year's profit.

The volume figures for the Scotch brands have improved compared to 2009, with Teacher's increasing by 8% to 1.9 million cases sold and Laphroaig also by 8% to 185,000 cases. In the bourbon category, Maker's Mark exceeded one million cases sold for the first time in its history.

Inver House Distillers

Inver House, a subsidiary of ThaiBev, could report on an impressive increase in net sales for the year ending 31 December 2010. A strong demand for their range of single malt and blended Scotch resulted in a rise by 19% to £63m. One of the most successful brands was Old Pulteney where volume went up 22% and value 34%. The company made significant gains in USA, Russia and Travel Retail during 2010 but in spite of this, net profits dropped by 3.5% to £6.8. The reason for this, according to the company, was increased investment in marketing and distribution.

The big brands

In 2009 sales of most of the big brands declined while cheaper whiskies enjoyed a healthy growth. One year later the scene had changed. Low-key brands continued to grow but it also marked the return for most of the top brands.

On the single malts list, the first place still belongs to Glenfiddich. A couple of years ago they were very close to reaching 1 million cases as the first single malt, but has since declined slightly due to the recession. In 2010 sales were still an impressive 954,000 cases. The struggle for the second place has, for the last 8 years, been between Macallan and Glenlivet. During 2010, the owners of Macallan could report a very impressive increase which handed them a second place with 700,000 cases sold while Glenlivet occupied the third place with, as it looks, just a few thousand cases less. After these top three there is a huge

Photo: William Grant & Sons

Glenfiddich shows no sign of giving up the number one spot as the most sold single malt in the world

gap to the rest. Glen Grant has succeeded to retrieve the fourth place with 328,000 cases in 2010 while Glenmorangie and Cardhu has had a tough fight regarding place five and six with 280,000 cases sold each. Aberlour comes in at place seven with a little more than 200,000 cases and Laphroaig (185,000 cases), Balvenie (182,000 cases) and Bowmore (163,000 cases) complete the top ten list.

If Glenfiddich is the dominant player in the single malts segment, there is an even more obvious leader amongst blended Scotch. Johnnie Walker turned a loss of 11% during 2009 into an increase of almost 10% in 2010 with a total of 15.9 million cases sold. Like last year, the number two spot is held by Ballantine's with 7.3 million cases but after that we see some changes. J&B (4.9 million cases), having fought against bad market conditions in its main market Spain, was pushed down to fourth place, while William Grant's (5 million cases) climbed to third place. In place five, with an impressive increase of 16% to 4.5 million cases is Chivas Regal followed by Dewar's (3.3 million cases), Famous Grouse (just under 3 million cases), Bell's and William Peel (both 2.5 million cases) and finally Label 5 (2.3 million cases).

As always, this ranking shows just the Scotch whisky brands. If we look at whiskies produced in North America, the number one spot is held by Jack Daniel's (Tennessee whiskey) with almost 10 million cases, followed by Jim Beam (Bourbon) with 5.3 million cases, Crown Royal (Canadian) 5 million cases, Seagram's 7 Crown (American blended whiskey) 2.4 million cases and Black Velvet (Canadian) with 2.1 million cases.

Finally, let's have a look at the Indian whiskies. This is a category where volumes are really high

due to the fact that India is the country where most whisky is drunk. The most popular and the top selling whisky in the world, all categories, is Bagpiper with 16.4 million cases sold in 2010. Number two, Officer's Choice, is one of the biggest climbers during 2010 with an increase of 33% to 16 million cases. After that follows McDowell's No. 1 (14.3 million cases), Royal Stag (10.4 million cases) and Original Choice (10.3 million cases).

Changes in ownership - mergers and acquisitions

The past year has, as usual, been filled with ownership changes within the drinks business but as this is being written (September 2011) no mega-deals have been made like the one which occurred in 2005 when Pernod Ricard acquired Allied Domecq or in 2001 when Pernod Ricard and Diageo split up Seagram Spirits & Wine amongst each other. There might be a large deal up someone's sleeve within the not too distant future though. Fortune Brands has declared that they will sell off two of their areas of business to be able to focus on the third – Beam Global Spirits & Wine which will then trade under the name Beam. In May 2011 they had found a buyer for their golf business and there were prospects that Home & Security would be sold off in a few months' time. The wine & spirits part would be left with big brands such as Teacher's, Laphroaig, Jim Beam, Maker's Mark, Sauza and Courvoisier. Several reviewers believe that this mix, which together makes up the world's fourth largest premium spirits company, will be far too interes-

The battle for Jim Beam Bourbon (and other brands owned by Beam) is due to start later in 2011

ting not to attract quite a number of bidders. For competition concerns it is likely to believe that in case of a purchase, it would have to involve a couple of interested parties.

Diageo could possibly be one of those interested. The company has very strong funds in contrast to their archrival, Pernod Ricard, who still has a huge burden of debt after buying Absolut Vodka and has furthermore declared through their CEO, Pierre Pringuet, that "...in the medium-term, we want to be seen as a consolidator...". Furthermore, Diageo lacks an important segment in their product mix that Pernod Ricard has, namely cognac (if you don't count the 34% share that the company holds in Hennesy) and they also don't have a bourbon in the portfolio. Courvoisier and Jim Beam would therefore be the perfect match.

Regardless of what happens to Beam Global, Diageo has not been on the lazy side when it comes to corporate take-overs. The interest has mainly been directed at emerging markets like Asia and Eastern Europe. At the beginning of 2010 Diageo bought another 4% of the shares in Sichuan Chengdu Quanxing Group which made them the main shareholder. Through a very complex ownership this meant that Diageo was forced (which, of course, was Diageo's plan from the start) to place a bid on Shui Jing Fang, one of Chinas largest spirit companies with 32% of the Chinese market. Foreign ownership of Chinese companies is always dependent on an approval from the Chinese authorities but positive signs were sent out at a meeting between the UK Prime Minister, David Cameron, and the Chinese Premier, Wen Jiabao, at the end of June. The deal will end up costing Diageo £610m.

Shui Jing Fang is one of China's largest spirits producers

Photo: Diageo

Diageo had also turned their eyes to Eastern Europe and Turkey. In February 2011, a deal was signed where Diageo acquired Turkey's leading spirits producer, Mey Içki, at a cost of $2.1bn. Mey Içki is the leading seller of the Turkish raki spirit and also produces vodka and whisky. But the brands are not the sole interest of Diageo but also the distribution net which can be used for their own products. A couple of months later, Diageo tried to strengthen their position in Eastern Europe as well, when they attempted to buy Stock Spirits – the leading spirits company in Poland and the Czech Republic and also producer of the number one vodka in Italy, Czysta de Luxe. A month later, however, Diageo withdrew from the negotiations because they thought the company was overvalued.

Like Pernod Ricard, United Spirits in India has been faced with economic difficulties since the purchase of Whyte & Mackay in 2007. The financial situation has however improved and in January 2011 the company bought Pioneer Distilleries with a distillery east of Mumbai. Just two months later a new deal was announced when United Spirits bought a 41% stake in the bulk spirits manufacturer, Sovereign Distilleries. The company's main product is ENA (Extra Neutral Alcohol) which forms an important part of Indian Blended Whisky.

Another of the big companies was in a spending mood during 2010. In October Bacardi paid €128,5m to get Frangelico, Carolans and Irish Mist from William Grant & Sons. This was a consequence of W Grant's acquisition of the Irish C & C Group six months earlier, where the goal was to get their hands on Tullamore Dew and then to sell off the brands that did not fit their portfolio.

In November 2009, Edrington announced that they were going to mothball their Tamdhu distillery in Speyside. Since it was clear that Edrington had no intentions to restart the distillery again in the future, a lot of rumors have flourished regarding who could be the potential buyer of the distillery. At the end of June 2011 it was final that Ian Macleod Distillers would take over Tamdhu distillery and the brand for an undisclosed sum. Apart from being an independent bottler, they also own Glengoyne distillery which was bought from Edrington in 2003. Ian Macleod's intention is to start up the production at Tamdhu during 2012, but the adjacent maltings will remain closed.

Last year we could report regarding the strenuous situation at Belvedere S.A., one of the biggest French spirits producers, with brands such as Sobieski vodka and William Peel blended Scotch in the portfolio, as well as Marie Brizard which was acquired in 2006. The company found themselves with a debt of €375m and the only way out seemed to be to sell Marie Brizard and the other two brands. Several competitors prepared their bids but, suddenly, a French court ruled that the company get the benefit of credit protection (similar to Chapter 11 in the USA). This continued until spring 2011 when another court decided to revoke the protection because "the company has not respected the conditions of a recovery plan". The end for the company seemed near but the story did not end here. At the beginning of July yet another court placed the company under creditor protection once more and it remains to be seen what will now happen. Although rather unknown outside of France, William Peel is the biggest blended Scotch on the French market and is placed 8 on the global sales list with 2.5 million cases sold in 2010.

Global protection for Scotch whisky is strengthened

Scotch whisky can only be made in Scotland! At least if Scotch Whisky Association (SWA) makes the rules. The trade association for the Scotch whisky industry has long fought for that to be the case all over the world. Within the EU Scotch whisky has already been awarded Geographical Indication (GI) status, which makes it illegal for any member state to produce or sell whisky produced outside Scotland using the name Scotch whisky. The general idea of GI is to prevent other whiskies (or indeed spirits) to benefit from the reputation of Scotch and thereby undermining the integrity of the category.

SWA has no way of enforcing these rules in other countries, but will have to work through negotiations to achieve brand protection.

Recently, such negotiations have been successful in a number of countries. It started with Malaysia and Thailand where the GI status was achieved at the beginning of 2010. By November of 2010, the Chinese government agreed to protect Scotch whisky on the same terms and in June 2011, two very important export markets for Scotch, namely South Korea and India, announced that they had approved Scotch whisky as a GI product. Both countries are among the top ten export markets for Scotch whisky and India alone increased by 40% during 2010 to 40 million bottles. The latest country to recognise the uniqueness of Scotch whisky was Turkey in July 2011.

The GI protection does not refer to the name Scotch only but also serves as protection against misleading elements such as images of pipers and the Highlands.

New, revived and planned distilleries

Annandale Distillery
In May 2010 consent was given from Dumfries & Galloway Council for the building of the new Annandale Distillery. The old one was closed in 1921 and in December 2008 the site was bought by Professor David Thomson and his wife, Teresa Church, with the aim to resurrect this, the southernmost distillery in Scotland. Work on the

Construction work on Annandale Distillery in the Lowlands began in June 2011

restoration began in June 2011 with the two old sandstone warehouses which will be restored to function as two-level dunnage warehouses. The mash house and the tun room will need a complete reconstruction while a new still house will be built. The remains of the old still house have been uncovered by archaeologists and will be preserved for the future. David also has plans to start using the old maltings as well, to malt locally sourced barley, but that will probably not be for another five years. Meanwhile, the old maltings will house a visitors centre.

As for the equipment (the original ones have all disappeared), this will be made by Forsyth's in Rothes. In July 2010, Malcolm Rennie, who managed Kilchoman distillery on Islay, joined the company as Distillery Manager. Together with Jim Swan, he created the design and the first delivery will be the mash tun, milling equipment and equipment for grain storage. The equipment specification, as it currently looks, will be one semi-lauter mash tun (2.5 tonnes), six wooden washbacks (12,000 litres each), one wash still (12,000 litres), one intermediate still and one spirit still (4,000 litres each). The planned output is 250,000 litres per annum. According to David's plans, the first production run could be in December 2012 with the distillery open to public by late spring 2013.

Kingsbarns Distillery

Fife will get its third distillery sometime soon if everything goes as planned. The first two are the huge grain spirit complex Cameronbridge and the small farm distillery, Daftmill. Kingsbarns Company of Distillers, spearheaded by Greg Ramsay and Doug Clement, are behind the new plans. Greg, who is from Tasmania, met Doug when they were working with establishing the Nant Distillery in Tasmania. Their idea is to build a distillery in the vicinity of St Andrews, home of golf and an area with thousands of visitors each year but lacking a whisky distillery. Greg and Doug have consulted Bill Lark as advisor. He is the owner of Lark Distillery in Tasmania, godfather of modern whisky-making in Australia, and advisor to several other whisky companies in his native Australia. The idea is to convert a farm-stead on the Cambo Estate which has been home to the Erskine family since 1688 and is owned today by Sir Peter Erskine. The distillery will have one pair of stills (to be built in Tasmania) and the capacity will be around 100,000 litres per year. The latest report was that they had received planning permission in March 2011. After that a second round of share offer to potential investors was released but due to the current economic climate, this proved harder than anticipated. Currently, the owners are looking for investors to help kickstart the distillery.

Falkirk Distillery

The construction of the first distillery in Falkirk, since Rosebank was closed in 1993, came to a halt temporarily in autumn of 2009 after the plans had

The 18th century East Newhall Farm Steading - the chosen location for Kingsbarns Distillery

been approved by the local council in spring of 2009. Objections were raised by Historic Scotland that the distillery would be built too close to the Antonine Wall. The Wall was built in 142 AD to stop Caledonian tribes attacking the Romans and it was given World Heritage Status in 2008. However, in May 2010 Scottish ministers gave the final approval arguing that the distillery would not interfere with the wall but could boost tourism to the area instead.

Falkirk Distillery Company, owned by Fiona and Alan Stewart, is behind the £5m project. The facilities will include a visitor centre, restaurant and shops apart from the distillery itself and could create up to 80 jobs. The Stewarts hope to be able to use the name Rosebank for their whisky but the trademark is owned by Diageo who, from time to time, release bottlings under that name from existing stocks. Diageo have stated that the trademark is not for sale even if the Stewarts are hopeful for a change once the stocks of Rosebank have drained

Dingle Distillery
Permission to build a distillery in Dingle, County Kerry, Ireland was applied for in autumn 2008 and was granted in March 2009 by Kerry County Council. The people behind it, Porterhouse Brewing Company and Jerry O'Sullivan, managing director of Southbound Properties, planned to convert an old creamery into a distillery, at a cost of €2.9m. Initially, it was said that the distillery would be up and running in late 2009 but the production start was postponed.

In 2010, the former business partners went their separate ways. Jerry O'Sullivan started planning for a brewery at the old creamery site. In summer 2011 brewing commenced and they also have plans to distil whiskey on site.

The people from Porterhouse Brewing Company, Oliver Hughes and Liam LaHart on the other hand, found a new location, also in Dingle. The plan is now to turn an old saw mill into a whiskey distillery with the express purpose to start distillation in late 2011 or early 2012. Meanwhile, a gin still has been acquired and production of organic gin and vodka is already taking place.

Barra Distillery
The classic film, Whisky Galore, based on the equally classic novel by Sir Compton Mackenzie, was filmed on the island of Barra in the Outer Hebrides. It is a story of the SS Politician which was stranded in 1941 and 264,000 bottles of whisky which were among her cargo were lost. The island where the ship went missing was in fact Eriskay, a smaller island to the north of Barra, but that did not deter Peter Brown who had moved to Barra from Edinburgh 12 years ago. He wants to build a distillery there and is convinced that the connection with the film location will be favourable for the business.

In November 2005, the Loch Uisge reservoir on the west of the island was acquired in order to secure water supply for the future distillery. Future

casks have been sold to the public since early 2008 and most of the plans regarding building and construction are ready. In July 2010, Peter Brown bought all the shares owned by Andrew Currie (of Arran Distillery fame) who had been part of the project since its inception. The original idea was to start building in autumn of 2009, but the recession has made funding difficult and the future for the distillery is now uncertain.

Investments

Three years ago, Diageo closed Kilmarnock bottling plant, Carsebridge cooperage and Port Dundas distillery. As a part of that operation, it was decided that the bottling plant in Fife should be expanded and a new cooperage in Cambus should be built. The £86m expansion of the bottling plant in Leven is now well under way. Construction started last year but came to a halt in November when the contractor, ROK, went into administration. A new company was hired and work was resumed in January 2011. The building was finished in summer 2011 and the whole project will be completed during 2012. The site will become one of the world's largest bottling plants for spirits with a capacity of 35 million cases per year. The replacement cooperage for the one closed in Carsebridge also opened summer 2011 at Cambus, Clackmannanshire.

But Diageo's investments during 2010/2011 were not just about replacing closed sites. In June 2011 it was announced that £9.5m would be spent

Diageo's new cooperage in Cambus

on an upgrade of the existing bio-plant at Dailu-aine. The increased capacity at Dailuaine handling the by-products from distilling, creates the possibility of increasing the capacity of production at Diageo´s distilleries. Another £10m will therefore go towards increasing the capacity at Caol Ila, Glen Ord and a number of Speyside distilleries. The total increase in capacity will be 10 million litres of alcohol.

An investment in storing and blending capacity announced by Dewar´s in 2008 continued during 2010/2011. By the end of December a total of nine warehouses had been built at a site at Poniel in South Lanarkshire, each with a capacity of 72,000 casks. A further three warehouses are under construction as from 2011 and will be completed by early 2012. The final goal is to have a total of 18 warehouses holding 1.3 million casks. The full capacity will not be used by Dewars´ themselves, but will be rented out, for example, to Diageo.

One investment for William Grant & Sons was damage control in the wake of the disastrous events on 7th January 2010. Heavy snowfall caused a number of warehouses to collapse with the result that 230,000 casks of maturing whisky became "homeless". In August 2011, four of the warehouses had been completely rebuilt, nine had been repaired and a completely new warehouse had been constructed. When the many casks were brought back from temporary warehouses, it was discovered that only six casks had been destroyed!

Whyte & Mackay, owners of among others Dalmore and Isle of Jura distilleries, have invested in the visitor centres at the respective distilleries. Jura visitor centre got a £100,000 facelift designed to replicate a traditional Hebridean bothy while £1m was invested in the visitor centre at Dalmore, which re-opened in summer 2011.

Another investment presented in 2008, is the bioenergy plant in Rothes where draff from the whisky production will be burnt together with woodchips to generate enough electricity to supply 9,000 homes. The project was initiated by Combination of Rothes Distillers (CORD) which is an association of whisky distillers in and around the town of Rothes. When first announced in 2008, the cost was estimated at £24m but has now spiralled to £50m. The goal is to have the plant ready by 2013.

The new visitor centre at Dalmore distillery

Photo: Whyte & Mackay

One of many warehouses on Glenfiddich Estate that were damaged in January 2010

Photo: William Grant & Sons

In May 2011 Irish Distillers (owned by Pernod Ricard) presented plans to increase the capacity at Midleton Distillery in Ireland. Midleton is already a huge distillery with a capacity of 33 million litres of alcohol per year, but which could increase to 60 million litres within two years. The cost will be €100m and would also include another 20 warehouses on a new site near Midleton distillery, which already has 38 warehouses. An important reason for the increase in capacity is the heavily escalated demand for Jameson, the most sold Irish whiskey in the world. In 2010 the brand reached 3 million cases with one third being sold in the USA.

Bottling grapevine
(see pp 278-281 for a detailed listing)

Let´s start the roundup with the very first bottling from the latest distillery in Scotland. In October, *Abhainn Dearg* on the Isle of Lewis released their *3 year old* – a limited unpeated bottling. Another first was Kilchoman, when they added *Kilchoman 100% Islay* from their own maltings to the range of bottlings made from Port Ellen malt. To continue with the smaller distilleries, *Edradour* released the sixth edition of the peated *Ballechin* as well as a *26 year old PX sherry finish*, the last from the 1985 stock. On to the big boys, where *Glenfiddich* launched a new addition to the duty free range with *Age of Discovery 19 year old Madeira cask finish* while *Macallan* presented the exclusive *MMIX*, also destined for duty free.

Tullibardine has made a habit of releasing old vintages and 2011 was no exception. Three

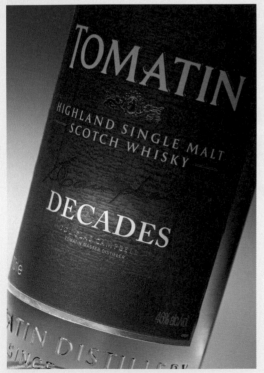

Tomatin Decades - in honour of Master Distiller Douglas Campbell

vintages from *1962, 1964* and *1976* as well as a *1992 wood finish* from Ch Lafite casks pleased the customers. Bill Lumsden, Head of Whisky Creation at Glenmorangie, could present a labour of love with his *Glenmorangie Pride*. The whisky is 28 years old with 10 years of extra maturation in Sauternes casks – the longest extra maturation for any Glenmorangie whisky.

Highland Park had, as always, an interesting mix of new releases. *Leif Eriksson*, matured in American oak, and *Vintage 1978* both went to travel retail while the *18 year old Earl Haakon* concluded the trilogy which started two years ago. From Springbank came *Longrow 18 years old* and *Hazelburn Sauternes 8 years old* as well as a rumour that the legendary *Springbank 21 year old* might be up for a relaunch sometime during 2012. From Campbeltown over to Islay, where *Bowmore* released a *1982 Vintage* as well as the third edition of the popular *Tempest*. From Ardbeg came *Alligator* which had matured in heavily charred casks, hence the name and *Laphroaig* moved their *Triple Wood* from the duty free range to a general release and substituted it with *Laphroaig PX*. *Caol Ila Moch* was the first official bottling from the distillery without an age statement and, as usual, an *unpeated Caol Ila* was released as part of Diageo´s Special Release. In the same launch came a *32 year old Brora*, the oldest distillery bottling from that distillery ever and also *Port Ellen 32 year old*. Diageo continued with a *25 year old Knockando* from first fill sherry casks, a *21 year old Rosebank*, a *40 year old Glenury Royal* and finally, perhaps the biggest surprise of them all, a rare *20 year old Port Dundas* single grain.

Dalmore has excelled in extremely rare (and expensive) bottlings these past few years and this continued in 2011 with *Astrum*, distilled in 1966 with an 18 months finish in Gonzales Byass casks. But there were affordable bottlings from the distillery as well – three new releases in the *Rivers Collection (Spey, Tay* and *Tweed)* are sold to help support the conservation of the rivers in Scotland. In 2010, a limited release from *Balvenie* called *Tun 1401*, delighted many whisky lovers. It was made up of six different barrels from 1966 to 1988 and in 2011 it was time for the *second edition* of this master piece from David Stewart. *Tomatin* distillery decided to celebrate Master Distiller Douglas Campbell´s 50th year at the distillery with *Tomatin Decades* – a whisky containing single malt from each decade Douglas has worked at the distillery. And while we are talking about anniversaries – Glenfarclas celebrated 175 years in the business by launching *Glenfarclas 175th Anniversary* containing whiskies from six decades dating back to the 1950s and *Chairman´s Reserve*, made up of four casks with a combined age of 175 years.

The people at Dewar´s released a *single cask Aberfeldy* in July with another two coming later in the year and they also let us know that at least one new bottling from *Royal Brackla* is due for next year. From *Benromach* came a a *2001 Hermitage wood finish*, a *cask strength*, also from *2001*, matured in first fill bourbon casks and a *30*

The Balvenie's Malt Master, David Stewart, nosing a sample of Tun 1401

Photo: William Grant & Sons

year old matured in sherry butts while Tomintoul released the oldest bottling from the distillery so far – a *Vintage 1966* and also a new *21 year old* for the core range.

The owners of *BenRiach* and *GlenDronach* distilleries usually keep themselves pretty occupied with new bottlings and 2011 was no exception. For BenRiach, this meant *twelve vintages* from 1971 to 1993, a *45 year old single cask* from 1966 and the unusual *Firkin Cask* with 32 years in a 45 litre Firkin cask. From *GlenDronach* came a *21 year old* for the core range, *eleven vintages, four wood finishes* and a *1968 single cask*. *Arran* distillery released the second edition of the peated *Machrie Moor*, the third edition of *Icons of Arran* (called

The Westie) and the *11 year old The Sleeping Warrior*. Sweden got an exclusive bottling of a *Vintage 1995* from *Balblair* (for sale also in duty free) and a *Vintage 1993* went to the French and Russian markets. Another InverHouse distillery, *Knockdhu*, released *anCnoc 1996 Vintage* and announced that their oldest distillery bottling ever, a *35 year old*, was due in 2012. *Glenglassaugh* also bottled a *35 year old* as the first in a series called *The Chosen Few* and late 2011 saw the first *3 year old* from the new owner's production.

The extremely rare BenRiach Firkin Cask 32 years (only 40 bottles)

Port Dundas 20 year old and Benromach 30 year old

Independent Bottlers

The independent bottlers play an important role in the whisky business. With their innovative bottlings, they increase diversity. Single malts from distilleries where the owners' themselves decide not to bottle also get a chance through the independents. The following are a selection of the major companies. All tasting notes have been prepared by Ian Buxton.

Gordon & MacPhail ....www.gordonandmacphail.com

Established in 1895 the company which is owned by the Urquhart family still occupies the same premises in Elgin. Apart from being an independent bottler, there is also a legendary store in Elgin and, since 1993, an own distillery, Benromach. There is a wide variety of bottlings, for example *Connoisseurs Choice, Private Collection, MacPhail's Collection* and *Pride of the Regions*. Many of the bottlings have been diluted to 40%, 43% or 46%, but the series *Cask Strength* obviously, as the name implies, contains bottlings straight from the cask. Another range called *Rare Old* consists of unusually old single malts which quite often come from closed distilleries as well. The Gordon & MacPhail warehouses in Elgin contain probably the largest collection of matured malt whisky in the world which was a prerequisite for the 2010 launch of the world's oldest single malt ever bottled – a 70 year old *Mortlach*. This was the first release in a new range called *Generations* and was followed in March 2011 with the release of a *Glenlivet 70 year old* together with another five bottlings of Glenlivet from the 1950s to the 1990s. There are also large volumes of *Macallan* dating all the way to 1940 enabling the release of a special range of whisky from this distillery called *Speymalt*. Several blended whiskies, e. g. *Ben Alder, Glen Calder* and *Avonside* are also found in the company's range.

Mortlach 15 year old, 43%
Nose: Big sherry wood nose but not obtrusive; raisins; prune juice; ripe fruits; fresh and grassy; aniseed/fennel.
Palate: Initial hit of pepper and spices; warm, mellow; toffee; opens up with water to reveal sherry layers; lots of body and weight. Lemongrass.
Finish: Sustained finish with gentle slow fade; smoke drifts in at the end.

Ardmore 1991, 57.8%
Nose: Sweet orange notes; dusty perfume bottles.
Palate: Immediately appealing, oily mouthcoating; waves of zesty citrus then alcohol strength takes over; ripe bananas; loads of vanilla and spice, some smoke emerging with water.
Finish: Aromatic woods, cedar and pine on long-lasting finish. Plenty of depth and cohesion.

Berry Bros. & Rudd ....www.bbr.com

Britain's oldest wine and spirit merchant, founded in 1698 has been selling their own world famous blend, Cutty Sark, since 1923. Berry Brothers had been offering their customers private bottlings of malt whisky for years, but it was not until 2002 that they launched *Berry's Own Selection* of single malt whiskies. Under the supervision of Spirits Manager, Doug McIvor, some 30 expressions are on offer every year. Bottling is usually at 46% but expressions bottled at cask strength are also available. The super premium blended malt, *Blue Hanger* is also included in the range. So far, five different releases have been made, each different from the other. The fifth edition was a mix of one cask each from Glenlivet (1978), Dufftown (1982), Mortlach (1991) and Cragganmore (1997).

2010 turned out to be an exciting year for BBR. First it sold Cutty Sark blended Scotch to Edrington and obtained *The Glenrothes* single malt in exchange.

A strategic partnership with American Anchor Brewers & Distillers, best known for Old Potrero single rye in a whisky context, was announced in summer of 2010. Anchor Brewers & Distillers will assist BBR in selling part of their range in the USA.

Blue Hanger 5th release, 45.6%
Nose: Big sherry wood nose; Christmas cake; port wine hints; ripe fruity pears; vine fruits; rich and full. Rich, mellow and full bodied. Spicy with water, with fruit at the back.
Palate: Mouth coating; preserved plums; hyacinths; some old whiskies in here; careful with the water, only a few drops go a long way. Sip and savour slowly.
Finish: Vanishes quite quickly. Salty aftertaste.

Signatory Vintage Scotch Whisky

Founded in 1998 by Andrew and Brian Symington, Signatory lists at least 50 single malts at any one occasion. The most widely distributed range is *Cask Strength Collection* which sometimes contains spectacular bottlings from distilleries which have long since disappeared. Another range is *The Un-chill Filtered Collection* bottled at 46%. Andrew Symington bought *Edradour Distillery* from Pernod Ricard in 2002.

Ian Macleod Distillers ....www.ianmacleod.com

The company was founded in 1933 and is one of the largest independent family-owned companies within the spirits industry. Gin, rum, vodka and liqueurs are found within the range, apart from whisky and they also own *Glengoyne* and *Tamdhu* distilleries. In total 15 million bottles of spirit are sold per year. Single malt ranges like *The Chieftain's* and *Dun Bheagan* are single casks either bottled at cask strength or (more often) at reduced strength, always natural colour and unchill-filtered. There are two *As We Get It* expressions – Highland and Islay, both 8 year olds. Bottled at 40% are the five *MacLeod's Regional Single Malts* (one for every region and Campbeltown is not included). The blended *Six Isles Single Malt* contains whisky from all the whiskyproducing islands and is bottled at 43%. A recent development of this is the limited Pomerol finish. Finally, *Smokehead*, a heavily peated single malt from Islay, was introduced in 2006. There is also a *Smoke-head Extra Black 18 years old* and *Smokehead Extra Rare* (which basically is a 1 litre duty free bottling of the 12 year old).

Smokehead Extra Black 18 year old, 46%

Nose: Petrol, like a gas station. Rubbery; medicinal, antiseptic notes; bitter orange; stale Christmas nuts; burnt toast.
Palate: Drying; mouth puckering; intense. Opens with water to reveal citrus and floral notes. Damp cellars and old wood, beaten earth floors.
Finish: Flattens and ends abruptly. Oily.

MacLeod´s Islay 8 year old, 40%

Nose: Maple syrup; toasted bitter almonds; marmalade orange sweetness; mixed Christmas spices; cloves. Thin, wispy distant smoke; aromatic sweetness; burnt toffee
Palate: Damp, autumn leaves. Smoke impact more pronounced. Marzipan / toffee sweetness. Damp ash.
Finish: Fades quickly, leaving a mouth coating smoke and forest fire note.

Blackadder International ....www.blackadder.se

Blackadder is owned by Robin Tucek, together with John Lamond. Apart from the *Blackadder* and *Blackadder Raw Cask*, there are also a number of other ranges - *Smoking Islay, Peat Reek, Aberdeen Distillers, Clydesdale Original* and *Caledonian Connections*. One of the latest brands in the Blackadder family is *Riverstown* aiming especiallay for the Asian market. The company has also been known for bottling some unusual expressions of *Amrut* single malt. All bottlings are single cask, uncoloured and unfiltered. Most of the bottlings are diluted to 43-46% but Raw Cask are always bottled at cask strength. Around 100 different bottlings are launched each year.

Duncan Taylor ....www.duncantaylor.com

Duncan Taylor & Co was founded in Glasgow in 1938 and in 2001, Euan Shand bought the company and operations were moved to Huntly. The company bottles around 200 expressions per year. The range includes *Rarest of the Rare* (single cask, cask strength whiskies of great age from demolished distilleries), *Rare Auld* (single cask, cask strength malts and grains with the vast majority aged over 30 years), *Peerless* (a unique collection of single malts over 40 years old), *NC2* (mainly single casks, 12-17 years, non chill-filtered at 46%), *Battlehill* (younger malts at 43%) and *Lonach* (vattings of two casks from same distillery of the same age to bring them up to a natural strength of over 40%). *Auld Reekie* is a 10 year old vatted malt from Islay, which is similar to *Big Smoke*, although the latter is younger, more peated and available in two strengths, 40% and 60%.

In the blended Scotch category, Duncan Taylor is well represented by the *Black Bull* range. The brand was trademarked already in 1933 and Duncan Taylor took over the brand in 2001. The range consists of a *12 year old* and a *30 year old*, both with a 50/50 malt/grain ratio. New editions to the range are *Black Bull 40 year old* (now with its second edition), containing 90% malt whiskies (i. a. Bunnahabhain, Glenlivet and Tamdhu) and *Black Bull Special Reserve No. 1*.

Another addition to the Duncan Taylor range involves the concept of re-racking the whisky from larger casks (hogsheads or barrels) to the smaller quarter casks (ca 125 litres) or octaves (ca 60 litres). This will speed up the

maturation due to the higher whisky to wood ratio, i. e. the whisky is more in contact with the oak. The whisky is allowed to be in the smaller casks for a minimum of 3 months before it is bottled.

Black Bull 40 year old, 41.9%

Nose: Bitter almonds; lemon rind; honey; allspice; pear drops.
Palate: Wood, liquorice, spice box; opens up to reveal sweetness and wine notes. With water some honey and floral flavours, but add sparingly.
Finish: Some bitter notes re-emerge, then honey sweetness.

Black Bull Special Reserve, 46.6%

Nose: Wine notes; then lemon and lime; heather; slightly spirit. Quite 'closed'.
Palate: Mouth coating ramble through sweet, then salty and astringent. Black pepper.
Finish: Quite long, very consistent and fades gently without breaking up.

Master of Malt ....www.masterofmalt.com

One of the biggest whisky retailers in the UK, Master of Malt also have ranges of its own bottled single malts. One range is called *Secret Bottlings* and are bottled at 40%. No distillery names appear on the label. Instead, the region is highlighted (40 year old Speyside, 12 year old Lowland etc.). The bottlings are very competitively priced, not least the older ones. A 50 year old Speyside is only £249.95. Master of Malt also bottles single casks from various distilleries. Some of the latest are a 27 year old Dailuaine, a 36 year old Inchgower and 20 year old North British grain whisky. The people behind Master of Malt have also come up with the brilliant idea to sell single malts (and other spirits) in 30 ml bottles. They call it *Drinks by the Dram* and it gives the customer an opportunity to sample a whisky before they buy it. At the moment there are more than 300 different drams to choose from.

Speyside 50 year old, 40%

Nose: Tar, oak wood, seaweed to the fore; some full fruity vanilla sweetness develops. Cake baking aromas.
Palate: Balsamic impact dominates at first; meat extract notes and dark oranges; Christmas spices – from a very old sherry cask perhaps? No sign of woodiness, still surprisingly fresh. Best neat, or with very small addition of water.
Finish: Fades rapidly.

North British 20 year old, 55.8%

Nose: Initial impact understated; pear drops, aniseed.
Palate: Almonds; white chocolate; nougat; honey nut muesli; mint sharpness dances on the tongue.
Finish: Spices; slightly oily aftertaste.

Douglas Laing & Co.....................www.douglaslaing.com

Established in 1948 by Douglas Laing, it is currently run by his two sons, Fred and Stewart. One of their most talked about ranges is *The Old Malt Cask* which contains rare and old bottlings. More than 100 different expressions can be found regularly in this range where bottlings are diluted to 50%. Some malts are released in an even more exclusive range – *The Old and Rare Selection* (sometimes also referred to as *Platinum Selection*), offered at cask strength. A third range is called *McGibbon's Provenance*, often aged around 10-12 years and almost always diluted to 46%. The *Premier Barrel* range, was initially designed for the gift market and consists of single malts bottled in ceramic decanters.

What started as a one-off with a blend of Macallan and Laphroaig single malts, has now turned into a small range of its own called *Double Barrel*, where only two malts are vatted together and bottled at 46%. The most recent in that range is a bottling of Mortlach and Laphroaig. In May 2009, the company launched *Big Peat*, a vatting of selected Islay malts (among them Ardbeg, Caol Ila, Bowmore and Port Ellen) and also bottled at 46%. Sometimes some very old and rare single grains are released in the *Clan Denny* range. Douglas Laing & Co also has a range of blended whiskies in which *John Player Special, The King of Scots* and *The McGibbon Golf Range* are the biggest sellers.

Double Barrel Mortlach/Laphroaig, 46%

Nose: Creamy toffee ice-cream; warm and sweet. Slight rubber hints with water
Palate: Assertive, explosive peat smoke; oily and mouth coating; big smoke waves with water; old books; leather; smoke dominates over time. Mortlach appears dwarfed in the vatting.
Finish: Spicy and peppery, quite complex, layered and evolves to a sustained smoke coda.

Clan Denny Speyside, 46%

Nose: Instantly appealing; honey; toffee and lemon. Bakewell tart (marzipan). Light smoke. Fresh and floral: an aperitif whisky.
Palate: Initial spice notes; warming. Caramel and vanilla come through with water. Smooth, soft, chewy liquorice.
Finish: Very consistent. Warming and long.

Wm Cadenhead & Co...............www.wmcadenhead.com

This company was established in 1842 and is owned by J & A Mitchell (who also owns Springbank) since 1972. The single malts from Cadenheads are neither chill filtered nor coloured. When it comes to whisky, they work essentially with three different ranges; *Authentic Collection* (cask strength), *Duthie's* (diluted to 46%) and *Chairman's Stock* (older and rarer whiskies). *Duthie's* was launched in 2009 and replaced the previous Original Collection. The range was named after a cousin of William Cadenhead who ran the company from 1904 to 1931 and who was largely responsible for the great reputation as a bottler Cadenhead's enjoys today. A chain of ten whisky shops working under the name Cadenhead's can be found in the UK, Denmark, The Netherlands, Germany, Poland, Italy and Switzerland.

Compass Box Whisky Co ....www.compassboxwhisky.com

The company was started by John Glaser with a past in the wine trade and, later, in Diageo working with premium malts. Most of the people within the whisky industry acknowledge the fact that the cask has the greatest influence on the flavour of the final whisky, but none more so than John Glaser. His philosophy is strongly influenced by meticulous selection of oak for the casks, clearly inspired by his time in the wine business. But he also has a lust for experimenting and innovation to test the limits, which was clearly shown when *Spice Tree* was

launched in 2005. For an additional maturation, Glaser filled malt whisky in casks prepared with extra staves of toasted French oak suspended within the cask. Scotch Malt Whisky Association deemed this non-traditional and threatened with court action unless the production was halted. Glaser had to give up but returned in 2009 with *Spice Tree II* with the difference that the controversial casks had been equipped with new French Oak heads to achieve the same effect.

The company today divides its ranges into a *Signature Range* and a *Limited Range*. *Spice Tree* (a blended malt), *The Peat Monster* (a combination of peated islay whiskies and Highland malts), *Oak Cross* (where Glaser uses casks of American oak but fitted with heads of French oak), *Asyla* (a blended whisky matured in first-fill ex-bourbon American oak) and *Hedonism* (a vatted grain whisky) are included in the former.

The Limited range consists of *Hedonism Maximus, Lady Luck* (a vatted malt made up of old Caol Ila and Imperial), *Flaming Heart* (a vatted malt with a second maturation in new French oak), *Canto Cask* (a series of single cask bottlings) and two special versions of previously released expressions to celebrate the 10th anniversary of the company; *Double Single* (where an 18 year old Glen Elgin is blended with a 21 year old Port Dundas) and *Hedonism* (a single grain from Invergordon distilled in 1971). A third range was added in summer of 2011 when *Great King Street* was launched. The range will offer blended Scotch with a 50% proportion of malt whisky and using new French oak for complexity. The first expression was called *Artist's Blend* an was bottled at 43%.

Great King Street: Artist's Blend, 43%

Nose: Vanilla fudge, with the oily grain also apparent. Kumquats.
Palate: Lots of oak, vanilla, applecake and spice layers. Soft and rounded, plenty of body. Honey sweetness opens out with water. Orange chocolate.
Finish: Spice notes develop over time, fades gently and consistently.

The Spice Tree, 46%

Nose: Sherry notes; glace cherries; blackcurrant leaves; honey. Lime flowers.
Palate: Creamy and yet citric at the same time. Complex spice development; fresh cut pears; sandalwood; buttery. Delightfully well balanced.
Finish: Lemon peel; saltiness; lingers and spice notes develop towards the end. Reminiscent of a margherita.

Murray McDavid ....www.murray-mcdavid.com

Established in 1995 by Mark Reynier, Gordon Wright and Simon Coughlin. Murray McDavid makes three to four releases a year, averaging 25 expressions per time. The range is highly selective and all casks are chosen by Jim McEwan who has more than 40 years experience in the whisky industry. Unlike most independent bottlers, the bottlings are vattings of four or five casks (same age) at 46% without chill filtration or tinting. The range can be divided into three categories: – the *Murray McDavid* range, the *Mission* range (unusual aged stock) and, finally, the *Celtic Heartlands* range – exceptionally old or unique casks from the sixties and seventies.

Speciality Drinks.......................www.specialitydrinks.com

Sukhinder Singh, known by most for his two very well-stocked shops in London, The Whisky Exchange, is behind this company. Since 2005 he is also a bottler of malt whiskies operating under the brand name *The Single Malts of Scotland*. He has around 50 bottlings on offer at any time, either as single casks or as batches bottled at cask strength or at 46%. In 2009 a new range of Islay malts under the name *Port Askaig* was introduced, starting with a cask strength, a 17 year old and a 25 year old. In summer 2011 the 17 year old was replaced by a 19 year old.

Elements of Islay, a series in which all Islay distilleries are, or will be, represented was introduced around the same time. The list of the product range is cleverly constructed with periodical tables in mind (see www.elements-of-islay.com and below) in which each distillery has a two-letter acronym followed by a batch number. New releases during 2011 have been for example Pe_4 (Port Ellen) and Lg_3 (Lagavulin).

Port Askaig 19 year old, 45.8%

Nose: Sweet and floral; orange blossom; grassy and hay-like; soap notes. Dry heat, like sauna coals. Vanilla notes with water. Swimming pool chlorine.
Palate: Flaccid. Dry, powdery paper.
Finish: Peppery. Lemon notes.

Elements of Islay Lg_2, 58%

Nose: Salty; soft, heathery sweetness; charcoal; pine forest. Wet paper with water; smoke arrives on nose; citrus hints; floral.
Palate: Initial honeyed palate, with wave of smoke following to back of the mouth. Barbequed meats.
Finish: Salty, mouth drying. Astringent.

Dewar Rattray.................................. www.adrattray.com
This company was founded by Andrew Dewar and William Rattray in 1868. In 2004 the company was revived by Tim Morrison, previously of Morrison Bowmore Distillers and fourth generation descendent of Andrew Dewar, with a view to bottling single cask malts from different regions in Scotland. All whiskies are bottled at cask strength, without colouring or chill filtration. To give customers a choice, a new range of single malts bottled at 46% was recently introduced. A 12 year old single

malt named Stronachie is also found in their portfolio. It is named after a distillery that closed in the 1930s. Tim Morrison bought one of the few remaining bottles of Stronachie and found a Highland distillery that could reproduce its character. The distillery in question was shrouded in secrecy until 2010, when it was revealed as Benrinnes in Speyside. Each Stronachie bottling is a batch of 6-10 casks from Benrinnes. The 12 year old Stronachie was joined in 2010 by another expression – an 18 year old. In 2011, Dewar Rattray introduced a new range of blended malts. The first was a limited release named Rattray´s Selection Batch 01, containing whisky from four single sherry butts from Auchentoshan (1991), Balblair (1990), Benrinnes (1989) and Bowmore (1981). The second release, Cask Islay, came in October 2011. It is a blended malt, bottled at 46% and the thought is to compete with the likes of Smokehead and Big Peat.

In September 2011, the company opened A D Rattray´s Whisky Experience & Shop in Kirkoswald, South Ayrshire. Apart from having a large choice of whiskies for sale, there is a sample room and a cask room. The plan is to have a new spirit collection from every distillery in Scotland and samples from as many different types of casks and ages from as many distilleries as possible.

Stronachie 18 year old, 46%

Nose: French nougat; light, nutty nose; subtle but complex floral notes. Candle smoke.
Palate: Some subtle lemon marmalade notes; nuttiness at back of palate; warming vanilla and toffee flavours. Slight rubbery, burnt flavours. Smooth mouthfeel, very gentle on the palate.
Finish: Quite short, smoke and leather.

Rattray´s Selection Batch No. 1 19 year old, 55.8%

Nose: Salted cheese and dried fish (hot smoked salmon). Light peat smoke with fruit notes behind.
Palate: Old wood; stale cellars; wet leather; salty. Musty, damp paper and over-ripe mushrooms.
Finish: Drying, fades quickly.

Periodic Table of Elements of Islay from Speciality Drinks

Ar_6	Bn_6	Br_6	Bw_6	Cl_6	Kh_6	Lg_6	Lp_6	Ma_6	Pe_6	Pl_6
Ar_5	Bn_5	Br_5	Bw_5	Cl_5	Kh_5	Lg_5	Lp_5	Ma_5	Pe_5	Pl_5
Ar_4	Bn_4	Br_4	Bw_4	Cl_4	Kh_4	Lg_4	Lp_4	Ma_4	Pe_4	Pl_4
Ar_3	Bn_3	Br_3	Bw_3	Cl_3	Kh_3	Lg_3	Lp_3	Ma_3	Pe_3	Pl_3
Ar_2	Bn_2	Br_2	Bw_2	Cl_2	Kh_2	Lg_2	Lp_2	Ma_2	Pe_2	Pl_2
Ar_1	Bn_1	Br_1	Bw_1	Cl_1	Kh_1	Lg_1	Lp_1	Ma_1	Pe_1	Pl_1

Creative Whisky Company .....www.creativewhisky.co.uk

David Stirk, who has worked in the whisky industry for the last 15 years, started the Creative Whisky Co in 2005. He is also author of The Distilleries of Campbeltown and of features in most editions of Malt Whisky Yearbook. Creative Whisky exclusively bottles single casks, divided into three series: The *Exclusive Malts* are bottled at cask strength and vary in age between 8 and 40 years. Around 20 bottlings are made annually. *Exclusive Range* are somewhat younger whiskies, between 8 and 16 years bottled at either 45% or 45.8%. Finally, *Exclusive Casks* are single casks, which have been 'finished' for three months in another cask, e. g. Madeira, Sherry, Port or different kinds of virgin oak. The Creative Whisky Company is currently experimenting with English Ales finished in ex-whisky casks.

Adelphi Distillery ....www.adelphidistillery.com

The Adelphi Distillery, one of the largest whisky distilleries in Scotland at the time, ceased production in 1902. The name was revived in 1992 by the great-grandson of the last owner, Jamie Walker, who established the company as an independent bottler of single cask single malts. He then sold the company in 2004 to Keith Falconer and Donald Houston, who recruited Alex Bruce from the wine trade to act as Marketing Director. Their whiskies are always bottled at cask strength, uncoloured and non chill-filtered. Furthermore, a decision was made to work only with ex-sherry or ex-bourbon casks, meaning that wood finishes from any other type of casks are out of the question. Adelphi bottles around 50 casks a year. Unusual for an independent, Adelphi has an on-line shop on their website. The company affords its customers the opportunity to join the Adelphi´s Dancey Man Whisky Club which has special offerings for its members, discounts and first choice of the latest releases. A new warehouse was recently constructed om the company´s family farm in Fife, including a bonded area and a bottling line. This means that the company now has complete control of the operation from tasting the samples, purchasing the casks through to bottling, packaging and shipping.

Dailuaine 27 year old, 58.1%

Nose: Loads of sherry wood; resins; leather; cedar wood; dried fruits; dark orange marmalade; Christmas cakes and spice. Old piano wood.
Palate: Oily and mouth coating; one for the hill; soft and honey sweet; with water reveals more layers, smoke and mint. A big, punchy whisky.
Finish: Peppery, fades gently but holds together.

Linkwood 26 year old, 57.6%

Nose: Big raisin, plum and spice cake. Cedar wood.
Palate: Initially very intense; dominates the back of the mouth; sweet and peppery; cedar wood. Opens up with water to reveal cut apple, heather honey, spices, ripe melon.
Finish: Lengthy and sustained; rewards careful sipping.

Wemyss Malts ....www.wemyssmalts.com

This family-owned company, a relatively newcomer to the whisky world, was founded in 2005. The family owns another three companies in the field of wine and gin. Based in Edinburgh, Wemyss Malts takes advantage of Charles MacLean´s experienced nose when choosing their casks. There are two ranges; one of which consists of single casks bottled at 46% or 55%. The distillery name is not used on the label, instead, the names are chosen to reflect what the whisky tastes like, for instance, *Red Berry Cream*, *Ginger Compote*, *Honey Harvest* and *Smoke on the Sea Shore*. All whiskies are unchill-filtered and without colouring. The other range is made up of blended malts of which there are four at the moment – *Spice King*, *Peat Chimney*, *Smooth Gentleman* and the recently introduced *The Hive*. When first introduced in 2005 they were bottled at the age of 5. Four years later the range was expanded with 8 year olds and in 2010 with 12 year olds. The latter were first released in duty free markets in India and Thailand and then in other markets in 2011. In summer 2011 the fourth member of the range was launched – *The Hive* – a 12 year old with a Speyside signature malt. All the blended malts are bottled at 40%.

Spice King 8 year old, 40%

Nose: Sweet caramel; warm honey; vanilla; heather; Christmas spices; dried fruits.
Palate: Smooth; dark brown sugar; rich and warming; hints of dried pears; raisins; develops greater complexity with water. An undercurrent of spice notes.
Finish: Long lingering sweetness; very smooth and warming.

Peat Chimney 8 year old, 40%

Nose: Toffee; lemon drizzle cake; distant pine smoke; toffee apple; sweet; Oddfellows (sweets).
Palate: Initially quite harsh and astringent; peppery; orange peel; wood polish. Cigar box.
Finish: Short finish, fades quickly with a peppery bite.

Glenkeir Treasures ....www.whiskyshop.com

The Whisky Shop, the biggest whisky retail chain in the UK, recently opened their 17th shop in Birmingham. The company was founded in 1992 and was bought by the current owner, Ian Bankier, in 2004. Apart from having an extensive range of malt (and other) whiskies, they also select and bottle their own range of single malts called Glenkeir Treasures. Once a cask has been chosen it is re-racked into smaller oak casks which are then put out for display in each store. The whisky is bottled to order and the customer can also try the whisky in the shop before buying. Glenkeir Treasures come in three bottle sizes – 10, 20 and 50 cl and is bottled at 40%. The current range consists of Aberlour 12, Ben Nevis 15, Deanston 12, Ledaig 9, Linkwood 12 and Macallan 18 year old.

Malts of Scotland ....www.malts-of-scotland.com

This is one of the more recently established independent bottlers. Thomas Ewers from Germany, bought casks from Scottish distilleries and decided in the spring of 2009 to start releasing them as single casks bottled at cask strength and with no colouring or chill filtration. At the moment he has released circa 70 bottlings from a 5 year old Bunnahabhain to a 38 year old Glengoyne. He also has two expressions called *Glen First Class* (a Glenfarclas) and *Glen Peat Class* (a vatting of Ardbeg, Laphroaig and Bowmore), both bottled at 50%. Another new series is *Amazing Casks*, dedicated to very special and superior casks. According to Ewers, there are several hundreds of casks from more than 60 distilleries maturing in the warehouse.

Scotch Malt Whisky Society .... www.smws.com

The Scotch Malt Whisky Society, established in the mid 1980s and owned by Glenmorangie Co since 2003, has more than 20,000 members worldwide and apart from UK, there are 15 chapters around the world. The idea from the very beginning was to buy casks of single malts from the producers and bottle them at cask strength without colouring or chill filtration. The labels do not reveal the name of the distillery. Instead there is a number but also a short description which will give you a clue to which distillery it is. A Tasting Panel selects and bottles around twenty new casks the first Friday of every month. The SMWS also arranges tastings at their different venues but also at other locations. The society produces an excellent, award winning members magazine called Unfiltered.

Mackillop´s Choice .... www.mackillopschoice.com

Mackillop's Choice, founded in 1996, is an independent bottler owned by Angus Dundee Distillers (owner of Tomintoul and Glencadam distilleries). The brand is named after Lorne McKillop who selects the casks. The whole range is single casks with no colouring or chill filtration. Some of the bottlings are at cask strength, while others are diluted to 40 or 43%. Among the latest new bottlings (released in summer 2011) are Bowmore 1989, Mortlach 1987, Tomintoul 1981, Tomatin 1965 and Linlithgow 1982.

Scott´s Selection .... www.speysidedistillers.co.uk

Speyside Distillers in Glasgow are the owners of Speyside distillery but also has a wide range of whisky brands in their domains. One of them is Scott´s Selection, a range of single cask malt whiskies, previously selected by the Master Blender Robert Scott, who is now retired. Emphasis is placed on whisky distilled in the 70's and 80's and some unusual distilleries such as North Port, Linlithgow and Convalmore are represented. Perhaps the most interesting bottling is a single grain, North of Scotland 1973. This was the grain distillery that the founder of Speyside distillery, George Christie, had built in 1958 and has since closed down in 1980. More single grains were released in 2011; Girvan 1964, Invergordon 1964 and the very rare Port Dundas 1965. All the whisky in the Scott's Selection range are bottled without colouring or chill-filtration and at cask strength. There is an additional range of single malts in the company, Private Cellar, but these are all diluted to 43%. In addition to single malt Speyside Distillers produces a range of blended whiskies, such as Glen Ross and Scotchguard.

The Whisky Agency .... www.whiskyagency.de

The man behind this company is Carsten Ehrlich, to many whisky aficionados known as one of the founders of the annual Whisky Fair in Limburg, Germany. His experience from sourcing casks for limited Whisky Fair bottlings led him to start as an independent bottler in 2008 under the name The Whisky Agency. He is currently working with three ranges; *The Whisky Agency* with five series of whiskies released so far – *Butterflies, Sharks, Fossils, Flowers* and *Liquid Sun* – the names alluding to the motif on the labels, *The Perfect Dram* (three series with four expressions each) and *Specials* with some unusual bottlings, for example a Tomatin 1967 sherry butt.

Distilleries owned by Independent Bottlers

Benromach - Gordon & MacPhail

Edradour - Signatory

Bruichladdich - Murray McDavid

Glengoyne - Ian Macleod Distillers

Tamdhu - Ian Macleod Distillers

Glencadam - Angus Dundee

Tomintoul - Angus Dundee

Speyside - Speyside Distillers

New bottlings

It is virtually impossible to list all new bottlings during a year,
there are simply too many and sometimes it is difficult to find information on them.
In this list we have selected 500 that were released from late 2010 until autumn 2011.
All bottlings (except for certain official ones) are listed with year of distillation, age,
finish or special maturation (if applicable), alcohol strength and bottler.
Read more about the major independent bottlers on pages 272-277.

Aberfeldy
1997	14		58,1% OB
1999			60,9% BA
1994	16		50,0% DL

Aberlour
a´bunadh batch #36			60,1% OB
1989	21		57,5% CAD
1990	20		50,0% DL
1998	12		46,0% DL

Allt-a-bhainne
| | 18 | | 54,7% CAD |

Ardbeg
Alligator			51,2% OB
1994	15		53,0% IM
1999	12		43,0% IM
1994	16		57,0% CAD
1991	20		48,3% DL

Ardmore
1992	18		48,6% IM
1999	12 Ch Palmer		53,5% IM
1992	18		46,8% DR
2003	7		58,4% AD
2003	8		58,2% AD
1992	18		50,7% AD
1996	15		50,0% DL

Arran
Icons of Arran Westie			46,0% OB
Machrie Moor sec ed			46,0% OB
The Sleeping Warrior			54,9% OB
	12 cs		54,1% OB
1998	12		57,4% CAD
1997	13		46,0% DR
1996	15		50,0% DL
1998	12		46,0% DL

Auchentoshan
1975			46,9% OB
1999	11		58,0% OB
Valinch			57,5% OB

1999	11		46,0% CAD
1990	20		55,9% DR
1990	20		50,0% DL
1997	13		50,0% DL
1998	12		46,0% DL

Auchroisk
| 1990 | 21 | | 50,0% DL |

Aultmore
1997	13 Sherry		50,2% IM
1997	13		46,0% CAD
1982	28		56,1% DR
1982	28		57,6% AD
1989	21		51,8% DT
1990	20		50,0% DL

Balblair
1995			43,0% OB
1993			43,0% OB
1991	19		46,0% DR
1990	20		50,0% DL

Balmenach
| | 22 | | 51,4% CAD |
| 1983 | 27 | | 50,0% DL |

Balvenie
| Tun 1401 batch 1 | | | 48,1% OB |
| Tun 1401 batch 2 | | | 50,6% OB |

Banff
1976	34		53,8% CAD
1975	35		42,5% DT
	35		42,4% DL

Ben Nevis
1971	40		45,8% DL
1995	15		50,0% DL
1998	12		46,0% DL

Benriach
| 1971 | 40 | | 49,8% OB |

1972	39		40,1% OB
1976	34		57,8% OB
1977	34 PX sherry		54,3% OB
1978	32 Virgin oak		50,9% OB
1979	31 Peated		50,3% OB
1980	31 Virdin oak		49,8% OB
1984	26 Peated		54,3% OB
1989	22 Sauternes		49,1% OB
1989	22 Virdin oak		50,6% OB
1992	19 Tawny		55,6% OB
1993	18 Barolo		56,1% OB
1978	Firkin Cask		40,1% OB
1966	45		OB
1991			57,9% BA
1992	18 Madeira		54,5% CAD
1991	19		46,0% DR
1996	15		50,0% DL
	27		52,4% DL

Benrinnes
| 1996 | 14 | | 56,1% DR |
| 1992 | 19 | | 50,0% DL |

Benromach
Peatsmoke 4th ed.			46,0% OB
2001		Hermitage	45,0% OB
2001 cs			59,9% OB
	30		43,0% OB

Bladnoch
| Distiller´s Choice | | | 46,0% OB |
| 1992 | 18 | | 50,0% DL |

Blair Athol
1986	25		54,5% IM
1986	25		52,9% AD
1990	21		50,0% DL
1999	11		46,0% DL

Bowmore
1982			49,6% OB
10 Tempest 3rd ed			55,6% OB
15 Laimrig 2nd			54,4% OB
1989			58,0% BA
	11		58,5% CAD

1990	20		50,2%	DR
1989	21		50,2%	DR
1998	12		61,9%	AD
1998	12		46,0%	DT
1989	21		50,0%	DL
1996	14		50,0%	DL
1987	23		59,1%	DL
2000	10		46,0%	DL
	10		58,4%	DL

Braeval

1996	14		43,0%	IM
1998	12		43,0%	IM
1990	20		50,0%	DL

Brora

	32		54,7%	OB

Bruichladdich

	10			OB
1990	21 Micro Pro.		48,2%	OB
1998 Ancien Regime			46,0%	OB
2001 Rennaisance			46,0%	OB
1991			53,5%	BA
1989	22		46,0%	IM
	20		50,0%	DL

Bunnahabhain

	14	Cognac	59,6%	OB
2000	10	Barolo	56,8%	IM
1998	12		53,4%	AD
1997	13		57,2%	AD
1979	31		46,5%	AD
1997	13	Peated	54,6%	SIG
1979	32		46,9%	DT
1978	32		54,3%	DL
1990	21		50,0%	DL
1997	14		50,0%	DL
2001	9		46,0%	DL

Caol Ila

Moch			43,0%	OB
	12	Unpeated	64,0%	OB
Feisle Isle 2011			64,3%	OR
2000			58,8%	BA
1996			60,3%	BA
1984	26		50,5%	IM
1991	20	Port	60,1%	IM
1997	13		43,0%	IM
1999	11	S. Giovese	46,0%	IM
1997	13	Jam. rum	43,0%	IM
1997	14	St Etienne	46,0%	IM
1995	15		46,0%	CAD
1991	20		53,4%	CAD
2000	10		46,0%	DR
1982	28		56,0%	AD
2001	9		60,7%	AD
1983	27		59,7%	SIG
1983	27		52,7%	DT
1980	30		50,0%	DL

1990	21		50,0%	DL
1980	30		50,0%	DL
1996	14		50,0%	DL
2001	10		46,0%	DL

Caperdonich

1996	14		51,7%	CAD
1995	15		60,4%	DR
1982	28		50,0%	DL

Clynelish

1995			46,0%	BA
1992	17		56,7%	CAD
1995	15		46,0%	CAD
1997	14		59,5%	AD
1992	18		46,0%	SIG
1995	15		56,6%	SIG
1997	13		56,8%	BB
1997	13		50,0%	DL
1990	21		50,0%	DL
1982	28		50,0%	DL

Cragganmore

1989			54,1%	BA
1989	21		53,5%	BB
1993	18		55,3%	DT
1991	19		50,0%	DL
1997	13		50,0%	DL

Craigellachie

1999	12	Ch Palmer	46,0%	IM
1998	12		43,0%	IM
2002	8		60,1%	DR
1991	20		52,0%	DR
1998	11		43,0%	SIG
1999	12		46,0%	DL

Dailuaine

1999	12	Barolo	43,0%	IM
1999	12		46,0%	IM
1999	11	S Giovese	43,0%	IM
1983	27		58,1%	AD
1973	37		50,6%	BB
1983	27		50,0%	DL
1997	14		50,0%	DL

Dalmore

1966	40	Astrum	42,0%	OB
1995		Castle Leod	46,0%	OB
Spey Dram			40,0%	OB
Tay Dram			40,0%	OB
Tweed Dram			40,0%	OB
1991	20		59,0%	OB
1997			46,0%	BA
1996	14	S. Giovese	43,0%	IM
1989	21		51,4%	CAD
1990	20		59,1%	SIG
1990	20		50,0%	DL
1999	12		50,0%	DL

Deanston

1994	15		50,0%	DL

Dufftown

1982	28		50,0%	DL

Edradour

	12	Caledonia	46,0%	OB
	26	PX Sherry	47,8%	OB
2003		Chardonnay	46,0%	OB
2003		Sauternes	46,0%	OB
2003		Burgundy	46,0%	OB
2003		Bourbon	57,4%	OB
Ballechin 6th ed.			46,0%	OB

Fettercairn

2000	10		46,0%	DL

Glenallachie

1995			60,3%	BA
1972	38		50,0%	DL

Glenburgie

1998	11		43,0%	IM
1998	12		43,0%	IM
	17	Rum	56,0%	CAD

Glencadam

	21		46,0%	OB
1989	21		55,1%	CAD
1990	20		58,15	DR

Glendronach

1971	40	PX	48,5%	OB
1972	39	Oloroso	49,9%	OB
1972	39	Oloroso	54,4%	OB
1978	32	Oloroso	53,3%	OB
1989	21	PX	54,1%	OB
1989	21	PX	53,5%	OB
1990	20	PX	50,1%	OB
1991	19	Oloroso	55,4%	OB
1992	19	Oloroso	59,2%	OB
1993	18	Oloroso	54,9%	OB
1994	17	Oloroso	60,1%	OB
21 Parliament			48,0%	OB
1968				OB
1995	15		50,0%	DL

Glendullan

1999	11	Ch Palmer	43,0%	IM

Glen Elgin

1985	24		44,9%	DL

Glenfarclas

175th Anniversary			43,0%	OB

Chairman´s Reserve   46,0% OB
Family Casks

Glenfiddich
1974	Vintage Res.		OB
	19	Madeira	40,0% OB

Glen Garioch
1986		54,6% OB
1994		53,9% OB
1990	20	54,9% AD

Glenglassaugh
	35	49,6% OB
	3	OB
1986	Dod Cameron	45,3% OB
1974	Jim Cryle	52,9% OB
1968	Bert Forsyth	44,9% OB
1967	Walter Grant	40,4% OB

Glengoyne
1987	24	54,8% OB
1998	12	46,0% DR
1998	12	46,0% DL

Glen Grant
	25		43,0% OB
1993	17		55,6% DR
1975	35		50,0% DL
1975	36	Brandy	54,0% DL
1985	25		58,1% DL
1995	15		50,0% DL

Glengyle
Kilkerran Work in Pr. 46.0% OB

Glen Keith
1995	16	Barolo	43,0% IM
1995	15	S Giovese	46,0% IM

Glenlivet
Master Dist. Reserve		40,0% OB
1940	70	45,9% GM
1954	55	50,6% GM
1963	47	40,6% GM
1974	36	50,1% GM
1991	19	54,4% GM
1976		47,2% BA
1977		49,4% BA
1995	15	46,0% SIG
1976	34	46,0% BB
1977	34	50,0% DL
1992	17	50,0% DL

Glenlossie
1992	18	56,6% DR
1975	35	49,7% BB

Glen Mhor
1982	55,5% BA

Glenmorangie
1981	28	Pride	56,7% OB

Glen Moray
	10	Chard.	40,0% OB
1998	12		46,0% CAD
1986	24		53,2% DT
1991	19		50,0% DL

Glen Ord
	15		57,3% CAD
1989	21		50,0% DL
1997	14		50,0% DL
1999	12		46,0% DL

Glenrothes
1995			43,0% DR
1988			52,5% BA
1998	13	Ch Palmer	46,0% IM
1998	12	Barolo	50,2% IM
1997	13		48,0% IM
1990	20		53,0% DR
1990	20		58,6% AD
1989	21		56,1% SIG
1969	41		44,2% DT
1990	21		56,8% DL

Glen Scotia
	11	red wine	58,0% CAD
1992	19		59,6% DR
1992	18		50,0% DL

Glenspey
1999		59,8% BA
1977	24	52,0% DR
1997	14	50,0% DL

Glentauchers
2000		46,0% BA
1998	12	56,1% CAD
1981	30	56,8% SIG

Glenturret
1995	15	53,0% CAD
1979	31	51,6% SIG

Glenugie
1977	32		55,5% OB
1980	30		50,0% IM
1977	33	Oloroso	57,2% SIG

Glenury Royal
1970	40	OB

Hazelburn
2002	8	Sauternes	55,9% OB

Highland Park
1978		47,8% OB
Leif Eriksson		40,0% OB
18 Earl Haakon		54,9% OB
1992	18	46,0% CAD
1992	18	58,6% DR
1984	26	53,6% DR
1995	15	55,4% AD
1997	13	58,0% AD
1998	12	58,2% AD
1998	12	46,0% DL
1996	14	50,0% DL
1978	33	55,7% DL

Imperial
1995	16	50,0% DL

Inchgower
1982	29	54,3% IM
1974	35	56,4% DR
1982	28	56,2% BB

Inverleven
1973	36	48,8% OB

Jura
1996 Feis Isle 2011		54,0% OB
2000	11 Rum	46,0% IM
1996	13	43,0% IM
1992	18	48,8% DL
1999	11	46,0% DL

Kilchoman
Winter 2010	46,0% OB
Spring 2011	46,0% OB
100% Islay	46,0% OB
4	46,0% OB
5	46,0% OB

Knockando
1985	25	43,0% OB

Lagavulin
12	57,5% OB

Laphroaig
PX Cask		48,0% OB
Cairdeas Ileach Ed.		50,5% OB
1998		56,4% BA
1997	14	43,3% IM
1994	16	55,2% CAD
1986	25	60,65 DR
1998	25	63,9% DR
1995	16	59,4% SIG

OB = Official bottling from the owner, AD = Adelphi Distillery, BA = Blackadder, BB = Berry Brothers, CAD = Cadenhead, DL = Douglas Laing, DR = Dewar Rattray, DT = Duncan Taylor, GM = Gordon & MacPhail, IM = Ian MacLeod, MM = Murray McDavid, SIG = Signatory, SD = Speciality Drinks

1997	13	Latour	46,0% MM
1999	10	Lafite	46,0% MM
1998	12		58,9% BB
1999	12		50,0% DL
1989	22		58,5% DL
1993	18		50,0% DL
1992	19		50,0% DL
1996	15		50,0% DL
1999	12		50,0% DL
2001	10		46,0% DL

Linkwood

1984	26	55,9% DR
1989	21	55,8% DR
1984	26	57,6% AD
1991	19	57,1% BB
1982	28	50,0% DL
1984	26	50,0% DL
1989	21	50,0% DL
1997	13	50,0% DL

Littlemill

| 1991 | 19 | 50,0% DL |

Lochside

| 1989 | 21 | 48,2% DL |

Longmorn

1988			57,0% BA
1997	13	Barolo	43,0% IM
	16		53,5% CAD
1996	14		46,0% DR
1992	18		55,6% AD
1990	21		53,3% AD

Macallan

Macallan MMIX		48,0% OB
Royal Marriage		46,8% OB
1990		51,3% BA
1989	21	50,9% CAD
1995	15	46,0% DR
1993	17	53,7% AD
1968	34	40,2% MM
1997	12 Latour	46,0% MM
1979	32	53,2% DL
1990	21	50,0% DL
1990	20	50,0% DL
1995	15	50,0% DL

Macduff

| 2000 | 9 | 61,1% DR |
| 1990 | 21 | 50,0% DL |

Mannochmore

| 1997 | 13 | 50,0% DL |

Miltonduff

| 1998 | 61,4% BA |

1987	23	50,0% IM
1980	30	44,5% DR
1998	12	46,0% BB

Mortlach

1998	13	Ch Palmer	46,0% IM
1998	12		43,0% IM
1995	14		43,0% IM
1993	18		46,0% IM
1992	18		46,0% CAD
1994	16		54,2% CAD
1995	16		51,7% DR
1997	14	Yquem	46,0% MM
1992	18		58,1% DL
1997	13		50,0% DL

Octomore

| Octomore 4_167 | 62,5% OB |
| Octomore 4.2 | OB |

Port Charlotte

| PC 9 | 59,2% OB |

Port Ellen

1979	32	53,9% OB
1982	28	50,0% IM
1979	31	52,1% DL
1983	27	50,0% DL

Pulteney

| 1990 | 20 | 56,9% CAD |

Rosebank

1990	21	53,8% OB
1990	20	46,0% IM
1990	20	52,9% CAD
1991	19	46,0% SD
1990	21	50,0% DL

Royal Brackla

| 1999 | 11 | 46,0% DL |

Royal Lochnagar

| 1997 | 13 | 50,0% DL |

St Magdalene

| 1982 | 28 | 50,0% DL |

Scapa

| 1993 | 17 | 50,0% DL |

Speyside

| 1993 | 17 | 61,2% SD |

Springbank

| 11 Local barley | 57,9% OB |

Strathisla

| 1998 | 12 | 43,0% IM |

Strathmill

1976	35	44,0% DR
1986	24	58,6% AD
1975	36	44,1% DL
1993	16	50,0% DL

Talisker

	34	OB
	25	45,8% OB
	30	45,8% OB
2001	10	50,0% DL

Tamdhu

1994	16	Fino	46,0% IM
1989	22		55,0% DR
1980	30		55,5% DR
1984	26		48,8% AD
1989	21		50,0% DL

Tamnavulin

1989	21	57,4% DR
1989	21	52,7% DT
1989	21	50,0% DL

Teaninich

| 17 | 53,8% CAD |

Tobermory

| 1995 | | 59,1% BA |
| 1995 | 15 | 50,0% DL |

Tomatin

	30	46,0% OB
Tomatin Decades		46,0% OB
1970	40	44,3% DL

Tomintoul

	21	40,0% OB
1966		43,0% OB
10 Ballantruan		50,0% OB
1967	44	47,0% DR
1989	21	50,0% DL

Tormore

| 1990 | 62,0% BA |

Tullibardine

1962		41,8% OB
1964		42,1% OB
1976		50,2% OB
1992	Ch.Lafite	46,0% OB
1990	21	46,0% DR

OB = Official bottling from the owner, AD = Adelphi Distillery, BA = Blackadder, BB = Berry Brothers, CAD = Cadenhead, DL = Douglas Laing, DR = Dewar Rattray, DT = Duncan Taylor, GM = Gordon & MacPhail, IM = Ian MacLeod, MM = Murray McDavid, SIG = Signatory, SD = Speciality Drinks

Whisky Shops

AUSTRIA

Potstill
Strozzigasse 37
1080 Wien
Phone: +43 (0)664 118 85 41
www.potstill.org
Austria's premier whisky shop with
over 1100 kinds of which c 900 are
malts, including some real rarities.
Arranges tastings and seminars and
ships to several European countries.
On-line ordering.

BELGIUM

Whiskycorner
Kraaistraat 16
3530 Houthalen
Phone: +32 (0)89 386233
www.whiskycorner.be
A very large selection of single
malts, no less than 1100 different!
Also other whiskies, calvados and
grappas. The site is in both French
and English. Mail ordering, but not
on-line. Shipping worldwide.

Jurgen's Whiskyhuis
Gaverland 70
9620 Zottegem
Phone: +32 (0)9 336 51 06
www.whiskyhuis.be
An absolutely huge assortment of
more than 2,000 different single
malts with 700 in stock and the rest
delivered within the week. Also 40
different grain whiskies and 120
bourbons. Online mail order with
shipments worldwide.

Huis Crombé
Engelse Wandeling 11
8500 Kortrijk
Phone: +32 (0)56 21 19 87
www.crombewines.com
A wine retailer with a heritage dating back to 1894 and now covers all
kinds of spirits. The whisky range is
very nice where a large assortment
of Scotch is supplemented with
whiskies from Japan, the USA and
Ireland to mention a few. Regular
tastings in the shop.

CANADA

Kensington Wine Market
1257 Kensington Road NW
Calgary
Alberta T2N 3P8
Phone: +1 403 283 8000
www.kensingtonwinemarket.com
With 400 different bottlings this is
the largest single malt assortment in
Canada. Also 2,500 different wines.
Regular tastings in the shop.

DENMARK

Juul's Vin & Spiritus
Værnedamsvej 15
1819 Frederiksberg
Phone: +45 33 31 13 29
www.juuls.dk
A very large range of wines,
fortified wines and spirits. Around
500 single malts. Also a good
selection of drinking glasses. On-line
ordering. Shipping outside Denmark
(except for Scandinavian countries).

Cadenhead's WhiskyShop Denmark
Vestergade 21
5000 Odense C
Phone: +45 66 13 95 05

Silkegade 7, kld
1113 København K
Phone: +45 33 39 95 05
www.cadenheads.dk
Whisky specialist with a very good
range, not least from Cadenhead's.
Nice range of champagne, cognac
and rum. Arranges whisky and beer
tastings. On-line ordering with
worldwide shipping.

Whiskydirect.dk
Braunstein
Carlsensvej 5
4600 Køge
Phone: +45 7020 4468
www.whiskydirect.dk
On-line retailer owned by Braunstein Distillery. Aside from own
produce one can find an assortment
of 200 different whiskies, including
own single cask bottlings.

Kokkens Vinhus
Hovedvejen 102
2600 Glostrup
Phone: +45 44 97 02 30
www.kokkensvinhus.dk
A shop with a complete assortment
of wine, spirit, coffee, tea and
delicatessen. More than 500
whiskies are in stock, mostly
single malts. They are specialists
in independent bottlings. On-line
ordering for shipments within
Denmark.

ENGLAND

The Whisky Exchange (2 shops)
Unit 7, Space Business Park
Abbey Road, Park Royal
London NW10 7SU
Phone: +44 (0)208 838 9388

The Whisky Exchange
Vinopolis, 1 Bank End
London SE1 9BU
Phone: +44 (0)207 403 8688
www.thewhiskyexchange.com
This is an excellent whisky shop

established in 1999 and owned by
Sukhinder Singh. Started off as a
mail order business which was run
from a showroom in Hanwell, but
since some years back there is also
an excellent shop at Vinopolis in
downtown London. The assortment is huge with well over 1000
single malts to choose from. Some
rarities which can hardly be found
anywhere else are offered much
thanks to Singh's great interest
for antique whisky. There are also
other types of whisky and cognac,
calvados, rum etc. On-line ordering
and ships all over the world.

The Whisky Shop
(See also Scotland, The Whisky Shop)
Unit 1.09 MetroCentre
Red Mall
Gateshead NE11 9YG
Phone: +44 (0)191 460 3777

11 Coppergate Walk
York YO1 9NT
Phone: +44 (0)1904 640300

510 Brompton Walk
Lakeside Shopping Centre
West Thurrock, Essex RM20 2ZL
Phone: +44 (0)1708 866255

7 Turl Street
Oxford OX1 3DQ
Phone: +44 (0)1865 202279

3 Swan Lane
Norwich NR2 1HZ
Phone: +44 (0)1603 618284

7 Queens Head Passage
Paternoster
London EC4M 7DY
Phone: +44 (0)207 329 5117

25 Chapel Street
Guildford GU1 3UL
Phone: +44 (0)1483 450900

Unit 35 Great Western Arcade
Birmingham B2 5HU
Phone: +44 (0)121 212 1815
www.whiskyshop.com
The first shop opened in 1992 in
Edinburgh and this is now the
United Kingdom's largest specialist
retailer of whiskies with 16 outlets.
A large product range with over 700
kinds, including 400 malt whiskies
and 140 miniature bottles, as well
as accessories and books. The own
range 'Glenkeir Treasures' is a
special assortment of selected malt
whiskies. On-line ordering and
shipping all over the world except
to the USA.

Royal Mile Whiskies
3 Bloomsbury Street
London WC1B 3QE
Phone: +44 (0)20 7436 4763
www.royalmilewhiskies.com

The London branch of Royal Mile Whiskies. See also Scotland, Royal Mile Whiskies.

Berry Bros. & Rudd
3 St James' Street
London SW1A 1EG
Phone: +44 (0)870 900 4300
www.bbr.com/whisky
A legendary shop that has been situated in the same place since 1698. One of the world's most reputable wine shops but with an exclusive selection of malt whiskies. There are also shops in Dublin and Hong Kong specialising primarily in fine wines.

The Wright Wine and Whisky Company
The Old Smithy, Raikes Road, Skipton North Yorkshire BD23 1NP
Phone: +44 (0)1756 700886
www.wineandwhisky.co.uk
An eclectic selection of near to 1000 different whiskies to choose from. 'Tasting Cupboard' of nearly 100 opened bottles for sampling with hosted tasting evenings held on a regular basis. Great 'Collector to Collector' selection of old and rare whiskies plus a fantastic choice of 1200+ wines, premium spirits and liqueurs. International mail order.

Master of Malt
2 Leylands Manor
Tubwell Lane
Crowborough
East Sussex TN6 3RH
Phone: +44 (0)1892 888 376
www.masterofmalt.com
Independent bottler and online retailer since 1985. A very impressive range of more than 1,000 Scotch whiskies of which 800 are single malts. In addition to whisky from other continents there is a wide selection of rum, cognac, Armagnac and tequila. The website is redesigned and contains a wealth of information on the distilleries. They have also recently launched "Drinks by the Dram" where you can order 3cl samples of almost 400 different whiskies to try before you buy a full bottle.

Whiskys.co.uk
The Square, Stamford Bridge
York YO4 11AG
Phone: +44 (0)1759 371356
www.whiskys.co.uk
Good assortment with more than 600 different whiskies. Also a nice range of armagnac, rum, calvados etc. On-line ordering, ships outside of the UK.
The owners also have another website, www.whiskymerchants.co.uk with a huge amount of information on just about every whisky distillery in the world and very up to date.

The Wee Dram
5 Portland Square, Bakewell
Derbyshire DE45 1HA
Phone: +44 (0)1629 812235
www.weedram.co.uk

Large range of Scotch single malts (c 450) with whiskies from other parts of the world and a good range of whisky books. Run 'The Wee Drammers Whisky Club' with tastings and seminars. On-line ordering.

Mainly Wine and Whisky
3-4 The Courtyard, Bawtry
Doncaster DN10 6JG
Phone: +44 (0)1302 714 700
www.whisky-malts-shop.com
A good range with c 400 different whiskies of which 300 are single malts. Arranges tastings and seminars. On-line ordering with shipping also outside the UK. Was known as Mainly Malts before they joined with a local wine shop.

Chester Whisky & Liqueur
59 Bridge Street Row
Chester
Cheshire CH1 1NW
Phone: +44 (0)1244 347806
www.chesterwhisky.com
A shop that specialises in single malt Scotch and American, Irish, Japanese and Welsh whisky.There is also a good range of calvados, armagnac and rum and the shop has its own house blend, Chester Cross Blended Scotch Whisky, as well as three casks for tasting and bottling in the store.

Nickolls & Perks
37 Lower High Street, Stourbridge
West Midlands DY8 1TA
Phone: +44 (0)1384 394518
www.nickollsandperks.co.uk
Mostly known as wine merchants but also has a good range of whiskies with c 300 different kinds including 200 single malts. On-line ordering with shipping also outside of UK

Gauntleys of Nottingham
4 High Street
Exchange Arcade
Nottingham NG1 2ET
Phone: +44 (0)115 9110555
www.gauntley-wine.co.uk
A fine wine merchant established in 1880. The range of wines are among the best in the UK. All kinds of spirits, not least whisky, are taking up more and more space and several rare malts can be found. The monthly whisky newsletter by Chris Goodrum makes good reading and there is also a mail order service available.

The Wine Shop
22 Russell Street, Leek
Staffordshire ST13 5JF
Phone: +44 (0)1538 382408
www.wineandwhisky.com
In addition to wine there is a good range of c 300 whiskies and also calvados, cognacs, rums etc. They also stock a range of their own single malt bott-lings under the name of 'The Queen of the Moorlands'. Mailorders by telephone or email for UK delivery.

The Lincoln Whisky Shop
87 Bailgate
Lincoln LN1 3AR
Phone: +44 (0)1522 537834
www.lincolnwhiskyshop.co.uk
Mainly specialising in whisky with more than 400 different whiskies but also 500 spirits and liqueurs and some 100 wines. Mailorder only within UK.

Milroys of Soho
3 Greek Street
London W1D 4NX
Phone: +44 (0)20 7437 2385
www.milroys.co.uk
A classic whisky shop in Soho now owned by the retail wine merchant Jeroboams Group. A very good range with over 700 malts and a wide selection of whiskies from around the world. On-line ordering for shipping within the UK.

Arkwrights
114 The Dormers
Highworth
Wiltshire SN6 7PE
Phone: +44 (0)1793 765071
www.whiskyandwines.com
A good range of whiskies (over 700 in stock) as well as wine and other spirits. Regular tastings in the shop. On-line ordering with shipping all over the world except USA and Canada.

Cadenhead's Whisky Shop
26 Chiltern Street
London W1U 7QF
Phone: +44 (0)20 7935 6999
www.whiskytastingroom.com
Used to be in Covent Garden but moved and was expanded with a tasting room. One in a chain of shops owned by independent bottlers Cadenhead. Sells Cadenhead's product range and c 200 other whiskies. Regular tastings and on-line ordering.

The Vintage House
42 Old Compton Street
London W1D 4LR
Phone: +44 (0)20 7437 5112
www.sohowhisky.com
A huge range of 1400 kinds of malt whisky, many of them rare or unusual. Supplementing this is also a selection of fine wines. On-line ordering with shipping only within the UK.

Whisky On-line
Units 1-3 Concorde House, Charnley Road, Blackpool, Lancashire FY1 4PE
Phone: +44 (0)1253 620376
www.whisky-online.com
A good selection of whisky and also cognac, rum, port etc. On-line ordering with shipping all over the world.

Constantine Stores
30 Fore Street
Constantine, Falmouth
Cornwall TR11 5AB
Phone: +44 (0)1326 340226
www.drinkfinder.co.uk
A full-range wine and spirits dealer with a good selection of whiskies

from the whole world (around 800 different, of which 600 are single malts).Worldwide shipping except for USA and Canada.

FRANCE

La Maison du Whisky
20 rue d´Anjou
75008 Paris
Phone: +33 (0)1 42 65 03 16

6 carrefour d l´Odéon
75006 Paris
Phone: +33 (0)1 46 34 70 20

(2 shops outside France)

47 rue Jean Chatel
97400 Saint-Denis, La Réunion
Phone: +33 (0)2 62 21 31 19

The Pier at Robertson Quay
80 Mohamed Sultan Road, #01-10
Singapore 239013
Phone: +65 6733 0059
www.whisky.fr
France's largest whisky specialist with over 1200 whiskies in stock. Also a number of own-bottled single malts. La Maison du Whisky acts as a EU distributor for many whisky producers around the world. Four shops and on-line ordering. Ships to some 20 countries.

GERMANY

Celtic Whisk(e)y & Versand
Otto Steudel
Bulmannstrasse 26
90459 Nürnberg
Phone: +49 (0)911 450974-30
www.whiskymania.de/celtic
A very impressive single malt range with well over 1000 different single malts and a good selection from other parts of the world. On-line ordering with shipping also outside Germany.

SCOMA - Scotch Malt Whisky GmbH
Am Bullhamm 17
26441 Jever
Phone: +49 (0)4461 912237
www.scoma.de
Very large range of c 750 Scottish malts and many from other countries. Holds regular seminars and tastings. The excellent, monthly whisky newsletter SCOMA News is produced and can be downloaded as a pdf-file from the website. On-line ordering.

The Whisky Store
Am Grundwassersee 4
82402 Seeshaupt
Phone: +49 (0)8801-23 17
www.whisky.de
A very large range comprising c 700 kinds of whisky of which 550 are malts. Also sells whisky liqueurs, books and accessories. The website is a veritable goldmine of information about the whisky business and especially so when it comes to photographs of distilleries. There are 7500 photos of 168 distilleries. On-line ordering.

Cadenhead´s Whisky Market
Luxemburger Strasse 257
50939 Köln
Phone: +49 (0)221-2831834
www.cadenheads.de
This first Cadenhead shop outside of the UK was established in 2001. Good range of malt whiskies (c 350 different kinds) with emphasis on Cadenhead's own bottlings. Other products include wine, cognac and rum etc. Arranges recurring tastings and also has an on-line shop.

Cadenhead´s Whisky Market
Mainzer Strasse 20
10247 Berlin-Friedrichshain
Phone: +49 (0)30-30831444
www.cadenhead-berlin.de
Good product range with c 350 different kinds of malt with emphasis on Cadenhead's own bottlings as well as wine, cognac and rum etc. Arranges recurrent tastings.

Malts and More
Hosegstieg 11
22880 Wedel
Phone: +49 (0)40-23620770
www.maltsandmore.de
Very large assortment with over 800 different single malts from Scotland as well as whiskies from many other countries. Also a nice selection of cognac, rum etc. Orders can be placed on-line or through Email and telephone.

Reifferscheid
Mainzer Strasse 186
53179 Bonn / Mehlem
Phone: +49 (0)228 9 53 80 70
www.whisky-bonn.de
A well-stocked shop which has been listed as one of the best in Germany several times. Aside from a large range of whiskies (among them a good selection from Duncan Taylor), wine, spirit, cigars and a delicatessen can be found. Holds regular tastings.

Whiskywizard.de
Christian Jaudt
Schulstrasse 57
66540 Neunkirchen
Phone: +49 (0)6858-699507
www.whiskywizard.de
Large assortment of single malt (over 500) and other spirits. Only orders on-line, shipping also outside Germany.

Whisky-Doris
Germanenstrasse 38
14612 Falkensee
Phone: +49 (0)3322-219784
www.whisky-doris.de
Large range of over 300 whiskies and also sells own special bottlings. Orders via email. Shipping also outside Germany.

Finlays Whisky Shop
Friedrichstrasse 3
65779 Kelkheim
Phone: +49 (0)6195 9699510
www.finlayswhiskyshop.de

Whisky specialists with a large range of over 700 single malts. Finlays also work as the importer to Germany of Douglas laing, James MacArthur and Wilson & Morgan. There is an impressive listing of 700 bottlings of Port Ellen on the website (The Port Ellen Archive). Shop in Friedrichsdorf as well as on-line orders.

Weinquelle Lühmann
Lübeckerstrasse 145
22087 Hamburg
Phone: +49 (0)40-25 63 91
www.weinquelle.com
An impressive selection of both wines and spirits with over 1000 different whiskies of which 850 are malt whiskies. Also an impressive range of rums. On-line ordering with shipping also possible outside Germany.

The Whisky-Corner
Reichertsfeld 2
92278 Illschwang
Phone: +49 (0)9666-951213
www.whisky-corner.de
A small shop but large on mail order. A very large assortment of over 1600 whiskies. Also sells blended and American whiskies. The website is very informative with features on, among others, whisky-making, tasting and independent bottlers. On-line ordering.

World Wide Spirits
Hauptstrasse 12
84576 Teising
Phone: +49 (0)8633 50 87 93
www.worldwidespirits.de
A nice range of c 500 whiskies with some rarities from the twenties. Also large selection (c 1000) of other spirits.

WhiskyKoch
Weinbergstrasse 2
64285 Darmstadt
Phone: +49 (0)6151 99 27 105
www.whiskykoch.de
Christopher Pepper and his wife Marion own this combination of a whisky shop and restaurant. The shop has a nice selection of single malts as well as other Scottish products and the restaurant has specialised in whisky dinners and tastings.

Whisk(e)y Shop Tara
Rindermarkt 16
80331 München
Phone: +49 (0)89-26 51 18
www.whiskyversand.de
Whisky specialists with a very broad range of, for example, 800 different single malts. On-line ordering.

Single Malt Collection
(Glen Fahrn Germany GmbH)
Hauptstraße 38
79801 Hohentengen a. H.
Phone: +49 (0)77 42 -857 222
www.singlemaltcollection.com
A very large range of single malts (c 600). Newsletter. On-line orders. Shipping also outside Germany.

Kierzek
Weitlingstrasse 17
10317 Berlin
Phone: +49 (0)30 525 11 08
www.kierzek-berlin.de
Over 400 different whiskies in stock.
In the product range 50 kinds of
rum and 450 wines from all over
the world are found among other
products. Mail order is available
within Germany.

House of Whisky
Ackerbeeke 6
31683 Obernkirchen
Phone: +49 (0)5724-399420
www.houseofwhisky.de
Aside from over 1,200 different
malts also sells a large range of
other spirits (including over 100
kinds of rum). On-line ordering with
shipping also outside Germany.

Whiskyworld
Ziegelfeld 6
94481 Grafenau / Haus i. Wald
Phone: +49 (0)8555-406 320
www.whiskyworld.de
A very good assortment of more
than 1,000 malt whiskies. Also has a
good range of wines, other spirits,
cigars and books. Also on-line
ordering.

World Wide Whisky (2 shops)
Eisenacher Strasse 64
10823 Berlin-Schöneberg
Phone: +49 (0)30-7845010
Hauptstrasse 58
10823 Berlin-Schöneberg
www.world-wide-whisky.de
Large range of 1,500 different
whiskies. Arranges tastings and
seminars. Has a large number of
rarities. Orders via email.

HUNGARY

Whisky Net / Whisky Shop
Kovács Làszlò Street 21
2000 Szentendre
(shop)
Veres Pálné utca 8.
1053 Budapest
Phone: +36 1 267-1588
www.whiskynet.hu, www.whiskys-
hop.hu
A whisky trader established in 2007.
In the shop in downtown Budapest
one finds the largest selction of
whisky in Hungary. Agents for
Douglas Laing, Cadenhead,
Bruichladdich and Glenfarclas
among others. Also mailorder.

IRELAND

Celtic Whiskey Shop
27-28 Dawson Street
Dublin 2
Phone: +353 (0)1 675 9744
www.celticwhiskeyshop.com
More than 70 kinds of Irish whiskeys
but also a good selection of Scotch,
wines and other spirits. On-line
ordering with shipping all over the
world.

ITALY

Cadenhead's Whisky Bar
Via Poliziano, 3
20154 Milano
Phone: +39 (0)2 336 055 92
www.cadenhead.it
This is the tenth and newest addition in the Cadenhead´s chain of
shops. Concentrating mostly on the
Cadenhead´s range but they also
stock whiskies from other producers.

THE NETHERLANDS

Whiskyslijterij De Koning
Hinthamereinde 41
5211 PM 's Hertogenbosch
Phone: +31 (0)73-6143547
www.whiskykoning.nl
An enormous assortment with more
than 1400 kinds of whisky including
c 800 single malts. Also whisky-
related items like decanters, books
etc. Arranges recurring tastings.
The site is in Dutch and English.
On-line ordering. Shipping all over
the world.

Whisky- en Wijnhandel Verhaar
Planetenbaan 2a
3721 LA Bilthoven
Phone: +31 (0)30-228 44 18
www.whiskyshop.nl
A wide selection of wines and spirits
with 1300 whiskies of which 1000
come from Scotland. Email orders.

Wijnhandel van Zuylen
Loosduinse Hoofdplein 201
2553 CP Loosduinen (Den Haag)
Phone: +31 (0)70-397 1400
www.whiskyvanzuylen.nl
Excellent range of whiskies (c
1100) and wines. Email orders with
shipping to some ten European
countries.

Wijnwinkel-Slijterij
Ton Overmars
Hoofddorpplein 11
1059 CV Amsterdam
Phone: +31 (0)20-615 71 42
www.tonovermars.nl
A very large assortment of wines,
spirits and beer which includes more
than 400 single malts. Arranges
recurring tastings. Orders via email.

Van Wees - Whiskyworld.nl
Leusderweg 260
3817 KH Amersfoort
Phone: +31 (0)33-461 64 26
www.whiskyworld.nl
A very large range of 1000 whiskies
including over 500 single malts. On-
line ordering.

Wijn & Whisky Schuur
Blankendalwei 4
8629 EH Scharnegoutem (bij Sneek)
Phone: +31 (0)515-520706
www.wijnwhiskyschuur.nl
Large assortment with 1000 different whiskies and a good range of
other spirits as well. Arranges recurring tastings. On-line ordering.

Versailles Dranken
Lange Hezelstraat 72-76
6511 Cl Nijmegen
Phone: +31 (0)24-3232008
www.versaillesdranken.nl
A very impressive range with more
than 1500 different whiskies, most
of them from Scotland but also a
surprisingly good selection (more
than 60) of Bourbon. Arranges recurring tastings. On-line ordering.

NEW ZEALAND

Whisky Galore
66 Victoria Street
Christchurch 8013
Phone: +64 (3) 377 6824
www.whiskygalore.co.nz
The best whisky shop in New
Zealand with 550 different whiskies,
approximately 350 which are single
malts. The owner Michael Fraser
Milne, has also founded The Whisky
Guild which has, as one of its aims,
to produce exclusive single cask
bottlings for members. There is also
online mail-order shipping within
New Zealand.

POLAND

George Ballantine´s
Krucza str 47 A, Warsaw
Phone: +48 22 625 48 32
Pulawska str 22, Warsaw
Phone: +48 22 542 86 22
Marynarska str 15, Warsaw
Phone: +48 22 395 51 60
Francuska str 27, Warsaw
Phone: +48 22 810 32 22
www.sklep-ballantines.pl
These four shops have the biggest
assortment in Poland with more
than 360 different single malts.
Apart from whisky there is a full
range of spirits and wines from all
over the world. Recurrent tastings
are arranged and mail-orders are
dispatched.

RUSSIA

Whisky World Shop
9, Tverskoy Boulevard
123104 Moscow
Phone: +7 495 787 9150
www.whiskyworld.ru
Huge assortment with more than
1,000 different single malts, mainly
from independent bottlers. It also
stocks a selection of rare and old
whiskies. The range is supplemented
with a nice range of cognac,
armagnac, calvados, grappa and
wines. Tastings are also arranged.

SCOTLAND

Gordon & MacPhail
58 - 60 South Street, Elgin
Moray IV30 1JY
Phone: +44 (0)1343 545110
www.gordonandmacphail.com
This legendary shop opened already
in 1895 in Elgin. The owners are

perhaps the most well-known among independent bottlers. The shop stocks more than 800 bottlings of whisky and more than 600 wines and there is also a delicatessen counter with high-quality products. Tastings are arranged in the shop and there are shipping services within the UK and overseas. The shop attracts visitors from all over the world.

Royal Mile Whiskies (2 shops)
379 High Street, The Royal Mile
Edinburgh EH1 1PW
Phone: +44 (0)131 2253383

3 Bloomsbury Street
London WC1B 3QE
Phone: +44 (0)20 7436 4763
www.royalmilewhiskies.com
Royal Mile Whiskies is one of the most well-known whisky retailers in the UK. It was established in Edinburgh in 1991. There is also a shop in London since 2002 and a cigar shop close to the Edinburgh shop. The whisky range is outstanding with many difficult to find elsewhere. They have a comprehensive site regarding information on regions, distilleries, production, tasting etc. Royal Mile Whiskies also arranges 'Whisky Fringe' in Edinburgh, a two-day whisky festival which takes place annually in mid August. On-line ordering with worldwide shipping.

The Whisky Shop
(See also England, The Whisky Shop)
Unit L2-02
Buchanan Galleries
220 Buchanan Street
Glasgow G1 2GF
Phone: +44 (0)141 331 0022

17 Bridge Street
Inverness IV1 1HD
Phone: +44 (0)1463 710525

11 Main Street
Callander FK17 8DU
Phone: +44 (0)1877 331936

93 High Street
Fort William PH33 6DG
Phone: +44 (0)1397 706164

Shop Unit 1
Station Road
Oban PA34 4NU
Phone: +44 (0)1631 564409

Unit 14
Gretna Gateway Outlet Village
Gretna DG16 5GG
Phone: +44 (0)1461338004

Unit RU58B, Ocean Terminal
Edinburgh EH6 6JJ
Phone: +44 (0)131 554 8211

Unit 23
Princes Mall
Edinburgh EH1 1BQ
Phone: +44 (0)131 558 7563

www.whiskyshop.com
The first shop opened in 1992 in Edin-burgh and this is now the United Kingdom's largest specialist retailer of whiskies with 16 outlets. A large product range with over 700

kinds, including 400 malt whiskies and 140 miniature bottles, as well as accessories and books. The own range 'Glenkeir Treasures' is a special assortment of selected malt whiskies. On-line ordering and shipping all over the world except to the USA.

Loch Fyne Whiskies
Inveraray
Argyll PA32 8UD
Phone: +44 (0)1499 302 219
www.lfw.co.uk
A legendary shop with an equally legendary owner, Richard Joynson. Joynson is known as a person with a high degree of integrity who does not mince his words on whisky matters. The range of malt whiskies is large and they have their own house blend, the prize-awarded Loch Fyne, as well as their 'The Loch Fyne Whisky Liqueur'. There is also a range of house malts called 'The Inverarity'. Loch Fyne Whiskies also publish the highly readable 'Scotch Whisky Review' which previously was produced by Joynson but now has authorities such as Charles MacLean and Dave Broom on the staff. Also on-line ordering with worldwide shipping.

Single Malts Direct
36 Gordon Street
Huntly
Aberdeenshire AB54 8EQ
Phone: +44 (0) 845 606 6145
www.singlemaltsdirect.com
Duncan Taylor, one of Scotland's largest independent bottlers, also has a shop in Huntly. In the assortment is of course the whole Duncan Taylor range but also a selection of their own single malt bottlings called Whiskies of Scotland. Add bottlings from other producers and you end up with a good range of almost 700 different expressions. Also has an on-line shop with shipping worldwide. The website has information on the production of whisky and a very comprehensive glossary of whisky terms.

The Whisky Shop Dufftown
1 Fife Street, Dufftown, Keith
Moray AB55 4AL
Phone: +44 (0)1340 821097
www.whiskyshopdufftown.co.uk
Whisky specialist in Dufftown in the heart of Speyside, wellknown to many of the Speyside festival visitors. More than 500 single malts as well as other whiskies. Arranges tastings as well as special events during the Festivals. On-line ordering with worldwide shipping.

The Scotch Whisky Experience
354 Castlehill, Royal Mile
Edinburgh
Phone: +44 (0)131 220 0441
www.scotchwhiskyexperience.co.uk
The Scotch Whisky Experience is a must for whisky devotees visiting Edinburgh. An interactive visitor centre dedicated to the history of

Scotch whisky. This five-star visitor attraction has an excellent whisky shop with almost 300 different whiskies in stock. The shop is open to the general public and not only to those who have taken the whisky tour. Do not miss the award-winning Amber Restaurant.

Cadenhead's Campbeltown Whisky shop (Eaglesome)
7 Bolgam Street
Campbeltown
Argyll PA28 6HZ
Phone: +44 (0)1586 551710
argyll.wmcadenhead.com
One in a chain of shops owned by independent bottlers Cadenhead. Sells Cadenhead's products and other whiskies with a good range of Springbank. On-line ordering.

Cadenhead´s Whisky Shop
172 Canongate, Royal Mile
Edinburgh EH8 8BN
Phone: +44 (0)131 556 5864
www.wmcadenhead.com
The oldest shop in the chain owned by Cadenhead. Sells Cadenhead's product range and a good selection of other whiskies and spirits. Arranges recurrent tastings. On-line ordering.

The Good Spirits Co.
23 Bath Street,
Glasgow G2 1HW
Phone: +44 (0)141 258 8427
www.thegoodspiritsco.com
A newly opened specialist spirits store selling whisky, bourbon, rum, vodka, tequila, gin, cognac and armagnac, liqueurs and other spirits. They also stock quality champagne, fortified wines and cigars.

Robbie's Drams
3 Sandgate, Ayr
South Ayrshire KA7 1BG
Phone: +44 (0)1292 262 135
www.robbiesdrams.com
A whisky specialist with over 600 whiskies available in store and over 900 available from their online shop, including a large range of Irish, Japanese and American Bourbons. Specialists in single cask bottlings, closed distillery bottlings, rare malts, limited edition whisky and a nice range of their own bottlings. Worldwide shipping.

The Whisky Barrel
PO Box 23803, Edinburgh, EH6 7WW
Phone: +44 (0)845 2248 156
www.thewhiskybarrel.com
Online specialist whisky shop based Edinburgh. They stock over 1,000 single malt and blended whiskies including Scotch, Japanese, Irish, Indian, Swedish and their own casks. Worldwide shipping.

Scotch Malt Whisky Society
www.smws.com
A society with more than 20 000 members worldwide, specialised in own bottlings of single casks and release between 150 and 200 bottlings

a year. Orders on-line for members only. Shipping only within UK.

Drinkmonger
100 Atholl Road
Pitlochry PH16 5BL
Phone: +44 (0)1796 470133

11 Bruntsfield Place
Edinburgh EH10 4HN
Phone: +44 (0)131 229 2205
www.drinkmonger.com
Two new shops opened in 2011 by the well-known Royal Mile Whiskies. The idea is to have a 50:50 split between wine and specialist spirits with the addition of a cigar assort-ment. The whisky range is a good cross-section with some rarities and a focus on local distilleries.

Luvian's Bottle Shop (2 shops)
93 Bonnygate, Cupar
Fife KY15 4LG
Phone: +44 (0)1334 654 820

66 Market Street, St Andrews
Fife KY16 9NU
Phone: +44 (0)1334 477752
www.luvians.com
Wine and whisky merchant with a very nice selection of more than 600 malt whiskies.

The Maltman
(S. R. & E. Barron (Dyce) Ltd.)
119 Victoria Street, Dyce
Aberdeen AB21 7BJ
Phone: +44 (0)1224 722208
www.maltman.co.uk
A good range with over 350 malts in stock, including a 'Collector's Corner' with rare malts. There is a mail order service, but not on-line. Only shipping within the UK.

Robert Graham Ltd (3 shops)
194 Rose Street
Edinburgh EH2 4AZ
Phone: +44 (0)131 226 1874

Finlay House
10-14 West Nile Street
Glasgow G1 2PP
Phone: +44 (0)141 248 7283

Robert Graham's Treasurer 1874
254 Canongate
Royal Mile
Edinburgh EH8 8AA
Phone: +44 (0)131 556 2791
www.whisky-cigars.co.uk
Established in 1874 this company specialises in Scotch whisky and cigars. They have a nice assortment of malt whiskies and their range of cigars is impressive. On-line ordering with shipping all over the world

Whisky Castle
Main Street
Tomintoul
Aberdeenshire AB37 9EX
Phone: +44 (0)1807 580 213
www.whiskycastle.co.uk
Whisky specialist situated in the heart of malt whisky country. With over 500 single malts, the specialisation is in independent bottlings. There is also a mail order shipping worldwide with the exception of USA.

SWITZERLAND

P. Ullrich AG
Schneidergasse 27
4051 Basel
Phone: +41 (0)61 338 90 91
Another two shops in Basel:
Laufenstrasse 16
Unt. Rebgasse 18
www.ullrich.ch
A very large range of wines, spirits, beers, accessories and books. Over 800 kinds of whisky with almost 600 single malt. On-line ordering. Re-cently, they also founded a whisky club with regular tastings (www. whiskysinn.ch).

Eddie's Whiskies
Dorfgasse 27
8810 Horgen
Phone: +41 (0)43 244 63 00
www.eddies.ch
A whisky specialist with more than 700 different whiskies in stock with emphasis on single malts (more than 500 different). Also arranges tastings.

World of Whisky
Via dim Lej 6
7500 St. Moritz
Phone: +41 (0)81 852 33 77
www.world-of-whisky.ch
A legendary shop situated in the Hotel Waldhaus Am See which has an also legendary whisky bar, the Devil's Place. The shop, run by Christian Lauper, stocks almost 1,000 different whiskies and has a good range of other spirits such as rum, cognac and armagnac. There is also a World of Whisky Malt Club and mail order.

Glen Fahrn (4 shops)
Glen Fahrn N°1 "the origin"
Fahrnstrasse 39
9402 Mörschwil
Phone: +41 (0)71 860 09 87

Glen Fahrn N°2 "the pearl"
Oberdorfstrasse 5
8001 Zürich
Phone: +41 (0)44 520 09 87

Glen Fahrn N°4 "the store"
Glen Fahrn Germany GmbH
Hauptstrasse 38
79801 Hohentengen a.H.
Germany
Phone: +49 (0)7742 857 222

Glen Fahrn N°5 "the hotel"
Bernstrasse 7
3280 Murten
Phone: +41 (0)26 678 81 91
www.glenfahrn.com
A wide range of spirits, fortified wines and champagnes. A large selection of whisky, with over 600 from Scotland. On-line ordering. Ships within Switzerland and to adjacent countries.

Scot & Scotch
Wohllebgasse 7
8001 Zürich
Phone: +41 44 211 90 60
www.scotandscotch.ch
A whisky specialist with a great selection including c 560 single

malts. Mail orders, but no on-line ordering.

Angels Share Shop
Unterdorfstrasse 15
5036 Oberentfelden
Phone: +41 (0)62 724 83 74
www.angelsshare.ch
A combined restaurant and whisky shop. More than 400 different kinds of whisky as well as a good range of cigars. Scores extra points for short information and photos of all distilleries. On-line ordering.

Cadenhead´s Whisky & More
Mittlere Gasse 15
5400 Baden
Phone: +41 (0)56 222 04 44
www.cadenheads.ch
A new member of the chain of Caden-head´s stores with a nice range of whiskies, especially Cadenhead´s. Also rum, cognac and other spirits.

USA

Binny´s Beverage Depot
5100 W. Dempster (Head Office)
Skokie, IL 60077
Phone:
Internet orders, 888-942-9463 (toll free)
Whisky Hotline, 888-817-5898 (toll free)
www.binnys.com
A chain of no less than 26 stores in the Chicago area, covering every-thing within wine and spirits. Some of the stores also have a gourmet grocery, cheese shop and, for cigar lovers, a walk-in humidor. The whisk(e)y range is impressive with 700 single malts, 120 bourbons, 40 Irish whiskeys and more. Among other products almost 200 kinds of tequila should be mentioned. Online mail order service.

Traverso´s
2097 Stagecoach Road,
Santa Rosa, CA 95404
Phone: +1 707 542-2530
www.traversos.com
Traverso's Gourmet Foods was estab-lished by Charles Traverso in 1922 and today specialises in food, wine and liquors. They have a very nice range of malt whiskies with regular tastings in the shop.

Park Avenue Liquor Shop
292 Madison Avenue
New York, NY 10017
Phone: +1 212 685 2442
www.parkaveliquor.com
Legendary whisky shop already estab-lished in 1934. A very large assortment of wine and spirits with 400 different expressions of single malt.

Statistics

The following pages have been made possible thanks to kind cooperation from three sources – Euromonitor International, The Scotch Whisky Industry Review and Scotch Whisky Association.

Euromonitor International is the leading provider of global strategic intelligence on consumer markets, with regional offices in Chicago, Singapore, Shanghai, Vilnius, Santiago, Dubai, Cape Town, Tokyo, Sydney, Bangalore and a network of 800 in-country analysts worldwide. For more than 39 years, Euromonitor has published internationally respected market research reports, business reference books and online information systems, providing strategic business intelligence for the world's leading FMCG multinationals. For more information visit **www.euromonitor.com**

The Scotch Whisky Industry Review 2011 is written and compiled by Alan S Gray, Sutherlands Edinburgh. It is now in its 33rd consecutive year and provides a wealth of unique business critical information on the Scotch Whisky Industry. Copies can be obtained from Sutherlands Edinburgh, 61 Dublin Street, Edinburgh EH3 6NL. Details also on the website **www.scotchwhiskyindustryreview.com**

Scotch Whisky Association (SWA) is the trade association for the Scotch Whisky industry. Its members account for more than 95% of production and sales of Scotch Whisky. Their main objective is to promote, protect and represent the interests of the whisky industry in Scotland and around the world. They also produce a plethora of statistical material covering production and sales of Scotch whisky. More information can be found on **www.scotch-whisky.org.uk**

Whisk(e)y forecast (volume & value) by region and sector 2010-2015

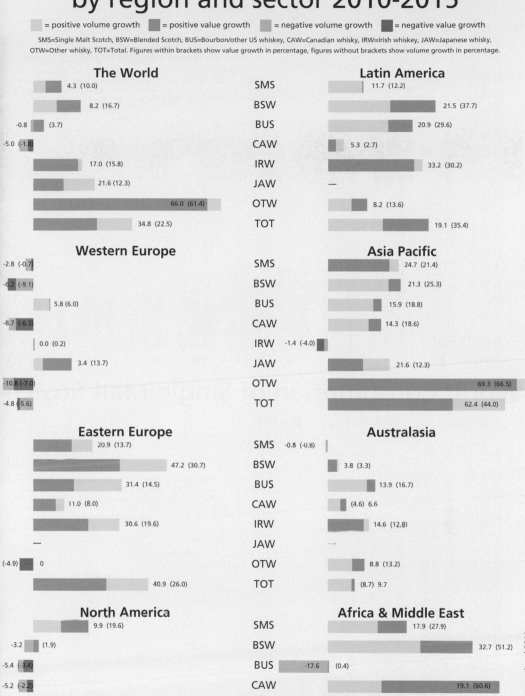

■ = positive volume growth ■ = positive value growth ■ = negative volume growth ■ = negative value growth

SMS=Single Malt Scotch, BSW=Blended Scotch, BUS=Bourbon/other US whiskey, CAW=Canadian whisky, IRW=Irish whiskey, JAW=Japanese whisky, OTW=Other whisky, TOT=Total. Figures within brackets show value growth in percentage, figures without brackets show volume growth in percentage.

The World

SMS	4.3 (10.0)	
BSW	8.2 (16.7)	
BUS	-0.8 (3.7)	
CAW	-5.0 (-1.8)	
IRW	17.0 (15.8)	
JAW	21.6 (12.3)	
OTW	66.0 (61.4)	
TOT	34.8 (22.5)	

Latin America

SMS	11.7 (12.2)
BSW	21.5 (37.7)
BUS	20.9 (29.6)
CAW	5.3 (2.7)
IRW	33.2 (30.2)
JAW	—
OTW	8.2 (13.6)
TOT	19.1 (35.4)

Western Europe

SMS	-2.8 (-0.7)
BSW	-6.2 (-9.1)
BUS	5.8 (6.0)
CAW	-8.7 (-6.3)
IRW	0.0 (0.2)
JAW	3.4 (13.7)
OTW	-10.8 (-7.0)
TOT	-4.8 (-5.6)

Asia Pacific

SMS	24.7 (21.4)
BSW	21.3 (25.3)
BUS	15.9 (18.8)
CAW	14.3 (18.6)
IRW	-1.4 (-4.0)
JAW	21.6 (12.3)
OTW	69.3 (66.5)
TOT	62.4 (44.0)

Eastern Europe

SMS	20.9 (13.7)
BSW	47.2 (30.7)
BUS	31.4 (14.5)
CAW	11.0 (8.0)
IRW	30.6 (19.6)
JAW	—
OTW	(-4.9) 0
TOT	40.9 (26.0)

Australasia

SMS	-0.8 (-0.8)
BSW	3.8 (3.3)
BUS	13.9 (16.7)
CAW	(4.6) 6.6
IRW	14.6 (12.8)
JAW	—
OTW	8.8 (13.2)
TOT	(8.7) 9.7

North America

SMS	9.9 (19.6)
BSW	-3.2 (1.9)
BUS	-5.4 (-3.4)
CAW	-5.2 (-2.2)
IRW	31.7 (38.0)
JAW	—
OTW	—
TOT	-3.5 (1.5)

Africa & Middle East

SMS	17.9 (27.9)
BSW	32.7 (51.2)
BUS	-17.6 (0.4)
CAW	19.1 (60.6)
IRW	41.5 (37.4)
JAW	11.5 (9.7)
OTW	10.9 (6.3)
TOT	23.5 (43.9)

Source: © Euromonitor International 2011

World Consumption of Blended Scotch

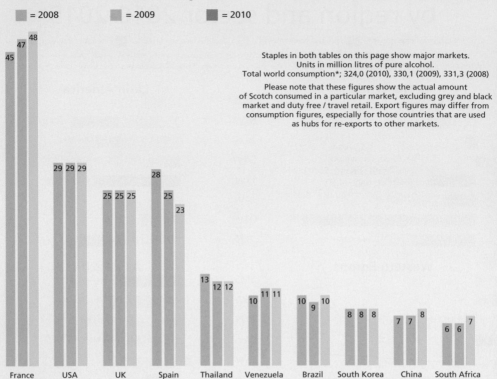

■ = 2008   ■ = 2009   ■ = 2010

Staples in both tables on this page show major markets.
Units in million litres of pure alcohol.
Total world consumption*; 324,0 (2010), 330,1 (2009), 331,3 (2008)

Please note that these figures show the actual amount
of Scotch consumed in a particular market, excluding grey and black
market and duty free / travel retail. Export figures may differ from
consumption figures, especially for those countries that are used
as hubs for re-exports to other markets.

France: 45 47 48
USA: 29 29 29
UK: 25 25 25
Spain: 28 25 23
Thailand: 13 12 12
Venezuela: 10 11 11
Brazil: 10 9 10
South Korea: 8 8 8
China: 7 7 8
South Africa: 6 6 7

Source: Euromonitor International 2011 and for* Scotch Whisky Industry Review 2011

World Consumption of Single Malt Scotch

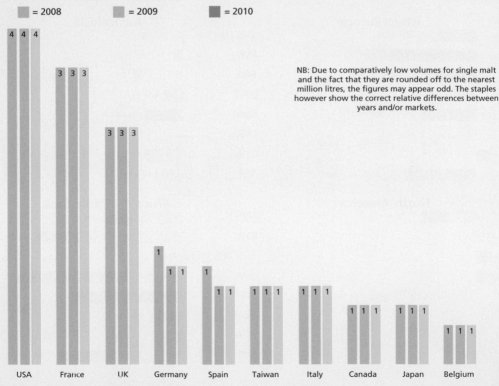

■ = 2008   ■ = 2009   ■ = 2010

NB: Due to comparatively low volumes for single malt
and the fact that they are rounded off to the nearest
million litres, the figures may appear odd. The staples
however show the correct relative differences between
years and/or markets.

USA: 4 4 4
France: 3 3 3
UK: 3 3 3
Germany: 1 1 1
Spain: 1 1 1
Taiwan: 1 1 1
Italy: 1 1 1
Canada: 1 1 1
Japan: 1 1 1
Belgium: 1 1 1

Source: Euromonitor International 2011

The Top 30 Whiskies of the World

Sales figures for 2010 (units in million 9-litre cases)

Bagpiper (United Spirits), Indian whisky — 16,39
Officer's Choice (Allied Blenders & Distillers), Indian whisky — 16,00
Johnnie Walker (Diageo), Scotch whisky — 15,90
McDowell's No. 1 (United Spirits), Indian whisky — 14,32
Royal Stag (Pernod Ricard), Indian whisky — 10,39
Original Choice (John Distilleries), Indian whisky — 10,32
Jack Daniel's (Brown-Forman), Tennessee whiskey — 9,95
Old Tavern (United Spirits), Indian whisky — 9,08
Ballantine's (Pernod Ricard), Scotch whisky — 6,18
Imperial Blue (Pernod Ricard), Indian whisky — 6,11
Jim Beam (Beam Global Spirits & Wine), Bourbon — 5,30
Crown Royal (Diageo), Canadian whisky — 5,00
William Grant's (William Grant & Sons), Scotch whisky — 4,99
J&B Rare (Diageo), Scotch whisky — 4,90
Hayward's (United Spirits), Indian whisky — 4,65
Director's Special (United Spirits), Indian whisky — 4,54
Chivas Regal (Pernod Ricard), Scotch whisky — 4,50
8PM (Radico Khaitan), Indian whisky — 3,94
Dewar's (Bacardi), Scotch whisky — 3,27
Jameson (Pernod Ricard), Irish whiskey — 3,17
Director's Special Black (United Spirits), Indian whisky — 2,88
Blenders Pride (Pernod Ricard), Indian whisky — 2,82
Kakubin (Suntory), Japanese whisky — 2,79
McDowell's Green Label (United Spirits), Indian whisky — 2,53
Bell's (Diageo), Scotch whisky — 2,50
William Peel (Belvédère), Scotch whisky — 2,50
Seagram's 7 Crown (Diageo), American blended whiskey — 2,40
Label 5 (La Martiniquaise), Scotch whisky — 2,27
Gold Riband (United Spirits), Indian whisky — 2,25
Black Velvet (Constellation Brands), Canadian whisky — 2,07

Source: Drinks International, Millionaires Supplement (Euromonitor International)

Exports of Scotch Whisky

= volume in million litres of alcohol   = value in £ million (inflation adjusted)

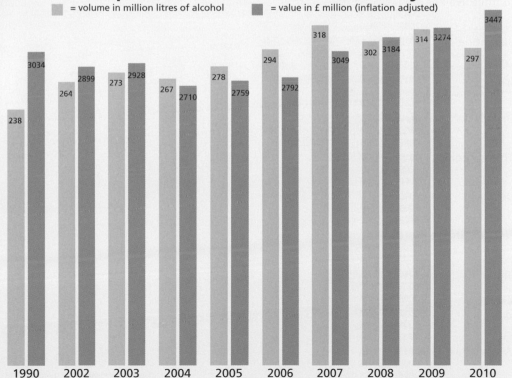

| 1990 | 2002 | 2003 | 2004 | 2005 | 2006 | 2007 | 2008 | 2009 | 2010 |

Source: Scotch Whisky Association and Bank of England

Top 10 Scotch Whisky Single Malt brands world market share %

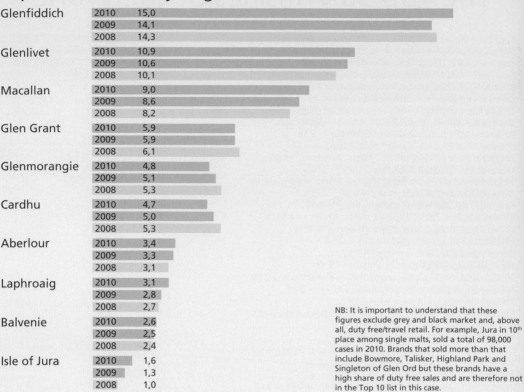

Glenfiddich	2010	15,0
	2009	14,1
	2008	14,3
Glenlivet	2010	10,9
	2009	10,6
	2008	10,1
Macallan	2010	9,0
	2009	8,6
	2008	8,2
Glen Grant	2010	5,9
	2009	5,9
	2008	6,1
Glenmorangie	2010	4,8
	2009	5,1
	2008	5,3
Cardhu	2010	4,7
	2009	5,0
	2008	5,3
Aberlour	2010	3,4
	2009	3,3
	2008	3,1
Laphroaig	2010	3,1
	2009	2,8
	2008	2,7
Balvenie	2010	2,6
	2009	2,5
	2008	2,4
Isle of Jura	2010	1,6
	2009	1,3
	2008	1,0

NB: It is important to understand that these figures exclude grey and black market and, above all, duty free/travel retail. For example, Jura in 10th place among single malts, sold a total of 98,000 cases in 2010. Brands that sold more than that include Bowmore, Talisker, Highland Park and Singleton of Glen Ord but these brands have a high share of duty free sales and are therefore not in the Top 10 list in this case.

Top 10 Scotch Whisky Blended brands world market share %

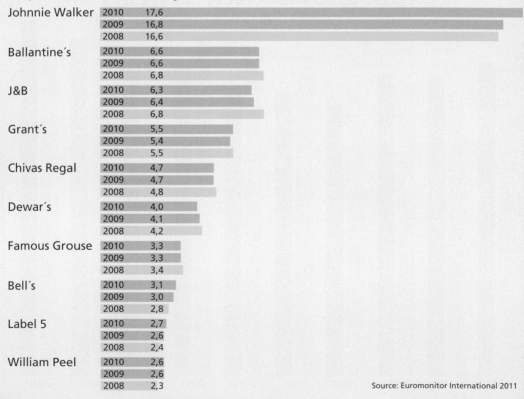

Johnnie Walker	2010	17,6
	2009	16,8
	2008	16,6
Ballantine's	2010	6,6
	2009	6,6
	2008	6,8
J&B	2010	6,3
	2009	6,4
	2008	6,8
Grant's	2010	5,5
	2009	5,4
	2008	5,5
Chivas Regal	2010	4,7
	2009	4,7
	2008	4,8
Dewar's	2010	4,0
	2009	4,1
	2008	4,2
Famous Grouse	2010	3,3
	2009	3,3
	2008	3,4
Bell's	2010	3,1
	2009	3,0
	2008	2,8
Label 5	2010	2,7
	2009	2,6
	2008	2,4
William Peel	2010	2,6
	2009	2,6
	2008	2,3

Source: Euromonitor International 2011

Distillery Capacity

Litres of pure alcohol, Scottish, active distilleries only

Roseisle	12 500 000	Speyburn	2 000 000	Glen Garioch	1 000 000
Glenfiddich	12 000 000	Ben Nevis	1 800 000	Tobermory	1 000 000
Glenlivet	10 500 000	Glenlossie	1 800 000	Arran	750 000
Macallan	8 750 000	Pulteney	1 800 000	Glengyle	750 000
Caol Ila	6 400 000	Auchentoshan	1 750 000	Glen Scotia	750 000
Ailsa Bay	6 250 000	Glen Elgin	1 700 000	Springbank	750 000
Glenmorangie	6 000 000	Knockdhu	1 650 000	Oban	670 000
Glen Grant	5 900 000	Bruichladdich	1 500 000	Speyside	600 000
Dufftown	5 800 000	Scapa	1 500 000	Benromach	500 000
Balvenie	5 600 000	Glendronach	1 400 000	Royal Lochnagar	450 000
Glenrothes	5 600 000	Glenspey	1 400 000	Glenturret	340 000
Miltonduff	5 500 000	Balblair	1 400 000	Bladnoch	250 000
Ardmore	5 200 000	Glencadam	1 300 000	Kilchoman	110 000
Glen Ord	5 000 000	Knockando	1 300 000	Edradour	90 000
Tomatin	5 000 000	Ardbeg	1 150 000	Daftmill	65 000
Kininvie	4 800 000	Glenglassaugh	1 100 000	Abhainn Dearg	20 000
Glentauchers	4 500 000	Glengoyne	1 100 000		
Teaninich	4 400 000				
Clynelish	4 200 000				
Glenburgie	4 200 000				
Tormore	4 100 000				
Allt-a-Bhainne	4 000 000				
Braeval	4 000 000				
Craigellachie	4 000 000				
Loch Lomond	4 000 000				
Tamnavulin	4 000 000				
Royal Brackla	4 000 000				
Auchroisk	3 800 000				
Mortlach	3 800 000				
Aberlour	3 700 000				
Dalmore	3 700 000				
Glendullan	3 700 000				
Aberfeldy	3 500 000				
Linkwood	3 500 000				
Longmorn	3 500 000				
Mannochmore	3 450 000				
Dailuaine	3 400 000				
Macduff	3 340 000				
Tomintoul	3 300 000				
Cardhu	3 200 000				
Glenallachie	3 200 000				
Aultmore	3 000 000				
Deanston	3 000 000				
Glenfarclas	3 000 000				
Inchgower	2 900 000				
Laphroaig	2 900 000				
Benriach	2 800 000				
Tullibardine	2 700 000				
Talisker	2 600 000				
Benrinnes	2 500 000				
Blair Athol	2 500 000				
Bunnahabhain	2 500 000				
Highland Park	2 500 000				
Strathisla	2 400 000				
Glenkinchie	2 350 000				
Fettercairn	2 300 000				
Strathmill	2 300 000				
Glen Moray	2 300 000				
Lagavulin	2 250 000				
Dalwhinnie	2 200 000				
Jura	2 200 000				
Balmenach	2 000 000				
Bowmore	2 000 000				
Cragganmore	2 000 000				

Summary of Malt Distillery Capacity by Category

Category	Litres of alcohol	% of Industry	Average capacity
Speyside (44)	178 200 000	60,1	4 050 000
Islands (7)	10 570 000	3,6	1 510 000
Highlands (30)	75 740 000	25,5	2 525 000
Islay (8)	18 810 000	6,4	2 351 000
Lowlands (5)	10 665 000	3,6	2 133 000
Campbeltown (3)	2 250 000	0,8	750 000
Total (97)	**296 235 000**	**100**	**3 054 000**

Summary of Malt Distillery Capacity by Owner

Owner (number of distilleries)	Litres of alcohol	% of Industry
Diageo (28)	92 170 000	31,1
Pernod Ricard (12)	51 100 000	17,2
William Grant (4)	28 650 000	9,7
Bacardi (John Dewar & Sons) (5)	17 840 000	6,0
Edrington Group (4)	17 190 000	5,8
Whyte and Mackay (4)	12 200 000	4,1
Pacific Spirits (Inver House) (5)	8 850 000	3,0
Beam Global (2)	8 100 000	2,7
Moët Hennessy (Glenmorangie) (2)	7 150 000	2,4
C L Financial (Burn Stewart) (3)	6 500 000	2,2
Campari (Glen Grant) (1)	5 900 000	2,0
Tomatin Distillery Co (1)	5 000 000	1,7
Suntory (Morrison Bowmore) (3)	4 750 000	1,6
Loch Lomond Distillers (2)	4 750 000	1,6
Angus Dundee (2)	4 600 000	1,6
Benriach Distillery Co (2)	4 200 000	1,4
J & G Grant (Glenfarclas) (1)	3 000 000	1,0
Tullibardine Distillery Ltd (1)	2 700 000	0,9
La Martiniquaise (Glen Moray) (1)	2 200 000	0,7
Nikka (Ben Nevis Distillery) (1)	1 800 000	0,6
Bruichladdich Distillery Co (1)	1 500 000	0,5
J & A Mitchell (2)	1 500 000	0,5
Ian Macleod Distillers (Glengoyne) (1)	1 100 000	less than 0,5
Scaent Group (Glenglassaugh) (1)	1 100 000	- " -
Isle of Arran Distillers (1)	750 000	- " -
Speyside Distillers Co (1)	600 000	- " -
Gordon & MacPhail (Benromach) (1)	500 000	- " -
Co-ordinated Developm. (Bladnoch) (1)	250 000	- " -
Kilchoman Distillery Co (1)	110 000	- " -
Signatory Vintage (Edradour) (1)	90 000	- " -
Francis Cuthbert (Daftmill) (1)	65 000	- " -
Mark Thayburn (Abhainn Dearg) (1)	20 000	- " -

Do you want to find out more in detail where the different distilleries are situated? We suggest that you pay a visit to **www.maltmadness.com/whisky/map/Scotland/** where you will find a very nice, interactive map made by Johannes van den Heuvel. Another favourite is found at **bit.ly/cgpHsX** where Steffen Bräuner has plotted all the Scottish and Irish distilleries and from there you can also access his maps of distilleries in North America and the rest of the world.

ORKNEY ISLANDS

Wick

NORTH HIGHLANDS

Isle of Lewis
129

SKYE

Barra
1

Kyle of Lockalsh

Inverness

SPEYSIDE

Loch Ness

Aberdeen

CENTRAL HIGHLANDS

Fort William

EAST HIGHLANDS

WEST HIGHLANDS

MULL

Oban

Pitlochry

Loch Tay

Dundee

Loch Lomond

Perth

St. Andrews

JURA

ISLAY

Stirling

Glasgow

Edinburgh

ARRAN

Campbeltown

Ayr

THE LOWLANDS

Dumfries

Stranraer

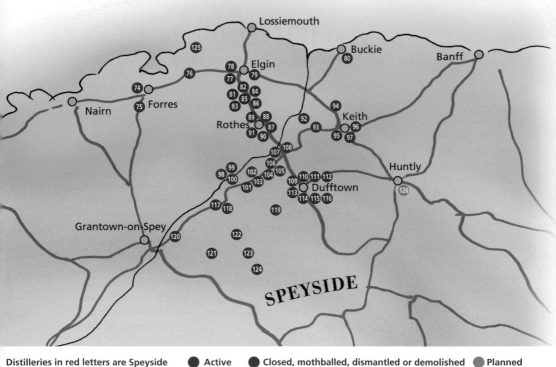

Distilleries in red letters are Speyside ● Active ● Closed, mothballed, dismantled or demolished ● Planned

Index

Bold figures refer to the main entry in the distillery directory.

Index

Bold figures refer to the main entry in the distillery directory.

Index

Bold figures refer to the main entry in the distillery directory.